PENGUIN BOOKS

LOCAL GOVERNMENT IN

Tony Byrne was born in 1937 and went to school in Liverpool. He took a degree in economics at the University of Bristol, and in government at the University of London. He has taught in schools in Liverpool and Somerset, was an adult education officer and an examiner for the Yorkshire and Humberside Council for Further and Higher Education, and is now lecturer in government, law and social administration at the Somerset College of Arts and Technology in Taunton and at the University of Plymouth. For some years he was chairman of the Taunton Marriage Guidance Council and has been secretary of the Taunton Workers' Education Association. His other books are *Social Services Made Simple* and *British Constitution Made Simple*, both written with the late Colin Padfield. As a semi-professional musician, he lectures on jazz and plays the saxophone with a local band.

TONY BYRNE

LOCAL GOVERNMENT IN BRITAIN

Everyone's Guide to How It All Works

SEVENTH EDITION

PENGUIN BOOKS

PENGUIN BOOKS

Published by the Penguin Group
Penguin Books Ltd, 27 Wrights Lane, London w8 5TZ, England
Penguin Putnam Inc., 375 Hudson Street, New York, New York 10014, USA
Penguin Books Australia Ltd, Ringwood, Victoria, Australia
Penguin Books Canada Ltd, 10 Alcorn Avenue, Toronto, Ontario, Canada M4V 3B2
Penguin Books (NZ) Ltd, Private Bag 102902, NSMC, Auckland, New Zealand

Penguin Books Ltd, Registered Offices: Harmondsworth, Middlesex, England

First published 1981
Second edition 1983
Third edition 1985
Fourth edition 1986
Fifth edition 1990
Reprinted with revisions 1992
Sixth edition 1994
Seventh edition 2000
10 9 8 7 6 5 4 3 2 1

The artwork for all the figures throughout this book
was prepared by Nigel Andrews at Capricorn Design

Set in 10/12.75 pt Monotype Baskerville
Typeset by Rowland Phototypesetting Ltd, Bury St Edmunds, Suffolk
Printed in England by Clays Ltd, St Ives plc

In memory of C. F. P.

'. . . local self-government is the life-blood
of liberty', (J. L. Motley, *The Rise of the
Dutch Republic*, 1853)

CONTENTS

LIST OF TEXT FIGURES

LIST OF TABLES

GLOSSARY
See also Index

Abatement the withholding of central grant to a local authority: see Holdback, below

ACA the area cost adjustment to grants whereby account is taken of the variations in the cost of providing of local services, e.g. as between rural and urban areas

ACC The Association of County Councils: one of several societies of particular types of local authority (p. 469)

Accountability the condition of being held responsible and answerable for decisions and actions (or inactions) which affect others and which are usually undertaken on their behalf: typically officers are accountable to councillors (members) and the latter are accountable to the local populace and electors (p. 62)

Action Zones areas, usually in towns/cities, where public, private and other resources are concentrated to combat multiple deprivation (p. 578)

AEF Aggregate External Finance (replaces Aggregate Exchequer Grant; see p. 349)

Agency where a public sector body performs a service on behalf of another (usually for reimbursement, and based on a 'service level agreement' or SLA)

Agenda 21 see Local agenda 21

AMA The Association of Metropolitan Authorities: a local authority association, for those in metropolitan areas (p. 469)

ARD Acquired Rights Directive (see TUPE below).

Association of London Government (ALG) the local government association for London authorities (p. 469)

Audit the checking of local councils' income and expenditure to detect errors, abuse, waste or illegality (p. 395)

Balanced council where no party has an overall majority of seats; otherwise known as 'hung council' or 'NOC' (no overall control) (p. 250)

Balances accumulated surpus of income over expenditure which are held in reserve for spending (usually on capital items); also known as 'Reserves' (p. 392)

BCA see Credit Approvals

Beacon councils are those which have been identified as having shown excellence in their performance and thus provide models for others to follow; they are 'rewarded' with extra powers and funds as a result (p. 596). (There are also some beacon schools which are to set an example to others.)

Benchmark a measure or standard used as a criterion for judging services (p. 594)

Best value is the principle of providing and continuously improving services to clear standards, covering both cost and quality by the most economic, effective and efficient means available (p. 593)

BIDs Business Improvement Districts (p. 366)

Billing authorities are the councils which collect council tax (p. 354)

Block grant central government's financial aid to local authorities; it is 'unhypothecated', i.e. it is not directly allocated to particular services; it forms the major part of the Revenue Support Grant (p. 351)

Borough (or in Scotland, **Burgh**) an old term still used to denote certain (mainly urban) local authorities entitled to have a mayor (or provost) instead of a chairman of the council, and other minor privileges. In England, such Borough (or district) councils may be metropolitan (of which London Boroughs are a particular case) or non-metropolitan (p. 47)

Budget requirement is the amount a council estimates as its planned spending after deducting any funding from fees and use of reserves; it is met from government grants, business rates and council tax. It is this figure which is 'capped' (see below)

By-laws legally enforceable regulations created by the council and which help to control social life in the local community (p. 76)

Capital expenditure spending on 'real' and costly items (highways, land, housebuilding, machinery etc.), cf. current or revenue expenditure (on wages, heating, etc.) (p. 381)

Capping the placing, by central government, of an upper limit on the proposed budget and council tax levied by local authorities; formerly known as rate-capping (p. 360)

Cash limits the maximum allowance made (usually by the government) for increases in the cost of expenditure due to inflation (prices and wages increases) (p. 429)

Caucus the inner group of a political party (p. 167)

CCN the County Councils Network (p. 473)

CCT compulsory competitive tendering, the requirement that local authorities invite firms to bid for contracts to supply services otherwise provided directly ('in-house') by the authority itself (p. 345)

Challenge funding finance from the central government for which councils have to make reasoned applications or 'bids', e.g. Capital Challenge, City Challenge, etc. (p. 386)

Chief Executive Officer (CEO) a chief local official who acts as head of the local authority's team of chief officers; they often head their own department and may sometimes be entitled Chief Administrative Officer, General Manager or Director of Administration (p. 299)

CIPFA the Chartered Institute of Public Finance and Accountancy, comprising accountants and financial managers from local government and the public services; publish data and journals and help in the development of SSAPs (see below)

Circular a government document sent to local authorities for the purpose of explanation or guidance, on legislation etc. (p. 428). (But note there are also 'circulars' sent out to local authorities by the local authorities' associations, and others sent to local parties by party central offices.)

Clawback The mechanism whereby 'excess' spending of a council results in some loss of grant for payments of council tax benefit (p. 591)

COG Chief Officers' Group or management team (p. 307)

Collection funds local authority financial pools comprising receipts built up from government grants, council tax and business rates (p. 338)

Commissioner for Local Administration (CLA) popularly known as the 'ombudsman', he or she is responsible for investigating complaints against local councils (p. 412)

Community charge a flat rate tax or levy; otherwise known as resident's charge or poll tax, now defunct (p. 363)

Community council a very local and small-scale form of local government, found in Wales and Scotland (p. 522)

Community politics concern and action involving very local issues at street or neighbourhood level (p. 529)

Corporate management a system whereby senior administrators (especially chief officers) and/or councillors regularly meet to determine, and coordinate, the execution of policy through a unified or collective approach (p. 255)

COSLA the Convention of Scottish Local Authorities (p. 470)

Council tax a tax for local authorities; levied on each household according to value of property but allowing a 25 per cent discount for single adult households, and perhaps other reductions (p. 369)

Creative accounting the use of financial devices and procedures (such as adjusting allocations and nomenclatures) to present expenditure accounts in such a way as to maximize grant entitlement and to minimize or escape government spending (capital or revenue) limits or penalties (p. 383)

Credit approvals authorization by the government for councils to borrow; can be Basic (BCA) or Supplementary (SCA) (p. 384)

Derogation a special relaxation or redetermination of the government's council tax cap

DETR the Department for the Environment, Transport and the Regions; the central government department which deals most with local authorities in England

Devolution the handing over of power from the centre to other bodies; such devolution may be legislative or administrative or financial (or all three, as with the Scottish Parliament). The central government and Parliament may devolve power (to regional bodies, local authorities, quangos, etc.; so may local authorities) (p. 69)

DFEE the Department for Education and Employment

Direct labour (DLO) use of a council's own workforce, instead of an outside contractor; also Direct Service Organization (DSO) (p. 345)

Director a local authority chief officer such as Director of Social Services (p. 260)

Employers' Agency negotiates on pay and conditions (p. 284)

Financial year the period from 1 April in one year to 31 March in the following year

Four Cs apply in Best value: Challenge, Compare, Consult, Compete (p. 594)

GLC the Greater London Council; the former top tier of London's government, abolished 1986 (p. 120)

GLA the Greater London Authority (p. 123)

GREA Grant Related Expenditure Assessment: a central-estimate of what each local authority needs to spend; it helps determine (block) grants to councils (p. 351); but see SSA below

HIPS Housing Investment Programmes: what the government agrees councils should spend on housing (building, repairs, renovation grants); may alternatively refer to Health Improvement (pp. 383, 595)

HMI Her Majesty's Inspector (p. 427)

Holdback the withholding of some of the (block) grant to those councils which exceed the spending targets set by the government (p. 548)

Hung (or balanced) council where no party has an overall majority; there is no overall control (or NOC) (p. 250)

Hypothecation the allocation of funds to particular items (p. 385)

ICSA the Institute of Chartered Secretaries and Administrators

IDA the Improvement and Development Agency, advises councils on management and operational good practice (p. 284)

ILEA the Inner London Education Authority: a special body, abolished in 1990, which was responsible for education in part of the Greater London area (p. 118)

INLOGOV the Institute of Local Government Studies, part of Birmingham University (p. 290)

IRRV Institute of Revenues, Rating and Valuation (p. 290)

LAFS the annual Local Authority Financial Settlement in which spending and government grant aid is determined (p. 374)

LASS local authority (personal) social services department(s) (p. 100)

LBA the London Boroughs Association (p. 431)

LCC London County Council (p. 114)

LGA the Local Government Association (p. 470)

LGMB Local Government Management Board (p. 284)

Local agenda 21 derives from the 1992 international agreement on environmental protection and sustainable development; involves local strategies to incorporate this principle into local policies and activities (70 per cent of councils are so committed)

Local authority associations groupings of councils of the same type (p. 470); the LGA is more general

Local income tax (LIT) a proposed council tax on income-receivers (p. 361)

Metropolitan a conurbation area containing metropolitan districts (or boroughs) and, until 1986, metropolitan counties (p. 47)

MPO the Managerial and Principal Officers association

NALGO a trade union: the National and Local Government Officers' Association (now UNISON) (p. 284)

Neighbourhood councils very local, non-executive, semi-official bodies (p. 526)

Net expenditure gross or total spending on a service from which is deducted or offset income from charges (and, in some definitions, specific grants) (p. 335, 551)

NLGN the New Local Government Network, a pressure group seeking to modernize and enhance local government

NOC no overall control (p. 162)

Non-domestic rates (or NNDR) a tax on business properties; known as the unified business rate, it is determined by the government and its proceeds distributed to local authorities (p. 364)

OFSTED Office for Standards of Education, the schools inspection service (p. 595)

Ombudsman see Commissioner above

OMT Officers' Management Team (p. 260)

Partnership the forming of an association or relationship between a council and another agency in the community, typically through a contract as with a business or voluntary organization, but often too with public sector bodies such as the NHS and other councils (p. 561)

Penalties loss of grant where a council exceeds GREA and/or target (p. 547)

Performance indicators (PIs) the measures used to assess the efficiency and effectiveness of councils' service provision (p. 593)

PFI is the Private Finance Initiative whereby private capital is brought in to local (and central) government projects (p. 387)

PIs are Performance indicators (p. 593)

Planning gain the benefit or asset that a local authority may derive from negotiations with developers who seek planning permission, e.g. a leisure facility (pp. 95, 384)

Policy and Resources Committee (P and R) the main committee of the council; here councillors are responsible for overall policy, management and finance (p. 258)

Poll tax a local tax or levy, collected from those listed on the register of residents or electors, see community charge above (p. 363)

PORPs politically restricted posts for officers (p. 297)

PPPs Public–Private Partnerships (p. 387)

Precept the council tax collected by charging authorities (district councils) on behalf of county councils, parish/community councils or for joint authorities/boards (p. 354)

Prescribed expenditure allocation (PEA) the blocks of capital expenditure allocated to local authorities by the government (p. 384)

Private Finance Initiative or **PFI**: see above

Privatization contracting out councils' work to private firms (p. 344)

PSS social services department of the local authority (p. 100)

PTAs Passenger Transport Authorities (p. 93)

PWLB the Public Works Loan Board: a government body which makes loans to local authorities (p. 382)

Qualgo quasi-local government organization; a form of 'quango' or semi-independent board in the field of local (as opposed to central) administration such as the ILEA, Police and Fire Authorities and Passenger Transport Authorities (p. 109)

Quango quasi-autonomous, non-government organization, a non-elected public sector body, semi-independent of the state (p. 5)

Rate-capping the placing of an upper limit on councils' or joint boards' rates/precepts; now budget-capping or council tax-capping (p. 360)

Rates a tax on property levied by councils for their own or (as a precept) others' revenue; based on property's (rateable) value (p. 354)

RDA Regional Development Agency, created in 1999 to promote economic growth, investment and training in eight regions plus London (p. 532)

Reserves see Balances

Resident's charge a local tax collected from those living in the area of a local authority; similar to community charge/poll tax (p. 363)

Residuary bodies panels or groups of government appointees who handle and wind up the remaining affairs and commitments of the abolished metropolitan county councils and the GLC (p. 52)

Revenue budget the main financial statement of a local authority containing details of planned revenue income and expenditure for the forthcoming year, often supported by information relating to previous years and projections for the future

RSG Revenue Support Grant (sometimes known as Standard Spending Grant) (p. 352)

Safety net the transfer of funds from gaining authorities to losing authorities in the early years of introducing the system of the unified business rate and community charge (p. 369)

SAUS the School of Advanced Urban Studies, part of Bristol University

Section 137 expenditure which is permitted (up to a maximum per head, e.g. £4.50) for anything which is in the interests of the area but not otherwise authorized (p. 78); largely superseded under the Local Government Act 2000

Section 151 officer the chief finance officer (p. 302)

Shire the non-metropolitan county (p. 46)

SIGOMA Special Interest Group of Municipal Authorities (p. 473)

Single regeneration budget (SRB) one of the Challenge funding arrangements for which councils bid (usually on the basis of a comprehensive scheme and involving a partnership) (p. 535)

SOLACE the Society of Local Authority Chief Executives (p. 304)

Special responsibility allowances payments to councillors with additional duties (p. 212)

SRB see Single regeneration budget above

SSA or Standard Spending Assessment is the basis of the system for distributing government grants to local authorities, such that each can achieve a standard level of service within the total grant the government can afford; the SSA for each service and each council takes account of local authorities' differing needs (through a formula which identifies population size, structure etc); the government's estimate of what local authorities should spend to achieve a common level of service provision (p. 352)

SSAP Statement of Standard Accountancy Practice describes methods of accounting (approved by the accountancy bodies), a number of which are being developed for particular application to local authority accounting practice

SSD local authority social services department (p. 100)

SSG Standard Spending Grant (also known as Revenue Support Grant) (p. 352)

Stakeholder members of the community who have a particular interest in the activities of the local authority such as service users, employees, partners, suppliers (p. 388)

Standards Committee in each council oversees conduct and helps enforce discipline. (Standards Commissions are independent bodies which reinforce the work of Standards Committee) (p. 229)

Sustainable development economic and social activity which seeks to avoid or minimize damage to the environment

Surcharge a financial penalty on those responsible for illegal spending (p. 396)

Supplementary rate (or precept) an extra levy, in addition to the regular, annual local tax (p. 548)

SWD local authority social work department (Scotland) (p. 100)

Taper the diminishing proportion of grant attracted by a council's spending when it exceeds a threshold level (p. 547)

Target a guideline level of council expenditure set by the government (p. 547)

Transitional relief (or community charge reduction) government subsidy to reduce the community charge/poll tax for those who would otherwise experience excessive increases

TUPE the Transfer of Undertakings (Protection of Employment) Regulations (p. 544)

Unified business rate (UBR) see non-domestic rates (p. 364)

Unitary single tier and all- or most-purpose authorities (p. 55)

Ultra vires beyond the powers; illegal (p. 75)

VFM value for money (p. 400)

WLGA the Local Government Association of Wales (p. 469)

ZBB Zero Base Budgeting; theoretically it implies analysing or justifying any expenditure at all on a service/function and starting from scratch, cf. Programme Budgeting (PPB) more used in times of economic growth and incrementalism (p. 390)

PREFACE TO THE FIRST EDITION

There is much public ignorance of and misunderstanding about local government: according to one survey, some 20 per cent of the British public cannot accurately name a single local government service. But local government is not unique in this respect, judging by the similar results produced by surveys of public understanding of the national government, the EEC and the legal system.

Such widespread ignorance, sometimes referred to as 'political illiteracy', may be understandable if not excusable. It takes energy, persistence and patience to master the intricacies of any large organization, be it the Ford motor company, the National Health Service or a government department such as the Ministry of Agriculture.

This book seeks to provide a reasonably clear and up-to-date account of what local government is, what it does and how it does it. I have aimed to achieve a balance between description and analysis, between law and practice and between institutions and issues. Being based essentially on secondary sources, the book makes no claim to originality, nor does it attempt to contribute to theory.

In writing this book, I have had in mind a number of overlapping groups of reader:

(1) the *consumer* who needs to know how local political decisions affect him or her;

(2) the *activist* who, as a citizen, wants a part in the decision-making process;

(3) the *student* who seeks an understanding of local government as part of his or her academic studies;

(4) the potential or *new entrant* to local government who wishes to know something about the world of the local authority.

It is ambitious to try to satisfy all these groups, and in a book of this size one can hope to do little more than provide an outline and an introduction to certain themes. I have treated the subject in a fairly conventional way, and I make no apology for this, since the book is intended as an introductory text. Detailed references, and a bibliography of more specialized works, are provided for the benefit of those who wish to pursue the various themes and issues in greater depth. Some of the works mentioned, such as Stanyer's *Understanding Local Government*, are highly original and commendable.

Comments or questions from readers will be welcome so that the text can be suitably amended at a later date.

Local government is a branch of public administration, and its study helps to form one of the 'social sciences': that is, studies which seek to apply to social affairs the scientific methods of observation, comparison and conjecture. But social science is not an exact science and there are many areas where ideas about relationships and the causes and consequences of events remain inconclusive. There are many 'ifs and buts' because we are dealing with a world (human society) which lacks certainty or uniformity; it is dangerous therefore to generalize. This is perhaps especially true of local government in Britain, which includes 500 principal local authorities and covers such different territories as England, Scotland and Wales, highlands, lowlands, conurbations, market towns and seaports. Each area and local authority is unique: it has its own traditions, history, problems and social structure . . . in short its own political culture.

However, as the late Professor J. Mackintosh said, the study of political institutions and theories connected with it depends on the patient accumulation of instances. Furthermore, local authorities do have many common features and are subject to a number of common influences and constraints, not the least important of which is the law. Consequently we can say that a local government 'system' does exist and we are able (with caution) to suggest some general tendencies which operate within it.

One thing which can be said with certainty is that local authorities live in exciting times! Nationally, our economic performance has faltered and we have sought salvation (at least in part) by joining the

Common Market. At the same time, a diminished faith in our political system has been manifested both in a review and reform of a number of our institutions (the civil service, the House of Commons, the National Health Service) and in our adoption or contemplation of certain exotic devices (ombudsmen, referendums, proportional representation, a written constitution).

Local government has not escaped scrutiny: indeed it can claim to have had more than its fair share of searching inquiry over the past twenty years; and since the 1960s local authorities have undergone substantial changes in their structure, in the allocation of responsibilities and in their internal organization. Confidence and optimism, sustained and reflected in their expanding budgets, have given way to retrenchment of spending plans and reductions in services. Local authorities have (perhaps only for the moment) been spared the challenge posed by devolution, but they are experiencing a longer-term and less conspicuous threat. This has been described as 'de-localization' and it is caused by the loss of certain services, the greater quest for equal (national) standards and the insinuation into local politics of national parties and pressure groups. In these ways local authorities are being homogenized – just as our town centres are losing their local character by the spread of national chain stores and building societies. However, there may be some gains from these developments, and in any case they are still far from complete.

Students, councillors and officers have had to cope with these developments, and it has not always been easy. This book deals with a number of them. Its preparation has been stimulating for the author, but it would have been an impossible task without the generous assistance of a number of friends, colleagues, specialist practitioners and students (past and present). My debt to published work will be obvious to the reader. I have also received helpful information and documents from central and local officials in England, Wales and Scotland. In particular, however, I wish to acknowledge the help I have received from the Rt Hon. Edward du Cann, MP; from Brian Bailey, John Blackmore, John Chant, Mike Dearden, Mr S. E. Harwood, John Pentney, David Perrin, Brian Tanner, Barry Taylor, Phil Trevelyan and Colin Vile (all of Somerset County Council); from Don Alder, Michael Clark, John Davis, Mr I. Locke, Mr S. Price, Mike

Porter and Derek Rumsey (all of Taunton Deane Borough Council); and from Rosemary Morris (Kent County Council). I am confident of the accuracy of their answers: I only hope I have asked the right questions. Any errors of omission or commission are entirely mine and while I have tried to make it entirely up to date, the book has come to fruition at a time of considerable change in local government.

I am also grateful to David Hencke of the *Guardian* and David Peschek of Local Government Information Services for advising me on certain sources, and to David Smith of the Conservative Central Office for allowing me access to local government records.

I should also like to thank my teaching colleagues Barrie Foster and Russell Pearce; the library staffs of the Somerset College of Arts and Technology, Bristol and Exeter Universities and Taunton library (in particular Bryan McEnroe); the NJC for allowing me to quote extracts from their scheme; and the Controller of HM Stationery Office for his permission to reproduce material from official sources.

Neil Middleton of Penguin Books has been most considerate in regard to unavoidable delays over deadlines. And his encouragement and help have been most welcome.

Finally, I must thank my wife Sari and my children Celie and Dan for their support and for enduring my more than usual preoccupation and periods of silence.

Tony Byrne   *Taunton, February 1981*

PREFACE TO THE SECOND EDITION

An American wit, parodying Lord Acton, has opined that 'Government is boring; Local Government bores absolutely'. Many people in local government would it were true! They seek more settled times – a return to normalcy, where they can get on with administration and the delivery of services, instead of adapting to the latest change and awaiting the next one. Professor Stewart's description of local government as 'the government of difference' is perhaps more apt, though for unfortunate reasons.

The exciting times referred to in the First Edition of this book have continued and this new edition takes account of the related causal and consequential changes (up to January 1983). The book was originally scheduled as a reprint with corrections. Fortunately I was able to take advantage of the opportunity to thoroughly revise the text and bring it up to date; I am grateful to the publishers for agreeing to this.

I must also express my gratitude to a number of people who have contacted me or otherwise communicated their generous and encouraging remarks about the first edition, or have provided me with additional information or perspectives. In particular I wish to thank Professor George Jones of the London School of Economics, William Thornhill of Sheffield University, Professor Ken Newton of Dundee University, Professor D. E. Regan of Nottingham University, John Gyford of University College London, Alan Parker of Teesside Polytechnic, Mr K. J. Bridge, Chief Executive, Humberside County Council, and Arthur Godfrey of the *Local Government Review*. I am also grateful to Peter Stuart of Somerset County Council Law Library, Bryan McEnroe of Taunton Library, Stuart Macwilliam of Exeter University Library and Phil Lawton of Somerset Health Authority.

For local government watchers there has been a lot to see in the past two years – legislation, legal battles, resource restrictions and service reductions. Unfortunately our sights are being narrowed here by government economy measures. Thus as part of the 'Rayner exercise' in cutting 'waste' in public expenditure, the OPCS has now ceased to collect and collate the local government election returns; consequently, after forty years, it is now impossible to follow trends and patterns in local government voting turnout. This, in itself, is not a vitally important matter; but it is another indication of the unfortunate recent tendency to down-grade Local Government in Britain.

Tony Byrne   *Taunton, January 1983*

PREFACE TO THE THIRD EDITION

It is tempting to suggest that for local government in Britain George Orwell's choice of the year 1984 was remarkably prescient, for 1984 saw the passage into law of the Rates Act. This permits, for the first time, the limitation of local councils' rates by (Big Brother) central government; and eighteen local authorities have been selected to have their rates thus capped in the year 1985–6.

As this legislation proceeded through Parliament there was massive protest and lobbying, and considerable opposition among MPs, including many prominent members and former leaders of the Government's own party; indeed one former (Conservative) Secretary of State for the Environment described the legislation as 'a deplorable Bill which raises major constitutional issues. It is a classic example of elective dictatorship' (Geoffrey Rippon, House of Commons, 22 December 1983).

With the Government's overwhelming majority (of 144 seats) in the House of Commons, parliamentary opposition is weak and frustrated, and as a result many detect that the task of opposition has, at least to some extent, shifted out to local government. In so far as this is (or is perceived to be) true, it helps to explain the acrimony which has characterized local–central relations in recent years – and is likely to continue, with arguments over rate-capping and derogation, and over targets and grants: already a number of councils are threatening to 'do a Liverpool' and deliberately to refuse or delay the declaration of a rate/budget. And 1985–6 will witness the debacle over the abolition of the metropolitan authorities and the redistribution of their responsibilities; members (especially Labour members) in metropolitan counties are resigning or threatening to resign their seats in order to force by-elections and thus test public opinion on the issue in the hope of embarrassing the Government and discrediting its plans.

Such is the continuing pace of change in the world of local government that I have found it necessary to undertake a further revision of the text, for which opportunity I am grateful to Penguin Books. However, I have left some of the figures unaltered either because the recent changes are not significant, or (as with the election turnout figures) because the data is unfortunately not available.

Tony Byrne   *Taunton, September 1984*

PREFACE TO THE FOURTH EDITION

So much continues to happen in the world of local government that to blink is to miss something – legal judgments, elections, nominations for rate-capping, financial brinkmanship, changes in party control, fluxing conventions – and, of course, the annual (at least) Local Government Act (there have actually been twelve such Acts since 1979).

Ideally, therefore, to observe local government in Britain, one needs a compound eye, for local government is not a single entity. Local authorities may exhibit a number of common features, and there is an underlying legal framework. But the essence of local government – and ultimately its *raison d'etre* – is its diversity, as local authorities serve differing communities. Local government might be described as 'bespoke' government in respect of local policy choices and decisions, and local procedures and practice – at least in theory, if not practice.

In practice, there are strong forces at work which are seriously undermining this potential for local choice and diversity. John Banham, the Controller of the Audit Commission, has described Britain as 'a highly centralized society with a central government machine that lacks – and inevitably will always lack – the information, skills and attitudes to manage the services for which ministers are nominally accountable to Parliament . . . The public expenditure process and Parliamentary procedures perpetuate the myth of central control. The mythology is dangerous since it simultaneously encourages delusions of competence at the centre and a dangerous, dependent attitude at the local level . . . Indeed public administration in Britain appears to combine the worst of all worlds: most of the costs associated with centrally managed economies but few of the potential benefits. The choice is clear: replicate in Great Britain the present administrative arrangements in Northern Ireland, or devolve much more power, responsibility and accountability to the local level. From a management point of view, least (central) government is best government' (*Public Administration*, Winter 1985).

He might have added that it is also best from a democratic point of view. Indeed, recently, Patrick Jenkin, the former Secretary of State substantially responsible for the abolition of the metropolitan counties and the GLC and for the introduction of rate-capping, has himself spoken of '. . . a greater and greater degree of centralization . . . that measure of central control is really hostile, inimical to what local authorities stand for. They ought to be substantially independent bodies. The more that central government tries to influence them the less efficient the system has become.'

Things might change. Particularly important here is the system of local government finance. To quote John Banham again, he describes it as 'a most ghastly shambles . . . one of the biggest administrative bog-ups it's been my misfortune ever to see . . . part of a system that's generating waste and inefficiency at local level on a scale that I find deeply depressing.' The opposition parties are highly critical of the grant system, and the Government itself has announced proposals for changing it.

Meanwhile, in this new edition, I have tried to incorporate a number of the recent events and changes. I would like to thank my wife Sari for her painstaking revision of the index, and for her vital support throughout.

Tony Byrne   *Taunton, May 1986*

PREFACE TO THE FIFTH EDITION

Since the first edition of this book there have been over fifty pieces of
legislation dealing with local government. Despite recent reassurances
from local government Ministers that there is to be a period of stability
and consolidation, there are already signs of further Government-
inspired change for local authorities – in finance (in response to
problems with the poll tax), in functions (planning, pollution, waste
disposal) and perhaps in structure. This is very unsettling for those
who just want to get on with the job of providing public services.

Yet government is about change and how to manage it. It is
said that good management copes with change, better management
anticipates change, and the best management creates change (though
presumably not just for its own sake). Certainly, local authorities
experience their own organic or self-induced change – in party politics,
in local problems, in their own management arrangements, for
example.

This new edition seeks to take account of such changes, and also
those arising from the Local Government Finance Act 1988 and the
Widdicombe Report (1986), with its consequential Local Government
and Housing Act 1989.

I wish to thank Peter Stuart, Somerset's Law Librarian, for his help.
And my debt to those who write and concern themselves with the place
of local government in Britain today is at least partially acknowledged in
the References and Further Reading section.

Tony Byrne   *Taunton, May 1990*

Note on 1992 revised reprint In this reprint, I have made a number
of amendments and additions – such is the volatile state of local

government. A fuller treatment will be given in the next edition: the General Election should by then have resolved some uncertainties.

Tony Byrne   *Taunton, February 1992*

PREFACE TO THE SIXTH EDITION

It would be trite to remark that much has happened in and to local government since the previous edition of this book. With 150 pieces of legislation affecting local authorities since 1979, change has become endemic. Some of the changes are continuations of existing developments – contracting out, opting out, etc., whilst others are new, or rather repeats of earlier policies, such as the introduction of a new system of local tax, the redistribution of responsibilities and, above all, the reorganization of the structure of local government.

Before the last General Election (1992) a prominent government minister, Chris Patten, declared that local government needed a reorganization 'like a hole in the head'. By the time this new edition is published the legislation will have determined the details of the new structure for Scotland and Wales, and the fate of the English authorities will be settled soon after.

Once the reorganization has taken place (no simple or quick matter) local government may be able to look forward to a period of relative calm. The Prime Minister said he wishes to see an improvement in general–local relations and a renaissance in local government. The introduction of the Secondment Initiative Programme and the government's newly established (1993) regional offices should facilitate better understanding and coordination with local authorities – all perhaps made easier with a (long-heralded) revival in the economy.

This is not to suggest that problems will not remain – inadequate sources of local tax, loss of functions to non-elected bodies, etc. This makes it all the more regrettable that the reorganization has not been accompanied by a fundamental examination of the role of local government and its financing. If there is a calm, it may be short-lived.

Tony Byrne   *April 1994*

PREFACE TO SEVENTH EDITION

It doesn't get any easier. But then, it's never dull either!

In the 1990s, local government has been the focus of an unprecedented amount of research attention – in particular by the Commission on Local Democracy, the Joseph Rowntree Foundation, the Local Government Management Board, the Economic and Social Research Council, the Fabian Society, the DETR, the Local Government Commission in England and the Scottish Commission on Local Government. Some of this is ongoing and more will emerge from the Local Authority/Research Council Inititative (LARCI). One tangible result is the volume of legislation, with a dozen bills affecting local government in the current session of Parliament.

I have tried to incorporate their major findings in this new edition. It also seeks to deal with the developments in structure, party politics, management and finance which have occurred since the early 1990s, and to anticipate further changes, especially those resulting from the government's ten-year modernization programme. Many in local government are quite optimistic that there really is to be a new and better relationship or partnership with the central government, though others feel disappointed or are reserving judgement.

I am indebted to many people and organizations who have helped supply me with material, some of which is reproduced by permission, and the copyright for which is retained by them. Responsibility for any errors or inaccuracies is mine.

Tony Byrne   *Taunton and Plymouth, January 2000*

RECENT LANDMARKS

1966-9 Royal Commissions on Local Government in England (and Redcliffe-Maud Report) and Scotland (Wheatley Report)

1967 Maud Report on Management in Local Government

1970 Local Authorities Social Services Act – social services departments created

✗1972 Local Government Act (1973 in Scotland) – reorganized structure

1972 Bains and Paterson Reports on management in the new authorities

1973 National Health Service Act – from 'tripartite' to 'unified' structure; local authorities lost health function to Area Health Authorities.

1974 Local Government Act – Local Commissioners (ombudsmen) created (1975 in Scotland)

1976 Layfield Committee Report on Local Government Finance

1976 Education Act – compulsory comprehensive schools

1976 'The party's over' (Anthony Crosland, Secretary of State)

1978 'Organic Change' White Paper – proposed increasing the role of city councils

1979 Education Act – rescinds 1976 Act

1980 Local Government Planning and Land Act – introduced block grants; competitive tendering; compulsory sale of council housing

1980 Education Act – parent governors; parents' right to choose school

1981 Spending targets and penalties introduced

1982 Local Government Finance Act – supplementary rates abolished; Audit Commission established

1982 Housing Benefit introduced

1984 Rates Act – introduced rate-capping

1985 Local Government Act – abolished GLC and Metropolitan County Councils

1985 Local Government (Access to Information) Act

1986 Widdicombe Report on the Conduct of Local Authority Business

1987 Abolition of Domestic Rates etc. (Scotland) Act – introduced community charge or poll tax

1988 Local Government Act – further compulsory tendering of council services

1988 Local Government Finance Act – community charge/poll tax for England and Wales; and national business rates

1988 Education Reform Act – local financial management in schools; power to opt out of LEA control; national curriculum; polytechnics independent of LEAs

1988 Housing Act – opting out; 'pick a landlord/tenant'

1989 Local Government and Housing Act – Government's response to Widdicombe Report: restricts officers' political activities; requires parties to share committee seats; bans councils' rent subsidies

1989 Children Act – introduces a new statutory framework for local authorities' work with children and families

1990 National Health Service and Community Care Act – removes local authority representation on health authorities; local authorities given the lead role in arranging the provision of social care in the community

1990 Environmental Protection Act – increased responsibilities for local authorities

1991 Criminal Justice Act – implications for local authorities' costs

1992 Local Government Act – Commission to review structure and electoral arrangements in England's non-metropolitan areas

1992 White Paper on structure of local government in Wales

1992 Local Government Finance Act – abolishes community charge/poll tax, introduces council tax

1992 Education (Schools) Act – sets up independent inspection system (OFSTED); schools to be inspected every four years; school performance indicators to be published

1992 Further and Higher Education Act establishes further education and sixth-form colleges as corporations independent of LEAs (in 1993)

1993 White Papers (two) on police – to be managed more independently by police authorities; councillor representation to be reduced to one half

1993 White Paper on structure in Scotland and (a second) in Wales

1993 Trade Union Reform and Employment Rights Act – provides for Careers service to be privatized

1993 Leasehold Reform, Housing and Urban Development Act – extends sale of council houses through rents-to-mortgage scheme; council tenants' rights to repairs made statutory; sets up Urban Regeneration Agency

1993 Education Act – promotes school opt-outs to grant-maintained (GM) status; sets up Funding Agency for GM schools; sets up Schools Curriculum and Assessment Authority (SCAA); inefficient LEA schools to be subject to take-over by specifically appointed bodies ('commissions')

1993 Working party report on councils' internal management

1993–4 Reports by Local Government Commission on the structure of local authorities in parts of England

1994 Local Government (Wales) Act – reorganized into 22 unitary authorities

1994 Local Government etc. (Scotland) Act – reorganized into 32 unitary authorities; water transferred to three separate bodies

1994 Police and Magistrates Courts Act – implements 1993 proposals

1996 Report by House of Lords' Select Committee 'Rebuilding Trust'

1997 Local Government (Contracts) Act confirms councils' powers to enter into contracts for private provision of services and assets (including PFI and capital items)

1997 Local Government and Rating Act – enhances powers of parishes; removes rates exemption from Crown property.

1997 Referendums on devolution in Wales and Scotland

1998 School Standards and Framework Act – limits infant classes to 30; requires nursery education provision; sets up Education Action Zones; abolishes Grant Maintained schools and re-casts schools into Community, Voluntary and Foundation categories; allows local ballots to abolish Grammars; allows more parents on to Governing bodies and LEA committees; requires LEAs to draw up education development plans; empowers Minister to take over failing LEAs and individual schools

1998 Government of Scotland Act – sets up devolved Parliament and Executive in Scotland with first elections in 1999

1998 Government of Wales Act – sets up devolved Assembly and Executive in Wales with first elections in 1999

1998 Regional Development Agencies Act – sets up bodies to oversee regional planning and economic strategy

1998 Referendum on London government

1998 Public Interest Disclosure Act – gives protection for those who report colleagues' corrupt behaviour

1998 Human Rights Act – incorporates the European Convention on Human Rights into UK Law

1998 Crime and Disorder Act – creates formal role for local authorities in community safety and anti-social behaviour initiatives

1998 White Paper, *Modern Local Government; In Touch with the People*

1999 White Paper, *Modernizing Social Services*

1999 Local Government Act – abolishes general capping; introduces system of Best Value (in 2000)

1999 Greater London Authority Act – creates elected mayor and assembly, with first elections in 2000

2000 Freedom of Information Act – gives a statutory right of access to information held by public bodies and imposes a duty to publish information

2000 Local Government Bill – allows local authorities to promote the economic, social and environmental well being of their areas, and develop comprehensive community strategies; removal of some central regulations; general introduction of new political management systems; new standards of conduct arrangements; allows for changes in election sequence; repeals Section 28 on publicity about homosexuality; abolishes surcharge

2000 Representation of the People Bill – introduces rolling electoral registers; allows flexibility in voting times and venues

2000 Political Parties Elections and Referendums Bill – sets up Electoral Commission to deal with boundaries and procedures for registration of parties and for referendums

1

WHAT LOCAL GOVERNMENT IS

In Britain, we all live in a local authority area – perhaps two or even three! The aim of this book is to uncover what many regard as the mystery of what these organizations are, what they do and how they do it.

The governance of a modern society is an enormous task. In Great Britain, for example, half of the nation's annual income flows through the hands of the government, and some 20 per cent of the labour force are employed in the state sector. Government is, therefore, a big and complex business.

For this reason most countries find it necessary to decentralize their administration, in other words to arrange for services to be provided and decisions to be made away from the centre or capital and 'in the field' or locally. Such decentralization can take a number of forms. The simplest is known as *deconcentration*, whereby the officers of the central government (the civil servants) are dispersed into local and regional offices such as the local tax or benefits office. Another simple form is *functional decentralization*, in which a particular service or function is hived off from the central government to a semi-independent organization commonly referred to as a 'quango' (quasi-autonomous non-governmental organization). Among their estimated 5,000, examples include the Post Office, the Arts Council, the British Council, the Gaming Board, the Housing Corporation, the Rural Development Commission, NHS Trusts, the Higher Education Funding Council and Police Authorities. *Regional devolution* (or regionalism) is more complex and involves the limited transfer by the central government of political and administrative authority to a regional body, such as the Scottish Parliament or the Welsh Assembly and their executives. Local government is an example of such devolution, but on a more local basis. Local government is self-government involving the administration of public affairs in each locality by a body of elected representatives of the local community known as the local authority (or council). Although subject to the central government in many ways, local authorities possess a considerable amount of responsibility and discretionary power.

Local government, then, is one of a number of forms of decentralization. This fact helps to explain why it can be so confusing: it resembles so many other administrative structures to be found in the modern state – ministries, departments, authorities, boards, corporations, agencies, bureaux, councils and so on. Consequently it is not surprising that many people mistakenly believe, for example, that local authorities run the hospitals (which are actually the responsibility of appointed Health Authorities or self-governing trusts) or think that social workers are paid by the Minister responsible for social services (in fact they are employed by the local authorities, who pay their salaries out of the rates and council tax). The situation has become much more diffuse in recent years. Consequently, the concept of *local governance* has emerged to reflect the fact that local areas are governed by a range of bodies, not just the 'local authority' or the 'council'.

Features of local government

There are, however, a number of characteristics which mark out local government as a distinctive form of public administration. Thus local government is *elected*. Although some areas (parishes and communities) are small enough to need only a simple meeting of all the local people, most local authorities consist of representatives chosen by the members of the community at properly constituted elections. These elected members form the local 'council', which then recruits the full-time paid staff of the authority, including engineers, accountants, teachers, clerks and bin-men. These employees resemble the State's civil servants and are organized at the town hall or county hall into departments such as the Education Department, the Housing Department or the Social Services Department.

It follows that local government is *multi-purpose*: every local authority

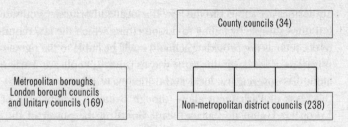

Figure 1 *The structure of British local government (since 1995/8)*

has many jobs to do and a variety of services to provide. An individual local authority may be responsible for the provision of schools, homes for the elderly and training centres for the disabled; fire services; road building and maintenance, and traffic management; and the control of the environment through the regulation of building and land development. By contrast, the 'quangos' and public corporations tend to be concerned with just one particular service or field of activity, such as health (the Health Authorities, the Food Standards Agency), culture (the Arts Council, the BBC) or racial discrimination (the Commission for Racial Equality).

The third feature of local government is the *local scale* of its operations: each authority has responsibility in its own area only. As we have seen, some of these areas (the parishes and communities) are very local in scale. But most of the more important authorities operate over the area of a county or over a small or large district (within or between counties).

Fourthly, local government has a quite clearly *defined structure*. This consists of either two tiers (made up of 34 large county councils plus 238 smaller district councils), or 169 single-tier councils. These all constitute the 'principal' local authorities, as illustrated in Figure 1 (though the diagram does not represent a hierarchical or power relationship between the two tiers). In addition, though not shown here, many parts of the country have parishes or communities making up a modest third tier.

The next feature of local government is that it is *subordinated* to the national authority, which is Parliament. Local authorities come into existence as a result of legislation passed by Parliament, and all such authorities are subject to the law. If a local authority steps outside the law (for example by failing to do something which the law requires it to do, such as not providing schools) it will be liable to the rigours and sanctions of the law in the same way as private people are. Parliament alone has sovereignty: local authorities exercise power to the extent that Acts of Parliament allow (though Britain's membership of the European Union now places some limits on the power of the UK Parliament).

Although local authorities carry out those responsibilities handed on to them by Parliament, it is misleading to see them simply as agents acting for the central government in the administration of certain services. While subject to certain controls operated by the central government, the local authorities work in partnership with it, and they possess a freedom and initiative which justifies their being described as bodies exercising local *self*-government.

Enabling them to do this, and the last important feature of local government, is the *local tax system*, comprising (from 1993) a local council tax on residents and a rate (or property tax) on businesses. Locally determined taxes (in the form of 'rates') have been collected by local authorities for centuries. Although local taxation has not been the chief source of local government incomes in recent years, it is still important (see Chapter 11) and provides local authorities with some degree of independence and flexibility.

Local government forms part of the administrative structure of the country, and it may be useful, before going further, to summarize the work of the two other main components of this administrative structure, namely central government and the quangos.

Central government and the quangos

Central government is composed of about a hundred Ministers of the Crown, responsible to Parliament. Most of them are elected MPs (from the majority party in the House of Commons), though some will be peers (members of the non-elected House of Lords). The central government forms the executive branch of the nation's political system, and it is headed by a Cabinet of senior Ministers, under the leadership of the Prime Minister. Central government is national, not local, and has to take the whole country into its consideration, administering services uniformly across the nation. Thus the services carried on are national, not local, in scale. The necessary finance is derived by the Treasury from national taxation.

Civil servants are recruited to carry out government policies and administer the statutes passed by Parliament. They are both advisers to the government and administrators of government policy. Although the main government departments (or Ministries) are in London (for the most part in the district of Whitehall), there are regional and local offices in the main towns and cities of Britain. So we have Ministers, each heading a government department, and civil servants or officials who are directly responsible to the Ministers. Each department has a hierarchical structure of civil servants ranging from the permanent secretaries at the top advising Ministers personally, down to the assistant clerical and administrative officers, who help to put the laws and regulations into effect at the community level (for example, by assessing and collecting income taxes, issuing licences, passports, keeping records, etc.).

Quasi-governmental organizations or 'quangos'* are independent agencies set up to perform some service or to administer a public sector activity free from direct government control (though subject to some restraints exercised by Ministers, who are responsible to Parliament). There are between 5,000 and 6,500[1] such bodies, and in addition to those mentioned (p. 1) examples include the Countryside Agency, English Nature, universities, the Regional Development Agencies, the national Tourist Boards, the British Library Board, the Royal Fine Arts Commission, the National Mobility Office, the Further Education Funding Council, the Museum Commission, British Waterways, the Atomic Energy Authority, the Independent Broadcasting Authority, and Remploy. At over £60 bn, quangos collectively are

---

* Quango is an acronym for quasi-autonomous, non-government organization. The term originated in the USA and referred to private businesses, such as the armaments industry, which depended overwhelmingly on government contracts. The term is now used more generally for appointed public bodies. Also sometimes known as Non-departmental public bodies (NDPBs) and as Extra-governmental organizations (EGOs), Non-elected agencies and as Non-elected public service organizations.

responsible for one fifth of public sector spending,[2] which is nearly as much as local authorities (see Chapter 11).

The role of these organizations varies. They may be *advisory* (for example the Qualifications and Curriculum Agency, or the British Safety Council); *executive* (the Business and Technical Education Council, the Bank of England or the Public Works Loan Board); *industrial–commercial* (the Post Office or British Nuclear Fuels); *promotional* (the Training Boards, English Heritage, the Millennium Commission, the Research Councils or the General Practice Finance Corporation); *regulatory* (the Competition Commission, OFWAT or OFSTED); *coordinating* (the National Blood Authority or the Environment Agency); *semi-judicial* (the Commission for Racial Equality, the Scottish Mental Welfare Commission or the Health and Safety Commission); or they may be *conciliatory* in function (the Advisory Conciliation and Arbitration Service or the Central Arbitration Council). Many in fact combine several roles and are therefore difficult to classify. For example, the Postal Services Commission is promotional and regulatory, in the commercial setting.

The number and variety of these organizations and bodies reflect the range of activities which fall within the sphere of 'government' in its widest sense. At the beginning of the last century, the main task of government was internal peace and defence against external enemies. Gradually government has widened its view and extended the scope of its activities, particularly with the development of the Welfare State and the 'managed' economy.

The financing and degree of control over these bodies exercised by government Ministries varies considerably. Most of the boards or managing committees, however, are appointed either by the Prime Minister or a Minister, and they are given a general responsibility defined in either a charter (like the BBC and the Arts Council) or a statute (like the Countryside Agency, the Local Government Commission, the Commission for New Towns and most of the others). The staff of these bodies are not civil servants as such, but they are public sector employees (of the particular corporation, commission, authority, council or board). Nevertheless, the ultimate political responsibility rests with the government Minister.

Quangos are given considerable freedom from direct government control so as to keep politics out of their day-to-day operations since this would be irrelevant or prejudicial to their various ostensible functions, whether commercial (as with the nationalized industries such as the Post Office) or cultural (such as the BBC) or semi-judicial (such as the Charity Commission).

While the creation and use of such extra- or quasi-government bodies is not new (going back to the nineteenth century or earlier), there has been a significant increase in recent years (at both national and local levels) with the consequence that elected self-government has been significantly superseded by such non-elected specialized bodies. This development, combined with 'privatization', the growth of partnerships and the increase in government control has, in effect transformed the situation: instead of *local government*, with the predominance of governmental activity undertaken by elected local councils, we now have *local governance* where there is greater plurality of provision and control, via local authorities, government departments, private and voluntary bodies, joint ventures and quangos.

The general administrative structure in Britain is summarized in Figure 2 on p. 9.

The justification for local government

Local government has existed for so long that it is difficult to imagine its disappearance. However, its experience in recent years has threatened not just its vitality but its viability. Consequently, it is worth considering some of the reasons which are advanced to justify its existence.

(1) Local government is seen as an *efficient* method of administering certain services. This efficiency is explained on one or more of the following grounds: (a) local authorities consist of members who are drawn from the local populace and who therefore have local knowledge or sensitivity and a commitment and responsiveness to the local area and its people; this specifically local focus makes for effective mediation of the different and conflicting interests (planning, traffic, school closure etc.) within the community; (b) local authorities are multi-purpose

bodies and can therefore, theoretically, secure a greater degree of coordination and policy integration: for example, since the same council may be responsible for planning, roads and housing, the liaison between these different services and departments is easier and closer; (c) public administration generally benefits from the existence of local authorities because they off-load responsibilities from central government departments and the civil service, who would otherwise be overburdened with work.

(2) Having a fair degree of independence, the local authorities can take initiatives and *experiment*: they can seek a variety of solutions to society's problems. In this way they may innovate and pioneer new services or methods of administration, and successful ideas may be spread to other authorities. For example, in 1847 Liverpool Council made the first appointment of a Medical Officer of Health; other authorities followed suit later. Similarly, certain cities in the late nineteenth century (notably London and Birmingham) developed the first council housing. More recently, individual local authorities have originated such schemes as devolved budgets to schools, free birth control, comprehensive education, mobile libraries, neighbourhood mediation, sale of council houses, community care packages, bottle banks, advice centres for housing or consumer affairs, rents-to-mortgages and free bus travel and special housing for pensioners; many local authorities, or even government, have since adopted these ideas.

(3) Local government can be said to encourage citizenship or *democracy* and to promote 'political education' in its widest sense. It does this by involving large numbers of people in the political decision-making process as electors or councillors. While people may find the affairs of a modern state too large and complex to understand, they will perhaps more easily and naturally participate with their neighbours in helping to manage local community affairs:

Nowhere has democracy ever worked well without a great measure of local self-government ... Where the scope of the political measures becomes so large that the necessary knowledge is almost exclusively possessed by the bureaucracy, the creative impulses of the private person must flag.[3]

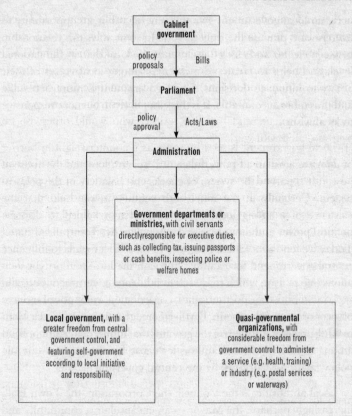

Figure 2 *British administrative structure*

In Britain, there are currently some 22,500 local government councillors, that is, members of the public who are elected to the principal local authorities.* A significant proportion of these are members of social groups which are distinctly under-represented in national politics, for example women and manual workers. Furthermore, experience in local government has frequently proved to be a stepping-stone to national politics: as many as one third of MPs are or have been local councillors.

Councillors of course are elected, and the frequent elections which

* In addition, there are some 10,000 parish or community councils.

occur in local government give the general public an opportunity to exercise and practise the right to vote. In some ways this relationship between elector and elected is closer at the local than at the national level, and helps to create an awareness among local voters of their ability to influence decisions. Local government is more accessible and thus more accountable. It is therefore likely to be more responsive to local wishes.

(4) Local government is seen by some as a counterweight, a barrier or *defence* against an all-powerful central government and the abuse of power; it is part of the system of checks and balances in the political system. Certainly in the nineteenth century it was held that the existence of a strong local government system helped to disperse political power and diminish the danger of an over-centralized state.[4] Today we tend to see local government more as a means to influence central government; for example, through the local authority associations (see p. 470), which may seek to influence government policy in such matters as transport subsidies, conservation, rural postal services or economic development. Furthermore, the diffusion of decision-making power is justified on the grounds that numerous errant policies among a variety of local authorities cause less harm than one big policy failure or 'cock-up' by the central government.

(5) Local authorities – the Council, the Corporation, the Town Hall, increasingly perhaps, the Mayor – can encapsulate a community and represent its *identity*. It can do this better than, say, a local major business or the football team because it is more comprehensive in scope. But mainly it is because it is subject to popular control, and *local* control stimulates local pride and identification.

(6) Local government may be justified simply on the grounds of *tradition* – that it has from time immemorial been a part of the British way of life, part of our heritage and of our culture. A more sophisticated view is that of Edmund Burke (1729–97): 'That which *is* must be good because it has stood the test of time.'

(7) Finally there is support for local government from those who, like the American Founding Fathers of the eighteenth century, believe that there should be no taxation without *representation* – that since local

authorities have the power to impose taxes (the council tax), the tax-payers should be represented on the body which determines how that money should be spent. This is a fundamental precept of parliamentary government (and has been since the signing of Magna Carta in 1215). Many feel it is equally applicable at the local level of government.

The Widdicombe Committee Report on *The Conduct of Local Authority Business* summarizes the case thus:

The value of local government stems from its three attributes of:
(a) pluralism, through which it contributes to the national political system;
(b) participation, through which it contributes to local democracy;
(c) responsiveness, through which it contributes to the provision of local needs through the delivery of services.[5]

This is an important statement since it emphasizes the governmental or politcal function of councils. For too long there has been a tendency to 'view local government almost exclusively as an instrument for the delivery of services'.[6] It goes on to add the comment that 'Local government has no independent right to exist. Its continued existence is based on the contribution it can make to good government. It needs to be able to demonstrate that it is a more effective means of government than local administration.'

The critics of local government

However, the case for local government is not overwhelming or unanimous: there exists a contrary view, especially that of the 'centralists', who are critical of its existence on a number of grounds:[7]

(1) Local government allows a variation in the standard of provision of local services which may be regarded as inequitable or unfair in an age of equality, or at least equality of opportunity. For example, in operating the '11-plus' examination and selective secondary education, some authorities allowed half of their secondary pupils to go to grammar schools, while in other areas the figure was only 20 per cent. Similar variation may be found in other areas of education (such as in the extent of the provision of nursery or adult/community education)

and in other services, such as the provision of special housing for the elderly, hostel accommodation for the mentally disordered, youth services, or the levels of provision of home helps, occupational therapists and social workers.

(2) Doubt is cast on the efficiency of local government administration. Many authorities are felt to be too small to be effective in the provision of some or all of their services (see p. 49). In addition, there is scepticism about the amount of coordination and integration of services which is achieved in practice within local authorities. Moreover, the speed of modern communications means that central government can be as effective in dealing with local problems even though local government is nearer.

In addition local government is seen as either too bureaucratic or too party political to be efficient or sufficiently responsive to public opinion. An alternative to central government takeover or intervention here is seen in the privatization of local services.[8]

(3) Though local authorities may be progressive and pioneer new services, equally they may drag their feet and be closed to new ideas and change. Thus local government is criticized as encouraging narrow, parochial or 'parish pump' attitudes and policies.

(4) Finally there is the danger of exaggeration and over-idealization. The notion that local government acts as a bastion against excessive state power and as a catalyst to the release of simmering community participation may be far too ambitious a claim. In practice, as we shall see later (Chapter 12), the central government exercises considerable control over the policies of local government, and the general public shows a considerable lack of enthusiasm for local government matters.

Arguments or views such as these may convince some people that local government should be abolished altogether.[9] In practice, the main consequence has been a loss of responsibilities to private business and quangos, and a tendency to closer control and supervision of local authorities by the central government. The government of Tony Blair has promised a 'new deal' and partnership for local government which may alter this.

2

AN EVOLVING SYSTEM

The British are renowned for their respect for tradition. The British system of government is equally famous for its reliance on conventions and unwritten codes of behaviour, in preference to formal written codes which often purport to be immutable. Change, however, is inherent in laws and constitutions, as it is inherent in life. The way in which local government has adapted to changing circumstances is the subject of this chapter.

History has imprinted itself with particular clarity on our system of local government. Understand our history and you go a long way towards an understanding of the present local government system, for we still have the same essential forms (for example, committees), the same basic geographical divisions (such as counties and parishes), the same sort of local leaders (the councillors) and the same sort of offices (such as mayors and provosts) as we have had for centuries. All the main elements have evolved to meet the new challenges of a complex society and to ensure sensible democratic government.

Before 1800: the early system

The feudal system in England lasted until the sixteenth century. It was based on land tenure or holding, with the king, as lord paramount, granting tracts of land to barons, nobles or bishops, who in turn granted portions to freemen. It was a social order or hierarchy, each person having duties towards or rights over those above and below. Central government was carried out by the king with his *curia regis* (or council). Justice was administered by judges, holding the king's commission, who visited the localities to supervise local administration and ensure justice, order and peace.

Local government grew out of the local communities of parishes, townships (some of which were boroughs) and counties, the boundaries of which were found even in Anglo-Saxon times. The local communities formed naturally, and leaders (such as the hundredman, the shire reeve or sheriff, and the Justice or Conservator of the Peace) emerged or were appointed by the king to help to carry out the basic tasks of the local communities – the prevention of crime, punishment of offenders, the provision of poor relief and welfare, the control of nuisance, the management of common lands and property, etc.

These essential local government activities were in fact dealt with by various bodies: self-help groups, voluntary associations and sometimes commercial undertakings. Formal legal authorities, what today we would call 'local authorities', provided a fourth agency, but they were not necessarily the most important, and in many areas the units of civil government merely filled in the gaps left by the other bodies.

In the course of time, many of the non-statutory bodies (charities, guilds, the Church and the manor) declined, and many of their functions were taken over by the nascent local authorities. From the late Middle Ages, around the fifteenth century, three types of civil authority became firmly established: the parish (based on the church parish), the shire (county) and the corporate town (borough or burgh).

The parish became responsible for local law and order (appointing a local constable), for providing common amenities (through a surveyor of highways) and for dealing with social distress (through overseers of the poor). These officers were elected or served on a rota basis. Some general supervision was exercised by the 'vestry', a local committee which in some places was elected and in others was appointed or self-selected. Further oversight was provided by Justices of the Peace (appointed by the Crown), who exercised authority on a county-wide basis. They were responsible for checking local affairs and administration, inspecting accounts and making appointments, but they had direct responsibility for such matters as highways and bridges, weights and measures, as well as the traditional duties of maintaining the peace and punishing petty crimes.

The corporate towns (called 'boroughs' in England and Wales, 'burghs' in Scotland) were those urban areas which had at some time obtained a charter from the Crown entitling them to certain privileges. These included the right to establish their own administration (in the form of a 'corporation'), to own corporate property (guild halls and town halls) and to have a separate 'bench' of magistrates or JPs; they may also have been entitled to call themselves 'cities'.

This was the picture, much simplified, of local government at the end of the eighteenth century. The real picture was very complex, however, and there were many variations among the regions and areas. In some areas charities were strong and active; in others responsibilities had been taken over by special statutory bodies (precursors of today's quangos), such as Turnpike Trusts (to build and maintain roads) or Improvement Commissioners (to provide water, lighting or sanitation). And there was considerable variation in the method of election or selection of officers, vestries and corporations. A generalization that can safely be made, however, is that the 'system' was rudimentary, and by today's standards many local authorities were inefficient and corrupt, though not uniquely so.

Over the course of the next two centuries local government appears to have undergone three distinct phases of development, which we now consider.

1800–1880: stress and improvisation

By the beginning of the nineteenth century the impact of industrialization and urbanization was becoming clear. Problems of poverty, disease, crime and squalor were demanding attention.

The response was substantial, though piecemeal and sometimes reluctant,[1] so that by the mid nineteenth century there was more active concern about the problems of society than there had been at any time before. However, it was a community response rather than an official response: private enterprise developed estates and provided water and gas; voluntary groups and charities provided schools, housing and hospitals; self-help and pressure groups urged the provision of parks and other cultural and social amenities.

From the official side it was soon apparent that the existing authorities could not cope with the problems they were now facing. The parishes were too small or inept, and they began to lose some of their traditional functions to higher authorities. For example, in England and Wales the inadequacy of the parish constables led to the setting-up of police forces in the boroughs in 1835 and in the counties in 1839 and 1856 (all modelled on the Metropolitan Police, created in 1829). Similarly, being unable to cope with the mounting social distress, the parishes lost their individual responsibilities for poor relief in 1834, when the Poor Law Act placed this responsibility on to groups (or 'unions') of parishes, which then operated under *ad hoc* elected Boards of Guardians.

Such *ad hoc* (or special-purpose) authorities were not new: a number of Turnpike Trusts and Improvement Commissioners had been created by Local (or Private – see p. 80) Acts of Parliament in the eighteenth century. These bodies proliferated in the nineteenth century (often by-passing the existing public authorities), so that we find local commissions or 'boards' for cleaning, paving or lighting the streets, for road building, for slum clearance, sewers, burial and for water supply.

Furthermore, general Acts of Parliament led to the creation of more *ad hoc* bodies, just as the Poor Law Amendment Act 1834 had created Boards of Guardians. Local health boards were set up under the Public Health Act 1848, highways boards under the Highways Acts 1835 and 1862, and elementary school boards under the Education Act 1870. Each of these local boards had its own elected body (the board itself), its own officials and its own rates.

Some existing local authorities showed initiative and foresight: they promoted local Acts and obtained the powers to take action themselves.[2] There was thus some administrative tidying-up, as corporations, and especially Boards of Health, took over some of the functions of the Improvement Commissioners.

In addition, there were some attempts to reform local government in the towns, since it was the towns which were most affected by economic and social changes (including an astonishing growth in population[3]). In 1835 the Municipal Corporations Act, affecting 178 corporate boroughs in England and Wales, was passed. In an attempt to remove corruption and inefficiency, the Act required the corporations to be elected by ratepayers, to hold council meetings open to the public and to have their accounts regularly audited. In this way, a uniform constitution for most (about two thirds) of the boroughs was established.

The Municipal Corporations Act 1882 added another twenty-five old boroughs to this scheme, and in the meantime all new boroughs (some sixty-two were created between 1835 and 1876) adopted this form of local government. Uniformity was enhanced by the Public Health Act 1872, which *required* the establishment of health authorities throughout England and Wales – whether they took the form of borough councils (for the towns and cities), Boards of Health (for urban areas) or Boards of Guardians (for rural areas) – and the obligatory performance of health functions and responsibilities.

But a number of the old corporations had gone unreformed and had dwindled into insignificance as the *ad hoc* bodies assumed real power. In other towns and villages there was no common pattern either: the vestry, manorial officers, guardians, Improvement Commissioners, charity trustees, Justices of the Peace, all jostled each other for authority. Consequently local government was fittingly described in the 1870s as 'a chaos of areas, a chaos of authorities and a chaos of rates'. The structure was the product of a continuous patching-up exercise: it was not purpose-built.

1888–1930: the period of ascendancy

Such chaos as existed in England and Wales before 1888 was described and condemned by the Royal Sanitary Commission (1868–71), and there was some attempt at improving and tidying up the situation by the Public Health Act 1872, which divided the country into *rural* and *urban* areas for the purpose of public health services such as sanitation. But the demand for a more thorough-going reform had been growing since the 1830s. In particular there was a call to set up in the counties a form of representative government similar to that established for the boroughs. The call was resisted by the country gentry, largely because of fear of an increased rate burden which they thought would result from a more open and more active county government.

The Reform Act 1832 had revised the allocation of parliamentary representatives to reflect the changed distribution of the population. In removing the parliamentary franchise from many ancient boroughs ('rotten' or 'pocket' boroughs), the effect was to leave the disfranchised boroughs somewhat powerless and exposed. Hence the reforms of the Municipal Corporation Act 1835 (see p. 16). In a similar way, the Reform Act 1884, by extending the parliamentary vote to agricultural workers, threw into sharp relief the anomaly of the non-elected character of the county authorities composed of Justices of the Peace. Consequently the Local Government Act 1888 created elected *county councils*, based largely on the existing counties.[4] Initially their responsibilities were limited to highways, asylums, weights and measures and police, but these were increased substantially over the next forty years.

The Local Government Act 1888 also created *county borough councils*. These were to be all-purpose authorities, independent of the county councils and based on existing boroughs. The criterion for their creation was population: a town with a population of 50,000 or more could claim county borough status. Some eighty-two towns[5] did so, much to the dismay of the county MPs, who had originally sought a qualifying figure of 150,000 population. Those boroughs which failed to gain county borough status remained as non-county boroughs and became *district councils*, for local government purposes, within the counties.

The rationalization of the local government structure was largely completed by the Local Government Act 1894. This created elected *urban district councils* (UDCs) and *rural district councils* (RDCs), which were based on consolidated sanitary districts. Like those of the *non-county borough councils*, the main functions of the district councils were public health and highways.[6] Under the same Act, *parishes* were revived by the creation of parish councils, which, except in parishes of under 300 electors (where they might simply have meetings of all parishioners), were elected.

The system of local government was completed in 1899 when twenty-eight *metropolitan borough councils* were established for the London area, which had at that time the largest city population in the world. In 1888 a separate London county area had been created by removing parts of Middlesex, Kent and Surrey, and the *London County Council* was established on a similar basis to other county councils. In 1899 the 'district' authorities were added, with the City of London (the square mile in the heart of London) being left as a separate authority in deference to its unique character and tradition.

Local government now had an established structure which was based on rational principles and provided a large measure of uniformity. In addition, all local authorities (councils) had a constitutional basis and operated on openly democratic lines. The stage was set for the local government system to enjoy some fifty years of ascendancy. It enjoyed increased status in the eyes of the general public, it became a pathway to a desirable career, and, above all, the central government was increasingly willing to entrust it with important responsibilities.

Some of these responsibilities were simply transferred from existing local government bodies when the new authorities were set up: in 1888 the county councils and county borough councils acquired the administrative functions of the Justices of the Peace, which covered rating, licensing, asylums, highways, weights and measures and police. Similarly, some of the JPs' functions were passed on to the new district councils in 1894, though the districts' most important functions came in the same year from the transfer of the functions of the public health and highways boards. Further important transfers were soon to follow. In 1902 the School Boards (see p. 16) were abolished, and in their place local authorities set up committees (known as 'local education authorities') to provide schools and other educational services such as meals (introduced in 1906) and medical inspection (introduced in 1907). Under the Local Government Act 1929 the Boards of Guardians (see p. 16) were abolished and their functions transferred to local authorities, who created Public Assistance Committees to continue the Guardians' former financial and welfare services.

Meanwhile new responsibilities were being assumed by the state, and many of these were placed in the hands of local government. In 1890 local authorities were permitted to build low-cost houses, and in 1919 they were given central government subsidies to encourage them to do so (as a result of which 1 million council houses were built in the years 1919–39). Under the Town Planning Act 1909, local authorities acquired the power to control the use and development of land, and while the legislation was modest in its provisions, it was greatly

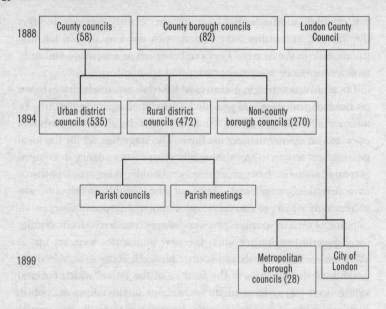

Figure 3 *Local government in England and Wales at the end of the nineteenth century*

strengthened in 1919 and was extended to rural areas under the Town and Country Planning Act 1932.

Following the Unemployed Workmen's Act 1905, local authorities were permitted to anticipate the creation of a national network of Labour Exchanges by setting up local labour bureaux to help the unemployed to find work. (They could also finance the voluntary emigration of those out of work.) The same legislation strengthened their powers to spend money on public works for the purpose of creating jobs, a scheme originated in 1886 by Joseph Chamberlain. For school-leavers, the Education (Choice of Employment) Act 1910 allowed local education authorities to make special provision for advising and placing young people in employment (later to become known as the Youth Employment Scheme or the Careers Service).

During this period, local authorities were also providing employment opportunities directly, as a result of their expanded trading activities. There was considerable development by local government, by means of the Private Bill procedure (see p. 80) of what are usually called 'public utilities' – public transport, water, electricity and gas supply – although some of this apparent expansion was due to 'municipalization', that is, the takeover of private enterprise provision by local authorities. Apart from these activities there was considerable variety in the nature of municipal enterprises, which included the provision of a racecourse (Doncaster), a municipal bank (Birmingham), river ferries (Birkenhead), a telephone system (Hull), a civic theatre (Manchester) and numerous crematoria, slaughter-houses and dock undertakings.

In the meantime, local authorities' powers in respect of health – already well established in the environmental field (see pp. 15–16) were being extended to personal services. These included the provision of sanatoria for tuberculosis (1921) and community care services for the mentally subnormal (1913) and the mentally ill (1930). Concern at the welfare of children and young people found expression in the Midwives' Act (1902), the Children's Act (1908) and the Maternity and Child Welfare Act (1919), all of which had an immediate effect on the role and scope of local authorities.

Thus, over a period of some fifty years local government enjoyed something of a 'golden age', the symbol of which was the Local Government Act 1933. This was a consolidating measure, designed to clarify, confirm and in effect set the seal on the constitution, structure, powers and functions of local government in England and Wales.

1930–74: the period of 'decline'

For the next forty years, local government was in retreat: it no longer assumed such pride of place in the career orientation of bright school-leavers; it was losing status in the eyes of the public and became the subject of a number of unlikely sounding television serials; its management processes came in for criticism when the aldermanic system, the proliferation of committees and the ethos of 'Buggin's turn next' were contrasted with foreign systems and in particular with modern business management.[7] But the more tangible evidence of a decline lay in four other directions:

(1) *Loss of functions.* As the result of a policy of nationalization, local authorities lost their responsibilities for electricity and gas supply when these were taken over by state electricity and gas boards in 1947/8. Local government had never been the sole provider of these services, but its role was a substantial one, supplying about one third and two thirds respectively of the nation's gas and electricity consumption in 1945. Similarly, under post-war legislation (notably the Water Act 1945) many local authorities lost their responsibilities for water supply, as smaller water authorities were absorbed by the larger local authorities or joint water boards. Between 1945 and 1970 the number of water undertakings shrank from 1,250 to about 300. Under the Water Act 1973, English and Welsh local authorities lost all responsibility for water and sewerage to regional water authorities* (which subsequently became private water companies in 1989).

These developments have been described as a return to the *ad hoc* system of the nineteenth century. But this resurgence is not confined to the field of public utilities. Under the National Health Service Act 1946, all local authority hospitals (about 1,700) together with voluntary hospitals (about 1,300) were transferred to Regional Hospital Boards. Under the National Health Service Act 1973 local government lost the remainder of their personal health services (including vaccination, health visiting, district nursing, ambulances and health centres) when these were transferred to the newly created *ad hoc* Regional and Area Health Authorities in order to create a more unified (and uniform) health service.

Similar developments occurred in the field of social security, for while local government inherited the function of public assistance (or poor relief) from the Boards of Guardians (see p. 16) when they were abolished in 1929, the local authority Public Assistance Committees which administered the system within the local government soon found themselves deprived of clients (whom they could barely afford to support) when, in 1934, the central government set up its own *ad hoc* Unemployment Assistance Board. In 1948 this became the National Assistance Board (then, in 1966, the Supplementary Benefits Commission, and subsequently Income Support in 1986–8), and it removed

---

* This happened in Scotland in 1995.

from local government almost completely the function of public assistance.

Further instances of the transference of local government functions to *ad hoc* bodies may be cited: under the River Boards Act 1948 (extended by the Water Resources Act 1963) the control of river pollution became the responsibility of River Boards. Under the Road Traffic Act 1930, the responsibility for licensing passenger road services passed from local authorities to regional traffic commissioners. The Transport Act 1947 transferred many canals and harbours to the British Transport Commission, and under the Transport Act 1968 special Passenger Transport Authorities have been established to manage the provision of local buses and trains in the larger urban areas (see p. 93).

However, the re-emergence of semi-independent public boards was not the only way in which local authorities lost functions. The central government itself has taken over direct responsibility for a number of services, for example the building and maintenance of trunk roads (under the Trunk Roads Acts 1936 and 1946) and rating valuation (under the Local Government Act 1948). For a short time, 1972–4, local authorities in effect found that central government had become responsible for the determination of council housing rents (under the Housing Finance Act 1972).

It is felt by some that another element in this aspect of local government 'decline' is the upward transfer of functions from the lower-tier authorities to the upper-tier ones. This has occurred most clearly in the case of the district councils. Although there were some exceptions, in 1944 district councils lost to the county councils their responsibility for providing elementary schools; in 1946 they lost their health and police functions, and in 1947 their fire services and planning functions.

This transfer between tiers has occurred in another sense. Under the direction of the Home Secretary, the number of police forces in Britain has been reduced from over two hundred in 1946 to fifty today. This is partly a consequence of the transfer from district to county councils under the 1946 Police Act. But it is also due to the fact that many police forces became administered by joint committees of neighbouring county councils (for example the Devon and Cornwall Constabulary).

(2) *Failure to attract new functions.* It has been suggested that local authorities have failed to acquire certain new responsibilities to which they would seem to have a claim. Under the New Towns Act 1946, the development of New Towns (such as Cumbernauld, Milton Keynes and Cwmbran) was placed in the hands of appointed boards instead of the proximate local authorities, and for nearly twenty years (1959–77) it was intended that the New Towns when completed should be transferred from the Development Corporations to the New Towns Commission rather than to local authorities. (This was changed in the 1977 Act and local authorities now acquire the New Towns' assets and management when they 'mature', though some authorities have been apprehensive about the costs involved.)

In 1949, under the Special Roads Act, the government announced plans to build motorways. It was not, however, the major local authorities who were to be responsible but the Ministry of Transport (operating through Road Construction Units). In 1967, in pursuance of a policy to preserve and enhance the environment, the Countryside Commissions were set up. Yet their functions (of encouraging the provision and development of facilities for open-air recreation) could perhaps have been undertaken by local authorities, if necessary through joint committees.[8] In 1965, under the government's National Plan, regional economic development machinery was established, in the form of Regional Planning Boards and Councils.[9] Although local authorities had representatives on these Planning Councils, at the time of their creation it was felt that local government was again being overlooked and by-passed. Indeed, in a leading article entitled 'Exit the Town Hall', *The Times* said, 'It is beginning to look as if confidence in it [local government] and practice of it may prove to be a passing phase in British political evolution.'

(3) *Loss of financial independence.* One of the characteristics of local authorities is that they have the power of taxation (see p. 354) and are thus able to finance their activities. Rates have never been the sole source of income, however, as local authorities have also received income by way of rents, sales, service charges, fines and legacies. Since the nineteenth century, beginning with police grants, local authorities have also received grants from the central government. Between the

1930s and the 1970s the proportion of this grant revenue in local authority budgets grew substantially, as the figures in Table 1 indicate. As a result, it is argued, local authorities have lost much of their independence – 'he who pays the piper calls the tune'. (See Chapters 11 and 12.)

(4) *Increased central control.* In the course of the twentieth century, the central government has sought to control the activities of local authorities in a number of other ways. Legislation in the 1940s, setting up the post-war health, education and welfare services, required local authorities to submit their proposed schemes (for the administration and development of these services) to the Minister, or else gave him or her wide discretionary powers over local authorities undertaking those services. The central government has also developed substantial powers to intervene in local authorities' appointment of senior officers, to inspect certain local government services and to determine the charges which local authorities make for certain services. In addition, the volume of informational and advisory documents from the central government (called 'circulars') increased in such a way as to give the central government considerable additional powers of persuasion and influence over the affairs of local government. The situation is well illustrated by the career of Aneurin Bevan. He is said to have been elected to Tredegar Urban District Council (in 1922) only to find that power resided in the county council. Having got himself elected to Monmouth County Council (1928), he found that power had gone to the central government. Subsequently he went there (1929) becoming Minister of Health (1945) and thus responsible for local government!

A number of explanations have been put forward to account for the apparent decline of local government. Firstly, it is suggested that rates as a source of income are inadequate: they lack 'buoyancy', that is to say that they do not automatically produce a higher yield in revenue as incomes rise generally (see p. 357). As a consequence local authorities have of necessity come to rely more and more on central government grants.

Secondly, local authorities lost another source of income when gas and electricity were nationalized. The notions of nationalization and

Table 1 *Local government income (revenue account)*

| Year | Grants | | Rates | | Other | |
	£m	%	£m	%	£m	%
1933	122	27	149	33	176	40
1953	469	36	443	33	413	31
1963	1,158	37	1,031	33	901	29
1973	4,422	45	2,682	28	2,660	27

Source: Local Government Finance (the Layfield Report), HMSO, 1976, Table 25; W. A. Robson, *Local Government in Crisis*, Allen & Unwin, 1966, Table 1.

centralization are normally associated with the rise of socialism. The Labour Party was swept to power in 1945 (remaining in office until 1951) and while Labour is usually seen as an ally of local government (having historically developed many of its roots there) this time its commitment to central state ownership outweighed its predisposition to municipal enterprise.

Thirdly, the notion of equality had been gaining general approval throughout the century. The privations and camaraderie of the Second World War gave it a substantial boost. Thus, following the Beveridge Report (1942),[10] the Welfare State was established. Social security and health services were unified and centralized to secure more uniform and equal treatment throughout the nation. And to the same end the activities of local government in the fields of education, welfare and housing became subject to greater central government oversight.

Fourthly, the radical doctrine of state intervention in the economy, usually associated with the economist J. M. Keynes (1883–1946) and often referred to as 'Keynesian economics', became official government policy during and after the war. In 1944 the government pledged itself to a policy of full employment (in contrast to the heavy unemployment of the 1930s) and this required 'budget management' by the government, that is to say that in times of threatened depression the government would spend money to boost the economy, even if it meant that its budget was in deficit and not balanced with income from taxation. Conversely, where demand in the economy was excessive and inflation threatened, the government would seek to reduce state expenditure and perhaps private spending too, for example through higher taxes, tighter credit facilities and higher interest charges. This is generally known as fiscal and monetary policy. Local authorities have inevitably been caught up in this new 'demand management' role of government as they are big spenders, and in this way they have lost some of their freedom and autonomy.

Fifthly, local government may be said to have 'declined' because of its outmoded structure, which was mainly established in the nineteenth century, when the population was much smaller and population settlement quite different. At that time there were few if any suburbs, nor was there a 'drift' of population such as we have experienced in this century towards the South and East. Increased mobility, especially with the spread of motoring, and modern transport and communications, has made the nineteenth-century local government boundaries meaningless. In many ways, therefore, the structure was out of date from its inception: boundaries were wrongly drawn (for instance, county boroughs were made too small) and with the possible exception of London (see p. 115) insufficient account was taken of the nascent conurbations (the large urban areas, which stretch around the cities of Birmingham, Manchester and Glasgow, for example).

Coupled with this was the notion that local government units were too small to be efficient. Business enterprise had shown that 'bigger is better' in the sense that economies could be achieved in large-scale units – increasing the size of production unit can lower the unit costs (just as a double-decker bus can carry twice as many people as a single-decker but still only needs one driver and four wheels). Thus 'the process of technical change, by making such economies possible, encourages a shifting of responsibility for particular functions from lower to higher levels of government'.[11]

Assessing the fortunes of a private company or the business sector in general can be a fairly objective and precise exercise: one can refer to profits records, balance sheets, etc. It is much more difficult to make a similar evaluation of local government, which is very subjective and open to varying interpretations.

In the previous pages we have indicated some ways in which local government generally has declined since the 1930s, in contrast with its expansionary and optimistic phase from the later nineteenth century. However, we must beware of the danger of exaggeration. It could be argued that a number of the functions lost by local government were not very significant. For example the central government, in building motorways and taking over trunk roads, became responsible for less than 5 per cent of the nation's public highways; local authorities have retained responsibility for the remainder. Overall, it is not unreasonable to suggest that local authorities have retained their most important functions, and indeed they have markedly expanded their provision of these, as for example in the fields of education, leisure and the welfare services.

In addition, local government has acquired some new or enlarged responsibilities: for instance in the environmental field (including planning, town development, pollution control and civic amenities) and in the field of welfare (such as children's services, consumer protection and community care for the mentally disordered). As a result of these developments, local government expenditure in the 1950s and 1960s increased not only in real terms but also as a proportion of total national expenditure (see Chapter 11).

Moreover, we must distinguish the substance from the shadow. Extensive central government control exists in law, but how much is exercised in practice? For example, although s/he has the power to do so, only rarely does a Minister issue general directions to local authorities (and not always successfully even then – see p. 433).

In so far as local government has experienced a decline in the ways described in this chapter, this *in itself* is not to be decried, for society changes and the machinery of public administration must change accordingly. What appears as a loss to local government may represent a net gain to society: thus the removal from local government of public assistance or gas supply may provide the greater benefits of lower costs and less uneven standards of service.

Finally, it may be added that local government has to some extent suffered at its own hands – by failing to take advantage of existing permissive powers and by failing to adapt itself and its structures to changing circumstances. It has also been suggested that too many authorities have developed a culture of 'submissive dependence' on central government.[12]

Scotland

The development of local government in Scotland quite closely parallels that of England and Wales. However, the relatively large number of burghs and their tradition of local self-rule provided Scotland with a more pervasive framework on which to build the structure of modern local government.

Burghs, like the English boroughs, were established in the Middle Ages as trading communities. Their primary function was to make profits and so supplement the king's revenues, but they were also set up to extend royal influence within the kingdom. In time many of these burghs flourished and grew into towns, and councils of burgesses were entrusted to collect the revenues and regulate trading practices. Subsequently they began to assume responsibility for the management of local affairs generally. Alongside these 'royal' burghs there developed a considerable number of 'barony' and 'regality' burghs, established by landowning Scottish nobles and bishops and having similar trading privileges. By the end of the sixteenth century, there were some 350 burghs of one kind or another in Scotland.

The Church, in the form of the 'kirk session' (similar to the English parish vestry – see p. 14), had long taken upon itself the responsibility for caring for the helpless poor and for providing some school education. In practice the cost of these services was met largely from church collections. But they were also partly financed from rates levied on the property owners (or 'heritors') of the parish. Assessment for rating was undertaken by committees of local landowners in each county, known as 'commissioners of supply'. Gradually the functions of these magnates widened to include such matters as the establishment of police forces, registration of electors and the management of roads, though in some cases the responsibility was shared with the Justices of the Peace.

So in the eighteenth century there was a rudimentary form of local government in both the urban and rural (or landward) parts of Scotland. But, as in England and Wales, Scottish local affairs in the late eighteenth and early nineteenth centuries suffered from the twin defects of corruption, due to the closed, self-appointing system of selecting councillors, and of impotence in the face of the problems

arising from rapid industrialization, population growth and urbanization.[13] One consequence was that the larger, mainly royal, burghs
were reformed: under the Burgh Reform Acts 1833 these councils were
made subject to open election.[14] Many burghs, however, remained
unreformed until 1900 (see below).

A second consequence was the creation of numerous *ad hoc* bodies.
In the smaller burghs, alongside the old councils, popularly elected
commissions were set up to provide police and basic improvement
services, such as sanitation, lighting and water. Following the Police
Acts of 1850 and 1862 new (non-burghal) towns were allowed to
establish similar multi-purpose police commissioners, and by the end
of the nineteenth century there were about one hundred such 'police'
burghs.

In 1845, following a Royal Commission report, elected parochial
boards were established to take over responsibility for the relief of the
non-ablebodied poor. Subsequently, these boards became responsible
for certain aspects of public health. In 1857 local boards were set up
to take care of the mentally disordered. And under the Education Act
1872, locally elected school boards were formed to administer the new
system of popular education.

In 1889 elected county councils were established in Scotland which
took over most of the functions of the commissioners of supply and
the JPs (both of which remained in being, partly to administer the
police through joint committees), together with some of those of the
ad hoc bodies. Similarly, under the Burgh Police Act 1892 the functions
and relationships between the police commissioners and the burgh
councils were clarified and rationalized. The reform momentum continued under the Town Councils (Scotland) Act 1900, when *all* burghs
were required to have regularly elected councils, each headed by a
'provost' (or mayor) and 'bailies' (aldermen). At a lower level, elected
parish councils were created in 1894 and given responsibility for poor
relief.

For administrative purposes county councils were obliged to delegate
a part of their responsibilities to county road boards (appointed by the
county council) and to district committees, comprising representatives
from the county council, town councils and parish councils and responsible for roads and public health. Consequently, despite some measure

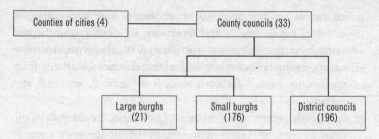

Figure 4 *Local government in Scotland 1929–74*

of rationalization, Scotland's local government in the early twentieth century was a complex network consisting of 200 town councils (the burghs), 33 county councils, 869 parish councils, nearly 1,000 school boards and a host of police commissions, county road boards, district committees and joint standing committees.

However, this complex structure was somewhat simplified by the Education (Scotland) Act 1918, which replaced the school boards with thirty-eight education authorities based on the counties and large burghs. And finally, the whole local government structure was re-cast by the Local Government (Scotland) Act 1929, under which:

(1) The various types of burghs were reduced to two, 'large' or 'small', depending on whether their population exceeded or fell below 20,000. (Towns with under 700 inhabitants lost their burghal status. In 1947 this figure was raised to 2,000.)

(2) The four largest burghs (Glasgow, Edinburgh, Dundee and Aberdeen) became 'counties of cities' (all-purpose authorities like county boroughs in England) and they, together with the county councils, became responsible for the provision of school education.

(3) Parishes, district committees and standing joint committees (with their commissioners of supply) were abolished and their functions transferred to the county councils.

(4) District councils were set up in the landward (rural) areas.

(5) The rates of the various authorities were combined into a consolidated county and burgh rate.

(6) Functions were divided between the county councils and the more local authorities: (a) the large burghs were responsible for all *except*

education and valuation; (b) small burghs were responsible for housing, public health and amenities; (c) district councils had statutory responsibilities for amenities (parks, allotments, entertainments, footpaths) but might also receive delegated authority from the county council for such services as lighting, sewerage and refuse.

(7) As a consequence of the division of functions, the councils of the counties were to contain representatives from the town councils of the burghs.

Like local government in England and Wales, the Scottish system had its critics. The need for structural revision was officially recognized in 1963, when the government published a White Paper, *The Modernisation of Local Government in Scotland* (Cmd 2067). This was not acted upon because, following a change of government, a Royal Commission was appointed in 1966 (under the chairmanship of Lord Wheatley) to undertake a thorough-going review of local government in Scotland. This Commission thus ran parallel to the Royal Commission, under Lord Redcliffe-Maud, which was considering local government in England (see pp. 42, 50).

3

THE STRUCTURE OF LOCAL GOVERNMENT

The structure of British local government is not simple. Not only are there various types of elected council, but within each type or category, there may be a variety of titles or nomenclatures. Recent changes (outlined later, p. 69) have not helped here, with the result that to be called a 'city' or a 'county' or a 'borough' does not necessarily give an indication of the status of that authority.

What can be said, however, is that British local government today has a dual structure, comprising *single-tier* authorities (in Wales and Scotland, in the metropolitan areas* and in the unitary councils located in a number of the shire areas of England) and the *two tiers* of counties and districts (in the shires of England). About half of the population lives within each system. This is a relatively new arrangement. After almost a century of near stability, the structure of local government has been subject to quite frequent and substantial change, as indicated by a succession of Local Government Acts – in 1972 (affecting England and Wales), 1973 (Scotland), 1963 (London), 1985 (London and the six metropolitan counties), 1992 (England), 1994 (Scotland and Wales). The current structure is also the product of a great deal of criticism, inquiry, debate, argument – and politics.

As we saw in the previous chapter, the old structure, established mainly at the end of the nineteenth century, had become out of date and inappropriate to twentieth-century circumstances. It was increasingly seen as an incubus and has been blamed for local government's loss of functions and general decline.[1] The words of the Royal

---

* Since 1986, London and the metropolitan areas have consisted of single-tier boroughs (plus joint boards). Since May 2000 there is an elected mayor and Assembly – a second tier – for the whole Greater London area. See Chapter 5.

Commission on Local Government in Scotland could have referred to the whole country: 'Something is seriously wrong with local government ... the system is not working properly ... At the root of the trouble is the present structure of local government.'[2]

The old structure: 1888–1975

Until the reforms of the 1960s and 1970s, local government in Britain comprised three different structures:

(1) The single-tier all-purpose authorities called 'county boroughs' in England and Wales, and 'counties of cities' in Scotland. About 15 million people, or about 25 per cent of the population, lived under this system in 1965.

(2) The two-tier system that existed in the administrative county of London, the London County Council (LCC) having responsibility over the whole area for such functions as education, planning, health and welfare, and the twenty-eight boroughs having responsibility for public health and housing. About 3 million people, or about 5 per cent of the population, lived in the LCC area in 1965. (About 8 million, or 15 per cent, lived in the area of Greater London. See Chapter 5.)

(3) The three-tier system of the counties, districts (including urban district councils, rural district councils and non-county borough councils – see p. 18), and parishes which operated in the remainder of Britain[3] and thus covered about 40 million, or about 70 per cent of the population. Under this system, the county councils had responsibility for the broader functions of education, planning, welfare and police, and the district councils for public health, housing and amenities. Within the RDCs, parishes held meetings of all parishioners or, where the population was large enough (200 or over), formed councils with responsibility for such things as allotments, footpaths and recreation grounds, some of these being exercised concurrently by the RDC.

The faults which have been detected in this structure over the course of the century are numerous. They may be summarized as follows:

(a) Many local authorities had become too small, with the consequence that they were unable to provide some of the services expected of them,[4] or they provided inferior services.

(b) There were great disparities in the sizes of local authorities of the same type. In 1966, out of a total of 140 top-tier local authorities in England and Wales (outside London), twenty-two had populations of over 500,000 and forty-one had populations of less than 100,000. Similarly, at district level, out of a total of 1,298 local authorities ninety-five had populations of over 50,000 while 184 had populations of less than 5,000. As a result, many top-tier local authorities were actually smaller than some second-tier authorities, so that population size was no longer an accurate guide to the status or functions of a local authority. (In Scotland, this was less of a problem because in 1929 the Scottish burghs were revised to take some account of population variations. See p. 31.)

(c) The structure no longer reflected the social geography of the nation: what may have been appropriate for the later nineteenth century no longer suited Britain in the second half of the twentieth. Movements in the population and developments in transport and communications, electricity, housing and medicine made many local government boundaries seem irrelevant and redundant. For example the distinction between town and country (as exemplified in the county council–county borough and the rural district–urban district bifurcations) no longer seemed appropriate, as people were regularly moving between the two environments for employment, leisure or education: they were no longer distinctive communities. A similar situation existed in the conurbations, where there were collections of separate local authorities and no authority with an overall responsibility or perspective.

(d) The division of functions among local authorities inhibited their effective performance. This occurred in two ways. Firstly, some services were complementary to one another, but their close liaison and coordination was obstructed because responsibility for them lay in the hands of different local authorities. For example, housing was the responsibility of the district councils while welfare functions – accommodation for the homeless, care of the elderly, community services for the mentally and physically handicapped – were carried out by the county councils. Secondly, the *same* function could be divided among different local authorities, and this fragmentation could reduce its effective performance, as, for example, in the area of the comprehensive planning and control of land development and transport.

Generally, therefore, it was felt that there were too many local authorities (about 1,500, excluding parishes) and that larger units would be more effective and more economic. Furthermore the existing system was regarded as confusing for the public, especially since it was compounded by complexities such as delegation, joint schemes and *ad hoc* provision.[5]

Some of these anomalies were inherent in the sense that they were allowed into the original structure. For example in 1888 four county boroughs came into existence with populations well below the statutory requirement of 50,000 (see p. 18). But most of them have arisen as a result of social and economic developments. It is perhaps surprising that the system did not respond to such changes and adapt itself to them. We consider this in the following section.

Attempts at reform 1900–1966: England and Wales

The local government structure created at the end of the nineteenth century did not remain completely unaltered until the reorganization of the 1970s. The founding legislation did allow for boundaries to be changed and for councils to be merged or altered in status. The process was quite cumbersome, involving the relevant local authorities, the central government and, for major changes, Parliament. But the system was used, and it led, for example, to the creation of twenty-one new county boroughs and over a hundred county borough boundary changes in the years 1889–1925. These changes cost the county councils an estimated 3 million loss of population and some £14.5 million loss of rateable value (revenue). It thus caused them considerable anxiety and heightened the enmity which existed between town and country authorities.

The consequence was a full-scale inquiry in the form of the Royal

Commission on Local Government 1923–9. Essentially, this had two consequences: (1) it stemmed the growth of county boroughs by recommending that the minimum population be raised from 50,000 to 75,000 (enacted in 1926); (2) it led to a massive reduction in the number of district authorities (UDCs and RDCs) from 1,606 to 1,048 during the years 1931–7.[6] This followed from the Royal Commission's recommendation (enacted 1930) that county councils should be *required* to conduct a review of the district authority areas. Nevertheless, the central government was moved to comment that 'the changes have not in every case been as comprehensive as would have been wished'.

The 1939–45 war prevented the issue of reform being taken any further, but in 1945 the government appointed a five-man Local Government Boundary Commission to 'consider the boundaries of local government areas in England and Wales (except London) and related questions such as the establishment of new county boroughs'; their objective was to secure 'individually and collectively effective and convenient units of local government administration'. They were also advised to take account of such factors as community of interest in the localities, their physical, economic and social characteristics, financial resources and local opinion.

The Commissioners felt that they had been given plenty of instructions but not enough powers. In their report for 1947 they made some very trenchant criticisms of the local government structure, and on the ground that a major disorder demanded drastic treatment they went beyond their terms of reference and recommended a substantial reorganization. Their proposals included: (1) two-tier county systems (like that of London – see p. 112) for the conurbations; (2) most-purpose authorities for the medium-sized towns (like the Scottish large burghs – see p. 31); (3) a uniform system of district councils formed from the UDCs, RDCs and boroughs. But the government, in the form of the Minister of Health, Aneurin Bevan, in effect rejected the report and the Commission was later dissolved.

In taking this action, the government declared that it was not the right time to introduce far-reaching changes in local government structure; in effect, the government wanted to get on with the more pressing job of post-war reconstruction. It also acknowledged the fact that the various types and tiers of local government were at odds with one another over the direction which reform should take, since inevitably one authority's gain was another's loss. This divergence of opinion was revealed most clearly in 1953, when the local government associations (the organizations representing the different types of local authority – see p. 470) held a number of joint conferences and issued reports. These reports were largely concerned with defending and espousing the virtues of their own particular types of local authority, and generally supporting the existing system with some modifications. However, the Association of Municipal Corporations, representing the county boroughs and non-county boroughs, was alarmed at the others' suggestion that county boroughs with populations of under 75,000 (nineteen of them) should be demoted, while no new county boroughs should be created without a population of at least 100,000. In reply, the AMC advanced the figure of 50,000 as the population minimum for county borough status.

The government sought to cool tempers among the local authorities by announcing that it had faith in the existing system and did not propose to embark on any extensive reform. 'The present system has, over many years, stood up to the severest tests. It responded well . . . There is no convincing case for radically reshaping the existing form of local government in England and Wales.'[7]

The Local Government Commissions 1958–65

Nevertheless some changes were needed and to this end the government set up two Local Government Commissions (for England and for Wales) under the Local Government Act 1958. They were to be advisory, not executive; that is, they could propose changes but the government and Parliament would make the decisions. They were also given some general guidelines, based substantially on an amalgam of the local authority associations' earlier proposals. Thus, in what were called 'General Review Areas', the Commissioners could propose changes in the area and status of county councils (which would then review district council areas) and county boroughs (taking 100,000 as a loose population criterion for the latter). In the five 'Special Review Areas', based on the conurbations apart from London, the English

Commission could be more assertive and (1) deal with *all* the local authorities, (2) re-distribute functions, and, in particular, (3) propose 'continuous counties' (counties in which there would be no 'islands' of independent county boroughs) where they thought it appropriate.

For a number of reasons, the work and achievements of these Commissions were limited. In the first place, their terms of reference were inadequate: in one sense they were too vague and in another too restricted (for example, by excluding the consideration of functions in the General Review Areas). Secondly, the procedure was cumbrous, providing as it did for innumerable consultations and opportunities to raise objections, so that delay was inevitable and inordinate (some reports took up to four years to produce[8]). Furthermore, a number of the recommendations were rejected outright (those of the Welsh Commission for example – see p. 41). Finally, the English Commission was prematurely dissolved in 1965 when the government announced its intention to set up a Royal Commission, under Lord Redcliffe-Maud, to undertake a more fundamental review of local government. (The Welsh Commission had already completed its work – see below.)

Nevertheless, a number of reports were issued[9] and some changes took place. For the General Review Areas, proposals were made to revise a number of county boundaries and to amalgamate some of the smaller counties. Similarly, boundary changes were proposed for county boroughs, with some demotions and new creations. For the Special Review Areas, apart from some adjustments to the boundaries and status of counties and county boroughs, the 'continuous county' system (an urban two-tier system like that in London) was recommended for Tyneside and South East Lancashire, while a joint board of neighbouring county councils was recommended for Merseyside.

Some of these recommendations were accepted by the government and became operative. For example, the Isle of Ely was merged with Cambridgeshire and a number of county boroughs were created, including Torbay, Luton, Solihull and Teesside. Other proposals were rejected, either outright (such as those for Wales) or after sustained protest and inquiry (such as the proposed abolition of Rutland County). The remainder languished and lapsed when, in February 1966, the setting-up of the Royal Commission was formally announced.

It has been suggested that 'the significance of the period from the

Second World War to the passage of the Local Government Act 1958 is that it was a period of great changes in local government, *except* in the structure of local government'.[10] As we have seen, the structure has not changed fundamentally throughout the century (until the 1970s). We now consider why this is so.

Why reform was delayed

Despite the fundamental changes in society and the mounting pressure for structural reform, local government remained substantially unchanged until the 1970s (except for London – see p. 115). This may be partly explained by exigencies, such as the costs involved in reorganization, the pressures on governments' legislative timetables and the problems caused by war and reconstruction. Nor was there any real fervour from the general public.

Secondly, there was no agreed alternative: a number of schemes were proposed of more or less equal appeal (or repugnance). Differences of opinion were bound to arise as some groups sought to promote *efficiency* (which frequently meant larger or single-tier units), while others sought to emphasize and enhance the cause of *democracy* (which often amounted to the retention of small local authorities, usually in a two-tier structure), while *community* identity was also espoused (and involved trying to match the structure boundaries to the varying social units, people's sense of place or networks of town, rural area, shire, village, etc.), and yet others pursued the goal of *simplicity* (which implied a uniform pattern of authorities). In other words, the whole basis of reform was in dispute and implied deadlock or compromise (as exemplified in the numerous boundary changes outlined above).

Finally, there were political reasons for delay. Any reform was bound to threaten some interests, and every local authority or group of authorities sought to justify its own continued existence. The government at Westminster could not afford to ignore or alienate large blocks of local government opinion. (A more cynical view was that the central government preferred to keep local authorities small, numerous and divided in order to sustain a dominant position.) Moreover, party politics were involved, since changing local government authorities and boundaries could affect the composition of constituencies and so large numbers of local government votes and party majorities.[11] In fact, it appears that when reform did appear it was to a large extent the result of pure chance.[12] Before examining this reform, it is appropriate to consider developments in Wales's local government structure.

Wales

The Local Government Commission for Wales (see p. 38) produced a draft report in 1961. It recommended the reduction of counties from thirteen to five. Following considerable protest, it deliberated further and revised its recommendations to seven new counties. Again there was strong reaction from the local authorities, and indeed the Commission itself was not entirely happy with its own conclusions, as it felt that its terms of reference were somewhat inadequate: '. . . we cannot help wondering whether, had we been allowed to consider at least the redistribution of functions, we might not have done a better job.'[13]

In response, the government thanked the Commission for its report, but rejected its proposals. It then acknowledged the limitations of the terms of reference by setting up a departmental inquiry (under the Welsh Office) in 1965 to consider the functions and finance, as well as the boundaries, of local authorities in Wales. Despite the inauguration of a Royal Commission in England in 1966, it was decided to persist with the Welsh inquiry, and in 1967 a White Paper was published.[14] This proposed that the county boroughs should be reduced from four to three, the counties from thirteen to five, and the districts from 164 to thirty-six. The scheme also proposed the introduction of an appointed Welsh Council with advisory functions.[15]

Inevitably, with various ideas for reform going before the English Royal Commission, it was felt that the proposals for Wales were premature. Subsequently, the proposals were changed, partly as a result of the Royal Commission's report (see below) and partly as a result of a change of government following the General Election of 1970.

The Royal Commission (Redcliffe-Maud) Report 1969

Local government is the only representative political institution in the country outside Parliament; and being, by its nature, in closer touch ... with local conditions, local needs, local opinions, it is an essential part of the fabric of democratic government. Central government tends, by its nature, to be bureaucratic. It is only by the combination of local representative institutions with the central institutions of Parliament, that a genuine national democracy can be sustained.[16]

Thus did the Royal Commission on Local Government in England 1966–9 (led by Lord Redcliffe-Maud) defend the concept of local government. It went on to say that a local government system should possess four qualities: the ability to perform efficiently a wide range of important tasks concerned with the well-being of people in different localities; the ability to attract and hold the interest of its citizens; the ability to develop enough inherent strength to deal with national authorities in a valid partnership; and the ability to adapt itself to the process of change in the way people work and live. These qualities were missing from English local government, which was found to be suffering from four structural defects, namely:

(1) The local government areas did not fit the pattern of life and work of modern England, and the gap was likely to widen with social, economic and technological changes.
(2) The fragmentation of England into seventy-nine county boroughs and forty-five counties, exercising independent jurisdictions and dividing town from country, had made the proper planning of development and transportation impossible. The result had often been an atmosphere of hostility between county boroughs and counties and this had made it harder to decide difficult questions on their merits.
(3) The division of responsibility within each county between county council and a number of county districts, together with the position of county boroughs as islands in the counties, meant that services which should have been in the hands of one authority were frag-

mented among several, making it more difficult to meet needs comprehensively.

(4) Many local authorities were too small in size and revenue and consequently lacked qualified manpower and technical equipment to be able to do their work well.

Furthermore, and partly as a consequence of these failings, there were deficiencies in local government's relationships with the general public, who saw local government as too complex and irrelevant to their daily lives, and with the national government, who doubted the ability of local governors to run local affairs and consequently restricted their activities.

As a result of this analysis, the Royal Commission members were unanimous in their view that the structure needed changing, and there was near unanimity on the principles which should underlie the reformed structure. These stated that local authority areas must be so defined that they enable citizens and their elected representatives to have a sense of common purpose. Consequently,

(1) The areas must be based upon the interdependence of town and country.

(2) In each area, all environmental services (planning, transportation and major development) must be in the hands of one authority. These areas must be large enough to enable these authorities to meet pressing land needs, and their inhabitants must share a common interest in their environment.

(3) All personal services (education, personal social services, health and housing) must also be in the hands of one authority.

(4) If possible both the environmental and the personal groups of services should be in the hands of the same authority: through the allocation of priorities and coordinated use of resources, this single authority can relate its programmes for all services to objectives for its area considered as a whole.

(5) Authorities must be made large enough to be able to command the resources needed for the efficient provision of services.

(6) The size of authorities must vary if areas are to match the pattern of population, but a minimum of around 250,000 is essential.

(7) On the other hand, authorities must not be so large that serious

managerial problems arise or elected representatives cannot keep in touch with constituents. Consequently a maximum of around 1 million is appropriate as a general rule.

(8) Where the area required for environmental services contains a very large population, a single authority for all services would not be appropriate; here, responsibilities must be divided between environmental and personal services and allocated to two operational tiers of authority.

(9) The new local government pattern should as far as practicable stem from the existing one.

In trying to determine the appropriate units for the new local government structure, the Royal Commission was thus laying down four criteria: efficiency, democracy, the pattern of living and the existing structure of local government. These were not all necessarily compatible. For example, research for the Royal Commission had shown that there existed some 130–140 areas which could be described as coherent socio-geographic units (that is, having patterns of living which combined town and country). But these areas were of varying sizes and were generally too small for the effective performance of the main services. The Royal Commission therefore had to strike a balance between the claims of efficiency, democracy, community and continuity.

In striking this balance, the Royal Commission concluded that most of England should be divided into fifty-eight areas, each having a population in the range of 250,000 to 1 million with a *single-tier* or 'unitary' authority to carry out all the local government responsibilities (that is, it would resemble the county borough system). In three other areas of England, all densely populated conurbations, the environmental group of services would have to deal with such large populations that a single authority would be too unwieldy, too difficult to control democratically and, for the purposes of the personal services, too remote. In these 'metropolitan' areas therefore, a *two-tier* structure was recommended (somewhat like the London system of local government – see p. 116). The top-tier metropolitan authority would be responsible for the mainly environmental services, while the smaller metropolitan district authorities were to provide the more personal services.

In addition, the Royal Commission recommended two partial or non-operational tiers of local government. At very local level, 'local councils' were to be elected with the duty of representing local opinion and perhaps with some powers to provide some local services. At the regional level, eight 'provincial councils' were to be set up to represent the main local authorities in those regions and be responsible for drawing up the provincial strategy and planning framework within which the main authorities would operate.

Reactions to these radical proposals were mixed. The Association of Municipal Corporations (representing the boroughs and county boroughs) accepted the report to some extent. The Labour Party endorsed most of the proposals, although the Labour government's projected legislation[17] included plans to increase the number of metropolitan areas to five and to defer its decision on provincial councils until the Royal Commission on the Constitution had reported.[18]

Hostile comment came from those, notably the Rural District Councils Association and the County Councils Association, who argued that the large unitary authorities would be remote, bureaucratic and unresponsive to local needs, and that the proposed local councils were inadequate, a mere sop to satisfy the demands for local democracy. In effect, these critics were saying that unitary authorities were government but not local, that local councils were local but not government, while the provincial councils were neither local nor government. Instead they favoured a two-tier system of local government throughout England.

They were not alone in this. Many other critics thought that the Royal Commission had sacrificed democracy in the pursuit of consistency and of efficiency (even though, as others pointed out and the Royal Commission acknowledged, there was no conclusive evidence that larger units of administration were more efficient). Indeed the Royal Commission did not produce a unanimous report, for one member wrote a powerful memorandum of dissent[19] because he believed that the main report had given too much weight to the principle of concentrating responsibilities into single-tier authorities, but that in making these areas the appropriate size for effectiveness (between 250,000 and 1 million) it had undervalued the important principle of population settlement. He felt that his colleagues on the

Commission had compromised in the wrong direction and had gained the worst of both worlds, as many of the proposed areas would be too small for environmental services and too remote for personal services. His own proposals for a two-tier structure (plus local and provincial councils) sought to give greater recognition to the 'facts of social geography' (rather like the Royal Commission on Scotland's local government – see p. 60) by creating small regional authorities, to exercise mainly strategic functions, and district authorities, for the more personal services.

In June 1970 the Conservative Party won the general election and local government reform was back in the melting pot. The Conservatives were anxious to avoid unitary authorities for a number of reasons. In the first place there was no great enthusiasm from any quarter – for many of the public the whole exercise was somewhat remote, and most people were at least used to the two-tier system (only 25 per cent lived in county boroughs). For members and officers, the unitary system threatened possible redundancy. For a number of Conservative MPs, the parliamentary constituency changes which may have resulted from the proposed local government reforms appeared unwelcome (especially where a rural constituency might be merged into an adjacent city). Fear of amalgamation and perhaps loss of political control also caused a number of county councillors to press the new government to retain the two-tier structure.[20]

Then in 1971 the government published its own proposals,[21] which accepted the two-tier system for the metropolitan areas, but rejected completely the unitary authorities which had been proposed for the rest of England. Instead, the whole of England (and Wales[22]) was to have a two-tier system. The first tier was to be based largely on existing counties; the main change was to occur at district level, in the second tier. None of the proposals applied to London (see Chapter 5).

The Local Government Act 1972

Under this Act (operative from April 1974) the eighty-two county boroughs were abolished outright. The fifty-eight *county councils* in England and Wales were reduced to forty-seven (thirty-nine in England

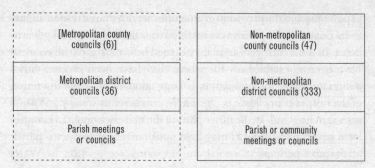

Figure 5 *Local government in England and Wales (outside London) 1974–86*

and eight in Wales), with populations ranging from 100,000 (Powys) to almost 1.5 million (Hants), and responsible for most of the planning, protective and personal services. Within these counties, 1,249 borough, urban and rural district councils were replaced by 333 *district councils* or *boroughs*[23] (of which Wales had thirty-seven). Their populations ranged from 422,000 (Bristol) to 18,670 (Radnor), and these councils are responsible for such services as housing, environmental health and amenities. However, a number of responsibilities, such as planning and amenities (parks and museums etc.), became shared between the two sets of authorities.

The Act also created six *metropolitan counties* (Greater Manchester, Merseyside, West Midlands, Tyne and Wear, South Yorkshire and West Yorkshire), ranging in population from just over 1 million (Tyne and Wear) to 2.7 million (West Midlands) with their councils responsible for the broad environmental services (planning, transport, highways). Within these metropolitan counties were created thirty-six *metropolitan districts* (or *metropolitan boroughs*)* ranging from 173,000 (South Tyneside) to over 1 million (Birmingham), with their councils responsible for most functions such as housing, education, welfare and environmental health. A number of other services, such

---

* Many of these are cities, a status conferred by the monarch (advised, these days, by the Home Secretary). The traditional criterion (up to 1884) was possession of an Anglican cathedral or bishop; these days the criteria are less clear – vide the fourteen cities created in the twentieth century – though the main ones are population size and regional significance.

as planning and the provision of amenities, were a shared responsibility.

In England, the parish was retained as a third tier of local government. In those districts where they existed before 1974, parish councils have been re-established. Elsewhere they have been created either automatically (if the population is large enough) or at the discretion of the district council (see p. 47). There are currently some 7,200 *parish councils* in England. In the other parts of the non-metropolitan counties local government electors may hold parish meetings to discuss parish affairs and perhaps to take some decisions (see p. 518). In Wales the situation is similar except that parishes have been replaced by 'communities', which are entitled to have community meetings and/ or community councils with a role similar to that of parishes in England, acting as a forum and a voice for the locality. In particular they can claim to be consulted on planning applications, and they may opt to exercise control over the provision of allotments, burial grounds, footpaths, bus shelters, recreation grounds and street lighting. Altogether, throughout England and Wales (though not in every district – see p. 526) there are about 11,000 parishes and communities, of which about 8,000 have elected councils. Collectively, they are known as 'local councils' to distinguish them from the larger 'principal' authorities (see p. 518).

Reorganized but not reformed?

The Local Government Act 1972 substantially altered the face of local government in England and Wales. Apart from the creation of the six metropolitan areas (with their county and district borough councils) and the reduction in the number of county districts by 75 per cent, the county borough 'islands' were abolished; some of the smaller counties disappeared through amalgamation (especially in Wales); some new counties were created; and there were innumerable boundary changes (only five counties retained their territories completely intact). It was widely anticipated that these changes would promote efficiency and improve services while at the same time retaining an ample measure of democratic control and involvement:

There is considerable advantage in having units of population sufficiently large to provide a base for ... effective organization and a high quality of service ... The Government obviously must seek efficiency, but where the arguments are evenly balanced their judgement will be given in favour of responsibility being exercised at the more local level.[24]

However, the critics of the reorganized system were legion. The substitution of the two-tier system for the proposed unitary authorities did not assuage the feelings of those who felt the new system to be remote and insensitive. In some areas the prescribed antidote became poisonous, as parish and town councils acted as a focus and rallying point for old local loyalties so that the hoped-for melding of new communities was slow to develop.

A different kind of criticism came from those on the left of British politics. They saw the reorganization as a stratagem for the greater centralization of power – in two directions: firstly from local to central government, and secondly from significant levels of working-class participation and influence to the more exclusive, elitist influence of the business and professional sectors of society.[25] In effect, the capitalist state is seen as mopping up pockets of resistance which local councils represent (see p. 706, note 65).

Most of the criticisms, however, tended to point in the other direction – that, broadly speaking, the scale of reorganization was inadequate and far too many small authorities remained and exercised vital responsibilities (such as education and social services). Even the metropolitan counties were felt to be too small in that their boundaries had been drawn too tightly around the urban areas, thus incorporating too little of the rural hinterland.[26] This arrangement to some extent reinstated the town–country dichotomy (see Chapter 10) and hindered successful planning and housing programmes, which often require inter-authority co-operation. Relations between local authorities were also soured in other ways, in particular by the division of responsibilities under the 1972 Act. The most contentious area here was that of 'concurrent' powers, where both tiers were given responsibilities for the same service (notably planning, but generally too in the provision of amenities). This caused considerable resentment and hostile relationships in many parts of the country (see p. 467). A further criticism concerns the effectiveness of the county or regional tiers. They were supposed to exercise a broadly strategic role, but this was made difficult by the fact that they did not control the administration of so many services – those which lay in the hands of the districts and of *ad hoc* bodies. This was particularly the case in the metropolitan areas.

Apart from any other consideration, the system of sharing responsibilities (compounded by 'agency' arrangements – see p. 86) added to the public confusion about local government. The reorganization was intended to 'de-mystify' the system for the person in the street by making the structure simpler and clearer, but the creation of a double two-tier system, the complicated division of services (not just as between the metropolitan and the non-metropolitan areas, but between England and Wales) and the proliferation of names (including boroughs, cities and town councils) made the system apparently as complex and perhaps irrelevant as ever. This criticism would appear to be reflected in the fact that election turnout did not improve after the reorganization (see p. 144).

Finally, there was the government's removal from local government of personal health services and responsibilities for water provision.[27] This not only added to public confusion, but also suggested a continued lack of confidence in local government by the central government – in contrast to the aspirations of the Royal Commission, which declared:

The whole Commission is unanimous in its conviction that if the present local government system is drastically reformed, its scope extended to include functions now in the hands of nominated bodies and the grip of central government relaxed, England can become a more efficient, democratic and humane society.[28]

The reorganized system of local government was essentially an evolution from the system established in the late nineteenth century, and in this respect it carried with it the virtues of that system. But it also had many of its defects. The reorganized system did work, but there were many who believed that it did not meet the major problems that local government has to face as effectively as a more radically reformed system would have done.

Consequently, the system was soon under review again.

Abolition of the metropolitan counties

Based on the White Paper *Streamlining the Cities* (1983), and following lengthy and controversial debate, the Local Government Act 1985 abolished the metropolitan counties and the GLC in April 1986. In eliminating these upper tier authorities, the Government sought to 'remove a source of conflict . . . save money . . . [and] provide a system which is simpler for the public to understand' (Para. i. 19).

Underlying the proposals was the government's view that those authorities were created (in 1972 and 1963 respectively) at a time when resources seemed plentiful and that there was a need for strategic planning to cater for continuing growth. But since the 1970s growth has faltered and 'incrementalism' (spending) has been replaced by 'decrementalism' (cuts). Thus the government aimed (1) to reduce public sector spending, (2) to improve efficiency (or value for money) and (3) to attack the 'national overhead' through cuts in the civil service, the removal of one tier of the NHS (see p. 460) and by setting higher revenue targets for nationalized industries. Abolition of the upper tier of metropolitan local government was seen as local government's contribution to this general objective and to the government's prime objective to 'tackle inflation and to improve efficiency in all sectors of national life'.

The government saw metropolitan counties as secondary and superficial; they had 'too few functions' which resulted in their finding it 'difficult to establish a role for themselves' – indeed they had sought to encroach on those of the borough councils, thus producing 'conflict and uncertainty'. Worse had been their inclination to 'promote policies which conflict with national policies which are the responsibility of central government'. Thus the capital offence of the metropolitan counties was to 'consistently exceed [the] targets' of expenditure set by the government. In abolishing these large top tier authorities, the government also claimed to be bringing local government closer to the people by distributing their functions to smaller, more local authorities, i.e. the borough councils. In the event, the responsibilities of the metropolitan county councils (and the GLC) were transferred not only to the boroughs but also to a number of ad hoc joint boards, including joint police authorities, joint passenger transport authorities and joint fire and civil defence authorities (for most of which one of the constituent councils has assumed the role of the 'lead' council), and to 'residuary bodies' (authorities appointed to handle and wind up those responsibilities which could not otherwise be allocated). In the case of London, the arrangements were particularly complex and confusing (see p. 122). Thus, it may be doubted whether the reorganization really did make local government less remote in these areas, with only about 20 per cent of the metropolitan counties' expenditure being transferred wholly to the boroughs as such. And, consequently, it is something of a misnomer to describe these councils as single-tier or 'unitary'.

Furthermore, a study of the relationships between the tiers in the metropolitan areas showed that reports, of inter-tier/authority conflict had been exaggerated.[29] It showed that conflict had occurred, but that it was limited to certain functions and areas only, and further, that there was already evidence to suggest that the new arrangements would experience similar problems.[30] Moreover, private management consultants have suggested that the government's assertions about the metropolitan authorities' excessive spending were overstated and misleading, and that abolition would produce no significant savings.[31] Another study[32] concludes, 'Notwithstanding the criticisms directed against them, the extent to which their activities are constrained by non-local factors and their apparent lack of legitimacy, the Metropolitan Counties cannot be regarded as redundant . . . due consideration must be given to the difficult circumstances in which they have had to operate, to the fact that historically they have been operating for an extremely short period of time, and to the fact that people's selective memories of the system they replaced are strong . . . Our conclusion then must be that the case for Metropolitan Counties remains a powerful one.' As *The Times* (1 August 1985) commented, 'A convincing case for abolition has yet to be made with intellectual vigour and sufficient fact . . . ministers will seem to believe that in this matter assertion can substitute for argument.'

Others have interpreted the reorganization as pure political opportunism, with a Conservative government removing seven strongholds of Labour power and opposition. Indeed Edward Heath, a former

Conservative Prime Minister, declared the reform to be 'the greatest act of gerrymandering* in the last 100 years of British history.' (See also pp. 109, 121.) However, apart from London (see p. 123), there seems no prospect at the moment (early 2000) of a restoration of metropolitan county councils, despite the Labour party's total opposition to their abolition. But other significant changes have occurred and others are under way or in prospect.

The 1990s and beyond: further change

Having overturned the Labour government's proposals for a system of single-tier councils in 1970 (see p. 46 above) and replaced them with their own two-tier structures, the Conservative governments of the 1980s and 90s set about undoing or reversing those very arrangements. The first wave of 're-reform' occurred (as outlined above) in 1986 with the abolition of the metropolitan county councils (and the GLC, another creation of a Conservative government in 1963; see p. 46). Then in the mid-1990s, the two-tier county/district system was swept away throughout Wales and Scotland and replaced with a uniform system of 'unitary' authorities (though with a variety of titles or designations, especially in Wales). At the same time, in England, there was a similar but more limited reorganization. (In many respects, the changes have been a return to the 1960s system of county boroughs (see p. 18 above) and thus a restoration rather than a reformation.) The overall effect was to reduce the number of principal councils from 514 to 441 (with England 387, Wales 22 and Scotland 32).

Unlike the 1960s, there was less obvious need for structural change in the 1990s. But in 1991, triggered by the violent reactions to the poll tax/community charge (see p. 369) there was a flurry of government proposals for local government reform covering finance, management and structure – all largely driven by the new Secretary of State, Michael

---

* i.e. the manipulation of boundaries for party political advantage. An alternative is to manipulate the social – and voting – composition of wards, e.g. through housing policies. See the *Independent*, 20 July 1989, and p. 536 below.

Heseltine. Consultative papers were issued outlining new (unitary) structures for local government in Scotland (see p. 66) and Wales (see p. 68) and England.

For England the intention was to replace many of the county/ district arrangements with unitary (single-tier/all-purpose) authorities, as was taking place in Wales and Scotland. But instead of a prescriptive blueprint, the government sought opinion by setting up an independent inquiry in the form of a Local Government Commission (1992–5). Under the chairmanship of Sir John Banham, a former head of the CBI and of the Audit Commission (see p. 399), it was to review the structure, boundaries and electoral arrangements of all the main councils (except those in London and the metropolitan areas). Under the Local Government Act 1992, the Commission (an independent body of thirteen people drawn from a cross-section of councillors, administrators, academics and private business) was duly appointed by the Secretary of State for the Environment, and given guidance on procedure – publicity, consultation, timings and drafting, together with policy guidance – to heed local loyalties and preferences, costs and benefits, history and traditions, accessibility, responsiveness and democracy. Above all, the changes, if any, should 'better reflect the identities and interests of local communities and secure effective and convenient local government'. In general, therefore, the criteria are those of efficiency, simplicity, community and democracy.

Thus taking account of local opinion and loyalties and of submissions from local authorities and other interested parties, the Commission was to outline proposals (including, perhaps, the status quo) for each area and then put these out for wider consultation before a final report and recommendations were submitted to the Minister.

The Consultative Paper stated a clear preference for a structure based on unitary (i.e. single-tier) authorities.[33] It was argued that this, by replacing the two-tier system, would reduce bureaucracy and operating costs, improve coordination of services and improve visibility and people's understanding and thus increase accountability. It also suggested that in some areas the 1974 reorganization had not settled down or been accepted. Thus it proposed that some existing or merged districts could become all-purpose authorities; in others it might be the county council assuming sole responsibility. However, there was to be no wholesale abolition of districts or counties, so that in some areas the two-tier system might well continue if this was thought best. (Within all of this, the roles of parish and town councils were to be enhanced.) Originally, the reformed structure was to be in place in 1994, but this was delayed.

Unlike the Royal Commission of 1966–9, there was little explicit attempt to identify an optimum or 'right size' for the new authorities. This was partly because the notion itself was very questionable[34] (as it had been even in the 1960s), but mainly it was because the whole place and purpose of local government was facing uncertainty. The government's policy of compulsory tendering (CCT; see p. 345) meant that local authorities were contracting out many of their services (and themselves contracting in size) as they increasingly became 'enablers' rathers than direct providers. Size was becoming less relevant. Thus in recent years we have seen a greater tendency among local authorities to cease trying to be entirely self-sufficient and to work together in partnership with the private and voluntary sector (and with one another) to deliver services. The scene has also been changing as services are not only contracted out (and in – see p. 345) but also as they choose to or are required to substantially 'opt out' of local government responsibility altogether (as for example with transport, grant maintained schools or housing) and as functions have transferred to quangos (such as TECs* and UDCs: see p. 555). This, alongside its varied criteria and somewhat uncertain terms of reference, might help to explain why the Commission produced such mixed results. 'The guiding philosophy behind this bizarre reorganisation process remains unfathomable, if it exists.'[35]

The outcome of the review and the government/legislative response (in the form of Parliamentary/Statutory Orders) was very mixed or 'hybrid'. The two-tier shire counties were reduced from 39 to 34, with Avon, Cleveland and Humberside being abolished outright and Berkshire retained in name only (for ceremonial purposes, somewhat like the metropolitan counties after 1986). Counties lost territory to the 46 newly created unitary authorities. Most of these 'unitaries' were

* In Scotland, TECs are called LECs – Local Enterprise Councils.

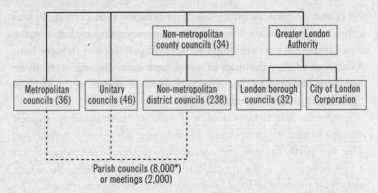

*This number is likely to increase as communities (especially in urban areas) take advatage of the new power to form local councils under the Local Government and Rating Act 1997 (see p. 519.)

Figure 6 *Local government in England 2000*

based on (sometimes enlarged or merged) urban district areas (often cities and many in effect becoming restored county boroughs, but with the added complication of joint arrangements for certain services, such as fire). A few former (pre-1974) counties (Hereford, Rutland, East Riding) were restored, but unusually for counties, as single-tier authorities. Overall there was a reduction of councils in England from 404 to 387, with a resultant loss of over a thousand councillors, down to a total of some 20,000, and a consequential increase in the size of authorities. Thus, where English councils had an average population of 37,000 in 1975, this had risen to 113,00 by 1996 and to 121,000 in 1998.* This contributes to what has been described as 'the democratic deficit'[36] in British politics. The new authorities came into operation in groups over the period 1995–8. The current pattern of local government in England is thus:

* In the reorganized areas in England, Wales and Scotland altogether, there was a reduction of 31 per cent in the number of councillors (= 2,240). Average population per council rose from 29,000 in 1975 to 129,000 in 1998. By contrast in other democratic states averages range from 29,000 (Sweden), 14,000 (Australia), 6,700 (Italy), 2,700 (Germany) to 1,320 (France): see *The Conduct of Local Authority Business* (Widdicombe Report), vol. 4, HMSO, 1986. In Britain councillors represent an average of 1,800 electors; in Europe the average ranges from 250 to 450

34 County Councils (with 2,471 members)

33 London Borough Councils (with 2,068 members) + Greater London Authority (25 members + mayor)

36 Metropolitan Borough Councils (with 2,478 members)

238 English District Councils (with 10,820 members)

46 English Unitary Councils (with 2,433 members)

The result was a disappointment for many, such as those who aspired to unitary status, to those who sought some consideration of a regional element and those who wished to see some reduction in quangos (through transfer of responsibilities to local authorities). The scale of the changes is nothing like what was expected or envisaged at the beginning of the process of review. Indeed, while the Commission's original proposals amounted to the creation of nearly 100 new unitary councils, most of these recommendations were subsequently reversed (especially in response to public opinion)[37] and the status quo prevailed. Consequently, many have concluded that the exercise was a huge waste in terms of cost*, time, disruption and anxiety[38] and that it was perhaps doomed from the start[39]; indeed it was to some extent undermined at the outset when the chairman of the Commission declared that 'if it aint broke, don't mend it!'

Others have variously described the review as 'a costly farce . . . futile . . . a bizarre can of worms . . . an inept process . . . shameless as much as shameful . . . off the rails . . . a loose cannon . . . unequivocable failure . . . an object lesson in how not to do things . . . predetermined conclusions . . . based on assertion rather than evidence . . . symbolic legitimation . . . a messy compromise which hardly satisfied anyone'.[40] In particular it was criticized as working in a vacuum (in not being able to consider the fundamental place or purpose of local government), and of seeking to protect party seats[41] Consequently some blame the government, especially for providing uncertain terms of reference and for its attempts to interfere by referring back recommendations and seeking to steer the review by changing the guidelines (which subsequently went to judicial review where in January 1994 the High

---

* Various estimates have been given, e.g. £15m for the review process and £1.3bn for the subsequent changes, though also savings have been estimated at £50m p.a. See *Independent* 18 January 1995.

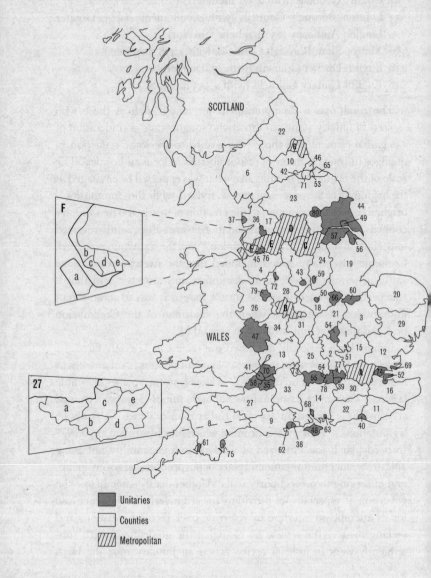

Figure 7 *Local government areas of England*

County councils in England and population

1	Bedfordshire CC	524,100
2	Buckinghamshire CC	632,500
3	Cambridgeshire CC	645,100
4	Cheshire CC	956,600
5	Cornwall CC	486,400
6	Cumbria CC	483,200
7	Derbyshire CC	928,600
8	Devon CC	1,009,900
9	Dorset CC	645,200
10	Durham CC	593,400
11	East Sussex CC	590,400
12	Essex CC	1,528,600
13	Gloucestershire CC	58,400
14	Hampshire CC	1,541,500
15	Hertfordshire CC	975,800
16	Kent CC	1,508,900
17	Lancashire CC	1,384,000
18	Leicestershire CC	867,500
19	Lincolnshire CC	584,500
20	Norfolk CC	745,600
21	Northamptonshire CC	578,800
22	Northumberland CC	307,700
23	North Yorkshire CC	556,200
24	Nottinghamshire CC	993,800
25	Oxfordshire CC	547,600
26	Shropshire CC	406,400
27	Somerset CC	460,400
	a) West Somerset DC	32,200
	b) Taunton Deane BC	99,400
	c) Sedgemoor BC	103,300
	d) South Somerset DC	152,300
	e) Mendip DC	99,500
28	Staffordshire CC	1,031,100
29	Suffolk CC	636,300
30	Surrey CC	1,018,000
31	Warwickshire CC	484,200
32	West Sussex CC	702,300
33	Wiltshire CC	654,500
34	Worcestershire CC	676,700

Unitary councils in England and population

35	Bath and NE Somerset	158,700
36	Blackburn with Darwen	136,600
37	Blackpool	146,000
38	Bournemouth BC	151,300
39	Bracknell Forest	95,900
40	Brighton and Hove	155,000
41	Bristol City	374,300
42	Darlington	98,900
43	Derby City	218,800
44	East Riding of Yorkshire	310,000
45	Halton	123,700
46	Hartlepool	90,400
47	Herefordshire	167,200
48	Isle of Wight	130,000
49	Kingston upon Hull City	265,000
50	Leicester City	270,500
51	Luton	171,700
52	Medway Towns	240,800
53	Middlesbrough	146,000
54	Milton Keynes	200,000
55	Newbury	136,700
56	NE Lincolnshire	164,000
57	North Lincolnshire	153,000
58	North Somerset	177,000
59	Nottingham City	363,500
60	Peterborough City	153,100
61	Plymouth City	243,400
62	Borough of Poole	133,000
63	Portsmouth City	174,700
64	Reading	128,900
65	Redcar and Cleveland	144,000
66	Rutland	32,500
67	Slough	107,000
68	Southampton City	196,900
69	Southend on Sea	169,900
70	South Gloucestershire	220,000
71	Stockton on Tees	178,000
72	Stoke on Trent City	244,600
73	Swindon BC	177,300
74	Thurrock	131,400
75	Torbay	98,400
76	Warrington	82,500
77	Windsor and Maidenhead	132,500
78	Wokingham	139,200
79	The Wrekin	143,400
80	City of York	174,700

The shaded areas (of the recently abolished Metropolitan County Councils) contain the following Metropolitan Districts/Boroughs: **A** Greater London – comprises 32 London Boroughs: see p. 116. **B** West Midlands – comprises Birmingham City (1,006,000), Coventry City (305,000), Dudley MB (309,000), Sandwell MB (294,000), Solihull MB (201,000), Walsall MB (263,000), Wolverhampton MB (248,000). **C** South Yorkshire – comprises Barnsley MB (224,000), Doncaster MB (293,000), Rotherham MB (255,000), Sheffield City (529,000). **D** West Yorkshire – comprises Bradford City (475,000), Calderdale MB (194,000), Kirklees MB (381,000), Leeds City (717,000), Wakefield City (317,000). **E** Greater Manchester – comprises Bolton MB (263,000), Bury MB (263,000), Bury MB (179,000), Manchester City (439,000), Oldham MB (220,000), Rochdale MB (205,000), Salford City (231,000), Stockport MB (288,000), Tameside MB (221,000), Trafford MB (216,000), Wigan MB (312,000). **F** Merseyside – comprises (a) Wirral MB (336,000), (b) Knowsley MB (157,000), (c) Liverpool City (481,000), (d) Sefton MB (295,000), (e) St Helens MB (181,000) . **G** Tyne and Wear – comprises Gateshead MB (204,000), Newcastle-on-Tyne City (278,000), North Tyneside MB (195,000), South Tyneside MB (157,000), Sunderland MB (297,000).

The Merseyside area (F) is highlighted to illustrate the district/borough pattern in the metropolitan areas. For similar purpose Somerset is highlighted.

Court declared the change unlawful). And at least five different/ successive Cabinet ministers had a direct hand in the review and adjusting its direction. Others blame the Commission for lacking a clear set of principles for reform and exercising too personal and subjective an approach. As a result of criticism and frustration the Chairman of the Commission himself became critical, threatened to resign and was subsequently replaced. He too concluded that the process had been 'messy and confusing. But it worked . . . better than we had any right to expect'.[42] Meanwhile, the government lost some of its enthusiasm for the whole exercise and the likely costs of upheaval.

There was also considerable in-fighting among the councils under review, and there is still a great deal of 'forgiving and forgetting' to be done. The political parties too have been divided over the issue, especially locally. But in general Labour and Liberal Democrats went along with the review; both had themselves in earlier years proposed unitary councils. Labour, in particular, had proposed a programme of 'organic change' in 1979, under which there would be a limited redistribution of responsibilities in favour of the larger urban non-metropolitan districts (such as Bristol, Nottingham or Hull)[43]. But they did criticize the government over its failure to consider a regional dimension, which they favoured,[44] as well as accusing it of gerrymandering in its reform of Wales and Scotland (see below).

Scottish local government 1966–96: from Royal Commission to no commission

The Royal Commission 1966–9

The Royal Commission on Local Government in Scotland 1966–9 (under Lord Wheatley) praised the work of the local authorities in Scotland, but found the structure of local government to be gravely defective:

Something is seriously wrong with local government in Scotland . . . the local government system is not working properly – it is not doing the job that it ought to be doing. At the root of the trouble is the present structure of local government. It has remained basically the same for forty years, when everything around it has changed. (paras. 1 and 2)

More specifically it pointed to the following defects:

. . . local authorities on the whole are too small. The boundaries pay little heed to present social and economic realities. Services are often being provided by the wrong sorts of authorities and over the wrong areas. The financial resources of authorities do not match their responsibilities. (para. 3)

And as a result:

. . . the services that local government provides do not operate as well as they should. Staff are not always deployed to the best advantages. Plans . . . are often not fully realized. Friction tends to build up between neighbouring authorities because of an artificial conflict of interest, created by the structure of local government and nothing else. The ratepayer's – and the taxpayer's – money is frequently wasted on maintaining two or more separate organizations where one would do perfectly well. Some important services have outgrown the structure, and have had to be taken away from local authorities altogether. (para. 4)

Thus the faults are similar to those diagnosed for England's local government (see p. 42). Not unexpectedly, the overall consequences are also similar:

Looked at as part of the machinery for running the country, local government is less significant than it ought to be. It lacks the ability to speak with a strong and united voice. Local authorities have come to accept, and even rely on, a large measure of direction and control from the central Government. The electorate is aware of this . . . The question is being asked . . . whether . . . local government is worthwhile maintaining at all. (para. 5)

The Royal Commission answered this last question with a firm 'yes' – 'local government of some kind is absolutely indispensable' – but only if it is fundamentally reformed.

The Royal Commission believed that the structural defects 'were so deep seated that surface patching would not do'. Consequently, the reforms were to be thorough-going and were to rest on a foundation of solid principle which would allow the new structure to (a) function as a whole and (b) be capable of coping with future social changes and demands on local government.

In order to provide the groundwork for such a system, the Royal Commission then set down four basic objectives of reform:

(i) Power: Local government should be enabled to play a more important, responsible and positive part in the running of the country – to bring the reality of government nearer to the people [and in particular away from central government].

(ii) Effectiveness: Local government should be equipped to provide services in the most satisfactory manner, particularly from the point of view of the people receiving the services. [This implies a reallocation of functions for discharge at appropriate levels.]

(iii) Local democracy: Local government should constitute a system in which power is exercised through the elected representatives of the people, and in which those representatives are locally accountable for its exercise. That is, local councils should be genuinely in charge of the local situation and elected local councillors really answerable for its actions.

(iv) Local involvement: Local government should bring the people into the process of reaching decisions as much as possible, and enable those decisions to be made intelligible to the people. (paras. 126–160)

These were to be the ideals of the new structure as a whole. But in the quest for appropriate *units* of local government, the Royal Commission emphasized three criteria:

(1) Functional viability. The Royal Commission examined the main functions (actual or potential) of local government and, after considering the scale on which they should be discharged and the extent to which they could be combined in the same hands, drew conclusions about the size of area, population and resources requisite for each. On this basis it said there was a *prima facie* case for three levels of local government (regional, intermediate and local).

(2) Correspondence with communities. It was felt important to match authorities with communities as closely as possible. After examining the social geography of Scotland, the Royal Commission concluded

that a pattern existed, made up of four types of community – the region, the shire, the locality and the parish.

(3) Democratic viability. Local authorities must have a sufficient range of functions to create local interest and provide opportunities for councillors to exercise real choice while at the same time keeping the councillors' duties within the compass of ordinary members of the public serving in a part-time capacity.

Clearly these criteria were not entirely compatible. Some sort of compromise was inevitable. In order to avoid fragmentation and to ensure that all local authorities had a sufficient range of functions, the Royal Commission rejected the idea of a four-fold structure to match the four-level community. Instead it sought to concentrate responsibility on just two sets of local authorities. This would have the added virtue of consistency – of as uniform a structure of authorities as could be achieved without undue violence to the pattern of communities.

The final result of the analysis[45] was the recommendation of a two-tier structure consisting of:

(1) Seven regional authorities, based on an amalgamation of existing counties and ranging in population from 2.5 million in the West Region to 145,000 in the South West Region;

(2) Thirty-seven district authorities, based on counties and counties of cities which had been enlarged and/or partitioned;

(3) At a very local level community councils could be set up throughout the new districts where there was sufficient local/popular support. They would have no statutory powers and would not be local authorities as such. Essentially their role would be a representative one: to give expression to the views of the community. They would also be entitled to do anything to improve the amenity of the area, and indeed might act as agents for the local authorities in the day-to-day running of certain services.

(4) Responsibilities would be divided between the two sets of authorities. The regional authorities would be responsible for transportation, water, sewerage, drainage, education, social work, housing and police; the districts for environmental health, libraries, building control and licensing. Functions such as planning, parks and recreation would be shared between them.

The Conservative government at Westminster made no radical changes to these recommendations – as it had to the Royal Commission report on English local government – partly because the proposed scheme fitted in with that party's preference for a two-tier system of local government, and partly because they had less at risk politically in Scotland than in England.

Nevertheless the government did respond to the criticism that the district authorities would be too few, too remote and too restricted in function. Consequently the number of districts was increased and they were given more responsibilities (notably housing). In addition, the island authorities were given a separate, virtually all-purpose (region *and* district) status, and another two regions were added to the seven proposed. (Some of these changes were forced on the government during the Bill's passage through Parliament.)

The Local Government (Scotland) Act 1973

The resulting Act created, with effect from May 1975:

(1) Nine regions, each with a Regional Council, and ranging in population from under 100,000 in the Borders to nearly 2.5 million in the Strathclyde region, and in area from 500 square miles in Fife to 10,000 square miles in the Highlands.

(2) Three island councils, two with populations of about 20,000 one with 30,000.

(3) Fifty-three districts, each with a district council and ranging in population from 856,000 in Glasgow to just over 9,000 in Badenoch and Strathspey in the Highland region.

Functions were divided between the two sets of authorities largely as recommended by the Royal Commission, except that housing became a function of the district authorities and the island authorities were each given responsibility for most functions (except fire and police services, for which purposes they combine with the Highland Regional Council).

Provision was made for the creation of community councils along the lines recommended by the Commission. (By 1979 some 1,343 such councils had been approved by the government.)

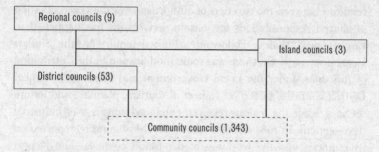

Figure 8 *Local government in Scotland 1975–95*

Predictably, the regional tier has been criticized as too big and remote; as over-bureaucratized, cumbersome and inefficient; as varying too greatly in area, population and resources.[46] The huge Strathclyde region (containing half of Scotland's population) came in for particular criticism.

The Royal Commission had anticipated some of the criticisms, saying for example that while the Strathclyde region was big, it nevertheless did comprise a meaningful and identifiable community.[47] Furthermore, it stressed that democracy could be enhanced rather than diminished by increasing the size of the local government unit:

It is when local government operates at the scale which its services demand that true local democracy emerges; because that is the point where power and responsibility can be properly entrusted and where the administration of services can be responsive in the right way, that is through pressures from within [the local authority] rather than from without [from central government]. (para. 162)

However, the expectation that the bigger and more powerful local authorities would stimulate a greater public participation was disappointed: voting turnout and the contesting of seats did not noticeably increase since the reform, apart from an initial improvement in the first elections in 1974[48] (see p. 147).

The other main criticisms were directed at the distribution of functions, and in particular at the transference of housing and refuse disposal from the regions to the district councils[49] and the souring of relations between the two tiers of authorities over the vexed question of shared responsibilities for certain services (as has happened in England and Wales). Following a limited inquiry by the Stodart Committee 1979–81, there was some modification in the distribution of functions under the Local Government and Planning Act 1982. District councils 'gained' in respect of tourism, planning and leisure services, while the regions received enhanced powers over industrial development. In 1984 another committee (Montgomery) reported on its inquiries into the workings of the island councils. The Report applauded the operation of these most-purpose authorities and recommended that their powers be consolidated and perhaps extended (e.g. into airport management).

The 1990s and beyond: a double reorganization

A consultation paper on local government in Scotland was issued in 1991 (alongside those for England and Wales, see p. 53 above). It contained some very general proposals, the only firm commitment being to the retention of the three island councils. The paper suggested a preference for the unitary model (again on grounds of efficiency and democracy), but left the details of number, size and powers for (limited) public consultation. It also suggested that police and fire services should be organized on a larger scale than other local services, and that water and sewerage may be best dealt with by independent authorities. Many people in Scotland feared that the latter implied water privatization (as had occurred in England and Wales in 1989) and there was protest at that prospect.

The Government had indeed considered privatization of water as part of its reform. However, in the end it announced (in July 1993) that water and sewerage were to be transferred to three separate appointed bodies and thus away from direct provision by local authorities. On local government structure, the nine regional and fifty-three district councils, together with the three island councils, were to be replaced by twenty-five new unitary councils, subsequently revised up to thirty-two (see Figure 9) i.e. a 50 per cent reduction overall, with the consequent loss of 450 councillors (down to 1,245) – which is fewer than those in Wales whose population (at 3 million) is smaller than that of Scotland (5 million), and which thus continues the pattern of apparent disparity in local representation among the different parts of Britain.* Prior to the reforms of 1974/5, the criticism was that of over-representation, with some district councils having fewer than 200 or even 100 residents (see *Municipal Yearbook* 1973).

The proposals for Scotland received considerable criticism – from those who saw no point in the reorganization and from those who wanted an independent commission (as in England) and viewed the Minister's plans as a political ploy to manipulate party advantage. The former Liberal Party leader, Sir David Steel, called the proposals 'corrupt'. The local authorities' association COSLA described the plans as 'tendentious and insulting' and, along with the Labour Party and the trade union UNISON, pursued a policy of non-cooperation. Nevertheless, the reorganization went ahead under the Local Government etc. (Scotland) Act 1994. The councils were elected (on a 'shadow' basis in 1995) with a turnout of 44.9 per cent, and became operative in April 1996.

In practice the 1995 elections proved disastrous for the Conservative Party (p. 162). There was little evidence of gerrymandering, and furthermore, it is suggested that even public consultation through a Commission would have produced a similar structural outcome.†

Unlike England and Wales, Scottish local authorities have a consistency of nomenclatures: they are all known simply by their proper names (as Stirling Council, Fife Council, Highland Council, etc., though there are, understandbly, a few 'Cities'). On the other hand, like England and Wales, the clear pattern of unitary councils is clouded by the existence of a number of secondary authorities, i.e. appointed or indirectly elected joint bodies – for example, for water (3), fire (6), police (6) valuation (10).

Again, like Wales (but not England, yet?) Scotland has a separately elected body, the Scottish Parliament (elected May 1999) and an executive or Cabinet headed by a 'First Minister'. Of the 129 members

---

* The average population per council in Scotland is 153,000 – cf, 128,000 in Wales and 121,000 in England.
† G. Boyne *et al. Local Government Reform*, LGC Communications, 1995.

(MSPs, sitting in Edinburgh) 73 are elected in the normal (simple majority) way and the remainder elected through proportional representation, in multi-member constituencies (based on the constituencies for the EU elections). They are elected for four years.

As in Wales, there has been concern that the new Parliament may draw powers away from local authorities, though a Commission (McIntosh)[50] was appointed to consider this situation and subsequently a concordat was agreed (similar to that in England: see p. 574). There is also the prospect that some elements of non-elected governance (i.e. quangos) may become subject to democratic, if regional rather than local, control.

1990s and beyond: local government in Wales

The pattern and experience of local authorities in Wales has been closely bound up with that in England. There have been divergences when they became subject to different reviews, as in the 1960s. The differences have become more obvious in the 1990s. Not only did English local government alone have a Commission of inquiry, but the result of recent changes is that, while English local government has become (more) hybrid in form, that in Wales now has a uniform structure of single-tier authorities.

The government's consultation paper on the structure of local government in Wales (1991) was quite prescriptive. Pursuing the government's quest for unitary local government (and for the same reasons as those given on p. 54 above) the paper proposed the replacement of the existing eight county and thirty-seven district councils with twenty unitary authorities deriving from existing boundaries (though it provided alternative plans for thirteen to twenty-four councils). Subsequent White Papers (1992 and 1993) outlined a revised scheme, though in the end that too was altered. Consequently, under the Local Government (Wales) Act 1994, twenty-two unitary authorities were created (see Figure 10), i.e. 50 per cent fewer, with the consequential loss of some 700 councillors (from 1,977 to 1,273). About half of them are based on former districts, many traditional county names have been restored and some cities (Cardiff, Swansea) regained control of their own affairs as pre-1974 (see p. 34). Thus there was much support for the reorganization, if not for the actual process. But there was also hostility (including from the Labour Party and the trade unions) and there was much negotiation with the Welsh local authority associations (see p. 470) before the legislation emerged in its final form. Following ('shadow') elections in April 1995 (with a voting turnout of 48 per cent), they came into operation in April 1996.

However, the picture is not quite as tidy as it may seem. In the first place (as with the English unitaries) there is some joint provision of services, in the form of three fire authorities for Wales; there are also a number of area committees (based on former, 'unitary-aspirant', districts) with some service responsibilities. Secondly, (again like England only more so) there is no consistency of names: there are some 'counties' (such as Cardiff County), some 'county boroughs' (such as Bridgend County Borough), while others just use their proper name (such as Gwynedd Council) and there is a 'City and County' (of Swansea). The third complication arises from *devolution*. Under the Government of Wales Act 1998, Wales now has a new tier of government (since 1999) in the form of an elected Assembly/Senedd in Cardiff.

With an annual budget of £7 bn, the Assembly and its Executive deal with matters formerly the responsibility of the Welsh Office, which include education, health, social services, housing, transport, agriculture, roads, planning, economic development and local government. Of the 60 members, 40 are elected in the normal way while 20 are elected through a system of proportional representation (based on party lists of candidates). Members of the Welsh Assembly (MWAs) are elected for four years.

Unlike Scotland, the Assembly is not a 'Parliament' and its powers are limited to secondary legislation. This is partly because there has been a longer history of close links with England and the desire for statehood is apparently less strong than Scotland's. (This was perhaps demonstrated in the referendum of October 1997, when just 50.1 per cent turned out to vote, and the result was 50.3 per cent in favour of devolution and 49.7 per cent against – a difference of just 7,000 votes! In 1979 a similar referendum was lost 47 per cent to 12 per cent.)

For local authorities in Wales, the concern is the relationship with

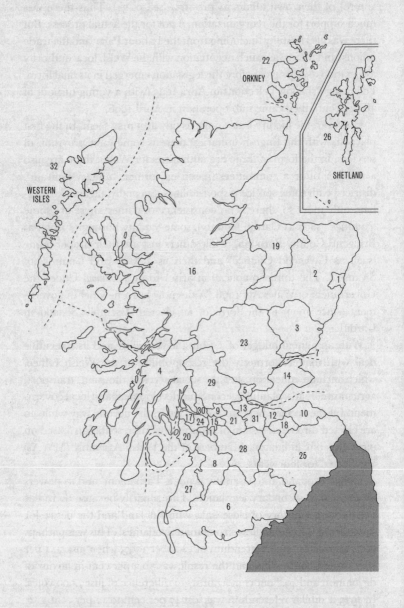

Figure 9 *Unitary authorities of Scotland*

Population	(1991)		Population	
1 Aberdeen City	219,100	17	Inverclyde	90,000
2 Aberdeenshire	226,500	18	Midlothian	79,900
3 Angus	111,300	19	Moray	85,000
4 Argyll and Bute	89,300	20	North Ayrshire	139,200
5 Clackmannanshire	46,700	21	North Lanarkshire	326,700
6 Dumfries and Galloway	148,000	22	Orkney	19,900
7 Dundee City	155,000	23	Perth and Kinross	131,800
8 East Ayrshire	124,000	24	Renfrewshire	177,000
9 East Dunbartonshire	110,000	25	Scottish Borders	105,300
10 East Lothian	85,500	26	Shetland	22,500
11 East Renfrewshire	86,800	27	South Ayrshire	114,000
12 City of Edinburgh	447,500	28	South Lanarkshire	307,400
13 Falkirk	142,500	29	Stirling	82,000
14 Fife	351,200	30	West Dunbartonshire	97,800
15 City of Glasgow	618,400	31	West Lothian	147,900
16 Highland	207,500	32	Western Isles	27,800

the Assembly. Does it represent a threat or an opportunity? The outcome, to some extent, will be in their own hands since many MWAs will be current or ex-councillors. But the situation has received some attention in the form of a Partnership Committee with members drawn equally from the Assembly and local authorities, which seeks good relations between them.

A note on boundary reform

Governments in Britain are not often accused of gerrymandering (i.e. the manipulation of boundaries for party electoral advantage), especially in the case of local government. Electoral areas (names, size and boundaries of wards and divisions, numbers of councillors, etc.) have, by law, to be reviewed on a regular basis every 8–12 years in the case of Scotland (under the Local Government (Scotland) Act 1973 as amended by the Local Government etc. (Scotland) Act 1994), and every 10–15 years for England and Wales under the Local Government

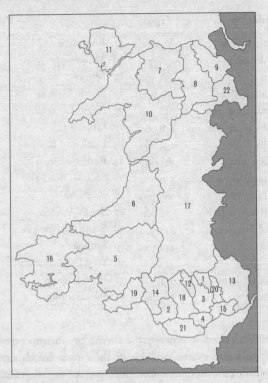

Figure 10 *Unitary authorities of Wales*

Blaenau Gwent County Borough	73,200	Monmouthshire County	86,248
Bridgend County Borough	131,500	Neath Port Talbot County Borough	139,459
Caerphilly County Borough	169,100	Newport County Borough	137,300
Cardiff County	315,040	Pembrokeshire County	114,400
Carmarthenshire County	169,108	Powys County	124,400
Ceredigion County	70,400	Rhondda Cynon Taff County Borough	241,313
Conwy County Borough	110,600	Swansea, City and County of	230,100
Denbighshire County	90,400		
Flintshire County	145,300	Torfaen County Borough	90,400
Gwynedd	118,000	Vale of Glamorgan	119,500
Isle of Anglesey County	67,055	Wrexham County Borough	125,200
Merthyr Tydfil County Borough	57,300		

Act 1972. Under the legislation of 1972 and 1973, three permanent Local Government Boundary Commissions were created for this purpose, each comprising about half a dozen people (usually from an academic, civil service or judicial background). In England the role was taken over by the Local Government Commission, which could direct to the Minister, undertake *ad hoc* reviews of structure and status of particular areas or authorities (which it did, for example, in the case of Southport in 1997 when it sought, unsuccessfully, separation from Sefton MB). The Political Parties Elections and Referendums Bill 2000 will replace the LG Commission with one of the four Boundary Committees of the newly-formed Electoral Commission.

A note on local government in Northern Ireland

Following the Report of the Review Body 1970 (Macrory), local government in Ulster was reorganized into twenty-six District Councils and nine Area Boards. The district councils are responsible for local environmental services (noise and smoke control, food hygiene, abattoirs, pests, refuse, street cleaning, cemeteries), for entertainments and recreation (museums, sports facilities), licensing and consumer protection, and for markets and gas undertakings. Councillors are elected for four years at a time, by way of proportional representation (using the Single Transferable Vote method, with electoral wards grouped into district electoral areas).

Of the area boards, four are responsible for health and social services and five for education and libraries. They are made up of 30–40 per cent district councillors and the remainder appointees of the Minister. For housing there is an appointed Housing Executive, and there is a single Fire Authority. The other services are run directly by the Department of the Environment for Northern Ireland.

Following the 'Good Friday' agreement in 1998, the political situation in Northern Ireland seems to be moving into a totally new non-violent era. The new elected Assembly and the power-sharing executive are in the process of taking over responsibilities and there is every prospect of local authorities assuming more autonomy and more genuine local self-government.

4

THE SERVICES OF LOCAL GOVERNMENT

Local government has a number of functions – providing a voice for the local community, acting as a counter-weight to the central government, supplying local services, levying taxes, regulating activities, recruiting people into the political process and off-loading the central administration. More briefly we can say that local government has a *political* (or representative) role and an *administrative* (or executive) role. In this chapter we are concerned with the latter.

The principle of 'ultra vires'

An essential element of any democratic system of government is the rule of law: that government is not arbitrary or unrestrained but operates according to the law of the land, and members of the government are not 'above the law' but are subject to the law just as are ordinary members of the public. But there is a difference.

Professor Finer tells of a wry joke which circulated in Soviet-controlled Eastern Europe:

In Britain everything that is not prohibited is permitted. In West Germany everything that is not permitted is prohibited. In France everything that is prohibited is permitted. In the USSR everything that is permitted is prohibited. (S. E. Finer, *Five Constitutions*, Penguin, 1979)

Whilst these are/were all exaggerations, they contained an element of fact. And as far as British local government is concerned, local authorities are in the 'German situation' i.e. as public bodies.

Local authorities in Britain are subject to the rule of law. Before they can act (impose charges, build schools, make by-laws, acquire property, etc.) they must be able to point to the statutory authority (normally an Act of Parliament) which authorizes such actions. If a local council were to take action which was not sanctioned by the law (say by opening a chain of fish shops) or if they exceeded their lawful powers (providing a laundry service where they were only permitted to provide public wash-houses[1]), they would be acting illegally, or *ultra vires*. When a court finds a local authority thus acting beyond its powers, it will declare these actions illegal and may punish members or officers of the authority (see p. 405). In contrast, private organizations or individuals can act in any way whatsoever as long as it is not forbidden by law. We can do what is not prohibited; local authorities can do only what the law explicitly allows them to do: what is permitted.

However, local authorities do have some freedom to act. In the first place, besides those powers explicitly conferred on them, there are those which are derived by *reasonable implication* or inference – powers which facilitate the discharge of their explicit powers. Thus under Section 111 of the Local Government Act 1972, local authorities may legally do whatever is 'reasonably incidental' or conducive to the discharge of their legal responsibilities – such as employing and training staff, acquiring property or equipment*, etc. Secondly, while Acts of Parliament mostly require local authorities to undertake certain 'mandatory' duties (such as building schools, housing the homeless, setting a budget, dealing with refuse, street lighting or land use), some statutes merely allow local authorities to exercise optional or permissive powers as they see fit (such as providing museums and leisure facilities, or promoting economic development). Thus local authorities have a certain discretion as to which services to provide.

Thirdly, there is an element of discretion about *how* local authorities carry out their functions. Thus councils can themselves decide the

---

* But this does not mean 'in connection with', which is too broad or vague. Further, in the exercise of their powers (particularly their discretionary powers – granting licences etc.) local authorities are expected to act 'reasonably'; otherwise they may be deemed to be acting *ultra vires*. In the Wednesbury Corporation case (1948) it was suggested that reasonableness implies that relevant matters are taken into account and irrelevant ones are excluded, and that decisions are not made in bad faith or for improper purposes, nor should they be just plain arbitrary.

form,[2] scale or level of service provision (e.g. providing meals on wheels seven days a week, or twice). They can decide the level of charges (nominal or full-cost), and they can determine the method of provision – whether by themselves directly (or 'in house'), through a voluntary organization (such as the Red Cross or WRVS) or by contracting out (say, to a catering firm). The Government may lay down certain minimum standards and may set maximum and minimum levels for charges, and in the 1980s the scope of councils to determine the method of provision became more limited as a number of services were made subject to competitive tendering (CCT) with the result that many councils had to contract out the provision of services to private firms. Stringent regulations on compulsory competition are currently being reduced as CCT is replaced with Best Value (see p. 591), though councils will still often be expected to contract out where this provides best value in the delivery of services to the community.

In addition to providing services, local authorities have a *regulatory* role (indeed, this is the essence of all government). Thus local councils are responsible for granting (or refusing) licences for taxis, public entertainment, market trading, etc., and for registering (and approving) private welfare homes and child-minding. Furthermore, they can exercise a general regulatory power over the community through by-laws. These are as much the law of the land as Acts passed by Parliament*, but are of local application only (e.g. prohibiting cycling on footpaths, banning dogs from beaches or parks, determining the opening times of parks or banning the consumption of liquor in public places). Such laws have to be approved by the Minister (who may indeed provide models for councils to adopt where appropriate).

Fourthly, a local authority has the freedom to spend a certain sum of money for any purpose which in its opinion would be to the benefit of the area (except where this runs counter to other statutory provisions). Such discretionary spending is restricted by law. Initially, when the scheme started in 1963, such expenditure was limited in amount in any one year to the product of a 1d rate (see p. 444), raised to 2p under the 1972 Act (Sec. 137) (Sec. 83 of Scotland's 1973 Act)[3]

---

* Indeed they are only authorized by legislation, mainly the Local Government Act 1972, Section 235.

and known as the 'free tuppence' or 'Section 137' spending. With the abolition of domestic rates (in 1989: see p. 444) such expenditure is determined by a statutory maximum figure per head of local population. These prescribed limits are periodically adjusted by the Government Orders so that currently the figures are £1.90 in shire counties or districts, £3.55 in metropolitan and London boroughs and £3.80 in unitary areas (and some metropolitan boroughs).* In practice, councils do not always make use of this power (in full or at all). Thus in recent years, councils have been spending 31 per cent of what is permitted (compared with only 7 and 17 per cent in 1982 and 1983 respectively, though some councils – 28 per cent – spend nothing). In all, spending here amounts to only 0.5 per cent of total expenditure by local authorities.[4] Councils tend to use it for economic development, low-rent workshops, etc., for community safety or for grants to voluntary bodies. While it provides a degree of flexibility within the *ultra vires* framework, councils find it of limited importance given the scale of financial limit relative to their total expenditure and to the main issues they face. Consequently, they would like to see the limits removed or their replacement by a power of general competence.†

The justification of the *ultra vires* principle is that it protects the community against possible tyranny, extravagance and hare-brained or politically motivated adventures by its local council. Some even feel local authorities have too many powers already, e.g. when it comes to planning or licensing or banning 'raves' and certain films (such as Westminster's ban on *Crash* in November 1996). And further, that Section 137 expenditure may be abused.[5] However, it could be argued that the ballot box is a sufficient safeguard and that the operation of the *ultra vires* rule is too restrictive. Professor Keith-Lucas has written, '. . . our local councils are narrowly limited in their powers and duties. There is a lack of enterprise among them, and a feeling in many people's minds that they are unimportant and rather dull'.[6] Apart from thus inhibiting enterprise, voting turnout and council membership, it

* Under Discretionary Expenditure Limits Order S.I. nos. 40 and 41 of 1993; 651 and 5504 of 1995. Councils also have other constricted powers for economic development under the LG and Housing Act 1989, Section 33.
† See below, and *Local Authority Activity under Section 137*, DETR, 1999.

was argued strongly by the Maud Committee[7] that the principle of *ultra vires* 'robs the community of services which the local authority might render . . . encourages too rigorous oversight by the central government . . . contributes to the excessive concern over legalities'. (And it was pointed out that foreign systems of local government do not have such restrictions.)

The private business sector can also be adversely affected by this rule, as in 1991 when the House of Lords declared local authorities' interest-rate swaps (or 'swaptions'; see p. 408) to be illegal, with the result that a number of banks lost large sums of money. (See too the Allerdale case, 1997.) Following a subsequent investigation, the Legal Risk Review Committee (Alexandra) recommended the abolition of *ultra vires* in its 1992 report *Reducing Uncertainty – The Way Forward*. In practice the situation has been eased in that the Local Government (Contracts) Act 1997 clarifies the ability of councils to enter into contracts, and in October 1998 the House of Lords declared that the rule precluding recovery of money paid under a mistake of law should cease to be (see: *Kleinwort Benson Ltd v Lincoln City Council*, 1998). However, in general there is still considerable uncertainty about the application of *ultra vires* (see *Local Government Chronicle*, 9 July 1999, p. 18).

The Maud Committee recommended that local authorities should be given a *general competence* to do whatever in their opinion is in the interests of their areas, in addition to what is already specified in legislation and subject to their not encroaching on the duties of other governmental bodies and to safeguards for the protection of public and private interests. A similar recommendation was made by the Royal Commissions on local government in England (Redcliffe-Maud) and Scotland (Wheatley) in 1969. Others take a similar view,[8] including the Liberal Democrat and Labour parties (the latter is proposing a partial implementation; see Chapter 15). The Widdicombe Committee (see p. 185), however, took the opposite view, as did the Audit Commission in its comment on the Alexandra report (above).

Official response to this suggestion has (until the LG Bill 2000, see Ch. 15) taken the form of a marginal increase in the power of local authorities to spend money for the benefit of their inhabitants (i.e. Section 137, see above). However, the Local Government Act of 1972 did make provision for local authorities to acquire statutory powers somewhat more easily (through the rationalization and consolidation of many private Acts and making them of general application to local authorities, as happened through the Local Government Miscellaneous Provisions Acts of 1976 and 1982). We now therefore consider the acquisition of powers by local authorities.

The source of powers

As we have seen above, local authorities are required to operate according to the law. Parliament is the source of law, but there are different kinds of law which can apply to local government. The most important derives from *Public Acts* (the most usual kind of legislation). Some of these Acts, such as the Local Government Acts of 1972 and 1973 or the Local Authority Social Services Act 1970, apply specifically to local government. Others deal with a general service or function and confer powers on local authorities along with other official bodies, as did for example the Education Act 1944, the National Health Service Act 1946 and the Housing Finance Act 1972. Most of these Acts are introduced (as Bills) by the Government. But some legislation affecting local authorities may be originated by backbench MPs, as *Private Members' Bills*. Recent examples include the Traffic Calming Act 1992 and the Local Government (Overseas Assistance) Act 1993, both of which enhanced local authority powers.

There are some Acts which permit local authorities to exercise certain powers if the authorities themselves formally 'adopt' them and thus choose to exercise them. These are usually called 'adoptive' or 'enabling' Acts. An example is to be found in connection with the licensing of private hire vehicles in the Local Government (Miscellaneous Provisions) Act 1976. However, they are of relatively little importance these days.

An individual local authority (except a parish or community council) wishing to extend the range of its powers beyond those conferred by public legislation can promote a *Private Bill* in Parliament. The procedure involves special meetings of the council, compulsory advertisement and public announcement, and the engagement of legal counsel for part of the parliamentary proceedings; it is thus complex, lengthy and costly,[9] and only about ten local authorities a year promote such Private (or 'Local') Acts.* For example, the Southampton Corporation Act 1960 empowered that local authority to construct a bridge across the River Itchen; the Abingdon Market Place Act 1978 allowed that authority to ban vehicles from the market place in order to help conserve the historic town centre; the Kensington and Chelsea Corporation Act 1977 enables that borough to ban the leaving of refuse outside commercial premises, and also empowers it to carry out the work necessary for the maintenance of the external decoration of any listed building or any building in a conservation area; the Cornwall County Council Act 1984 provides the power to ban dogs from beaches; the Birmingham City Council Act 1985 allows city-centre motor racing; and the Greater Manchester (Light Rapid Transit System) and the Greater Nottingham (Light Rapid Transit System) Acts, 1994 allowed these city councils to construct local railways.

Finally, local authorities can seek to extend their powers by applying to the Secretary of State (the Minister), who has the authority, delegated to him/her by Parliament, to confer certain powers or duties. In most cases the Minister will have to submit such *orders* for parliamentary approval. Parliament seldom rejects such Ministerial Orders, though they are often challenged (for example by other local authorities) and may be amended.[10] But in many cases s/he alone has discretion, for example, if a local authority is seeking power to acquire property by compulsion, the 'compulsory purchase order' needs to be confirmed only by the Minister. Similarly local traffic management regulations and parking restrictions only require the Minister's approval. And this is generally the case with local *by-laws* whose overall purpose is that of 'good rule and government and for the suppression of nuisances' (Local Government Act 1972, Sec. 235) (such as the behaviour of people in libraries, unauthorized tipping of waste or sticking posters, etc.). Clearly by-laws are similar to Private/Local Acts, but they are quicker and cheaper. The main difference in application is that by-laws tend to be narrower in scope and 'negative', in that they prohibit activities whereas Local Acts permit them – such as allowing motor

* There have been 26,500 local Acts in the period 1797–1994 See: *The Chronological Table of Local Legislation 1797–1994*, HMSO, 1996.

racing (Birmingham), allowing loans from abroad (Somerset) or acqui-
sitions of art collections (Plymouth).

Who does what

In examining the reorganization of local government in Chapter 3 we
had an indication of the division of responsibilities among the various
tiers and types of local authority. It may be useful at this point to draw
the threads together before analysing the various functions in further
detail. Table 2 attempts to do this.

Simply stated, most local authorities are responsible for most local
public services. But many local services are the responsibility of central
government departments, quangos and semi-public bodies as well as
voluntary organizations and perhaps even private firms – not to
mention the devolved governments of Scotland and Wales. Many of
the services for which local authorities are responsible are in the hands
of the same local council, as many local authorities are now 'unitary'
or single-tier, all-purpose bodies (following the reorganization of the
1990s; see Chapter 3 above). However, this situation is not only quite
new but even now is by no means universal; not only are there various
joint or inter-authority arrangements (see p. 109 below), but one half
of the population of England is still served by a two-tier system of
local government – the county/district council arrangement* (see
Figure 6, p. 56). Such a two-fold structure has actually predominated
in local government since the nineteenth century, and though subject
to some criticism (of manifesting unnecessary complexity, confusing the
public, duplication and inadequate service coordination) it managed
(largely) to withstand the review by the Local Government Commission
in England 1992–4 (on grounds of local identity and the public's
aversion to disruption). In Wales and Scotland, the two-tier system
was simply replaced with a unitary system without an open review
process.

Consequently over most of England, the functions of local government are undertaken by two parallel sets of local authorities – county

---

* Parishes form a lesser third tier; these are dealt with in more detail in Chapter 13.

councils and district councils. While this is explained largely by history, there is an underlying rationale in that the 'bigger' services are administered by the 'bigger' authorities. Broadly, the functions are allocated between the two main tiers on the basis of operational efficiency and cost-effectiveness. Thus it is both cheaper and more effective to have responsibilities such as strategic planning and fire services operated over fairly large areas. Similarly it was strongly argued by the Redcliffe-Maud Report[11] and the Wheatley Report[12] that the education service should be administered over an area containing at least 200,000–250,000 people in order that such authorities should have at their disposal 'the range and calibre of staff, and the technical and financial resources necessary for effective provision' of the service. On the other hand services such as allotments, public health and amenities can be effectively administered over smaller areas, and are thus the responsibility of district (and even parish/community) authorities.

There is, however, no universal agreement about this general distribution of functions. There is even less agreement about such services as housing, waste disposal and social services (social work): on operational grounds a good case could be made out for their being administered by either tier; and indeed there were variations in the tier responsibilities among the different different parts of Britain until 1996 when Wales and Scotland 'went unitary'. Table 2 shows the current pattern.

However, the scale of operations is only one criterion. In the allocation of responsibilities, regard has rightly been given to the need for democratic control and responsiveness to local needs. Furthermore, in practice, the rationality of the system has been undermined by the respect which has been paid to history and tradition: for example, the district authorities in England and Wales not only have long experience (and expertise) in housing but also have substantial political influence which they could use to defend themselves against any threatened loss of the housing (or other) function.

Another complication is that the allocation of responsibilities among the local government tiers is not clear-cut: many responsibilities are *shared*. Shared responsibilities can take a number of forms, including (1) *concurrent provision*: whereby several types of local authority all provide the same service, such as car parking, amenities or caravan sites; (2) *joint provision*: whereby several local authorities join together by forming a joint committee or board for the provision of a common service, such as crematoria or communications (for instance, the Forth Road Bridge Joint Board, a combined provision by the West Lothian and Fife Councils or the Devon-Cornwall Tamar Bridge); (3) *shared but divided provision*: whereby several tiers are responsible for a service, but each is responsible for a separate part or aspect of that service, as with refuse collection and disposal (in England) and planning development and control;[13] (4) *reserve powers*: as in the case of housing (and, until recently, planning control), whereby the English county councils may assume responsibility under certain circumstances (for such undertakings as providing houses for certain employees, such as police or teachers); (5) *claimed powers*: whereby certain responsibilities are initially allocated to one set of authorities, but may be claimed by individual local authorities from another tier, such as the district councils in England, which can claim to maintain unclassified roads in urban areas;[14] (6) *agency powers*: whereby a local authority can arrange (by mutual agreement) for another local authority to carry out functions on its behalf and be suitably reimbursed. This power to delegate or transfer responsibility is widely available, except that it is specifically prohibited in the case of education, social services, finance (other than tax collection and valuation) and diseased animal control. It is quite widely used, but it varies considerably among both local authorities and services. For example, many district councils have agency agreements to maintain highways and street lighting for county councils and for the provision or maintenance of sewerage for water companies. Services may also be transferred when an authority defaults (see p. 425).

Local authorities have a number of other joint arrangements for the provision of services. These include statutory joint authorities, boards or joint committees, joint forums, lead authorities and arm's-length suppliers (see p. 108).[15]

Further complications arise from the fact that in some cases non-providing local authorities must be advised and consulted about matters relating to certain services. For example, parishes and community councils must be consulted about planning matters by the appropriate planning authority. Similarly, district authorities are normally given representation on bodies that are the responsibility of the counties (as in the case of school governing bodies).

Table 2 *The responsibilities of local authorities*

	England Metropolitan		England Non-Metropolitan		London		Scotland, Wales & England	
	Joint Authority	Borough/District Councils	County Councils	District Councils	Borough Councils	Greater London Authority	Joint/Special Authority	Unitary Councils
Social Services		●	●		●			●
Education		●	●		●			●
Libraries		●	●		●			●
Museums and Art Galleries		●		●	●			●
Housing		●		●	●			●
Planning – Strategic		●[3]	●			●		●
– Local		●		●	●			●
Highways		●	●		●	●		●
Traffic Management		●	●		●	●		●
Passenger Transport[5]	●		●			●	●	●
Playing Fields and Swimming Baths		●		●	●			●
Parks and Open Spaces		●		●	●			●

Refuse Collection

Refuse Disposal

Consumer Protection

Environmental Health

Police[1]

Fire[2]

1 Police Authorities often (always in Scotland and Wales) cover several local authority areas. While local authorities as such no longer provide this service, councillors still form a slight majority of Police Authority members.

2 Fire services are often (always in Scotland and Wales) provided jointly by local authorities, and some have statutory appointed boards to run them.

3 Strategic planning in metropolitan boroughs and many unitary councils is coordinated by joint committees.

4 Refuse disposal is often a joint rather than a single council provision.

5 Apart from shared membership of special/joint authorities, councils may assist in provision through subsidies.

6 In Scotland, water and sewerage services are provided by Water Authorities whose membership includes councillors.

Enough has been said to illustrate the main point: that while it may be possible to indicate in a broad way the allocation of responsibilities among local authorities, for any particular local authority its range of responsibilities will depend on its status, the use it makes of agency and claiming powers, and the use it makes of its permissive powers – all of which will depend in turn on its size, local needs, finance, party politics and the vitality of local voluntary organizations and pressure groups.

The range of services

The range of local government responsibilities is extensive (especially compared to local government in European countries).[16] It is no exaggeration to say that it provides services 'from the cradle to the grave'. Table 2 gives a stark indication of this, and Table 18 (p. 337) shows the relative importance of each function in terms of expenditure. The wide range of activities is well illustrated by the fact that some public information booklets produced by local authorities to outline their functions contain up to 1,000 separate headings. Here we shall try to put some flesh on the bare bones by describing some of these responsibilities in more detail. We can conveniently group them into five categories (Table 3), though it is not always easy to decide the allocation of some services.

(1) Protective services

Protective services seek to protect the citizen from various dangers.

(a) *Police*. The organized provision of local police services has been a local government responsibility since the mid nineteenth century, but since the Police Act 1946 about 150 small local forces have disappeared as they were amalgamated and became combined.* Consequently the 150,000 police personnel are now organized into just 51 forces (39 in England, 4 in Wales and 8 in Scotland) and they are no longer directly

---

* In 1850 there were 226 constabularies in England and Wales, 13 of which had just one policeman.

Table 3 *Categories of local government services*

Protective	Environmental	Personal	Recreational	Commercial
Police, Fire	Highways	Education	Sports	Markets
Consumer	Environmental	Careers	facilities	Transport
protection	health	Housing	Museums,	Smallholdings
Diseases of	Transport	Social work	galleries	
animals	Planning	Homes	Theatres	
Licensing	Parking	Aids	Camp sites	
Emergency		Meals		

superintended by a separate committee of the local authority like other local services (see Chapter 9). This is partly a consequence of their becoming joint or combined forces, but it is also due to the notion that policing should not be at risk of interference by local politics. As a result, the Home Secretary has considerable powers of inspection and regulation of all local police forces, and must approve the appointment of chief constables. Police forces are also substantially (50 per cent) funded by the central government (Home Office) as the police are both servants of the Crown and employees of police authorities.

Local management of the police is now therefore in the hands of separate, free-standing police authorities (which, apart from government grant, fund themselves by way of 'precepts' on the relevant councils: see p. 352). In Scotland, these are constituted from appointed local councillors, but in England and Wales (under the Police and Magistrates' Courts Act 1994) elected councillors constitute only a bare majority of the police authority, i.e. nine out of the usual seventeen members, with three magistrates and five independent members. Clearly there is concern at the diminished role here of elected local members as such. But there is further unease about the limited remit of the police authority, which is essentially confined to responsibility for maintaining the police force (funding, equipment, buildings, etc.) and for appointing the chief constable. The latter is responsible for the efficiency, conduct and the general operational management of the force and consequently many committee members' questions and probings are allegedly blocked and deflected by the chief constable on the grounds that members are trespassing into his operational territory or that revealing certain information would be contrary to the public interest.

(b) *Crime and public safety* is no longer just a police function, especially as the broader notion of community safety developed in the 1980s. Under the Crime and Disorder Act 1998 local authorities are required to work with police and other organizations to develop crime-reduction strategies. But in an attempt to reduce crime and the fear of crime, local authorities have increasingly sought to inhibit and remedy the causes of crime and anti-social behviour. Many have formed community safety teams, usually in partnership with the police, voluntary bodies, business and the Church, and have conducted crime surveys and audits. (More controversially, some have gone further and established their own uniformed quasi-police patrols or employed private security controls.) Specific areas have received particular attention through Estate Action (for certain housing areas), Town Centre Management and Neighbourhood Watch schemes, and the use of cctv has become widespread (often using competitive 'Safer Cities' and 'Challenge' government funding).

However, community safety, properly done, is an all-embracing, or corporate, policy – concerned with poverty, unemployment, training and education, as well as more obvious aspects such as litter, drinking bans, vandalism and graffiti control, adequate lighting and maintenance of public spaces, suitable public transport, drug-abuse programmes and perhaps victim and witness support. Thus regeneration, housing and community development are important aspects, including conditional tenancies and building and environmental architecture (to 'design out' opportunities for crime). So too is employment and 'employability' creation, which involves not just economic development, education and training but such aspects as truancy and school exclusion, bullying and discrimination, basic literacy programmes, youth services and parenting guidance/instruction.

A number of authorities pioneered this aspect of local provision in the 1980s (such as Birmingham, Strathclyde, Hammersmith and Fulham) and it is now widespread in one form or other. Under the

Crime and Disorder Act 1998 it has become mandatory, along with targets for crime and disorder reductions (and the introduction of anti-social behaviour orders, for noisy neighbours and troublesome youths, and night-time curfews on children under ten). Along with anti-poverty policies (which an LGMB survey showed were operated by some 25 per cent of councils in 1995) it will be reinforced by local authorities new powers to 'promote the economic and social wellbeing of their areas' (*Modern Local Government: In Touch with the People*, White Paper, 1998).

(c) *Fire.* The provision by local authorities of fire-fighting services was not generally obligatory until 1938. Under the Local Government Acts of 1972 and 1973, fire authorities are required to cooperate and assist one another and, like police services, fire brigades may be amalgamated under a single chief fire officer; this is especially so in unitary authority areas (and thus there are just eight fire authorities in Scotland and three in Wales). Apart from fire-fighting and rescue, fire authorities are also concerned with fire prevention, and under a number of statutes (notably the Fire Precautions Act 1971 and the Health and Safety at Work Act 1974) a wide variety of premises (residential, educational, leisure and employment) are required to obtain fire certificates. These are issued by the fire authority (county councils, the boroughs' joint boards, unitary councils) if they are satisfied that adequate fire precautions and safety facilities (such as fire escapes, alarms, fire doors) exist. Local authorities may provide loans to enable such adaptations as are necessary. In the first instance, it is normally the district authorities who (in the pursuance of building regulations) inspect and require the occupier of premises to obtain fire certificates.

(d) *Consumer protection.* Local authorities appoint inspectors (often known as trading standards officers) whose task it is to test the weights and measures of local trading concerns and to take legal proceedings against fraudulent traders and similar offenders – those giving short measure, for example. In recent years their work has extended into other areas of trading practice, such as charges and credit facilities and false or misleading descriptions of goods and services. Consequently, local authorities are empowered to make purchases locally for test purposes, and inspectors have the right of entry to premises.

Local authorities have similar powers in relation to their food and drug responsibilities, which include the enforcement of regulations regarding the production and sale of food and drugs – their purity, safe storage, labelling and fitness for consumption. For this purpose local authorities appoint inspectors and many will also appoint a qualified public analyst. Inspectors have the right of entry to premises and the right to take food samples for testing. Under the Food Act 1992 and the Environmental Protection Act 1990 local authorities took over much of the responsibility of the Health and Safety Executive (for example in the control of pesticide use in commercial premises).

Local authorities are empowered to set up consumer advice centres. These provide general pre-shopping and post-shopping advice to consumers, assessing product claims and facilitating the investigation of complaints. There is considerable variation across the country in what is provided here, and some local authorities rely on local voluntary provision (by Citizens' Advice Bureaux, for instance). This variation is due partly to financial stringency but also to differences of principles and politics: councillors have varying opinions about how far local authorities should go in advising consumers on appropriate purchases and how far it is the proper role of local authorities to take a pro-consumer stance and campaign against questionable trading practices.

(e) *Diseases of animals*, such as tuberculosis, BSE, swine fever, foot and mouth or rabies, can be directly or indirectly injurious to humans. Consequently, legislation seeks, through local authorities, to control such disease by regulating the movement of livestock and by promoting certain preventive measures (such as sheep dipping). Local authorities issue licences for the movement of animals, and farmers must keep records of such movements.

(f) *Licensing* has already been mentioned. Broadly it takes two forms: (i) Licensing which seeks merely to regulate certain trades or activities, such as pawnbroking, money-lending, taxis, massage treatment, gun-ownership, street-collecting, cinemas, theatres, employment agencies, riding stables, kennels, sex shops, gaming establishments, child-minding or private nursing homes. Such licensing or registration normally involves inspection or compliance with particular regulations (such as safety facilities or refraining from exhibiting certain films). (ii)

Licensing which involves regulation, but also provides a source of revenue or local taxation, such as dog licences (until 1988), waste-disposal licences or licences required for killing or dealing in game. The amounts of money raised here are very small.

(2) Environmental services

Environmental services control and improve the physical environment.

(a) *Environmental health* is perhaps the best known and most firmly established local government function (see Chapter 2). Although in 1974 local authorities in England and Wales lost their responsibilities for the supply of water and main sewerage to *ad hoc* water authorities, they have for instance in recent years become responsible for smoke and noise abatement, the regulation of caravan sites, the control of poisonous waste disposal and the enforcement of health and safety at work regulations. Their more traditional responsibilities, undertaken by environmental health officers (often on the basis of by-laws), include: the control of nuisances (such as waste tips, insanitary or overcrowded premises, unfenced mines and quarries) and offensive trades (such as glue-making, fat-extraction and tanning); the enforcement of building regulations (which lay down criteria for the construction and design of buildings, including such matters as the adequacy of drains, insulation and accessibility); refuse collection, street cleaning and the instituting of proceedings against litter offenders; the provision of public toilets; the provision of cemeteries and crematoria (and the disposal of dead bodies where no one else can be found to be responsible); and the control of vermin (by requiring or perhaps undertaking the destruction of vermin – most commonly rats, mice and lice – affecting persons or premises).

Many of these activities aim at preventing the outbreak of disease. When an outbreak of a 'notifiable' infectious disease (smallpox, diphtheria, typhoid, cholera, dysentery or anthrax) does occur, local authorities have the duty to inform the local health authority. Local authorities also have powers to prevent the spread of diseases through disinfection of premises and people and the compulsory removal to hospital of infected persons.

(b) *Highways, traffic and transport.* Roads take a number of forms and local authorities are involved in all of them. Motorways are the responsibility of the central government,[17] which organized their construction through Regional Construction Units (which then broke down into sub-units run by local authorities and acting as agents for the central government). RCUs were disbanded in the early 1980s (with much of their remaining work being contracted out to private contractors). Trunk roads are also the responsibility of the central government, but it is normal practice for local authorities to act as agents and undertake their building, maintenance, lighting and speed restriction. When such roads become 'de-trunked' (as when a parallel motorway is built) they become the full responsibility of the local authorities. The county councils have often lobbied for the outright responsibility for trunk roads to be transferred to local authorities.

All other public roads and bridges are the responsibility of local authorities, mainly the county and unitary councils. District councils have the right to claim responsibility for the maintenance of urban non-classified (i.e. less busy) roads; in practice they often undertake maintenance of these and other roads as agents of the (county) highways authorities. Responsibility for lighting may be similarly delegated, as may the provision of pedestrian crossings, footpaths, seats, shelters, speed limits, etc. Such agency agreements are often preferable to the claiming arrangement (see p. 83), as the latter can give rise to discontinuous or patchy coverage of responsibility.

Traffic management involves responsibility for such devices as signals and roundabouts and for regulations such as those covering one-way streets, speed limits and the prohibition of certain vehicles. They are the responsibility of the highway authorities, but may be delegated along with highway maintenance. Decisions concerning street parking restrictions rest with the highway authority, but district authorities may provide off-street parking in their own right. Local authorities have a statutory duty to promote road safety and the prevention of accidents. For this purpose they usually appoint a road safety officer who organizes publicity to encourage road consciousness and the formation of local voluntary groups (for cycling, motor-cycling proficiency, etc.), often in conjunction with the police and the schools.

Local authorities may provide passenger transport services, though this has changed considerably since deregulation in 1986 (under the Transport Act 1985) and it now mainly occurs in the metropolitan and some unitary authorities.[18] Metropolitan boroughs are responsible (through joint boards or Passenger Transport Authorities) in their areas, while in London responsibility rests with London Transport (a statutory corporation which provides public transport services through contracts with private bus companies and through its own subsidiary London Underground Ltd; it is accountable to the Greater London Authority – see Chapter 5). Otherwise councils have some responsibility for coordinating and rationalizing such provision, for which they seek financial support through Transport Planning Packages or TPPs. Some local authorities have formed transport companies to run buses – there are currently eighteen municipal and seven PTA bus companies. Others own airports. More generally they may be involved in such aspects as the management of bus shelters, the supply of timetables, school transport and transport for those with special needs. Councils also assist by way of concessionary fares and through grants (including subsidies for the running of mini-buses in rural areas).

There is considerable government support for local authority road schemes, substantially approved on a 'package' basis, with councils encouraged to submit bids (through TPPs) for packages of measures covering both roads (including priority facilities for bus lanes, priority traffic lights, etc.) and public transport. The government White Paper, *Modern Transport*, July 1998 seeks to encourage more partnerships with private bus companies; it also allows local authority charges for workplace parking and urban motoring to reduce traffic congestion and encourage the greater use of public transport.

(c) *Planning*. Britain is a small and densely populated country. Land space is limited and its use needs to be carefully monitored, guided and, if necessary, controlled in the interests of the community as a whole. This is the realm of town and country planning, an essentially twentieth-century function of local government.

Planning is important, therefore, because it affects the way individuals dispose of their property (land) and because it affects their living environment. Broadly, local authorities are charged with responsibility for the preparation of plans, the control of development and the conservation of the environment.

There are two types of plan, 'structure plans' and 'local plans', and in non-metropolitan shire England these are the separate responsibility of the county and the district council respectively. 'Structure plans' set out for a ten-year period the broad policy or strategy of the local authority for the use of land in the area of the county. They cover such concerns as the lines of proposed roads, the sites of public buildings and open spaces, and the allocation of areas for such uses as housing, schools, agriculture and commercial premises, and they thus imply an element of economic planning. These plans are based on a survey of various factors, including population, economic activity, communications and traffic, each of which is likely to affect the scale and nature of land use and development. In drawing up its structure plan, the local authority must consult other appropriate bodies (including constituent district councils and neighbouring councils) and must submit the plan to the Secretary of State for approval.

'Local plans' cover smaller areas, filling in the details, and are also submitted to the Secretary of State, but do not necessarily require confirmation (though s/he may require alteration, and where a plan is 'called in', it is suspended). Local plans have, where appropriate, to be certified by the county council as conforming to the structure plan. Metropolitan and London boroughs have 'unitary development plans' which combine local and structure plans. This also applies to unitary authorities, though in most cases they have to work on a joint basis with the surrounding or neighbouring council(s) via a joint committee.

All of these plans must be well publicized and there must be ample opportunity for objections from the public.[19] The consequence of objections is a public inquiry or a local hearing or, in the case of structure plans, 'an examination in public'. The final decision rests with the Secretary of State, in the case of structure plans, and with the local planning authority in the case of the local plan (unless the Secretary intervenes, by 'calling it in').

Having settled their plans, local authorities are then responsible for the implementation of those plans through the process of the control of development. All development – from the big housing estate or shopping centre to the individual house extension or conversion, and the location and size of advertisements – must obtain, through planning applications, planning permission[20] from the local council. Where such permission is refused or involves unacceptable conditions, appeal may be made to the Minister who may hold an inquiry, usually through an inspector (or in Scotland, a reporter) before making a decision. There are some 650,000 such appeals a year in England and 40,000 in Scotland, and most are dealt with by correspondence. Where there is an inquiry the Minister rarely overturns the decision of the local authority. (In some cases, involving matters of national, regional or technical importance, the Secretary of State may appoint a Planning Inquiry Commission.)

Planning often appears to be a rather negative exercise, and planners are sometimes characterized as 'inverted Micawbers', waiting for something to turn down. However, town and country planning has many overtly positive aspects. Local authorities may acquire land (perhaps through compulsory purchase orders) with a view to its development either directly or by attracting industry (through the provision of loans or factory space). They also have powers to reclaim and improve derelict land. In both these respects the powers of councils in the inner urban area are especially great; one of these is the possibility of 'planning gain' or betterment, where private developers provide amenities (e.g. a public park or play space) for the authority in recognition or as a condition of planning approval.

Councils also have certain powers related to conservation. They can require special planning applications for the demolition or alteration of 'listed buildings' (those listed as of special architectural or historic interest or importance). Trees and woodlands may be protected by local authority 'preservation orders'. Local planning authorities may make grants or loans available for the maintenance of listed buildings. Finally, councils are empowered to preserve and enhance the natural beauty of the countryside by creating country parks and setting up nature reserves. They are also responsible for the recording and protection of rights of way. A number of their conservation functions are exercised in conjunction with the Countryside Agency.

(d) *Emergencies*. Local authorities have made some sort of provision for the possibility of Britain being involved in a war, such provision normally including the formulation of an emergency plan, (though a number of councils dragged their feet after declaring themselves 'nuclear free zones'). They also have contingency plans for natural disasters or hazardous conditions, such as abnormally heavy snowfalls, floods or extensive oil pollution. Under such circumstances, the emergency planning officer would be responsible for the coordination and execution of the appropriate services (perhaps in conjunction with outside bodies, such as the armed forces or health services).

Environmental services often seem dull in the sense of their being devoid of conflict and controversy. There are good reasons for this – we can normally expect the bins to be emptied, the dead to be buried or the public lavatory to function without a fuss. On the other hand there are many areas of dispute in this field. In the area of planning, apart from issues such as compulsory purchase or refused planning applications, there are the larger-scale issues of planning blight, the damage caused to communities by large-scale green-field housing or redevelopment and the running down of town centres (e.g. as a result of too many out-of-town superstores), etc., which give rise to neighbourhood action groups and civic societies. In the field of transport, there are the problems of routing, parking and pedestrianization, and the broader questions of social need and loss of amenity. Questions of highway design, road crossings (at school/peak traffic times), car parking and lighting are being raised in relation to the incidence of crime, especially against women and children.

(3) Personal services

Personal services seek to enhance personal welfare.

(a) *Education*, taken as a whole, is the local authorities' most costly service (see p. 337). Their basic responsibility laid down in the Education Act 1944 and 1996 (England and Wales) and 1945 (Scotland) and the Education Reform Act 1988, is to provide, without charge, adequate primary (including nursery) and secondary education for the 9.5 million schoolchildren in Britain (in some 35,000 schools, of which 5,000 are secondary). This implies the provision and staffing of schools, the enforcement of regular school attendance and the provision of transport and maintenance and clothing grants for the children. Other welfare services include the supply of milk, meals and child guidance services, as well as special arrangements for the education of disabled or special needs children at home, in hospital or in schools.

State schools are 'maintained' by local education authorities (LEAs). Many of these in England and Wales – about one third – are known as 'voluntary' schools, implying their foundation by a voluntary organization (usually the Church) which continues to exercise a management role in spite of dependence on LEA financial support. The management committees or boards of governors of schools and colleges have been reformed (following the Taylor Committee Report 1977 and the Education Acts 1980 and 1986) to include (alongside the LEA appointees) a stronger representation of members of the public, both (elected) parents and (co-opted) business people (see p. 235). Under the Education Reform Act 1988, the governors have important new powers. In particular, they now have the responsibility for managing their school/college budget, under the system of LMS – local management of schools or (under the 1998 Fair Funding scheme) devolved funding. In the early 1990s some governors went further, under the Act, and, following a vote among parents, they opted out of LEA control and became grant-maintained (GM) by the central government through a funding agency. In 1993, there were 1,500 such schools. But under the School Standards and Framework Act 1998, they have been brought back into the mainstream as 'foundation' schools, alongside the other LEA 'community' and 'voluntary' schools. (Under the School Standards and Framework Act 1998, the remaining 140 grammar schools face the possibility of demise as and when local parents are balloted on the issue.)

Beyond the secondary school stage, LEAs were until 1993 responsible for the provision of courses in tertiary or technical colleges, sometimes known as colleges of further education, and in sixth-form colleges. In 1993, all these (500) colleges became independent of local authorities and set up as state corporations (quangos, in effect). Local authorities (on a joint or 'pooled' basis) up to 1990 were also responsible for part of the higher education system in the form of polytechnics and monotechnics. Under the Education Reform Act 1988 these have now become self-governing and have been re-titled universities, and are thus funded through the Higher Education Funding Council. Councils also provide grants for students entering post-school courses.

Despite the trauma of public expenditure cuts in recent years, there is still much talk of 'continuing education' – the opportunity for those who wish to go on learning after leaving school, or who fared badly in school and need a second chance, or who need to keep up with and adapt to economic and technological change in society. Apart from further education, what is known as 'adult education' plays an important role here, especially for those whose schooling finished early (and about one quarter of Britain's population left school before the age of fifteen). Except for some formal and examination-orientated studies, adult education is largely associated with so-called leisure-time classes – needlecraft, cookery, woodwork and art, for example. In recent years a fusion has occurred between adult education and youth services (but often also including schools, voluntary groups and volunteer tutors and parents), giving rise to 'community education'.

The main educational issue of the 1960s, however, was the comprehensive school. The post-war system of segregating secondary school children according to the results of tests given between the ages of ten and eleven (the '11-plus') was increasingly condemned as unfair and elitist. By the mid 1970s most LEAs had 'gone comprehensive', and the Education Act 1976 sought to compel the remaining LEAs to do likewise. However, the Conservative government's Education Act 1979 restored to local authorities their freedom to determine their own system of secondary education. In doing so the government was also attempting to enhance parental choice (of their children's schools) and parental participation (in the management of those schools, as governors). However, over the past twenty years it is in the field of nursery and primary education especially that parents have been encouraged to participate, as helpers and quasi-'teachers'. At the same time, the policy of designating certain parts of towns as 'educational priority areas' (EPAs) was an attempt to equalize educational opportunities by diverting extra resources to areas of deprivation: see p. 578.

Freedom is a strong feature of the British education system, for although the Secretary of State is required 'to promote the education of the people . . . and secure the effective execution by local authorities, under his control and direction, of the national policy' of education, in practice LEAs are given a substantial degree of autonomy. The British system of education is perhaps the most decentralized in Europe. However, this can have its disadvantages in that it may create too great a variety (of teaching methods, of subjects, of exam standards). The periodic discoveries of low levels of literacy and numeracy gave rise to the 'great debate' on education and the greater monitoring of standards, with demands for closer links with the world of industry. These developments have moved government policy in the direction of greater curriculum uniformity. Under the Education Reform Act 1988, a national curriculum (consisting of three core subjects – English, Maths and Science – and seven foundation subjects) was introduced, together with universal assessment and testing (or SATs) at the ages of 7, 11, 14 and 16. (The national curriculum is to be revised in 2001.) Under the School Standards and Framework Act 1998, the provision of nursery education is now mandatory, and infants' class sizes are limited to a maximum of 30.

(b) *Careers*. Most councils have had long experience in providing employment services for young people. Since the Employment and Training Act 1973 all local (education) authorities are required to provide vocational advice and guidance for pupils and students attending educational institutions (except universities) and an employment service for those leaving or having recently left such schools and colleges. Today, however, the careers service is no longer an exclusive service of local authorities and is more a partnership organization in which Technology and Enterprise Councils (TECs) are a major element (but see the Learning and Skills Bill 2000).

(c) *Personal social services* are concerned with the social welfare of people of all ages and conditions, but their main attention is focused on the more vulnerable groups in society – the elderly, children and the disabled. Broadly speaking, local authorities are required to promote social welfare by making available advice, guidance and assistance, and by providing a range of facilities. These facilities include residential homes or hostels and foster care; day-time care, training and occupation centres; help in the home, including laundry, meals and practical aids; and the support and advisory work provided by social workers, be it on an individual (casework) or group basis, or in a community setting (working with voluntary and tenants' groups).

Traditionally the emphasis has been placed on residential care and even today 50 per cent of welfare expenditure takes this form. However, since the 1950s, increasing emphasis has been given to the concept of 'community care'. Thus, in order to avoid or postpone the need for residential care of the elderly, community support has been broadened by way of home helps, aids and adaptations, special equipment, recreational facilities and help with travelling. Special 'sheltered' housing schemes have also been developed (in conjunction with housing authorities and voluntary associations). Consequently, only about 3 per cent of persons of retirement age are in residential or hospital care.

Similar forms of provision, including facilities for occupational therapy and sheltered employment, have been developed for the physically and mentally disabled (i.e. those with special needs and/or learning difficulties), often in cooperation with local voluntary groups. The intention here is to provide rehabilitation and reduce the numbers in long-stay hospitals and homes, in order to avoid segregation and the danger of institutional neurosis (or over-dependence) and also to lower costs.

There has been a significant increase in expenditure on these community services over the past twenty years, following the Social Work (Scotland) Act 1968, the Local Authority Social Services Act 1970, the Chronically Sick and Disabled Persons Act 1970 and the Disabled Persons Act 1986, and partly as a result of central pressure on councils to provide for the mentally disordered, with the inducement of 'joint funds' from the NHS. This has been greatly reinforced by the NHS and Community Care Act 1990 (operative, mainly, from 1993), which seeks to shift the emphasis of welfare from hospitals and residential care to domiciliary and community care. (There is also a change in the form of provision, with local authorities themselves being less responsible for actual provision and more for arranging (through contracts) for others (private and voluntary bodies) to provide – a clear manifestation of the 'purchaser–provider' split, so evident in the NHS; see below.) However, there are many wide variations in different local authorities' provision, due in part to differences in resources, but also to differences in councillors' values, priorities and political wills. The mixed result is sometimes described as 'territorial injustice'.

Similar difficulties exist in the provision of services for children. Recent legislation (e.g. the Children Act 1989) is placing extra demands on the local authority social services departments. Apart from their traditional role as provider of care for children deprived of normal family life (through fostering and residential care in community homes), they have now to devise comprehensive adoption facilities, provide a thoroughgoing monitoring system to prevent child-abuse, and supervise young offenders in the community on a caring rather than a punitive basis. Some of these services will only be adequately developed as more resources become available to the personal social services.

(d) *The National Health Service.* The NHS, until its reorganization in 1974, was a tri-partite organization: one arm (the hospitals) was administered by appointed hospital boards; another arm (the family practitioner services) was administered by appointed local executive councils; and the third arm was administered by local authorities, who were responsible for a number of health services including health centres, home nursing, health visiting, maternity and child clinics, school medical services, family planning, vaccination and ambulances. Local government lost responsibility for these services when they transferred (in 1974) to Scottish Health Boards (15) and English and Welsh Regional (14) and Area (98) Health Authorities. The 98 Areas became 201 District Health Authorities (DHAs) in 1982 (though many have merged, or joined with Family Health Services Authorities, and have become Health Commissions, and subsequently Primary Care groups).

These health authorities are responsible for most health services.[21] They are appointed bodies and have always included members drawn from local authorities, though this has now ceased under the NHS and Community Care Act 1990. This Act also initiated the separation of responsibility for arranging provision from actual supply of service (as with community care, above). Consequently, health authorities purchase or commission services from the providing units (e.g. hospitals) on the basis of contracts, and so most hospitals have become NHS trusts. This is another example of the internal market or purchaser–provider split. Half of the DHAs have geographical boundaries that broadly match those of the main local authorities. This co-terminosity – greater before 1982 – was deliberate and aimed to facilitate liaison between local government and the health services. Furthermore, in order to promote the coordination of health and welfare services (especially for groups such as the elderly, the mentally disordered and discharged hospital patients) joint consultative committees, joint planning teams and jointly financed projects have been established. Another aspect of the NHS is of particular interest to local government: the Community Health Council or, in Scotland, Local Health Council. There is such a local health council for every health district. Their purpose is to monitor the health services and represent to the health authorities the views of the consumer. By law at least half of the members of health councils must be drawn from neighbouring local authorities.

Thus local government has a continuing interest in the nation's health services. This is perhaps inevitable, since the boundary between health and welfare service is not clear-cut, and many people felt that a reorganized and strengthened local government system could be strong enough to take over responsibility for the NHS.[22] While this now seems out of the question in the immediate future, the idea is by no means dead and buried (and it has been partially revived by the Griffiths Report on *Community Care* (1988) and since).[23]

(e) *Housing* covers a wide range of services, some of which could be said to fall within the environmental and protective fields. Thus, as an adjunct to public health, local authorities have long been empowered and (through subsidies) encouraged to clear slums and re-develop or rehabilitate whole areas (known as 'general improvement areas' and 'housing action areas'). Similarly they have developed powers to control overcrowding. In general, their principal statutory duty is to undertake periodic reviews of housing conditions in their areas.

It was in response to the need to rehouse persons displaced by slum clearance that council housing was introduced in the nineteenth century. However, it was not until general subsidies began after 1919 that the building of council houses began on a large scale. Local authorities currently provide about a quarter of housing accommodation in Britain (i.e. they own about 5 million houses or flats).

Central government grants have been paid to encourage local authorities to provide housing. They are also intended to reduce rent charges to tenants. However, when it was felt that such subsidized rents were too indiscriminate and wasteful, the Conservative government passed the Housing (Finance) Act 1972 which required local authorities to charge 'fair' (generally higher) rents, but with reductions for those on low incomes. This policy was welcomed in many quarters as fair, rational and long overdue, as well as contributing to a reduction in state expenditure. Elsewhere (generally on the Left) it was condemned as inflationary, exploitative and profiteering, and also autocratic, since local authorities were no longer free to decide their own rents. Councillors at Clay Cross (Derbyshire) actually refused to implement the law and were displaced by housing commissioners, appointed by the Secretary of State. These councillors were saved from threatened imprisonment by the Labour government, which restored local authorities' housing powers in 1975. However, the other main part of the 1972 Act was left intact. This is the scheme whereby tenants in *privately* rented accommodation receive rent allowances according to their income. Rents are settled (if necessary with the assistance of rent officers and rent panels) and the role of local housing authorities is to process tenants' claims and disburse the appropriate allowances (for which they are largely re-imbursed by the government). Since 1982–3, rent rebates and allowances became known as 'housing benefits'.

In recent years governments have tended to give added emphasis to the policy of housing conservation and improvement. Local authorities are responsible for the distribution of housing renovation grants and for ensuring that any conditions attaching to them are complied with. Generally speaking the grants are payable for housing conversions (into flats, for instance) and for improvements (like the installation of amenities such as running water or a WC or thermal insulation). Local authorities have the power to compel owners to improve their properties. The most important grant condition concerns future occupation: in order to prevent abuse, restrictions are placed on the immediate future use or occupation of the improved properties. In addition certain grants are not payable if the property exceeds a certain rateable value. Overall the number of such grants increased substantially in recent years, from 128,000 in 1968 to 200,000 in 1980, but have since declined and there is now a waiting list.

The most controversial aspect of housing has been the sale of council houses (see Norwich case, p. 702). Since 1980 it has become incumbent on local housing authorities to sell some of their housing stock (at a discount of up to 60 or even 70 per cent). The broad objective is to extend the property-owning element of our democracy. However, critics point out that there should always be a sizeable proportion of rented accommodation (which the private sector is failing to provide) and that the private sector can be left to supply adequately for owner-occupation. Also, in recent years, local authorities (except in Scotland) have been restricted to using only a limited proportion (25 per cent) of the proceeds of house sales (worth £5 billion) for new building (which has fallen significantly), the remainder being used for debt repayment. In addition, local authorities already promote owner-occupation through the provision of mortgage advances (up to 100 per cent in some cases), by guaranteeing the repayment of loans from building societies and, most recently, through rents-to-mortgages schemes.

Under the Housing Act 1988, council tenants now have the right to opt out of their local authority tenancy and transfer to another landlord, where the latter is prepared to take over the housing stock and manage the property in a 'social' (rather than purely commercial) manner. The transfer can only take place if a majority of tenants on individual housing estates vote in favour. Over 40 local authorities have transferred their entire housing stock and some 200,000 houses have thus transferred to housing associations or not-for-profit housing companies, some of which have been set up by local authorities themselves (to give them greater flexibility, especially in the raising of capital finance – approaching some £3 billion by 1996. Some councils have also released themselves from debt in this way).

Local authorities have other important housing responsibilities. These include the provision and control of caravan sites and the ancient responsibility of providing accommodation for the homeless. Since the Housing (Homeless Persons) Act 1977 (as amended by the Housing Act 1985) the responsibility (currently affecting some 120,000 households) has been transferred to local housing authorities from social service departments. Another more recently developed 'welfare' service is the local authority provision (either direct or indirect) of housing advice and aid centres. As part of the policy of community care (see p. 100) housing authorities have been placing emphasis on the provision of housing for special needs.

(4) Amenity services

Amenity services provide for citizens' leisure time and, more than any other, tend to be taken for granted, mainly because they have long been provided by local government and have become very closely identified with it – museums, art galleries, parks and gardens (now including country parks), libraries and playgrounds are typical examples. Many were established in the nineteenth century, the formative years of local government, and their foundation stones and commemorative plaques bear the names of many civic leaders of earlier generations.

The past thirty years have witnessed a significant growth in leisure time, and local authorities have made an equally significant contribution to the provision of facilities for active forms of recreation, either indirectly through grants and assistance to sports clubs, or through the direct provision of facilities such as sports centres, swimming baths, squash courts, ski slopes and skating rinks as well as the longer-established bowls, golf, tennis and other recreational grounds.

On the cultural and entertainments side, local authorities have continued to subsidize art galleries, museums and exhibitions in addition to making their own direct provision, and their library services have diversified into such areas as information provision, audio-visual materials, sound archives and special services for the disadvantaged groups.

There has been a noticeable expansion too in the number of municipal theatres, and in local authorities' promotion of groups and festivals of drama, music, crafts and dancing as well as such events as regattas, flower and agricultural shows, particularly in areas where local authorities are promoting tourism and holiday-making. For this purpose they may also provide long-distance footpaths, camp sites and perhaps hotels and restaurants. Since the Local Government Acts of 1972 (England and Wales) and 1973 (Scotland), the financial limits on local government expenditure on such entertainments have been removed. But tight budgets often place limits on such provision.

(5) Trading services

(a) *Trading services* are services for which local authorities make commercial charges. While councils charge fees for a large number of services, including adult education, day nurseries, school meals, residential care, home helps, car parks and sports facilities, these charges are generally below the full economic cost and are often scaled to take account of users' ability to pay. Apart from housing, such charges bring in only about 15 per cent of the costs. Consequently they are substantially financed by local taxes and central government grants (see Chapter 11) and are not classified as *trading* services. What distinguishes the trading services is, firstly, that their charges aim substantially to cover costs (in aggregate they cover about 90 per cent of costs) and, secondly, these charges do not normally allow for differences in the incomes of users, such as farmers who pay to sell their livestock at municipal markets. (In addition it may be added that it is only the profits and losses of the trading services – and unlike other services, not their gross income and expenditure – which are brought into account in the general revenue fund: see Ch. 11.)

Local authority trading activities are limited by the Local Government (Goods and Services) Act 1970 which essentially allows them to trade only with other public sector bodies (otherwise they may face legal action on grounds of *ultra vires*). The reason is to avoid public monies being put at risk. However, the government is currently reviewing this. In the meantime, a number of rather unusual municipal trading ventures have been allowed including Birmingham's bank, Hull's telephone system and Doncaster's racecourse, but more generally they include allotments and smallholdings, markets, civic airports, conference and exhibition centres, estate development and beach undertakings.

The importance of trading services has declined, especially since the nationalization of gas, electricity and water. And there is a general reluctance to involve local government further in competition with private enterprise, partly for political reasons (to avoid 'creeping socialism') and partly for economic reasons (to avoid the waste of inefficient management). Such arguments are not conclusive and are examined further in Chapter 11.

(b) *Economic development* Not all local trading activities manage or even aim to make a profit and may regularly be subsidized by the council. Some are perhaps run at a loss because they bring wider benefits – such as making the area more lively and attractive, which enhances local property values and job opportunities (and so local revenues). The best illustration of this is local authorities' attempts to attract commercial enterprises to their areas through offering low-rent, ready-available buildings and sites, purpose-built units, transport links, skilled labour and educational facilities (sometimes using Section 137 money: see p. 78). For example, in the 1970s, the Greater London Council set up a technology centre where newly formed companies could develop their ideas for new products. That represents one important aspect of local authorities' involvement in economic development (often these days in conjunction with the local TEC or LEC and perhaps local chambers of commerce), and frequently using EU or government funding (through the Single Regeneration Budget, City Challenge and English Partnerships).

Attracting business investment, especially large-scale (Toyota, Siemens, Philips, Lloyds, etc.) has been criticized as simply 'shuffling the pack' since where a local authority 'wins' others lose, so there is no overall benefit. Also, there may be little local gain in so far as the incoming business brings its own re-located workforce or uses non-local suppliers. Consequently some local authorities have tried to create employment by setting up their own companies and cooperative businesses. And some try to promote small business formation by ethnic minorities, women and long-term unemployed through the provision of capital, training, advice and facilities (such as creches and managed workspaces). Local authorities have also responded positively to the government's 'New Deal' and 'Welfare to Work' programmes, Regional Development Agencies (long a feature in Wales and Scotland) should help to coordinate and reinforce local efforts (as Government Offices for the Regions have also been doing since 1996).

(6) Legal services

Legal services do not fall within the mainstream of local authority responsibilities, but there is a connection. While in Scotland the probation service is part of the social-work department's role, in England and Wales the only link is through local authorities having to help finance, and perhaps help compose, probation committees which organize the service locally. Similarly, local authorities contribute to the running costs, and perhaps the membership, of the magistrates' committees which manage the magistrates' (JPs) courts and youth courts, and the coroner service. Local authorities administer the registry of births, marriages and deaths. Elected councillors also help to constitute various local tribunals and appellate bodies, such as those that deal with appeals on school placements and property valuation and council taxes.

A note on joint provision

The Local Government Act 1985 abolished the metropolitan counties (see p. 51) and the GLC (see p. 121) in 1986, and redistributed their responsibilities among the local authorities in these areas. Most of the functions of the metropolitan counties were transferred to the metropolitan borough councils (which thus became the sole principal local authorities in these areas). A number of the functions (planning, highways and traffic management, waste disposal) require that there is considerable coordination, cooperation and sharing of specialist staff resources by the boroughs. However, certain functions – those of a 'county-wide' nature (i.e. police, fire, civil defence, public transport) – were transferred to statutory joint authorities or boards (or what are becoming known as 'qualgos': quasi-autonomous local government organizations). Much the same happened in the reorganization of local authorities in Wales and Scotland in 1995/6, and to a lesser extent in England when the unitary authorities were created 1995–8.

Joint *boards*, unlike joint committees, are corporate bodies created under law by Ministers and/or Parliament, not by councils themselves. Unlike joint *committees*, boards have a 'life' of their own (i.e. they continue in being regardless of changing membership); they can hold property, levy charges or precepts and raise loans. Either way, such arrangements have been criticized for creating public confusion, for fragmenting what should be a coherent approach to urban problems, and for diminishing accountability and democracy by further manifesting the 'corporate state' (or 'corporatism') where governmental decisions are made by organized bodies on behalf of the public, who may have little or no say, or control. It is also widely believed that bodies such as these tend to be wasteful of expenditure.

5

LONDON'S LOCAL GOVERNMENT

London's system of local government has a number of distinctive features – a consequence of its importance as the nation's capital and of its preponderant size. With a population of 7 million, London contains nearly one in seven of the nation's population.

Local government in London has always posed difficulties owing to the rapid and continuous growth of its urban population. An immediate problem is to determine what and where exactly London is. Up to the nineteenth century, for local government purposes, it consisted essentially of the ancient City of London: the square mile of heartland which was governed by a Corporation consisting of aldermen, sheriffs, liverymen, freemen and justices – all functionaries of medieval origin. Around this nucleus lay the ancient counties of Middlesex, Kent, Surrey and Essex, which were governed by JPs and parish vestries. The increasing urban development of London led to the creation of numerous *ad hoc* authorities – turnpikes trusts, Commissioners of Police, Boards of Guardians, and Boards of Commissioners with powers of sewerage, paving and water supply – all operating over limited areas. Thus by the mid nineteenth century there were some 300 such bodies (with about 10,000 members) all functioning in the area which became known as the 'metropolis' owing to its substantial population growth and urbanization. (In the period 1801–61 the population increased from 865,000 to 2.8 million in the area subsequently covered by the LCC.)

The Municipal Corporations Act 1835 (see p. 16) had not applied to London. Instead, because of its special problems, London was the subject of a separate report by the Royal Commission on Municipal Corporations in 1837. This considered the feasibility of placing London directly under the jurisdiction of the central government. On balance the report recommended a system of local self-government for London by extending outwards the authority of the City Corporation. This was not acted upon, but in 1854 another Royal Commission reported and emphasized the problems created by a multiplicity of unco-ordinated authorities and communities within the vast urban sprawl of the metropolis and its surroundings, promoted by the railway development of the mid nineteenth century. However, this Commission rejected the notion of a single elected council for the whole of the London area on the grounds of size: that local government should be based on local knowledge and a community of interest, neither of which, it felt, would be possible with a single authority. London was more a collection of communities. The result was a compromise. Under the Metropolis Local Management Act 1855 a two-tier system was to replace the haphazard arrangements then existing. An area of 75,000 acres (containing 2.8 million people) was clearly defined. It contained ninety-nine parishes, but most of these were grouped into districts, each under a district board. These vestries (fifteen) and district boards (twenty-three), together with the City, which remained unchanged, were to continue as the primary units of local government in London, with responsibility for local sewerage and drainage, paving, lighting and street cleaning. Superimposed on this pattern of authorities was a new central body, the Metropolitan Board of Works. It had forty-five members, indirectly elected from the constituent parish vestries and district boards, with a term of office of three years, and it was given responsibility for main sewers throughout the metropolis. However, it was to become more than just a sanitary authority, for subsequently it acquired responsibility for (and achieved some notable successes in) flood prevention, fire services, housing provision, building controls and street improvements. It also had a supervisory role in relation to the public health activities of the primary authorities.

However, such control was weak and did not prevent some dereliction of responsibility by the vestries and boards. The Board of Works lacked authority (being indirectly elected) and failed to inspire civic pride. Furthermore its position was undermined by the continued existence of a number of *ad hoc* authorities within its territory. These included the Metropolitan Asylums Board (established 1867), which arranged for the grouping of Boards of Guardians and their provision of accommodation and hospitals; the London School Board (established 1870), with responsibility for the provision of state elementary schools in London; and the Port of London Sanitary Authority (established 1872), providing for public health in the dockland areas. Meanwhile, water supply was in the hands of nine private companies and gas in the hands of three more.

Subsequently there developed a movement for the reform of local government in London. Various pressure groups were involved – the Municipal Reform Association (founded 1866), the London Municipal Reform League (1881) and perhaps above all the Fabian socialists, who saw London as pioneering a 'brave new England' of municipal enterprise (otherwise known as 'gas and water socialism'). Such notions aroused the hostility of the City and the fears of those who foresaw the ignorant masses holding sway over the richest and most prestigious city in the world. Consequently, the argument became not whether to rationalize the government of London, but how to do so, and in particular which tier or level of authority was to predominate – the county or the district authorities.

The reform of local government in London took place as a result of the insistent pressure of those who argued that, like every other town, London should have a directly elected body to represent ratepayers. But the more immediate reasons were (1) the alleged corruption and investigation of the Metropolitan Board of Works (in 1888) and (2) the fact that the rest of English local government was being reorganized (see p. 18). However, the reform was controversial and modest in scope, partly because of the widespread fears and opposition of those who foresaw a socialist London re-creating something approaching the Commune, the left-wing revolutionary government which ran Paris in 1871, after the Franco-Prussian war. Thus under the Local Government Act 1888 an elected London County Council (of 124 councillors and twenty aldermen) replaced the Metropolitan Board of Works and became responsible for its functions. But the new LCC was given few additional powers, and its area of administration, to be known as the Administrative County of London, covered only the Metropolitan Board of Works' former territory, despite the growth of population. Furthermore, the forty-one vestries and district boards plus the City remained untouched, thus detracting from the authority of the LCC to speak for London – a situation which was exacerbated by the continued existence of numerous *ad hoc* bodies including the Metropolitan Asylums Board, the Boards of Guardians, the Metropolitan Police, Burial Boards, School Boards and the Thames Conservancy Board.

Despite its inauspicious beginnings, the LCC soon grew in stature, partly because of its endeavours and achievements, and partly because of the eminence of its members, such as Lord Rosebery, who became Liberal Prime Minister in 1894–5, and Sidney Webb, a leading member of the Fabian Society. Socialist members[1] and non-members called for greater powers for the LCC. They wanted a municipal takeover of water, gas, transport and the docks. They also envisaged a programme of action to deal with housing, unemployment and land speculation. In the process, they sought the abolition of the numerous vestries and boards in their midst.

These proposals were offensive to Conservative opinion and, following the recommendations of a Royal Commission Report of 1894, but partly also under pressure from the larger vestries themselves, the government passed the Local Government Act 1899. This Act reorganized the lower tier of London's local government by replacing the mass of vestries and boards with twenty-eight municipal boroughs, each with an elected council. (The City remained unaffected.) They were given significant responsibilities for public health, housing, libraries, recreation and rating, and the whole arrangement seemed clearly aimed at reducing the power of the LCC by enhancing that of the boroughs: a counterweight to the actual or threatened excessive power of the top tier. Consequently, the Act was criticized as having, in effect, broken up London into a collection of twenty-eight power centres (or 'Birminghams'), and further that, being artificial creations, these centres lacked any civic identity of the sort that Birmingham and other county boroughs could reasonably claim.

However, it would be inaccurate to see the London boroughs as county boroughs (see p. 18). They were really a new genre of local authority: something more than town councils but less than county borough councils. Equally the LCC was unique as a county council, for it lacked some of the powers and authority which other counties possessed. Nevertheless, in the course of time, its prestige mounted, and in parallel with other local authorities in Britain the LCC became responsible for a whole range of functions, some of which were new, such as planning (1909) and education welfare (1907), and some of which were transferred from *ad hoc* bodies, such as school education (1902) and health and welfare services (1930).

Meanwhile, the population pattern was changing (see Table 4). The population of inner London (the 117 square miles of the LCC area) stopped growing in the twentieth century and indeed began to fall. The surrounding area of nearly 600 square miles (outer London – the area which covered that originally designated to the Metropolitan Police in 1829) continued to grow rapidly.

Developments in electricity, slum clearance, transport and communications were increasing the mobility of the population and thus reducing the validity of the administrative boundaries and the division of responsibilities. Under the impetus of the LCC, the concept of 'metropolitanism' began to emerge: the idea of a government for Greater London as a whole (both the inner and the outer areas) and having responsibility for services such as public health, planning, housing and transport, on the grounds that these could be effectively handled only by a single authority operating over the wider area.[2] As if to demonstrate the point, in 1933 the LCC's transport functions were transferred to the London Passenger Transport Board, a new *ad hoc* body with responsibility for services in and beyond the Greater London area.

In 1940, the Royal Commission on the Distribution of the Industrial Population (Barlow) drew attention to the growth of London, which was being accelerated by the 'drift' of the population to the South and East. Also, the problems of reconstruction after the war, coupled with the increase in commuting[3] between inner and outer London, were threatening the integrity of the Green Belt (the zone of protected countryside surrounding London) and led to the urgent consideration of a strategy for planning in the London region.

The immediate result was the Abercrombie Plan of 1944, which recommended the creation of a ring of small new towns around London and the setting-up of a regional planning board. But planning was not the only problem, and clearly something more comprehensive was needed.

Table 4 *The population of London*

	City of London	Inner London*	Outer London†	Greater London conurbation
1801	128,269	959,310	157,980	1,117,290
1851	127,869	2,363,341	321,707	2,685,048
1901	26,923	4,546,267	2,050,002	6,596,269
1951	5,324	3,347,956	5,000,041	8,347,997
1961	4,767	3,492,879	4,499,564	7,992,443
1971	4,245	3,031,935	4,420,411	7,452,346
1981	5,893	2,496,756	4,199,252	6,696,008
1991	4,100	2,530,500	4,359,400	6,889,900

*Comprising the County of London after 1888 and the inner boroughs after 1965.
†After 1965 the outer London boroughs.
NOTE: this Table is based on the official (Census) definition of Inner London, comprising 14 boroughs; it thus differs slightly from the area of ILEA (see p. 119).

In 1945, while the Boundary Commission looked at the rest of England and Wales (see p. 37), a special committee under Lord Reading was appointed to inquire into and advise on the local government problem within the County of London. But this committee was soon disbanded when it was realized that the scope of the inquiry was too narrow and the problem of London government needed to be considered within a regional context. This wider inquiry took the form of a Royal Commission (known as the Herbert Commission).

The Herbert Commission (1957–60)

London had outgrown its nineteenth-century local government structure. In recognition of this fact, the Royal Commission on Local Government in Greater London (1957–60) was to examine the Greater London area, within and beyond the LCC area, and it therefore included those built-up areas which identified with London but technically formed part of the separate counties surrounding London (the 'Home Counties'[4]). Thus the social unit of Greater London was not reflected in its local government structure: services were administered by seven county councils, three county boroughs, twenty-eight London boroughs, the City Corporation and seventy-one UDCs, RDCs, and non-county boroughs, apart from half a dozen *ad hoc* authorities. As the Royal Commission commented,

The machinery is untidy and full of anomalies. There is overlapping, duplication, and in some cases gaps . . . The fact that local government in London does manage to hang together and avoid breakdown says much for the British knack of making the most cumbrous machinery work . . . judged by the twin tests of administrative efficiency and the health of representative government the present structure . . . is inadequate and needs overhaul. (paras. 286, 696) . . . none of these major functions [except environmental health] can be discharged best by the local authorities which exist under the present structure of local government, and . . . some of them cannot be adequately discharged at all. (para. 672)

The report of the Royal Commission, published in 1960 (Cmnd 1164), was unanimous in its recommendations for change. Its detailed proposals for a two-tier structure were based on the principle of having as many services as possible concentrated in the hands of the borough councils, except where these could be better performed over the wider area and thus by an 'umbrella' or supra-borough authority. This body was to be the Greater London Council. The Commission recommended that:

(1) The London County Council and the Middlesex County Council be abolished and replaced by a Greater London Council (GLC) whose jurisdiction would also include the metropolitan areas of Essex, Kent, Surrey and Hertfordshire together with the county boroughs of Croydon, East Ham and West Ham. The area thus created would cover about 600 to 800 square miles and contain some 8 million people.

(2) Within that area covered by the GLC, the existing local authorities were to be reduced from ninety-five to fifty-two, to be called Greater London boroughs (except the City, which was to retain its ancient identity).

(3) Greater London boroughs were to have responsibility for the local

services of housing, health, welfare, libraries and non-major roads. The GLC would exercise the wider, strategic, functions of fire, ambulances, main roads and refuse disposal. In education and planning the GLC would be the main authority, but the boroughs would have executive powers, that is the GLC would draw up the development plan for Greater London, but the boroughs would deal with local planning applications; in education, the GLC would be the local education authority, owning the schools and appointing teachers, but the day-to-day running and maintenance of the schools would rest with the boroughs. The GLC would also have some concurrent and supplementary (shared) powers in the fields of housing, open spaces, sewerage and drainage where these functions cut across or involved several boroughs, such as large housing and redevelopment schemes or the very large London parks.

The government responded favourably to the report, though it did propose some amendments. Reactions elsewhere were more hostile: some, such as Middlesex, sought to preserve their own existence; others, such as the LCC, were afraid of the upheaval to services which the reorganization would cause; and inevitably there were fears, especially in the Labour Party, about the threat to party fortunes. An independent panel considered the local authorities' comments and there was further acrimony and review as the Bill went through Parliament. The result was the London Government Act 1963 (which came into operation in 1965). Under the Act:

(1) An area of local government, somewhat smaller than that suggested by the Royal Commission, was designated as Greater London. It was to have an elected council of a hundred councillors (reduced to ninety-nine in 1973) and sixteen aldermen – special councillors. (They were abolished in the GLC in 1977 and in the London boroughs in 1978.)

(2) The area was divided into thirty-two London boroughs (plus the City), each with an elected council comprising councillors and aldermen.

(3) Functions were allocated largely as recommended in the Royal Commission report,[5] with the notable exception of education. Since the boroughs were now to be fewer and larger than originally

envisaged, it was felt appropriate to give them responsibility for education. However, in order to preserve the unity of the education services built up by the LCC, it was decided that the inner London boroughs would not individually control education. Instead, in that area (the original LCC area) education would be administered by a special committee of the GLC, called the Inner London Education Authority (ILEA), consisting of members of the GLC from inner London, together with a representative from each of the twelve inner London borough councils (who were responsible for rate-funding the service).

Various criticisms have been levelled at the reform outlined above. There were those who thought that the reorganization did not go far enough, and that the boundaries of the GLC area had been too tightly drawn, and others who argued for a regional structure for the local government of London and the South-East. At the other extreme were those who genuinely believed that no major reorganization was necessary.[6] In between were those who felt that the allocation of functions was unsatisfactory and that inadequate attention had been paid to the functions of the *ad hoc* bodies.

Nevertheless, the new London system was, to some extent, used as a model for the reorganization of local government in the other conurbations of England (see p. 47). And a subsequent study of the London system of local government concluded that 'neither the best hopes nor the worst fears of the protagonists in the discussion which preceded the reforms appear to have been justified . . .' and on balance 'the new system represents a distinct advance in the evolution of London's government'.[7] Clearly, the study envisaged further change and drew particular attention to the problems caused by the sharing of responsibilities between the two coordinate tiers of authority (the GLC and the boroughs). This problem was reiterated in the Marshall Report in 1978.

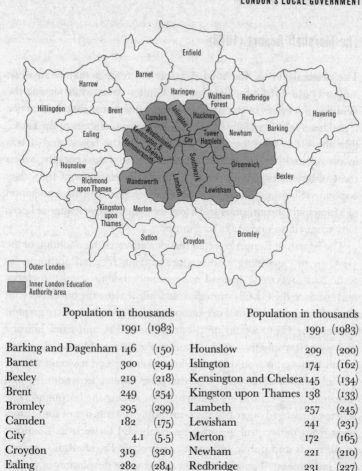

	Population in thousands			Population in thousands	
	1991	(1983)		1991	(1983)
Barking and Dagenham	146	(150)	Hounslow	209	(200)
Barnet	300	(294)	Islington	174	(162)
Bexley	219	(218)	Kensington and Chelsea	145	(134)
Brent	249	(254)	Kingston upon Thames	138	(133)
Bromley	295	(299)	Lambeth	257	(245)
Camden	182	(175)	Lewisham	241	(231)
City	4.1	(5.5)	Merton	172	(165)
Croydon	319	(320)	Newham	221	(210)
Ealing	282	(284)	Redbridge	231	(227)
Enfield	263	(263)	Richmond upon Thames	164	(160)
Greenwich	214	(216)	Southwark	227	(215)
Hackney	188	(186)	Sutton	171	(169)
Hammersmith and Fulham	156	(150)	Tower Hamlets	168	(144)
Haringey	212	(204)	Waltham Forest	218	(215)
Harrow	204	(199)	Wandsworth	265	(258)
Havering	233	(240)	Westminster, City of	188	(184)
Hillingdon	237	(234)			

Figure 11 *Greater London and the London boroughs*

The Marshall Report (1978)

The original aim of the 1963 Act was to create a mainly strategic authority (the GLC) for the Greater London area, while leaving the delivery of services in the hands of others (the boroughs). In practice it had been felt, especially by the Conservative members of the GLC, that the GLC's strategic role had gone by the board and it was involving itself in too many other activities. Consequently, when the Conservatives gained power in the GLC elections of 1977, they appointed Sir Frank Marshall, a lawyer, ex-chairman of the Association of Municipal Corporations and a former Conservative leader of Leeds City Council, to undertake an inquiry.

The Marshall Report rejected the idea either of the abolition of the GLC or of expanding it to a wider-ranging regional authority (as some had suggested). Instead its recommendations sought to clarify and enhance the GLC's strategic role while leaving the boroughs with local executive functions. For example, to deal with the areas of greatest dispute, the GLC would drop out of the ILEA and from housing provision. It would thus concentrate on the setting of broad objectives for all London; it would oversee local policies; and it would assume overall control of resources (authorizing capital expenditures and distributing the central government grant among the boroughs). The scheme envisaged other transfers, including the transfer of some functions from the central government to the GLC (such as London's trunk roads and public transport – especially British Rail – pricing and investment). The plan thus involved some devolution of power: from the central government to the GLC and from the GLC to the London boroughs. As *The Times* concluded, the report was 'a constructive attempt to find a useful and clearly defined role for the GLC in the middle of the sandwich of power'.[8]

Abolition of the GLC: the Local Government Act 1985

In 1979 the Conservatives won the General Election and replaced the Labour Government; conversely (but being in mid-term, quite typically) in 1981 Labour won control of the GLC from the Conservatives. The new government in effect ignored the Marshall Report, and instead stumbled into a much more radical and controversial policy: the abolition of the GLC. First, in 1980 the government set up an inquiry into the future of the ILEA – much to the chagrin of most of the (Labour) inner London boroughs. The inquiry followed an earlier report by a group of London Conservatives, which referred to ILEA's poor educational standards and lack of democratic and financial responsibility and urged its dismantlement. In 1981 the government announced that the ILEA was to be retained, but this did not stop the argument or the uncertainty.

Second, in December 1981, the House of Lords declared the GLC's transport subsidy – known as 'Fares Fair' – to be excessive and illegal, thus confirming Lord Denning's earlier judgment in the Court of Appeal. Apart from the immediate financial turmoil, this decision brought allegations that the Lords and the judiciary were being political and helping the government to implement its public expenditure (local government cuts) policy. The case had been brought by Bromley Borough Council and also illustrated an element of the conflict which could arise between the London boroughs and the GLC when their party complexions differed – and when ratepayers baulk at the GLC's precept (see p. 354). But the issue also increased calls for the removal of GLC responsibility for transport.[9] This took place in 1984 when London Transport was replaced by London Regional Transport (a 'quango' appointed by the Transport Secretary)[10] because under the GLC 'transport services were not integrated, not economic and . . . not efficient' (Secretary of State for Transport in the debate on the London Regional Transport Bill 1983). There are currently (1999) proposals for the privatization of the underground railway.

Finally, there was mounting pressure for the total abolition of the GLC – partly from those who wished to see its functions transferred to the boroughs (as housing virtually has been); partly from those who saw it as merely duplicating the functions of other authorities; and from those who argued that it was redundant since it had so few responsibilities, having lost planning responsibility for the docklands area to a development corporation in 1980 and losing transport to London Regional Transport (LRT) in 1984.

In the White Paper *Streamlining the Cities* (1983), the government declared that the GLC (and the metropolitan counties) represented 'a wasteful and unnecessary tier of government'; it lacked functions and *raison d'etre*, especially since its policing (by 'the Met') is the direct responsibility of the Home Secretary and responsibility for London Transport (run by the GLC since 1969) had been transferred to London Regional Transport. In addition, the GLC was deemed the nation's principal 'over-spender' (i.e. above the government's target guideline) to the extent that it had lost entitlement to any government block grant (see pp. 147ff.). Within this context, the villain of the piece was the radical and outspoken leader of the (Labour) GLC Mr ('Red Ken') Livingstone. So the rationale behind the abolition of the GLC was an unfortunate mixture of politics, personality, economics and administration.

In April 1986, under the Local Government Act 1985, the London boroughs (plus the City of London) took over responsibility from the GLC for most of its functions, but special arrangements were laid down for many of these. Thus strategic planning was undertaken by the boroughs through a joint Planning Advisory Commission and, where appropriate, under guidance of the Minister. For many of the transferred functions, the Minister required adequate cooperative arrangements among the boroughs and exercised reserve powers where such cooperation was lacking (thus five Waste Regulation Authorities were formed for refuse disposal). Thirdly, for certain services (e.g. fire and civil defence) statutory joint boards (comprising borough councillors) were established. Under the Education Reform Act 1988, the ILEA was abolished (in 1990) and its responsibilities transferred to the constituent inner London boroughs (which received specific grants to facilitate their new role).

The GLC's responsibility for land drainage and flood protection went to the Thames Water Authority; the Arts Council became responsible for the South Bank complex and the GLC's responsibility for listed buildings and conservation was transferred to the Historic Buildings and Monuments Commission. Further allocations involved the Sports Council, the Theatre Trust, the Lee Valley Regional Park Authority and central government itself. Finally, an appointed London Residuary Body (LRB) was made responsible for those items that could not easily be transferred elsewhere (GLC debts, superannuation, properties, etc.).

Thus, London became unusual among capital cities in not having its own elected metropolitan government. Instead, it was subject to administration by some seventy to eighty different bodies (according to definition); indeed one estimate in 1994 put the figure at 270.[11] (For example there are sixteen waste disposal bodies: four statutory, twelve in the hands of the boroughs, but with eleven of them formed into three voluntary groups, together with a London-wide waste regulatory body.) This has caused confusion amongst the public and has diminished accountability. It is doubtful if any real savings have resulted and problems have arisen from the lack of coordination.[12] Such a situation was unlikely to last and it was not long before all the main political parties, to varying degrees, were developing ideas for a regional London-wide body of some kind.

The new government of London

In July 1997, the newly elected Labour government began to fulfil its pre-election promise of a new authority for London by publishing a Green Paper, *New Leadership for London* (Cmd 3724), followed in March 1998 with the White Paper, *A mayor and assembly for London*. A referendum in May 1998 endorsed the proposals (with 72 per cent support, though the turnout was only 34 per cent). Consequently the Greater London Authority Act 1999 created a directly elected, full-time, executive Mayor, accountable to an elected 25-member Assembly (the Greater London Authority), both elected and operative from July 2000. All are salaried and serve a four-year term of office (i.e. until May 2004).

The aim of the new arrangements is to overcome some of the problems arising from the abolition of the GLC by providing a strategic lead and overview (i.e. not additional service provision). Consequently, the London boroughs will continue to be responsible for the provision of most local services, alongside the various *ad hoc* agencies and authorities. But there should be more integration and partnership, and the appointed bodies will become more accountable. In brief, 'the mayor will lead and the assembly/GLA will check'. Together, their brief covers the London-wide issues of transport, economic regeneration, crime, fire and emergency services, waste, environment, planning, arts, tourism and sports – for which purposes some powers are being handed down from the government (planning, police) and new bodies are being formed. Of particular importance are four functional bodies, which report to the GLA: (i) Transport for London (TfL), with members appointed by the mayor and responsible for transport and traffic management; (ii) the London Development Agency (LDA), appointed by the mayor and, like those in the rest of England, responsible for economic development and sustainable growth; (iii) the London Fire and Emergency Planning Authority, with members appointed by the mayor from the London Boroughs and the GL Assembly; and (iv) the Metropolitan Police Authority, which thus replaces Home Office responsibility* and, like other police authorities (see p. 88), has a bare majority of elected members (i.e. the 12 appointed by the mayor from the Assembly).

The Mayor is elected (in a huge constituency of 5 million) by the Supplementary ballot (see p. 275) and is responsible for setting broad policy objectives and coordinating the work of the agencies. S/he is responsible for the budget (of £3.3bn, mainly government grants) and its allocation, i.e. allocating the expenditures of the city-wide services of police, transport, fire, etc.). S/he is also responsible for the appointment of their boards (following Nolan committee requirements of prior public advertisements).

The Assembly/GLA is responsible for monitoring the performance of the various service agencies and that of the mayor (and his cabinet). The budget requires its approval (and maybe amendment) as do the various mayoral board appointments. The 25 members are elected through a mixed (Additional Member) system of voting (like the Scottish and Welsh Assemblies) with 14 being elected by the 'normal'

---

* The Police Commissioner is appointed by the crown via the Home Secretary.

simple majority method (in constituencies based on combined boroughs) and 11 'additional' members elected on a proportional party list system*. Up to 10 may be appointed to sit in the Mayor's cabinet (or office, which may include a further two political advisers).

Inevitably, there has been opposition, especially from those who supported the abolition of the GLC. The boroughs in particular fear a diminishing role and encroachment (e.g. on to their planning powers or on to 'strategic' main roads). Other concerns have to do with a growing bureaucracy and rising costs, and perhaps the rise of populist politics. There are criticisms too about the balance (or imbalance) of Mayoral–Assembly power† or the over-dependency on central funding and lack of financial flexibility (with the Scottish Parliament having income tax powers while the GLA has the more limited option of revenue from tourism and pollution taxes).

The GLA is an untypical local authority – the more so because it is the first to have a general power (under Section 25 of the GLA Act) to promote the economic and social development of the community (subject to its not impinging on responsibilities of other authorities). It is also the first to have a directly elected executive mayor, full-time paid members and election deposits, and perhaps electronic voting. In so far as it is successful, it will provide a model for local government in Britain for the twenty-first century though the process of selecting their mayoral candidates by the Labour and Conservative parties proved a very inauspicious beginning.

* With the result that voters have four votes: two to choose the Mayor and two to choose two Assembly members (MLAs).

† The Mayor's powers of patronage/appointment are held to exceed those even of the Prime Minister or the Queen: see *The Times*, 5 January 2000.

6

LOCAL GOVERNMENT ELECTIONS

We have seen that one of the main features of local government is that it is elected. The members of local authorities – the councillors – are chosen by popular ballot, in keeping with the democratic nature of Britain's system of government. Both in theory and in practice, the electoral system in Britain's local government displays a number of democratic features – the right to vote is widespread, as is the right to stand as a candidate; the administration of elections is impartial and uncorrupt; there is plenty of advance notice about elections; the ballot is secret, and it is simple. Finally, the result of the election is direct and immediate: the composition of the council is changed to reflect the voters' preferences, the candidates who gain the majority of votes being deemed elected and becoming councillors for a fixed period of 'office'.

On the other hand, there are a number of aspects of local government elections which diminish its democratic impact. They include the low turnout at the polls; the numerous uncontested seats; the ignorance and confusion about such things as 'warding' or 'election by thirds'; and the possible injustice of the simple majority system of choosing winners. We examine these aspects in more detail below.

The administration of elections is the responsibility of the Returning Officer, usually a senior officer who often doubles as Registration Officer (see below). S/he is responsible for advising voters of the pending election and the location of the polling stations or (in Scotland) polling places. S/he also appoints polling officers, who distribute the ballot papers and supervise the polling stations (mainly schools, village halls, public buildings, etc.). The Returning Officer oversees the counting of the votes and declares the winners. S/he must also receive the nominations of the candidates and check their qualifications and their election expenditures (see p. 133).

The boundaries of local authorities are not determined by those authorities: this is the responsibility of the Local Government (Boundary) Commissions (see above, p. 73), appointed but impartial bodies who are also responsible for reviewing the electoral districts within local authorities (called 'divisions' and 'wards') in response to population changes. The objective is to have councillors representing more or less equal number of electors (both as between authorities themselves and between wards/divisions within authorities) so that imbalances can be rectified and votes have equal weighting or importance, and councillors do not have inequitable workloads).* To achieve this the Commission may seek to change the number of councillors or, more likely, redraw the boundary lines. But this has to be done sensitively – not just because of party allegiance and voting transfer consequences, but voters could find themselves in different electoral wards or divisions voting for new councillors on new issues. The Commission has to take account of electors' sense of community-identity (which can affect readiness to vote) and of councillors' capacity for representing large and sparse areas.

The right to vote

There is a widespread franchise in local elections; indeed the right to vote is almost universal. Anyone who is at least eighteen years of age† and a British subject (or a citizen of the Irish Republic or of the Commonwealth or the European Union) is entitled to vote. But certain people may be disqualified: those detained in psychiatric institutions; convicted prisoners; and persons convicted of corrupt and illegal practices in elections.[1] In order to vote, however, an elector's name must appear on the local authority's Register of Electors. This Register

---

* e.g. In 1998, each Birmingham councillor had an average of 6,235 electors compared with a figure of just 780 in Berwick-upon-Tweed. Before the review in Somerset 1998–9, the councillor in Bridgwater East represented 10,000 electors while in Dulverton it was under 4,000. It is a particular problem in metropolitan areas where many people have migrated from the inner cities to the suburbs and ward changes have not caught up.

† Scotland is considering sixteen for certain local elections: see p. 600.

(which is used for national as well as local elections) is compiled each year by the Electoral Registration Officer of the council (usually, in the shires, a senior official of the district council). S/he lists the names of residents in the electoral area who are of voting age on the qualifying date (10 October), together with 'attainers' – those who will reach voting age during the following twelve months. (In the City of London, non-residents may register to vote on condition that they occupy property there with a rateable value of at least £10 p.a. Known as the 'business vote', this additional qualification had applied to all local authorities prior to the 1969 Representation of the People Act.) The Register is published in draft form (in about December) and, following appeals over omissions and exclusions or other errors, the final Register is published and is ready for use on the following 16 February. This will lapse with the new 'rolling' system, whereby electors register as they become eligible, under the Representation of the People Act 2000.

Voting

Voting is simple enough – a matter of marking an 'X' against the name of one of the candidates listed on the ballot paper (unless there are several seats to be filled, in which case a number of Xs will be required – see p. 134). The Representation of the People Act 1969 allowed candidates to add to their names a short description (in no more than six words) of themselves and what they stand for. In practice that often means simply stating the candidate's party or putting the word 'Independent'. This has helped to remove some confusion and erroneous voting, especially in those constituencies, such as Wales, where several candidates might have the same surname (such as Jones or Thomas).

Voters who cannot attend the poll (at the local polling station, which is open 8 a.m. to 9 p.m. – compared to 7 a.m. to 10 p.m. for General Elections) are allowed to vote by post if they have moved house after the qualifying date, if they are ill or disabled and housebound or if they are engaged in religious observance for the day of the election. Electors who are working outside Britain, such as fishermen or military service personnel, are allowed to vote by proxy, that is they can nominate a person to vote on their behalf. The Representation of the People Act 1985 extended absent voter rights to holidaymakers, and to parish/community council elections. On average about 2 per cent of electors vote by post or proxy, and an estimated 7 per cent of adults (i.e. 2.5 million)[2] do not register for voting and are therefore not entitled to vote – a figure which may have increased with the introduction of the poll tax/community charge, and could affect marginal seats (see p. 369); indeed in 1993, the Office of Population, Censuses and Surveys (OPCS) estimated that one-fifth of the electorate was missing from the register in inner London and in 1998 a MORI Poll indicated that 36 per cent of 18–24 year-olds had not registered: see Appendix 17. There is some dissatisfaction with the registration system as so many people move house and fail to vote (by post or by making the journey to their former home polling area) – hence the 'rolling' reform.

The winner

The winner of an election is determined on the basis of 'the first past the post' (FPTP) – a simple majority is all that is required. Thus if there are three candidates and they receive votes as follows – Ellington 4,000, Basie 3,000, Herman 2,000 – Ellington is declared the winner. The same system is used in the General Election for Members of Parliament and it has come in for severe criticism in recent years on the grounds that:

(1) It exaggerates victories and distorts the true results. Thus in our example, while Ellington had 4,000 votes and was declared the winner, he actually had more electors 'against' him (the 5,000 who voted for the other two candidates). The distortion is magnified if we introduce political parties: for example suppose that Taunton is divided into five electoral divisions for the purpose of electing five councillors to Somerset County Council. Suppose also that Ellington is a nominee of the Conservative Party, and that in the other four divisions his party colleagues were equally successful (that is, they each had simple but not overall majorities). That would result in a 'clean sweep' for the

Conservative Party in representing the Taunton area, and the other parties would be completely unrepresented even though they attracted sizeable voting support. Thus, for example, in 1998 Labour won all the seats on Wansbeck council, and in 1996 won all 60 seats on Stoke council – a clean sweep, though other parties polled over 20 per cent of the votes. In 1990 the Liberal Democrats won 92 per cent of the seats in Richmond with only 46 per cent of the vote and in the same year, with 27 per cent of the vote, the Conservatives won just one seat (out of 24). In Islington in 1982 Labour won 51 of the 52 seats with only 51.9 per cent of the vote.[3]

Conversely, it is not unusual for candidates to win seats with 25 per cent of votes cast or even less.[4] And, in practice, parties may gain most votes yet fail to gain power (a majority of seats) in the council, e.g. in Croydon in 1994, Labour won 40 seats with 39 per cent of the votes compared to the Conservatives' 30 seats with 42.5 per cent of the votes.

(2) It creates upheavals whenever power changes hands. Thus, when a council changes hands from say Conservative to Labour, there is a lurch in policy in such matters as secondary school organization, council house rents or concessionary bus fares.

(3) Somewhat contradicting the previous point, it is argued that the simple majority system creates permanent majorities on local authorities – areas come to contain 'safe' Labour or Conservative councils. Consequently it may be that complacency or even corruption develops because there is no effective opposition.

The remedy for such defects in the voting system is often held to be some kind of *proportional representation* (PR), in which parties would be allocated seats in proportion to the volume of votes they attracted. This would be fairer and it might well produce coalition councils which could avoid lurches in policy and break up the stranglehold which some parties exert on some councils (such as those above; see too Table 7) as well as providing some real choice. On the other hand, it might add to public confusion and obscure accountability and a clear choice for voters, since there may be no clear party majority: unscheduled bargaining and deals would be struck between the party groups. In the allocation of (proportional) seats, the power of the party over the candidate/councillors is likely to increase. Problems would also arise at by-elections[5] where a vacancy occurs through death or resignation.

However, the anomalies and distortion of results produced by the present voting system is giving rise to a groundswell of opinion in favour of change. After all, a system of PR has been used for many years in Northern Ireland's local elections and now features in elections for the Greater London Authority and for the Parliaments of the EU, Wales and Scotland. Even under the existing FPTP system in Britain, one third of councils (see p. 160) have no clear party majority – they are 'hung' or balanced – yet they operate successfully (see Chapter 9). The government has not ruled it out for local elections, but much depends on its decision about Parliamentary elections following the Jenkins Report in 1998. Alternatively, councils could (should?) be allowed to decide for themselves which system is to be used.

The right to stand

A candidate must be at least twenty-one years old and be a British (or Irish, Commonwealth or EU) citizen. In addition, he or she must possess one of the following qualifications:

(1) be registered as an elector for the area;
(2) have occupied land or property in the area for at least twelve months prior to nomination;
(3) have his/her main or only place of work in that area for at least twelve months prior to nomination;
(4) have been resident in the area for the previous twelve months, or within three miles in the case of the parish/community council in England or Wales (requirements for Scottish communities vary).

On the other hand, a candidate (or elected councillor) may be *disqualified* if he or she:

(1) is (or has within five years of the election been) a declared bankrupt;
(2) as a member of the council has been found to have caused loss or

deficiency by wilful misconduct or incurred or authorized expenditure which is unlawful and exceeds £2,000;[6]

(3) has been found guilty of an offence which leads to a prison sentence (without option of a fine) of at least three months;

(4) has been found guilty (in his local authority area) of the criminal offence of corrupt and illegal practice at an election (this would include such actions as bribing or using undue influence on an elector, impersonation, hiring vehicles to convey electors to the polls, indiscriminate sticking of posters or exceeding permissible election expenses – see p. 133);

(5) becomes a paid employee of the local authority (though there are certain exceptions here; for example, state school teachers can be co-opted on to committees (see p. 235) and as an employee of the county he or she can be a member of a district council even though that authority appoints members to the County Education Committee).

All these disqualifications except (5) last for varying lengths of time, but most typically for five years. It is perhaps surprising that members found guilty of corruption (receiving bribes, non-disclosure of a financial interest etc. – see p. 220), are not subsequently disqualified unless they come into category (3). (Councillors can be dismissed if they fail to attend for council business for a continuous period of six months, or, as part of the Code of Conduct, (see p. 225) they have misused council property/resources for personal or party political purposes.)

Perhaps the most controversial of these disqualifications is (5), and many people (especially trade unionists) have argued for a relaxation of this part of the law. It is said, for example, that it is unreasonable to exclude council employees while allowing local businessmen such as estate agents, architects, building contractors etc. to qualify, since the latter may have just as much to gain from influencing council policy. The issue was considered by the Committee on Conduct in Local Government 1974 (see p. 224), which concluded that on balance it should remain unchanged. The rule reflects a more general principle, the 'separation of powers',[7] in that it attempts to avoid the situation in which a councillor who is in the employment of his own local authority might be tempted to manipulate policy to his own advantage (for example in the grading of posts). To make doubly sure, a councillor may not become an employee of his authority within twelve months of his ceasing to be a member.

In 1986, the Widdicombe Committee Report *The Conduct of Local Authority Business* found some 16 per cent of employed councillors working for (other) local authorities or 'twin-tracking' (especially teachers). The Committee was concerned here about such political activity by senior officers and its compromising effects on their ability to serve and advise their employing authority with impartiality. It smacked of self-advancement, nepotism and 'jobs for the boys'. Consequently, the Committee recommended that such officers should be disqualified from being councillors. Thus, under the Local Government and Housing Act 1989, senior employees of local authorities (some 50,000)[8] may not be elected members of *any* council (nor may they engage in political activities of any kind; see p. 295), though exceptions may be permitted. Such posts are therefore 'politically restricted' (in similar fashion to that of civil servants).

Election expenditure

Candidates in parliamentary elections are required under the Representation of the People Act 1985 to put down a 'deposit' of £500 (£600 for the European Assembly election) as an indication that they are contesting the election seriously; the money is returned if they achieve not less than 5 per cent of the total poll. This requirement does not apply to local government elections (except for candidates for the Greater London Assembly), but candidates are required to produce the written support of a proposer and seconder and (except in parishes and communities) eight other electors for that area. Candidates are also required to nominate an election agent (they can if they wish act as their own agent) whose function is to assist in the election campaign, but who is specifically charged with keeping an accurate record of the candidate's election expenditure. These accounts must be submitted to the returning officer, who will check to see that the statutory limits have not been exceeded. The object of these restrictions is to equalize election chances between rich and poor candidates. Currently, the limits for candidates are £205 per ward or electoral division plus 4p per elector.[9]

The electoral sequence

Normally we do not know more than a few weeks in advance the date of a forthcoming General Election for Members of Parliament: the decision rests with the Prime Minister (the only limitation being that a Parliament must not go beyond five years before it is dissolved and faces re-election). Local councils, however, have a fixed term of office, so that their election arrangements follow a regular sequence (apart from by-elections – see note 5 – and exceptions which occur as a result of boundary changes), and local government elections normally occur on the first Thursday in May.

All councillors are elected for a fixed term of office of four years. In most local authorities (counties, parishes, London boroughs, all Welsh councils) councillors are elected *all together* every fourth year. (In Scotland it is every third year, though in 1999 it was extended to four years to coincide with the first elections for the new Scottish Parliament. The McIntosh Commission (p. 599) commended the three-year cycle.) This is known, variously, as 'whole council', the quadriennial the 'county' or the 'all out' system. For the purpose of these elections, the local authorities are divided into electoral 'divisions' or 'wards'[10] some returning one member, others two or three. In the metropolitan districts, *one third* of the councillors are elected in each of the three years when there is no county election. This is known as 'election by thirds' (or the system of 'partial renewal' or of 'rolling elections' or simply as 'annual elections') and the local authority is divided into wards with each ward returning (usually) three councillors (or a multiple of three according to the size of the council). Non-metropolitan district councils and unitary councils in England may themselves choose which of the two systems to adopt. If they opt for the whole council system (and most – two thirds – have) they normally hold these elections in the mid-term year of the counties. Thus the election sequence runs as Table 5.

Each of the two systems has claims to superiority. It is argued by its supporters that the system of elections 'by thirds' has the merit of keeping in closer touch with public opinion, as there are (annual) elections in three years out of four. Also there is greater continuity in council policy and administration as new members of the council will form only a minority and can be 'shown the ropes' by existing councillors who form the majority. Some would claim that this system of gradually changing the composition of councils prevents the full-time officials from 'getting on top' by browbeating new and inexperienced councillors. But it has been argued more cynically that the system of election by thirds is favoured only because the frequency of elections is a device to keep local party machines in motion. In practice (apart from metropolitan districts) it is the larger towns, such as Bristol, which have opted for the 'thirds' system: these areas have a longer tradition of local party politics.

Against this system, and in favour of 'whole council' elections, is the argument that elections can be frustrating where they provide only for partial change: that it takes three or four years for a complete change to occur. Apart from frustration and disillusionment, it may be that the public get confused by these partial elections, and perhaps their frequency reduces public interest (for example, compare election turnout in counties with metropolitan councils). Certainly elections cost the councils time and money* in terms of the formal electoral arrangements and the need to recast the membership and chairmanship of committees and representation on outside bodies. (They also cost the candidates and parties in electioneering, with the thirds system making it a virtually continuous activity.)

Just as the arguments are well balanced, so too is public opinion. A survey for the Widdicombe Committee showed that 47 per cent of the public favour the whole council system, while 44 per cent prefer to vote for part of the council each year.[11] And the Widdicombe Committee itself recommended the county system,[12] as did the Local Government Commission in its recent reports on structure. Whilst this is also the Conservatives' preferred system, the Labour Party are

---

* e.g. Fowey Town council has 1,850 electors and raises £8,000 in council tax. In 1998 it spent £1,500 on a council by-election (in which 500 people voted).

Table 5 *The local elections cycle in Britain*

	1994	'95	'96	'97	'98	'99	2000	'01	'02	'03	'04
English county councils				√				√			
Metropolitan boroughs	1/3	1/3	1/3		1/3	1/3	1/3		1/3	1/2?	1/3
Some English unitaries	1/3	1/3								1/3	1/2?
Some shire districts	1/3	1/3	1/3		1/3	1/3	1/3		1/3	?	1/2?
Most shire districts		√				√				√?	
Most English unitaries		√				√				√	1/3?

English/Welsh parish/community councils	.	.	√	.	.	.	√	.
London borough councils	√	.	1/3?	.	.	.	1/3?	.
Greater London Authority (GLA)	.	.	.	.	√	.	.	.
Welsh unitary councils	√	.	.	√	.	.	√	.
Scottish unitary councils	?	.	.	?	.	.	√	.

NOTES: Some councils may not conform to this schedule owing to boundary changes, etc. Welsh and Scottish elections may be altered by their respective Assembly/Parliament after 2000. In Scottish communities elections vary considerably.

The government plans to change elections in most English councils in the new millennium (see Chapter 15); the precise date is to be decided. The pattern in the future *could* look like that shown above, with all counties and shire districts alternately electing half of their councils every two years, and all unitaries and London boroughs having elections by thirds.

in favour of having annual elections in local government, and the government is intending to implement this following the Local Government Act 2000: see Table 5 and Chapter 15.

Voting behaviour

Since elections in Britain are conducted on the basis of secret ballot, we cannot know who votes, how they vote or why they vote as they do (or do not). We must rely substantially on social survey evidence, which is inevitably somewhat limited and patchy. It is also often inconsistent.

A survey for the Maud Report[13] suggested that those with the most favourable attitudes to voting are 'likely to be men, to come from the middle age group (35–64), to come from socio-economic groups 1 and 2 and to have had more than a primary type education'. Those with less favourable attitudes are 'likely to be women; to be under 35 and over 64; to be semi- or unskilled manual workers; and to have had only an elementary or secondary education'. When the same survey investigated those who said they had voted at the last local elections, it found a close relationship to the attitude findings, except that there was no difference in (claimed) voting between men and women (although a MORI poll in 1993 indicated that young women were least interested in politics and least likely to vote). Other surveys[14] confirm some of these findings, particularly the research for the Widdicombe Committee.[15] Thus, in general:

(1) *Age* seems to make a difference in preparedness to vote: people under thirty-five appear to be less likely to vote than their elders. (It may be, of course, that older people exaggerate their declared readiness to vote in response to survey questioning. In a MORI poll in 1998, 52 per cent of 18–24 year olds said they never voted in local elections, while 73 per cent of pensioners claimed to do so: see Appendix 17 and MORI report in *Local Government Chronicle*, 6 August 1999.)

(2) *Sex* seems to make no difference (there is no 'gender gap'), as men and women appear equally likely (or unlikely) to vote, though

young married women appear to be the group least likely.

(3) *Class* generally appears to make little difference in influencing the propensity to vote (somewhat in contrast to America, where studies suggest that the middle class are more ready to vote than the working class). But there is some evidence of a greater readiness to vote in more affluent (especially metropolitan) areas.[16]

(4) *Activists*, that is party members and those who identify with and are strongly committed to a party, show (unsurprisingly) a greater than average inclination to vote.

(5) *Owner-occupiers* are more likely to vote than are tenants who rent their accommodation (This differential is largely attributable to tenants in private accommodation rather than council houses, and is likely to be associated with length of residence and mobility (and hence the age differential, above). The homeless and rough sleepers are least likely to vote since many are not, and probably cannot be, registered (though some local authorities are accepting make-shift and unorthodox locations as 'addresses' for the purpose of registration) and the Representation of the People Act 2000 now legalizes such registration.

(6) *Mobile* people, especially recent newcomers to an area, are less disposed to vote in local elections. More specifically, a report in 1992 showed differentials among those who claimed to vote varying by length of residence as: under one year 23 per cent, one to five years 39 per cent and over ten years 54 per cent.[17]

(7) *Race.* Black Britons seem to vote less often than whites, while Asian turnout is average or over.

(8) *Cognisance.* People also seem more likely to vote if they *know* the candidate(s), and they are more likely to vote *for* any candidate they know!

It may be noted that 'voting behaviour' can involve more than merely voting. There is the activity of registering to vote, and evidence suggests that, overall, some 7–10 per cent of adults may not be so registered (with perhaps up to 20 per cent in Inner London). Non-registration is particularly high (30–50 per cent) among young people, the unemployed and the black and Asian community. Reluctance to pay the community charge/poll tax may have exacerbated this problem – indeed it is estimated to have deterred 350,000 potential (and largely non-Conservative) voters.[18]

It is important to bear in mind that these are no more than tendencies drawn from a few local surveys. Any individual local election can reveal considerable variations in behaviour patterns. One particularly interesting development in recent years is the apparent emergence (or restoration) of local factors in voting for councillors. Much has been said and criticized about the overbearing influence of national attitudes and trends on local elections (e.g. how people feel about Thatcherism or New Labour, the capability of Tony Blair or Margaret Thatcher, or the state of the economy will be manifested in how they vote for local authority councillors). And there is much evidence of such local impact by national politics (see p. 176). But there is evidence too that *local* issues are often influential, as in the success of low poll-tax councils in the 1990 elections. There is evidence of differential voting and a lack of general swing for or against a particular party in different areas (e.g. an examination of local election results across London boroughs soon confirms this). Such differences are perhaps becoming increasingly significant (see p. 177), hence the (not unwelcome) difficulty of discerning national or general swings and trends in local election results.

Polling and voting turnout

One well-documented area of electoral behaviour is that of turnout. An examination of the electoral statistics shows considerable variations in this pattern of voting between different parts of Britain (for example Wales compared with England); different types of local authority (for example ex-metropolitan county councils compared with non-metropolitan county councils in England); different (individual) local authorities of the same type; and the same local authority at different times.

One of the factors which affects turnout is the existence of political parties. Generally, it is believed that parties boost popular participation in elections (through canvassing, greater publicity, etc. – see Chapter 7). However, this can be offset where parties dominate or monopolize

particular authorities;* here elections can be seen as foregone conclusions and of relatively little importance, though in recent years
voting patterns have become more volatile: more voters have become
'floaters' and less attached and allegiant to particular parties so that
even 'safe' seats are changing (party) hands (as with the collapse of
Conservative control of so many counties in the 1993 elections). In
contrast, it is evident that polling tends to be higher where seats are
marginal and the result is uncertain;[19] here votes and voters really
count and are likely to generate greater party competition (such as
increased canvassing). In any particular area, of course, much will
depend on the vitality and resources of local parties, and on the level
of people's identification with parties.

The data in Table 7 indicate some regional and national differences
in relative turnout/polls and the contesting of seats. Table 8 displays
similar differences in party orientation. More detailed information
shows other interesting differences in the (local) political cultures of
England, Wales and Scotland and their sub-areas. For example, in
Scotland the three Island councils consist entirely of Independents,
and 20–25 per cent of districts in Wales and Scotland were run by
Independent before they became unitary in 1995. (Non-partisan politics
is a notable feature of parish and community councils.)

It was suggested earlier (p. 135) that too-frequent elections may
cause a decline in local political interest. If this were so, we would
expect to see a lower turnout of electors in those local authorities,
notably metropolitan districts, that hold annual elections (using the
thirds system) as compared to those authorities, such as counties, that
hold elections every fourth year. The figures in Table 6 give some
support to this view, since up to 1990† the metropolitan districts

* For example in 1992 Labour held 63 of the 66 council seats in Barsley MB and 17
of the 20 seats in Monklands DC (Scotland), whilst in Castle Point DC the Conservatives
held 37 of the 39 seats. In 1996 Labour won *all* 60 council seats in Stoke on Trent and
47 of the 48 seats in Newport CB, and in the same year they had all 60 seats in Newham
and 47 of the 50 in Barking and Dagenham, 69 of the 72 seats on Wigan council, 58 of
60 seats in Kingston upon Hull City, 65 of 66 in Rotherham, 61 of 63 in Wakefield, all
46 in Wansbeck, 33 of 33 in Lincoln City, 44 of 45 in Mansfield, 38 of 39 in Stevenage;
Liberal Democrats had 25 of the 26 seats in Oadby and Wigston.

† After 1988, the metropolitan districts became single-tier authorities with the abolition
of the metropolitan county councils (and the GLC).

Table 6 *Average turnout in recent sub-national elections*

	Mean (%)
Luxembourg	93
Sweden	90
Australia* (compulsory)	85
Italy	85
Belgium	80
Denmark	80
Germany	72
France	70
Spain	64
Ireland	62
Portugal	60
Israel	57
Netherlands	54
New Zealand*	53
Poland	43
Great Britain*	40
Australia* (optional)	35
Canada*	33
USA*	25

*Indicates use of a non-PR electoral system.
Source: C. Rallings, M. Temple and M. Thrasher, *Community Identity and Participation in Local Democracy*, Commission for Local Democracy, 1994.
NOTE: There is a higher turnout in some countries because of proportional and compulsory voting, as indicated. But also most countries have smaller local authority areas than in Britain, and arguably their local authorities have greater autonomy.

consistently polled below 40 per cent while the counties and London boroughs mainly polled over 40 per cent. On the other hand, those non-metropolitan districts which elect their council by thirds experience turnouts which exceed those of the metropolitan districts – for example in 1978 the average was 42.3 per cent (compared to 36 per cent for the metropolitan districts) and in 1979 the figure was 77 per cent (compared to 74.4), perhaps because they are smaller and constituents identify more closely with them. Nevertheless, within the non-metropolitan districts, the turnout is higher (up to 7 per cent higher) in those districts polling every four years.[20]

Clearly, there are other factors influencing events. One such general factor is the size of the ward/division; the smaller the ward, the higher the poll, due, at least in part, to a closer identification with the area. It may also be due to a familiarity with the candidates: people are inclined to vote for people they know (what has been termed the 'Friends and neighbours' effect[21] – though there is a risk in small wards of non-contested elections as individuals decline to stand in order to avoid giving offence to known candidates or incumbents.[22] (Parish councils perhaps exemplify this, having an average poll of 44 per cent.)

Another factor is almost certainly the incidence of non-contested seats. In general, turnout tends to be higher in those authorities where a larger proportion of wards/divisions are left uncontested: in other words, where there is a fight it will tend to be a good one.[23] Two other important influences seem to be population size and stability of population. The larger the local population, the lower the turnout tends to be. And a mobile and changing population will also lower the turnout.[24]

The most striking and apparently consistent feature of the statistics in Table 6 is the *low level* of turnout by voters[25] – indeed so low as to damage local government's claim to manifest legitimate local democracy.[26] At around 40 per cent, the poll is low in comparison to that in parliamentary elections (which have ranged from 72 per cent to 84 per cent since 1945). The exceptions were 1979 and 1997, when the local and parliamentary elections were held simultaneously: electors simply put their 'X' on two ballot papers instead of the usual one. Consequently, the local poll rose dramatically (though not surprisingly) in those years. But thereafter, the average local turnout returned to its norm of around 40 per cent. Thus, in 1985 the average (for England and Wales) was 41.1 per cent (from 75.8 in 1979) and in 1998 (for England) the poll was only 30 per cent (from 71.5 in 1997)*. Clearly, the reorganized

* In 1999 the average poll in England was 32 per cent. It was higher in Wales (46 per cent) and Scotland (59 per cent), partly, at least, because local elections coincided with the elections for their National Assembly/Parliament.

Table 7 Local government elections: principal authorities in Britain (selected years)

Area/Type of authority	Year	Total of electors	Total of councillors	Councillors returned unopposed		Councillors elected	Electors in contested areas	Total poll	% poll
	(1)	(2)	(3)	returned unopposed (4)	% returned unopposed (5)	(6)	(7)	(8)	(9)
ENGLAND – counties	1973	19,354,642	3,129	396	12	2,731	17,386,510	7,399,655	42.6
	1977	20,195,908	3,129	376	12	2,753	18,397,510	7,795,341	42.3
	1985	22,211,838	2,005	33	1.6	1,969	22,032,571	9,020,828	41.0
	1989	—	—	64	2.1	3,005	—	8,794,061	39.2
	1993	—	—	60	2	2,998	—	8,392,804	37.2
	1997	—	—	33	1.5	7,203	—	—	73.2
Non-metropolitan (or shire) districts	1973	19,354,642	13,560	1,665	12	11,879	17,416,523	6,730,483	38.6
	1976	20,228,191	13,614	2,207	16	11,388	17,082,398	7,569,057	44.3
	1978	3,000,429	1,989	47	7	628	2,487,184	1,053,301	42.3
	1979	20,807,223	13,510	2,269	19	9,840	17,186,806	13,216,753	76.0
	1987	—	—	—	11.3	—	—	—	44.0
	1988	—	—	—	4.3	—	—	—	41.6

1990	—	~	—	3.7	—	—	—	48.6
1991	—	—	—	12.4	10,110	—	9,802,201	48.1
1992	—	—	—	3.4	—	—	—	38.3
1994	—	—	—	—	—	—	—	42.6
1995	—	—	—	—	—	—	—	41.8
1996	—	—	32	2.0	1,528	—	2,313,217	37.2
1998	—	—	—	—	—	—	—	30.8
1999	—	—	522	6	—	—	—	35.5
Metropolitan districts								
1973	8,327,570	2,514	66	3	2,445	8,204,197	2,744,195	33.4
1976	8,466,953	2,517	13	0.5	838	8,116,271	3,151,964	38.8
1978	8,482,364	2,517	7	0.3	930	8,327,862	3,099,025	36.1
1979	8,652,318	2,508	9	0.4	978	8,291,576	6,174,319	74.4
1982	—	—	—	—	—	—	—	37.6
1983	—	—	—	—	—	—	—	41.2
1984	—	—	23	—	—	—	—	38.6
1982	—	—	—	—	—	—	—	37.6
1986	—	—	—	2.9	—	—	—	39.3
1987	—	—	13	—	—	—	2,754,650	44.0
1988	—	—	16	2.1	—	—	—	38.8
1990	—	—	53	6.4	—	—	3,816,525	46.3
1991	—	—	37	4.5	—	—	—	40.8
1992	—	—	—	1.5	—	—	2,754,650	32.5

1994	—	—	—	—	—	—	—	39.0
1995	—	—	31	3.5	842	—	2,736,069	33.8
1996	—	—	34	3.9	836	—	2,467,478	30.5
1998	—	—	—	—	—	—	—	24.8
1999	—	—	11	1.3	—	—	—	26.1
London boroughs								
1974	5,300,915	1,867	22	1	1,845	5,182,440	1,893,009	36.0
1978	5,195,451	1,908	0	0	1,908	5,111,143	2,213,507	43.3
1982	5,095,833	1,914	2	0.3	1,912	5,090,625	2,233,386	43.8
1986	5,113,730	1,914	3	0.1	1,911	5,107,386	2,321,072	45.4
1990	—	—	—	0.5	—	—	—	48.1
1994	—	—	—	—	—	—	—	46.0
1998	—	—	—	—	—	—	—	34.6
Unitary authorities								
1996	—	—	3	0.5	658	—	648,421	34.6
1997	—	—	4	0.4	1,044	—	1,811,600	69.7
1998	—	—	—	—	—	—	—	27.8
1999	—	—	11	0.9	—	—	—	31.5
WALES – counties								
1973	1,982,126	578	109	19	468	1,647,836	906,830	55.0
1977	2,055,109	578	122	21	456	1,714,085	874,323	51.0
1985	1,966,449	494	129	26	364	1,460,874	752,723	45.8

Districts								
1989	—	—	145	22	504	—	730,905	44.0
1993	—	—	111	18	502	—	678,203	38.2
1973	1,982,126	1,521	281	18	1,240	1,690,233	847,131	50.0
1976	2,046,375	1,513	316	21	1,194	1,709,809	909,300	53.0
1979	2,084,700	1,521	396	27	1,119	1,675,048	—	77.0
1987	—	—	—	—	—	—	—	40.7
1988	—	—	—	—	—	—	—	42.1
1990	—	—	—	—	—	—	—	45.8
1991	—	—	—	27	1,367	—	—	53.4
1992	—	—	—	—	—	—	—	33.8
Unitary								
1995	—	—	—	20	1,272	—	926,216	48.8
1999	—	—	200	15.7	—	—	—	49.7
SCOTLAND – regions and islands								
1974	3,704,758	507	77	15	430	3,445,472	1,708,792	50.1
1978	3,809,212	508	134	26	374	3,356,403	1,509,476	45.0
1982	3,881,552	520	110	21	410	3,586,549	1,540,773	42.9
1986	3,948,194	524	8	15	435	3,754,717	1,711,040	45.6
1990	—	—	—	8.5	—	—	—	45.9
1994	—	—	—	—	—	—	—	45.6
Districts								
1974	3,655,775	1,110	223	20	887	3,173,701	1,636,859	52.1
1977	3,735,784	1,114	247	22	867	3,230,280	1,540,280	48.2
1980	3,808,438	1,123	289	25	834	3,184,075	1,469,496	46.2
1984	3,887,914	1,152	250	22	902	3,387,754	1,493,280	44.1

1988	—	—	—	—	—	—	45.5
1992	—	—	—	13	—	—	41.4
Unitary authorities	1995	—	52	4.3	1,161	1,702,473	44.9
	1998	—	—	—	—	—	27.8
	1999	—	—	56	4.6	—	59.4

Source: Office of Population Censuses and Surveys Electoral Statistics; Registrar General (Scotland) Annual Reports (adapted); J. M. Bochel and D. T. Denver, *The Scottish Regional/District Elections,* Dundee University (various years); *Scottish Government Yearbooks,* Edinburgh University; C. Rallings and M. Thrasher, *Local Elections Handbook(s),* LGC, www.lgcnet.com; London Boroughs Association and London Research Centre; individual local authorities.

NOTES: In 1979, 1997 and 1999 local government elections coincided with the Parliamentary or Assembly election. Apart from any other consideration, this meant that the polling stations were open for an hour longer than normal.

The figures in columns (4) and (6) do not always add up to those of column (3) because some elections are held only for part of the council, and also because some seats may be left vacant, as when an election is cancelled (countermanded) due to death of a candidate.

For data on elections in the (now defunct) Greater London Council and the metropolitan county councils, see Table 6 of earlier editions of this book (up to and including the fourth edition, 1986).

After 1986 the government stopped collecting and/or publishing local electoral data. Consequently, the statistics presented above are drawn from a variety of sources.

(post-1974) local government system has not succeeded in attracting voters as had been hoped by some advocates of reorganization in the early 1970s[27] (see Appendix 3). The introduction of the community charge/poll tax was intended to raise public interest in local government and boost turnout, and there was some increase in polling, for example in the metropolitan districts where there was an increase from 38.8 per cent (in 1988) to 46.3 per cent (in 1990). But there was no significant change in the Scottish regions/islands and even the rise in the metropolitan districts' turnout* was short-lived (see Table 7).

The low polls in local government elections are widely held to reflect a lack of interest, and local electorates are derided as apathetic. In the elections for the London County Council in 1946, the poll was just 26 per cent and in 1956 it was 31 per cent for the London borough elections. More recently, following the exceptionally low turnout for the English 1999 local elections (32 per cent) and 1998 (30 per cent) and individual figures such as 21 per cent in Stoke, 18 per cent in Kingston upon Hull and 17.4 per cent in Wigan, together with polls in some wards – in Stoke, Liverpool and Sandwell for example – of 10 per cent or less, the press declared that 'the Apathy party' had won! There may well therefore be some truth in the assertion. An inquiry for the Maud Committee (1967) showed that among those who did not vote in local elections were substantial proportions of electors – over 20 per cent in some places – who said they were not interested in local elections or they did not know, or did not know enough, about the election taking place.[28] In a National Consumer Council survey in 1995, 66 per cent said they knew 'just a little or hardly anything' about their local council. A survey for the Widdicombe Committee (1986) revealed 34 per cent who did not know who to vote for because local elections are so complicated.[29] (One surprising finding of recent analysis, however, is that very few – only one per cent – of the non-voters abstain from voting on a regular basis; the 'serial abstainer'

---

* The rise may have been due more to the publicity surrounding the controversial introduction of the tax rather than the local incidence of the tax itself, especially since there is evidence that rate-paying seems 'to make no difference to the level of electoral participation' (C. Rallings *et al.*, *Community Identity and Participation in Local Democracy*, CLD, 1994, p. 23). More generally it is suggested that turnover varies with economic growth: see *Comparative Political Studies*, December 1996.

is a rare species, most behave only intermittently in this respect.)[30] It also concluded that Britain's local election turnout 'is almost bottom of the international league table'. This has been well documented[31] as Table 6 illustrates. A survey in 1991 made a similar point but also suggested that the number of people who think their vote is effective in deciding how their locality is governed has fallen since 1965[32] from 77 per cent to 60 per cent in 1985; by 1994 it had fallen to 54 per cent.[33]

However, instead of blaming the public for their ignorance or apathy, perhaps we should look elsewhere for an explanation. It may well be, for example, that people see local authorities as essentially administrative rather than decision-making bodies, so that it little matters to electors who sits on the council: even if the election totally changes the composition of the council, the administrative end-product will be the same. Rightly or wrongly, council decisions may be seen as not very important, since it is felt that the central government and Parliament make the strategic decisions (hence the impact of national politics on local elections – see p. 176). At local level, much policy-making is often seen as no more than an adjustment here and there – whether to raise the fees for adult education classes by 50p rather than £1; which of the libraries is to be closed down; what kind of comprehensive school system or sheltered housing design to adopt. These are administrative details which may be of interest to councillors and officers, but are hardly issues of principle to excite the general public. In the nineteenth century the 'improvers' battled with the 'economizers' to persuade the public of the need for municipal provision of water, public health or building controls, but perhaps all the battles of principle have been won, so that now local authorities can be run on a simple care and maintenance basis.

Yet there *are* issues in local government, and policy decisions *can* give rise to considerable argument – and high polls (see p. 663, note 25). Current and widespread examples include the sale of council property, concessionary bus fares, direct service provision versus contracting out ('privatization') and rate/council tax levels.[34] While there may be no specifically Conservative or Labour way of paving the streets, for example, even here awkward political questions remain to be dealt with: whose street is to be repaved first? Who will get the contract? Why not spend the money on a sports hall or keeping open a threatened day centre instead? As Professor George Jones has said,

Political parties are not artificially imposed on local government. They grow out of a local environment, and competition between them reflects clashes of local interests and views on public policies. They differ in their attitudes as to what is prudent spending, over priorities, the pace of development of services, and over who should receive what benefits. Such differences involve differing concepts of equality and liberty, different attitudes about who is deserving or the under-dog and about the scope of public collective activity and enterprise.[35]

To a considerable extent, the current centrally-imposed expenditure constraints have reintroduced the nineteenth-century argument, only these days it has been more a matter of the 'cutters' versus the 'preservers' of services (see p. 159 below).

Why, then, does the low turnout persist? A third of non-voters say there's no point in voting because it wouldn't make any difference* – partly because the central government controls so much of what local authorities do (see MORI survey in *Local Government Chronicle*, 5 June 1998). Some people blame the councillors – 'they're all the same, so what's the point?' The Widdicombe survey (Vol. 3) found 66 per cent who believed that 'the people you vote for say they'll do things for you but once they're in they forget what they've said'. Others blame the complexity of the local government system. There is the confusion caused by the voting system(s), which is compounded where elections occur out of sequence (as when boundaries are changed) or where the districts' partial elections coincide with the whole council elections of the parish/community (often involving many of the same candidates). About 20 per cent (in the MORI survey 1998) are disenchanted by what they regard as an unfair voting system (as p. 130 above) and especially the incidence of local party predominance or monopoly (such as those exemplified on p. 130 above and sometimes referred to as 'fiefdoms' or 'rotten boroughs'). A non-proportional electoral system which almost invariably exaggerates the representation of the leading party to the detriment of smaller parties, and which has been reinforced

---

* Only 54 per cent of people believe that elections decide how things are run locally, yet 60 per cent claim to vote for their local council! See *Local Government Chronicle*, 6 August 1999, pp. 8 and 17.

over the years by an increasingly 'winner take all' response to even the narrowest electoral victory, is almost bound to discourage the participation of at least marginal voters.[36]

Another possibility is that the low poll is a deliberate and adverse comment on local government performance (and perhaps reports of sleaze) – that people are voting with their feet. Yet the converse may just as well be true: that people are basically satisfied with the services provided and do not therefore wish to promote any significant changes. Indeed the Widdicombe survey (Vol. 3) found a high level (70 per cent) of satisfaction and support for local authorities. Thus, the low poll may be seen as an accolade for local government. In 1996 this very point was made to a Parliamentary committee by Robert Worcester, the chairman of the opinion-polling organization MORI, when he reported that 49 per cent of respondents (in a 1995 survey) said they were satisfied or very satisfied with the way their local authority was doing its job. (A survey in Scotland in 1994 gave a figure of 80 per cent: see *Municipal Journal*, 27 February 1998, p. 14.)

Rather than take too rosy or pessimistic a view of election turnout, perhaps we need to adjust our perspective. It may be argued, for example, that the 70 per cent turnout in the General Election is an unreasonable paradigm – after all, General Elections occur infrequently and are accompanied like *national* issues by a lot more publicity and 'bally-hoo'; there is far more personalizing in national politics, with the media concentrating on the party leaders in particular (there are usually no such obvious leaders in local authorities – though this will change to the extent that local authorities adopt the system of directly elected mayors as in London). Many people may thus be turning out to vote for rather superficial or synthetic reasons. Besides, voting in a General Election may be held to be a civic duty (like filling in one's tax return) and this attitude has not yet penetrated to local elections. Is it fair, then, to compare local with national elections? Perhaps the 40 per cent figure is a good indication of a genuine interest in politics in Britain. After all, polling in the elections for the European Parliament has only averaged 36–39 per cent (and local election turnout in the USA and Canada is, on average, 25 and 33 per cent respectively). It might even be argued that the local government figure is a *desirable* level of participation, since too avid and active an interest in politics can be politically destabilizing and dangerous.[37]

Furthermore, it may be argued that elections should not be seen as the sole or even the principal criterion of political interest. The vigour of the local press and other media, the growth of 'consumerism' in the form of welfare rights groups or direct action events (rent strikes, marches, road-crossing demos, sit-ins), the formation of local pressure groups such as civic societies or education campaigns – all of these indicate a vitality of local political awareness and commitment, but using methods which supplement or substitute for the electoral system: after all, polling is only one means of gathering opinions.

Improving voting turnout?

Some analysts and commentators have detected an improvement in local voting turnout, though the evidence is patchy, inconsistent and even contradictory: to some extent it depends on the time-frame.[38] There may also be a possible (artificial) influence from changes in the registration process – with less committed voters removing themselves, as indicated on p. 129, and other bogus entrants being removed by more careful registration officers[38] – both of which would tend to improve the poll-to-register figure. Whatever the improvement, if any, there is still considerable concern at the low level of voting. Consequently a number of innovations are being tried or proposed to improve turnout: see Appendix 17. These range from such short-term, mechanistic or technical measures as improving the appearance and content of polling cards, longer polling hours, voting at supermarkets, etc. to the more fundamental or longer-term aspects, such as political education, reforming internal management, instituting elected mayors, reducing central controls and introducing some key changes in the local electoral system, including proportional representation (PR)*

---

* There is some evidence to suggest that PR could increase turnout by 7 per cent: see *European Journal of Political Research*, 18, 1990. And in 1998 a MORI poll found 44 per cent of people who found councils 'remote and impersonal' and said a PR system would make them more likely to vote: see *Local Government Chronicle*, 29 May 1998. But Professors Rallings and Thrasher are sceptical: see *Local Government Chronicle*, 3 September 1999, pp. 12–13.

(see Chapter 7, p. 157). These are dealt with more fully in Chapter 15 which deals with a host of reforms facing local government in the new millennium.

Lack of candidates

Less defensible is the large number of uncontested seats in local government elections. The figures in Table 7 show that the proportion of uncontested seats in recent years has amounted to over 20 per cent in many areas (especially in the Welsh and Scottish districts – indeed in the Scottish Island and Highland elections, even recently the figure has been over 40 per cent[39]). But the emergence of a strong third party (the Social, now Liberal, Democrats) in 1981, has led to more electoral contests, and in 1982 the overall figure was only 1 per cent.[40] In the 1998 elections (England), there were over 13,000 candidates, and an average of 2.6 candidates per contested seat. Overall, there were 36 unopposed seats, i.e. less than 1 per cent, – 6 per cent in 1999 – though the figures vary locally. In the local elections in Wales in 1995 only 12 per cent of the wards were contested by three or more party candidates compared with almost 50 per cent* in England (and half of Welsh councils have 75 per cent of members from one party). (By contrast it is worth noting that some 13 per cent of councillors are members of more than one council, with as many as 28 per cent in some types of authority. Even 10 per cent of councillors in full-time employment find time to serve on more than one council.[41]) Also, earlier in the century, the figures were often much worse: in 1934 in the county elections for Kent, only 20 per cent of seats were contested; in Cornwall only 3 of the 65 had elections and in Cumberland there were no elections for the county as there were only 38 candidates for the 40 seats! In 1967 the Maud Report commented that 'Recruitment of candidates . . . was a problem in almost all the authorities we visited. In some areas it was difficult if not impossible to find sufficient people of even the minimum calibre considered adequate willing to accept nomination.'[42] The Committee found that over 40 per cent of members

---

* This figure rose to 76 per cent in the 1999 elections.

of principal authorities had been returned without having to contest elections. 'It seems likely that about one in three of county councillors and about one in two of rural district councillors have never had to fight an election.'[43] (See Appendix 3.) In some areas, local parties have sought to overcome the shortage of candidates by openly advertising for them.

By contrast, in General Elections, despite higher costs and more demanding campaigns, there is no shortage of contestants: no constituency has fewer than three candidates. In the elections of 1979 there were 2,576 candidates for the 635 seats, in the 1992 election there were 2,948 candidates for 651 seats and in 1997 there were 3,591 candidates for 659 seats.[44]

Why is there any shortage of public-spirited citizens willing to run for election locally? Many explanations have been put forward, and these are dealt with in some detail in the next chapter. Here it will be sufficient to say that there are two main reasons:

(1) Many of those who have *been* members give up for reasons of time; loss of income; frustration with the methods and controls or with party politics; mobility, especially in pursuit of a career.
(2) Many members of the public do not seek to *become* councillors because they think it might interfere with their business interests or their voluntary activities elsewhere; they are insufficiently informed about local government; or they are just not interested.[45]

In response to such attitudes a number of proposals have been made to try to improve the situation.[46] These include:

(a) the internal reorganization of local authorities by streamlining committees and departments, concentrating responsibility and making greater use of management services – all with a view to making council membership less time-consuming and less frustrating (see Chapters 10 and 15);
(b) reducing the degree of Whitehall interference in local government, and giving local authorities a greater general competence (see Chapter 12);
(c) providing more publicity about the activities of local government through open meetings, improved facilities for the press and

publication of discussion papers, and a greater encouragement to schools to include local government studies in their curricula (see Chapter 13);

(d) improving the image of local government, partly through (c) above, and partly through such changes as compulsory retirement from membership at the age of seventy and the removal of antiquated procedures, ceremonies, dress etc;

(e) increasing the opportunities for membership by increasing the scope for release from employment to undertake council duties;

(f) the provision of training for councillors;

(g) the payment of full- or part-time salaries.

Some of these suggestions have, or are being acted on, especially at or following re-organization. And there is some evidence of improvement, for example in the county councils, the proportion of non-contested seats fell from a figure of about 50 per cent in the 1950s and 1960s (see Appendix 3) to a figure of 12 per cent in the 1970s and below 2 per cent in the 1980s. But this has been accompanied (causally?) by a growth of local parties, and across local government generally, bearing in mind that the number of local authorities has been altering (from 1,500 in 1972 to 440 today) and the number of members similarly reduced (from 42,000 to 23,000) it would be surprising if the recruitment picture had not improved with fewer seats to fill.

However, the proportion of seats which remain uncontested is still significant. And many of those which are contested give a limited choice, e.g. in 1995 only 12 per cent of the wards in Wales were contested by three or more parties. It may be that service on the newer, larger authorities is more demanding of councillors. But it may also be that the local government changes were too much for some of the older or longer-standing members, who have complained about the authorities becoming too big, too remote, too managerial or too bureaucratic. In terms of the 'brave new world' of efficient local government and in terms of attracting members of the 'right calibre', this shedding effect may have been no bad thing. But many felt that, in the process of change, local government was losing its 'soul': it was being seen purely as a mechanism for effective administration and the delivery of services (the 'instrumental' view). What was being overlooked or devalued was its 'organic' aspect: that local government should be seen as an extension or a natural expression of the community.

It has also been argued that current participation levels at least provide a fair reflection of society; that there is perhaps a danger in trying to increase overall participation rates, as this may result in a disproportionate increase in influence by one class or interest.[47] How far local government is attracting the right people and fairly reflecting the community is examined in Chapter 8. But it may be said here that it is important that local authorities comprise a good cross-section of the community: after all, politics is about dealing with social problems (those which cannot solve themselves) and social problems are, ultimately, *everyone*'s problems – they are ours. Therefore to improve councillors' reflection of society it may be suggested that (i) the image and standing of local government be improved to make it more attractive; (ii) the image of councillors be changed, such that they are not perceived as 'different to us' and therefore exclusive; (iii) there is more information about local government, about how to become a candidate (including self-nomination?); and about support services (such as training, allowances, childcare facilities, aids for those with disabilities). Such efforts should be especially directed towards the under-represented groups.

So far we have considered the formal organization of local government – that which is based on law or long established precedent. We now turn to examine part of local government's 'unwritten constitution'[48] – an informal, but increasingly crucial, element in local authorities: political parties.

7

THE POLITICAL PARTIES

It is very difficult to assess the real extent of party politics in local government, partly because it is changing (especially in the 1970s as a result of reorganization), but mainly because of the problem of definition* – when does a group of like-minded councillors become a 'party'? Is a group of active campaigners who seek but lack representation on the council a political party? Do labels always mean what they say – for example how many 'Independent' members are really disguised party supporters, and how many of those councillors bearing party labels really participate on a party basis?[1] See too p. 185.

The vast majority of local government decisions involve no party politics.[2] Yet in some authorities they obtrude into virtually every issue, no matter how minor or routine,[3] and will vary so considerably among the different types of local authority and the different areas of the country that generalization is difficult. Much will depend on:

(1) whether the local parties are branches of national parties (Labour, Conservative, Liberal Democrat, Plaid Cymru, Scottish Nationalist, etc.) or

(2) are purely local organizations, not connected with a national party (ratepayers' associations, residents' or tenants' groups, etc.);

(3) the personalities, experience and motives of the councillors, especially the local party leaders;[4]

* Definition will become more necessary in so far as we move to a system of proportional representation (PR) as there is then a greater likelihood of votes going explicitly to parties. A step in this direction occurred with the Registration of Political Parties Act 1998 which aimed to deal with the confusion caused by party names (sometimes a deliberate ploy by candidates, using such labels as Literal Democrat or Conversative!) The Act establishes a Registrar for elections using PR and s/he can refuse to register certain party applications. See too the Political Parties Elections Bill 2000.

(4) the political culture,[5] traditions and conventions of the local area.

Consequently, the local party system can take a number of different forms (see p. 160) only one of which resembles our traditional Parliamentary system. These are:

(a) *one-party monopolistic:* where a party holds an overall majority of seats (80 per cent or more) and maintains that position over a long period;
(b) *one-party dominant:* where one party persistently has a majority of seats of about 60 per cent and over;
(c) *two-party:* where the leading party has no more than 60 per cent of seats and there is genuine competition from another party, with the reasonable possibility of power changing hands between the two rival parties (as is basically the situation in British central government);
(d) *multi-party:* where third and other parties have at least 10 per cent of seats and power is shifting among the parties following elections or is held jointly in coalitions (several parties combining to form an alliance and thus together enjoying a majority position). These may be known as 'hung' (or balanced) councils; where there is mutual hostility and a failure to cooperate, the parties exercise only a negative form of 'power';
(e) *non-existent:* where the majority of the council, around 60 per cent or more, are non-partisan (that is, independents); party members of the council are in a minority and perhaps divided into several small parties.

Within these categories may be found a host of others – for example where parties fight elections under their own labels but drop their separate identity within the council chamber. Parties will vary enormously in the extent to which they exercise discipline over their members, appoint party 'whips' (the party business managers, who resemble school 'prefects') or hold party meetings to predigest council business. Some parties are no more than loose groupings, perhaps bound together by a vague philosophy or a particular issue or by a dominant personality. Like national parties, local parties are outwardly monolithic but inwardly fragmented and often fall out among

Table 8 *Party systems in local government, 1998 (1992, 1998 and 1979)*

	Number of LAs				%				Definition
Non-party	14	(36)	(41)	(81)	3	(7)	(8)	(16)	60 per cent or more seats held by Independents
One-party monopolistic	81	(51)	(64)	(52)	18	(10)	(13)	(10)	80 per cent or more seats held by one party
One-party dominant	119	(134)	(173)	(187)	27	(26)	(34)	(36)	60–80 per cent seats held by one party
Two-party	54	(100)	(87)	(109)	12	(19)	(17)	(20)	Two parties, with the leading party having not more than 60 per cent of seats
Multi-party	173	(193)	(146)	(92)	39	(38)	(28)	(18)	Third party or parties having 10 per cent or more seats
	441	(514)	(514)	(521)	100	(100)	(100)	(100)	

Based on information from *Municipal Year Books* and press reports.

NOTE: The number of councils fell with the abolition of the GLC and Metropolitan County Councils in 1986 and reorganizations 1995–8.

themselves over policy issues in order to protect a sectional interest, a locality or a particular service. This is often the case where there is a dominant party; in practice that party may divide into several feuding or rival semi-parties or factions (as happened most publicy for example in the 1990s in the Labour parties of Glasgow and Walsall when members were actually suspended from the official party by the national party executive).

The variety of party systems is rich in local government. The pattern is illustrated, though not completely, in Table 8 (which accepts at face value the labels supplied by the local authorities).

Table 9 shows the state of party control of councils in 1999; it is of course, a snapshot.

Local party politics in the past

It is often suggested, usually by critics of party politics, that parties are something new to local government: a twentieth-century phenomenon. This is not an unreasonable belief, for to some extent it was the Labour Party, seeking to create a power base, which penetrated local (urban) politics and established at large the devices of party organization, discipline and local policy programmes; these devices were new to local government,[6] and the other parties were slow to copy them. But the concept and experience of political parties were not new. Acknowledged historians of local government have stated: 'By 1890, it would indeed be difficult to find any great English town . . . with a municipal council elected on other than party lines.'[7] Numerous studies attest to the vitality of party politics in nineteenth-century local government – in Leeds, Sheffield, Exeter, Liverpool, Manchester and Oldham for example, where the parties were in conflict over such issues as public health expenditure,[8] municipal transport, education and its relationship to religion. The broadest division was between the 'improvers', who wanted to spend along the lines of the 'gas and water socialists', and the 'economizers', who did not. Such a division was well illustrated by the London County Council virtually from its inception in 1889, when the 'Radicals' (or 'Progressives') clashed with the Conservatives (or 'Moderates') over just this issue.[9] What is mainly

Table 9 *Party control and composition of councils 1999*
(i) Political control of local authorities in Britain 1999 (1992, 1988 and 1979) respectively

Overall majority of seats on each council held by:	England				Unitary councils	Total
	County councils	District councils	Metropolitan District councils	London councils		
Labour	8 (9) (5) (3)	60 (82) (61) (53)	29 (26) (29) (20)	18 (13) (16) (14)	29	144 (130) (111) (90)
Conservative	8 (19) (11) (39)	59 (88) (139) (164)	0 (2) (1) (11)	4 (12) (10) (18)	3	74 (121) (161) (232)
Other	2 (0) (1) (0)	20 (27) (3) (9)	3 (0) (0) (0)	2 (3) (2) (0)	4	31 (30) (6) (9)
Independent	0 (0) (0) (1)	6 (14) (24) (27)	0 (0) (0) (0)	1 (1) (1) (1)	0	7 (15) (25) (29)
NOC	16 (11) (22) (2)	93 (85) (69) (43)	4 (8) (6) (5)	8 (4) (4) (1)	10	131 (108) (101) (51)
Total	34 (39) (39) (45)	238 (296) (296) (296)	36 (36) (36) (36)	33 (33) (33) (34)	46	387 (404) (404) (411)

'Other' refers mainly to Liberal Democrats, though in some areas it includes local parties (such as Ratepayers' or Residents' Associations), and it includes nationalist parties in Scotland (SNP) and Wales (PC). Some seats (about 50) are vacant.

Tables based on information from *Municipal Year Books* and press reports and the *LGC Elections Centre*, University of Plymouth.

NOTES: The discrepancy between the NOC (no overall control) or mixed system of Table 8 and the multi-party of Table 9 arises from different definitions – a multi-party system can have a majority party. Variation in number of councils arises from the abolition of the GLC and Metropolitan County Councils in 1986 and the creation of unitary councils in 1996.

Overall majority of seats on each council held by:

	Wales			Scotland			Gt Britain
	Unitary councils	County councils	District councils	Regions and Islands	Unitary councils	District councils	Total
Labour	8	(5) (4) (3)	(17) (16) (16)	(4) (4) (4)	15	(22) (24) (6)	167 (178) (159) (119)
Conservative	0	(0) (0) (1)	(1) (3) (2)	(0) (0) (2)	0	(5) (3) (9)	74 (127) (167) (246)
Other	4	(0) (0) (0)	(1) (3) (5)	(0) (0) (0)	2	(4) (5) (9)	37 (35) (14) (23)
Independent	2	(1) (2) (3)	(10) (9) (8)	(5) (5) (4)	4	(13) (11) (16)	13 (44) (52) (60)
NOC	8	(2) (2) (1)	(8) (6) (6)	(3) (3) (2)	11	(9) (10) (13)	150 (130) (122) (73)
Total	22	(8)	(37)	(12)	32	(53)	441 (514) (514) (521)

(ii) Councillors by political party 1999

	Scotland	Wales	London	Metropolitan	Counties	Districts	Unitary	Total
Labour	550	562	1,050	1,680	743	3,323	1,232	9,140
Conservative	108	74	539	295	885	3,702	545	6,148
Lib Dem	156	95	301	449	496	2,438	553	4,488
Ind/Others	203	295	182	55	79	1,267	105	2,186
PC/SNP	205	242	–	–	–	–	–	447
Total	1,222	1,268	2,072	2,479	2,203	10,730	2,435	22,409

new to twentieth-century local government is the form rather than the fact of party politics.

However, it is apparent that in the course of the last eighty years party politics have become much more widespread in local government especially as a result of reorganization in the mid 1970s. On the evidence of the last few years, this trend is continuing. This is illustrated in Table 10. Consequently, parties are now so well established in local government that they form a third 'pillar' alongside the councillors and the officers. This has been most clearly acknowledged in the government's current reforms to local authorities' political management arrangements (see Chapters 9 and 15).

Prior to the reorganization of the 1970s, the smaller and more rural authorities were the ones least likely to operate on party lines. It was anticipated that this situation would change as the rural authorities were merged with the urban and as the smaller authorities were thus enlarged. The figures indicate the extent to which this has occurred, though they cannot tell us how active these parties are or whether they are no more than old wine in newly labelled bottles – perhaps no more than electoral ploys. (It may also be that erstwhile Independent members have taken off their masks of neutrality and openly adopted the party label to reveal their true affiliation.) We must therefore examine the consequences of party politics in local government.

It should be noted that some parties are rather 'invisible' in that, while they fight elections and gain votes, they do not win enough seats to run councils. For example, the Green Party currently has 22 council seats.

The operation and effects of local party politics

As so often elsewhere in local government, it is difficult to make safe general statements about the role of party politics – so much will depend on the local party system, the local political culture and the influence of personalities. Broadly, it can be said that parties have three roles – electoral, educative and governmental. The existence and the form of political parties is likely to affect local authorities in the following ways:

Table 10 *Local authorities run on party lines* (as a percentage of all local authorities of that type)*

	1998	1992	1988	1983	1979		1972
County councils	100	98	96	92	92	Council councils (England and Wales)	59
London councils†	97	97	97	97	97	London councils	97
District councils (England and Wales)	—	93	90	90	88	County borough councils	99
District councils (Scotland)	—	77	79	72	70	Scottish county	
Regions/islands	—	58	58	50	67	councils	68
Metropolitan boroughs	100	100	100	100	100	Scottish burghs	43
English unitary	100					Non-county	
Scottish unitary	88					boroughs/	
Welsh unitary	82					rural boroughs	63
English districts	96					Urban district councils	70
						Rural district councils	27

*i.e. at least half of the councillors on the council openly belong to a party (see Table 8).
†The City of London Corporation is the only non-party authority.
Source: Municipal Year Books and press election reports.

(1) *Elections*. There are a number of likely effects here. In the first place, the existence of party competition is likely to reduce the number of uncontested seats.[10] Even where the seat is 'safe' and the likely result is well known (a fact which will probably deter the Independent), a rival party is likely to field a candidate if only to 'wave the flag' or give new candidates their first experience of elections.

Secondly, the existence of parties will influence the number and composition of the candidates who stand for election. As we shall see (p. 194), a large proportion of councillors have said that they entered local government at the suggestion of a party. And it is far easier to fight an election on a party 'ticket' than organize and finance your own campaign. Thus parties are responsible for the entry of many members to local government office: they are important agencies for recruitment.[11] In many, especially urban, areas, party competition is keen and so too is competition to stand for election. For this purpose, the candidate has to be selected and nominated by his/her party (usually by a relatively small committee of the local party). Who we as electors can vote for is therefore often determined for us by the party machines. And while there may be some guidance from the national party on policy, on campaign procedure or in respect of choice of candidates, local parties are usually free to follow their own judgement (or prejudices). Some choose intellectuals or those from a professional background; some choose the party loyalist regardless of background; and others may prefer the ideological 'hardliner' or those who are union-sponsored.

Thirdly, election turnout is likely to be higher where there is a party contest. This is partly because voters can easily recognize or identify (national) party labels, whereas it requires considerably more effort to discern individual non-party candidates and their election 'platforms'. The better turnout[12] is also a consequence of the better election organization and greater publicity which the parties are likely to foster – for example in informing the public about the issues, the candidates and even simple things such as the location of the polling stations. (Not that this increased turnout is necessarily a good thing, for example if people have simply turned out to vote like zombies, lacking awareness and without considering the issues or seeking to exercise any real sanction over the elected representatives.)

(2) *Public interest.* We have already seen how parties are likely to encourage members of the public to participate as candidates or as electors. In addition it is likely that the parties will help to stimulate interest in local government affairs by spreading knowledge about issues and personalities, and indeed even by performing an 'educative' or civic awareness role by providing information about such basic

aspects as the structure and functions of the local authority. (Such a consequence would be mainly as a by-product of the campaign.) Much of this information may get little further than its own party members, though even this is not insignificant as a step to public participation. But in the process of campaigning, canvassing, sloganizing and conducting arguments through the local press and other media, the parties will have some impact on the stimulation of public awareness and interest.

(3) *The authority's operation and policy decisions.* This is the most difficult area in which to make general statements, since so much will depend on the number of parties; their 'style' (structure, discipline, outside links etc.); the local traditions and experiences; the size of the council and the size of the authority's area; whether there is a majority party etc. Here we must deal in general tendencies, and many of these are based on the operation of local parties in the more established 'political' urban areas. These have developed a broadly 'Westminster' pattern of party politics which can provide a useful model for the study of local party politics generally. One finding for example, is that Labour councils, are most likely to provide services to members (Thomas Report: see note 62, p. 683 below), although the more recently ascendant Liberal Democratic party is probably at least as well organized in this respect.

It is common practice for Labour, Conservative, Liberal Democrat, SNP, etc., councillors to form themselves into party 'groups' within their local authorities. Such groups, depending on their size, will often appoint officers – chairman, whip, secretary, leader (if not the chairman) – from among their own members, and perhaps a policy committee (sometimes called the leader's coordinating committee). Inevitably, there is a more or less close relationship between the group and the local constituency party (especially in the Labour Party) and members of the latter may actually attend and speak (though usually not vote) at group meetings. (These 'outsiders', together with the group's officers, form what is called the party 'caucus'.[13]) However, this relationship varies among local authorities. It also varies among parties in that Labour, compared to the Conservatives, has a much more systematic and structured relationship set down in the model standing orders originally drafted by the national party organization in

1930. These purport to give the local party some potentially significant influence over the local groups' policy-making powers. In practice, that influence appears to be limited or variable, and is complicated by the cross-membership of councillors who are also active members and office-holders in their local party. Most party groups meet less than once per month (though Labour groups tend to meet more often; see Widdicombe Report, Research Vol. 1).

What is the *role* of the party group? It is here that we observe the significant impact of parties on the operation of local authorities. The functions of the party group are numerous[14] and may include:

(a) Choosing members to serve on various committees, to act as chairmen of those committees, to choose the leader of the party group and to nominate the mayor/chairman or provost/convenor of the council, where this is separate from leader. In about 5 per cent of councils the majority party does not take all the committee chairmanships and in 13 per cent they do not take a majority of seats on all committees; 20 per cent have committees comprising only majority party members, though these committees are usually deliberative rather than executive; see Widdicombe Report, Research Vol. 1. (In the case of Regina v. Greenwich London Borough Council, ex-parte Lovelace, June 1989, it was held that it was lawful for a council – in effect the majority party – to remove from its committees councillors who were opposed to the policy of the council and replace them with others.) Under the Local Government and Housing Act 1989, committees have been required to have a membership reflecting, *pro rata*, the party composition of the council (though informal one-party committees could operate). However, under the Local Government Act 2000, this general requirement is to cease as the Committee system is fundamentally reformed: see Chapter 15);

(b) formulating policies for the various council services;

(c) determining the group's attitude to policy proposals which emerge from other sources – especially from chief officers of the authority and from committee reports and recommendations. In this task, individual differences can be thrashed out in the privacy of the group meeting, so that in council or committee meetings all members of the group will speak and vote according to the party 'line';

(d) determining tactics regarding debates, votes and other procedures at council and committee meetings;

(e) enforcing discipline and helping to present a united front in the public activities of the council;

(f) keeping members informed and primed, especially on the work of committees (since most members will sit on only a few such committees);

(g) scrutinizing existing policy and administration, and perhaps dealing with constituents' complaints;

(h) as a consequence of several of the above points, helping to promote the coordination of the authority's policy and administration.

Many of these activities resemble those of Parliament, and in some respects the local party groups go further than the parliamentary parties, for example in the holding of 'epitome' or dress-rehearsal meetings (prior to council and perhaps committee meetings) at which they vet committee minutes and reports, determine their party 'line' on policy and devise their tactics – who is to speak, in what order, whether they will move for a referral back etc. The result is that the subsequent council or committee meeting will have been pre-empted: the proceedings will be cut and dried and the result a foregone conclusion.

However, not all party groups will attempt to pursue all those objectives. This is obviously the case where no party has a clear majority as in the many 'hung' councils (see p. 250) which have emerged since the 1980s. Here there is a greater tendency to compromise or cooperation (though it is important to distinguish between the *effectively* hung and those – about half – where it is *nominal*, such as where Conservatives or Liberal Democrats get sufficient regular support from Independents to enable them to govern as with a majority). But even where a majority does exist, there may be strong differences within the party which disciplinary threats or patronage blandishments cannot overcome. Thus, where party cohesion is weak, there can be frequent conflict between members from different districts of the authority[15] or among different age groups (the young Turks v. the old guard) and perhaps, above all, between members of different committees – especially over such issues as economies and where cuts should fall.[16] Further, while it may be frequent practice for the majority party, by virtue of its superior numbers, to assume a majority on the key committees and to monopolize the key posts (the chairmanship of committees and perhaps of the council),[17] not all such parties take full advantage of their opportunity.[18]

Party discipline is more crucial[19] where party majorities are marginal, and it is here that we find the greater use of 'a rigid and comprehensive whipping system'. However, there has been a general increase in the control of local parties and party groups by the national parties, especially Labour.[20] And paradoxically it was the overly large majorities of some local Labour parties (and their 'internal strife, complacency and, in a few cases, a failure in public standards'*) which led the national party to tighten its grip locally (including a more rigorous system for the vetting and selection of local candidates, for their more systematic training and preparation for office and for their greater freedom to expose and 'whistleblow' wrongdoing). The situation has therefore changed since the 1970s when central party control was less evident or systematic,[21] (though there appears to be some variation as between councils having frequent/annual as opposed to all-out quadriennial elections – the latter having some greater autonomy).[22]

Generally the Conservatives claim to have little truck with many of what they see as inflexible and restrictive party devices[23] such as 'whipping' (e.g. only 23 per cent of Conservative party groups in power always vote together at council meetings, compared with 59 per cent for Labour; see Widdicombe Report, Research Vol. 1, 1986) and while there may be more need for a formal structure and discipline in the Labour Party (for ideological and other reasons),[24] even here there have been considerable variations among local Labour groups. By analogy, just as the Labour Party at national level has long tried to

---

* John Prescott, Deputy Leader of the Labour Party, at their local government conference 1998. At the 1999 Labour Party conference, it was announced that the whipping system would be removed or relaxed in the new management/committee structures: see p. 272 and Chapter 15.

settle the issue of the proper relationship between the Parliamentary Labour Party and the mass party outside (especially as manifested in the party conference), so there are numerous local disputes over the same theme – how autonomous is the local group, and how independent-minded can individual councillors be allowed to be?

Similarly there are variations in the extent to which local party groups initiate policies. Some groups have policy or advisory committees which act as a source of policy ideas, and it has been claimed that 'in many authorities operating on party lines the party group makes a more significant contribution than any single "constitutional" committee towards general policy initiation'.[25]

On the other hand, many party groups appear to be so overwhelmed with the size and complexity of their existing programmes that they are unable to disentangle themselves and think in broad and longer terms (with the result that much policy often emerges from individual committees or service officers/managers). The introduction of policy committees and the notion of corporate management (see p. 253) were intended to change this (as is the prospect of a community leadership role: see Chapter 15). Another driving force has been the emergence of a younger, better educated and more assertive (and more full-time) cohort of councillors.[26] In the meantime, we may conclude with Gyford that

party Groups provide a useful means of exchanging information between members, of pleading cases before a sympathetic audience, and, if effectively organized, of securing the passage through committee and full council of approved recommendations, whatever their source. They also serve to encourage debate and criticism and to ensure, through the existence of Minority Groups, that local Government enjoys the equivalent of a Parliamentary Opposition . . . They find it more difficult to operate as co-ordinating devices and as policy initiators.[27]

These limitations are even more apparent in those local authorities where the party system is less developed. And in local government generally it is worth repeating that a great deal of business is not transacted on party lines. 'In committees and sub-committees free discussion and even "cross-voting" is quite common and on many issues there is little evidence of party discipline.'[28]

Regarding *policies* and ideology, it may be said that generally, in local government, the Conservative Party has been associated with policies of economizing in service provision, especially to keep local taxes low, the disposal of unnecessary council assets and in particular the contracting out of services. The Labour Party has been more strongly associated with maintaining the levels and the in-house provision of services, urban regeneration, the promotion of economic development and equal opportunities initiatives and the 'hard left' see their duty as one of redistribution from the 'fat cats' to the 'losers in life'.[28a] The Liberal Democrats are characterized by a strong commitment to improvements in the environment, to community politics and a wish to bring services closer to the communities for whom they are provided. A graphic illustration of their different attitudes is displayed in the policy on homosexuality. Section 28 of the Local Government Act 1988 prohibits councils from 'promoting homosexuality . . . [and] the teaching of the acceptability of homosexuality as a pretended family relationship'. Labour's Local Government Bill 2000 is repealing this Conservative law.

Political parties: curse or blessing?

There is some evidence to suggest that Labour control of a local authority will tend to increase the levels of that authority's expenditure on education, housing and welfare services, in contrast to expenditure when the Conservatives are in control.[29] Thus in terms of the size and the composition of a local authority's provision, which party is in control is clearly important. However, as we have seen, the mere existence of parties can have very significant effects on the working of local government. The question is whether these effects are desirable or not. The arguments are extensive and quite evenly balanced. Here we must content ourselves with a resume of the main points.

The arguments *in favour* of parties in local government can be grouped as follows:

(1) *Participation.* As we saw earlier (p. 165), parties help to mobilize voters. Turnout tends to be higher where parties contest local elections,

partly because of the better organization and publicity which they bring. But it is largely due to the fact that parties simplify and crystallize the main issues for the general public. Parties present a publicly known set of principles and policies, as local party manifestos are becoming much more common. At the very least party labels will provide instant indicators of the candidates' policy orientations – what they stand for (or against). In contrast, for electors to sift through a collection of Independents' election addresses is to expect too much from the real world.

We also saw (p. 164; see also p. 194) how parties help to recruit council members and reduce the number of non-contested seats. It is also worth pointing out that membership of local government tends to be more representative of the community than is the House of Commons[30] (or the British component of the European Assembly). It is unlikely that local authorities would draw on such a cross-section of the community if it were not for the recruiting activities of the parties. In general then, the smaller proportion of uncontested seats and higher turnouts are the by-products of party competition.[31]

(2) *Public interest.* We have pointed out that parties can help to stimulate and sustain a general interest in local government (p. 165), though it is difficult to gauge the extent of this. Again, at least, the party 'ding-dong' at council/committee meetings provides plenty of copy for the local press, and to a lesser extent local radio and television.

(3) *The working of the council.* The main advantage claimed for parties here is the coherence they can bring to the work of the authority. Parties are 'organized opinion' and where they hold a majority position within the council they can provide a programme of internally and mutually consistent policies. This is much more difficult to achieve in an authority of Independent members; such councils often lack a sense of direction and are prone to complacency as there is no challenge from party competition. Consequently, their efficiency has been called in question.[32] And there is the added gain of responsibility: with a single party holding a majority and in office, the electors can pin responsibility for the authority's achievements and failures fairly and squarely on the shoulders of that party: it alone may be held accountable in debates, public meetings and above all at election time when people

can vote for or against the incumbent 'team' of party councillors.

It is also claimed that having parties in the council chamber helps to diminish the possibility of domination by officials: parties will have their own views on policy and perhaps some research facilities with which to challenge official reports.[33] Issues like council house sales, education priorities, transport policy etc. can receive deeper and more structured analysis than would be the case in the non-party authority (an argument which resembles the one that favours the entry of 'political advisers' or 'departmental cabinets' into central government). Party groups keep members better informed and may also enhance regularity of attendance at council meetings (as members' absences often have to be explained to the party whips). In a number of councils, the leader (i.e. head of the majority party) and committee chairmen form a policy group (or semi-formal 'cabinet').

(4) *Central government relations.* For many years local government has suffered from central government policies. Supporters of party politics point out, however, that in terms of local government's relations with the central government the existence of local parties can facilitate some influence in an upward direction. Members of local party groups – many of them respected and influential figures within the national parties – can have the case for local government raised in Parliament either directly (where the councillor has become an MP) or through sympathetic MPs of their own party, and this may be particularly effective for the party whose national leaders constitute the central government (see p. 703, note 44).

However, the advocates of parties perhaps claim too much. To a large extent this is because they take the 'ideal-type' two-party system as their model. In practice it cannot be assumed that parties will produce majorities, and thus the pursuance of consistent policies and constructive opposition cannot be assured. The benefits of local party government will depend on the nature of the local party system. Besides, as we have seen (p. 170), parties often take little initiative in the development of policy, and some of the claimed advantages of parties have been obviated by internal reforms of local authorities (see p. 255). Furthermore, in terms of elections, it is not necessarily the case that parties increase the poll, and even where they do so, it is not necessarily a good thing since many can be induced to cast their vote through blind loyalty or prejudice and in complete ignorance of the points at issue. The arguments *against* parties can be considered under the following headings:

(1) *Participation*. Parties distort the composition of councils by squeezing out the Independents: the bearing of a party label has become the necessary if not sufficient condition for election success. Apart from voters' actions, there is a certain amount of self-selection (or denial) here as independent-minded people will be deterred from local politics by the party regimentation and the 'rail-roading' of decisions in the council chamber. Others are discouraged from standing, not because they are non-partisan but because they do not wish to reveal (e.g. in election campaigns) their affiliation for social or business reasons. This latter group may be small (the Maud Committee believed it to be only 1 per cent), but they are significant because they represent sections of the community (such as business or professional people) which arguably should be adequately represented.[34] In 1998, SOLACE were concerned that talented potential councillors are deterred by parties (*Municipal Journal*, 3 April 1998, p. 3)

In general it is said that the Independent can make a useful contribution to council decisions: they have freedom to assess issues on their merits and can more effectively relate issues to their own localities (rather than to the official party line). They also claim to be able to act as 'honest brokers' within the system. But, in practice, the path of the Independent tends to be a lonely one as they are few in number and they have little 'clout' in decision-making as their individual vote counts for little and they may be less well briefed.

Another aspect of this issue arises from the fact that, in the process of selecting candidates, parties may use the wrong criteria – rewarding loyalties and services to the party and perhaps thereby overlooking those with the desirable qualities of a councillor (see p. 201). The whole process may also create cynicism if it appears to degenerate into a self-perpetuating clique arrangement – especially likely where one party dominates the council.

(2) *Elections*. Where one party does so dominate, electors may be discouraged from voting because they see the result as a foregone

conclusion. Where parties have a stranglehold majority* – as is the case in 200 out of 441 authorities – and there is no effective opposition, the area in effect becomes an entrenched one-party state and people can be turned off from voting as their vote is felt to be so insignificant.

However, perhaps the greatest indictment of parties in this field is the impact of national issues. Rightly or wrongly electors identify local party groups with the national parties and either vote for their party election after election through blind loyalty and without regard to local issues, or they switch their voting support among the local parties in response to the actions (or inactions) of the central government party: in effect it is national rather than local politicians who are being held accountable on local election day. Thus a general dissatisfaction with the Thatcher government, or say its foreign policy (e.g. supporting the USA over its bombing of Libya in 1986), will be reflected in a uniform swing against Conservative councillors throughout the country regardless of their individual worth and irrespective of local issues. See Appendix 1 for graphic illustration of this.[35]

Professor Miller found that over four-fifths of the electorate vote in accordance with their national political preferences when they voted in local elections:

Local effects seem to move about one tenth of local voters away from their national preferences and toward 'less political' candidates (Alliance and others . . .). And local influences may determine the local choice of another tenth of local voters who have no national preference.[36]

Local elections thus become miniature general elections,† and good councillors are penalized along with the bad if their party is out of favour nationally: the councillor becomes 'protest fodder' and the

---

* After the 1995 elections, half of the councils in Wales had 75 per cent of their members drawn from one party.

† This likelihood is said to be increased by the fact that elections for local government do not normally occur at the same time as Parliamentary elections, so voters cast their votes more critically because the 'honeymoon' with the government has faded. This un-synchronized voting is also held to explain the regular local government tensions with central government, as each is elected by a different constituency and is likely to differ in political complexion.

quality of local government is jeopardized. It is an abuse of the local ballot, and it undermines the credibility of local government. Furthermore, 'those who treat local polls as surrogate general elections are merely playing the centralist game'.[37]

The close relationship between national trends and local voting patterns appears to be further confirmed by recent events. In 1981 a series of spectacular Parliamentary by-election successes by the Social Democrat/Liberal Alliance was accompanied (though somewhat less spectacularly) by Alliance gains in local elections. Then in 1982 we witnessed the 'Falklands factor' – when the widespread national support for the government's policy of armed retrieval of the Falklands carried unusually large numbers of Conservatives to victory in the local elections. Similarly in 1992–3 there were sensational Liberal Democrat victories in Parliamentary by-elections followed by outstanding gains in the county council elections. Similarly, after a series of sweeping gains in local elections 1994–6, Labour won a massive victory in the General Election of 1997.

It could be argued that such local impacting of national trends is not unreasonable now since so much of what local authorities do (or not do) is attributable to the national government, as a result of its centralizing tendencies, especially since the 1970s, i.e. central government *can* be held accountable for local circumstances, and with local authorities so lacking in autonomy, voters may just as well use their local vote to express their view of the government.[38]

However, within local elections (including those mentioned above) there are many aberrations and unexplained variations. The results of the 1997 General Election are instructive here. Like 1979, it was an unusual election in that local elections took place at the same time – there were 'synchro-elections'. Yet on both occasions there is evidence of voters 'splitting their ticket', i.e. voting for different parties at the same time in each election. In some areas in 1979 there was a difference of 15 per cent and 1997 showed a general differential of nearly 22 per cent (mainly benefitting the Liberal Democrat candidates).[39] A MORI poll found 10 per cent who intended to vote Conservative or Labour in the 1997 General Election but said they would vote Liberal Democrat in the local election.[40] Another analysis concludes that 'it seems clear that many more electors cast votes for different parties at the 1997 general and local elections than had done so at the comparable contests in 1979'.[41]

In the 1997 General Election, whilst the Liberal Democrats gained a record number of MPs, at the same time they lost many seats and a number of councils in the simultaneous local elections. Conversely in other areas the local government vote for Liberal Democrats was 10 per cent higher than their comparable Parliamentary vote (*The Economist*, 17 May 1998). Indeed, among local elections generally, there are many deviations from putative trends. Why does a party improve its vote by 15 per cent in one local authority area (Sheffield) but lose 9 per cent in another locality (Plymouth), and another party lose 3 per cent in Sheffield but gain 22 per cent in the Wirral election?[42] Such variations can occur as a result of a number of factors – candidate personality, party campaign, council performance, local controversy, council tax rise, etc.[43] So there is a danger in generalizing about local results, turnouts and trends; not only are there considerable variations among individual council results (in turnout, party allegiance, etc.) but there are significant (and fascinating) variations *within* local authorities, i.e. differential patterns or trends in party support or 'swing' and in turnout as between wards or divisions of the same local authorities. It does appear that local issues are actually becoming a more significant factor in local elections: that with the limitations on resources since the mid 1970s, difficult *local choices* are having to be made about priorities, what services to cut, which staff to shed, which client groups to disappoint.[44] And in two recent analyses around 50 per cent of respondents claimed to vote in local elections on the basis of local rather than national issues.[45] Intense involvement with parochial issues – known as 'community' or 'pavement politics' – has long characterized the Liberal approach (see p. 529), and as multi-party politics and 'hung' councils become more commonplace, so does the importance of local factors, including the level of rates or council tax.[46] In the 1990 elections there was the 'London effect', in which low poll tax Conservative boroughs bucked the trend to Labour.[47] In fact London provides a good (though not unique) illustration of the fact that it is misleading to characterize local elections as merely an opinion poll or referendum on the national government and that national trends sweep all before them. In London, adjacent boroughs often display dramatically different results and deviate significantly from the national trend. For example in the local elections of 1998, Brent and Lambeth saw a 7 per cent swing from Conservative to Labour; yet in Hillingdon there was an equal swing in the opposite direction. In Harrow, the Liberal Democrat vote fell by 10 per cent, while in Islington, it rose by 14 per cent.[48] An analysis of the 1994 London elections concludes that,

London's local elections remain resolutely local. However powerful national and regional trends, voters will be swayed by local factors . . . [in the] London results . . . [are] many different currents and eddies of electoral fortune . . . There are no uniform swings across London; the reputations of individual councils, concerns about local controversial issues and the impact of central government policies will affect each borough differently . . . Londoners vote in local elections along local lines. (*London Borough Elections 1994*, London Research Centre, 1994)[49]

In their more general research Professors Rallings and Thrasher conclude that,

The conventional wisdom that local elections are little more than state-sponsored opinion polls can be disregarded. Variations in performance between parties asnd candidates are simply too great to explain other than by local people making locally relevant choices . . . Many people do consciously vote for the person or a local policy or on the record of their local council. They will often do so while retaining a national party allegiance in conflict with their current behaviour. (*Parliamentary Affairs*, April 1988)

. . . Local elections provide opportunities for movements away from any national pattern or trend. Behaviour and outcomes vary among and even within local authorities. Local issues and concerns can influence the vote over either the entire area of a council or in individual wards. Similarly, party campaigns and the personality of the candidates can have a clear impact on the result. Everything that has been written about the 'denationalization' of British politics in recent general elections applies, except even more so, to the local electoral arena. (*Local Elections in Britain*, Routledge, 1997)

And further,

There is increasing evidence that parliamentary voting intentions are less reliable in forecasting local electoral outcomes . . . Despite the growing influence of national parties in local politics, it does appear that voters are quite capable of discriminating between candidates on the basis of the particular electoral context. (*Parliamentary Affairs*, January 1999)

(3) *The working of the council.* The criticisms in this area are numerous. Firstly, party-based councils are prone to treat too many items of business as party issues (see p. 168).[50] This may not only prevent the issues being dealt with on their own merits (as national policies are adopted in doctrinaire fashion by local party groups much to the particular chagrin of Independents), but it may slow down the whole process of decision-making and implementation, as parties seek to obstruct and score points off one another. There is the danger of too much party bickering and not enough civil engineering! This is especially likely in a multi-party system where no party has a majority (and causes some officers to regard the hung council situation as 'sheer hell').[51] For example, hung councils often have to spend much time choosing between three (party) budgets (though it may be said in favour of the hung council that at least the parties have to confer together to reach decisions, even if it takes longer. See Chapter 9). There is the added danger that deadlock in the council chamber can result in power slipping into the hands of the officials.

Secondly, and conversely, wise decision-making can be jeopardized because chief officers (to preserve their impartiality) are normally absent from the meetings of party groups and cannot therefore provide the sort of guidance and advice which they would be called on to give at council and committee meetings in non-partisan authorities. Where there is a party system, the party group decisions are often final, the council/committee meeting becomes a formality and officials are too late to make a contribution (for example it is suggested that the GLC's legal conflict over its fare subsidies could have been avoided if it had been more fully advised by its officers).[52] Furthermore, where the official does make a contribution to the council/committee discussion he will often feel frustrated by seeing his/her advice ignored and decisions being made 'on the nod' (for a graphic illustration, see p. 331; see too note 22, p. 718).

Thirdly, where control of the council is subject to frequent, see-sawing change of party control (every four years at 'whole-council' elections), policy lurches can be time-consuming and wasteful, and again may be very frustrating to the officers and staff, as well as the local population (as in Tameside's switchback on comprehensive schools – see p. 433).

Fourthly, party political control of councils brings the risk of central government interference. Individual or groups of councils may suffer intervention, grant penalties, manipulation of spending approvals (SSAs) – even abolition – by governments, due to central government party bias (see p. 377).

Fifthly, the party system is condemned as undemocratic. As in Parliament, the elected members are expected to 'leave their minds outside the chamber' and slavishly obey the dictates of the party caucus. They cannot exercise their independent powers of judgement: once the party decision is made – even where a majority by only one vote had decided the issue – party solidarity requires members to toe the party line. Free speech is stifled and individual initiative is dampened; council debates become sterile, set pieces; minds are closed and decisions are pre-determined. Such party solidarity is incumbent on group members. Loyalty may be demanded (through disciplinary mechanisms which can threaten expulsion and political career progression) or expected (as a result of obligation or repayment for use of party label and electoral assistance) or is inherent (as activists and holders of party principles and beliefs). But such party loyalty can clash with individual conscience or, perhaps more importantly, with loyalty to the local community and electors: do councillors represent their party group or their constituents? Such group allegiance is more explicit in the Labour and Liberal Democrat Parties, but is no less expected of Conservative councillors once they are in office.[53]

The criticism has even greater poignancy in so far as the local party is run by long-established cliques and elders and where there is an input to decision-making from outside, either in the form of the manufacture of policies by the parties' national headquarters or in the form of the 'outsiders' sitting in caucus meetings (see p. 166). (There is no such right for the local party to sit in at Conservative group meetings, and generally Conservatives and Liberal Democrats are less subject to strong central party organization or direction.)[54]

What has been of particular concern recently is the abuse of power by majority – especially dominant or monopoly – parties. These concerns include the use of council funds for apparently party political purposes and 'advertising' (e.g. the GLC's anti-abolition campaign, and the campaign against rate-capping; in 1985 Bristol council (Labour) was criticized for holding a free – 'on the rates' – public seminar on social security reform as it was seen merely as a vehicle for publicizing the Labour Party's views on that subject).

Another concern is the virtual cornering or hijacking of decision-making procedures to exclude, perhaps completely, minority party groups (see p. 326) or even some of its own members, as allegedly happened in Liverpool's (Militant) Labour Party (and prompted an inquiry by Labour's head office in 1986). In 1976 the Salmon Commission on Standards in Public Life (see p. 223) warned of the dangers of one-party rule in local government. 'Not only are such authorities at particular risk of the absence of effective opposition which can scrutinize their decisions, but investigations and the making of complaints . . . may also be inhibited by the feeling that there is no way round the local "party machine".' Such situations create a 'democratic deficit',[55] somewhat like Parliament under the Conservatives in the 1980s or under Labour domination after the 1997 election. (Such 'one-party local states', however, do not always last: only 10–15 per cent survive for more than twenty years).[56]

The 1990s have witnessed numerous cases of actual or alleged local party corruption and bad behaviour (including expenses fiddles, foreign trips, junketing-for-votes and questionable planning approvals or deals with developers). Some have resulted in official police or auditor inquiries and perhaps legal action (as in the case of councillors' fraudulent claims for expenses in the Labour-dominated council of Blaenau Gwent and 'homes for votes' gerrymandering in Conservative Westminster; see p. 356). Others have led to (Labour) party investigations, expulsions and suspensions (of individuals or even the whole district party) – as in Hackney, Glasgow, Paisley, Monklands, Doncaster and Hull.

Parties are the glue of politics. They are also the poison. They put loyalty above truth. They are the extension into peacetime of the lies, corruption and ruthlessness of war . . . They are one-time democrats yearning to be oligarchs.

No nation's public life is so polluted by party as Britain's. (Simon Jenkins, *The Times*, 14 October 1998)

With the politicization of local government it is alleged that a number of councils have become 'poisoned' by ideological politics and intolerance, with the result that councillors and/or staff are being bullied, harassed and intimidated, party supporters or sympathizers are given council houses or sinecure jobs (some as 'advisors'), other council posts (senior officers, head teachers, even gardeners) are determined by party affiliation or support, and it may even reach down to the determination of school syllabuses, or the purchase of books. Some councils have banned what they regard as obstructive or conspiratorial chief officer group meetings (see p. 307). And, following elections, new (party) administrations will often experience the early retirement of some chief officers as a result of disagreements or the fact that they were appointed by (and are identified with) the previous (party) administration. Other officers find it difficult having to be so guarded or circumspect in the advice they offer in case it offends the party leaders[57] and some chief officers have simply been bullied or dismissed.* And a further aspect has been the appointment to chief officer posts of partisan members of neighbouring councils (known as 'twin-track politicians': see p. 541).

More obvious is the influence of ideological considerations on policy decisions, with councils veering into areas which some commentators regard as inappropriate or irrelevant to local politics and which bring local government into disrepute (see note 19, p. 717), an example of which was the ban on the purchase of, or advertising in, certain newspapers by councils which sympathized with the printers in dispute in 1986 with News International. Such action by Derbyshire was declared illegal in 1990. (Other councils ban publications from their libraries for political reasons.) Concern has also been expressed about management (or technical) decisions being overlaid or influenced by

---

* A Labour Party document (August 1997) itself refers to its own disproportionately large number of councillors, to the existence of bullying (of councillors, colleagues and officers) and law-breaking – hence the reforms noted in Chapters 8 and 15. Seven chief executive officers in Scotland have left their posts since the 1995 reorganization, some of which is attributed to alleged bullying: see *Local Government Chronicle*, 11 December 1998, p. 5 and *Scotland on Sunday*, 6 December 1998.

political or ideological considerations in such areas as competitive tendering contracts or the local administration of services (decentralization or 'going local'; see pp. 517ff.), and school governors.[58]

Finally, political parties are often condemned for engendering artificial and unnecessary conflict, that 'the regular stirring up of political feeling in small communities is harmful'.[59] The implication here is that small communities are naturally consensual and in harmony.

Clearly a number of these points are based on exaggerations. For example, party discipline and 'rubber-stamping' is by no means universal even in those authorities with a developed party system, for not only are there different party systems but local parties operate in more or less their own unique way (e.g., in some authorities majority parties do not take majorities on all committees (see Widdicombe Report, 1986); or in some, party groups are formally constituted as council committees; and Widdicombe provided evidence of an actual decline in the partisan appointment of officers, though there is other evidence of increased party activity and regimentation.[60]

As regards the absence of chief officers from crucial group meetings, there is evidence of ways having been found round this problem[61] and besides, as we have seen (p. 171), most business is transacted without regard to party considerations. Under the 1989 Act (following Widdicombe; see p. 188) officers' terms and conditions of service have been amended (through LACSAB, see p. 284) to allow them to attend and provide advice to councillor party groups (including minor parties). Requests for such advice will have to pass through the chief officer who will be responsible for nominating the officers involved.

The assumption that the small community is more in harmony without political parties is even more questionable. Even if there were no parties, there would be conflicts of personality (among councillors or between officials and councillors); or clashes over sectional interests (such as tenant groups, allotment holders, out-of-town developers, shopkeepers, or over which area gets a fire station); or rivalry among territorial blocks (councillors from a formerly autonomous area forming a separate identifiable group within the council and protesting their area's relative neglect within the larger amalgamated unit of local government)[61]; or there may be functional competition between different committees and services. When 'independent' councillors thus form cliques or unspoken agreements we have an emergent or concealed party system. The 'open' political parties cannot create conflict from nothing: their aim in this respect (if indeed they are aware of having an aim) is to heighten people's awareness of issues and their relationship to those issues. Indeed local parties can help to overlay some of the local divisions and reduce petty squabbles and parish-pump attitudes. (Further, it may be argued that parties make a positive contribution to the well-being of the community, in that many councillors are initially recruited by the parties and subsequently move on to give service to voluntary organizations.)[62]

The assertion that there ought to be 'no politics in local government' and that the council should 'pull together in the best interests of the community' leaves two vital questions unanswered. First, what *is* the community? Is it the adult population? people who live in families? sport fanatics or culture vultures? motorists or pedestrians? Sunday shoppers or worshippers? And, second, what is *best*, and who decides what this is? Politics is about choice – 'who gets what' – and it is not at all obvious whether the town would benefit more, say, from the provision of a new sports centre or from the installation of central heating on a council housing estate. Parties may distort some of the issues, but they do not create them, and to a large extent they help to articulate and clarify them for the public at large. Above all, parties do not exist by command of the law: they exist because they attract popular support. If they were as dreadful as their critics suggest, Independent candidates would do far better in elections than is currently the case. In England and Wales in 1975 there were thirty-one councils wholly non-party or entirely composed of Independents; in total there were some 4,000 Independent or non-party members (17 per cent of all councillors). In 1998 there was only one such council (the City of London Corporation), and the number of Independents or non-party councillors had fallen to just 8.5 per cent of the total[63] (see Figure 12); Independents controlled just 16 councils in Britain, i.e. 4 per cent of the total of 441.*

* In preparation for the London elections in 2000, the London Alliance was formed to mobilize Indepoendent candidates; not only did it register as a party but it sought to promote a number of local policies some of which were by no means uncontroversial (such as decriminalizing drug usage).

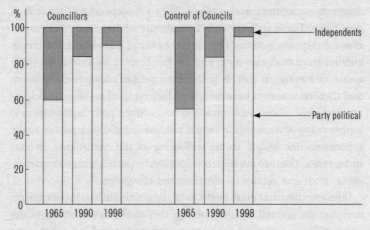

Source: based on figures in *Municipal Yearbooks*

Figure 12 *The decline of the Independent councillor*

However, such was the concern of the government about the developments in local party politics, that in 1985 it appointed the Widdicombe Committee to inquire into 'the practices and procedures governing the conduct of local authority business'.

The Committee confirmed that there had been an increase in party politics in local government and that local party politics had 'taken on a new intensity'. This took a number of forms, including an increased ideological orientation (e.g. with some 63 per cent of councillors now believing that their first duty is to implement the party's election manifesto); a greater polarization of the parties and an increased propensity to organize themselves within their authorities; a tendency to control officers more and to challenge established frontiers between members and officers;[64] and a greater penetration of national issues into council business.

Nevertheless, it found that there was still a considerable bipartisan approach to local administration, and that a number of important local inter-party agreements or conventions had developed to moderate the erstwhile conflict or potentially harmful consequences.[65]

In many authorities the Committee found a number of benefits in the party system, such as increased democratic choice, enhanced coordination, greater consistency, better accountability. But it also found cases of abuse and corruption, such as showing favour or allowing party considerations to influence staff appointments, planning permission, the allocation of services or the allocation of funds (e.g. to outside groups). It was also critical of councils wasting time scoring party points during council business and engaging themselves on national rather than local issues. Consequently, while the Committee expected to see a continuing trend towards political organization in local authorites, it did 'not regard this in itself as either desirable or undesirable'. But the growth of party politics has caused 'definite strains and stresses', and as a result the Committee concluded that there was a need to take account of this growth: to provide some formal recognition of local party politics and introduce some clarifying and regulatory measures.

Some of the Widdicombe proposals dealt specifically with party politics; others were more general in nature but did bear indirectly on party matters. Among its recommendations were:

(a) all decision-making committees should reflect the composition of the full council, and should comprise only elected members (or where non-elected members, such as co-opted members or advisers, attend, they should not vote);

(b) council meetings should provide opportunities for business chosen by minority parties and providing a period for question time;

(c) national parties should seek to ensure that local party groups: (i) keep a publicly available list of those attending their meetings; (ii) limit the number of non-councillors so attending and preclude their voting at such meetings; (iii) debar from attendance anyone disqualified from council membership following surcharge (see p. xix); and (iv) apply the principle of conflict of interests and disclosure at group meetings (as well as in normal council and committee meetings; see pp. 220ff);

(d) officials at the rank of principal officer and above should be barred from political activity (including holding office in a party, holding or standing for public elected office, canvassing or speaking/writing in party political debate);

(e) staff appointments should be based on merit and fair and open competition (with provision for an independent assessor in the selection of chief executives, for whom dismissal should only be permitted where at least two-thirds of council members concur);

(f) chief executive officers (see p. 299) should be legally responsible for all appointments, discipline and dismissal of staff below principal officer level, and also for initiating discipline and dismissal of staff above that level;

(g) local authorities should be allowed to attach staff to party groups (so long as they are clearly identified and are limited in numbers and seniority);

(h) officers should be allowed to attend party group meetings (provided requests from the groups are directed through the chief executive officer).

In an interim report (July 1985) the Widdicombe Committee recommended that local authority publicity of a party political nature should be made illegal, and that council's powers to issue publicity generally should be clearly confined, i.e. in effect to sections 142 and 111 of the Local Government Act 1972 (sections 83 and 69 of the 1973 Act in Scotland). The Committee commented that 'tone and presentation is important and it should be controlled . . . on matters of political dispute and sensitivity, it is wrong for public funds to be spent on material that is strident, sloganized or partisan in style'. But many (including some of the committee) disagree and feel that persuasion is a legitimate objective for councils when providing information; that central government itself uses persuasive information; or that the position of local government has changed so dramatically in recent years that constitutional principles and the law courts are no longer sufficient for its protection. Nevertheless, the government quickly pushed through the Local Government Act 1986 to prevent 'propaganda on the rates' (extended further by the Local Government Act 1988). The Act prohibits the financing or the publication by local authorities of material 'designed to affect public support for a political party'. The government is empowered to issue codes of recommended practice regarding content, style and distribution of local authority publicity. In effect the result was that local authorities could only seek to inform people, not to persuade them.

The government endorsed many of the committees' other recommendations and either commended them for action by the appropriate bodies (parties, local authority organizations and councils themselves) or legislated for them. In particular, points (a) and (d)–(g) were implemented by the Local Government and Housing Act 1989. Under (d) officers are identified as those who are chief officers or hold 'sensitive' posts that may involve giving advice to councillors, having contact with the public and media or exercising delegated discretionary powers, or more generally, those officers with salaries at or above the grade or salary scale of spinal point 44 (i.e. currently about £25,000 per annum). Collectively these – some 47,000 – form the 'politically restricted' (or 'PORPS') group of officers. Whilst (e) applies generally, there is no special provision for chief executive officers. Similarly, (f) applies in so far as an officer (rather than necessarily the chief executive) is identified and he or she is responsible for staff appointments up to the level of the politically restricted group, while in matters of discipline and dismissal, councillors would continue to be involved (subject to certain safeguards); recommendation (g) was originally rejected on the grounds that 'it is inappropriate for local authorities to employ at public expense staff whose purpose is to undertake political support duties for a particular party group or councillor rather than serve the council as a whole'[66] (especially as they would have to be available to all party groups), but these have now been approved, though limited to a maximum of three per authority and with a salary maximum (in 1999) of £25,000 per annum. Item (h) was accepted (see p. 296).

Thus political parties come in for considerable criticism and blame. Some critics of political parties in local government find solace in the thought that, as the standards of services become more uniform throughout the nation and as control by the central government is extended, so the scope for local party politics diminishes. Whether this optimism is justified is doubtful, but they also like to comfort themselves with the thought that the extensive nature of party politics in Britain reduces the scope for what many people see as a far more sinister phenomenon – the pressure group (see p. 473).

8

THE COUNCILLORS

There is something of a shortage of people willing to stand for election as councillors. As we have seen, in some areas there have been as many as 50 per cent uncontested seats for major local authorities, and even today, the overall figure can reach 20 per cent. In addition, there are a number of vacancies on the local authorities of Britain – council seats which remain unfilled because no one is willing to serve (although some of these vacancies are temporary – the result of death or resignation and awaiting a local by-election). In 1991, Secretary of State Michael Heseltine publicly proclaimed that 'it is getting harder to attract people to serve on councils. Not just people of the necessary calibre – it's often difficult to attract anyone at all. And it's affecting all parties.' A report in 1993 predicted an 'approaching precipice' in the recruitment of councillors[1]

Who'd be a councillor?

Such deficiencies are not altogether surprising considering the disadvantages of being a councillor. Chief among these is the time it consumes. Councillors spend much time on their public duties – on average 74 hours per month, perhaps very much more (see p. 206). This can cut severely into his or her social life. It can also interfere with business and earnings. Others find it a physical and mental strain, and many councillors find their duties frustrating. This may be the result of experience with the administrative machinery – the limited powers of local authorities, restrictions by the central government, delays in reaching or implementing decisions or difficulties in obtaining finance. But for many people – 93 per cent – the notion of being a councillor simply doesn't occur to them.

Among the more important reasons for people not seeking to become councillors are lack of confidence to play the councillor's role, insufficient time and having never contemplated seeking election. Probably there are deeper reasons for this indifference; a lack of interest in local politics and public affairs; the low standing and salience of local government; cultural change that devalues public service; the general public unwillingness to involve themselves in local affairs; and a lack of strong attachment to the localities in which many people live. All play a part.*

Alternatively, the reluctance to serve may be the result of bad relationships with other councillors, either on a personal level or via party politics – the Minister (above) blamed 'the local politicking that Labour has introduced into the culture of local authorities over the last two decades'. Others may be put off by what they see as hostility or ignorant attitudes of the public. We get some idea of the scale of these difficulties from Table 11, which is based on a survey of councillors.²

There are other reasons why people are unwilling to enter or remain in local government service. For some, the times of meeting³ are inconvenient – for example, evening meetings may not suit those who dislike night driving, while afternoon meetings may be awkward for housewives and mothers. Meetings at any time may be difficult for those in full-time employment and attendance may involve some loss of income. Although the Employment Protection (Consolidation) Act 1978 (as amended by the Employment Rights Act 1996) requires employers to allow their employees to take reasonable time off (not necessarilly paid) to attend public duties, it may be done grudgingly, jeopardize promotion prospects and create friction with colleagues.⁴ A survey by the MSF union found considerable variation among employers as to what constituted 'reasonable' time off: some allowed less than three days, others more than fifty-two days; and there were corresponding differences in attitudes to involvement in public duties,

---

* See *The Impact of Releasing People for Council Duties*, DETR, 1998, p. 10. A survey by the LGMB at the time of the 1998 local elections showed 27 per cent of councillors did not seek re-election (often after just one or two terms) mainly because of the time commitment (though 11 per cent cited the erosion of local government's influence as the reason). Overall, 40 per cent of councillors have under five years' service.

with the result that 34 per cent of employees surveyed felt their careers were damaged.[5] One suggestion is that in so far as employers are reluctant to allow councillors time off to perform their council duties (which is a particular deterrent to those at the beginning of their careers) it may be feasible to consider making payments of councillors' allowances (see below) directly to employers.[6] However, a more recent survey suggests that this is not such a great problem, with employers allowing their councillor employees, on average, over half a day a week and paying two-thirds of them in full (despite most of them being ignorant of the the 1978 Act!).[7]

The Widdicombe Committee (above) found private employers compared well with the public (State) sector, though it found wide differences in practice among the former and urged a more positive and flexible approach; they also found manual workers in particular had problems with lost earnings and getting time off. (In view of the apparent abuse by some councils in granting virtually full-time paid leave of absence, the Committee recommended that there be a statutory upper limit on paid leave which public sector employers may grant employees for council duties, and the government, under the Local Government and Housing Act 1989, imposed a maximum of 208 hours p.a.

Some potential councillors are put off by the increasing complexity of council business, the central controls and financial constraints and having to cut budgets and reduce services, or the perceived vilification of local government by the central government,[8] and others may be put off by their image of local government (parochial, bureaucratic, corrupt, etc.). Further (as we have seen in Chapter 6 above), some local seats are so safe, either in personal or in party terms, that it is regarded as a hopeless task to fight an election there. An additional obstacle or deterrent – criticized at the time by ethnic minority groups – appeared in 1998 when the Labour Party introduced some basic tests of literacy and numeracy as well as financial probity and integrity for its local government candidates (after discovering that over 10 per cent were unable to read or add up properly).

Although professional and business/managerial occupations appear to be well represented in local government;[9] there is a feeling in some quarters that many potential councillors from such a background are

Table 11 *Councillors' probable reasons for eventually giving up council work, and ex-councillors' reasons for leaving*

	Councillors'* probable reasons for giving up %	All ex-councillors' reasons for leaving %	Ex-councillors' (under 65) reasons for leaving %
Personal reasons:			
Ill-health/tired/found it a strain	22	23	} 21
Old age	21	7	
Interference with business or family life	17	14	15
Amount of time given	5	18	25
Moving from area	5	13	16
Became MP	1	—	—
Council reasons:			
Frustrations of party system	5	8	} 22
Frustrated by other aspects of local government organization	12	13	
Other answers/not answered	12	4	1
Total	100	100	100
(Numbers)	(1,044)	(401)	(289)

*Excluding those who said: 'Can't think of anything.'
Source: *The Management of Local Government* (Maud Report), HMSO, 1967, Vol. 2.

lost to local government on account of their mobility, especially in the pursuit of their careers. However, while there is clearly something in this, a study in Bristol[10] suggested that many such people are lost to local government because they prefer to give their services to voluntary organizations (partly because it affords greater status), or they become members of the growing number of quangos (which may be more powerful, better paid or more party-anonymous, cf. pp. 5–6) or join single-issue pressure groups (see Chapter 13).

It may be thought that the problem was eased in so far as the various reorganizations of local government reduced the number of councils and thus councillors (by as much as 50 per cent in Wales and Scotland in the 1990s; see Chapter 3). Certainly we have seen an increase in the number of contested seats, and there has been a rise in the number of candidates per seat contested (from two in the early 1970s to three today, 'though such figures tell us nothing about the quality and motivation of those candidates').[11]

However, a reduction in the number of councils and councillors is not good for democracy, especially since (excluding parishes) Britain already has fewer councillors than many countries abroad. For example, whereas in Britain there is one councillor per 2,500 of the population, in most European countries the figure is below 500. (In France councillors constitute 1 per cent of the population and as John Stewart says, 'They are embedded in the local community'.[12]) In addition, and not surprisingly, the result of reorganization has been to increase councillors' workloads: in Scotland, for example, on average councillors now spend 46 hours per week on council business compared to 31 hours in 1983 and 27 hours in 1993.[13] This can have consequences not just for recruitment and retention (or turnover) but also for the composition and the representative nature of councillors (see p. 195 below). (A number of these issues was considered by the working party on councillors in 1993; see p. 270 below.) Thus there is a preponderance of non-working and of older, retired people serving as councillors. The government is concerned about this and would like to see the profile change and become generally younger.[14] Yet paradoxically perhaps it is the deterrent pressure on full-time workers, as well as more convenient hours, which has helped more women to find a place as local councillors (see below).

In spite of these obstacles, why are so many people willing to become councillors? For example, in 1998, there were over 13,000 candidates, i.e. about three per seat. According to one survey[15] only a minority of councillors themselves had the idea of standing: these were often driven to seek election in order to promote or campaign against a specific issue. For others it is a consequence of coming from a political family background. But most – over three-quarters – said they were asked to stand, and most of these said they had thought little or not at all about becoming councillors beforehand. About one third had been asked to stand by political parties and another third by personal friends or acquaintances. Others were asked by organizations such as trade unions (which may 'sponsor' them, as they do MPs),[16] or religious, welfare, business or civic groups. Thus most seem to be passive or even reluctant recruits, at least initially. Once elected, there are a number of *satisfactions* to be gained from being a councillor.

(1) One of the most important seems to be that of giving service to the community. (Some may treat it as a form of apprenticeship before standing for Parliament. In the 1992 General Election a record number of parliamentary candidates – 880, or almost 50 per cent – came from a local government background, either as current or ex-councillors. In 1997, some 60 per cent of the new MPs had local government experience. This may be an indication of local government's growing importance as a national political issue; see Chapter 14.) Such Parliamentary links and 'dual mandates' should be useful as a means of facilitating better knowledge and understanding, (though MPs apparently soon relinquish their councillor roles).[17]

(2) There is a certain prestige attached to being a councillor (although the Maud Report doubted the importance of this these days).[18]

(3) Many find satisfaction, especially manual workers,[19] in council work (decision-making, leadership, involvement) as a contrast and compensation for their paid employment (which may be more routine and undemanding or lacking authority). Retired members may find it a substitute for their former employment. And the hen-pecked husbands or intimidated wives may find it a compensation for their lack of status at home.

(4) The town hall has been described as 'the best club in town' and many councillors do find that membership of the council can enhance their private and social life. Such satisfactions are reflected

in the fact that 12 per cent of councillors serve on more than one council (with a 'dual mandate'), and between 45 and 68 per cent sit on voluntary and public bodies (including school boards of governors).

Portrait of the councillor

There are about 23,000 councillors in Britain's principal local authorities – about 1 per 2,500 of the population (plus some 70,000 parish and community councillors). Like MPs they are elected as local representatives. But just how *representative* of their community are they? How typical are they of the person in the street?

The pattern varies somewhat among communities and types of local authority – for example, London borough councillors tend to be younger and Welsh councillors older, than the national average councillor; there are fewer women councillors in Welsh and Scottish councils. Overall, the picture[20] reveals that councillors are not a cross-section of the community: they are *un*typical. Compared to Britain's population as a whole, councillors tend to be:

(1) *older* – the average age of councillors (in England and Wales) is 55.6. 50 per cent of councillors are over the age of fifty-four, and less than 5 per cent are under thirty-five years of age; this contrasts with the national population figures of 34 per cent aged fifty-five and over, and nearly 30 per cent aged between twenty-one and thirty-four; while 22 per cent of the population are retired, for councillors the figure is 35 per cent (compared to 20 per cent in 1965 and 25 per cent in 1985),[21] though much of this increase is due to earlier/younger retirement. There has been a significant fall (from an already small proportion) in those under thirty-five. And, arguably, the time involved tends to skew the composition towards the retired and unemployed.

(2) *male* – though the figure of 27 per cent for females is a distinct and progressive improvement, from 12, 17 and 19 per cent in 1964, 1976 and 1985. This figure for Scotland is 23 per cent (from 20 per cent in 1992)[22] and the figure for Wales is 20 per cent. (As a result

of the 1997 General Election, women MPs rose from under 10 per cent to 18 per cent).

(3) *owner-occupiers* – 85 per cent of councillors own their home, compared to 60 per cent for the population as a whole;

(4) *white collar* in occupation – just under 14 per cent currently work manually or in a craft; 60 per cent are managers, technicians and professionals; the rest are in education or office work. About 40 per cent have jobs in the State sector.[23] (Between 40 and 60 per cent also serve on public boards, in charities and as school governors.)

(5) *better educated* – one in three has a degree and/or professional qualification. And by way of comparison, in 1985 while 20 per cent of the population experienced education at A level or above, the proportion of councillors was 40 per cent;

(6) *better paid* – in so far as those in employment come disproportionately from the salaried occupations. Again, by way of comparison, earnings of occupied councillors (in 1976) were approximately one third higher than the national average: no doubt a reflection of their educational and occupational background, and age; in 1985, some 40 per cent of councillors had incomes of £10,000 or over, compared to the national average earnings figure of £9,000 p.a.

The overall average age of councillors was 55.6, though slightly higher in shire counties (57) and in Welsh authorities (57.8) and lower in Metropolitan districts (53.9) and London boroughs (52). Over half of councillors were in the age groups 45–54 (27.5 per cent) and 55–64 (29.5 per cent) and 11.4 per cent were aged 70 and over. While the older age groups are not significantly over-represented on councils, 25.1 per cent of the 65s and over were councillors, compared to 20.6 per cent of the general population. Only 4.4 per cent of councillors are under 35, which is a fall from 7 per cent in 1986[24] (despite a rise in that age group in the population) – so that, while there was some evidence to suggest that younger candidates were coming into local government between the surveys of 1964 and 1976 (see Table 13), this appears to have been reversed since. However, while 45 per cent of councillors are self-employed or in full-time employment, 8 per cent are in part-time employment, 3 per cent are unemployed and 35 per cent are retired. Nearly 25 per cent are full-time councillors (i.e.

Table 12 *Councillors by age, compared to general age structure England & Wales, 1997*

Age range	% of adult (over 21) population	% of councillors
under 25	8.1	0.2
25–34	21.2	4.2
35–44	19.1	13.6
45–54	17.8	27.5
55–59	6.9	14.9
60–64	6.4	14.6
65–69	6.0	13.7
70–74 } over 74 }	14.6	7.8 / 3.6

Source: First National Census, LGMB, 1998. See too *Municipal Journal*, 27 February 1998.

spending over 30 hours a week on council work) and thus often very reliant on their council allowances (see p. 210).

In addition, 11 per cent of councillors are disabled, 34 per cent have some responsibilities in caring for others (i.e. young children and other dependants) and 3 per cent come from ethnic minorities. (This last figure was 1.9 per cent in 1994. While the figure has improved, it is barely half of the 5–6 per cent for the ethnic population in Britain generally. However, its adequacy will depend on the composition of the local population such as Bradford or Birmingham. For example, representatives from ethnic minorities in the London boroughs have over 11 per cent of seats.[25])

The high proportion of councillors who are retired is often the focus of criticism. Yet the extra time they can give and the life experience they can bring should not be overlooked as valuable contributions.

These are national average figures: the social composition of any particular council will vary with local circumstances. For example, in rural areas farmers will tend to be well represented; in Labour-dominated areas there will tend to be more members from a working-

Table 13 *Councillors by age and gender*

Age-range	% of whole adult population 1985		% of councillors 1985		1976	1964
21–24	9.3	} 28.7	—	} 7	9	4
25–34	19.4		7			
35–44	18.8	} 34.1	19	} 44	17	15
45–54	15.3		25		24	26
55–64	15.5	} 27.8	27	} 46	30	31
65–74	12.3		19		19	19
75 and over	9.1	9.1	3	3	2	4
	100	100	100	100	100	100
Female councillors				19%	17%	12%

Sources: 'The Local Government Councillor', *The Conduct of Local Authority Business* (Widdicombe), Research Vol. 2, HMSO, 1986, Table 2.3; OPCS Monitor *Mid-1985 Population Estimates*; 'The Local Government Councillor', *The Management of Local Government* (Maud), Research Vol. 2, HMSO, 1967; *The Remuneration of Councillors* (Robinson), Vol. 2, HMSO, 1977.
NOTE: Figures for 1964 and 1976 refer to England and Wales; 1985 figures are for Britain. In 1998, the *First National Census of Councillors*, by the LGMB, gave the figure of 27 per cent for female councillors in England and Wales.

class background; there are more women councillors in metropolitan and London Boroughs.[26] Much too will depend on the turnover of councillors in the area, and on the method of recruitment (whether members are recruited through political parties, for instance, see pp. 164, 194) and their criteria – or bias – for selection.

It may be argued that our local councils should be more of a cross-section of the community: that only in this way can councillors really understand the issues and problems which are felt by the ordinary person in the street. For example, does the lack of women councillors (especially single mothers) explain the apparent inadequacy of nursery provision, while there is an arguably ample supply of municipal golfing facilities? In other words, better balanced councils would make for a better balance of services, of priorities and of justice. Current

Table 14 *Councillors by political party membership and age, gender, activity status, socio-economic group and income* (1985)

	Conservative %	Labour %	Liberal %	Independent %	Other* %	All Councillors %
Age: 60+	37	32	22	52	30	36
45–59	42	33	30	36	33	37
18–44	19	33	49	11	33	26
Gender: Male	78	83	79	81	81	81
Female	21	17	21	19	19	19
Activity status:						
Employed full- or part-time	64	59	74	47	67	60
Unemployed	2	8	3	1	2	4
Retired	24	22	13	40	30	25
Permanently sick/ disabled	—	2	—	1	—	1
Looking after a home	9	6	9	9	7	8
Other	—	1	—	—	—	1
Socio-economic group:						
Professional	11	6	15		5	9
Employers/managers	42	20	28	37	26	32
Intermediate non-manual	14	22	23	11	30	18
Junior non-manual	8	11	15	6	2	10
Skilled manual/own account non-professional	10	25	8	14	14	16
Semi-skilled manual	1	8	4	5	—	4
Unskilled manual	—	2	—	1	—	1
Armed Forces/NA	12	8	8	16	5	11
Income:						
£15,000+	25	7	18	14	33	16
£10,000–£14,999	22	23	29	17	2	22
£6,000–£9,999	23	28	23	27	25	26
Up to £5,999	22	38	23	29	23	28
None	1	1	2	2	—	1
Refused/NA	8	4	3	10	12	7
Base	(595)	(496)	(133)	(224)	(43)	(1,557)

*Includes Scottish Nationalist, Social Democrat, Plaid Cymru (Welsh Nationalist) and other parties.

Source: 'The Local Government Councillor', *The Conduct of Local Authority Business* (Widdicombe), Research Vol. 2, HMSO, 1986, Table 4.5.

illustrations are the campaigns for better planning and design, more road crossings, better lighting and cleaning, etc. to make the urban environment less hazardous or threatening to women and mothers with young children (who arguably are the greatest users of council services) or campaigns for more sports facilities and cycleways for younger people. A better balance in composition is not only fairer but it also improves the democratic legitimacy of councils. And in so far as it incorporates the skills, experience and perspectives of a wider range of people, it may improve both the quality of decisions and of the decision-making process.

On the other hand, it may be felt that the atypical (some would say elitist) composition of our local authorities has certain advantages – that age brings experience and wisdom; that certain occupations (especially business and managerial) bring useful contacts; and that, above all, managerial and administrative ability is necessary for the work councillors have to do (reading reports, committee work, dealing with the public, articulating interests and concerns, etc.).

Whatever the appropriate qualities of councillors and the desirability of their being a close cross-section of the community, it is most unlikely that we shall ever see such a reflection or balance on our councils. Apart from such problems as time availability, competence, confidence, etc.,[27] which may be soluble (see p. 219), the fact is that local government is about politics and increasingly party politics. And politics is a minority interest and activity; most people are just not interested ('it's a job for the politicians'), and it is difficult, perhaps impossible (even undesirable?)[28] to change. Besides, perhaps 'un-representative' people can effectively 'represent' others? (And there is also the contribution from officers who have a professional interest in and responsibility for their particular service area – housing, education, social services, etc. – and to the service users and complainants.) The Maud Committee[29] concluded that

It is neither possible, nor in our opinion is it desirable, that councils should in some way be representative of all the varying interests, economic groups, income or education levels in the community . . . The qualities of the member should be related to what he is expected to do . . .

The councillor's role

The duties of councillors are little stated in law. It has been described as the only job without a job description. To a large extent therefore they must turn for guidance to the conventions and practice[30] of their local authority. (Many of these will have been set out in the authority's standing orders – see p. 242.) Legislation – the Local Government Acts 1972 (England and Wales) and 1973 (Scotland) – does require their attendance at council meetings (see p. 132) and disclosure of financial interest (see p. 222). They have the right of access to the local authority's official documents in so far as this will enable them to carry out their responsibilities as a councillor (but see p. 233) and they can by law claim a financial allowance (see p. 211). Councillors' discussions enjoy 'qualified privilege' (i.e. complete freedom of speech in council/ committee meetings, except deliberate untruths which are motivated by malice). Normally it is understood that individual councillors have no lawful authority: that executive power is exercisable only by the council as a whole, as a corporate body (and operating within the powers given to them by law – see p. 76). Consequently all questions are decided by the vote of the members of the council, each voice and each vote counting equally.

However, local authorities have the power to delegate responsibility, and they frequently use it, especially in relation to committees (see p. 243). As a consequence of this and of other practices and conventions[31] in individual local authorities, the theoretical parity (of authority) among members is very different in practice. This is especially so with the development of parties, and more recently, with the establishment of the cabinet and mayoral system (see Chapter 15). Indeed the current reforms are pointing up, if not altering, the general role(s) of councillors: see Ch. 15.

Councillors will find that they have a variety of overlapping and perhaps conflicting roles and responsibilities. They are also subject to change as a result of contracting out (CCT) and partnership arrangements, and as a result of the current reform programme (see Chapter 15). They must therefore try to achieve a satisfactory balance among them. Thus, they are:

(1) *Representatives*. They are elected to represent a ward or division, but they are also expected to have regard for the interests of the whole of the local authority area. This dual role can be difficult, especially justifying it to local constituents[32] – a problem compounded in the case of the councillor who also sits on another council (see pp. 206 and 465).

(2) '*Ombudsmen*' or citizens' referees. As such they have to deal with, or 'trouble-shoot', problems and issues raised by individual constituents' grievances (such as school closures or allocations, adult education fees, road or council house maintenance, and planning permission).

(3) *Community leaders*. This is a wider aspect of the above, where councillors become 'democratic advocates' on behalf of their constituents, i.e. consumer watchdogs of all local services, public or private. Here, councillors can play an important role in monitoring the quality of services provided to their constituents by other agencies (such as the NHS). Agency representatives may be invited to address special council or committee meetings. Or, more usually, councillors are appointed to represent the authority on various outside bodies. This can provide important opportunities for councillors to exercise leadership and influence as well as being consumer champions and advocates and 'charter-seekers'. This would involve a combination of some of the above roles.[33]

(4) *Managers*. Here they must oversee the administrative machinery and service delivery of officers and staff, to see that it is fair (as above) and efficient. This includes their oversight of departments and separate boards/DSOs and contract arrangements whose services are subject to tendering (see. p. 244).

(5) *Policy-makers*, helping to shape policies and plans in the council and committees. In this and the previous role, they are expected to identify needs, set objectives and establish plans to meet those needs, and subsequently to review achievements (sometimes known as monitoring or 'progress chasing').

(6) Above all, councillors are *politicians*, seeking to manage and resolve conflicts. In pursuit of this aim, they will exercise some of their other roles – especially policy-making and the determination of service expenditures and priorities ('who gets what'). As such they

must be motivators and persuaders, trying to influence, sway, convince – be it their committee members, constituents or party fellows. Inevitably, many councillors will also adopt a narrower political role in having a commitment to a political party.

Analysing the role of the councillor in this way suggests a degree of fragmentation. Yet many aspects are congruent and reinforcing. For example, as a recent report states, 'The representative role of the councillor is indivisible from his or her role in policy formulation or the scrutiny of performance. The roles are mutually interdependent and inform each other.'[34]

In Parliament, some MPs become Ministers and shape government policy. Other MPs play a supporting role or, in the case of the Opposition, a critical and probing role (asking questions, making critical speeches, attempting to influence policy, especially through committee investigations, etc.). Finally, there are those MPs who are content to play a more passive back-bench part (going along with the party directives, raising constituency matters from time to time, etc.).

In similar fashion, councillors vary in the roles they play. Some, variously known as 'delegates' or 'tribunes',[35] are mainly interested in playing the representative role – dealing with complaints and speaking for particular areas or groups. This seems especially true of newer, less experienced, 'lighter' members. Others, known as 'statesmen' or 'trustees', will seek to play a more active part in policy-making, whether in broad terms (setting general objectives, determining priorities, etc.) or in the area of particular services, such as housing or education. Thus, in local government, we have something equivalent to the parliamentary front- and back-benchers, and to government and opposition, since 'the growth of political party organization within local government has significantly altered the role of the councillor. The fact that in many authorities there is a majority party – which forms the administration – and a minority party or parties which form the opposition, challenges the pretence that all councillors have equal power and equal responsibilities. In practice they do not, and not only in majority councils.'[36] (A recent survey of councillors[37] showed that 31 per cent had no special responsibilities or leading roles, such as council or party leaders, mayors, committee chairs, etc.) These differences are now being made explicit and are being insitutionalized in the government's current reforms (see Chapter 15). Essentially, councillors are being divided into *executive* policy-makers (manifested in the mayor and/or cabinet) and the *scrutinizing* councillors who are to represent the community and monitor the executive (like Parliamentary Select Committees and Parliament itself). The extra responsibility and time commitment of leaders, chairs, mayors, etc. is recognized in their financial allowances (see p. 209).

The demands of council work

Being a councillor is a heavy commitment: the Robinson Committee[38] (1977) found that on average a councillor spent seventy-nine hours a month on his duties. This is a significant increase since the Maud survey (1967) which found the average to be fifty-two hours – a reflection among other things of the fact that in 1974–5 the number of principal local authorities (i.e. excluding parishes/communities) was reduced from 1,857 to 521, and the number of councillors from 46,000 to 26,000. There were further losses in 1986 (700 fewer councillors) and in the 1990s the overall figure came down to 22,700*. The Widdicombe Committee Report on the *Conduct of Local Authority Business* (1986) showed that the average councillor was spending 74 hours a month on council business (though there were considerable variations among types of local authority, with Scottish regional/island councillors spending 129 hours per month compared to 58 for English shire district councillors). There is now clear evidence of further increases in the time spent by members on council business,† the most striking

---

* The UK councillor represents an average of 2,600 inhabitants compared to 116 in France, 250 in Germany, 400 in Italy and 600 in Spain (*Local and Regional Authorities in Europe*, No. 56, 1996).

† Barron (1991) gives a monthly figure of 137 hours for English county councillors; the surveys of Bloch (1992) and Rao (1994) for England and Wales showed 82 and 97 hours respectively. A study in 1993 gave figures of 94 and 64 hours per month for English county and district councillors respectively (K. Young and Rao *Managing Change*, Rowntree, 1993), and 111 and 98 for their Scottish counterparts. In 1983, the average figure for Scottish councillors was 124 hours (Martlew, 1988). In 1999, the figure for London councillors was 80 hours per month (*Municipal Journal*, 26 February 1999).

of which is that for Scotland where on average councillors spend $46\frac{1}{2}$ hours a week or 186 hours a month,[39] which would suggest that most are full-time councillors. The actual full-time figure for England and Wales is 24 per cent (defined as over 30 hours a week, LGMB Census 1998). It also showed that 12 per cent of councillors were members of other councils (a 'dual mandate'; cf. p. 437).

In 1998, a more modest, though still burdensome, figure of 16 average hours a week was revealed, but this is for councillors who are also in employment.* This also showed that of those in employment, 44 per cent worked in the public sector (cf. 25 per cent of general population).

The average figures inevitably conceal variations, and not just among different types of local authority (as illustrated above) who will, for example have different numbers of committees or differing frequency of meetings and different lengths of meetings (e.g. especially if they are 'hung' councils). Councillors will also (in spite of the work of the Boundary Commissions, see p. 73) have different areas (with travel implications) and different populations to serve (with workloads thus affected through surgeries, correspondence, lobbying etc.). There are variations too among individual councillors, since obviously they are not all equally devoted to their duties. For example, councillors who are retired from employment appear to give more time than do councillors who have a self-employed occupation. There is also some variation as between the parties and between the sexes, with women councillors spending 20 per cent more time on their council work than men.[40] Furthermore, being a leading councillor, such as mayor,[41] Lord Provost, committee chairman or party leader, obviously involves a far greater commitment. Thus in Scotland, leading councillors spend 70 hours a week on council duties compared to 50 for committee chairs and 38.5 for the backbench and opposition members.[42]

Table 15 gives a breakdown of the time spent by the average councillor on public duties. In more detail, they include:

(1) Council and committee meetings, including sub-committees. These involve attendance, preparatory work (reading relevant papers

* G. Courtnay *et al.*, *The Impact of Releasing People for Council Duties*, DETR, 1998.

Table 15 *Time spent by councillors on their public duties*

	hours per month
Attendance at council and committee meetings	21
Preparation for meetings	18
Travelling to meetings	7
Party meetings	5
Electors' problems	13
Meeting organizations on behalf of the council	8
Public consultation	2
Total	74

Electors (17%)   Attendance (28%)
Organizations (11%)
Consultation (3%)
Party (7%)
Travel (10%)   Preparation (23%)

Source: 'The Local Government Councillor', *The Conduct of Local Authority Business* (Widdicombe), Research Vol. 2, HMSO, 1986.
Note: Whilst the overall hours spent on council work has increased since 1986 (see p. 205), the allocation is little changed from that shown in the Table above; see for example *Municipal Journal*, 13 December 1996, pp. 13–15.

such as reports, etc.), attending party meetings, personal contacts, meeting council officers and travel.

(2) Dealing with electors' problems (especially housing matters) and holding 'surgeries' at which the councillor makes himself available for consultations by constituents, including pressure groups. Sometimes councillors will visit constituents and they may organize open forums on local issues of the day.

(3) Serving as a nominee of the council on other organizations, such as health authorities, school governors, joint committees, voluntary bodies, the Local Government Association etc.

(4) Miscellaneous duties, including conferences, training courses, meetings of local organizations (such as Age Concern, Round Table and Shelter), site visits, ceremonies, speech days, fetes and various other semi-social functions.

A 1991 survey showed the average time spent by councillors to be eighty-two hours per month,[43] and a later one puts the figure at ninety-seven hours.[44] But the average councillor is hard to find. The number of hours any one councillor will spend on duties will depend on a variety of factors – whether s/he is a member of the ruling party group, experience and seniority, the amount of time s/he is prepared to give, etc. Councillors may also serve on more than one council, especially in shire areas (e.g. 25 per cent of Somerset County Councillors are also members of District councils. Even 10 per cent of councillors in employment find time to serve on two councils).*

The number of years of service also varies. The 1986 Widdicombe Report drew attention to the development of the tendency for members to serve for only two terms. Thus by the mid 1980s, the number of councillors with ten years or more of council service was only a third, compared to nearly a half in the mid 1960s[45] In the 1990s one quarter of members had under three years of council experience, and indeed councillor *turnover* has become such that newly elected members can become chairs of meetings at the beginning of their term rather than having to serve a long apprenticeship as in the past. In general, there is a turnover or replacement of councillors of 30–50 per cent[46] and most of this is due to their deciding not to fight again rather than to electoral defeat.[47] In spite of this the evidence, at least up to the early 1990s, suggests that such voluntary retirement is not actually increasing.[48] However, the rate of turnover is a cause for concern since it affects council continuity and depth of experience (though it may have one advantage: more open attitudes to change; see *Portrait of Change*, LGMB, 1998).

Recent surveys[49] confirm the findings of the Maud Committee (Table 11 above) – that most councillors retire through age, ill-health, family pressures and work (either interference or relocation). The 1991 survey (above) showed that 42 per cent of councillors did not seek a second term of office due to the time commitment, the effect on job opportunities, the inadequacy of financial allowances and the lack of childcare facilities. The difficulty of combining employment with council service is obvious and there is evidence that fewer employed people are coming forward as councillors (with, for example, a fall

---

* *The Impact of Releasing People for Council Duties*, DETR, 1998.

from 60 per cent to 48 per cent before and after reorganization in Scotland; see *Municipal Journal*, 13 December 1996). Yet a surprising number do manage to integrate their work and council duties without overburdening themselves or their employers. Councillors in full-time employment manage to devote an average of 16 hours a week to council duties (60 per cent using an average of eight days of their leave to do so.[50]). On the other hand it has been suggested that there are fewer local businessmen willing to stand for election as councillors since local authorities are no longer (since 1990) responsible for business rates[51] (see Chapter 11).

However, political reasons were also significant, with councillors expressing feelings of frustration and disenchantment with their own council (parties, procedures, etc.) and with the debilitating effects of central government policies (finance, restructuring, services, etc.[52]) And with more services being contracted out, schools managing themselves, etc., councillors have felt they are losing much of their 'hands-on' role.

The problem of turnover reflects that of recruitment generally, and both impact upon the composition and quality of councillors. 'A significant proportion of retiring councillors were in the 35–44 age group and had served just one term of office . . . suitably qualified and able candidates were increasingly reluctant to be recruited onto the council.'[53] The situation may worsen as workloads increase as a result of the reorganization into fewer councils (thus introducing the paradox that fewer councils means fewer councillors needed, but fewer councillors forthcoming because of the increased time commitment!).

A recent review of local authorities found that 'the most common complaints . . . from councillors were not about the costs of being a councillor but about the time-consuming nature of their duties and the often unfocused nature of the debate in which they had to engage.'[54] A solution to this problem is for councils to review the way they manage their business. In so far as the problem is timing rather than just length of time involved, this implies altering the times (and places) of meetings (see p. 242), such as differentiating the use of meetings in different parts of the committee cycle (see p. 245) and varying the nature and purpose of committee meetings, by emphasizing different aspects of their role at different times – such as budget and policy framework, policy development and review, general debate, etc. This would provide a clearer focus for councillors. Councils should also consider how they structure their agendas and the clarity and quality of the information they provide. More fundamentally, councils should seek to avoid the duplication of decision-making – and this is what lies behind the current reforms; see Chapter 15.

Payment

In view of the considerable time which is involved in being a councillor it may seem reasonable to suggest that councillors should be paid for their endeavours. Yet up until the reorganization of local government in 1974–5, councillors received no payment as such, just expenses and loss of earnings allowance, which had been introduced on a systematic basis in 1948. This arrangement was superseded as a result of the Local Government Acts of 1972 and 1973 (since amended by the Local Government, Planning and Land Act 1980; see p. 212), when attendance allowances were introduced, and councillors in principal local authorities (that is, excepting parish and community councils) became entitled to claim an *attendance allowance* for approved duties up to a maximum (e.g. £18.25 per day in 1990). There were considerable variations among local authorities as to what constituted 'approved duties', but it was and remains normal practice to pay special non-taxable allowances to the chair of the council (the mayor, convenor or Lord Provost) to cover the extra cost (civic expenses) of high office. In addition all councillors could claim for travel and subsistence expenses necessarily incurred in the pursuit of council business.

The issue of payment has always been controversial. Members of the public are often quick to accuse councillors of self-seeking and not deserving of trust. Yet being a councillor can be costly: e.g. a 1977 survey showed about 40 per cent of working councillors lost pay if they stayed away from work, and about one in five of these lost as much as £50 or more a month, even taking attendance allowances into account. Overall, the cost of local authorities' expenditure on members' allowances and expenses amounted to £28 million in 1985 – or under 0.1 per cent of their total expenditure.

The Wheatley Report (p. 60 above) and the Robinson Committee

(1977) recommended a more substantial and uniform payment to councillors. In the words of the former, 'There is a job to be done, and the labourer is worthy of his hire.' It argued that a better system of payment would attract more people to stand for election: that in the light of 'the demanding and responsible nature of local government service . . . service given [ought no longer] to be its own reward' and that a standard system of payments would be far simpler and less invidious than the current arrangements.

The payment of councillors may have other merits. It might help to bring in a broader cross-section of the community (assuming this is desirable) and possibly a more committed, professional approach to the task (unpaid, part-time councillors can fend off criticism and can excuse any inept action or inactions on their part on grounds that they are after all only amateurs and are doing it for nothing anyway). It might also help to stimulate public interest in the work and workings of local government. Finally, it might be argued that the adequate payment of councillors would help to eliminate corruption by reducing the disparity between the financial position of so many councillors and that of their officials and of the businessmen they must regularly meet.[55]

However, the Robinson Committee rejected the notion of a full-time salary on the grounds that it

would irretrievably damage the voluntary principle . . . would endanger the relationship between elector and elected . . . would endanger the relationship between members and officers by tending to blur the well-established distinction between their respective roles . . . Further, we do not believe that public opinion is ready to accept the idea of full-time salaried councillors.[56]

It was also concerned about the likely cost.

While many of these points are by no means self-evident, it may be added that on the one hand such payments might attract the wrong sort of person on to local authorities, while on the other hand there is little if any evidence that payment would attract candidates: according to the Maud Report some two thirds of the elected members questioned thought that councillors should not be paid, and it did not appear that finance was a dominant influence on ex-councillors in giving up council work (see p. 192). In the survey of electors, only just over 10 per cent mentioned finance as a means of attracting more people into local government (and see p. 212).[57]

Consequently the Robinson Committee (1977) recommended the abolition of the current attendance allowance (both because it was unfair and because it was surrounded by public misunderstanding and suspicion) and its replacement by a multi-component system of payment. This was implemented in the the Local Government, Planning and Land Act 1980, whereby local authorities were empowered (though not required) to pay *special responsibility allowances* (SRAs) to certain (leading) councillors, such as committee chairmen. In addition, councillors had the option of claiming attendance allowances (as above) or alternatively of claiming a *financial loss allowance* (to compensate for loss of earnings caused by attendance at council meetings. In 1986 the Widdicombe inquiry found only 1 per cent of councillors claiming financial loss allowance, and only 43 per cent of councils paying special responsibility allowances, and under 1 per cent of councillors receiving more than £5,000 a year from all three types of payment (i.e. excluding travel and subsistence expenses).

The Widdicombe Committee was critical of this system on grounds of its complexity, uncertainty and its possibly encouraging unnecessary meetings. Consequently, it recommended instead that all councillors should in future be entitled to flat-rate annual payment (varying with type and size of council) plus, for 'key' councillors, special responsibility allowances (SRAs). Subsequently in 1990, under the Local Government and Housing Act 1989, the government introduced such a scheme, though limited by the Secretary of State to a global sum of £39m (increased in subsequent years). Councils were given an allocation varying with size and type of council and population from which they were to pay councillors a basic allowance and, where appropriate (for up to one third of the council), SRAs (though no member should receive over £8,120 (1993/4) in SRA). On top of this, councils could pay attendance allowances (up to a maximum of £21 per day).

The 1993 working party report, *Community Leadership and Representation: Unlocking the Potential*, criticized this three-fold scheme as too rigid. It recommended that authorities be given the freedom to set their own allowances, including payment for attendance at party group meetings. At the same time, the Labour Party made proposals for some councillors to become salaried. The working party report found little support for such a development. Indeed, while they accepted that payment does have a part to play, in general they questioned the 'extent to which improvements in the allowance system will of themselves or alone make people more likely to stand for election or stay on as councillors'.[58] But the idea has been recently reiterated in the 1998 White Paper, *Modern Local Government: In Touch with the People*, and indeed members of the Greater London Authority and elected mayors are salaried.

In 1995 the government decided to deregulate this aspect of local government. There is no longer an overall ceiling on what local authorities collectively or individually can spend on allowances* (subject to audit scrutiny; see p. 395) and there is no longer a set pattern for payments (though in Scotland, councils have a more self-regulated scheme in that they follow guidelines drawn up by Convention of Scottish Local Authorities, COSLA, based on local population sizes). Consequently, councils have altered the rates and bases of their allowances and some have discontinued certain kinds of allowance (especially the attendance allowance, which is criticized as unduly encouraging committee meetings and distorting the role of councillors, whilst at the same time not covering the many informal meetings they have to attend. The government is to abolish this payment completely.) Some councils have developed additional forms of allowance, such as childcare or other caring allowance.

However, this issue is not settled. There is a strong belief that the desire to perform public service should be the attraction rather than money and consequently councillors should be *compensated* for financial loss and not salaried. But many councillors regard the payments as derisory and a deterrent to recruitment, though only 15 per cent of retiring councillors gave poor allowances as their principal reason for leaving (LGMB councillor exit survey, 1999). They are also felt to be unfair as between councillors (such as those putting in more, but

---

* though the government did not make any more money available to local authorities in its annual grant. Overall expenditure has, understandably, increased from 0.1 per cent of total local authority expenditure to 0.7 per cent in 1996 (*Local Government Chronicle*, 19 June 1996, p. 15).

Table 16 *Allowances paid to councillors, 1998 (and 1997) (average figures)*

	Councillors £	Leaders £
All councils in England	3,669 (2,413)	7,749 (5,925)
English districts	1,739 (1,623)	3,471 (4,242)
London boroughs	2,914 (2,598)	6,152 (7,218)
English counties	3,603 (3,126)	6,605 (8,979)
Metropolitan boroughs	5,265 (4,621)	13,291 (12,702)
Unitary councils	4,824	9,228

Source: Local Government Chronicle, 29 May 1998, 16 May 1997 and May 1999.
(The highest paid leader in 1998, at Leeds City Council, received £26,932; but that was for an average 60–70-hour week!). Five leaders were paid over £22,000. On the other hand some leaders receive little more than £1,000 a year in allowances. And, for councillors, Tamworth Borough Council's basic allowance of £431, with an attendance allowance of £23.22 per meeting, is not untypical.)
Note: allowances in Scotland tend to be higher owing to their relatively higher time commitments (see pp. 205–6 above).

And it may be noted that the average Health Authority chairperson and the average HA member received (in 1996) £18,000–20,000 and £5,000 respectively. The highest paid appointee to a local quango (the Birmingham Heartlands UDC) received £27,365 for a 2-day week. It has been estimated that the average pro rata income of Welsh quango members is 20 times that of the average Welsh councillors (see *Municipal Journal*, 14 October 1994, p. 130).

unrewarded, hours), between councils (paying different rates) and between local authorities and other public bodies (especially some quangos, where the differences are so stark to those councillors who serve on both: e.g. a council travel allowance of 21p per mile and a police authority travel allowance of 36p per mile, for the same car!). Table 16 illustrates some of the differences and shows why many want to see a substantial rise in allowances (notwithstanding adverse public reaction or the danger of attracting people – of high or low calibre – for the wrong reasons). Others wish to go further and have full-time, salaried councillors* if only for leaders and committee chairs (as is

---

* MPs were not paid until 1911, until which time their service was seen as voluntary, public spirited, and disinterested.

common in France and Germany). The government is currently developing such a system (see White Paper, *Modern Local Government*, 1998), though it may be noted that in practice it is only endorsing the existing practice of a number of authorities where allowances are tantamount to a salary in recognition of the level of responsibility and time involved in being a (mainly leading) councillor. In 1986 just 1 per cent of councillors were full-time and lived on their allowances; today 25 per cent are full-timers (spending over 30 hours a week on council duties). In so far as the roles of councillors are identified as 'executive', as distinguished from 'representative', and separated accordingly, the former at least is likely to be full-time and salaried.

Training and support services

A frequent complaint from councillors is that 'on election they had only a limited idea of what the role of councillors was and no one told them what to do, how to do it or how to use the council's resources. They were given the minimum assistance possible provided they turned up to the necessary meetings.' Consequently it is small wonder that some first-time councillors become quickly disenchanted.

Alongside allowances and expenses, clerical and other support services are an important way of easing the burden on councillors (especially leaders). However, in general, there is little systematic *training* for councillors. Although most local authorities provide some form of general induction procedure for new members and perhaps some briefing on areas of special interests, such as housing, social services or the financial aspects of the authority's work. Some provide training which includes presentation skills and even (with an eye to the EU) foreign languages and some councils see training and support for their members as an essential ingredient of their pursuit of quality public service.[59] And the political parties and local government associations often make an important contribution with, for example, an induction course, media training and briefing on legislation. In 1997 the Local Government Information Unit launched a nationwide training and development programme which sought to address a range of issues facing councillors including personal effectiveness (such as time-management, delegation, negotiation and communication), management of meetings, the councillor as employer and legal aspects of members on outside bodies. In 1998 the Local Government Association ran courses to help councillors prepare for the new management structures and changing roles which are being brought in by the government (and had been anticipated by some individual councils) – see Chapter 15 below.

Similarly, the facilities and *support services* available to councillors to help them with their work vary considerably from one authority to another. It is possible for them to include secretarial and administrative assistance, such as typing correspondence, photocopying, filing, telephoning, making appointments, booking courses/conferences and publicity e.g. re: public meetings or surgeries. Some provide an office or workroom, perhaps a room for surgeries. A members' lounge is usual and is likely to contain some information resources – journals, handbooks, papers, maybe pcs. Research and other reports, official circulars, statistics, legislation, etc. may be held here or in a separate library or resource centre. Councillors may also be provided with equipment and materials for working at home – on-line pc, answering machine, fax, filing cabinet, stationery, etc.

In 1972 the Bains Report on local government management said 'Some authorities already provide some facilities for members, but in very few is there anything approaching a comprehensive service'.[60] There has been an improvement since then, but as the publishers of a book on councillor support services have said, 'Local government is the biggest business in the country, but all too often those who control it, the elected members, have to take decisions and make policy without a proper level of professional support services.'[61] Similarly, the Audit Commission's report on the role of councillors, *Representing the People*, 1997, was critical of the support given to councillors. In 1998, the value of expenditure on councillor support and training was £5 per head.*

One study suggests that the 'Councillor's role has been perceived as a part-time leisure activity rather than as a professional or career activity. As a result . . . the facilities to support the representational

* *Supporting Councillors*, LGIU, 1998.

role are limited.'[62] It is further suggested that while the task of local government is becoming more complex and demanding, such that the days of the dedicated amateur approach are no longer relevant, officers' needs have received attention to the neglect of members'. Consequently, it is recommended that there should be more systematic training for members (both induction and continuing) and more adequate support services (in the form of accommodation, transport, creches, secretarial assistance and information services). The most recent working group on local government management (see p. 264 below) suggests that the installation of such facilities as fax machines or word processors in councillors' homes or the costs of childcare should be clearly allowable expenses.

The growing politicization of local government led the Widdicombe Committee to state that

there is need for councillors and senior officers to develop a better understanding of each other's roles. Councillors need to understand and respect the delicate balance which officers must keep between serving the council as a whole and providing adequate advice to the majority party. Senior officers need to understand and respect the political aspirations of councillors . . . The scope for misunderstanding will always be greatest when a new council is elected . . . elections can result in 50 per cent or more councillors being new . . . there is a need for induction training for new councillors . . . and current arrangements are patchy . . .[63]

Consequently it recommended local authorities (in conjunction with the Local Government Management Board) to provide more training to secure better understanding by councillors and officers of each other's roles, responsibilities and aspirations. This was endorsed by the government.

Qualities and calibre

There has always been some concern about the quality of local government. In the nineteenth century fears were frequently expressed – by such worthies as J. S. Mill, Joseph Chamberlain, Beatrice Webb[64] – at the shortage of the right sort of person coming forward to serve on local councils. Such views continued to be expressed in the first part of the twentieth century, at a time when local government was becoming more significant and more demanding. In 1940, the Barlow Commission commented that

the calibre of those who administer the larger units of local government today is tending to decline. Councils and committees to be manned are numerous . . . the work is arduous, and volunteers of good administrative ability are not always easy to find. (*Report of the Royal Commission on the Distribution of the Industrial Population*, Cmd 6153, HMSO, 1940)

Such denunciations have become especially intense in the years since the Second World War. In 1948, a respected historian commented on 'candidates of illiterate speech and low social standing . . . tongue-tied [in council debates]'.[65] In 1960, a senior civil servant[66] averred that '. . . despite the first-class people there are on every sort . . . of local authority . . . by and large local government is not drawing as good a quality of councillor or as many outstanding leaders by way of councillors as it used to do'. In 1961, a professor of government wrote that '. . . our councils are filled with retired people, with women whose children have grown up, and with a few others who can afford the time, or see some particular advantage in being on the council'.[67] In July 1963 *The Times* headed an article 'Petticoat and Pensioner Rule in Council Chambers'.

Partly as a consequence of this onslaught, the government appointed the Maud Committee on the Management of Local Government (1964–7). Its terms of reference were 'to consider in the light of modern conditions how local government might best continue to attract and retain people of the calibre necessary to ensure its maximum effectiveness'. This implied that the government had confidence in the quality of current councillors (and officers), but that there were doubts about the immediate future.

These doubts were reinforced in the research work which was undertaken for the Maud Committee:

Many chief officers . . . thought that members were unable to grasp issues of any complexity . . . only a small minority . . . made any real contribution in committee . . . Instances were found of dismal standards of discussion . . .

Evidence of a decline in calibre is insubstantial. It does seem clear, however, that the increasing complexity of proposals for innovations are tending to increase the gap in understanding between member and officer, and . . . frequently . . . members take decisions without an adequate understanding of the issues involved.[68]

A former leader of the Greater London Council condemned the shortage of young, enthusiastic and discerning councillors (see p. 326). But, to be fair, the blame clearly did not always lie with councillors themselves; it was at least partly due to the fact that 'in many spheres, local government had become so highly technical that its intricacies were in large measure incomprehensible to the layman'[69] be it environmental planning, engineering and building techniques or finance and budgetary procedures. As the Salmon Commission put it, '. . . members [of local authorities] may enter public life with little preparation and may find themselves handling matters on a financial scale quite beyond their experience in private life'.[70]

The Maud Committee itself declared that it is difficult both to measure the quality of councillors and discover hard evidence for its alleged decline. It is like the current debate on educational standards – and part of the problem here is that the nature, context and aims of education itself have changed. While the quality of councillors is subject to criticism,[71] it is also open to praise[72] and it is tempered by the fact that the roles and context of councillors are quite unlike those of the past. For the Maud Committee, the 'jury was out' on this question. Instead, it looked to the future and suggested that councillors should possess the following qualities:

(a) The capacity to understand sympathetically the problems and points of view of constituents and to convey them to the authority and, at the same time, to interpret and explain the authority's policies and actions to those whom they represent.

(b) The capacity to understand technical, economic and sociological problems which are likely to increase in complexity.

(c) The ability to innovate, to manage and direct; the personality to lead and guide public opinion and other members; and the capacity to accept responsibility for the policies of the authority.[73]

To secure councillors with these qualities, it suggested a number of changes to the then existing practice, including compulsory retirement at seventy, training courses, greater opportunities for release from employment, review of the councils' meeting times, reduction in the number of committees and increased use of co-option. It also commended the reform of local government structure (which was at that time under review by a Royal Commission headed by the same chairman, now ennobled to Lord Redcliffe-Maud). But its main emphasis was placed on streamlining councils' committee and management systems and on a reduction in central government controls over local government. Some of these points have been dealt with above; others will be covered in later chapters.

Standards of conduct and corruption

If the 1960s were concerned with the quality of councillors, the 1970s were concerned with their integrity – or rather apparent lack of it. Such concern, however, is by no means a modern phenomenon: in 1834 the Royal Commission on Municipal Corporations (see p. 16) criticized the way members enjoyed rent-free use of municipal property, held entertainments at public expense and misappropriated corporation income. Throughout the nineteenth century there were numerous scandals involving the Boards of Guardians (see p. 16) and rumours of 'jobbery' in the granting of contracts. In 1888 the allegations of corruption in property development by the Metropolitan Board of Works were such that they led to the appointment of a Royal Commission of Inquiry. Then, in the 1920s and 1930s there was another upsurge of rumour and suspicion about the activities of elected Guardians and councillors – partly due to the supposed vulnerability of the growth in incumbents from poorer backgrounds.

In an attempt to prevent such abuses, the central government used the system of inspection (originally developed to improve efficiency in certain services – see p. 426), and local authority finances became increasingly subject to the professional audit (of their accounts) by the district auditor (see p. 395). Parliament has increasingly required councils to open their meetings to the public and press, and it has established local commissioners to investigate complaints of maladministration. Local authorities themselves have laid down codes of conduct in standing orders (see p. 225), and to promote greater openness they have established a number of public relations activities (see p. 506).

In addition a number of legal restraints have been placed upon councillors – notably (1) the disqualification of being an employee of the authority or for unauthorized expenditure exceeding £2,000 (see p. 131); (2) the duty to make a 'declaration of pecuniary interest'; and (3) the regulations against corrupt practices. As the other points are dealt with elsewhere, we shall briefly deal with the last two points here.

Pecuniary interest

Councillors are unique in public life in that their duties are of an executive nature and yet they are not responsible either to an employer or to an appointing authority: their responsibility to the electorate is tenuous to say the least. On the other hand, by the very nature of local government's functions, councillors are likely to encounter a conflict of interests between their own private interest or benefit and those of the community they represent (especially in such areas as planning decisions, awarding contracts or allocating council house tenancies). To help to guard against the temptations of such situations, it has long been a requirement[74] that councillors who have a direct or indirect financial interest in any matter which is before the authority must at the meeting where the matter is under consideration disclose the fact that they have an interest (except in certain cases – see below) and thereafter refrain from speaking or voting on the matter. Members must *declare an interest* as soon as practicable after the start of the meeting. Alternatively, where the interest arises because they or their spouse is a member, partner or employee in a business which has dealings with the authority, or they are tenants of authority property, they may give a general written notice of this interest; they need then make no oral disclosure at the meeting. A record or register of such notices and of disclosures made at meetings is kept by the authority and is open to inspection by members of the council (in England and Wales) or by local electors (in Scotland) (somewhat parallel to MPs' register of interests). Breach of this provision is a criminal offence; for example between 1964 and 1974 some twenty members were prosecuted for failing to disclose a pecuniary interest in the business before their council.

However, the law is not totally rigid in this matter, and the Secretary of State has the discretionary power of dispensation. He can (and does) remove from individuals or groups of members the ban on speaking and/or voting in council or committee, usually where the pecuniary interest is somewhat remote or where the incidence of disabilities would be such as to decimate the council or committee concerned. Such general dispensation has been granted, for example, to councillors who are tenants of council houses or have children at state (LEA) schools.

Corrupt practices

The Prevention of Corruption Acts 1906 and 1916 (and their predecessor, the Public Bodies Corrupt Practices Act 1889) were the product of the report in 1888 of the Royal Commission on the Metropolitan Board of Works (see p. 111 above). This report had stated that

it might have a wholesome effect if it were distinctly made a criminal offence to offer to any member or official of a public body any kind of payment, fee, or reward having any relation to the affairs of the body of which he was such a member or official, and also to make the person accepting any such payment ... amenable to the criminal law.

This legislation has no doubt had the desired salutary effect, but it has not of course eliminated corruption. In recent years, much publicity has been given to cases in which councillors have been convicted under that legislation for taking bribes in respect of the allocation of council houses or the granting of planning permission. The penalties include imprisonment, fine, surrender of the corrupt gift and disqualification from office (for example, between 1964 and 1974, sixteen members – and twenty-two officials – were convicted for such offences, or similar ones).

The most notorious prosecutions occurred in 1974, when a number of leading councillors in the North of England were imprisoned for corruptly securing lucrative contracts for a private architect, John Poulson. It was this 'Poulson affair' which jolted public opinion and gave rise to several official inquiries into standards of conduct in public life.

The first of these dealt with local government and reported in 1974;[75] the second, a Royal Commission (Salmon), ranged more widely and reported in July 1976.[76] Neither was unduly concerned at the extent of corruption. 'Our own judgement . . . is that standards of conduct in local government are generally high.'[77] 'We have heard no evidence to give us concern about the integrity and sense of public duty of our bureaucracy as a whole . . .'[78] But they do admit that corruption is difficult to measure. 'There is no objective way of making a true assessment of the amount of public sector corruption that exists now or whether the amount has changed over recent decades.'[79]

However, this view was not entirely supported by at least one member of the Royal Commission, who suggested that certain recently changing factors 'may have enabled corruption to creep into bodies which have rightly enjoyed a long standing reputation for very high standards of honesty and unselfish service'.[80] These factors included:

(a) the growth in power of certain councillors and committees as a result of changes in the planning and building functions of local government;
(b) the emergence of one-party domination in many authorities;
(c) the uncertain tenure of chief executive officers (in contrast to the older-style clerks), which might inhibit their pursuit of a suspicion of corruption by councillors, his employers;[81]
(d) the diminution in the degree of central government control of local government;
(e) the emergence of a 'Robin Hood syndrome', whereby, with the aim of providing services 'in the public interest', more quickly or adequately, members lose their patience with the ordinary processes of government and start to cut corners;
(f) councillors' lack of training, and their inadequate remuneration.

Despite their belief that 'the picture is still of an essentially honest service', the reports themselves saw no room for complacency, and they recommended a number of changes to improve the situation and reduce that minority who 'do not measure up to acceptable standards of probity in public life'. Broadly they sought to do this by (i) further discouraging corruption, for example by suggesting stronger penalties and recommending that, in charges of corruption, the burden of proof should rest on the defence (thus implying the presumption of guilt rather than innocence);[82] (ii) making it easier to investigate suspected corruption, for example by increasing police powers of access to information, including information held by the Inland Revenue and other official agencies.

For local government specifically, the more comprehensive recommendations are to be found in the report of the Committee on Conduct in Local Government (1974). This made the following proposals:

(a) Councillors (and officers) should be required to disclose a pecuniary interest orally whenever it arises (that is, exceptions would no longer be allowed) and to withdraw completely from the meeting.

(b) Such disclosures, withdrawals and dispensations should be recorded and be open to inspection by local electors (by councillors in the case of officers' disclosure).

(c) There should be a compulsory register of certain pecuniary interests of councillors (paid employments, local land holdings, company interests and tenancies of council property), to be annually revised and open to inspection by electors.

(d) Local authorities should have clear and well publicized arrangements for receiving and investigating complaints.

(e) In conjunction with the central government, local government should establish a national code of conduct based upon those principles which already govern the best practice among individual authorities.

(f) Political parties should ensure that rules of conduct in local authority party group meetings are no less strict than in those of the authority itself.

(g) Councillors (and employees) should treat their non-pecuniary interests (such as family ties) on the same basis as the law requires them to treat their pecuniary interests.

(h) Councillors (and employees) should ensure that hospitality given or received in connection with their official duties can always be justified in the public interest; and that official facilities or allowances to which they are entitled are used strictly for the purposes of their official duties.

The most immediate result of all these inquiries and suggestions was the joint publication by the local authority associations and the government of a National Code of good behaviour in local government. This reiterates a number of the recommendations and seeks specifically to guide the conduct of councillors and more generally to provide an explicit public standard by which local government can be measured by those outside it.[83]

That such action was desirable was not doubted by Richard Crossman, a former senior Minister, who wrote, 'The truth is that the moral standards of local government have declined until the relationship between members of public bodies and outside business interests are freely tolerated.'[84]

The Widdicombe Committee approved the current methods of overseeing members' interests, i.e. the 1972–3 legislation which dealt with pecuniary interests, and the Code of Conduct for non-pecuniary interests (such as friends, relatives or club membership). But it concluded that there should be more emphasis on openness, and proposed (like the 1974 Committee on Conduct and the Salmon Commission 1976) that there should be registers of members' interests placed on a statutory basis in order to enhance public confidence in the integrity of councillors. The government accepted this (see Local Government and Housing Act 1989, and p. 186), with the exception of non-pecuniary interests (which it felt would be too general and perhaps intrusive), though individual councils may set up such registers on a voluntary basis.

In addition, under the 1989 Act the Code of Conduct was given statutory force and now requires all councillors taking office to affirm that they will be guided by the Code in carrying out their duties and all councils will monitor and report regularly on whether councillors are observing the Code. However, events elsewhere have brought further changes.

In the 1980s and 1990s a number of cases of local government fraud were uncovered by the Audit Commission and there have been some well-publicized cases of political and financial corruption, 'sleaze' or ill-judged decision-making (in such areas as Glasgow, Doncaster, Westminster, North Cornwall, Bassetlaw, Warwick, Brent). In the case of Lambeth (1993) the Chief Executive identified numerous examples of unlawful activity in the council and 'improper behaviour on an unprecedented scale', including the awarding of contracts without competitive tender or proper approval, disregard for standing orders and codes of practice re: expenses claims and invoicing, inadequate financial record-keeping and a loss of management control. Some of these deficiencies were discovered by the District Auditor and the Ombudsman in the case of West Wiltshire (1990–91); the latter identi-fied a small group of councillors and officers who 'set aside account-ability and took decisions they were not empowered to make . . . [manifesting] . . . a serious breach of standards expected . . .'.*

In 1993 the Audit Commission uncovered over 100 local government frauds (of not less than £500 each) amounting to £2.5m, though about half of these were perpetrated by outsiders† against the councils. This is an increase from seventy-five cases in 1985 (worth £1.5m) – an increase which may be due to local authorities' difficulties (in compe-tition with the private sector) of recruiting strong financial staff. In some cases it is also suggested that it is due to left-wing Labour councils deciding to cut spending on their finance departments in order to use hard-pressed finance for front-line public services. But although a number of Labour councils (such as Lambeth, Hull, Redbridge, Ren-frewshire and Monklands DC) have been in the headlines for alleged fraud, nepotism or gross mismanagement, so too have some Conserva-tive-run councils (such as West Wiltshire DC and Westminster LB). In the 1990s, there were a number of cases (and prosecutions) involving former council staff who had set up companies and been awarded contracts to provide council services. In 1993, the Welsh local govern-ment Commissioner ('ombudsman' – see p. 409) severely criticized Brecknock district council over councillors who allocated council houses to their relatives in advance of other people on the waiting list.

---

* Report of the Local Ombudsman, No. 89/B/2325 1991.

† e.g. for 1996, the Audit Commission reported 1,475 proven cases of fraud and 21 cases of corruption affecting local authorities. But most are committed by outside persons against councils – 99 per cent in respect of fraud.

Since 1996 the auditor (and later police) have been to Doncaster (or 'Donnygate') investigating allegations involving millions of pounds and accusations of expenses fiddles and lavish entertainment, housing and planning irregularities and improper contracts. In 1997 one of the auditor's reports detailed behaviour which it called 'patently unacceptable in a public body', including pressure put on officers to award contracts without competitive tendering. There have been 16 arrests.

In 1998 the annual Report of the Audit Commission revealed a 'disturbing new trend' in theft and fraud among councillors and officers with internal corruption amounting to over £9m (an increase of over 40 per cent on the previous year) arising especially from increases in misappropriated revenues and corrupt claims for pensions and allowances. It pointed out that one-in-five councils still have no register of officers' interests or hospitality received by members, half have no anti-fraud strategy and a third have no effective arrangements for protecting whistleblowers (see p. 393).

The 'insider' offences were largely committed by employees (such as the obtaining of council goods by a purchasing officer, collaboration with a contractor to overcharge the council, or a housing benefits officer making payments to himself). In 1992 a city treasurer was imprisoned for making false expenses claims. See: *Protecting the public purse*, Audit Commission (annual).

Some of this increase could be explained in part by improved detection and perhaps by ignorance of local government law. Other explanations of this apparent decline in standards has been attributed to the volume and pace of changes imposed on local authorities and to the nature of many of such changes, including decentralization and delegation of financial and management responsibilities, the purchasing–contracting system, joint ventures, pressures to cut expenditures and the growth of management buy-outs. These created conflict of interests and loss of attention (and resources) to system control and greater opportunities for the less scrupulous.[85]

However, local government has not been alone in experiencing inappropriate, if not scandalous, behaviour. Between 1990 and 1994, the media uncovered a number of instances where MPs were abusing their position by asking Parliamentary Questions and making other connections for outside interests in return for payment – commonly known as 'cash for questions' or 'sleaze'. The result was the appointment of a committee of inquiry on 'Standards in Public Life', chaired by a judge, Lord Nolan. Its first Report recommended the disclosure of incomes and a Code of Conduct for MPs, together with the appointment of a permanent Select Committee and a Parliamentary Commissioner for Standards. These were soon implemented and the Committee turned its attention to appointed bodies, reporting in 1996. One result of the two Reports was the formulation of a 'common ethical framework'. This laid down seven principles of public life which now guide the behaviour of those holding public office, including local government (see Appendix 30). They are:

(i) Selflessness: decisions should be taken solely in the public interest.
(ii) Integrity: holders of public office should not place themselves under financial obligation to outsiders who could influence their work.
(iii) Objectivity: decisions on public business (such as awarding contracts or appointing staff) should be made on merit.
(iv) Accountability: holders of public office are accountable for their actions and inactions.
(v) Openness: decisions should be made as openly as possible.
(vi) Honesty: there is a duty to declare private interests.
(vii) Leadership: these principles should be supported and promoted by example and leadership.

The Committee then sought to examine how local government fitted into this framework – particularly in view of the changing role of local authorities, with the increasing tendency for services to be supplied in partnership with others or by outside bodies under contract. With local authorities responsible for millions of pounds of expenditure, and with the possibility of councillors being less able to cope (see Qualities and calibre above) there was the greater risk of mismanagement and perhaps corrupt practice/malpractice.

The Nolan Committee on Standards in Public Life reported on *Standards of Conduct in Local Government* in July 1997 (Cmd 3702–1). It concluded that 'Despite instances of corruption and misbehaviour, the vast majority of councillors and officers observe high standards of conduct.'

Nevertheless, it made a number of detailed recommendations and these were endorsed by the government in 1998 and formed the basis of a new ethical framework* to underpin standards of conduct in local government and (as the White Paper put it) to help 'the process of rebuilding trust between councils and their communities'. Thus under the Local Government Bill 2000:

– every council† is required to adopt a Code of Conduct (which replaces the existing National Code of Local Government Conduct which Nolan criticized). Councils in England will have some scope to adopt their own Code (as there is considerable variation in types of council here compared to Wales and Scotland), but all Codes must contain the General Principles of Conduct which derive from the Nolan Report to guide the (good) behaviour of those in public office (see Appendix 30). The key elements are provided by a Model Code (drawn up by the government in consultation with the Local Government Association and others. In Scotland and Wales the national Parliament/Assembly played a leading role.);

– every council is required to establish a public Register of Members' interests (maintained by the council's Monitoring Officer). Councillors who fail to register are subject to disciplinary procedures (though no longer subject to prosecution for criminal offence);

– councillors must not participate in the discussion or determination of matters in which they (or their partners) have a direct pecuniary interest; or in which they might appear to be at risk of bias by putting private considerations above the public interest; or in which they could be seen to be using their position as a councillor to secure preferential treatment for themselves or others. (Dispensations may be granted by the council and/or the Standards Board.)

– every council (except parishes) is required to establish a Standards Committee (containing one or two independent, non-councillor members) which works with the Monitoring Officer to advise the council

* See consultation paper, *Modernizing local government: A new ethical framework*, DETR, 1998.
† Parishes use the Code of their district council.

on the content of the local Code, arrangements for dispensations, training of councillors in matters of conduct and advising councillors on the treatment of personal interest and conduct matters generally;

– an independent Standards Board (together with an Adjudication Panel) which works through its investigating ethical standards officers to deal with breaches of the Code and has the power (subject to appeal) to impose penalties ranging from public censure, suspension (for up to three months) or disqualification (for up to five years). (Councils' Standards Committees have the power to reprimand and it is the function of the Monitoring Officer to take a view on whether an allegation appears to constitute a breach of the Code, and if so inform the Standards Board.)

– surcharge (or 'fine') of councillors and officers for wilful misconduct leading to financial loss by the council is to be abolished (though in cases of personal gain, restitution of financial loss may be obtained by way of compensation orders) (see p. xix on surcharge);

– the District Auditor's 'stop' power (over an authority's spending; see p. 399) is to be discontinued and replaced by warning or advisory notices. On the other hand auditors are to have more discretion to refuse to hear public objections to the council's accounts (subject to appeal) to avoid vexatious or time-wasting challenges;

– there is also a statutory duty on councils to adopt an Employees' Code of Conduct (based on a model approved by the government, which includes the restrictions on political activities; see p. 294). The requirements of this Code form part of the terms and conditions of employment and are enforceable through the staff disciplinary arrangements and employment law.

The government is also considering a reform of the criminal law of corruption and is proposing a new statutory offence of 'misuse of public office'. Clearly this will have significance for the interaction of the criminal law and local government disciplinary and enforcement processes. The roles of the Standards Board, the Ombudsman and the auditor need to be adjusted and coordinated to avoid confusion and duplication.

Planning is a particularly sensitive and difficult area of local government work, and is subject to its own framework of legislation and government guidance. Following the Nolan Committee's recommendations on this aspect and the government's endorsement of them, councils have been encouraged to provide specific training for members of planning committees and to draw up local planning Codes of good practice. Councils are now required to give reasons when granting planning permission (as well as for refusals) where the development proposals are significant.

The complete elimination of corruption is impossible – after all, corrupt dealings are conducted in secret and are therefore difficult to assess or prove. Codes of conduct and declarations of interest will have little impact on the dishonest, though they may dissuade the pliant. Periodically there is disquiet about the effects of freemason membership on those in public office, including allegations concerning council decisions or appointments and police promotion or inquiries, but there has been no conclusive evidence. Under the Public Interest Disclosure Act 1998, employees who disclose corruption ('whistleblow') at work are protected. In local government, they would normally proceed through a senior officer – Chief Executive or Monitoring Officer; but where they are unable to report their suspicions internally, they can use the Audit Commission as a point of contact, and in 1999 the AC set up a confidential hotline (01716 301019).

Political parties have played a part in dealing with corrupt or suspect practices, including member/staff harassment (e.g. in the 1990s the Labour Party has conducted a number of inquiries and suspended a number of its council members as a result; see p. 182). The parties have also tightened their rules about their members' competence and standards of behaviour in office. The Labour Party's 'Project 99' established local vetting systems for their candidates for political office whose criteria for selection included probity as well as loyalty and ability.

The Nolan Committee appreciated the role of the parties in this respect, but also pointed out the limitations (that not all councillors belong to a party and that parties may 'pull their punches' in their inquiries to protect its reputation and avoid giving ammunition to their opponents, etc.) and so emphasized the need for a more formal system of discipline. However, there is a fundamental dilemma: the introduction of greater scrutiny and regulations can seriously damage the morale and feeling of mutual trust within an organization.* In particular, it may inhibit the leadership and initiative of management. Before we turn to management, in the next chapter, perhaps we should conclude by putting local government corruption into perspective: local authorities are local, their activities are watched by the press, they are in many ways more open and exposed to public scrutiny than are government departments, 'quangos', political parties, charities and private enterprise. There may *appear* to be more corruption in local government simply because there is more light and more detection. And, overall, local and central government show a very high standard of probity relative to other sectors as far as fraud is concerned.[86] Indeed, it has been suggested that the reforms outlined above, are a 'bureaucratic sledgehammer to crack a few unethical nuts'.[87]

Access

A number of councils have set up closed one-party committees (sometimes with special rules or powers) which have excluded minority party members and denied them access to relevant records and information. In 1984, in the so-called Hackney case, the court declared that opposition councillors should not be barred from attending sub-committee meetings (see pp. 324 and 186; see too R. *v.* Sheffield City Council 1985).

However, it has long been the practice of local authorities to restrict access to council records exclusively to members of the relevant committees for reasons other than party political. This was highlighted in 1982 (in the so-called Birmingham case) when a councillor sought to examine the case file of a social services client. Lord Denning ruled that such files were only accessible to committee members. However, on appeal to the House of Lords, it was instead declared that 'a councillor is entitled by virtue of his office to have access to all written

---

* In 1999, one council (Renfrewshire) sought to tighten up the rules on probity by proscribing the acceptance of gifts from school children by teachers.

material in the possession of the local authority of which he is a member, provided he has good reason for such access'.

The Local Government (Access to Information) Act 1985 sought to clarify and extend the right of councillors to examine council documents, subject to certain limitations of confidential items. This Act* also increases the opportunities for public access to sub-committees and to council papers such as agendas, reports, minutes, letters, memoranda and other background documents. Some councils are accused of evading the law by forming informal working parties and secret panels or by charging excessively (and deterrently) for copies of documents. The Widdicombe Committee suggested that the former would be a not unexpected consequence of councillors being (wrongly) unable to develop policy options in confidence before presenting their final choice for public decision. The Committee therefore suggested that purely deliberative committees and sub-committees could be reasonably excused from the requirements of the 1985 Act. The government did not accept this suggestion (though the 1991 consultative document *The Internal Management of Local Authorities in England* was rather more persuaded; see p. 269). However, as a result of the decision of the Court of Appeal in R. *v.* Eden District Council ex-parte Moffat 1988, local authorities have reviewed their procedures to ensure that any of their bodies exercising executive power are designated as committees or sub-committees; further, they are admitting all councillors who wish to attend (member-level) working party and panel meetings, and requiring such bodies to consider closely their grounds for excluding the press and public when this occurs.

The Widdicombe Committee was also concerned that the law allows the council, and thus in effect the majority party, to determine whether a member needs to inspect a document or attend a meeting in order to carry out his or her duties, and further that the law enables councillors to have access to documents not available to the public and in which they may have a pecuniary interest. The government is amending the law in this latter respect and, in pursuit of open government, it has

---

* In practice this Act operates by adding clauses to the Local Government Acts of 1972 and 1973. In consequence, the Public Bodies (Admission to Meetings) Act 1960 – see p. 507 – is superseded except for parishes.

created statutory rights of access to personal records and health and safety information (including safety of food, transport, public places and consumer goods, and environmental health risks) and also extended rights of access to manually held files (though it only applies to information created after the new legislation is passed).

More generally, concern has been expressed that the 1985 legislation became too tightly drawn as it passed through Parliament. Originally it was intended to allow public access to any document relating to any matter discussed in public by the local authority, i.e. not just those relied upon in producing council reports. Some councils, however, have adopted the broader approach.[88] But others use exempted business (confidential items) as a device for disguising policy matters.

Non-elected council members

In addition to elected members (councillors) local authorities have often drawn in other members of the public by the appointments of (1) *aldermen* (though this office has now been abolished) and (2) *co-opted* members, neither of them directly or publicly elected.

(1) *Aldermen*, or in Scotland 'bailies', were elected to individual councils by existing councillors.[89] They had no special role as aldermen/bailies. They tended to be older and somewhat more prestigious than the average member. In some respects they were more 'powerful' in that they often chaired committees, and in England and Wales their term of office was twice that of ordinary councillors (six years instead of three years, before 1974).

For the most part aldermen were actual or former councillors (just as many members of the House of Lords are former MPs), though legally anyone who was qualified to stand for election as a councillor (see p. 131) could be appointed. However, their numbers were limited to a maximum of the equivalent of one third of the council (one sixth in the London boroughs): thus a council of twenty-one councillors could add seven aldermen to their number.

The aldermanic system was introduced mainly to secure a measure of stability and continuity, especially where the whole council could be replaced in a 'clean-sweep' election. In addition, it was justified on the grounds that it could bring on to the council persons of ability and experience who might have been unable or unwilling to gain a place through open election. However, the system was clearly undemocratic and there were some notable instances of abuse – a marginally superior party might shore itself up by taking all the seats on the aldermanic bench. Consequently, under the Local Government Acts of 1972 and 1973, the office of alderman/bailie was abolished (except in the Corporation of London).[90]

(2) *Co-opted members* (or '*additional' members*) are similar to aldermen in that they are chosen by the council itself (on the recommendation of its committees). The system of co-opting members is often used in parishes to fill council vacancies, or the appropriate district council may have to resort to co-option if the parish council is too low in membership through lack of candidates. The procedure is used in other local authorities to augment the membership of committees, but these co-opted persons do not become members of the local authority (the council) as such, though they can claim expenses and allowances.

Legally, any local authority committee (except the finance committee) or sub-committee may co-opt persons from outside the council, and normally the council will set down in its standing orders (see p. 242) its arrangements for co-option, such as the numbers and composition (for example a certain percentage of women on the social service committee). Some committees have been obliged to co-opt, because the law may require the representation of specific groups or interests, and without co-option the committees may be deficient in this respect, e.g. the 1944 Education Act required education committees to include people who were experienced in education or acquainted with educational conditions in the area. Existing councillors (such as teachers in private schools) may themselves fulfil this requirement but otherwise they needed to be co-opted.

In practice, co-option is now only a requirement in education in order to give statutory representation to the churches (who originated many of the 'voluntary' schools) and to parents (where, under education regulations, every LEA is required to have two to five elected parents). Where there is a statutory requirement to co-opt, co-optees become full members of their committees with powers to speak and vote (and may claim certain financial allowances). Where co-option is discretionary, it is left to each council to determine the status of such members, except that (under the 1989 Act), they are not allowed to vote.*

Rarely do co-opted members form a substantial proportion of committee membership. Legally they can comprise up to one third of the membership of most committees, but they can constitute up to 49 per cent of education and social services committees, and even 100 per cent of sub-committees, though they rarely ever do so. In 1965, there were about 16,000 co-opted members (i.e. one for every three elected members). In 1985, the number had fallen to 6,000 (or one for every four). It is not unknown (though rare) for a committee chair to be a co-opted member. However, co-opted members do not become members of the local authority (the council) as such; they are usually confined to the field of their committee.

There are two broad types of co-opted member: (a) a person chosen on an individual or personal basis as having expertise or local notability (perhaps as a long-serving ex-councillor) and (b) a person chosen as a representative of some outside interest – the Church, a teachers' union, a welfare society or the local chamber of commerce. In the case of 'representative co-option', the local authority will often leave it to the outside body itself to select the representative.

The sort of people who get co-opted to local authority committees are of a very similar mould to councillors themselves – which is not altogether surprising, since they must have the qualifications of a councillor[91] (see p. 131), and they are likely to be interested in council work and to know council members (perhaps as relatives). Some are chosen to provide them with a trial run at local authority committee work; others are chosen for party political reasons (and may as a consequence be subject to the party whip system). Allegations of party manipulation or of nepotism call in question the whole principle of co-option, hence the general loss of voting rights in 1989.

Briefly stated, the *advantages* claimed for co-option are as follows:

---

* Co-optees may vote on sea fisheries, superannuation and educational appeal committees.

(i) It can provide expertise (cheaply) which may be lacking among the members and the officials or which may be sought as an alternative or counter-weight to that of the local government officers. (In a rather similar way, some Ministers bring in 'outsiders' to their departments in Whitehall: hence they are sometimes known as 'advisers'.)

(ii) Outsiders can give a wider, perhaps fresher perspective and reduce the danger of parochialism; and, in so far as they are independent, they can help to diminish a preoccupation with party politics.

(iii) A larger number and a wider range of people can be brought into the political process, especially those who can give only a limited amount of time, or who would be otherwise deterred by having to go through the election process.

(iv) In the 'representative' form, co-option can promote the exchange of ideas with outside organizations and so enhance mutual under-standing and cooperation between them.

The *disadvantages* may include the following:

(i) The involvement of co-opted members may be regarded as undemocratic, not simply because they are not elected and are therefore not accountable to anyone, but because they may be appointed for purely party motives and may even include candidates who stood unsuccessfully in the election.

(ii) They may upset committee relations with the local authorities' own 'experts' – the officers – and indeed, in so far as co-opted members are unfamiliar with local government procedures, they may upset councillors with their biased or 'starry-eyed and imprac-ticable' ideas.

(iii) They may provide dangerous openings for pressure groups, with the consequent unreasonable distortion of priorities in individual local authorities' provision.

The Widdicombe Committee was critical of co-option on the grounds that it blurred the accountability of elected members and detracted from the democratic basis of local government, besides which it could distort the political balance of committees. It therefore proposed that co-option should be banned from all decision-making committees, though non-voting members or 'advisers' should be permitted. This was implemented in the Local Government and Housing Act 1989.

9

INTERNAL ORGANIZATION: THE COUNCIL AND ITS COMMITTEES

How local authorities organize themselves to carry out their responsibilities varies from one authority to another. But, despite recent changes, they follow a broadly similar pattern, and certain forms or procedures are universally adopted where they are required by law. Briefly it can be stated that all local authorities will conduct their activities through a council of all members, aided by a number of committees (comprising small groups of members), which work in close collaboration with senior officers, who are employed by the council and head the various departments of the council. This is illustrated by Figure 13. In this chapter we shall be mainly concerned with the work of the council and its committees. The officers and staff of local authorities are more fully examined in Chapter 10.

The council

By 'local authority' we mean that group of people who are elected to be councillors and form a council, the body which takes authoritative decisions for the local areas. But all councils delegate much of their work to smaller groups (committees) or to individuals (officers). Such delegation occurs because councils are too large to be effective decision-making bodies (some have over a hundred members), and council members, meeting only as a whole group, would not develop sufficient expertise. Further, most councils do not meet frequently (many meet only five times a year) and their meetings (of perhaps three hours' duration) do not give them enough time to exercise close supervision of the work of the many departments and employees of the council.

Consequently, most of the activity at full council is concerned with

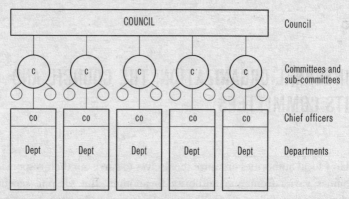

Figure 13 *Basic structure of a local authority*

(1) the ratification (through voting) of decisions and actions which committees have taken since the last full meeting of the council, and (2) the discussion of committee reports, analyses and recommendations which may then be approved, amended, rejected or 'referred back' for further consideration to the committee concerned.

The council itself will determine what or how much is delegated to committees and will often reserve to itself the more important policy matters. It thus remains the ultimate decision-making body. However, as the Bains Report (see below) pointed out, the way councils exercise that role differs widely from one authority to another. At one extreme the council receives and considers the reports and minutes of every committee: at the other extreme, members individually may receive the relevant papers but very little may go before the full council unless members specifically request it. In between these two types are those councils which receive and consider summary reports and may as a consequence debate major matters arising from them.

Council meetings are by law presided over by a chair, who must be elected annually by the council. They are variously entitled chair or mayor (in England and Wales), provost or convenor (in Scotland), according to the type of local authority. (In cities, they are Lord Mayor or Lord Provost.) However, most of the council discussion is led by the chairs of the various committees. Chief Officers also attend council meetings, but they do not normally speak: their role on these occasions is mainly a consultative one – to be 'on tap'. The other officials

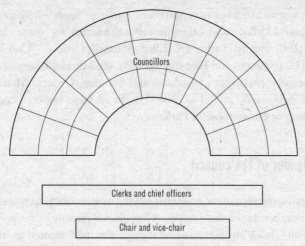

Figure 14 *A council setting*

present are the clerk or administration staff. They are responsible for distributing any relevant papers and for taking the minutes (a written summary) of the meeting. These minutes are subsequently open to inspection by the public.

One type of council setting is illustrated in Figure 14.

Council meetings

The frequency and timing of meetings are matters which are left largely to the local authorities themselves to decide. By law, all principal councils (that is, all except parishes and communities) must hold an annual meeting. Some authorities meet monthly or even more often; others meet only quarterly. The timing of meetings is an important consideration, as it can affect attendances. Urban authorities tend to meet in the evening; other authorities meet in the daytime for the convenience of councillors who have to travel long distances (e.g. the Western Islands council in Scotland meets for four days at a time), though this may present problems in getting release from employment.

Council meetings are formal affairs, and much ceremony may be attached to them – the civic mace may be carried and the chain of office worn. Meetings may start with prayers. Speech-making, the conduct of debate and other procedural matters are quite closely controlled, usually in what are called 'Standing Orders'.[1] (Under the Local Government and Housing Act 1989, the Minister is empowered to prescribe particular procedures and Standing Orders.) Members of the public may attend as observers. In all these respects, council meetings resemble those of Parliament.

The leader of the council

In Britain, the *chair* of the council is elected by councillors from among their number. He or she is not therefore elected directly by the people, as in the USA or Germany – though this will change as more councils adopt the elected or 'strong' mayoral system; see Chapter 15. Consequently (and partly because of the tendency to rotate the office) the office has been ceremonial rather than effective: the chair is traditionally a figurehead rather than a political force, unlike the council *leader*, who is normally head of the majority party. However, in some local authorities, the chair acquired a pre-eminence by way of social standing, hard work, experience or sheer ability.[2] As a result, the chair may develop a permanence and so combine *chairmanship* with *leadership* of the council. In many local authorities, usually those where parties are strongly developed, council leadership is openly and formally acknowledged (perhaps in standing orders). However, in these circumstances it may be difficult to combine this role with that of chair, since the latter requires a non-partisan approach, so that the roles of leader and chair will be separated and come to resemble that of (political) Prime Minister and (non-political) monarch. (The Speaker of the House of Commons plays such a non-political role; so do a number of national presidents, as in Germany or Italy.) It is also quite usual for there to be a council *leader of the opposition* (as in Parliament). However, unlike chairmanship, the office of leader is not statutory but is informal and based on convention and practice – again, this is changing as a result of current reforms; see Chapter 15.

Committees

The number, size, composition and powers of committees in any local authority are determined by each individual council and laid down in the Standing Orders. (The social services committee ceases to be statutory under the Local Government Bill 2000.) Generally, the functions of local government committees are to: (1) take particular interest in one aspect or area of the local authority's work (education or highways, for instance); (2) closely supervise the administration of that area; (3) formulate policies or lines of action; (4) deal initially with any problems which arise in its field of special interest.

Committees are usually required to report their discussions back to the full council. This may be something of a formality, simply in order to keep the council informed, as in cases where the committee is executive in nature, having been delegated the power actually to decide issues of policy (such powers were significantly increased in the Local Government Act 1972). But more usually the purpose is to gain approval of the council for the actions which the committee may recommend (closing certain schools, selling council houses, undertaking a redevelopment scheme, etc.). And, by law, certain matters cannot be delegated to committees: the power to raise loans or to determine the council tax rests with the council alone. Obviously, where a committee has to await the approval of the council before it can act, there is delay involved, but this may be regarded as a reasonable price to pay for greater democratic control. In such cases, the committees are advisory or deliberative rather than executive in nature. Nevertheless, they do a lot of the detailed groundwork and sifting on behalf of the council and have been aptly described as the 'workshops' of local government (though of course much of the work of local government occurs in the departments and among senior officers and increasingly by party groups; see Chapter 15).

Types of committee

There are many different kinds of committee in local government. The most usual categories are as follows:

(a) *Horizontal and vertical.* Those committees which concentrate on the administration of a single service (such as education or housing) are usually called 'vertical' (or service) committees. Other committees may be concerned with a particular function that directly affects many or all other council activities (though often having little contact with the general public), and because they cut across other services these are known as 'horizontal' (or functional) committees – finance or staffing, for example.

(b) *Special* and *standing.* Special (or *ad hoc*) committees are formed to deal with a particular problem (for instance, flood) or event (for instance, millennium celebrations) and are disbanded when circumstances permit. Standing committees are more permanent, being re-appointed annually to fulfil the roles outlined in (a) above.

(c) *Joint.* These are formed by two or more local authorities when they share an interest in some activity or problem (a bridge or airport or other amenity). It is common for there to be a joint committee of the county and district councils in shire areas. In many instances these committees are called 'boards' or 'authorities' – the Avon and Somerset Police Authority or the Glasgow Joint Transport Board for example.

(d) *Statutory.* While local authorities have considerable discretion as regards the committees they appoint, they have long been required by law to appoint *certain* committees. Before the reorganization legislation of 1972–3, the list of such committees was considerable; now it is just social services committees and (where appropriate) sea fisheries committees but this is to cease: see above.

Size and membership of committees

For the most part, membership of committees in local government is confined to currently elected members of the council, the councillors. (Co-opted members are an exception to this rule – see p. 234.) These members are allocated to committees by the full council, though much of this work is often done in advance by a special 'selection' committee (which usually consists of more senior councillors) or, behind the scenes, by parties. In this allocation process, arrangements vary among local authorities, though it is normal for some account to be taken of councillors' own preferences, the balance of the parties, the representation of wards or districts and the balance of age and experience of members. Where a party dominates the council, it will usually, and understandably, use its advantage to predominate in each of the important committees, though the Local Government Act 1989 brought in the requirement of proportional representation of parties on committees; however, this will not apply to executive cabinets (and their sub-committees) as they come into being: see p. 272 and Chapter 15.

The size of committees is a matter for the individual council to determine and there is wide variation. The desirability of having small and business-like committees needs to be balanced with the democratic desire to have a proper representation of areas and interests. The importance and even perhaps the popularity of a committee is likely to affect its size. As we have seen (p. 234), some committees will find it necessary to co-opt members from outside the elected membership of the council.

The operation of committees

Usually, the first task of a committee is to appoint a chair, though often this may be done for it by the whole council, and where there is a majority party the allocation of such positions is often a foregone conclusion.

Naturally, committees are usually smaller in membership than the full council. Committee meetings are less formal occasions than full council meetings, and officers are expected to play an active role by answering questions and giving advice and briefings. Indeed, a lot of committee time is spent hearing and reacting to the reports by chief officers on such matters as the council's budget, a housing development scheme, the community care plan or the planned closures of certain schools or homes. From such questions and discussions will emerge the committee's views, and these views, or 'resolutions', together with the 'minutes' (written summaries of the committee's proceedings) are usually submitted to the next meeting of the full council.

Just as the full council meets at regular intervals, so do committees – they go through a regular 'cycle' of meetings (though, like the council, they may have special or emergency meetings). By law, their meetings are open to the public, but for certain items a committee (and indeed the full council) can exclude the public and press by going into 'closed' session (meeting *in camera*). These items are usually of a confidential nature, such as those where a council is negotiating for property or where a housing committee is discussing rent arrears or evictions. On occasion, a member of the public may be invited to address a committee. (Whilst local government has no Official Secrets Act* such as that operating in central government, local authorities usually have a clause in their standing orders which prohibits the disclosure of council or committee matters until this is authorized by the council. For many matters the latter occurs in the normal course of events, e.g. in open council or committee meetings; and council minutes are made available for public inspection at the council offices or public libraries.) Under the Local Government (Access to Information) Act 1985,† council sub-committees became open to the public, subject to certain limitations concerning confidential or 'exempted' matters.

As we have seen (p. 221), when items occur at committee or full council meetings in which any councillor has a pecuniary interest, such as owning a property which the council may wish to acquire or running a business which it may wish to employ, he or she must declare an interest and take no further part in the discussion or voting on that item.

The role of chair

Chairs of committees do not merely control the conduct of committee meetings and speak on behalf of their committees at council meetings (like Ministers speaking in Parliament). They will be in regular contact with the departmental chief officers, especially prior to committee meetings. Occasionally they may call emergency meetings of the committee. And they may also, as its chair, meet members of the public – to explain the council's policy on school closures or housing rents, for example. The precise role of chair will vary among local authorities and may or may not be set out in their standing orders.[3] However, the mayor or any person presiding at a council meeting does

---

* Currently being replaced with the FOI Bill 2000.
† Technically, this amended certain sections of the Local Government Act 1972.

have the legal right to exercise a second or 'casting' vote and may, rather than act impartially, thus vote in accordance with the policy of his or her party (see R. *v.* Bradford City Council ex-parte Corris, May 1989).

Generally speaking, a committee chair's job is a responsible and onerous task. Between committee meetings a chair may have to deal with urgent issues – on lesser issues this power may be delegated to the relevant official – and take decisions on behalf of the committee (for which he or she will subsequently have to get its approval. This is known as 'chairman's action'. However, in a recent court case it was held that a chair is not legally entitled to take decisions alone (R. *v.* Secretary of State for the Environment ex-parte Hillingdon LBC, 1985). The Widdicombe Committee recommended that 'chairman's action' should be legalized, but the government disagreed, on the grounds that it would breach the essential local government principle of corporate decision-making and would undermine the proposals for proportionate representation on decision-making committees (see p. 185); instead it believed that councils should be able to convene small urgency committees (of, say, three members). This has inhibited local authorities' experiments with mayoral systems, and is currently being changed; see Chapter 15.

The pros and cons of the committee system

Historically, committees exist in local government because the modern local government system was largely preceded by a collection of *ad hoc* authorities (Boards of Guardians, Boards of Health, School Boards) which were more or less simply amalgamated when local authorities were created, so that the latter became a system of ready-made committees and departments. Furthermore, it has been convenient (and sometimes mandatory) for local authorities, on the acquisition of an extra responsibility, to create a committee (and a department) to administer that function.

There are, however, some more positive reasons for setting up committees:

(a) They off-load the full council, which can consequently spend less time on details and devote greater attention to overall policy matters.

(b) They can save the time of councillors, since different matters can be considered at the same time in the different committees – they can be dealt with in parallel rather than in series.

(c) Above all, committees allow councillors to have a real impact on decisions (in contrast to the limited influence which MPs exercise).

(d) Their existence can simplify the tasks facing the council through the division of labour and the specialization of responsibilities.

(e) Such specialization should facilitate greater knowledge and expertise by councillors (aided where appropriate by co-opted outsiders). This should also produce more effective supervision and control of the local authority's administrative areas.

(f) They open up decisions to public and opposition party scrutiny, and provide a forum in which officers and contractors can be openly called to account for their performance.

(g) Committees are generally smaller in size and their procedures are more informal, which may encourage councillors to speak more freely.

(h) Finally, committees provide a useful point of contact with the officials and help to keep them in touch with public opinion (though see p. 323) and they provide a forum in which officers and contractors can be openly called to account for their performance.

It is difficult to envisage local government trying to operate without committees, and many councillors would feel that they are not sufficiently involved unless they personally are a member of at least one committee.[4] However, committee systems can be abused and thus create problems. Among the principal *dangers* are the following:

(a) Rather than save time, committees may actually waste it. They may do this in a number of ways – by going into excessive detail and talking endlessly, by creating unnecessary sub-committees and working parties, by delaying decisions while waiting for another committee to make a decision which affects its work, and so on. Besides, there may be simply too many of them. They often grow without regular review, and as a result there may be overlapping and duplication of function. Committees may also be accused of diluting or clouding responsibility since no individual can be held accountable for their decisions.

(b) While committee members may become experts in the field of administration covered by their committee, they may also become narrow-minded and fail to see the work of the council as a whole. Indeed, there is the real danger of insularity (especially among vertical committees and their related departments), with members (and officers) identifying too closely with 'their' service: rivalry, jealousy and protectiveness may follow. Councils have usually tried to secure some coordination in the work of their committees and departments by various means, for instance through horizontal committees, such as finance, or by ensuring that there is cross-membership within the vertical committees (some members sitting on several committees). Some relied on the machinery of the political parties, and perhaps most assumed that the chief administrative officer – the Clerk – would provide a sufficient overview of the local authority's affairs. But in the 1960s these arrangements were increasingly felt to be inadequate – hence the setting-up of the Maud Committee (see p. 251).

(c) The real decisions are taken in private party group meetings in advance of the formal committee meetings. So the real decision-making is hidden from view (and accountability), and it renders the committee meeting a waste of time. This is a particular criticism by the Audit Commission in *Representing the People*, 1997.

(d) Routine committee meetings take up the time of councillors – about 50 per cent – and prevent them from developing more of a representational role, which is what they would prefer to spend more time (some 70 per cent of it) doing.[5]

It is in the light of these criticisms, and especially where committees are a source of delay, buck-passing or backstairs deals, that the government is reforming the system. Under its modernizing programme, the traditional committee system is to be abolished and there is to be a clearer and more explicit executive focus. This is like the 'Griffiths' management reform in the NHS in 1985 except that the local authority cabinet and/or mayor executive is to be balanced by the monitoring and scrutinizing roles of 'backbench' councillors and watchdog committees; see Chapter 15.[6]

The way committees and the council as a whole operate varies with the political structure of the council. The 'hung' or balanced council is of particular interest here.

Hung councils

It is difficult to generalize about the behaviour of local authorities: like people, each is unique in various ways. In regard to the operation of the council and committees, where there is a majority party in control (which, these days, is normal; see p. 163), the content and flow of business is largely at the disposal of the party: it 'calls the shots' and provides (additional) organization and (actual or potential) consistency. Where there is non-party control (very rare today with the virtual demise of Independents; see p. 184) or where no single party has control by way of a clear majority (i.e. there is no majority party in charge or NOC), council business has to be disposed of in a different (and often more complicated) fashion. This latter situation – being 'hung' or balanced (see p. 163 above) – faces one third of councils today.

Hung councils are a relatively new feature in local government, emerging in any significant number in the 1980s, especially with the rise of Liberal Democrats. In the late 1970s, the proportion of councils in 'balance' was about 15 per cent. Since then the figure has increased and now stands at 33 per cent (in 1995 it was 36 per cent). Some of these councils are only formally or arithmetically hung since in practice it may be quite obvious where control lies (e.g. where Independent councillors regularly give their support to one party so there is an effective majority). But generally, hung councils have to devise their own methods of coping and various forms of inter-party agreement have emerged, the more usual being:

(a) the minority administration, where the largest party tries to run the council, though it lacks an overall majority (which clearly can create difficulties). This currently operates in about a third of hung councils;

(b) formal coalition, where two or perhaps more parties agree to run the council and committees jointly. This involves reaching agreements on policies, priorities, chair and membership of committees, etc. Again this can be difficult to achieve, especially over a period of time when disagreements occur and may cause a breakdown and resort to one of the other alternative arrangements;

(c) informal power-sharing occurs, where parties agree to share committee chairs (perhaps on an alternating basis) but there is no formal agreement about policies, although there may be unspoken 'like-mindedness' (e.g. as has often occurred with Labour and Liberal Democrats);

(d) no administration, where policy-making is very pragmatic and often guided by the council officers. The chairing of committees may occur on a rotating basis and voting decisions can be knife-edge and unpredictable.

All such arrangements are relatively fluid and often change as party control changes following each election. In any one council, the precise arrangements and their stability will depend on a number of factors – the arithmetic of the situation; the electoral cycle; the attitudes, partisanship and cohesion of the parties; the ability and personality of the leaders and the senior council officials (especially the Chief Officer); and the history and culture of the authority, including the length (or expected length) of experience of balance or hung-ness.

Another influence is the attitude and guidelines issued by the national party. The Labour Party has been the most reluctant to enter into power-sharing, especially coalition, agreements and has sought to regulate the behaviour of Labour groups in that situation.[7] But local parties do not always conform to such guidance.

Being balanced or hung will have obvious effects on a council – on its procedures and ways of managing, on policy outcomes, on the budget in particular and on timing. On the *positive* side it is claimed that a hung council allows for more balanced, informed and extensive debate; greater access to information, to committees and to officials; greater consensus in decision-making and thus less extremism; and, generally, a more open and democratic process, where the outcomes are uncertain (and not party-predetermined), members have to listen and rational argument can be persuasive. But the potential *problems* are clear – longer meetings and delays or even paralysis in decision-making (e.g. having to consider three different party draft budgets – 'analysis paralysis'); one budget took seventeen meetings to agree!); fudged or weak, compromise policies, with an inclination to seek to please by taking the line of least resistance; lack of direction, consistency and of long-term strategy; increased party point-scoring; and perhaps above all, the loss of accountability to electors since no one party can be clearly held responsible for the council's actions.[8]

It is largely this last point which has caused governments to resist the call for fairer elections by way of proportional representation (PR). However, this situation may now be changing, with the partial use of PR in elections for the Scottish Parliament and the Welsh and London assemblies, and for European elections. The present government (1999) has promised to review the local government electoral system in the light of its response to the Jenkins Report (1998) which has recommended a partial PR system for Parliament.

The Maud Report

In the 1960s, there was concern about the organization and management of local government, and its possible effects on the ability of local authorities to attract and retain suitable councillors and staff. Consequently, in 1964 the government appointed a committee, headed by Sir John Maud, to investigate.

Its report – *Management of Local Government* (HMSO, 1967) – identified a number of serious deficiencies in the way in which councils were being run. Chief amongst these was the committee system. The inquiry found that many of the principal local authorities had thirty or more committees and forty or more sub-committees.[9] The same report showed that one large local authority sent out 700–1,000 sheets of official paper (agenda, reports etc.) each month to committee members. Consequently, preparation for, travel to and from, and attendance at meetings were making considerable demands on the time of members and officers. The Committee also expressed its concern that 'the association of each service with a committee, and of a department and a principal officer with both, produces a loose confederation of disparate activities, disperses responsibilities and scatters the taking of decisions'. It concluded:

The virtues of committees are, at present, outweighed by the failures and inadequacies of the committee system ... It becomes increasingly difficult for committees to supervise the work of the departments because of the growth of business, lack of time and the technical complexity of many of the problems. The system wastes time, results in delays and causes frustration by involving committees in matters of administrative detail. The system does not encourage discrimination between major objectives and the means to attain them, and the chain of consequential decisions and action required. We see the growth of business adding to the agenda of committees and squeezing out major issues which need time for consideration, with the result that members are misled into a belief that they are controlling and directing the authority when often they are only deliberating on things which are unimportant and taking decisions on matters which do not merit their attention.

Some local authorities had become aware of the deficiencies of their committee structure and their internal arrangements generally, and a number had undertaken interesting and sometimes controversial reorganizations (in Newcastle and Basildon, for example). Other local authorities had more conventional arrangements, but sought to achieve greater coordination through the creation of special 'policy' or 'management' committees or by enhancing the role of one of the horizontal committees. For example, the London County Council had a cabinet-like policy committee.

The Maud Committee may have been influenced by some of these developments. It was not only outspoken in its criticisms, but radical in its recommendations. It proposed that:

(1) Each local authority should create a small 'management board' of councillors (with 6–9 members) with considerable delegated powers. Its functions would be to provide leadership, develop policy, review progress and generally coordinate the work of the council (rather like the Cabinet at central government level).

(2) Committees and departments should be drastically reduced in number (a figure of six was suggested) and certain separate functions should be grouped.

(3) These committees would have deliberative rather than executive responsibilities (see p. 241).

(4) There should be a chief officer for each local authority who should have general management abilities which he should use to

    supervise and coordinate the work of other principal officers and
    their departments.

(5) More responsibilities should be delegated to officers, and members
    should generally become less involved in the day-to-day adminis-
    tration of services, decisions on case-work and routine inspection
    and control.

The Maud Report stimulated a great deal of interest and discussion.
But it also provoked much hostility: in whole or in part it was regarded
as too radical by many local authorities, who believed that their
particular system was already adequate to the task. Some argued that
the proposed management board would not only be undemocratic
but would clash with the principle of the 'collective responsibility' of
all councillors. Apart from this, many councillors were afraid of 'losing
control' to the officials or of becoming second-class councillors in
contrast to the 'elite' appointed to the management board.

    However, the Maud Report did cause some local authorities to
review their internal organization and procedures, and certain councils
began to introduce a number of diluted Maud-type reforms.[10] They
received added impetus from the publication of the two Royal Commission reports – the Redcliffe-Maud Report for England and the
Wheatley Report for Scotland – in 1969. Thus there was a reduction
in the number of committees and sub-committees;[11] central or 'policy'
committees were established; chief executive officers were appointed
or clerks had their positions enhanced to give them some formal
authority over other chief officers in the authority, who were formed
into management teams; departmental functions were amalgamated
or grouped and the 'directorate' approach was adopted, chief officers
becoming responsible for several areas of activity (such as planning
and transportation, or leisure and amenities).

    Such moves were encouraged in the 1970s as a result of the reorganiz-
ation of the local government structures and in particular by the tide
of support which accompanied the Bains Report and the Paterson
Report. These were the product of two committees set up in 1971 to
produce advice on management structures for the new local authorities
which were to be established under the reorganization Acts of 1972
(England and Wales) and 1973 (Scotland).

These two Reports were more favourably received than was the Maud Committee Report of 1967, for a number of reasons. In the first place they were not as radical as Maud: all councillors would continue to be substantially involved in the work of the council, as each was to have a place on at least one committee, and these were to continue to play an important part, and the controversial idea of a high-powered (some called it 'oligarchical') management board was dropped. Secondly, their recommendations were less dogmatic and presented local authorities with a number of alternative schemes (for the grouping of services, the number and role of committees, etc.) from which to choose. Thirdly, the Maud Report had educated (or 'softened up') local authorities to the idea of reform in their internal arrangements. Fourthly, local government was to be comprehensively reorganized and new internal structures would be required: experience of reforming Greater London (1963) had indicated that merely modifying existing structures would not be sufficient to meet the changed circumstances. This view was endorsed by both the Redcliffe-Maud and Wheatley Royal Commissions (1969). Finally, the Local Government Acts of 1972 and 1973 removed a number of the legal constraints on local government (concerning the compulsory appointment of officers and committees or the scope of delegation), which made it easier for the new authorities to adopt new management structures. However, it has been remarked that 'the extent to which the Bains Report has been accepted is in its own way both exciting and disturbing'.[12]

Bains, Paterson and the 'corporate approach'

The Bains and Paterson Reports of 1972 were very similar both in their general approach and philosophy, and in their detailed recommendations. Similarly they reflected many of the sentiments expressed in the Maud Report and in the Redcliffe-Maud and Wheatley Reports, though they provided more in the way of detail. Above all they emphasized the desirability of a 'corporate' (or integrated) approach to the management of local authority affairs, in contrast to the traditional, departmental approach (so strongly criticized by Maud – see p. 250), which lacked a sufficiently unified attitude towards the development of policies for the locality. Despite the coordinating role performed actually or potentially by senior officers (such as the clerk or the finance officer) or by committees (such as the finance committee), the Paterson Report concluded:

In general, the process of formulating policies and devising plans to implement these policies is carried out independently within the various service committees and their respective departments, each making separate recommendations to the full council. Although there is now widespread recognition that the activities of any one committee or department interact to a substantial degree with those of other parts of the organization, particularly in terms of their end-effect on the public, there is still very little in the way of formal coordination across the whole range of an authority's activities. (para. 3.5)

Furthermore, although the finance committee could exert some overall influence, its effectiveness was limited because

its members are no position to assess whether the sum total of the various departmental spending proposals really represents a cohesive programme geared to achieve the authority's objectives; they lack guidelines to assist them in reconciling the competing claims for the services for finance; they are concerned only with the financial implications . . . and not with the deployment of other important elements of resource necessary for the implementation of the programmes. (para. 3.6)

The two reports, then, are concerned with coordination, not merely to provide better services and prevent errors (such as housing estates lacking community facilities, or education and housing provisions being out of phase), but also to promote efficiency, avoid wasteful duplication and ensure value for money.[13]

However, there is a third reason for seeking the corporate approach in local government management. The perception of local government should not be

limited to the narrow provision of a series of services to the community . . . It has within its purview the overall economic, cultural and physical well-being of the community and for this reason its decisions impinge with increasing frequency upon the lives of its citizens ... Local government is about, and more important, for people. (Bains, paras. 2.10, 2.13)

Such overall responsibility and the interrelationship of problems in the community calls for the wider-ranging, less mutually exclusive, corporate approach. Such an approach is unfortunately limited by the fact that *other* public bodies are responsible for such matters as income maintenance, health services, training and (except in Scotland) social work with offenders. However, under the government's current reform programme, local authorities are being formally given a community leadership role. They now have the 'duty to promote the economic, social and environmental well-being of their areas' since they are 'the organizations best placed to take a comprehensive overview of the needs and priorities of their local ... communities and lead the work to meet those needs ... in the round' (*Modern Local Government: In Touch with the People*, para 8.1). Thus the aim is to develop a corporate approach across the whole range of community provision.

Corporate management

Both the Bains and Paterson Reports take as their basis a corporate approach to the management of local authorities. Management, generally, has been described as consisting of forecasting, planning, organizing, commanding, coordinating and controlling.[14] Corporate management aims at securing a unity to these processes, both individually and collectively. For local authorities this implies the development of comprehensive policies and cohesive programmes of action – a unified approach to the formulation and implementation of policies and plans to meet the needs of the community. As the Paterson Report puts it,

The ultimate objective of corporate management is to achieve a situation where the needs of a community are viewed comprehensively and the activities of the local authority are planned, directed and controlled in a unified manner ... (para. 5.3)

The Bains and Paterson Reports both outline management structures to support such an approach (see Figure 15). Thus they recommend that at *councillor* level:

(1) The number of committees should be reduced by organizing them on a 'programme area' basis, grouping together related activities in terms of their end-result (such as education + libraries + amenities, or transport + highways + planning). These programme areas should match the broad objectives of the local authority. Each of these spheres of activity thus would have its own objectives and programme for meeting them, and the committees would be responsible for each programme and the allocation of resources within it. Consequently, the committee structure would be directly geared to the needs and objectives of the authority, and a 'mini-corporate' approach would be developed at committee level rather than a single-service or departmental view. Such committees would continue to have policy-making and executive roles (they would not be merely advisory as Maud suggested).

(2) A central management committee – the Policy & Resources (P&R) committee – should be established to provide coordination and guidance to the council on overall policy, priorities, resource allocation and major programmes, to coordinate advice to the council, to exercise overall control over major resources and to coordinate and control programme implementation. For these purposes, it would have a close working relationship with certain committees, some of which might become its sub-committees.

(3) Area joint committees should be set up to plan and coordinate the provision of services which are closely related but separated (such as housing and social services in non-metropolitan areas) or provided concurrently (such as planning). These committees would consist of members from the county and district councils in the areas.

(4) At *officer* level, a chief executive officer (CEO) should be appointed to head the full-time officers' side of the local authority. He or she would become the council's principal official adviser on matters of general policy and would be responsible for securing coordination of advice on the forward planning of objectives and services, for the efficient implementation of policies and for ensuring that the authority's resources are most effectively employed.

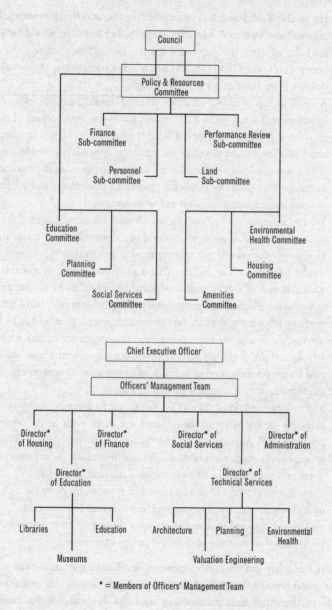

Figure 15 *Suggested committee and departmental structures (from the Bains Report)*

He or she would also be responsible for the maintenance of good internal and external relations.[15] His or her key role would be to lead the officers' management team (chief officers' group). As a general rule, the CEOs should not head departments, as this may detract from their other responsibilities.

(5) A small group of about six chief officers, should form the officers' management team (OMT). It would act as the counterpart of the members' policy committee (PRC),[16] providing a forum in which chief officers would develop a corporate approach and identity. This team would be responsible for the preparation of programmes in connection with the council's long-term objectives, and for the general coordination of their implementation.

(6) Where appropriate, departments should be amalgamated into 'directorates'. This grouping should not normally go as far as the grouping of committees (recommended in (1) above), since that might jeopardize the highly prized professionalism or expertise which is one of the strengths of local government or might give rise to some illogical groupings and to the problem of control. But, perhaps above all, drastic departmental groupings might lead to the re-creation of the one-committee/one-department link which so fostered the development of departmentalism in the past. Bains and Paterson indicated a number of alternative arrangements as guidelines, one of which is shown in Figure 15.

(7) More decision-taking should be delegated to officers, the general principle being asserted that 'issues are dealt with at the lowest possible level consistent with the nature of the problem'.[17] Thus, as a general rule, members would not normally be involved in detailed or routine low-level decision-making. Nevertheless, the 'constituency' role of members would require them to be aware of and sensitive to local needs and feelings, and consequently both reports recognized that members may genuinely have occasion to be involved in matters of detailed policy execution.

At the other extreme, both reports emphasize the important role of the full council. In spite of the delegation to officers, the enhanced role of the chief executive officer and the key role of the policy committee, the council is to remain the ultimate decision-making body in a real rather than a merely formal sense. It should provide 'a forum for public debate and for the open challenge and questioning of policy and its application' . . . it is 'the body in which the authority's broad objectives and the major commitment of resources should be fully discussed and decided'.[18] Councils should not degenerate into ritualistic talking shops or rubber stamps.

The central theme of the reports – that the whole of a local authority's activities should be carried out by a group of people all working towards the same general end – is incontrovertible and highly desirable, and seemed especially so at that time, when local authorities were about to become bigger and cover more diversified geographical areas. Furthermore, in a period of scarce resources, there is an obvious need for their rational allocation, for determining objectives and ordering priorities, and subsequently monitoring results for effectiveness. Not that this necessarily implied restraint or retrenchment: financial management, planning, personnel management and policy in general were to become much more positive and forward-looking instead of simply reacting to events on a piecemeal basis. In short, the multifarious roles of the local authority were to be seen in the round, as a totality. 'Problems do not arise in neat compartments or individual packages, but rather as a tangled, interrelated mass needing a corporate approach to solve them.'[19]

However, some *critics* quickly denounced the proposals as a 'bureaucrat's charter' and feared that members might become overawed with the new language and procedures and would find it difficult to counter the collective advice coming to them from the officers' management team and the chief executive officer. And there was the fear that the new corporate structures and processes might lead to the general public's becoming further mystified and confused about local government. Thus the changes were seen as a further manifestation of managerialism and technocracy at the expense of democracy (in the same way that many people allege that the country is really run by the civil service). In so far as it is true, one solution has been to increase the training and competence of councillors. Another approach has been to strengthen member control through the party group as 'the caucus strikes back' (see p. 167 and p. 181). But others have interpreted the changes as a 'dual elite' (of leading councillors and officers) takeover or dominance (see p. 330). Cynics detected a ploy for well-paid jobs and empire-building.

Others feared the new approach being implemented simply because it was fashionable, with local authorities setting up the machinery of corporate management without a proper understanding of how it should work. As Paterson says, corporate management is 'a total style of management, not merely an isolated technique' (para. 5.1). In particular, there was a fear that old attitudes and cultures would persist among committee members and officers, who would identify too closely with *their* service, neighbourhood, political party or interest. In contrast to the Maud Report, the Bains and Paterson Reports had made this more likely by compromising on the matter of committees and giving them an executive rather than a merely advisory or consultative role.[20] In so far as the policy committee consists of service committee chairs, and the officers' management team of departmental chief officers, effective corporate management could be severely jeopardized, as it would be difficult for these individuals to act otherwise than in a representative or partial capacity.

Similarly, the position of the chief executive in relation to the other chief officers was stated in somewhat ambiguous terms, and left open the question of the relationship between the chief executive and the other chief officers. As head of the paid service, how authoritative is the chief executive to be? Equally uncertain is the relationship between the chief officers and the management team, and, in particular, just how binding upon the officers the decisions of the management team should be. One thing has become clear, however, chief executives no longer have a predominantly legal background, with only 43 per cent being lawyers (compared with 68 per cent in 1975).

The corporate approach since 1974–5

Local authorities had many decisions to make about how far they would adopt the corporate approach and the ways in which they might adapt the Bains and Paterson models[21] to their circumstances.

In practice, they were adopted on a very wide scale, though there were differences of emphasis.[22] Some made adaptations, but others adopted corporate forms (names and titles changed) without a clear understanding of the requisite relationships and operations for it to ·work successfully: they gave the appearance of changing 'because it was fashionable' (Bains Report, p. 29). Consequently, these had the outward appearance of a reformed, corporate system but actually operated in the older, more traditional ways, with policy ideas emerging from the departments and the service committees, the policy committee and management team playing a relatively small coordinating role, and the chief executive liable to operate rather like his or her predecessor (the clerk) and being seen as no more than 'first among equals'. Within this arrangement, there was a tendency for the department and committee system to be in a one-to-one relationship: in effect, old wine in new bottles (or 'changing the door plates').

Other local authorities had the 'developed corporate approach'[23] with corporate structures operating in appropriate fashion with each part of the machinery fulfilling its proper role – the chief executive acting as policy adviser and director of the officers' management team, which becomes a corporate planning unit, acting in a directing relationship to the individual departments. Similarly, the policy and resources committee acts as 'custodian of the plan', seeking to assert itself over the service or programme committees. Other councils fell in between these two broad types, and exhibited features of both.

The existence of these and other variations is in no way surprising. As the research report says, corporate management 'is a phrase to which people react in emotional rather than rational ways'.[24] Certainly many councillors were suspicious of the new mechanisms and similarly, a number of chief officers were concerned that their particular service might suffer as a result of the corporate approach. Consequently, the assumption of a corporate form of management often became a façade hiding regular inter-committee or departmental battles. Indeed, corporate management has been applied in so many different ways and with so many different levels of understanding that it has 'become a phrase to which it is increasingly difficult to give a real meaning'.[25]

There appears, in fact, to have been something of a retreat from corporate management. Some local authorities unthinkingly adopted the form or machinery of corporate management without the appropriate attitudes and processes. Subsequently, when it did not appear to be working, it was deemed a failure and partly or wholly abandoned. A number of chief executives have either been dropped or have assumed departmental responsibilities. Many policy committees failed to develop real authority or power. In 1993, the Working Party report on internal management, *Community Leadership and Representation: Unlocking the Potential*, declared that while 'most authorities already have a policy committee which explicitly provides strategic direction to guide the running of the authority's affairs and sets out the authority's vision for local people . . . [others] need to use their policy committees specifically to identify what they want to achieve for their communities, and how it can be achieved' (para. 4.11(i)). More recently the Audit Commission had reported the burden 'placed on councillors, often unproductively, by committee meetings' (*Representing the People: the Role of Councillors*, Audit Commission, 1997, reiterating some of the criticisms from its previous report *We Can't Go Meeting Like This*, 1990) – though the average number of committees is now only seven (*Portrait of Change*, LGMB, 1998) compared to twelve in 1967.* And the government is currently urging councils to move their committee structures 'away from the traditional functional structure and towards looking at strategic issues . . .' (*Modernising Local Government: Local Democracy and Community Leadership*, DETR, 1998).

Councils committed to the 'corporate revolution' were to some extent, frustrated or diverted by a number of other developments. It is perhaps unfortunate that these management reforms should have coincided with restraints on public expenditure and strong pressures on local authority resources. And subsequent fluctuations and uncertainties in finance (with changes in grant revenues and tax-capping; see p. 544) jeopardized or obviated corporate planning and goal-setting; crisis management often took over.

Second, the trend towards greater accountability in local government has led to the development of *decentralization*, with patch systems, neighbourhood offices (even neighbourhood chief executive officers;

---

* Maud Committee Report, vol. 5, HMSO, 1967. The average number of sub-committees is just coming back down to 12, which was the average in 1967[26], though there is a significant growth in informal decision-making working parties/groups which may undermine any committee streamlining.[27]

see p. 514). Clearly such arrangements can weaken or jeopardize corporate management; indeed one view is that decentralization is 'the very antithesis of corporate management'.[28] A third development involves opting out or the transfer of various local authority services to government-appointed agencies or quangos, such as Housing Action Trusts, Urban Development Corporations or the Grant Maintained Schools Trust – which further undermines the corporate concept.[29] Third, there is competitive tendering and the *contracting-out* of services (see pp. 306, 344), which in itself need not present a threat, but which in practice often appears to do so:

The name of the game for the service chief officer will be survival ... Coordination and the subordination of interests to achieve a wider benefit to the local authority or local community will not win contracts . . . [the officer's] ambition will be more heavily focused on his own service, and he will not be prepared to accept those compromises demanded in the name of the community or the wider local authority interest, if he will lose the contract.[30]

One consequence of this is that service managers will demand additional services, information, advice and skills from their central departments – finance, personnel, legal – which, if they are not forthcoming adequately enough, they may seek to develop themselves or buy in from outside. More generally competitive tendering and contracting out the responsibility for service delivery has created significantly new organizational and management structures and cultures for local councils. The main change has been in response to the need to separate the roles of client and contractor within the authority (the so-called 'purchaser–provider' or 'client–contractor' split). The *clients* are those within the council who are purchasing the service(s) and are responsible for drawing up the contract, specifying quantities, standards, frequency, etc. and monitoring delivery and costs. The *contractors* are those who produce and deliver the agreed service. The latter may be private or voluntary organizations, external to the council. Or, where the council wins the bid (or tender) to deliver a service (cleaning, catering, refuse collection, etc.), the council's own (in-house) staff will provide the service through their Direct Labour or Service department or organization (DLO/DSO). The separation of these roles may take the form of separate contractor departments or be within the same department but using separate, arm's-length units or boards. In addition, internal markets have developed as budgets have been devolved and departments charged for central services (administration, finance, legal, communications, etc.). As a result, local authorities have become somewhat fragmented or balkanized and new types of managers have appeared. (See Chapter 10.)

Reforming internal management in the 1990s and beyond

After the initial wave of reforms in the 1970s, changes in organization and management bubbled on among individual local authorities on a quite wide, if unspectacular, scale. The 'management of change' had become 'the change of management'. Some of this was *ad hoc*, as a result of a change of party control or the employment of a new Chief Executive. Others were the result of new management ideas* coming from the private sector, from the Local Government Management Board and the Audit Commission, from management schools (such as INLOGOV) and from within local authorities themselves, some of which were the result of new approaches to the public service concept (such as 'getting closer to the customer'). Others were a consequence of developments in information technology or simply attempts to make savings. A more general 'change driver' was, as we have seen above, competitive tendering, together too with the loss or voluntary transfer of responsibilities (via delegated school budgets, opting out by GM schools, sale of and transfer of council houses, joint ventures and partnerships and the creation of TECs and UDCs; see p. 555). Another factor has been the various reorganizations of local government (in the mid-1980s and mid-1990s) which had direct effects or at least implications (such as greater inter-tier cooperation) even for councils which were not formally changed.

All of these required or stimulated renewed consideration of man-

---

* Such as visioning, mission statements, developing core values, service plans, business and performance plans, target-setting, costs centres, devolved budgets, ownership, empowerment, re-engineering, de-layering.

agement structures and processes. Thus councils have slimmed down or merged committees and departments*; they have created more multi-purpose directorates and changed the roles of chief officers. A few have created two-tier committees (strategic and service) or alternatively have dispensed with committees altogether, perhaps operating more through advisory panels, working parties, task forces and project teams. Some councils have sought to rationalize the committee process rather than structure by introducing 'differentiated' agendas and cycles, such that all committee meetings no longer concern themselves with *every* aspect of committee work (policy, performance review, routine decisions etc.)[31]

In the 1990s, management reform has also been motivated by the emergence or greater commitment to what are called the 'wicked issues' or policy challenges – of unemployment, youth disaffection, drugs, poverty, crime and public safety, traffic congestion, the environment, urban regeneration and sustainable development – which cannot easily be fitted into the traditional structures and ways of working. As Professor John Stewart put it they 'cannot be tackled without working across boundaries, learning new ways of working, thinking holistically and encouraging people to change their behaviour'. Such issues also go beyond the individual council and require a corporate community and partnership approach (police and health authorities, plcs, etc.). This situation is reinforced by the new funding opportunities which fall awkwardly across traditional departmental structures – such as EU grants, Capital Challenge and the Single Regeneration Budget (SRB). (See p. 381.)

As a result, many councils have renewed the quest for corporate management, strategic planning and a 'seamless' or 'joined-up' provision of services. Some have altered some of their council meetings to discuss general issues (such as community safety) or the 'state of

---

* Between 1989 and 1994, the average number of committees has fallen from 7.4 to 5.6 (it was over 13 in 1967) and the average top management team fell by one to 6.7 officers; working parties on the other hand have increased by 50 per cent (*Portrait of Change*, LGMB, 1996). It has been suggested that overall there has been more innovation in professional management than in political (i.e. councillor) management owing to the Local Government Act 1972 which requires councillors to take decisions collectively (*Local Government Chronicle*, 16 January 1998, pp. 14–15).

the city', etc. But most have or are reviewing their political and professional management structures. Thus for example:

The Council is undergoing fundamental change, with the aim of becoming a more corporate, forward looking organisation . . . New Committee structures have been put in place. A new Directorate structure has been agreed, and an Executive Management Team appointed with the task of providing creative and corporate management leadership . . . a programme to transform the organisational culture is under way . . . (Sheffield City Council, 1998)

The County Council's internal management structure has recently been reorganised . . . The revised structure is designed to break down departmental boundaries and encourage cross-service working . . . encourage greater flexibility and innovation . . . The County Council has recognised that the achievement of its aims requires a change of culture . . . A management of change programme has begun to address that issue . . . (West Sussex CC, 1997)

The breaking down of barriers both between external agencies . . . and between departments and service areas within the Council itself, is of paramount importance . . . Significant strides are also being made towards corporate management . . . as we work towards a genuinely corporate organisation . . . Our corporate aims and objectives . . . provide the overarching framework within which all policies, priority budgeting and service planning processes are subsumed . . . (Manchester City Council, 1998)

. . . proposals for new management and committee structures . . . and more systematic arrangements for corporate working include . . . a new Corporate Vision for the Council . . . Four strategic Directors . . . A new Strategic Management Team . . . A new emphasis on corporate working instead of 'Departmentalism' . . . Four main committees will no longer be linked to departments but will broadly reflect the service group responsibilities of the Strategic Directors . . . A replacement of the Policy and Resources Committee by a Policy and Strategy Committee to concentrate on setting the broad direction . . . and with a strong monitoring and scrutiny role . . . A Joint Management Board or 'Cabinet' . . . to co-ordinate the work of the council. (Northamptonshire CC, 1997)

The report [*Waking up the Sleeping Giant*] . . . sets out a management vision for the City Council changes to the corporate priorities and the principles of restructuring . . . One of the fundamental requirements . . . is a shift towards greater corporate working and corporate responsibilities . . . This will help us to develop a seamless service for our customers . . . (Newcastle City Council, 1997)

We are developing Conditions of Service to encourage staff to work creatively across traditional boundaries, and with other agencies. We are creating a Corporate Centre . . . because the Council is increasingly needing to work in new partnerships – both internally and externally . . . The corporate centre will provide a focus for work which needs temporarily to be 'uncoupled' from mainstream services in order to give the necessary intensive attention, and in order to catalyse collaboration between different services specialists and different external agencies (Somerset CC, 1998)

Governments have also been instrumental in encouraging (if not requiring) management developments in local government. Thus:

(1) Under the Conservatives, in 1991, Michael Heseltine, as Secretary of State for the Environment, expressed concern at the shortage of people willing to become councillors. In large part he blamed 'the procedural wrangles, the proliferation of committees and the scheming that goes on in smoke-filled rooms . . . [which] . . . have all discredited the system. There are simply too many councillors spending too much time – achieving too little'.[32] The speech had been preceded by the government's publication of a consultative document, *The Internal Management of Local Authorities in England.** This provided a wide range of options for organizing (and improving) the management of councils and implied that local authorities, where appropriate, may experiment and adopt a variety of committee and management arrangements. These could include a cabinet–backbench system, elected mayors or appointed council managers. The paper raised questions as to the desirability of delegated powers for chairmen, salaries for councillors, referendums on local spending and the power to dissolve councils and hold elections as appropriate. The wisdom of having two different election systems (of 'thirds' and 'whole council') was also questioned. The objectives of any subsequent change in

---

* Similar documents were issued for Wales and Scotland in 1993.

management arrangements should be to promote more effective, speedy and business-like decision-making; enhance scrutiny of decisions; increase interest in local government by the public; and provide councillors with greater scope for their constituency work.

Of those who responded to the consultation paper, nearly half were in favour of leaving the present arrangement unchanged. Subsequently a working party (comprising councillors, officers and representatives of the local authority associations, the Audit Commission, the LGMB, civil servants of the Department of the Environment and a professor of government) was set up to review and report on current management practice in local government, to consider suggestions for change received in response to the consultative paper and to suggest possible experimental models of internal (or 'political') management. In explaining its role, the Working Party report (*Community Leadership and Representations: Unlocking the Potential*, 1993) says:

In all areas of the public sector new management styles are being developed to deal with new roles and new circumstances. Local government is at the forefront of these changes ... the increasing ... diversity of provision ... opens up opportunities for choice and improved services. The local authority has to look not only to its traditional role as provider of services but also to one where the emphasis is now more on specifying requirements, coordinating functions and monitoring performance. The existing committee structure and many features of common practice grew up as the best way of managing service provision; it may not be the best way of running an authority, with a new role, in the 21st century.[33]

The working party recommended that all local authorities should review their committee and internal management arrangements to assess the extent to which they are appropriate for achieving the review's main objectives of strengthening the role of all elected members and developing the framework for effective leadership within local authorities.

After outlining a number of current management arrangements (formal and informal) currently operating in various local authorities, the report illustrates a number of management models which, given due government approval where necessary, local authorities may (voluntarily) experiment with, according to local circumstances. (The

Bains Report was felt to have been somewhat overprescriptive.) These models may be executive or non-executive in orientation. Of the former, some – such as the directly elected single- (mayor) or multi-member executive – are not recommended, largely on the grounds that such systems could confuse accountability and create difficulties in the relationship between the executive and the separately elected council (i.e. a potential clash of supremacy or of mandates) as well as making it difficult to ensure political neutrality of officers with two masters. Other models include the single-party policy committee with a limited range of executive powers; the lead-member system where – like government Ministers – senior councillors have delegated control and executive powers over aspects of the council's services; the 'cabinet' system, the membership of which has individual and collective executive powers; and the 'strong political executive', drawn from the council but (like a collective presidential system) having a separate legal entity and taking many (even all) decisions on behalf of the council.

The advantages claimed for these executive' models are that they would provide clear political direction for the authority, make clear where accountability lies, provide a more efficient, quicker and coordinated decision-making process, and provide a confidential forum for the ruling group to test the range of policy options with its official advisers. In their annual report for 1992, the local government Commissioners (ombudsmen) for England also endorsed the idea of separating councils' decision-making process from that of scrutiny (along the lines of Parliamentary select committees).

However, such proposals are unlikely to find universal support, and the most obvious objection will come from the councillors who find themselves excluded from the executive body, however constituted.[34] Whilst recognizing this problem, advocates of the 'cabinet' system suggest that backbench councillors could have enhanced area-advocacy and consumer-advocacy roles together with a degree of rotation or alternation with the frontbench roles[35] and greater investigatory powers (through Parliamentary select committee-type scrutinies).[36]

The Working Party also felt that there was a strong case for councils experimenting with a non-executive or advisory committee, which should be single party (where there is a majority) or multi-party (dominant party coalition). On the grounds that 'most major policy decisions in practice are taken not by the full council, its committees or sub-committees but elsewhere within the ruling group . . . or in consultation with the leadership of other groups . . . the majority party . . . through its leading members and especially its leader, is a de facto executive . . . Formal authority may rest with the full council, or with the committee . . . [but] the real authority rests with individuals.' The result is that, due to the law and other formalities, councillors often 'spend unnecessarily long hours in meetings which purport to take decisions which in reality have been taken elsewhere'. By aligning appearance with reality 'there should be clearer policy guidance and recommendations being issued to executive committees'. Clearer accountability will be achieved, since 'such a system would also clarify the source of recommendations being put to committees'. Hence it is recommended that councils should be allowed (notwithstanding the 1989 Act (see p. 185)) to establish such deliberative committees on a formal basis.

(2) Under the ('New') Labour Government, early in 1998, a number of discussion or consultation papers was published with the general title *Modernising Local Government*. The subsequent White Paper, *Modern Local Government: In Touch with the People* (Cmd 4014) appeared in July 1998.

In its consideration of the internal (or political) management of local authorities, the thoughts of the government were heavily influenced by the Working Party Report 1993 outlined above; indeed some of the wording is virtually identical. In fact some of the wording and a great deal of the general thrust and suggestions/sentiment derives from the Maud Report 1967, so in some respects we are back to the future!

Traditional committee structures, still used by almost all councils, lead to inefficient and opaque decision-making. Significant decisions are, in many councils, taken behind closed doors by political groups or even a small group of key people within the majority group. Consequently, many councillors . . . have little influence over council decisions.

Councillors also spend too much time in committee meetings which, because the decisions have already effectively been taken, are unproductive. Councillors attend too many council meetings. The evidence is that many wish to spend more time in direct contact with those they represent . . . the emphasis ought to be on bringing the view of their community to bear on the council's decisions, and on scrutinising their performance ... Equally there is little clear political leadership ... caused by the structures in which [council leaders] work. People often do not know who is really taking the decisions. They do not know who to blame or who to contact with their problems. People identify most readily with an individual, yet there is rarely any identifiable figure leading the local community. [*Modern Local Government: In Touch with the People*, p. 25]

Consequently, the government applauds those authorities which have reformed their decision-making processes – cutting committees, reducing their sizes and frequency of meetings – which leaves more time for councillors to consult and represent their citizens, which some have enhanced by introducing different forms of decentralization. Other councils are urged to follow suit. But the government wants them to go further and to clearly separate the role of councillors into that of *executive* and *representative*. The former implies responsibility for proposing the council's policy framework and its implementation; the latter implies representing constituents, sharing in policy and budget decisions, suggesting policy improvements and scrutinizing the executive's policy proposals and actions.

Such a separation would improve (i) efficiency since a small executive 'can act more quickly, responsively and accurately to meet the needs and aspirations of the community'; (ii) transparency, since it will be clearer who is responsible for decisions 'and the scrutiny process will help to clarify the reasons for decisions and the facts and analysis on which policy and actions are based'; (iii) accountability, as 'increased transparency will enable people to measure the executive's actions against the policies on which it was elected. Councillors will no longer have to accept responsibility for decisions in which they took no part. That should sharpen local political debate and increase interest in elections to the council.'

The government's reform proposals draw upon models of local government decision-making operating in other countries where the executive–representative separation of powers or functions is more common (just as the Maud Report had admired them thirty years ago). Whilst councils have some scope to undertake management reforms, the government aims, under the Local Government Act 2000, to increase their freedom to introduce such changes. And, like the Working Party Report 1993, it provides illustrations and options (see Appendix 24)* including, in particular:

(a) a directly elected mayor (or, in Scotland provost) with a cabinet, where the mayor is elected by the local community, separately from the council. The mayor then selects a cabinet from among the councillors who would become local 'ministers' with powers to take executive decisions and be responsible for particular portfolios or aspects of the council's work, under the policy and management leadership of the mayor, like the new system in London;

(b) a cabinet with a leader, where the council would elect (and where necessary de-select) a leader, and the leader (in effect, an indirectly elected mayor) *or* the council would select a cabinet;

(c) a directly elected mayor and council manager, where the mayor would give a political lead to an officer or 'manager'. Strategic policy and day-to-day decision-making are delegated to the latter, while the role of the mayor is to provide guidance and leadership (i.e. the relationship is like that of a company non-executive chairman and his/her chief executive or director-general).

The Local Government Bill 2000 also allows for possible direct election of members of the executive cabinet, either collectively or individually to identified posts or responsiblities (like directly elected local 'Ministers').

In all these (and other) arrangements, the role of the 'backbench' councillor is to scrutinize the executive, to propose amendments to policies and budget proposals and to represent their electors. The council as a whole would be responsible for the final determination of the policy framework and budget, the council's general decision-making (or political management) structure and for the appointment of chief officers. Thus it is up to councils themselves to decide their internal management and organizational structures and this will vary, especially according to the local party system (majority, hung, domi-

---

* In practice there are many varieties of such executive systems: see for example *New Forms of Political Executive in Local Government*, LGMB, 1998, and the Working Party Report, *Community Leadership and Representation: Unlocking the Potential*, DOE, 1993. See, too, S. Leach, 'Cabinets in Local Government', *Parliamentary Affairs*, January 1999.

nant, etc.). Following more detailed guidance from the government on these and related matters (including freedom of information), councils are required to draft proposals for their own decision-taking arrangements and a timetable for their implementation. Such proposals are then (like the mayor–assembly system for London; see p. 129) to be subject to popular approval by way of a binding referendum. A petition (of 5 per cent of the local electorate) can also require a council to institute the elected mayor system where it is not already proposed, and where a council is unduly slow in coming up with its management proposals, the ministers can impose a referendum related to one of the management models outlined above. Some councils have anticipated and exemplified such proposals/reforms by abolishing traditional committees (such as Education: see *Times Education Supplement* 18 June 1999) and by establishing cabinet-type committees and (e.g. in the case of Hammersmith and Fulham LB and Lewisham LB) an indirectly elected 'strong' or executive mayor. Where the directly elected mayor system is adopted, the election is held in the fourth or 'fallow' year when there is no election for one third of the council.

Elected (or 'strong') mayors

The executive mayoral (or provost) system is the alternative most favoured by the government and is being pressed on local authorities. (And using London as the model, the Supplementary vote system* is to be used.) Those in favour of the 'strong' or executive (or 'political') mayoral system argue that, in addition to the gains of improved decision-making and efficiency, transparency and accountability

(i) such figures can become influential enough with government ministers and MPs to redress the balance between local and central government;

---

* Under this system voters indicate their preference for candidates. Where a candidate gets 50 per cent or more of the first preferences s/he is elected. If none receives 50 per cent, all except the top two candidates are eliminated and appropriate second preferences on their ballot papers are allocated to the remaining candidates, of whom the one with the most votes wins.

(ii) the election campaign and focus would be on named individuals and this could increase public awareness of local government and improve voter turnout;

(iii) voters would be more influenced by local factors and issues rather than national ones;

(iv) such a high-profile job makes it attractive to a wider range of people, and it may enhance the calibre of those taking part in local politics; the mayoral role may rival that of the MP (certainly their electorates would be different), giving mayors a stronger mandate or legitimacy;

(v) where the mayor is elected directly by the people at large (rather than being the creature of the majority party as council leaders are now), s/he can more clearly focus on the interests and aspirations of the community, i.e. look outwards rather than looking inwards (to their party group on whom they currently depend);

(vi) the power of the party caucus and local entrenched cabals may be reduced as individual mayors, with a large personal vote, exercise independent judgement.

Professor Regan summarizes the case when he says

Since *all* on a local council are responsible for both executive and legislative responsibilities *none* is clearly accountable for either. The public cannot clearly apportion blame and credit for the stewardship of the council's services when their elected representatives comprise a largely undifferentiated group ... Democratic accountability ... requires more concentrated and visible executive responsibility. Local government is a headless state ... Given that most people do not have a deep interest in local politics ... executive responsibility ... needs to be dramatised, clarified and exposed instead of diffused and obscured by the committee system. Such highlighting ... would be best achieved by focusing it upon *one person*. (D. Regan *A Headless State*, University of Nottingham, 1980)

A nationwide survey in 1996 showed 75 per cent of the public was in favour of introducing such a system (W. Miller and M. Dickson, *Local Governance and Local Citizenship*, ESRC, 1996). And some local authorities have anticipated government policy/legislation and made radical changes to their political management systems, including a salaried executive (indirectly elected) mayor (Hammersmith and Fulham Council), cabinets (Kent CC) or quasi-cabinets such as the strategic committee (Southwark) or policy committee (Barnet LBC), scrutiny committee (Lambeth LBC) and, here and elsewhere, massive reductions in committees.

However, the whole idea of the strong mayoral system faces a number of serious objections:

– some see it as reducing democratic input into decision-making, and delegating power to an individual creates the potential for abuse of power ('Power tends to corrupt . . .').

– many councillors (especially backbenchers) fear becoming marginalized as decision-making is concentrated into fewer hands and as committees lose their potency. (Councillors already feel a loss of control as a result of contracting out services, devolved budgets and partnership arrangements.) This is reinforced by the government's suggestion that 'In the longer term . . . [these changes] . . . might suggest a reduction in the number of councillors on each council'.*

– there are those who fear a renewal of the central–local conflicts which occurred in the 1980s and which helped to undermine local authorities generally.†

– some dislike the 'Americanization' of politics, particularly the greater role of personality and personalization (with the intrusion of hype and irrelevant factors such as candidates' appearance, speech, dialect etc.) and a diminution of debate on key economic and social issues.

– similarly there are fears that the mayoral system is more prone to corruption and cronyism (and committees are more difficult to bribe than a single individual).

– others see a dilution of representation and perhaps erosion of parties, arguing that different sectors of the community (districts, ethnic group, etc.) cannot be embodied in a single person.

---

* *Modernising Local Government: Local Democracy and Community Leadership*, DETR, p. 33.
† It has already been suggested that attempts in 1999 to prevent Ken Livingstone becoming mayor of London were motivated by government fears of conflict.

– there is the danger of deadlock where the mayor and the council disagree; much depends here on the nature and balance of the powers of the mayor and the council (so that there could be an imbalance, with an over-strong mayor or an impotent one).

– how far should executive functions which involve quasi-judicial decisions (planning, licensing, appeals, etc.) rest with individual mayors?

– others are critical of what they see as the heavy hand of government virtually imposing this new system on local councils.

There are also those who feel that the criticisms of the committee system are excessive; that not only do council committees have many virtues (see above) but committees are prevalent in, say, the Cabinet and in Parliament, and in the latter, some (especially the Standing Committees) manifest/betray many of the faults or inadequacies attributed to those of local government.

Furthermore, the development of a system of directly elected local mayors raises the possibility of a directly elected First Minister for Scotland and for Wales . . . and perhaps an elected Prime Minister or President of the United Kingdom.

By late 1999, most councils had rejected the notion of the directly elected mayor, opting instead for the Leader–Cabinet model (see *Modernising Local Government: Taking the Initiative*, Local Government Association, 1999). But are there considerable misgivings that many councillors may feel that they no longer have 'a proper job' when all the internal reforms (including the separation of roles into executive and scrutiny) are in place: see Chapter 15 and *Local Government Voice* September 1999, pp. 4–6.

The government has sought to assuage the fears of councillors by pointing out that far from diminishing their role, it is actually enhanced by the new arrangement, since under the present system many councillors are in practice excluded from real decision-making (of/by the inner group) and have little power to challenge the decisions. Under the new system, councils are required to establish (multi-party) scrutiny committees of backbench councillors, whose duty is to review and question the decisions and performance of the executive and to offer alternative policies where appropriate. Councillors are able to spend more time in and with the community, collecting views and concerns – which is what many of them prefer.*

Their role will be to represent the people to the council rather than defend the council to the people. Each councillor will become a champion of their community defending the public interest . . . and channeling the grievances, needs and aspirations of their electorate into the scrutiny process. In-touch local councillors, aware of and responsive to the needs of those they represent, will have a greater say in the formulation of policy and the solving of local problems than they could have within current committee structures. (*Modern Local Government: In Touch with the People*, para. 3.43)

Councillors' roles may also be enhanced in so far as councils decentralize their structures, as the government hopes. And there is to be a review of arrangements for councillors' financial allowances, and more training and administrative support is to be provided, with some officers having the specific function of supporting backbench councillors (with briefings and research on local issues).

However, the new arrangements have caused misgivings amongst officers too, as it raises questions about politicization, divided loyalities/ responsibilities, security of employment, etc. We deal with the 'official' side of local government in the next chapter.

Before examining the work of local government officers, it is worth noting the obvious point that whatever form of decision-making and coordination, it is obvious that most of the work of local government is conducted in the 'field'. Most of us encounter local government on the roads, in the car parks, playing fields, sports halls, etc. And most of the staff employed in local government do not work at the headquarters (the Town or County Hall) but in a host of institutions and depots, area offices, nurseries, schools and colleges; hostels, homes, day centres; workshops, training centres; libraries, fire stations and building/engineering sites and stores. For example, it is estimated that 53 per cent of the population of Somerset come into contact with staff of Somerset County Council each day. We examine local government staffing in the next chapter.

* See *The Role of Local Government Councillors in 1993*, JRF, 1994.

10

INTERNAL ORGANIZATION: THE OFFICERS

The local government service is the local government equivalent of the civil service, consisting, that is, of paid employees whose job it is to carry out the policy decisions of the elected politicians. Local government officers are therefore 'bureaucrats' in the sense that, in the interests of efficiency and fairness, they are appointed and promoted on merit rather than fear or favour, and they do their work (such as allocating school places, grants or council houses) impartially and in accordance with the council's declared policy and rules of procedure. This is not to deny that they may become 'bureaucrats' in the pejorative sense of becoming slow, rigid, unsympathetic and, above all, exercising power without being held to public account. As we shall see, there are mechanisms and procedures which seek to minimize such undesirable tendencies.

The central government has a civil service of 500,000 employees (in 1979 it was over 700,000). Like the civil service, local government employment is large, with nearly 2 million employees (down from 2.3 million in 1979 – see Table 17). The wage bill amounts to 60 per cent of total local government expenditure. Unlike the civil service, however, it is not really one single service: each local authority recruits and employs its own staff. There is no single employing body, and local government officers cannot be posted from one part of the country to another, as a civil servant can. In practice, however, salaries and conditions of service have become substantially standardized throughout the country as a result of the emergence of national negotiating machinery, trade unions and the Local Government Training Board (subsequently the Local Government Management Board; see p. 384). Recent developments (allowing local authorities more flexibility to introduce performance-related pay and short-term con-

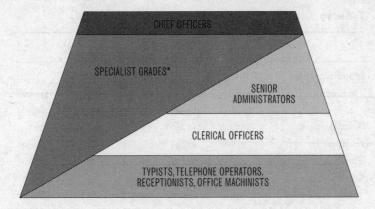

*Includes architects, accountants, engineers, public health
inspectors, social workers, technicians

Figure 16 *The structure of local government service*

tracts of employment, together with contracting out and out-sourcing,
etc.) are altering this situation.

Table 17 shows the large number of different kinds of employee in
local government. Traditionally, they are divided into officials or
'officers' (professional, technical and clerical staff, or 'white-collar
workers' – about 750,000) and 'servants' ('blue collar', or manual
workers, including refuse collectors, gardeners, cleaners or road workmen – about 700,000). Each group always had its own conditions of
service, superannuation provisions and negotiating machinery, but
this changed when 'single status' was instituted in 1997/8 so that
common conditions and a common pay scale or 'spine' applies to all
staff (referred to as 'the Green book').

However, there is a third group of employees whose existence is
crucial to local government but who are classified neither as officers
nor as servants. These are teachers, social workers, firefighters and,
until 1996, the police. In this chapter we are primarily concerned with
the first group, the officers: it is they (about 0.75 million) who form
what is known as the 'local government service'.[1]

The figures in Table 17 show a changing pattern in the distribution
of these different occupations. This is in response to a number of
factors including changing priorities (government or local authority),

Table 17 *Local authority employees (full-time or equivalent), 1979–98*

	1979	1984	1988	1993	1998
Education: teachers/					
lecturers	629,312	608,526	585,591	555,906[b]	445,900
others	467,058	424,740	439,635	410,356	365,000
Construction	155,336	132,897	131,738	94,356	72,700
Transport	31,688	27,694	3,813[a]	2,275	2,300
Libraries and museums	37,453	37,042	38,694	38,601	36,900
Recreation, parks,					
baths, tourism	97,767	87,026	99,415	85,093	80,200
Environmental health	25,200	23,397	24,248	23,681	20,900
Cleaning, refuse					
collection/disposal	60,852	51,035	47,372	32,093	35,200
Housing	54,256	62,073	70,858	76,068	77,500
Social services	234,653	251,562	273,186	282,972	284,600
Town and country					
planning	24,369	23,038	24,011	26,629	31,400
Fire service	45,892	46,204	47,315	47,576	45,700
Miscellaneous (finance,					
trading standards,					
etc.)	303,876	288,549	290,611	310,818	243,600
(Police inc. clerks,					
cadets, wardens)[c]	172,521	182,117	186,651	200,892	201,200
(Local courts and					
probation staff)[c]	17,599	21,600	24,319	27,197	24,600
Total (= 7% of					
national workforce in 1998)	2,358,686	2,267,500	2,286,327	2,214,513	1,970,700

Source: Employment Gazette (up to 1995); *Annual Abstract of Statistics*, 1998.

Occupational groups	
Chief officers	0·3%
Administrative, professional, technical and clerical	40%
Teachers, police, firemen	30%
Manual	30%
	100

[a]Reduction reflects creation of public transport companies in October 1986.
[b]Education figures reflect transfer of polytechnics from local government 1989; teachers and lecturers who transferred to further education corporations in 1993 reflected in 1998 figures.
[c]Not strictly part of the local government system; police were 'uncoupled' into separate Police Authorities under the Police and Magistrates' Courts Act 1994.

structural and functional changes (such as the decline in the school population, the transfer of polytechnics and colleges), competitive tendering and contracting out of services, the introduction of housing benefit, community charge and community care, etc. Of the total figure of 2 million, nearly 70 per cent are women. They far outnumber men in social services and education, though most are employed on a part-time basis

Negotiating machinery

Since 1944, local government has developed a national negotiating machinery known as the National Joint Council for Local Authorities Services. This comprises a number of separate committees, about forty in all, covering such occupational groups as firefighters, youth leaders, manual workers, engineering craftsmen and teachers. Their function is to negotiate national salary scales and conditions of service. There are thus two 'sides' involved – the employers (or management side) and the employees (the staff side). In practice, the employers' side is drawn from representatives of local authorities in the form of the Local Government Association (formed in 1997 from an amalgamation of separate associations for metropolitan, district and county councils), and the staff side from the trade unions such as the TGWU, GMBAT and especially UNISON (formed in 1993 through the amalgamation of the NALGO, NUPE and COHSE unions). In 1998/9, as a result of devolution, Scottish local authorities broke away from the NJC and formed their own negotiating machinery (affecting some 200,000 employees).

In the past the multiplicity of negotiating bodies made the negotiating machinery very complex and liable to create inconsistencies and unfairness, as well as being difficult to operate. However, the problems were reduced by the creation in 1948 of an advisory and coordinating body, the Local Authorities Conditions of Service Advisory Board (LACSAB). LACSAB, the Local Government Training Board (LGTB) and the Local Authorities Management Services and Computer Committee (LAMSAC; see p. 311) merged into the Local Government Management Board (LGMB) in 1991. In 1999 the LGMB divided into the Improvement and Development Agency (IDA, which deals with management, training, etc.) and the Employers Agency (which deals with matters of pay and conditions of employment, though it also provides information and recommendations on general legislation, reports on how national decisions are working out in practice and responds to requests for advice on specific issues. In addition, at regional level, there are local authority Provincial Employers' organizations which keep the national bodies in touch with local opinion on conditions of service matters. They also oversee and assist with the local implementation of national agreements and hear local disputes and staff appeals.

The terms and conditions of employment resulting from the negotiations – sometimes called 'Whitleyism' – are implemented by individual local authorities (except parishes and community councils, to which the agreements do not apply), although the agreements only provide guidelines for minimum rather than necessary conditions, and local authorities are free to improve conditions where they see fit. Individual local authorities negotiate with staff through their own Joint Consultative Committees. Where a local authority fails to meet the minimum agreed provisions, employees can appeal through the well-established machinery. It is perhaps ironic, though probably inevitable, that individual councils are advised on matters of implementation by their officers – that is by their employees!

Officers and conditions of service

In this chapter we are primarily concerned with the administrative and professional staff of local government – the officers. These comprise various grades and statuses: the professional and specialist officers; general (or 'lay') administrators; technicians; and clerical and other office staff. These are traditionally referred to as 'the APT & C' grades. Under the Local Government Acts of 1972 and 1973, local authorities are required to 'appoint such officers as they think necessary for the proper discharge by the authority of such of their . . . functions as fall to be discharged by them'. Certain officers are, however, required by law to be appointed: these include Chief Fire Officer, Director of Social Services, Education Officer, Registration/Returning Officer (for elections), public analysts, agricultural analysts and Inspectors of Weights and Measures. Local authorities are also required by law to designate officers for the posts of Head of the Paid Service, a Monitoring (or propriety) officer and Chief Finance Officer, in practice these roles may be combined except monitoring and finance offices. It is the responsibility of these three statutory officers to oversee the conduct of the council's affairs, and they have powers to warn or to insist on the consideration of some matter, or to delay decisions of the council because they detect some possible wrongdoing or misconduct (see p. 299 – though they can also exercise influence informally by encouragement and persuasion).

All such officers 'hold office on such reasonable terms and conditions . . . as the local authority think fit' (Section 112 Local Government Act, 1972). Some – the chief officers – have their own separate national negotiating machinery. But for the majority of local government officers their conditions of employment are determined by the National Joint Council, and these conditions are set out in a detailed scheme[2] sometimes called the 'charter' or 'purple book' (but now superseded by the 'green book'; see p. 281). This originated in 1946 and represented a breakthrough in the establishment of the principle of equal pay for equal work throughout the country (except for the GLC, which had its own scheme). In general local authorities have developed a reputation for being 'good employers' and setting an example to other employers of good practice in wages, employment conditions, equal opportunities, trade union recognition and training.

The National Joint Council is regularly negotiating and reviewing the scheme of conditions of employment. As a result there will be regular adjustments in hours, holidays, leave of absence, sickness payments and, above all, salaries. In 1998 it agreed the move to single status for white collar and manual staff.

Before 1946 the rates of pay varied haphazardly among local authorities, partly as a result of local trade-union pressure and partly as a consequence of local party politics. However, variations will still occur, partly because of local authorities' differing management structures and partly because of variations in the local employment situation. It is particularly likely where authorities abolish departments and replace them with trading agencies (as Berkshire CC did, for example, in 1992). Financial constraints and competitive tendering have also led councils to make their own pay settlements and introduce more flexibility via working hours ('flexi-time'); home-working, performance-related pay, and more flexible contracts of employment – e.g. 20 per cent of chief executives have fixed-term contracts. A number of councils (e.g. Harrow LBC) are breaking away from national agreements to develop their own local pay scales, in some cases to deal with the problem of excessive staff turnover (as in Kent CC, which has experienced a 20 per cent turnover in recent years).

A glass ceiling

Whereas women form the vast majority (70 per cent) of employees in local government, relatively few reach top positions. Such a situation is not confined to local government, though there have been improvements in recent years. Thus in the private sector women now constitute 15 per cent of top management and in the NHS there are 28 per cent female chief executives and general managers.[4] In local government, women constitute 8 per cent of the chief officers (i.e. department heads) and 14 per cent of deputy chiefs, while for the next ranks of senior and middle management, over two-thirds are men.

While such factors as prejudice and tradition may be affecting appointment and promotion processes, there may also be an element of self (de-) selection involved. Many women officers (and councillors) are deterred by the all- or predominantly-male environment in which they may have to work, and there is the problem of the long and often unsocial hours involved. The LGMB has encouraged local authorities to undertake equality audits and to improve opportunities, and there are some signs of improvement; for example, in 1991 women managers constituted only 4.9 per cent and 6.8 per cent of chief officers and deputies respectively (LGMB figures).

Salaries and grading

Until recently local government staff have been divided into distinct groups – Chief Officers, APT&C, Special classes, Miscellaneous and Manual. Apart from certain (designated) chief officers, all staff* now form part of a common 'green book' scheme and pay 'spine' or ladder. Within this, there are different grades and pay scales.

Administrative, professional, technical and clerical (APT & C) staff have salaries ranging (in 1999) over six scales from £7,218 to £17,319 for those doing *clerical* work (such as filing, typing, checking documents, processing claims for grants or other payments) or *technical* work (such as that of draughtsman, librarian, building inspector and engineering, laboratory, planning or accounting technician). The actual salary scale will vary according to degree of responsibility and level of work undertaken. Thus there is a salary range for *senior officers* of £18,000 to £20,022 and for *principal officers* of £20,346 to £25,245. These latter posts are available for the more experienced and qualified officers, and it is here that we find education officers, housing officers, planners, lawyers, accountants and engineers. Their work often involves controlling large or important sections of a department and the leadership

---

* There is also a separate Craft scale (the 'Red book') which ranges in pay from £9,258 to £11,709 and covers engineers, builders and electricians.

of teams of officers. At the top are the *chief officers* and *senior managers*, whose work involves giving advice on policy and managing whole departments or groups of departments. Their salaries can range from £26,952 to £85,000, but the actual levels will depend on the size of the local authority and its population. In England and Wales, chief executive officers have a separate salary scale from other chief officers, currently in the range £51,500 to £103,000 (though the highest paid, in 1999, was the Chief Executive of Liverpool, at £113,000).

These are the national scales (for 1998–9), which vary with size of population in the authority area. But the scales are only guidelines, and councils can agree to pay over the scale rates, some on the basis of performance-related pay. About 50 per cent of chief executives and 20–30 per cent of other chief officers are paid above the maxima in order to attract particular individuals*. It is not always easy to make comparisons as the figures may or may not include perks (such as a car) or performance bonuses.

Among those who do not belong to the traditional APC&T categories, there are social workers on £13,000–26,535, residential staff on £8,982–26,535 and day centre staff and managers with £8,679–25,884. Manual grades range from £8,376–9,891 (excluding bonuses).

Generally speaking, grading in all posts depends on such factors as experience and level of responsibility as well as qualifications. This gives each local authority some discretion in grading posts in relation to the national scheme.

---

* The Audit Commission has looked askance at some of the pay deals (with some shire district chief executives on six-figures salaries – see '*Paying the piper*, AC, 1995) and the legality of some has been questioned by the District Auditor (e.g. Goole in N. Yorkshire in 1996). This has led some to question the competence of amateur councillors to assess the quality and performance of professionals and, by implication, to control multi-million pound organizations.

Recruitment, appointment and promotion

Recruitment to local government traditionally relied on the grammar-school leaver. Before the Second World War local government provided an occupation opportunity with some status and security. Entrants were expected to study and gain professional qualifications (in law, engineering, housing administration, etc.). Since the war, local government has periodically faced competition from other employers and as a consequence has either had to lower its entrance requirements or has moved 'up market' to recruit A-level students and graduates.[5] The situation eased during the high (especially youth) unemployment of the 1980s, but demographic change has led to a falling off in the number of school-leavers and thus a return of the recruitment problem, exacerbated by the economic growth of the 1990s. Shortages have occurred in a number of areas – teachers, accountants, educational psychologists, social workers, IT and occupational therapy, though in other areas staff are being offered early retirement or redundancy (especially construction and engineering). Extra pay, 'golden hellos' and attractive employment packages are being offered in many authorities to combat the problem.

Appointment is based on (desirable) bureaucratic principles: the aim is to appoint on the basis of merit and eliminate the possibility of nepotism or favouritism. Any relationship between a candidate and a councillor or officer of the authority must be disclosed, and canvassing for an appointment is prohibited (though it still occurs).[6]

Promotion too is based on merit or performance as well as qualifications. Officers, especially young clerical entrants, are encouraged to move among departments in order to obtain a wider administrative experience. Officers are also generally encouraged to undertake approved courses of education and training to obtain qualifications, especially those in the administrative and professional grades: the aim is to develop certain skills and promote in officers a broader and more positive interest in their daily duties.

The education and *training* of local government officers has long been exhorted by the trade union UNISON (formerly NALGO[7]). And, although well developed (e.g. the Local Government Examinations

Board was established in 1945), it was given a substantial impetus with the setting-up of the Local Government Training Board in 1967, superseded by the Local Government Management Board (LGMB) in 1991, and now, since 1999, by the Improvement and Development Agency (IDA). By helping to spread the costs of training among local authorities, the aim was to deal with the problem of the small authorities which had difficulties in financing the training of their staff; it also aimed at stopping the less training-conscious authorities 'poaching' trained staff from other authorities.

The underlying purpose of this training is to increase the effectiveness of local government manpower. Training courses include induction, training in clerical skills, training for supervision, preparation for administrative and professional qualifications, and instruction in the principles of management. Some training is carried out at work itself or at home (through distance learning courses), but a great deal is given in colleges on a day-release or block-release basis. A number of higher management courses are provided by the University of Birmingham's Institute of Local Government Studies (INLOGOV) and at other universities such as Aston, De Montfort, SAUS, Sheffield Hallam and Warwick. However, while education and training have much expanded over the past fifteen years, its cost is now being more carefully counted, and there is a growing insistence that training and post-entry education should be job-related and effective, i.e. less purely academic and more geared to problem-solving and practical application, increasingly in the direction of business-related skills and the Investing in People programme. BTEC and National Vocational Qualifications (NVQs) focus on the development and testing of skills and competences, and professional bodies such as the ICSA and the IRRV place increased emphasis on financial and management information, systems management and marketing as well as developing strategies for greater business awareness, continuous professional development (CPD) and credit accumulation and transfer (CAT); CIPFA's new training scheme 'recognizes the realities of the new world in which we find ourselves'.[8] The highly regarded MBA has now been adapted to the public sector. In their recent revision of the qualifying scheme the ICSA perceive the needs of local government to be similar to those of the private sector, because of the more commercially oriented approach to local authority activities as manifested in CCT and contracting out, cost-centre management, service level agreements, business plans and internal trading accounts.

Security of tenure and standards of conduct

The substantial security enjoyed by local government officers is well known, and in the past has proved an attractive feature of local government employment. However, local government officers can be relegated, suspended or dismissed on grounds related to discipline or efficiency – for example, unauthorized disclosure ('leaks'), persistent lateness or absenteeism. Local government employees can also be made redundant – no longer an empty threat in these days of expenditure cuts, and an increasing number of staff are being employed on fixed-term contracts.

Local government officers must not only behave properly, but they must be seen so to behave. The APT & C scheme (p. 285) states:

The public is entitled to demand of a local government officer conduct of the highest standard and public confidence in his integrity would be shaken were the least suspicion . . . that he could in any way be influenced by improper motives.

As a consequence and to reinforce this general goal a number of precepts are laid down:

An officer's off-duty hours are his personal concern, but he should not subordinate his duty to his private interests or put himself in a position where his duty and his private interests conflict.

(An example might be taking on an inappropriate part-time job such as a local authority planner or architect undertaking technical or presentational work for an applicant for planning permission.)

No officer shall communicate to the public the proceedings of any committee meeting etc., nor the contents of any document relating to the authority unless required to do so by law or expressly authorized to do so.

If it comes to the knowledge of an officer that a contract in which he has any pecuniary interest . . . has been, or is proposed to be, entered into by the authority, he shall . . . give notice . . .

It is difficult to know how far employees live up to these standards. Statistics for the period 1965–75 showed that ninety local government employees (including forty dustmen and seventeen policemen) were convicted of offences under the Prevention of Corruption Act (see p. 222), and for the period 1967–79 about 1,000 cases of fraud were reported, though this 'does not indicate extensive dishonesty having regard to the scale of local government operations, and many of the sums [frauds] include very small sums'[9] (Most of the offenders here were those who generally handled small amounts of money.) More recently, in 1996, the Audit Commission declared that 'probity in local government is generally in good order', though by 1998 there had been a marked increase in fraud and corruption.* In 1998 there were 233,000 identified cases of fraud, amounting to £89m, though most of these involved 'outsiders', especially benefit claimants. 'Insider' fraud by staff (via such devices as creating false accounts or creditors and fiddling expenses) and corruption (through accepting bribes/gifts for contracts, grants, licences, reduced rent; disposing of assets; non-declaration of interests) amounted to nearly £4m in 1997–8. The (illegal) offering of gift vouchers as inducements to local officers who order products for councils appears to be quite widespread among major firms.

Opportunities for such behaviour may have increased as local authorities have become more decentralized and entrepreneurial, and with more officers operating council bank accounts and entering into contracts on behalf of the authority. Joint ventures, the creation of local authority companies and management buy-outs compound the problem. Consequently, following recommendations by the Nolan Committee[10] the government is introducing a statutory duty on councils to adopt an employees' Code of Conduct like that for councillors (see p. 223). This supersedes the previous voluntary code used in many councils and will form part of the terms and conditions of employment (with subsequent enforcement therefore through staff disciplinary pro-

* *Protecting the public purse*, Audit Commission, 1996 and 1998.

cedures as well a employment law). The Code includes the requirement for officers to register and declare relevant interests (in parallel with councillors) and the existing rules governing the political activities of certain senior officers (see p. 296). Nolan also recommended that local authorities should consider introducing restrictive covenants into the contracts of employment of officers. The aim would be to prevent staff who change jobs (into the private sector) from using (or abusing) their privileged (or 'insider') knowledge and previous contacts to advantage themselves and/or their new employers. This has now been agreed such that chief officers must not, within a year of leaving the council, work for any organization which could benefit from 'commercially sensitive information' the officer knows from his/her council job.

Furthermore, officers can be placed in awkward situations when they suspect or allege corruption among their colleagues or councillors: they risk possible victimization and pressure to resign.[11] This problem was considered by the Nolan Committee. It recommended that there should be a procedure for confidential disclosure – or 'whistleblowing' – within the management structure (perhaps through the monitoring officer) or if necessary by way of an external body (such as the district auditor, ombudsman or the new Standards Committee). The result has been the Public Interest Disclosure Act 1998 which protects 'whistleblowers' in general from detriment and unfair dismissal (provided they have reasonable belief that the information disclosed relates to a criminal offence, miscarriage of justice or damage to the environment).

Politics

Another potentially hazardous area for local government officers is party politics. The APT & C scheme declares that the officer

... should not be called upon to advise any political group of the employing authority either as to the work of the group or as to the work of the authority, neither shall he be required to attend any meeting of any political group.

A similar provision exists in the conditions of service of chief officers. The aim is to reinforce the political impartiality of the local government service, which, like the civil service, is expected to show disinterested loyalty to whichever political party group controls the council. The situation can be more difficult in local government because parties are a new phenomenon for many authorities, and because local government officers are responsible to the council as a whole rather than to the council chair or committee chairs. (Civil servants are responsible to individual Ministers, not to Parliament as such. However, the question is sometimes raised there whether the Opposition, or indeed MPs generally, should be briefed by officials.) Meanwhile, for local government the questions remain to be decided among the local authorities: should (chief) officers develop special relationships with the majority party and its leaders? Should they appear at party caucus meetings, as a growing number appear to be doing,[12] and if so on what conditions? How should they balance this relationship with the minority parties and the council as a whole? The government has recommended that officers' terms and conditions of service be amended to allow officers to attend party meetings (on request via the Chief Executive). Some councils have drawn up statements or protocols which define or guide the working practices of officers and party groups. The Nolan Committee recommended that all councils should do this.[13] The aim is to establish principles such that advice to political groups is given in a way that avoids compromising the officer's neutrality, the advice is confined to council (not party) business, relationships with a particular party do not create the impression of favouritism and information received by the officer should not (normally) be communicated to other parties.

There is thus a strong convention that local government officers, especially more senior staff, should refrain from open support of political parties. Otherwise members might lose confidence in the impartiality and objectivity of professional advice and may doubt the speed, enthusiasm or even the direction with which their decisions were being implemented by the officials. Similarly, members of the public might come to suspect that they were not receiving fair treatment from their local administrators. This is especially so since, unlike civil servants, local officers play a quite public role (in committees, etc.)

However, while we as a society restrict the political rights of local government officers, we compensate them with security of tenure: we do not (as in the so-called 'spoils system') change our officials when we change (by election) our council (though this may change under the mayoral system). Nor do we elect our officials (as in some parts of America, where they may elect their mayor and other officials). Like civil service employees, British local government officers are 'permanent' (subject to what has been said on pp. 285 and 291). And by law (under the Local Government and Housing Act 1989) all appointments to paid office must be made on merit. The issue arose because of an increasing tendency for councillors to become involved in the appointment of staff,[14] often using party political criteria.

Nevertheless, cases of alleged nepotism, improper practice and sectarian bias have occurred in some senior appointments the 1990s.[15] Consequently, members are now involved in the appointment of those officers in the politically restricted group (see below); and 'the proper officer' (i.e. the head of the paid service; see p. 299) is responsible for appointments outside that group. Members may continue to be involved in matters of discipline and dismissal, but must take into account the accompanying report of the proper officer.

Chief executive officers are protected against unjustified (and perhaps politically motivated) dismissal by law. Under the Local Government and Housing Act 1989 each local authority must appoint an independent assessor who must agree with any disciplinary action which the council proposes to take against the chief executive officer as a result of alleged misconduct. The Nolan Committee recommended that the same protection be extended to the other statutory officers (i.e. the monitoring officer and chief finance officer) as their particular powers (of restraint, outlined above p. 285 and p. 299) could make them vulnerable to retaliation by councillors, and all these officers (and others) may be subject to harassment for party political or other reasons. This has now been agreed for finance officers. Another recent decision (which aims to reduce improper behaviour) is to impose a restriction on chief officers seeking employment in the private sector (except where they have been made redundant from their council posts).

The law therefore also intervenes to keep officials away from party politics by making membership of a local authority legally incompatible with paid employment by that authority.[16] This does not altogether prevent an officer from becoming a councillor, since he or she may be free to stand for election and serve as an elected member for *another* local authority. Clearly this may jeopardize the principle of official impartiality, especially where the candidates fight the election under party banners. However, a concerned local authority can insist that an officer does not 'put himself in a position where his duty and his private interests conflict'. Indeed, under the scheme, senior officers must obtain the consent of the council before 'engaging in any other business or take up any other additional appointment'. But a number of cases in the 1980s caused concern[17] and invited the attention of the Widdicombe Committee. As outlined above (p. 187) the Committee recommended that senior officials should be barred from any political office (the so-called 'twin-trackers') and the government made provision for this in the Local Government and Housing Act 1989. Under regulations deriving from this Act, officers are deemed to fall into the *politically restricted* category if they hold senior posts and/or their work is of a sensitive nature, including staff who service committees and elections officers (who may even be restricted in what they are allowed to wear on election days in case the colour suggests political affiliation!) For senior post exclusions, a criterion salary level of spinal point 44 has been given (i.e. about £26,000 in 1999), though the Minister has the power to alter this, and also to declare exemptions. Not only may such officers not stand for political office (with the exception of parish/community membership) but (under their contracts of employment) they must desist from such political activities as canvassing at elections, holding office in a political party, or speaking or writing publicly on matters of party political controversy. However, officers may vote and belong to a party. They may also by request and through the chief officer, attend party group meetings to give professional advice. And others may be appointed (with a salary of up to £25,000 (1999)) in order specifically to assist and advise party groups. Such party *political advisers* are appointed on political criteria and are limited to a maximum of three per authority. (In 1994 they were employed in some forty local authorities.)[18]

Such restrictions are controversial and there have been attempts to challenge their legality. Judicial review in British courts 1991–3 failed. The case subsequently went to the European Court of Human Rights on the grounds of violating rights to freedom of expression and of assembly and to participate fully in the electoral process. In September

1998 the Court found no such violation and the restrictions declared lawful. The restriction, affecting some 40,000 officers, has become an issue again, especially in Scotland and Wales, where many officers have sought to become elected members of the Scottish Parliament or the Welsh Assembly. Consequently, the scope of politically restricted posts (PORPS) is likely to be scaled down.

It has also been argued that the ban on staff becoming elected members of their own local authorities is unjust. Apart from depriving some 2 million employees of their rights as citizens to take part in this form of civic life of their community, it denies both to local government and to the public the benefits of the pool of skill, experience and enthusiasm which such employees may possess. In addition it is argued that local government should follow the tendency of other forms of employment towards greater participation by employees in decision-making. (In practice, some local authorities such as Basildon, Slough and Hampshire have allowed manual and staff workers speaking rights at council and committee meetings.) The Widdicombe Committee on Conduct in Local Government (see p. 187) considered these arguments but concluded that it was in the public interest that the law should remain unchanged.

The role of local government officers

Local authorities have wide discretion in appointing officers (see p. 76), and officers are appointed on such reasonable terms as the authority thinks fit (p. 284), with conditions being agreed collectively through the National Joint Council, though these are not binding on individual authorities. The relationship between officers and councillors is not defined in legislation, but the National Code of Local Government Conduct recognizes that whereas councillors are responsible to the electorate, officers are responsible to the council, to give advice and carry out the council's work. Thus the primary task of local government officers is to implement the policy decisions of the council. In the Middle Ages everyone was expected to spend a few days in the year making up the local roads, whereas highway engineering today requires skill and training, as do all modern local government services – social work, housing maintenance, planning, architecture. The trend to specialization continues. Elected councillors themselves lack both the expertise and the time: hence they employ full-time paid officers and other staff.

Not all officers are directly concerned with the delivery of services. Many are providing back-up or support services. Just as local authorities have 'vertical' (or service) and 'horizontal' (or functional) committees (see p. 244), so they have vertical departments (such as the education department and the social services department) and horizontal departments (such as finance). Officials in the latter departments help only indirectly to implement policy. Their immediate function is to provide central support services for the other, 'delivering', departments.

A third and perhaps less obvious role of officials is to advise on policy. It is no longer possible these days (if it ever was) to say that members make policy and officers merely carry it out. Officers, especially senior officers, not only have experience and professional training: they also have a commitment to their service – whether in education, social work or engineering. As a result they will have ideas, pet schemes and ambitions which will inevitably be communicated to councillors, especially committee chairs. In some ways it is true to say that the members' task is to keep a rein on officials' enthusiasm and tell them what the public will not stand! Apart from the fact that ideas will emerge from the administrative process itself, administrative experience provides other lessons. Officers too will exercise a negative influence, checking members' exuberance and advising them what is not feasible (for legal, financial or other reasons) or warning them of possible snags and suggesting alternatives. This officer–member relationship is explored further below (p. 321).

The chief officers

Chief officers head the departments, or, in some cases, as 'directors', groups of departments. (The exception is the chief executive officer – CEO – who, following the Bains recommendation, in most local authorities does not have a department. See Chapter 9 and p. 306).

The Chief Executive Officer

While not mandatory, 90 per cent of authorities have a chief executive. (Among those which do not, North Tyneside, for example, has a collective executive of 5 joint Executive Directors instead.) While usually known as Chief Executive Officer, they are sometimes titled Managing Director, Head of Paid Service or Council Manager. In some authorities the CEO is no more than first among equals; elsewhere he or she* is genuinely in managerial control of the council's operations. The Widdicombe Committee considered that the post of CEO needed to be formalized and enhanced in order to improve corporate management, to secure a clearer relationship between officers and members, and to promote the interests of accountability and better management within the officer hierarchy. They recommend that (a) the post be made mandatory, (b) he should be designated as head of the authority's paid service, with overall managerial responsibility for the discharge of functions of officers, and (c) he be given additional responsibilities, such as securing proper party balance on committees, determining councillors' need to inspect documents or attend meetings, to advise on the legality of any proposed action by the council or to be involved in discipline of senior (as well as junior) staff.

In response, the government has rejected (a), but under the Local Government and Housing Act 1989 (sec. 5), now requires all principal authorities to designate an officer as *monitoring officer*. It is his or her duty to alert the council to any situation where the council or a committee/sub-committee or an officer may be about to do or may have done something unlawful, improper or which would constitute maladministration. For example in June 1998 the monitoring officer intervened in an unlawful appointment in Hillingdon LBC. (In some councils – about a third of them[19] – the post of monitoring officer is assigned to the CEO, but more usually it goes to the chief legal officer or council solicitor.) Such an action takes the form of a report, usually written in consultation with the CEO and the chief finance officer. This is sent to the full council, which must consider it within three

---

* There are now 35 women chief executives (one in Scotland); in 1989 there were just four.

weeks, during which time action on the identified, 'at risk' business is suspended. The 1989 Act also requires local authorities to designate an officer (usually the CEO) as *head of the paid service*, whose duty would be to advise the council on the coordination of its functions and the organization (including discipline and grading) of its staffing.

A chief executive's duties may include the following:

 (i) to act as head of the council's paid service, with authority over all other officers so far as this is necessary for the efficient management and execution of the council's functions;

 (ii) to act as leader of the chief officers' group (COG) and (through the policy and resources committee) as the council's principal adviser on matters of general policy and financial strategy. It is his responsibility as such to secure the coordination of advice on the planning of objectives and services, and to lead the management team in securing a corporate approach to the affairs of the authority generally. (In Bristol, he is actually entitled 'Policy Coordinator and Chief Executive');

 (iii) to be responsible, through his leadership of the COG, for the efficient and effective implementation of the council's programmes and policies, and for ensuring that the resources of the authority are most effectively deployed towards these ends;

 (iv) to review the organization and administration of the authority and make recommendations to the council (through the P & R committee) if s/he considers that major changes are required in the interests of effective management;

 (v) to be responsible, as head of the paid service, for ensuring that effective and equitable staffing policies are developed and implemented throughout all departments in the interests both of the authority and the staff;

 (vi) to be responsible for the maintenance of good internal and external relations.

Although they may have specific responsibilities as head of paid service (including mediation of disputes) they may also act as electoral officer and take responsibility in matters of emergency planning. The precise role of chief executives will vary – with the size of the authority and staff to be managed, with the party system (hung or dominant party), with personality (and that of council leader).[20] And it is not static, as circumstances change – thus the consequences of the growth of party politics is that CEOs have a bigger part to play in managing the political process and the interface between both elected members themselves in their party groups, and between members and the paid staff/officers. Similarly restrictions on local authority resources and problems in the local economy (closures, unemployment, etc.) have given CEOs an entrepreneurial function, especially in seeking to attract new investment into the locality. CEOs are also having to play a leading role in modernizing their councils.*

A not unrelated development has been the emergence of local 'governance', as new players have appeared (or been discovered) on the local scene – quangos, voluntary organizations, government agencies, plcs. As leaders of the community, local authorities are endeavouring to play a/the major role here and this requires the CEO to engage in a number of overlapping networks – consultative, negotiating, competitive, partnership, joint ventures, etc. – which will increase in so far as s/he is given specific duties relating to health and public safety as the government proposes[21] and as regional development agencies and assemblies develop. CEOs are having to look outwards more and develop a greater community focus. Further changes will occur as councils seek Best Value and perhaps 'Beacon' status but especially as they separate their executive function (cabinet/elected mayors) from the representative and scrutiny role (for example, the CEO post may become a political appointment).

In responding to change an important function of the chief officer is to help manage change, to provide leadership on strategic issues and motivate and develop the workforce. Many of these points will apply to other chief officers.

Other Chief Officers

The chief officer is primarily a manager and he or she must recognize that any major decision cannot be made without an impact on other services. In general, the role of the chief officer includes:

* See *Local Government Chronicle*, 9 October 1998, p. 70.

(i) membership of the chief officers' group (COG) or Corporate Management Team, which secures a corporate and forward-looking approach to the affairs of the authority (see p. 260);

(ii) responsibility for the efficient and effective implementation of the council's and committee's policies and programmes within his or her department or directorate and within the strategic plan;

(iii) acting as principal adviser to his or her committee;

(iv) responsibility for the maintenance of good relations with the community with regard to the service provided.

Under the Local Government Act 1972 local authorities are required to make arrangements for the proper administration of their financial affairs and to appoint one of their officers to assume responsibility (though not necessarily exclusively) for this. In practice most councils appoint a separate or dedicated Chief Finance Officer (CFO or Treasurer) though some 7 per cent of local authorities currently have a combined CEO and CFO post. Under the Local Government Finance Act 1988, each authorities' CFO has the responsibility of advising or warning the authority about any of its decisions which might involve unlawful action and/or expenditure (including that which exceeds the authority's resources). Such advice, in the form of an 'S 114' report is sent to every councillor of the authority and to the external auditor, and in effect stops further spending or doubtfully legal actions for up to 21 days (i.e. until the council has had time to consider them). In order to provide a system of checks and balances, this role cannot be combined with that of the monitoring officer above (though government recognizes that this may lead to a difference of opinion between the two officers on occasion).

The main roles of the CFO (who is required by law to be a qualified accountant) are financial strategy and planning, financial administration and stewardship, corporate management, supporting councillors and providing financial advice.* Their principal professional body is the Chartered Institute of Public Finance and Accountancy (CIPFA).

* See *Worth more than money*, Audit Commission, 1998.

Local authorities are closely bound by law (see p. 76) and consequently need to take special care in their actions. Up to the 1970s, councils had legally qualified Clerks to guide them in this respect. Today as we have seen it may be the CEO or CFO or Monitoring Officer (or all three) who play such a role, though on a day-to-day basis it falls to the authority's lawyer and his/her department. The latter have experienced a particularly busy time in recent years in advising councils on how to implement (or, innovate around or even resist) centrally driven initiatives – tendering and contracting, forming partnerships, PFI and companies, housing transfers, equal opportunities, child care, community care and special needs provision. As a result of the Local Government Act 1986, local authority law officers must help their councils to avoid publishing material which appears to be designed to influence public support for a political party ('propaganda on the rates'). The introduction of Best Value, the Nolan principles on probity and the incorporation of European Human Rights present new challenges. In these and other respects, they are assisted by their professional body the Association of Council Secretaries and Solicitors (ACSeS).

Although in any one day much of the work of chief officers is totally unpredictable, their work generally falls into four general areas or directions, each of which involves a combination of administration and politics, in the non-party sense of the word.

(1) Working within their own department. Here they exercise an administrative or managerial role – overseeing the execution of policy, being responsible for the allocation of work and the general standards and efficiency of working methods, staff appointments, discipline and general morale and leadership. Apart from managing the current work of the department, chief officers also see their role as a policy-formulating one (see p. 322). When the chief officer is heavily involved in working outside his department, some of this work, especially the management aspect, is likely to be shared with or devolved upon his deputies, who are most frequently appointed in the county authorities.[22]

(2) Working with other departments. This is likely to involve a lot of the chief officer's time in councils where the corporate approach has been developed and inter-departmental mechanisms have been instituted (such as officers' management teams and inter-departmental

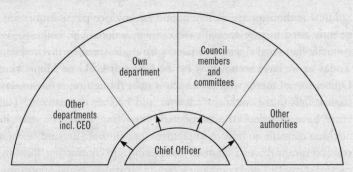

Figure 17 *A chief officer's domain*

working parties). This is particularly likely in the case of the larger authorities. A particular problem for chief officers is balancing the claims of their individual departments with those of the authority as a whole, but this is becoming increasingly important as councils seek to tackle the cross-cutting 'wicked issues' (see p. 565); the days when a local authority can do everything in isolation are gone.

(3) Working outside the department with other authorities and with other organizations and agencies – private, public and voluntary. Thus, like the CEO, this implies (increasingly) an ambassadorial role and involves relations with other local authorities (such as district councils) and liaison with the local offices of the departments of social security, education and employment, etc. and especially the government's ten integrated regional offices (created in 1994), and with semi-government bodies (such as the Health Authority or the Further Education Funding Council). Some chief officers have direct links with Whitehall departments or their regional outposts in, for example, discussions over educational matters, building programmes or local government finance. In addition many chief officers act as advisers to the local authority associations (see p. 469), they are frequently engaged in the activities of their own professional associations such as the Association of Directors of Social Services (ADSS) or the Society of Local Authority Chief Executives (SOLACE)* and

* There are many such bodies whose acronyms create a large alphabet soup: such as Society of Education Officers; LACOTS; SOCPO; ACSeS; IRRV.

all of them are expected to play some part in the public relations side of their department, including relations with the media and pressure groups. The actual amount of time involved varies among departments as does the extent to which they are involved in partnerships, joint schemes and funding, community forums and health, crime, environmental, etc. initiatives.

(4) Working with councillors. This occurs mainly in the formal setting of committees, but involves a considerable amount of time in preparations for committees, including the briefing of committee chairs before meetings. Again certain officers are more heavily involved than others: the treasurer or solicitor is called on to attend many committees. There has been considerable criticism of the extent to which members get involved in detailed aspects of administration. The Maud Committee poured scorn on those councillors who spent time with things like detailed aspects of administration (for instance, choosing furniture or colour schemes for homes or constituting selection committees for minor posts such as junior library assistant). The Committee urged greater delegation of authority to officers, with members concentrating on broader policy matters (especially in the management board – see p. 253) and on their representative or constituency roles (especially in their non-executive committees). More recently the Audit Commission and the government have criticized the time spent (wasted) by committees (and attendant officers), especially since so many decisions have been taken in advance by party groups. Similarly officers have become concerned about the extent to which members have become involved, and are increasingly full-time[23] with the consequence that not enough is delegated to officers (though in so far as committee cycles are lengthening*, the latter problem may diminish.

---

* The average frequency is 7 weeks, and 7.5 for council meetings; in 1967 the figures were 5 and 4.5 respectively. *Portrait of change*, LGMB, 1998.

Departmental reform

As we have seen above p. 254, the organization and management reforms of the 1970s, based on the corporate approach, were a mixture of the cosmetic and the real. Few local authorities adopted a thorough-going directorate approach (of grouping departments.) Most retained the traditional departmental/professional structure though perhaps slimmed down* and with some inter-departmental links such as pro-gramme teams (sometimes known as the matrix system).[24]

Change has been much more dramatic in the formal designation of a head of the officer structure. By 1975 only one major local authority in England and Wales had not appointed a chief executive officer.[25] Most of them had been given, at least formally, the responsibilities recommended by Bains and Paterson, with the important exception that a large minority had given their chief executive a department. These local authorities argued that a non-departmental chief execu-tive officer would become too detached and isolated. For the most part, their departmental responsibilities involve such central support services functions as personnel, management services, public re-lations, corporate planning and research. This is in contrast to the functions of the traditional and largely superseded Clerk's department, which was responsible for legal services, committee administration and electoral registration. The latter responsibilities are now usually in the hands of the local authorities' secretary or chief administrative officer.

In the appointment of chief executives, local authorities were urged[26] to have regard to managerial ability above all. Professional and techni-cal expertise and background should no longer be the main criterion (as in the appointment of other chief officers and as traditionally in the appointment of lawyers as clerks). The top local government post

---

* Such reductions continue, with the average number of departments and size of the management team falling from 8 to 7 and 7.7 to 6.3 respectively between 1989 and 1996 (*Portrait of change*, LGMB, 1998). 57 per cent of councils now have less than 6 members in their officer management team (CP, Whitford-Jackson, *New management structures in local government*, LGC/CIPFA, 1998).

therefore was to be an open field to officers from any background. Some envisaged a top place for 'lay' administrative officers (that is, officers whose work in local government is of a general administrative nature, like that of the top civil servants, rather than those who specialize in education, finance or engineering). In practice local authorities have tended to appoint from inside local government and often from the finance and (decreasingly) legal professions.[27]

A third area of change in the administrative arrangements at officer level is in the universal creation in the 1970s of officers' management teams (OMTs) or chief officers' groups (COGs). In the early 1960s these were rare; by 1970 more than half the local authorities had them; by 1975 all local authorities had them. There are, however, variations in the size of these teams, in the proportion of chief officers included and in the frequency of their meetings.[28] A few councils have developed joint councillor–officer management committees.

However, management teams failed to develop the corporate drive intended for them, largely because they were too large or CEOs developed (of necessity) stronger links with the political leadership of councils. And in general, as John Stewart has pointed out, much of the so-called corporate management has only reconstituted the old departmental or functional approach.[29] But structures and processes have also altered as a result of of developments in customer care and decentralization based on area and neighbourhood (see p. 517)[30] as well as loss of functions and externalization.

The new public management

Over the past twenty years there has been an increasing reorientation (or 'marketization') of the public sector, towards a greater private business style of operation (encouraged or initiated by the government via compulsory competitive tendering (CCT), the Citizen's Charter, VFM audits, etc., as well as the constraints imposed by such things as capping and cash limits). This has created what has been termed a 'private style of public management'.

CCT and other (often government) initiatives have generated the purchaser/provider (or client/contractor) split and the 'contract culture', with authorities becoming 'clients' buying (under agreed contracts) services or products from outside suppliers or from their own arm's-length organizations or companies (typically, direct service or direct labour organizations – DSOs or DLOs). In social services, many councils have set up not-for-profit companies to take over the running of their residential care homes. In education, LEAs, now compete with others, to become the providers of services (legal, payroll, psychological testing, etc.) for 'client' schools which now have control of their own 'devolved' budgets (formerly known as local management of schools or LMS).

With service (or 'vertical') departments having to demonstrate their real costs (i.e. without the often hidden subsidies of the central servicing departments), systems of interdepartmental charging have developed, 'cost centres' are being identified and time costing has been developed for the services of council solicitors, architects, etc. This has become more apparent with the application of CCT to professional white-collar jobs in local authorities. Some authorities have devolved central service functions to service delivery ('vertical') departments (who thus manage their own finances, personnel, etc.). And throughout local authority departments private business concepts and practices are being applied (such as value-added analyses, formulation of business plans, vision statements, etc.).

Departments have shrunk or begun to merge (e.g. education and social services) as work has been contracted out or services devolved/transferred – to schools (via LMS or through opting out), to housing associations, or perhaps to local community self-management (e.g. tenants). In some authorities, whole or large parts of departments have been transferred ('externalized') to the private sector (through 'outsourcing' contracts,[31] perhaps with the transfer of staff). Some councils have formed new departments by putting all their DLOs/DSOs together in one Contract Services Department. Hierarchies have become shorter as ranks of middle managers disappeared or as managers have been given greater autonomy and responsibility (for managing budgets, utilizing staff, as well as giving value for money and sustaining a clientele).

The trend to devolve responsibility to middle and first-line managers seeks partly to concentrate power in the hands of those who are closer to the consumer and partly to increase efficiency and effectiveness through greater flexibility of decision-making and the innovation and enthusiasm which can flow from the 'ownership' of decisions. As one chief executive officer has said, 'Good management will more and more be seen as removing barriers to colleagues' and subordinates' performance by enhancing their contribution and releasing their potential'.[32]

As a consequence, the role of officers (and members) is changing. Chief officers are developing a different relationship to their middle, more autonomous, managers. Chief executives are becoming managing directors,[33] and the management function is tending to divide – into those who specify and buy in or contract for services; those who provide services; those who monitor, inspect and regulate or audit services obtained; and those who are responsible for the overall strategy of the authority.

As a result of these changes and in so far as the contract culture and management 'revolution' continues, managers will need to acquire a range of skills. These include especially for the purchaser/client manager, those of policy development, negotiation, brokering, networking, communication and political awareness. Services/contractor managers need the skills of leadership and people management, business and marketing and operational management.[34]

Modern management, as developed in the private business sector, seeks to lead by example and the generation of a sense of purpose or 'mission', rather than, as in the past, control and constraint. Staff are to be motivated by sharing the goals or 'vision' of the organization. This sense of commitment allows the management system to become 'loose-tight', i.e. the structure can be loose (e.g. through devolution and decentralization) but there is still tight integration because of the common cause. In his book *Thriving on Chaos*, Tom Peters says, 'The boss with a vision is political in the very best and purest sense of that word. He or she . . . is constantly out "campaigning" – campaigning for the support, energy and wholehearted participation of everyone in the organization.' In so far as councils develop the government's current objective of community leadership, this perspective is extending beyond the local authority itself.

Thus overall, local authorities are becoming *less* centralized and hierarchical, monopolistic, professional-service focused and *more* customer focused, devolved and decentralized, competitive, flexible.

Quality

'A focus on quality has been one of the defining motifs of recent local government management'.* The 'mission' of local authorities is increasingly centred on the consumer and the quality of services provided to him or her. Competitive tendering and the threats of services opting out (schools, housing estates) has made councils more service conscious. So have the reports of the Audit Commission and the 'ombudsman'. Some local authorities had already been influenced and stimulated by private sector management practices and by the writings of such management 'gurus' as Tom Peters. They had begun to produce customer charters and service commitments before the government's Citizen's Charter of 1991. (For example, in 1990, the Audit Commission reported that two-thirds of councils employed staff to monitor service delivery.[35]) Nevertheless this has now generated considerable activity among local authorities in pursuit of the Charter's six principles of standards and performance, openness and clear information about services, choice and consultation of users, courtesy and helpfulness, straightforward avenues for complaint and putting things right, and value for money. Thus by 1992, over 90 per cent of local authorities had become or were becoming involved in quality initiatives[36] and by 1996 30–40 per cent had designated quality officers or working parties. A number of local authorities have been awarded the prestigious 'Charter Mark' as a result of their efforts (in 1992 there were eight, including Braintree DC, Bromley LB and Kent CC; in 1997 there were over a hundred).

Instead of measuring just costs or 'inputs', more attention is being paid to the 'outputs' or outcomes of local authority activity, especially those identified by performance indicators (see p. 317) and most have committee or departmental arrangements (and staff training) for per-

* *Portrait of change*, LGMB, 1998.

formance review.* And councils are committing themselves to the achievement of stated levels of service (aided by the specification involved in tendering and contracts), with redress or compensation to the public where standards fail. Competition generally has increased councils' concern for quality and customer satisfaction.* They have also set up complaints systems, but many seek to avoid complaints and prevent faults in service delivery by regular monitoring of results, developing systems audit and by creating quality circles and adopting quality standards such as BS 5750 and TQM.[37]

There are inevitably differing judgements and opinions on these developments. There are those who take a very positive, inspirational attitude, that change is inevitable if not good and local authorities should see problems as an opportunity and 'run with it',[38] and indeed there are calls to go further.[39] Others give cautious approval and see the public–private distinction as too stark or exaggerated.[40] Some see the Citizen's Charter as creating too narrow a focus,[41] seeing people as customers and not as citizens who have other, wider, civic interests beyond those of the consumer. There are sceptics who see the new 'private style of public management' as superficial – makeover management dreamed up by consultants – and amounting to no more than 'Have a nice day!', whilst others are very concerned at the effects of the importation of private-sector business methods and attitudes on the concept and practice of public service; it has been called 'ethic cleansing'.[42] Much more critical are those who detect a further manifestation of capitalist over other values, and see the management changes as 'managerialism' and disguised forms of discrimination or worker exploitation (i.e. through performance measurement, flexible arrangements for pay and conditions, etc.).[43] The government's quest for Best Value among local authorities will add another dimension (see Chapter 15).

* *Portrait of change.*

Management services

(1) Personnel management

The Bains Report argued that local government tended to lag behind industry and other areas of the public service in its recognition and development of the personnel management function:

There must be a greater awareness of the importance of personnel management in local government. Manpower is a leading resource of any authority and must be properly deployed. The appointment of the senior officer responsible for personnel management is crucial . . . (p. xv)

Personnel and establishment officers had traditionally confined themselves to the oversight and administration of salaries and conditions of service. Since the 1970s the Personnel function has received greater recognition in local government and now takes a wider and more positive approach in order to promote the effectiveness of (costly) human resources and to create opportunities for flexibility and change when it becomes necessary. Thus personnel management, or human resources management (HRM), should encompass manpower planning, recruitment techniques, training, career development and industrial relations (though there are some chief officers who regard it as somewhat negative or out of touch with their particular departmental needs, especially where they see staff as being employed by the department rather than by the authority as a whole)[39]/[40]. Indeed some departments prefer to perform their own personnel function, but it remains largely a centrally provided/corporate function.*

The Investors in People (IIP) programme is perhaps the most comprehensive approach to staff development of recent years. Over 75 per cent of local authorities currently participate in it and identify such benefits as improved communication, cultural change and improved motivation and morale (with 57 per cent of councils reporting the latter to be 'moderately high' or 'high and buoyant'.* Training and management development has been increasing significantly in

* *Portrait of change*, LGMB, 1997.

the 1990s (with most emphasis being placed on specific skill development).

(2) Management techniques

Local authorities have also taken a greater interest in other management processes, techniques and services. 1967 saw the creation of the Local Authorities Management Services and Computer Committee (LAMSAC). This body's function was to coordinate research, development and training, to establish a central information library and to act as a clearing house for local authorities. In 1989 it was decided to set up the Local Government Management Board (LGMB) by merging LAMSAC with LACSAB (the employers' coordinating body; see p. 282) and the Local Government Training Board. This took effect in 1991. However, in 1999, the LGMB was divided into two Agencies, the Employers' Agency (which is concerned with pay and conditions: see p. 282) and the Improvement and Development Agency (IDA). The function of IDA is to support local authorities to improve their performance by collecting and disseminating good practice in management, the implementation of Best Value, and training and development (for councillors, managers and workforce). It also acts as a 'trouble-shooter' where individual councils fail inspections or by request (e.g. Liverpool in 1999).

Management services help management to plan, control and improve the activities of the organization. Broadly their role is either to assist the planning and decision-making process or to promote the efficiency of execution and value-for-money (VFM) expenditure. Some of the services will be grouped and centralized in a Management Services Unit; others may be dispersed and utilized in individual departments. The following is a brief description of the main management techniques.[44]

Planning, Programming and Budgeting Systems (PPBS) have been defined as methods of establishing what an organization is aiming to achieve – what its *objectives* are; which *activities* contribute to these objectives; and what is actually being achieved, or what the *outputs* are (such as the number of old people rehoused or the miles of road re-surfaced) in relation to expenditure.[45] A similar technique is *management by objectives*

(MbO), which generally seeks to pinpoint key tasks and set work targets for officers.

More measurable or quantifiable forms of work may be set targets as a result of *work study*. As the name implies this involves the investigation of work processes and the various factors which affect their operation (such as the layout of the office) with a view to improving their efficiency. It is often used as the basis for incentive bonus schemes, in refuse collection for example. It may also be used for job evaluation and the grading of posts.

Organization and methods (O&M) is concerned with the structure of an organizational unit and the way in which that unit operates to achieve its objectives. It is often applied to administrative arrangements to secure more efficient methods, for example by simplifying procedures and delegating more routine clerical operations so as to enable the professional staff to devote more time to their professional work.

Operational research (OR) is used to establish a more rational or scientific basis for management decision-making. It uses complex mathematical techniques, and local authorities have received guidance from the Local Government Operational Research Unit (established in 1965). The technique has been applied to operations such as refuse disposal, purchasing methods and urban planning.[46]

Another decision-making technique is *cost-benefit analysis* (CBA). This attempts to go beyond the immediate direct (or primary) costs and benefits of a service or project by taking into account the indirect or 'external' costs and benefits. Many of the latter are intangible and difficult to measure, since they involve social considerations. For example, the relative financial cheapness of high-rise dwellings may be offset by the social costs of the possible family distress they cause. But this analysis does have the merit of extending perspectives, of reducing to statistical terms matters which would otherwise be the subject of unscientific value judgements and of facilitating detailed consideration of alternative courses of action.

Network analysis may be used once a new project has been approved. It aims at providing a plan of action by analysing the project into component parts and recording them on an arrow network diagram. The implementation stages and the inter-relationships of the various activities then become clear and the work – such as school building or engineering projects – can be programmed. This procedure can give rise to a number of ancillary techniques such as *critical path analysis* (CPA), *programme evaluation and review* (PERT) and *resources allocation and multi-project scheduling* (RAMPS).

Many of these procedures will involve substantial use of the computer. Its advantages stem from its ability to store masses of information and solve very complex problems with speed and accuracy. The creation and accessing of databases and the general process of information systems management is now commonplace. *Performance indicators*, and various financial information and management techniques, such as *performance review*, *policy reviews* and *zero-base budgeting* (ZBB),[47] are becoming more prominent (though only 56 per cent of local authorities regularly evaluate their activities.)*

One procedure which is apparently under-utilized is 'value-management' (or value-analysis/engineering) which is a combination of process analysis (or O&M), cost accounting, brainstorming and benchmarking. The aim is to identify the function and cost of each element of activity under review and to improve the relationship between cost and function or purpose, i.e. to improve 'value'.†

How efficient is local government?

It is not easy to measure local government efficiency, since there are no indices of success as there are in the business world (such as profits or market penetration figures). Local government has to satisfy three criteria:

(1) *Relevance:* Is the local authority doing the right thing, pursuing the right policies, providing the appropriate service? A local authority's operations may be highly efficient but they may be irrelevant to the problems to be solved. Should local authorities engage in such activities as housing, refuse collection or transport services or should these be left to private enterprise or other public bodies? The

---

* See *Made to Measure*, LGMB, 1998.
† See *Local Government Chronicle*, 20 September 1998, p. 14 and *The Times*, 30 January 1997, pp. 38–9.

answer to this will depend on one's moral and political values as well as economic considerations. There is no simple test of what is 'right' for local government[48] (see Chapter 14).

(2) *Effectiveness:* If it is accepted that local authorities should provide certain services, such as welfare for children or the elderly, they may still be wasteful of resources even if they are efficient in making such provision. This may be due to their pursuing the wrong policies which limit the effectiveness of the operations. For example, a local authority may be building residential homes more cheaply than ever before or more cheaply than other local authorities, but the institutional form of care may not be contributing much to the welfare needs of deprived children or the elderly.

(3) *Efficiency:* Having identified a correct course of action, the local authority must seek to operate efficiently so that its actions are in themselves not wasteful, extravagant or incompetent. There is certainly a danger of inefficiency in this sense, since local authorities do not have the financial discipline of the market: they cannot make losses since they have the power of taxation. Furthermore, how does one measure inefficiency or extravagance? How much time should a social worker spend with a client? How many hours per week should a GCSE student receive in tuition? Some guidance can be obtained by making comparisons with other authorities, but such comparisons are difficult because local authorities vary considerably in their physical, social and economic characteristics. Local authorities' internal audit (see p. 395) and the government's external audit[49] may provide a check, as they detect unreasonable expenditure. But traditionally their function is to investigate the legality of financial transactions (for example that the correct fees have been charged and collected).

The various management techniques outlined above seek to improve the efficiency of local government operations. But many people are sceptical of the progress in this field,[50] pointing to the growth in local government manpower and rising local government costs (reflected in the local tax levels). Much of this is, of course, due to inflation (labour costs absorb some 70 per cent of local government expenditure) and part is due to increased responsibilities which the government has placed on councils. Some is also due to improved conditions of service (itself enhanced by the growth in trade-union activity in local government). Reorganization in the 1970s, with its widespread upgradings and golden handshakes, also added to costs, at least in the short run.

Perhaps the most significant change which is taking place is in the area of programme or output budgeting. Traditional indicators of performance in local government have been in terms of inputs: in the size and funding of the authority and its services (and so to a large extent local authorities have been more interested in improving – that is, expanding – services than merely reducing rates/taxes). Much more attention is now being given to performance and output measurement. This involves the clarification of objectives and the devising of techniques to measure the achievement of those objectives. Expenditure is thus considered in terms of its purpose or the activity it finances, for example the tons of rubbish collected per dustman, or in housing, the number of dwellings improved to a planned standard, or in education, the number of children acquiring basic skills by a given age.[51] A very public and nationwide example is the publication of schools' test (SATs) and examination results.

However, useful as such steps are, there are problems, especially in defining suitable output measures for many services and in particular those of administrative personnel. Bains suggested that performance should be subject to annual review, and 60 per cent of authorities have established performance review systems; a lot more is being done in this area. Consequently, many more indicators are being devised, such as staff–student ratios, student retention (or drop-out) rates, area cleaned per hour, library-book stock or issues per head, numbers of visits, inspections or cases dealt with per week, speed of response to letters or complaints, etc. The pursuit of the '3 Es' (economy, efficiency and effectiveness) is not easy, and satisfactory performance indicators are difficult to devise in services where quality as well as quantity is important. But the Audit Commission regularly provides data to enable local authorities to compare their own performance with that of a group (or 'family') of authorities with similar features (e.g. see Appendix 15).

Following the Citizen's Charter and the Local Government Act 1992, the Audit Commission (see p. 399) has a duty to specify a list of performance indicators (PIs) which every local authority in England

and Wales is obliged to report annually. In 1993 the Commission produced a list of 152* such measures of performance (many of which are not new) and local authorities publish the specified information in local newspapers each year (see Appendix 15) or in their annual reports. (The Commission itself publishes summaries.) The Best Value process is requiring councils to undertake fundamental reviews of their services and provision, and value for money is critical (see p. 593).

Although local government is often denigrated for its inefficiency, in 1985 the Audit Commission concluded that 'the best of Local Government is better than the private sector and much better than the NHS or Whitehall at delivering services. This was endorsed by others – indeed in 1998 Tony Blair said that at its best, local government is 'brilliant' – and on the evidence of recent surveys, the general public seem well satisfied with the services provided by local authorities. Thus, the Consumers Association[52] found nearly two thirds of those interviewed thought local authority services were good value for money and four out of five were satisfied overall with the quality of their services. A survey for the Audit Commission[53] revealed 54 per cent were satisfied with council services. The Widdicombe Committee[54] found more than 70 per cent of respondents very or fairly satisfied with the performance of their councils, and a survey for Professor W. Miller[55] found a figure of 75 per cent. Furthermore, as Miller discovered, although there may be a general preference to cut services rather than raise rates, when voters 'are confronted with specific cuts in the big-spending services then they tend to favour the maintenance of those services'. Other surveys have found the same result† and a referendum in Milton Keynes in February 1999 showed a substantial majority voting for a 10 per cent rather than a 5 per cent rise in council tax (on a 45 per cent poll – much higher than the 26 per cent turnout in the previous local election).

Recent surveys confirm that there is a satisfaction rating of around 50 per cent,[56] and these compare favourably against other agencies (such as 18 per cent for the EU in 1996 and 34 per cent and 23 per cent for Parliament in 1996 and 1997 respectively). But some compari-

* Not all of which applied to each authority. The list has since been reduced.
† See P. Gooby-Taylor, *Welfare: Means to an end*, Macmillan, 1999.

sons have been distinctly unfavourable. For example, relative to the firm BT, public ratings were: 'reponsiveness to customer needs' 10 per cent / 56 per cent, 'open and honest' 6 per cent / 29 per cent, and 'communicates well' 11 per cent / 62 per cent* – all in favour of BT! Overall, there was evidence of improvement in public satisfaction over the decade from the mid-1980s (due largely to greater customer orientation and responsiveness). But there have been periods of deterioration too – during the the poll tax years and in the wake of various municipal corruption scandals, DLO bankruptcies and serious policy or management failures: see MORI poll in *LGC*, 26 November 1999. It is also possible that general satisfaction with council provision may be a reflection or spin-off of satisfaction with life in general.†

Nevertheless, council management has been criticized following the child-abuse revelations in Clwyd, Cleveland, Staffordshire ('pindown'), Orkney and Leicestershire, the interest-rate 'swaps' in Hammersmith and Fulham, and the financial losses or waste in the Western Isles and Brent councils. More recent have been the scandals of child abuse in care homes in North Wales and lapses in Coventry's procedures for dealing with at-risk children and their homecare costings for services for the elderly and disabled (as a result of which the government announced, in November 1998, that it was to take over much of local authorities' inspection and control systems.) There have also been some spectacular failures in education/schools (such as in Hackney and Calderdale).

Numerous reports by the Audit Commission have detailed failings in local authorities in a variety of areas, including rent arrears, special needs education, police, property management, support for the arts and surplus school places. And in 1995 it suggested that weak management and archaic work practices contributed to an estimated waste of £1bn (though much of the blame also lay with the government for 'imposing new and radical changes on to local authorities'.‡ In 1999, the AC criticized local authorities schemes for economic regeneration

---

* Most of the surveys indicate that councils are better regarded where they publicize themselves more.
† See H. Davis *et al.*, *New perspectives on local governance*, JRF, 1998.
‡ Audit Commission, *Paying the piper* and *Calling the tune*, HMSO, 1995.

as short term, fragmented and overlapping i.e. wasteful (see *A Life's Work*, Audit Commission, 1999). In 1998 *The Sunday Times* (15 March) estimated that local authorities are losing £1.5bn per annum as a result of uncollected council tax, rent arrears, unfilled school places, housing benefit fraud and empty houses (up to 2.7 per cent in England, from 1.9 per cent in 1992).

Like schools' examinations league tables, there may be good reasons for the considerable variations displayed by local authority Performance Indicators. Instant judgement (or condemnation) can be unfair. Nevertheless, the following examples are bound to raise questions as to: Why can one council complete the administrative procedures for all its special needs pupils within six months while others can only achieve it for 10 per cent of them? Why do some councils take twice the time (over 20 weeks) as others to re-let their houses? Why can some councils pay students grants on time and others can't? Why can one inner London authority process 99 per cent of council tax benefit claims within 14 days while another can only achieve 44 per cent? Why do some metropolitan councils achieve a 100 per cent inspection of food premises while others are below 50 per cent? Why do some authorities have higher proportions of 75-year-olds in residential care compared to others, or aim to deliver a bath to a home in two weeks while for others it is three months? Why do education administration costs vary from £17 to £167 per pupil? Why does rent arrears range from 2.6 per cent, in District councils, 3.6 per cent in Unitaries, 4.9 per cent in the Mets and over 10 per cent in London? And similar questions can be asked about the wide-ranging variations in charges. The government's programme of Best Value for local authorities is intended to root out inefficiencies and bring standards up to those of the best run councils (see p. 583). See too *Sunday Times* 11 April 1999, p. 12 and *The Times*, 24 January 1999, p. 8.

Local authorities face other problems in trying to give value for money. Councillors, as elected politicians, may wish to see reductions in overall expenditure and rates, but will urge particular expenditures, especially for their own localities.[57] And unlike their opposite numbers in the business world, the top managers (chief officers) are not autonomous: the chief executive officer does not have the authority of a managing director of a company or an American 'city manager' to 'hire and fire', and the chair of the council or of a major committee has nothing like the authority of the chair of a public company. Besides, broadly speaking, councils are anxious to avoid redundancies; as good employers, they are normally conscious of their responsibilities as regards the employment situation in their areas (though less so in recent years). But perhaps the biggest contrast to the business world is local government's system of dual management. We consider this below.

Member–officer relationships

Like Whitehall, local government is characterized by the system of 'dual management', i.e. the political management of the elected members and the executive management of the appointed officers. The traditional view of the relationship between members and officers is that of master and servant: the council issues orders and the officers carry them out. Such a view is based on the rational, democratic principle that councillors are elected to make policy decisions and the expert is engaged to execute those decisions. Furthermore, the law appears to support such a view: in the Bognor Regis case (1965) the QC conducting the inquiry concluded that

. . . if a Clerk is not answerable to his council he is answerable to no one. In my view he is the employee of his council and it is to them that his primary loyalty and duty lie and it is to them that he is answerable for his actions.[58]

In practice, the notion that the council formulates policy is substantially qualified by the fact that many responsibilities are delegated to officers (especially since the Local Government Acts of 1972 and 1973).* But a more important modification lies in the long-standing fact that local government officers advise the council and its committees. This is both inevitable and desirable: after all, the officers are full-time and permanent, and with training and experience acquire considerable expertise. Members can therefore scarcely avoid placing considerable reliance on their judgement: the range of policy and individual matters

* For illustration, see Appendix 13.

of administration is too great to be managed by part-time members. According to the Maud Report:

> In nearly two thirds of the authorities we consulted officers were said to make a significant contribution to the initiation of policy and in nearly a quarter they were said to play the major part.[59]

It is this advisory role which, in the words of the Bains Report, explodes 'the myth of policy being a matter for the elected members and administration for officers'.

> We do not believe that it is possible to lay down what is policy and what is administrative detail; some issues stand out patently as important and can be regarded as 'policy'; other matters, seemingly trivial, may involve political or social reaction of such significance that deciding them becomes a matter of policy and members feel that they must reserve to themselves consideration and decision on them. A succession of detailed decisions may contribute, eventually, to the formulation of a policy . . . policy making can arise out of particular problems when consideration of a new case leads to the determination of general guides to action which have a general application.[60]

Thus administrative details shade imperceptibly into policy and both officers and members therefore play a part in policy-making and in detailed administration. Bains refers to it as the 'dual nature of management' and likens it (in the words of one witness to the committee) to a scale or spectrum, with the setting of objectives and allocation of major resources at one end, moving through the designing of programmes and plans, to the execution of those plans at the other end. At all points on the scale, as in a partnership, both the elected and the official elements are involved, but to varying degrees. This may be illustrated as follows:

Policy/objectives   Members   Officers   Execution/administration

A question of trust

Clearly Councillors and officers need to be able to trust each other*
As the Nolan Committee said:

No local authority can function properly without a good relationship between
its councillors and its officers. Where the relationship breaks down, an atmosphere of suspicion or dislike can make it very difficult to devise and implement
policies in any consistent way ... but ... defining the precise boundary
between matters dealt with by officers and those by councillors was very
difficult. (*Standards of Conduct in Local Government, Standards in Public Life*, vol. 1,
Cmd 3702, 1997)

Yet there are built-in tensions to the relationship – as between experienced professionals and amateur politicians who sweep in and out on
the party political tide and often on a low turnout and/or majority.
As the 'experts', officers advise councillors. Like civil servants, their
advice is expected to be impartial or politically neutral. But it may be
too neutral; thus when councillors reject a policy recommended by
officers, the latter will feel that their ideas developed out of their
specialized knowledge and are politically neutral. But councillors may
not regard professional values as being neutral and will prefer policies
which are consistent with political philosophy (they may also be
concerned with the impact of policies on the electorate and so may
reject even a wise policy if it seems unattractive to voters). Consequently, senior officers need to work out measures which are in the
spirit of the ruling party, to develop a 'common mind' with the political
leadership (though clearly this is difficult in a hung council and would
be easier in others if the appointment of senior officers were to be
political). Another potentially difficult area is that of the 'stop' power
of the finance officer and the warning power of the monitoring or
chief executive officers (see p. 299).

---

* See *All You Need is Trust*, LGMB, 1998.

Points of contact

The member–officer relationship occurs in a number of settings. Some of these are *formal*, such as council meetings, committees, joint meetings with other local or regional and central authorities, and ceremonial occasions. There may, for example, be joint meetings of the officers' management team and the P & R committee, and many chief officers attend meetings of the P & R committee as a matter of course. *Semi-official* meetings take place at site visits, disaster areas (such as those damaged by flood) or in departments when a councillor calls in to discuss a constituency matter. And there is an increased tendency for chief officers to attend party group (caucus) meetings.[61] Finally, officers and members may meet *informally* at the club, in the pub or at civic socials (though as the National Code says, while 'mutual respect between councillors and officers is essential to good local government, close personal familiarity between individual councillors and officers can damage this relationship and prove embarrassing to other councillors and officers'.

It is usually assumed that the most important of these is the first, particularly committee meetings. At this level there is a close relationship between chief officers and committee chairs (and vice-chairs). This situation may be changing somewhat in so far as councils are setting up panels or 'working groups' of officers and members with the task of examining particular issues or areas in order to discover the facts or possible courses of action rather than make any decisions. In addition, in so far as programme committees have been formed, the committee chairs will each have to relate to a number of chief officers rather than develop a close working relationship with just one.

In the traditional setting, this close relationship between the chair and the chief officer was the result of their working in their particular service area (education, social services, finance, etc.). The chair would be in regular contact with the department; he or she may have had an office there, and would attend pre-committee briefing meetings (and perhaps agenda meetings) so as to be kept informed of latest developments before the formal committee takes place. And in the meantime he or she may be called upon to make decisions or approve the actions of the senior officers. Above all, as a consequence of their

respective roles and time commitment, there is a particularly close working relationship between council leaders and chief executives. (There
is some uncertainty and anxiety about the role and security of chief
executives as new management structures are introduced. It is felt that
management change may be the pretext for councillors to replace them
because 'they want a new face' or for party reasons; and their responsibilities to the minority groups and non-executive scrutiny committees
rather than to the executive cabinet or mayor may become unclear.)*

Where the power lies

Sir John Maud, himself an ex-civil servant, was concerned that
members were getting too involved in matters of day-to-day administration at the expense of the officers, whose capacities were thus being
under-utilized. Consequently the Maud Report recommended:

It is members who should take and be responsible for the key decisions on
objectives, and on the means and plans to attain them. It is they who must
periodically review the position as part of their function of directing and
controlling. It is the officers who should provide the necessary staff work and
advice which will enable the members to identify the problems, set the
objectives and select the means and plans to attain them. It is the officer who
should direct and co-ordinate the necessary action, and see that material is
presented to enable members to review progress and check performance.[62]

However, the situation seems to have got worse, with evidence 'that
suggests that councillors want their presence felt at far lower levels
within the organisation than had previously been the case'.†

In 1989, the Audit Commission suggested that the greater delegation
of decision-making to officers would reduce both costs and conflict.[63]
And in 1993 the working party report on internal management (see
p. 262 above) made recommendations which it was hoped would
'reduce the focus of attention by councillors on detailed administration
to enable them to concentrate on strategic issues' [para. 2.7] (though
with strengthened scrutiny and monitoring powers). The new statutory

* See *Local Government Chronicle*, 8 January 1999, p. 1.
† C. Exeter, 'Strained Relations', *Municipal Journal*, 29 Nov. 1996, pp. 14–15.

arrangements (in the Local Government Act 2000) for separating the roles of councillors (into 'strategists' and 'scrutineers/izers') is designed to achieve this.

However, more people see the problem not as one of too much interference in administration by members but rather as one of too much influence on policy by officials: that is, they see the problem as one of 'bureaucracy' or 'managerialism'. After all, members are amateurs (non-experts), they are part-time and they are (largely) unpaid. They can therefore be easily dominated by the full-time professionals, especially when they adopt the corporate approach, with its seemingly conspiratorial groupings, its somewhat alien language and its coordinated advice which is so pre-packaged, plausible and persuasive. There is evidence to suggest that the power of senior officers has increased at the expense of councillors as a result of such developments as competitive tendering and EU, as well the greatly increased use of working parties and working groups.[64]

Such dominance by officials may occur because of their superior knowledge, and this may be the product of the way central government relates to local authorities, i.e. dealing with officers rather than councillors, even to the latters' exclusion. For example, in 1982 government inspectors' (HMIs) reports on the effects of expenditure cuts on education provision in certain LEAs were sent to chief officers under conditions of such confidentiality that in some cases elected members were not given the information.[65] Councillors have also complained at being denied access to their local authority's committee proceedings and documents, though this has been substantially overcome by the House of Lords' ruling in the Birmingham case[66] and by the Local Government (Access to Information) Act 1985. (MPs have made similar complaints about their role in Parliament, although, unlike councillors, they have no direct responsibility for administration.)

Sir Horace Cutler, a former Conservative leader of the GLC (1977–81), declared that 'it is because we have not enough people with discernment that officials are able to take advantage of elected members and do very much as they please ... Paper is useful in baffling councillors when bureaucrats want to get their own way. Documents go on endlessly when it would be perfectly possible to reduce them to the important facts. As a result, policies can be manipulated and distorted so that they slip through in a totally different fashion from what was intended.'[67]

A more striking lack of trust between members and officers was vividly revealed in Walsall Borough Council in 1980. Here the Labour members suspected that when they gained office after the elections officials would undermine or thwart their policies. Consequently, to help secure the achievement of their manifesto objectives, they declared their intention of appointing only officers whose social awareness was 'akin to Labour philosophy'. (Such 'politicization' of officials is similar to the 'spoils' system operating in the USA, whereby the top levels of the civil service are replaced when a new party gains the Presidency. The Local Government and Housing Act 1989 now requires appointments to be based on merit alone (though the Widdicombe research showed that such partisan intrusion into the making of appointments was limited in scale).[68] A more moderate approach (which models itself on recent central government practices in Britain and longer experience in France) is being tried in some local authorities: here, special advisers are brought in to provide support services such as research and policy analysis and to advise the council (the majority party) on policy or to help keep policy running in line with party ideology or plans.

The general premise here then is that local government is run by officials; they are 'statesmen in disguise', and the existence of elected members merely provides a democratic veneer.

Such a view is no more tenable than that of the ever-meddling councillor. However, to say that the true situation lies somewhere in between is too simple. There may well be authorities which are substantially run by the officers; and there may be those in which weak or intimidated officers push upwards to councillors trivial administrative decisions. However, it is quite possible to have a combination of these situations so that councillors become heavily involved in routine administrative decisions (see p. 254) while effective control and initiation of major policy decisions rest with the officers. A chief officer has suggested that 'Local government is full of transvestites, members who want to take control of detail and officers who want to make policy.' Furthermore there can be variations among departments within the same authority. In one authority, although the housing manager could himself sanction all repairs and maintenance work below a total of £3.5 million, the children's officer could spend only £10 per case without reference to the committee.[69]

Undoubtedly officers can and do exert substantial influence, since most of the discussion at committee meetings is based on the reports drawn up by senior officers. Most of these reports are well-informed and often based on the guidelines of statute law or central government advice (circulars and official memoranda) which is the familiar province of officers. And although the reports often point out the implications of following certain policy lines or provide a number of options from which the committee may choose, the main themes underlying the reports are influential in the sense of tending to focus discussion and thus limit the range of thinking (especially if there is no alternative paper to consider). In this and other ways, officers, perhaps unconsciously, will filter the information which comes before members. In addition, officers attend committee meetings and they normally speak: indeed some may insist on speaking[70] – they might even have a greater moral claim to local knowledge than the more mobile, less native members. But they need not even speak in order to exercise some influence:

The reality of the formal proceedings of council and committee meetings is that the elected members meet in the presence of officers to consider reports prepared by the officers containing recommendations for action made by the officers. The meetings thus differ from other meetings . . . in that information and advice from experts is rendered in person whilst the process of decision-making is under way. This . . . offers to the officers the opportunity for the well-timed remark, the cautionary aside to the chairman, even the occasional sigh or grimace, which might prevent the councillors taking a decision unwelcome to the officers.[71]

As one chief officer has stated, councillors 'should be led to the right conclusion under the impression that they are arriving at it under their own steam'.[72]

Not all officers, however, are strong-minded or have a 'line' on policy: there may not exist a departmental view on policy, and still less likely is there to be a monolithic official view. Corporate management tends perhaps to encourage such a development, but it is far from being achieved, and it is by no means unknown for differences of opinion among officers to be displayed at committee meetings,[73] which can place the chair in an awkward situation.

The extent of official influence on policy-making is significantly determined by the role played by the committee chairs. They work closely with the senior officers, though how much one will influence the other will depend on personality, on mutual respect and on whether theirs is a close or an arm's-length relationship. In practice there is a range of such relationships, with some committee chairs taking a strong lead and severely limiting the officers' contribution, while others are prepared to play a backseat role, perhaps to the extent of appearing as mouthpiece or ventriloquist's doll to the chief officer. Some chairs surrender, others are captured.[74] Whether the chairs themselves carry influence with their committees will also vary. Some are respected, popular, acknowledged as leaders. Others are seen as party placemen. And in some authorities, they will tend to carry less weight if they have achieved office merely on the basis of 'Buggin's turn next'.

It used to be said that county councils are run by the officers and town councils by the members. The evidence for such a view was related to some extent to the existence or non-existence of political parties or the political zeal of members.[75] However, in so far as it was ever true, recent events will have an impact in that party politics are now more pervasive and reorganization has diluted the town–country distinction.

Party politicization has led to a greater 'hands-on' approach to the running or management of local authorities by councillors.[76] Apart from anything else this has meant councillors becoming more involved in 'routine' administration (agenda setting, vetting minutes, drafting committee reports), more assertive and proactive in committees and pre-committee briefings, and more active in and inquisitive about policy implementation (with more frequent visits to departments, to the extent that some, especially full-time, chairs virtually shadow or duplicate the chief officer). It has also meant officers being more drawn into the political process (attending party group meetings, help with manifestos, helping to find creative financial solutions).

Thus, compared to the past, there is now a certain amount of role-exchange or perhaps 'blur' (especially with the increase in full-time members). 'In some areas full-time members are getting close to an executive role and chief executives have been going out in a rather ambassadorial role representing the authority as an elected member or even elected mayor might'.* It remains to be seen whether or how the new management structures and differentiated councillor roles will affect this situation.

In general, however, it may be dangerous to try to make any sort of general statement about the relative importance to decision-making of officers and members. It is 'a fundamental error to believe . . . that one set of relationships exists throughout our infinitely variable local government system'.[77] That author goes on to suggest that the relationship depends on a number of characteristics including: (a) the range and size of the authority's service provision, (b) the degree of professionalism among its officers, (c) the existence of political party arrangements, (d) the sensitivity to local public opinion and (e) the extent of central government involvement. On the basis of these factors a range of possible situations is suggested, from those where 'the officer runs the show' to others where 'the party rules and officers do what they are told – or get out'. The emergence of more assertive parties is creating melting pots for many long-standing conventional arrangements and established practices (see p. 541) and there is evidence that it is placing a strain on member–officer relations.[78] This may be compounded by the shortening of councillors' time-horizons as the system of annual or more frequent elections is applied. (See below Chapter 15.)† That mistrust can exist between members and officers was illustrated in the local ombudsman's investigation (in December 1988) of the way in which Westminster London Borough council had disposed of cemeteries. He found maladministration arising from a failure to communicate between members and officers, and stated:

Members believed, or gave the impression that they believed, that some officers were intent on 'sabotaging' their policy of running the council on more businesslike lines. Officers felt that their service to the council . . . was not valued, and that members did not trust them . . . They felt that any suggestion that the ideas of the leading members should not or could not be implemented without amendment would be considered to be undermining

* *Local Government Chronicle*, 24 January 1997, p. 5.
† See too S. Leach *et al.*, *All you need is trust*, LGMB, 1998.

the majority party policy. But officers have a duty to give advice to all members even when they suspect it will be unpalatable. Here they failed in their duty.

Within any particular authority the relationship of officers to members will vary with local custom, convention and local political culture: in some authorities, officers will grow up with (or be sharply taught)[79] the notion that policy is councillors' business and officers must keep clear. This was graphically illustrated in Lambeth LB council in April 1992 when party political differences spilled over into the abuse and baiting of officers (the police were also called in to deal with a brawl between councillors!). A survey in 1992 showed that chief executives find dealing with councillors and political difficulties a stressful aspect of their work,[80] there is clearly a need for greater mutual understanding.[81] The relationship will also depend on personality, since, in practice, power is not shared equally even among members themselves. Chairmanships, council leadership, policy committees, in-groups and out-groups, etc. all have variable effects, and there are individual differences in members' sense of justice or mission, in their tenacity, in their time and devotion to duty. And there are also differences in their 'legitimacy' (their claim to act as decision-makers), especially since some councillors are barely elected and others not elected at all (see p. 153).

Finally the relative importance of members and officers will vary with the nature of the issue. Matters involving delicate human problems (such as rent arrears by single-parent families) may require the members' common sense rather than the officers' specialized knowledge. Similar considerations apply in controversial matters, likely to arouse strong feelings in the locality, such as the use of the Welsh language in Welsh schools. If, on the other hand, the question is highly technical in character, such as a flood-relief scheme or the purchase of a computer, the tendency is for members to accept the recommendations of the officers.

Rather than deciding whether it is one group or another which has the upper hand, some observers[82] suggest that it is both together, with senior councillors and officers forming a 'dual elite'. Clearly there is much in this interpretation, especially in view of the 'corporate revolution' of the 1970s. Some see the recommendations of the working party on internal management (see p. 268 above) as reinforcing this tendency (though the report does also seek to provide a balance by increasing the 'backbench' councillors' powers to monitor and scrutinize). However, the interpretation may be challenged[83] on various grounds. Firstly, it perhaps too readily assumes a cohesion or unity of view. As we have seen above, this is by no means assured. Secondly, there is the increased readiness of councillors in general, and of party-based councillors in particular, to assert themselves and challenge the official view and the chief officers' 'right to manage'. As the researchers for the Widdicombe Committee found:

. . . in a situation where quite clearly the political environment of local authorities is changing . . . it is almost inevitable that frictions between . . . the worlds of members and officers will be created.[84]

And

Whereas in the past chairmen (of committees) saw their role, in many instances, as that of persuading the group to accept lines agreed between themselves and the chief officers, they are now more likely to act as a channel in the opposite direction, from the group to the chief officer, advising that certain recommendations will not be accepted, or that alternative options should be investigated.[85]

Further

It is becoming increasingly common for members to expect free access to whomsoever they wish to talk to in a department, rather than to feel obliged to operate through a chief officer . . . There is a growing awareness that policies will be judged by those they affect not in terms of documents agreed in committee or council, but rather in terms of how they are delivered to service recipients.[86]

Thirdly, not only may backbench councillors exercise much influence in private party caucus meetings in devising the party programme, but they can and are likely to press for the full implementation of the manifesto policies[87] (with 63 per cent of councillors seeing this as their primary concern[88]). Fourthly, the experience of the recently hung or balanced councils suggests that much of the decision-making is the result (understandably) of inter-party negotiation and bargaining, with such dealings involving more than simply the party leaderships. The

role of the committee chairs is reduced and/or rotated and 'all members
... are politically active and politically important ... a no-majority
council enhances the roles of individual council members in decision-
making'.[89] Fifthly, there are inevitably inter-departmental conflicts or
rivalries, for example, differences over professional territory: does land
development 'belong' to the planners, architects or housing managers?
Is truancy properly an education or a social service matter? There
may be differences too over policy, for example whether to pursue a
more or less free market philosophy.

Finally, as suggested above, we must not too readily assume unity
within departments. It is becoming more apparent that chief officers
experience tensions and pressures from inside their own departments
as junior officials bring their own influences to bear (deriving perhaps
from their greater specialist expertise, more recent education and
training or their experience and contacts developed through area-
based administration). This is partly also a consequence of the more
consensual or human relations approach to management.

All this is not to deny a place to the 'joint elite' concept of power
relationships. But it is clear that power does not lie at any given point
in the British system of local government.[90] Instead there are a number
of actual or potential centres of power – the policy committee, the
officers' team, the individual chief officers or committee chairs (or
both together), the party group, the whole council, etc. So, rather than
seeing power as consisting of a hierarchy or series of concentric circles
spreading from a small apex or central point, it might be more accurate
to see local government power-points as consisting of a series or cluster
of more or less influential groupings, varying in size in relation to time
and issue. If, in general, councillors feel themselves to be somewhat
at a disadvantage in their relationship to officers, perhaps they should
do something about it by improving their own back-up services and
procedures, using such means as properly organized research, training
and secretarial services.[91]

The payment of allowances to members since 1974, the introduction
of special responsibility allowances to committee and council chairs
in 1980, and the more general payment introduced in 1990 (see p. 212),
provide some recognition of the fact that the work can no longer be
left on an amateur basis in the hands of relatively few councillors.[92]

11

FINANCE

In the nineteenth century there was a political conundrum about the constitutional status of the territory near what is now Denmark, called Schleswig-Holstein. At the time it was said that only three people really understood the correct position: one of these was dead, another had gone mad and the third had forgotten! Some people believe that local government finance is like this, especially the grant structure.

The scale of expenditure

Local government is big business. Councils spend nearly £75,000 million a year (£1,300 per person). This amounts to 25 per cent of all state spending and nearly 10 per cent of the National Income (GNP). They manage a total debt of £40,000 million and, as we saw in Chapter 10, local government employs 2 million staff (about one worker in ten in Britain works for local government). Local authorities are also big property owners, landlords and shareholders.

However, local government has not always been so important in economic terms. Although in 1951 it was responsible for spending about £1,300 million (about 9 per cent of GNP), at the beginning of this century the figure was only about £100 million (5 per cent of GNP).[1] Local government has grown as Britain committed itself to the idea of the Welfare State and as legislation has extended the responsibilities of local authorities in the fields of education, housing, social work, transport and the protective services.

Much of local government's expenditure is therefore a result of decisions by the central government and Parliament. For example the Education Act 1944 requires local education authorities to provide schools and teachers, and since the Children's Act 1948 they have been obliged to provide a service for deprived children. In addition the central government may lay down certain standards for those services which may be scrutinized by means of inspection (via Her Majesty's Inspectors, or HMIs). But local authorities also spend money in response to local demands and needs, whether expressed through elections and pressure groups or discerned by professional judgement. Certain services are optional, and local authorities decide whether and at what standard to provide them.

But even then local authorities do not have an entirely free hand to determine their levels of spending. They are faced with pressures which arise from their own local economic and social conditions (they may have a backlog of run-down areas to be cleared and re-developed or a growing number of old people to be accommodated), or from public expectations and aspirations about the appropriate levels of service (for example, as regards traffic congestion, street cleaning or school crossing patrols). Furthermore, local authorities are committed to certain expenditures under national pay agreements (see Chapter 8) and by joint financing (or 'pooling') schemes, such as with health authorities for community care.[2] Finally, there is the legacy of previous spending: if a local authority opens a new school or welfare home, it will be committed to paying for it for many years, for, even if it were closed down in order to save the running costs, loan charges would still have to be paid.

Capital and revenue expenditure

Analysing finance is fraught with difficulties and many of these are the result of the variety of definitions which exist – whether the figures are net or gross, whether depreciation has been taken into account, are the figures at factor cost or market prices (i.e. do they include VAT and other taxes?), are they indexed to allow for inflation, do they allow for rebates and benefits and for inter-authority transactions, etc. Thus can opponents quote different statistics to prove their point and both be right!

One of the key distinctions is between *capital* items and *revenue* items.

Expenditure for new roads, school buildings, libraries or residential homes is an example of what is called 'capital' expenditure. Such expenditure implies that the object of expenditure has a long life: it is an asset. Such items are usually very expensive: they involve a heavy outlay, and for that reason they tend to be financed largely from borrowed money (and so repaid over a long period). Short-lived items – fuel, typing paper, the manpower services of teachers etc. – are known as 'revenue' (or current) expenditure. They are consumed as soon as they are purchased or a short time afterwards, and thus are regularly re-purchased. Such items are paid for out of current revenues rather than borrowed money.

The distinction between capital and revenue items is not always clear-cut: some items could be classified either way (school books for example), but the distinction is important, for in general it is felt that an expensive asset – such as a sports centre or swimming pool, or a fleet of vehicles (refuse wagons or buses) – should in fairness be paid for by the beneficiaries – those who do or could use them. It would be unfair to spend £1 million on a new swimming pool and charge the full cost to the ratepayers in one year: many of those ratepayers will move away from the area or die while the asset continues to give service, and new residents (who will not have paid anything towards the pool) will move in and be able to make use of it. By borrowing money to purchase a capital item, a local authority can spread the cost (of repayment plus interest) over a number of years and so among the actual or potential beneficiaries. Consequently, capital expenditure is often financed by borrowing, (though the figure has fallen substantially in recent years as capital expenditure has fallen and loans have been repaid, especially as a result of government limits on the re-use of asset sale funds: see p. 384). Councils thus have a loan debt of £40,000 million (which costs them about £3½ billion a year (see Table 18). Most is owed to the government (i.e. to the Public Works Loan Board; see p. 382).

A high proportion of local government expenditure is thus committed in loan charges. As a result any move to cut government expenditure cannot be made 'across the board' (say 10 per cent off all items) because the debt interest expenditure is protected: it *must* be paid or local authorities will be defaulting on their creditors. The cuts must therefore

Table 18 *Local government gross expenditure (by service category), England, 1997*

Current/Revenue items			Capital items	
£m	%		£m	%
23,260	33	Education, libraries, arts, museums	900	14
5,000	7	Environmental services	1,100	17
3,430	5	Transport	1,200	18
11,250	16	Housing (including benefit payments)	2,500	38
10,400	15	Personal social services	200	3
8,960	13	Fire, police, probation	330	5
850	1	Sports and recreation	200	3
5,850	8	Other (including debt interest)	70	1
69,000	100	Total	6,500	100

Source: Local Government Financial Statistics, DETR, 1998.

fall more heavily on the other items of expenditure, that is on the services provided by the local authorities (though some of these too are protected, where they are statutory or compulsory, with the result that other services – the non-statutory – are particularly vulnerable).

Local government expenditure

Table 18 shows that local government is spending some £75,000 million a year. Within this total, the principal item of capital expenditure is housing (comprising about 40 per cent of that total). Current or revenue expenditure is dominated by education (comprising 33 per cent of that total).

There are considerable differences in the magnitude of expenditure among the different types and tiers of local authority. Among English authorities 30 per cent is spent by shire counties, 25 per cent by metropolitan authorities, 20 per cent by London boroughs, 15 per cent by unitary councils and 10 per cent by district councils. Similarly local

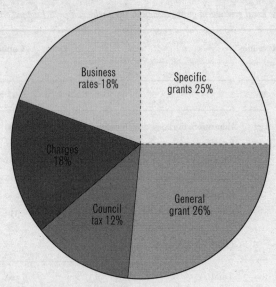

Figure 18 *Local government revenue (1997)*

authorities' income patterns vary considerably, with the shire counties for example depending a great deal more on grants than on local tax (precept) revenues.

Local government income

Local authorities derive their income from three main sources: (1) from the rents and fees they charge for services (car parks, residential care, etc.); (2) from grants or subsidies which they receive from the central government (housing subsidies, etc.); and (3) from local taxation (the rates or council tax). In addition they receive a number of miscellaneous revenues, such as interest and dividends, the proceeds of sales of land and property (such as council houses or county farms) and, for the purpose of capital items, by borrowing. Each of these is dealt with in some detail below, and their relative importance is shown in Table 19 and Figure 18. What the table does not show is how the

Table 19 *Local government income, England, 1997*

Current/Revenue			Capital	
£m	%		£m	%
		Central government funded		
12,700	18	Non-domestic/business rates		
18,000	26	Revenue support/general grant		
17,800	25	Specific/allocated grants	1,800	34
		Local authority funded		
8,600	12	Council tax		
13,100	18	Charges (including rents)		
		Sales of assets (houses, land etc.)	2,200	41
		Other	1,300	25
70,200	100	Total	5,300	100

Source: Local Government Financial Statistics, DETR, 1998.

pattern is changing over the years, notably the rise in the importance of government grants (for example from less than 30 per cent in 1951 to over 50 per cent) and the recent fall in local authority borrowing and the rise in (house) sales income.[3]

(1) Charges and miscellaneous incomes

Local authorities have long received small sums of money from a variety of sources – licence fees (entertainment and dog licences, birth, marriage and death certificates, etc.), library and parking fines or permits, interest on its loans to house purchasers and dividend receipts from its investments (of superannuation funds for example). Since the Lotteries Act 1976 local authorities have been able to run local lotteries for particular purposes or projects. These were quite successful initially, with 350 being registered with the Gaming Board[4] by 1979, with a turnover of £21 million. But they have since declined, with only about fifty in operation (mainly seaside towns) and dealing in sums of £30,000–50,000 a year.

Larger sums are derived, especially recently, from the sale of land and property[5] and from loan repayments from those who borrow from local authorities and from various external sources – the European Union (see p. 451), public bodies (such as the Sports Council), the government itself (see below) and the National Lottery.* Such is the importance of these sources that local authorities appoint specialist External Funding officers to pursue them, especially through the competitive bidding process (see p. 381). Thus, for example, using such sources councils have obtained various sums, including Westminster LBC £347m over three years to 1998, Norwich £51m and NE Derbyshire £273,000). (Education Action Zones have been created to improve standards in schools in disadvantaged areas. Groups of schools bid for this status which results in private–public management schemes. Apart from cash donations, there may be private sector management provision and advice, mentoring and sponsorship of books and equipment.)† Advertising in schools and elsewhere is another source which has helped to pay, for example, for extra teachers, crossing patrols, highway roundabouts, etc. Local authorities also benefit from a variety of disguised and difficult-to-quantify forms of income or expenditure savings such as planning gain and voluntary service, e.g. by staff who work unpaid hours, or parents who act as classroom assistants, etc., or by voluntary organizations. Some councils have made savings through their staff working at home (e.g. Birmingham saved some 10–20 per cent of office space by home-working, teleworking and 'hot-desking'), and one Scottish council has sought to save on staff expenses when they are away on council business by getting them to stay with friends or relatives!

Local authorities also receive substantial revenues from their *charges* on a whole range of services (an estimated 600). Broadly speaking there are three groups of charges.[6] (a) For *trading* or commercial services, which include industrial waste disposal, passenger transport, slaughter houses, harbours and docks, civic aerodromes and markets.

---

* There are some misgivings about Lottery finance, as not only does it usually require matching funding by the council, but there is the risk that council services will be usurped, e.g. when the Heritage Lottery Fund is used for urban parks, museums, regeneration projects, piers, etc., which are traditionally local authority responsibilities.
† 90 per cent of secondary schools have links with business.

Theoretically, as trading undertakings these should raise sufficient revenue from charges to cover costs, but in practice many do not achieve this and have to be subsidized. (b) For *personal* services, such as charges for home helps and for maintaining children or old people in care, or fees for adult/community education classes. Such fees will often take account of the individual's ability to pay[7] and seldom cover the full economic cost of the service. Some critics wish to see such charges abolished altogether on the grounds that they deter those in need, that they often involve high collection costs and that there are considerable inconsistencies and inequities in the various means tests for the different services. (c) For *amenities* such as baths, sports facilities, civic theatres and car parks. The level of charges here will depend on how far the local authorities take account of social criteria: should the ratepayer subsidize a laundry service, in the interests of the needy, or sports facilities, in order to encourage healthy pursuits? Equally, subsidized facilities may, by helping local business, encourage tourism and local prosperity. (Some socialists are critical of this arrangement, as it suggests the deliberate subsidizing of capitalist enterprises, in the same way as the nationalized industries have perhaps provided private enterprise with low-cost supplies.) Alternatively, hefty car-parking* fees (for example) may be used as a deterrent to traffic congestion or too rapid a deterioration of the highways; this is being encouraged by the government, which wants to see an expansion in public transport financed through councils taxing private parking and traffic entering towns. (d) For *regulation* services. These are perhaps the most irksome of charges as they are an additional imposition on those (like private residential care homes owners) who have to pay to be inspected and registered. Other examples include fees for planning applications and building control.

Each council has to make up its own mind about charges, and their extent and level can reflect the political control of the council. But in

---

* In 1996–7 local authorities raised £239m in parking revenue. Westminster LBC collected most, at £92m (£33m, net of costs) though some councils make losses. Income from on-street parking can only be spent on transport schemes; off-street parking revenue can be spent on any council service. Others are accused of seeking to maximize revenues from their parking fees or fines (though government guidelines state that councils should use these powers for traffic-managment purposes).

a number of services, the government requires charges to be levied and it may set levels or guidelines.

The single most important charging service is housing. However, for social reasons housing is a service which is (or has been until recently) substantially subsidized both by the central government (via subsidies) and by local authorities (from their rates). In 1976 council rents were meeting only 45 per cent of costs, compared with 75 per cent in 1966.[8] Since the 1980s, government policy has been to cause rents to rise to a more economic level.

It is sometimes suggested that more income could be derived from charges either by raising their level or by extending their scope.[9] Alternatively, local authorities may 'privatize' or 'hive off' some of their services to private firms. Councils can then collect their local tax to cover the costs of the contracted-out services; or they could allow the firms to collect normal commercial charges from the public.

Such charges would perhaps help to sort out those who really need the services from those who use them just because they are free and such charges, even nominal ones, may reduce other, consequential problems, such as road congestion. Indeed, charges are seen as a superior method of rationing scarce goods and services: they can provide choice and avoid (paternalist) allocation decisions by bureaucrats or politicians, and they can improve quality and efficiency of provision since users are paying direct. (In addition hidden subsidies would become exposed.)

Furthermore a review of local authority charging policy might help to remove some apparent anomalies, such as charging for day nursery care (under the social services department) but not for nursery schooling (provided by the education departments, the LEAs); or in the library service, not charging for books, but charging for recordings. A report by the National Consumers Council in 1995 was highly critical of the inconsistency of local authorities' charging policies, both in fee levels and fee applications (e.g. with some charging people on income support and others not).

Many would like to extend charges and/or private provision (though others are sceptical).[10] The government has seen charging as another method of increasing accountability, as 'an even more direct way of ensuring that local people can see what they are getting for what they are paying'.[11] But in reality there are great variations in the extent to which local authorities use charges. A joint report by the Audit Commission and the Social Services Inspectorate in 1998 showed home care for the elderly ranged from £7 an hour in Liverpool to £16 in Cornwall; local authority residential home fees nationally, range from £125 to £750 a week (*Key Statistics of Social Services*); a PSI survey (*Local Living Costs*, 1997) showed council house rents ranging from £82 per week to £19, meals-on-wheels (five per week) from £10 to £3 and schools meals (five a week) from £6.25 to £3.85; in 1999 Mencap revealed a ten-fold differential in day centre charges. (Mencap is also questioning the legality of these charges.)

The Local Government, Planning and Land Act 1980 allowed councils to charge for planning applications and appeals and for building regulations enforcement as well as allowing LEAs a free hand in deciding their charges for school meals (under the Education Act 1980) – though not for their lessons.[12] (It had also planned to allow LEAs to introduce charges for school transport, but this was defeated in the House of Lords on the grounds that the legislation would discriminate against rural families and religious groups.) The Education Reform Act 1988 and the Local Government and Housing Act 1989 extended the scope for charging in schools (for optional extras) and certain library services, as well as giving the Secretary of State a more general power to allow local authorities to impose charges.

Consequently during the 1980s, user charges for local services increased by over 100 per cent and, as a source of local government revenue, it rose from one eighth to one seventh of the total,[13] though among local authorities there is great variation here.* Charges currently apply to over 600 local activities, though this is not as extensive as in European countries. Hence the call for, and tendency towards, further charges, including from those who see charges as a fair system of finance because people pay only for what they receive (or perhaps

---

* For example, the AC/SSI survey above showed that Liverpool generated 4 per cent of its revenue fronm charges – cf. 28 per cent in West Sussex. Similarly, Mencap showed that, while half of authorities charged (varyingly) for day centres, half did not charge at all. Nationally, the proportion of Social Services revenue generated by fees ranges among authorities from 1 per cent to 30 per cent.

choose to receive); they are not paying into a communal chest from which others can draw.

However, a principal argument against charges is that they are unfair because not everyone can afford to pay, and they can cause hardship to low-income groups. This problem could be met through exemptions, discounts and government grants such as those paid for means-tested housing benefits. But this makes the system complicated and, like charging itself, it creates administrative costs (such as in the case of the poll tax which in some cases was costing pounds to collect pence). And with some 40–50 per cent of the population currently exempt or assisted on various grounds (age, income, disability) the potential for raising revenue is clearly limited.[14] Also some argue that charges may be morally offensive, that certain services (such as education) exist as human rights and therefore should be free. Also there may be wider social benefits from having, say, a community with general access to free or low-cost education, libraries, housing or transport, etc. Some even question whether local authorities should actually be raising (rather than spending) money *at all* (see note 13, p. 649, Bailey, p. 13).

The issue of *privatizing* local services involves the political question of the proper role of government in society; it is also very much a matter of economics and efficiency. Some councils have adopted the working methods of the commercial world (such as incentive bonus schemes in refuse collection) so that transfer to the private sector may involve no great advantage to the economy as a whole. But there is a widespread feeling, especially in Conservative circles, that much of the work conducted by local authorities could be more effectively undertaken by the private sector. Consequently, the Local Government, Planning and Land Act 1980 required councils to scrutinize and justify their use of direct labour (or DLOs – that is, where they employ their own staff rather than outside contractors for building or maintaining roads, parks and housing). DLOs were required to submit estimates or 'tenders' in competition with private firms and must achieve given rates of return (or 'profit') or face closure: in effect they became trading undertakings. Part of the motivation of the government for this policy was the 1978–9 'winter of discontent' when local public services were disrupted through industrial action and strikes. In 1985 a survey[15] showed that out of 510 replying, 190 councils had contracted out some of their services though some later brought them back 'in-house', so that the total value of such contracts (in 1987) was only £120 million. But later legislation on compulsory competitive tendering (CCT) altered this situation. The Local Government Act 1988 extended the number of local authority services which had to be put out to tender, i.e. the council's direct service provision must bid in competition with private contractors. These included refuse collection, cleaning of buildings and streets, catering, and the maintenance of grounds and vehicles. The Act allowed the Minister to designate other services (management of sports facilities was thus added). Although by 1993 private contractors had won only 17 per cent of the value of current contracts (of £1,753 million, ranging from 25 per cent for refuse collection to 3 per cent for catering),[16] the government estimated that the result of this injection of competition had been a cost saving of 6.5 per cent,[17] with perhaps £80 million being saved on refuse collection alone[18] (the Audit Commission believed more savings were possible[19]). By 1997 the proportion had risen to 27 per cent, and the estimated savings were about 20 per cent.[20] More recently, the overall estimate of savings is 9 per cent (see *Local Government Chronicle*, 21 March 1997). Under CCT there have been savings whether services are contracted out or not, but they tend to be greater where they are (see *Municipal Yearbook*, 1998, p. 129). By 1998 only 79 local authorities had no services contracted out, i.e. they had 100 per cent DLO/DSO provision. On the other hand, 50 councils had no DLO/DSO in-house contracts for any service.[21] Apart from savings, CCT also improved quality of services and customer care (*Portrait of change*, LGMB, 1996) partly, at least, because councils had to think about service standards for tenders specification. The Local Government Act 1992 (following the consultation paper *Competing for Quality*, 1991) identified the 'white collar' (i.e. professional and technical) occupations suitable for competitive tendering and 'market testing'; thus local authority lawyers, accountants, computer and personnel officers had to submit bids in competition with private firms for the work of the council. There were similar plans for housing management, police support services, vehicle fleet management, security services, school transport, parking services, theatre management, library services and construction-related services (such as engineering, architecture and estate management). However, much was delayed because of the 1992 Local Government Review and structural reorganization, and the advent of a new, Labour, government in May 1997 has led to the replacing of CCT with a policy of 'Best Value' (see p. 591).

(2) Government grants

The central government has been helping to finance local authorities since 1835, when grants in aid were introduced to assist local authorities in the cost of transporting prisoners. Subsequently grants were developed for local services such as police and education. Since they helped to finance the cost of particular services, they were known as 'specific' grants. One interesting and notorious form of grant was based on the 'payment by results' system, whereby teachers got paid according to their success in drilling their pupils in the 'three Rs' and getting them through their exams! (Some see the current grant mechanisms and teacher promotion/grading incentives as a partial return to this.)

Another unusual form of grant was the system of 'assigned revenues'. In 1888 local authorities were empowered to retain and utilize the proceeds of certain taxes (mainly licence duties) collected in their area. Thus tax revenues (sometimes known as 'whisky money') were diverted from the central government to local government. However, this form of financial aid proved to be too erratic in its distribution and insufficiently expansive to keep pace with local authorities' growing expenditures.[22] Consequently, local authorities continued to draw upon government grants. (However, the format of business rates since 1989/90 could be interpreted as a form of assigned revenue; see p. 362).

The character of grants began to change in the course of the twentieth century. Under the Local Government Act 1929, assigned revenues ceased (apart from a few licence fees, which still exist), and a number of specific grants were replaced by a 'block grant' – a sum of money not tied to any particular service and which the local authorities could use for spending as they saw fit. The aim of this new grant was to place a limit on the government's financial commitment to local government. From 1948 onwards, the block grant was paid only to those local authorities whose means (or rate resources) were below the national average. It was known as the 'exchequer equalization grant'.

In the meantime, specific grants[23] continued to grow in magnitude as services (such as education, housing and roads) expanded. Consequently, in 1958 the government replaced many of these with a new form of block (or 'general') grant. The equalization grant continued under the name of the 'rate deficiency grant'. Finally, in 1966 these two block grants, together with some of the remaining specific grants (for school meals and milk), were incorporated into a single 'rate support grant' (RSG), which formed the basis of our present system of grant aid up to 1989–90, when it changed to the Revenue Support Grant System (see p. 352). Before we examine the details of current grants, some general aspects must be considered.

(a) The justification for government grants

Government grants to local government may be justified on a number of grounds. In the first place, the central government will wish to encourage the development of certain services which are felt to be in the national interest (education, for example), and it may feel a moral obligation to assist local authorities financially where national legislation compels the latter to provide certain services. Secondly, government grants can help to even out the differences in resources between rich and poor authorities. Thirdly, grants may seek to compensate local authorities for their varying needs to spend, either because of the amount of need in their area (they may have many schoolchildren or old people) or because of the costs involved in meeting those needs (the population may spread thinly, for instance). Fourthly, government grants may seek to reduce the impact of local taxes. The latter are often said to be 'regressive' or unfair to the lower income groups. In so far as central government taxation is 'progressive' (taking proportionately more from the better off), government grants can partially help to balance the tax burden on the local taxpayer; indeed this was precisely one of the government's lines of defence in introducing the system of community charge or poll tax (see p. 362). Finally, the central government may pay grants to local authorities to compensate them for any restrictions it may have placed on their other sources of income: thus in 1929, when the government ceased to allow local authorities to collect rates from agricultural property, their lost income was made up to some extent in the new block grant. Since 1966, government grants have been used for the explicit purpose of keeping the local taxes down, at least in the case of the domestic local taxpayer (see p. 350); this was illustrated particularly in 1991 when £4.3 billion was transferred from local taxes to general value-added tax (VAT).

There is, then, a strong case for grants. But some would doubt the wisdom of local government's being so dependent on the central government. Grants to local government have increased substantially in this century: as a proportion of local government income they have increased from 15 per cent in 1913, to 34 per cent in 1950 and to 50 per cent in 1980. Ignoring income from fees, charges and other sources, the ratio of grants to local taxes changed from 51:49 in 1966 to 65:35 in 1980. In the 1980s this decreased, to 57:43 by 1987. But it has now reached, in effect, 85:15 – see p. 353.

One consequence of such grant aid is that the central government increases its control over local authorities. This appears to be a world-wide phenomenon and is perhaps an inevitable feature of modern society. It is not necessarily or totally undesirable (see p. 420), and for the most part it is not the principle which is in question but the lengths to which it has been taken. In some respects this has been recognized by government, which has sought to ameliorate the problem by changing the nature of its grants. It is widely felt that grants in general bring central control, grants in the specific form bring closer central controls[24] and they certainly appear to encourage the provision of particular services, which perhaps distorts local authorities' patterns of spending. It was partly for this reason – to give authorities more discretion – that specific grants were largely replaced by the block form. However, over the past fifteen years, there has been a revival in the specific form of grant such that in relative terms they now constitute some 25 per cent of current/revenue grants compared to 17 per cent in 1980. Some of these specific grants include those for which local authorities have to make bids to the government, for example for Capital Challenge, for rural transport (Rural Bus Challenge'), for inner city regeneration (in 'City Challenge') or crime prevention (under the 'Safer City' initiative). While these clearly benefit many councils, they also create a tendency to fragmentation or segmentation rather than a corporate view of resources, and also the potential for greater central control, as the outcomes of these discretionary grant bids hinge on the judgements of ministers and civil servants. They can also make planning difficult (and producing bid packages can be expensive for councils).

(b) The present grant system

Current grants to local authorities take four forms: (i) the revenue (until 1990, rate) support grant, (ii) specific grants for teacher training, under-fives education, services for travellers, HIV and Aids, community care, etc.), (iii) supplementary grants (for transport, for instance), and (iv) housing subsidies (which, like higher education awards and council tax rebates, are a special form of specific grant and are subject to a separate procedure).

(c) The rate support grant (RSG) 1966–90

Every year, central government departments and local authority associations have been meeting (in the forum of the Consultative Committee on Local Government Finance[25]) to agree a forecast of total 'relevant' expenditure[26] for councils for the coming year. This comprises all local government expenditure except mandatory payments such as student awards, rate rebates and housing subsidies (all subject to separate arrangements). The government would then decide what proportion of this total it was going to finance by grant: from 1977 to 1981 the figure was 61 per cent for England and Wales, and 68.5 per cent for Scotland,[27] and for 1986–7, it was 46.4, 66.8 and 56.1 for England, Wales and Scotland respectively. The resulting grant total was the 'aggregate exchequer grant' (or AEG) – now known as Aggregate External Finance. From this total were deducted the various small amounts for specific grants (for teacher training, housing improvement, etc.) and supplementary grants (for transport and national parks), both amounting to nearly 30 per cent of the total by 1990 (from 17 per cent in 1980). The remainder (70 per cent or more) constituted the rate support grant (RSG), which was distributed as a general or block grant and was not therefore tied to particular services.

For distribution purposes, the RSG has been divided into three elements: (i) the 'needs' element, which was designed to compensate local authorities for differences in the amounts they need to spend per head of population to provide a given standard of service. It was calculated by reference to a complex formula prescribed annually by the government and based upon an analysis of each local authority's past expenditure, together with some objective indicators of their expenditure needs (factors such as population, number of children, density, etc.); (ii) the 'resources' element, which sought to compensate for the disparities in local authorities' rates/tax resources. The government would prescribe annually a 'national standard rateable value per head' (in 1981 for example it was £178), and those rating authorities whose rateable value (see p. 354) fell below this figure (the majority) would receive payment in proportion to their rate deficiency. Taken together, and assuming local authorities to be providing a given standard of services, the 'needs' and 'resources' elements were to lead to an equalization of rate poundages (the standard rate in the pound which ratepayers have to pay, or Grant Related Poundage (GRP)). In other words these two elements should have enabled local authorities to provide similar levels of service without widely different rate burdens; (iii) the 'domestic' element, which was a form of rate relief for domestic ratepayers: householders thus paid less than industrial and commercial ratepayers, and the difference was made up to the local authorities in the 'domestic' rate relief element of the RSG.

The RSG has been the most important financial aid to local authorities, and while the needs and resources elements were largely a continuation of what existed before 1966 when this grant was introduced, the domestic element was new – a response to the then growing concern over the rises in rates. The result was that, while rates appeared to be rocketing, their impact on householders in real terms was barely altered since 1966. This (domestic) element was criticized on the grounds that it was inequitable, being paid on a flat-rate basis regardless of ratepayers' ability to pay. A second criticism was that, by disguising the true cost, it was wastefully drawing resources into the housing sector.

However, in general it was the other elements of the RSG which came in for criticism. In particular, the needs element was held to be unduly influenced by local authorities' past expenditure patterns, which may not be an accurate guide to local needs.[28] The resources element has been criticized on the ground that rateable values (the basis for this element) were not a fair reflection of property values.

Another more general criticism was that the formulae for RSG distribution could be manipulated by the party in government to suit its own purposes or in response to community pressure groups, with, in general, Labour diverting financial aid to urban areas at the expense of rural, and Conservatives doing the opposite (but see p. 377 and note 12, p. 673).

The Conservative government, however, sought to change the RSG for another reason: to contain local government expenditure. Under the Local Government, Planning and Land Act 1980, a 'block' (or unitary) grants system was introduced (for England and Wales only) whereby local authorities which spent in excess of their 'true needs' (i.e. as perceived by government) would not receive the same proportionate level of grant support as authorities which exercised restraint on their spending. The idea of a 'unitary' grant (combining into one the *needs* and *resources* elements) was commended by the Layfield Committee on Local Government Finance and was accepted by the government in 1977.[29] It has been seen as a means of penalizing the 'spendthrift' authorities without harming the others, for under the old RSG system, if some councils spent more than the government wished, the latter could take action only by reducing the whole level of its RSG (thus shifting the burden on to the rates of *all* local authorities). Under the 1980 scheme a 'block grant' was calculated for each local authority to cover the deficiency or gap between the cost of providing services comparable with those of similar authorities and the local rate revenue assuming the rate to be set at a particular level (the GRP determined nationally by the government). In effect, the government calculated what the local authority should spend; it then deducted what the standard (or GRP) rate poundage would produce, and the difference paid in grant. A local authority spending above its 'norm' (officially known as Grant Related Expenditure Assessment or GREA) would have to find more from the rates as its grant was reduced or tapered away. Grant fell as the GRP was increased by a 'multiplier' when spending exceeded GREA. Above a certain expenditure threshold, grant was disproportionately withheld.

Local authorities reacted strongly to this legislation. While perhaps having some general sympathy for the general aim of the proposal (to restrain overall local government spending), many authorities felt that extensive powers had been taken to control all local authorities for the sake of a few who acted irresponsibly. And in general it was felt that this was a dangerous attempt to substitute a 'national judgement' about local spending for the 'local accountability' of the authorities themselves (see p. 447). The new grant and rates system (see below and pp. 588) has not substantially changed this.

(d) *The revenue support grant (RSG)*

Under the Local Government Finance Act 1988 (operative from 1990) and the Abolition of Domestic Rates (Scotland) Act 1987 (operative 1989), domestic rates were replaced by the community charge (or poll tax; see p. 361), business rates were 'nationalized' (see p. 362) and the rate support grant was replaced by the 'revenue support grant' (RSG, also known as Standard Spending Grant (SSG)). The aim was to reduce the complexity of the system (for example by simplifying the needs calculation – the former expenditure assessment – from sixty-three indicators or measures to eleven) and to provide greater stability by avoiding the often substantial changes in grant allocation which could affect authorities from year to year. In 1993 the community charge was itself abolished and replaced by the council tax (see p. 369). But the grant system was unchanged.

The essence of the system is that the grant will compensate for differences between areas in their need to provide services (as measured by population and physical/social features, such as numbers in care, incidence of disability, children at risk, etc.), i.e. each authority will have a *needs assessment* or Standard Spending Assessment (SSA); in Scotland it is the Grant Aided Expenditure Assessment. An allowance will then be made for the authority's income from the business rate and its council tax (for which the government will assume a notional or standard level for each property band, and is thus known as 'council tax at standard spending' or CTSS). Thus:

Revenue Support Grant =

$$\text{Needs Assessment (SSA)} - \left(\begin{array}{c} \text{Business rate} \times \text{local population} \\ + \\ \text{Council tax} \times \text{local householders} \end{array} \right)$$

i.e. RSG = SSA − (UBR + CTSS)

For detailed illustration, see Appendix 18

Authorities whose needs are considered high (in terms of numbers of schoolchildren or elderly residents, for example) will attract higher needs assessments and grant. Thus, since the RSG aims to enable all local authorities to provide a common level of services (based on SSAs) the RSG is alternatively called the Standard Spending Grant (SSG). With the business rate revenue (see pp. 354, 364) being distributed nationally on the basis of population (the main criterion of need) and the grant based on needs assessment, then the council tax is the local authority's balancing item. The grant is fixed for the year (in contrast to the previous rate support grant entitlement, which could alter sharply for a local authority during the year or even later since it was based on actual expenditures). Thus the council tax is the variable item which the local authority itself can alter (unless it is 'capped'; see below).

These arrangements mean that if each local authority spends at the level of its SSA (see above), local authorities' council taxes will be identical for each property band (see p. 371 and Appendices 18 and 19): Where an authority chooses to spend more or is wasteful, the cost will be borne entirely by the (higher) council tax (and equally, underspending will reduce it), since RSG is normally unaltered.* Originally, in 1990, the RSG overall provided 50 per cent of local government expenditure (with UBR and community charge at 25 per cent each). But in the 1991 Budget, the government unexpectedly switched £4.3 billion on to central taxation (VAT) and increased the RSG such that, together with specific grants and revenue from business rates (NNDR or UBR; see below) central support to local authorities now provides some 80 to 85 per cent (according to definition). Thus the community charge (and subsequently the council tax) only had to raise about 15 per cent – thus easing, though not eliminating, its burden on local taxpayers.

It was also intended that the new grants system would not only be less complicated but also provide greater stability and clearer accountability, since changes in the community charge – now council

---

* Though local authorities' council tax grant will alter as more or fewer people become eligible for council tax benefit. The government is currently altering this; see p. 591.

tax – would be due to changes in local spending decisions and not (at least so it was intended) due to grant changes, as often was the case under the rate support grant system. But stability and accountability have been undermined by significant grant changes from year to year and also especially by a provision in legislation (originally the Rates Act 1984) which gives the Minister the power to limit any local authority's expenditure budget and thus to 'cap' the local tax level.

(3) Rates (substantially abolished 1989–90; see p. 362)

Rates are an important element in local government finance – partly because they have existed for centuries as the only local tax and have provided a substantial proportion of local authorities' revenue, partly because they still exist despite the fact that they have been significantly altered in recent years.

Rates are a form of local property taxation levied on property (real or fixed rather than personal) according to its value. They originated in the Middle Ages, and over the years new and separate rates were established to help to pay for separate services (public health, schools, the poor, highways, water, etc.). These were finally consolidated (see p. 17) into a single general rate in 1925 (although in England and Wales water and sewerage rates are still separately assessed and collected). Under the Rating and Valuation Act of that year certain types of local authority were classified as 'rating authorities'. Those which were not so named (counties and parishes in England and Wales; the districts and communities in Scotland) were to raise their finance by 'precepting' the rating authorities (the district councils in England and Wales; the regions and islands in Scotland): in effect this meant that the rating authorities collected the rate for the other authorities (and, since 1981, they also bore the cost of administration).[30] Since the abolition of local rates (see below) we now have 'billing' authorities and 'precepting' authorities. There have been substantial differences in the extent to which authorities depended on rate income.[31]

(a) Liability for rates

Technically, to be liable for rates, property (or 'hereditaments', as they are called) had to be occupied (though not necessarily in a personal sense: a house could be liable for rates if it was empty but contained furniture). However, since 1967 rating authorities had a discretionary power to rate empty properties if they were continuously empty for a given period, usually three or six months. (From 1981 the maximum rate on empty commercial property was 50 per cent; since 1984 empty industrial property has been de-rated.) Whether they decided to rate empty properties and whether they charged full or partial rates would depend on such factors as the administrative costs, the revenue product and whether they thought such an action would encourage owners to utilize the property more quickly or whether it might deter further development.[32] (It should be noted that local authorities themselves pay rates on their properties.)

Certain properties have been statutorily exempt from the payment of rates. The main ones include: (i) Crown property, such as government building, military premises, royal parks, etc. (in practice, the Treasury compensates rating authorities with 'contributions in lieu'); this exemption is now ceasing under the local Government and Rating Act 1997; (ii) agricultural land and buildings (except the farmhouse), which have been exempt since 1929 (worth £1 billion per annum today), when they were de-rated partly in order to lighten the farmers' burden at that time of economic difficulty; (iii) churches and other buildings used exclusively for religious purposes, charities and related organizations, public parks, police properties, lighthouses, sewers and pumping stations and foreign consulates. Disabled persons were granted rate relief on their properties where these had been specially adapted. In Scotland, industrial property was rated at only 50 per cent, in order to offset the generally higher rate poundages than in England and Wales.

(b) The calculation of the rate

The basic idea of the rating system is quite simple. All property in the area (apart from the exemptions) is given a valuation: this is the 'rateable value'. Every year the rating authority fixed a multiplier or rate in the pound (per pound of rateable value) and the occupier of that property paid rates at that poundage. Thus, if the rate was 80p and the property's rateable value was £200, the rates due were £0.80 × 200 = £160. The key elements therefore are rateable value and the rate poundage.

The valuation of property is undertaken by the Inland Revenue

(England and Wales) and by the Scottish Assessors' Association (although in 1991, valuation of domestic properties was undertaken, on behalf of the government, by estate agents to provide a set of capital values for the introduction of the council tax). Since the 1939–45 war regular revaluations should have taken place every five years, but in practice they have occurred at very irregular intervals except in Scotland.[33] Business properties have recently been revalued, with new valuations to taking effect in April 2000.

The valuation of property for rating purposes is based essentially on the market rent which the property could earn in the course of a year. From this gross or rental value is allowed the deduction of the notional cost of repairs and insurance, etc. For some properties (such as a town hall, school or cinema) it is extremely difficult to assess a rental value and so other bases may be used, such as capital values or profits records. Indeed the rental basis for ordinary purposes may be substantially distorted (for example, because of statutory rent controls) and the use of alternative criteria has been proposed, such as capital values or site values.[34]

Information on the valuation of properties is publicly available in the form of a valuation list (England and Wales) or roll (Scotland), which is usually held at the council offices. Individuals may appeal against the valuation of their property to the valuation court* and beyond that if necessary to the land tribunal. For businesses there is a high appeal rate of over 50 per cent. Any structural changes affecting a property's valuation will come to the attention of the local valuation officer normally as a result of the planning permission process.

The rate *poundage* (or simply 'the rate') is the amount per pound of rateable value which is collected from occupiers of property. Up to 1989–90 this rate was determined annually by the local authority (some being issued in the form of 'precepts' on the rating authorities – see p. 354). The basis of the calculation was as follows: each local authority estimates its expenditure for the coming year. (The financial

---

* Valuation courts, which decide appeals about rateable valuation of property, were reconstituted as Valuation and Community Charge Tribunals, as they dealt with appeals over the community charge. But since the introduction of the council tax in 1992, they are now known as Valuation Tribunals. There are 56 of them, dealing with 300,000 rating appeals and 80,000 council tax valuation appeals a year.

year runs from April to April). It deducts from this figure its known or estimated revenues from charges and grants. This leaves a sum – known as the 'rate-borne expenditure' – which has to be financed from the remaining source of income – the rating of property. The proportion of that rate-borne expenditure figure to the total rateable value in the local authority area (say 80 per cent) shows the poundage (80p) or 'rate' of tax necessary to raise the sum required.[35] Thus for individual ratepayers their property's rateable value multiplied by the rate produces their rate demand.

The rating system has been unpopular because it required lump-sum payments (usually twice a year) rather than regular (and smaller) weekly or monthly payments such as we use to pay income tax ('pay as you earn'). However, after the General Rate Act 1967, the system was modified to allow some rates to be paid in instalments of not more than ten monthly payments.

The same Act provided an incentive to pay in full by allowing local authorities to give discounts to those who paid promptly.

(c) Criticisms of the rating system

No tax is popular, but rates were particularly unpopular. This is partly because they had to be paid in advance and in a lump sum (even if they were paid in instalments, the demand arrived initially as a lump sum). But rates were also unpopular because the rate (poundage) received a lot of media attention when it was fixed (which usually meant increased) each year. So rates were an overtly painful form of tax. In this respect they differed from income tax and indeed most other taxes that ratepayers have to pay: the total yield from other taxes increases automatically as incomes or prices rise, but that from rates increases only when there is an appreciation in rateable values (following an infrequent, and well-publicized, revaluation survey). Consequently rates lack 'buoyancy' and the rate had to be altered regularly in order to increase the yield.

Rates were also unsatisfactory, as we have mentioned above, because their basis (the annual rental value) is inadequate or distorted. Furthermore, it is suggested that they may act as a brake on property improvement, owners being deterred by a threatened rise in their rates through increased revaluation.

However, the biggest criticisms of the rating system relate to its unfairness. In the first place, rate resources are very unevenly distributed among local authorities and are quite unrelated to their varying needs: hence the 'resources' element of the rate support grant (see p. 348). (It may be added, however, that no known form of local taxation could easily secure an even or fair distribution of resources.) Secondly, rates were said to be 'regressive', that is, relatively they bear most heavily on those with low incomes, since the rate demand was applied to the value of property, not to the occupier's ability to pay. One household may depend on a small income (say a pension), while another identical house, subject to the same rate demand, may enjoy the benefit of several larger incomes.[36] Thus they fail to take account of people's ability to pay.

This last criticism lost much of its force in recent years. This is partly because incomes are taxed nationally (some on a 'progressive' basis) and part of the proceeds help to finance local government in the form of government grants and so reduce local taxes. But mainly it is because since 1967 lower income groups were able to claim rate rebates, such relief varying with income and family circumstances. Rate demands therefore bore a closer relationship to incomes,[37], though there is strong evidence that many groups in society (especially private tenants) failed to claim this benefit, although entitled to it. (The same problems arise with council tax benefit. And there were others who were outside the rebate scheme although they may be on low income, such as, until 1988, owners of small commercial premises. Also, there is no provision for rebates on water and sewerage rates since the separate collections began in 1980–81.)

A further criticism is based on the 'beneficiary principle'. Here, rates are criticized because only the householder would pay the rates bill, while other members of the household would not be liable, and yet they could benefit from the services provided from the rates and may thus be encouraged to press for greater service provision without feeling any financial 'pinch' (see p. 368).

(d) Merits of the rating system

The rating system has a number of strengths. As a tax, it is simple to administer, difficult to evade and cheap to collect. The total yield of rates up to 1989 was substantial (equivalent to about a 10p income tax) and, being stable from one year to the next, it is reliable and predictable. In addition, since it is truly local in nature, it makes an impact (sometimes very painful) on the ratepayer, and is commonly seen (rightly or wrongly) as the payment for local services. It may thus have the merit of arousing an interest in local government affairs and promote the accountability of the councillors and officers who spend it. This was enhanced by the requirements under the General Rate Act 1967 that local authorities provide certain specified information with the rate demand, such as description of the property, its rateable value, the amounts in the pound spent on each principal service, etc. Such information has been expanded under subsequent legislation (see p. 392).

A further advantage of the rating system was that, by encouraging a fuller utilization of the household stock and discouraging households from occupying premises which are larger than they need, it helped to mobilize the supplies of housing. A small family or business occupying unnecessarily large premises would be inclined to move to a smaller property because of the relatively heavy rates which large premises attracted, and thus made space available for those better able to use it.

Apart from these technical advantages, there was also the perhaps surprising fact that domestic rates in general were a small proportion of households' disposable incomes – between 2 and 3 per cent,[38] (national taxes are some 40 per cent). This may help to explain why rates were not as unpopular as many people believe.[39] However, while domestic ratepayers have been protected by the 'domestic' element of the RSG and by rebates, industrial and commercial ratepayers (especially in England and Wales) have been less fortunate: while for the period 1966–74 the overall rate bill rose by 120 per cent, domestic rates payments rose by 80 per cent and non-domestic by 150 per cent. And among the 2 million non-domestic ratepayers businesses as such since 1969 have no local vote (although arguably business is well represented among the membership of most councils and other official bodies). On the other hand, businesses can offset their rates against other taxes (assuming profits are being made) and perhaps pass it on (in whole or part) in higher prices for their product.

(e) Reform of the rating system

Various proposals have been made to reform the rating system. One group of reforms seeks to increase the yield of rates, in particular by shifting the burden of de-rating from local authorities to the central government. Thus if the government sees fit to exempt agriculture or charities from rates, it should reimburse local authorities for the revenue foregone.[40] In effect this did happen indirectly through the resources element of the RSG, and in Scotland there was some direct recognition through the payment of a higher RSG to cover the rate relief of charities. However, some critics sought 100 per cent rate liability of all properties; anyone claiming hardship should then be able to approach the central government for financial assistance in the form of grants. A further suggestion is that property revaluation should occur more frequently (the Layfield Committee suggested three-yearly intervals) and that capital values should be used, in view of the narrow base which exists for rental comparisons (see p. 356).

These seem sensible suggestions, but there are technical problems in trying to value agricultural property or road bridges and tunnels, or undertake more regular revaluations. And the yield may be rather insignificant. But above all are the political problems involved in trying, for instance, to re-rate agriculture or charities. More generally, it is suggested that local authorities which rely heavily on local incomes tend to be parsimonious.[41] The government's immediate solution, introduced in 1984, was *rate-capping*, i.e. placing an upper limit on individual local authorities' rate levels when they reach a given point (in 1989 that point was 12.5 per cent above GREA). Then, in 1989–90, domestic rates were abolished – only to be (partially) restored in 1992 in the form of the council tax; see p. 367. Capping was retained.

Alternative sources or strategies

A second group of reforms has, over the years, been put forward to supplement, or to replace, the rating system.[42] These proposals have comprised a selection of local taxes, including petrol duties, sales tax, employment tax, vehicle duties, parking/congestion taxes and, above all, a local income tax. They have been regarded as unacceptable on various specific grounds, including the problems of collection, the scope for avoidance, the small yield, their regressive nature, their intrusion upon the government's revenue sources (and its control of tax levels and inflation), their uneven distribution among local authorities and the fact that such new forms of taxation would confuse the public and so jeopardize the delicate thread of accountability which runs between the council and the people.

Governments have usually rejected such proposals on the grounds that the time was 'not appropriate' for the introduction of new taxes.[43] An example of this was the (Labour) government's response to the report of the Layfield Committee, which dealt thoroughly and comprehensively with the subject of local income tax (LIT) – widely regarded as the most realistic potential source of local revenue. The Committee was set up in June 1974 in response to widespread public protest over the rises in rates that year: local government was seen to be particularly susceptible to the effects of inflation (some 70 per cent of its expenditure going on wages and salaries), while its rate revenues tended to be rather sluggish (i.e. they lack buoyancy – see p. 357). However, the Layfield Committee did not consider it feasible to abolish rates. Instead they proposed that a local income tax should be instituted as an additional source of local revenue. The objective was to 'foster the autonomy of local authorities by reducing their dependence on government grants and giving them sources of revenue they can more easily vary under their own control to meet their expenditure requirements'. (In 1993, the former deputy chairman of the Board of the Inland Revenue gave his support for the Layfield proposals, and suggested that, with recent developments in technology, many of the technical and administrative objections made against LIT had been overcome.) However, Chancellors of the Exchequer (and/or the Treasury) are reluctant to allow the instruments of economic management, especially direct taxation, to be diverted from their control – a point which was reiterated in the 1998 White Paper, *Modern Local Government* (p. 44).*

The government's response to Layfield was to deny that a large central grant did undermine local discretion over expenditure: the block grant (RSG) allowed local authorities the freedom to decide their own expenditure priorities. (This relationship of grant level and local autonomy was also reiterated recently.†) Consequently it saw no

---

* See too S. Jenkins, *The Times*, 16 December 1998.
† See *Local Government Chronicle*, 6 November 1998, p. 1.

need to introduce LIT, and indeed it went further and positively rejected it on the grounds that

> the freedom of local authorities to vary the LIT rate would have to be closely constrained so that it did not unduly complicate central government economic and financial management ... it seems highly questionable whether the majority of electors could be made aware of the LIT element in their normal PAYE deductions as to achieve the [Layfield] Committee's objective of securing an effective local discipline on local authority expenditure decisions.[44]

Another area of possible reform is the transfer of some local government services (such as the police or education) to the central government or alternatively the transfer of the cost of certain services (such as teachers' pay). The examples quoted are felt to be particularly appropriate because they are already subject to considerable government intervention. The latter proposal also featured in the 1979 Conservative and Liberal election manifestos. However, there are a number of serious objections to such transfers. In the first place it would lead to a further erosion of local government responsibilities or discretion, and if it were the costs that were transferred it would make councils appear even more as the agents of central government. Furthermore, it might be damaging to the service to have a divided responsibility (and it would inhibit local corporate management). The likelihood of greater public confusion would again endanger accountability. And in the end there might be no net financial gain for local government if the central government simply reduced its grants to compensate. Above all, however, the decision about whether a service should be administered locally or centrally ought to be decided on its own merits; it should not be seen merely as a device for easing local authority financial problems.[45]

Rates reform, the community charge and the council tax

The Conservative government of Mrs Thatcher had long pledged itself to abolish domestic rates. It considered a number of alternative revenue sources in a 1981 Green Paper,[46] including a local sales tax, a local income tax and a poll tax. All were rejected and rates were to 'remain for the foreseeable future [as] the main source of local income'.[47] Then in January 1986 the government published another Green Paper outlining its proposals to abolish domestic rates and introduce a poll tax (residents' or community charge).[48]

As we have seen above, rates have taken two main forms: (i) domestic; and (ii) non-domestic or business. Under the Abolition of Domestic Rates (Scotland) Act 1987 and the Local Government Finance Act 1988, domestic rates were abolished for Scotland (in 1989) and England and Wales (in 1990) respectively, and business rates have been fundamentally altered. Consequently, the Rate Support Grant became the Revenue Support Grant. (Northern Ireland was unaffected by these changes.)

(i) The domestic rate was replaced by a 'community charge' or poll tax (or 'service tax'). This was basically a flat-rate levy on all individual adults, determined by each council on an annual basis. Known as the *personal* community charge, a national target or model figure was set (e.g. in 1990 £278 (£300 Scotland, inc. water charge), in 1992 £257), though there were wide variations in the actual charge levels (for example, £438 in Edinburgh (including water charge), to £148 in Wandsworth). Furthermore, individual circumstances affected the amount paid:

(a) Some people (about half a million) were exempt entirely; these included hospital patients, people in care, prisoners, etc.

(b) Others were entitled to rebates/reductions of up to 80 per cent according to their income and savings. Full-time students and those on Income Support would automatically get 80 per cent rebate; they were thus bound to pay at least 20 per cent of the local charge (though Income Support levels were raised to allow for this). Transitional relief or charge reduction was given to those worst affected by the changeover.

(c) Some paid twice if they had a second home (unless it was used by someone else as their main residence); the charge here was the *standard charge*, and it was determined by the council in whose area the property is located.

(d) Those who moved frequently and used lodgings, hostels or houses of multiple occupation paid the *collective charge*. This would be a proportion of the personal community charge, depending on length of stay and was paid initially to the landlord with their rent.

In order to collect the community charge, local authorities (in Scotland the regional and island councils and in England and Wales, the boroughs and districts, collectively known as the 'charging authorities' – the others 'precept' on them; see p. 354) drew up community charge registers, based on people's completion and submission of a registration form. People could be fined for non-registration and the community charge registration officer could help compile the register by scrutinizing such local sources as library or education registers, council-house tenancy lists or the electoral register.

(ii) Non-domestic or business rates were retained but reformed. Instead of each local authority determining its rate level, the rate (poundage or national 'multiplier') is now set centrally and differently for Scotland, Wales and England and is the same throughout the individual nations; hence it is known as the *uniform business rate* (UBR), or national non-domestic rate (NNDR). The rate changes from year to year, but any increase cannot exceed the rate of inflation. In addition, rateable values are to be regularly up-dated every five years (the first of these in 1989 in England and Wales showed a seven-fold increase since the previous one of 1973). The latest business rates register began in 2000.

Certain business properties are exempt. These include agricultural land and buildings; fish farms; lighthouses; sewers; land and structures occupied by drainage authorities; municipal free parks; property used to provide occupations, training, workshops or welfare services for the disabled; property in Enterprise Zones. Local authorities have discretionary powers to give relief to non-profit making bodies (such as charities), to ratepayers suffering hardship (under the Local Government Finance Act 1988) and to village shops (under certain conditions; see Local Government and Rating Act 1997). Overall (in England) there are 1.6 million rateable properties (about 20 per cent in London compared to 5 per cent in East Anglia), with a total rateable value of £33 billion. Of these about a third are shops, producing about a fifth of total rates revenue; offices, warehouses and factories account for about 40 per cent of properties and rates product; schools, hospitals, etc. provide about 30 per cent, and public utilities (gas, electricity, water, railways, etc., whose rates are collected and pooled by central government) provide 7 per cent. In 1999–2000 (England), the rate was 48.9 p* (i.e. per pound of rateable value) compared to 47.4 p in the previous year. This tax burden amounts to about 5 per cent of turnover for half of business properties.

The money raised from the UBR and collected locally is transferred to a national pool and then shared out among councils according to the number of adults in their areas. Thus there is an element of redistribution of the uneven rateable property resources, and initially the North of England benefited most from the reform. But the scheme is criticized because as a tax it does not take account of businesses' differing abilities to pay, nor their differing benefits from council services (though local authorities must still consult local businesses about services (see p. 403)). Furthermore, by centralizing the tax, it reduces (further) local authorities' accountability for meeting business needs. But, above all, this system in effect removes from local government one of its own independent sources of income: it is virtually equivalent to an assigned revenue (see p. 346) or government grant.

It may be noted that the total yield from business rates has declined by 8 per cent in real terms over the ten years to 1998.[49]

Objectives of the reforms

The system of business rates was changed to a national(ized) pooling system in order to provide stability and equal treatment for businesses across the country. Previously some business had felt they were being exploited or 'milked' by local councils; this could distort competition and lead to relocation and uncertainty. Whilst the present government can see a case for restoring local discretion over business rates – to improve accountability and financial autonomy as well as enhancing local development and council–business relationships – it intends to keep the main elements of the current system. But councils are urged or expected to build effective partnerships with businesses and involve them in their expenditure planning arrangements and, more crucially,

---

* Businesses with a rateable value of under £10,000 receive a small business rebate of 0.9 per cent, so for them, the rate was 48 p.

they are *required* to consult with local businesses on the details of a scheme to allow councils to set a supplementary rate (or perhaps rebate) within centrally prescribed limits. If introduced, this supplementary rate (linked in value to the local council tax) would be used for local discretionary spending. (In some areas, known as Business Improvement Districts (BIDs), businesses volunteer to pay extra rates for additional local services.) The better councils ('beacons') are allowed to set an additional local rate (though small businesses are to be protected against any undue consequences of any of these local business rates).

For private households, the government's stated purpose of converting domestic rates to the community charge/poll tax was to spread the cost of local services wider and more equally. Under the financial system operating before 1989–90, about one third of local government expenditure was financed by central grants, a third by sales, rents and charges and a third by ratepayers. Of the last, business contributed more than domestic ratepayers; yet business as such had no vote to influence council spending decisions, i.e. there was a lack of accountability, and businesses (especially in some local authority areas) felt they were being charged excessive rates to help fund inappropriate local expenditures.

Of domestic ratepayers there were only 19 million compared to 27 million (income) taxpayers and 36 million adults. Among the 19 million ratepayers, 7 million were receiving full or partial rebate, i.e. rate reduction (see pp. 358, 429). Thus it was felt that a minority of adults were paying rates, thereby subsidizing the services enjoyed by others who would perhaps be inclined to vote for more local service provision because they would not be contributing (directly) towards their cost. It was intended that the community charge/poll tax would raise people's awareness of local spending and decision-making. Consequently it was anticipated that excessive council spending in particular, and perhaps their spending in general, would be reduced as more people felt the impact and baulked at the charge they were having to pay.

The impact of payment was to be enhanced in two important ways. Firstly, all charge payers would be issued with a 'ready reckoner' that indicated what the community charge norm (or target figure) was calculated to be: it was a guide or benchmark against which to judge the local council. Since the revenue support grant equalized between local authorities on the basis of assessed need (and the UBR crudely did the same) then a common or national level of charge should help finance a common or standard level of service. Consequently, to reinforce accountability, local authorities were required, with each community charge bill, to include details of the notional or standard level of community charge for which each local authority could provide a standard level of service. Thus charge payers would be able to compare this to their actual charge and so assess their authority's efficiency and/or spending decisions.

Secondly, as the income from the centre (RSG and UBR) was fixed, any increase in expenditure beyond SSA would (ignoring fee income) fall entirely on to the community charge. Since this was small (25 per cent) relative to grant (50 per cent) and UBR (25 per cent), any increase in expenditure (beyond the notional standard) would trigger a steep rise in the charge. This is known as the 'gearing' effect; in this case it is 1:4, i.e. a £1 rise in expenditure requires a 4-fold rise in community charge (since it is not grant-aided). At present, with council tax only raising 15 per cent of total revenue, the average ratio is in effect 1:7. (For some councils it is much higher, e.g. Tower Hamlets is 1:14.)

Each local authority was to be as well off after receiving its share of the UBR and the needs-weighted RSG as any other local authority, so the actual community charge would directly reflect the decisions of the council and (through the ballot box) the wishes of the community. Thus the community charge was designed to place the burden of financing marginal increases in expenditure fully on those who in general benefited from them.

Pros and cons

As a flat-rate charge, it was clearly regressive; since it took the same amount from each individual adult – milkman or millionaire – regardless of income or means, it would be a relatively greater burden on the poor. But the government rejected this criticism, pointing out that (ignoring fee revenues): (1) half of local authority income came from central government grant, which is substantially funded by progressive (heavier-on-the-rich) income tax, capital gains tax and death duties; (ii) a quarter of local income is paid by business; and (iii) about 10 million adults (and some businesses) were totally exempt or received rebates of up to 80 per cent (together with a top-up of Income Support for the remaining 20 per cent where appropriate). Thus it was claimed that the community charge was broadly related to ability to pay for those on low incomes.

A further justification drew on taxation theory. While with the development of progressive income tax it has become widely (though not universally[50]) accepted that taxes should be based on the principle of ability to pay, an alternative principle states that those who benefit from a service should pay for it. On the basis of this 'beneficiary principle' rates were, at least partially, a tax levied on property because property owners benefited from the prevailing services (law and order, highways, sewerage, lighting, gas, etc.). But these days, local services are more personal in nature (education, social services, libraries, etc.) and more widely utilized; hence the community charge or 'benefit tax'.

However, even on the beneficiary principle it could be argued that a fairer or progressive form of local taxation is justified. This arises from evidence that suggests that the higher-income middle-class members of society disproportionately utilize or benefit from community services.[51] In so far as this is true, it would suggest the introduction of some form of property or wealth tax or a local income tax.

A number of other criticisms have been made of the poll tax:

(a) Administration was an enormous problem: registering charge payers, keeping track of those who are mobile, securing payment, processing claims to rebate or exemption. Indeed, it was the 1983 White Paper *Rates* that rejected the poll tax option on the grounds that 'the tax would be hard to enforce . . . expensive to run and complicated'. Some estimates suggest that in inner-city areas, some 40 per cent of residents (or 1 million) move in the course of a year, and overall it is estimated that mobility creates a 'leakage' (in potential revenue) of up to 20 per cent. The cost (three times that for the old rates) increased significantly where people pay by instalments (and where there is an 80 per cent rebate, the cost of collection could exceed the revenue).

(b) There was concern at the intrusion into people's privacy, as questions are asked about cohabitation (which could affect liability to pay for another person) or about mental disability or imprisonment (for exemption purposes); and since the register was open to inspection, there were fears over confidentiality (for example among estranged battered wives or refugee students).

(c) There was the risk that people would be deterred from registering to vote in order to evade the tax – indeed there was evidence of considerable electoral non-registration,[52] and by encouraging evasion there was the side-effect of reducing general respect for the law.

(d) Although not legally liable for their payments, it is suggested that families may have discouraged their elderly or disabled relatives or their older children from living with them.

(e) On a wider front, it is believed that the new system may have contributed to the rise in house prices (since the tax – rates – had been removed) and the excessive or wasteful use of housing space.

(f) Finally, although enhanced accountability was one of the main objectives of the new system, this was undermined by widespread rebates (and safety nets[53]), by dubious SSAs, by the continued regime of 'capping' (see p. 360), by allowing one spouse/partner to pay for both (as with rates) and by the fact that many local authorities (such as counties) did not register or collect the charge direct: they precepted (see p. 355). The loss of independent business rate revenue also diminishes accountability.

It also appears that the old rating system was not so flawed, in that non-ratepayers' voting behaviour did not differ from that of ratepayers.[54]

The council tax

The consequences of the introduction of the poll tax/community charge were momentous. There were riots, massive refusals to pay, judicial review, attachment of earnings and benefits, rebellions by poll-tax payers over their surcharge for others' non-payments, threatened or actual imprisonments and warrant sales for non-payment, prosecutions under the Data Protection Act . . . followed by a sudden change in government policy on local finance. Mrs Thatcher was forced to resign, at least in part, over the tax issue. In November 1990 John Major became Prime Minister, and Michael Heseltine was brought back into the government as Secretary of State for the Environment, and thus responsible for local government affairs. He was critical of many of the injustices of the community charge and soon published a review of local finance in the consultation paper *A New Tax for Local Government*, which contained a review of local finance together with plans for further reform. Consequently, the Local Government Finance Act 1992 abolished (in 1993) the community charge/poll tax (on 41 million people) and replaced it with the council tax (on 22 million households).

The council tax is a tax on both the person (like the poll tax) and his or her property (like the rates), and is split equally between the two. It is based on the relative value of people's property and on the assumption that there are two people (adults) in the household. Where there are more than two, the tax bill is unaffected; but where there is only one adult (an estimated 7 million), the 'personal' part of the tax is halved and so there is a 25 per cent *discount* on the tax bill. In addition, there are categories of people (such as students, residents in welfare homes, those receiving child benefit, carers, those with severe mental impairment) who may be officially disregarded such that a number of multi-occupied houses count as having just one adult and receive the discount. There are also reductions for disabled people who have had their properties specially adapted/enlarged. Furthermore, about 700,000 dwellings are exempt or receive 50 per cent reduction (including empty or unfit houses, student dwellings, armed forces' accommodation).

The amount of tax varies according to the value of the property, for which purpose houses and flats are to be grouped into eight valuation bands (A to H) (see Table 20 and Appendix 14). Those in the top band pay about three times as much as those in the lowest. The property valuation, undertaken in 1991–2, was intended to be relative rather than absolute or actual, to provide a base for the tax.

Table 20 *Council tax bands (England)*

Band	Property value upper limit (£)	Proportion of tax for band D property (%)	% of homes in band (total + 20.7 m)
A	40,000	66.6	26
B	52,000	77.7	19
C	58,000	88.8	22
D	88,000	100.0	15
E	120,000	122.2	9
F	160,000	144.4	5
G	320,000	166.6	3
H	320,000+	200.0	1

NOTES: 1. The Council Tax for Standard Spending (CTSS) in England 1998–9 was £635.

2. Houses containing only one adult are entitled to a 25 per cent discount in each band. Discounts and exemptions apply in other special circumstances.

The average (for England) is about £80,000 (which is in Band D), where a household (in 1999) would pay around £798 if the council spends at government (standard spending) guidelines (though in practice the range for band D is £350 for Westminster to £669 in Bromley, £802 in Walsall and £1,171 in Liverpool. Those on low incomes get rebates of up to 100 per cent in the form of Council Tax Benefit. (In some authorities this benefit can amount to over 30 per cent of their CT revenue; on average a fifth of any increase in council tax is met by CT benefit. This is funded by a special government grant/subsidy; but see Chapter 15.)

Unlike the community charge, each household receives a single council tax bill. The owner-occupier or resident tenant thus normally pays, though joint owners or joint tenants would be jointly liable (as are husbands and wives or 'as married' partners). (In some cases the owner rather than the tenant is liable.) Unsettled disputes over liability or the level of the bill go to a Valuation Tribunal (see p. 356).

The business rates and grant systems were left unchanged by the 1992 Act except that grants are now paid separately to each tier. Grants, as we have seen, take account of the differences in the needs

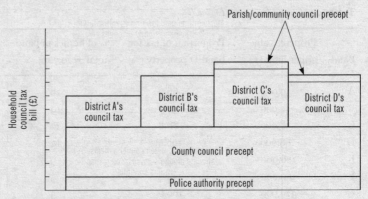

Figure 19 *Components of the council tax in a county*

and taxable capacity of each area. So if all local authorities spend at the level the government considers appropriate (i.e. the SSA level), the council tax would be the same across the country for all properties in the same value band. Having received its share of grants and NNDR income (which are paid into the local collection fund), each authority sets its own council tax (or precept). The council's tax demand should enable local taxpayers to be able to identify which local authority is responsible for each element of the council tax (see Figure 19).

Capping was retained in the 1992 Act, having, under the Local Government Finance and Valuation Act 1991, been extended to small-spending councils previously exempt. Capping overall has reduced local government expenditure by £1.2 billion (i.e. about 2 per cent), affecting such services as home help hours or school class sizes. But it has also reduced the council tax by 13 per cent (i.e. equivalent of £90 p.a. for a band D householder).[55]

The new council tax (CT) was welcomed by many as fairer, simpler, easier and cheaper to administer than the community charge/poll tax (CC/PT), where there is a continuing shortfall in collection (of £800m in 1996).*

The average cost of collection per household is about £17, compared to £23 per adult for council tax.† It is less easy to evade and more

---

* See *Local Government Financial Statistics*, DETR (annual).
† See: *Improving Local Financial Accountability*, DETR, 1998.

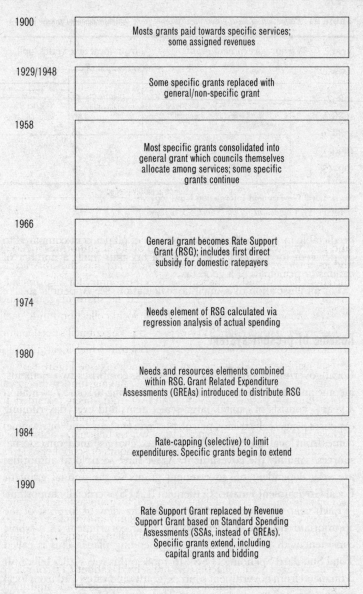

Figure 20 *The changing grants system*

Table 21 *Proportion of local government income from central and local funds*

Year	% from government grants	% from local taxes rates/poll tax/council tax
1980/1	59	41
1986/7	50	50
1988/9	54	46
1990/1	72	28
1992/3	85	15

Source: Local Government Information Unit, 1994.

predictable in yield (with a collection rate of 98 per cent compared to 93 per cent for CC/PT). The council tax thus fulfils a number of canons or principles of a good tax.

For an illustration of council tax calculation, see Appendix 19.

Resume of present system

Local government finance, like everyone's, comprises two elements, income and expenditure. The latter – amounting to some £75 million a year – consists of capital (large-scale) items and everyday running expenses (wages, electricity, petrol, postage, etc.), Income (or revenue) comes from local sources (rates, council tax, charges) and from external sources – mainly the government. As we have seen, local authorities are very dependent on government grants so the annual grant or Local Government Finance Settlement (LAFS) is crucially important.

Each year the government announces its view or forecast of the appropriate amount of spending for local government as a whole consistent with overall public (state) spending plans. This is called Total Standard Spending (TSS). In 1998–9 this was £48.2 billion. It is financed from government sources (grants and rates) and from local sources (council tax and reserves). However, TSS does not include many aspects of council spending such as (i) capital items, (ii) trading services, direct labour services (DLOs) and housing services, as these cover their costs through charges/rents and (iii) expenditure met from some specific grants, from sales and from fees, also largely self-financing. So there is expenditure inside TSS and expenditure outside TSS. They are financed differently in that the latter is financed from some specific grants and (mainly) local charges, while the former is financed from government grants, rates, council tax and council reserves.

The government also announces Standard Spending Assessments (SSAs) for each council, i.e. an assessment of the appropriate amount of revenue expenditure which would allow the authority to provide a standard level of service consistent with TSS. The calculation of SSAs is based on local socio-geographic factors or indicators – age composition, density, lengths of road, incidence of lone parenthood, ethnic and language mix, etc., as these indicate local need for services and local costs. The total of SSAs is similar to TSS but does not include some figures for specific and special grants included in TSS, i.e. TSS is greater than the sum of SSAs. The original and key purpose of SSAs is to provided a basis for distributing grants (RSG) among local authorities as, in effect, each SSA is each council's share of the TSS.

The government provides financial support for much of the TSS. This support is called the Aggregate External Finance (AEF), and it comprises Revenue Support Grant (RSG), rates collected from businesses (UBR or NNDR) and certain other grants (specific, supplementary and special). Thus the difference between TSS and AEF is the approximate amount local authorities need to raise through council tax if they are to spend at the level of TSS, i.e council tax for standard spending (CTSS). The RSG is distributed (using SSAs) so that, if all local authorities were to set their budgets and spend at the level of their SSA, then broadly the council tax would be the same for all properties in the same valuation band throughout England – see Appendix 19 for illustration. (The same process occurs in Wales and Scotland.) Thus the SSA is an estimate of local authorities' entitlements to general (RSG) government funding (i.e. excluding specific grants). It is a measure of each local authority's relative need to spend (within a fixed overall level of resources). It is not supposed to be an assessment of each council's (absolute) spending need; nor is it a spending edict or prescription (but see p. 377).

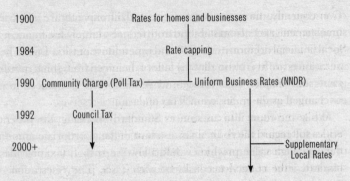

Figure 21 *Local taxes: the changing system*

A perennial concern of governments has been the overall size of local government spending: this is considered further in Chapter 14.

New Labour: further changes

In opposition, the Labour Party was highly critical of most aspects of the Conservative government's policies concerning local government finance and they promised major changes when they were returned to power. In its *Modernising Local Government* programme (February 1998) the new government stated that changes to the system of local government finance 'are needed to enhance local accountability, and reduce central government's involvement in local tax and spending decisions'.

As we have seen (p. 372), the council tax meets many of the requirements of a good tax. However, there are anomalies in the system.

A good tax will achieve a balance between the interests of local people and those of central government. It should be based on a strong link between a council's budget, the level of its tax bill and the cost and quality of services provided, while ensuring that it contributes to the achievement of national policy objectives. The present system has got the balance wrong. Local accountability is not strong enough and central government exercises its powers in a way that is disproportionate to achieving its objectives. (*Improving Local Financial Accountability*, Consultation Paper, DETR, 1998)

Consequently, the government is seeking to improve local community involvement and accountability, and reduce central intervention in local financial decisions (especially capping and grant variations). Local authorities are also to be allowed to levy their own, marginal, business rate (see Chapter 15). But central funding (RSG) is to continue unchanged as the mainstay of local finance.

While the council tax is seen as an improvement on the poll tax, critics still regard the council tax as unfair, mainly on the grounds that the very high value properties (Band H) escape high taxation. Also, like rates, the council tax lacks bouyancy (see p. 357), especially if revaluations (which cost £100 million) are delayed. (Some critics had also predicted problems of collection with the resistance to the poll tax having created a more general culture of non-payment; but there is little evidence for this, with the council tax having a collection rate of 95–98 per cent).[56]

Others question the validity and fairness of the Standard Spending Assessments. There are regular, criticisms of SSA methodology[57] – of what factors are taken into account and their relative weightings and thus which areas gain and lose,* together with the uncertainty created by the annual revisions of the SSA formula (the present government has now promised a three-year hold on further changes). Others object on principle – that assessment of local need should be left to those who are elected to represent localities.[58] The Audit Commission has criticized the use (or growing abuse) of SSAs, with service blocks becoming regarded as measures of appropriate expenditure and consequently the virtual hypothecation of grants, i.e. telling councils how much expenditure they should allocate to each service.†

The centralized setting of the business rate is similarly denounced. But most fundamental of all is the government's decision to maintain

---

* In 1998 for example one authority received £2,115 per primary pupil compared to £2,740 in another authority nearby (see *Times Educational Supplement*, 11 December 1998, p. 12). It has also been revealed that the government in 1990 deliberately manipulated SSAs to soften the introduction of the poll tax and the abolition of the Inner London Education Authority/ILEA: see *Public Administration*, Winter 1998. See too 'Targeting Benefits for Electoral Gain', *Political Studies*, March 1999: also *TES*, 14 January 2000, p. 11.

† See: *Passing the Bucks*, Audit Commission, 1994.

the present balance in the central–local division of local authority funding. In the 1991 Budget and subsequent legislation (The Community Charge (General Reduction) Act 1991), the government transferred an additional £4.3 billion to local government (funded by a 2.5 per cent rise in VAT). The result is that local authorities only raise 15 per cent of their net expenditure* from local taxes compared to the 85 per cent coming from central government. This severely undermines local government as a manifestation of local choice and decision-making. Local authorities have become 'mere Whitehall agents'.[59] This is compounded by the severe 'gearing' effect (see p. 367) it creates. Thus a 1 per cent increase in spending needs an 7 per cent rise in the council tax to pay for it. (In Wales, it is even higher, at 10 to 14 per cent, as the council tax raises only 7 to 10 per cent of revenue.)

The government recognizes a number of these criticisms, but the basic system is to stay in place. It is reluctant to make any significant changes because this would be disruptive and costly and because 'the council tax has been generally accepted and . . . there are clear tensions between maintaining the simplicity of the tax and any changes which might make it fairer. Any changes which result in the tax being more complicated could make the system harder for local taxpayers to understand and would detract from . . . local accountability'.† However, there is now to be more stability and predictability to the system in that aggregate levels of government grant are to be set out for three years at a time (rather than annually). In addition the annual revision of SSA grant distribution is to cease (pending a fundamental review over a three-year period, during which time the Census 2001 data becomes available). The aim is to avoid relatively small changes in government grant having disproportionate effects (especially through 'gearing': see p. 367) on local council taxes such that 'to local people it looks as if changes in their council tax bills are driven by the decisions of central government than by the decisions of their own councils . . . Greater local accountability depends on people understanding better

---

* This becomes 20 per cent when allowance is made for council tax benefit, transitional allowances, etc.

† *Improving Local Financial Accountability* DETR, 1998. In April 2000 councils were given the power to charge landlords of empty property a 50 per cent council tax (worth an estimated £18 million p.a.).

the link between their council's spending decisions and the council tax bills which they face.*

The major change is the abolition of 'crude and universal capping' under the Local Government Act 1999. However, the government has reserve powers to intervene and prevent excessive local budgets and CT increases. The government could 'cap' where the local expenditure was considered excessive or represented an excessive increase. (The normal criteria have been either a council's increase over its previous year's budget or its spending compared to SSA. In 1995–6 seven councils were capped bringing about a reduction in budgets of £24.4 million.) It is anticipated that this power to regulate council taxes (or precepts) will be rarely used, partly because of the new regime of Best Value and partly because of the improved dialogue and relationship between councils and their communities (the latter is dealt with in Chapter 15).

'Best Value' is a duty on local authorities to deliver services to clear standards – covering both cost and quality – by the most effective, economic and efficient means available. The policy of Best Value aims 'to improve the quality of local services and the efficiency and economy with which they are delivered. It will apply to all authorities and all services, and is intended to ensure sustained improvements in performance'.†

Under the Local Government Act 1999, local authorities are required to secure continuous improvements in the way their functions are exercised, having regard to economy, efficiency and effectiveness. For this purpose they must consult tax payers and service users; they must take account of national standards set by the government in such services as education and social services; and they are expected to liaise with other providers to share aims and visions, and to integrate services. Councils are required to undertake regular reviews of their service levels and methods with a view to setting performance targets and action plans to meet them. Each year they are required to prepare Best Value performance plans, which include objectives, assessments, reviews, performance indicators (PIs), performance standards (PS)

---

* *Improving Local Financial Accountability*, para 4.3.
† *Improving Local Services Through Best Value*, DETR, 1998.

and performance targets (PTs) and there have to be comparisons with other local authorities and previous years. Thus local people will be clear about the standards of services which they can expect to receive, and better able to hold their councils to account for their record in meeting them.

Performance plans are subject to inspection by the auditor who may send a report to the Audit Commission and the Secretary of State. Such inspections, where appropriate, will work with specialist inspections (such as those for education, social services or housing). The Secretary of State has considerable discretionary powers (including issuing statutory guidance) such that s/he can direct the Audit Commission to carry out inspections of authorities' compliance with Best Value requirements. Where there is failure s/he may initiate an inquiry or direct the offending authority to prepare (or amend) a performance plan, and a further consequence might be a requirement to put the service out to competition or even to transfer it to another authority or agency. The government envisages that intervention will be rare, especially since local authorities are being advised by the newly-established Improvement and Development Agency (of the former Local Government Management Board. (In Wales and Scotland the detailed arrangements rest with their respective Assembly/ Parliament.)

While Best Value is intended, from the year 2000, to replace the rigid regime of Compulsory Competitive Tendering (CCT), two points may be noted. First, clearly it is not a 'soft option' to CCT, though many authorities are embracing this new approach with enthusiasm (and bids to be nominated for the Best Value pilot projects were over-subscribed). Second, it does not rule out competitive tendering and much is likely to occur (indeed, where there is evidence that it is lacking, it could be made compulsory). Where it continues, the law has been amended so that non-commercial considerations may now be taken into account in awarding contracts (such as equal opportunities).

Capital finance

Capital expenditure is spending on items which have a long life, such as houses, vehicles, roads and schools. Such expenditures are traditionally financed by borrowing, but there are other sources (see Table 19, p. 339). These may include the setting up of companies to attract private capital (and have a freer management structure), the *sale* of assets (such as land or houses), money received in the *repayment* of loans by those who have borrowed from local authorities (for house purchase etc.) and revenue from investments and from *grants*. The central government provides (capital) grants to local authorities for such purposes as construction and repair of roads, schools and houses, for the purchase of property or derelict land, for adaptations (e.g. for the disabled) and for housing transfers to housing associations. (The Single Regeneration Budget is so-called because it has absorbed a number of previous grant-aided programmes including Capital Challenge, City Challenge and Estates Action. These along with others involve councils making competitive bids to the government, and one of the criteria for success is demonstrated efficient performance.) Local authorities also receive grant aid from the European Union for such purposes as industrial development or education and training. In addition, their capital expenditures are financed from Lottery funds, from joint ventures and Public–Private Finance arrangements (PFI; see p. 387) and the private sector may provide roads or traffic management schemes as a contribution for planning permissions ('planning gain'). In recent years local authorities have tended to finance more of their capital expenditure from *current revenues* (council tax, rates, charges, sales of assets, etc.) partly because it was cheaper (especially when interest rates were higher) and partly for political reasons.[60] (Legally they are obliged to set aside a proportion of revenue – known as Minimum Revenue Provision (MRP) – to repay debt. Currently it is 2 per cent of their borrowing for housing and 4 per cent of all other debt.) The Revenue Support Grant and the housing subsidies help councils to finance the cost of their capital expenditure, i.e. interest charges and repayment of loan.

Capital finance (like revenue finance) is subject to a control framework which covers (i) procedures for allocating capital resources to councils and (ii) regulations governing how they can utilize those resources.

Borrowing

Local authorities are empowered to borrow under the Local Government Acts of 1972 and 1973. There are many ways in which they may raise loans; which precise method they decide to adopt will vary according to current legislation[61] and policy, current financial conditions and the individual judgement (and politics) of the local authority. A large proportion of local government borrowing takes the form of loans from the Public Works Loan Board (PWLB), a government agency comprising twelve Commissioners (originally established in 1815) to lend to public authorities.* Under this arrangement each local authority is given a quota which it may borrow from the PWLB (and which it may exceed but at higher rates of interest). Otherwise, local authorities raise mortgage loans from the public, or they issue stock and bonds (these are regularly advertised in the press), or they can raise temporary loans (which do not need loan sanction – see below) such as bank overdrafts. Such borrowing may be expensive when local authorities have to compete with other borrowers and offer attractive interest rates. It can also, on occasion, be rather embarrassing, as when, in 1980, being in dispute with their local authority employers, the National and Local Government Officers' Association (NALGO) threatened to withdraw £2 million of short-term loans from fifteen councils which had borrowed from it! It may be safer and cheaper therefore for local authorities to build up their own reserve funds (for specific capital items) and balances, as indeed most do. Many of them also utilize their superannuation funds; thus, in effect, local authorities 'borrow' from themselves, and indeed a number of councils are net lenders. In recent years, local authorities' borrowing has fallen significantly, partly because of reductions in expenditure, but also due to their use of funds from assets sales (such

---

* Of total local authority debt of £56 billion in 1994 70 per cent was owed to the PWLB (See *Annual Abstract of Statistics*, HMSO).

as houses). Government policy has also required them to repay debts, such that in some years there has been overall debt repayment ('negative' borrowing). A number of local authorities are completely debt-free and have substantial reserves.

For capital grant and expenditure approval purposes, the government requires local authorities to draw up and submit their proposals; for example, 'Transport Policies and Programmes' (TPPs) for roads and transport, 'Housing Investment Programmes' (HIPs) for housing.

Loan sanction

Before 1980, the central government placed strict limits on the amounts which local authorities could borrow. This system of control was known as 'loan sanction'. Under this system local authorities had to obtain explicit permissions from the relevant government department (such as the DfEE) or DoH before they could borrow money, so that, for example, before raising a loan to finance the building of schools, an LEA had to apply for loan approval.

Under the Local Government, Planning and Land Act 1980, local authorities in England and Wales moved closer to the capital control system then operating in Scotland, whereby central approvals apply to programmes rather than individual projects, and related more to expenditure than borrowing. The new controls were intended to enable central government to ensure that the total of local authority capital spending each year was consistent with national expenditure plans (in previous years such planning had been too often frustrated[62]), while reducing central government involvement in detailed local capital spending decisions. However, the system did not work as the government anticipated. Together with the rate support grant system, it created a new profession or industry of creative accounting and finance (including such devices as sale and leaseback, advanced purchase, deferred purchase, barters, interest-rate swaps, re-definition/ allocation of prescribed expenditure, etc.) that, overall, has been wasteful and distorting.[63] Consequently the government moved back to control capital expenditure levels through control over borrowing.[64]

Under the Local Government and Housing Act 1989, local authorities now receive an annual *credit approval* or BCA (based on the government's perception of each authority's needs and spending power). Rather like Standard Spending Assessments, the government issues annual Capital Guidelines (ACG) to councils which broadly represent an authority's need for capital expenditure in the next year relative to the needs of other authorities. These allocations relate to five services areas (housing, education, social services, transport and other). An authority's BCA is calculated by adding up its ACGs and then deducting a proportion of its capital receipts (known as receipts taken into account or RITAs). As a result some councils receive no BCA.* The BCA can be used to finance expenditure on any service (though in practice there is an element of hypothecation in that spending is heavily influenced by ACGs). For particular services or projects local authorities may also receive Supplementary Credit Approvals (SCAs).

Local authorities can also use (i) a proportion of their accumulated capital receipts (from property sales) for capital expenditure, namely 25 per cent of house sales proceeds and 50 per cent of other sales receipts; each of these is currently producing about £600 million p.a. The remainder – known as 'set aside' – is to be used to redeem debt (some £40 billion and costing some £3½ million per annum) and/or for future capital investment, and (ii) any surpluses from current revenues.

Thus in effect, all capital expenditure must be set against a permission to borrow (the credit approvals), plus part of capital receipts (50 or 25 per cent) plus certain other receipts (for example from planning gain† and legacies).

While there appears to be some relaxation in direct controls, the indirect control remains and is perhaps more comprehensive in scope or actual coverage. Indeed the aim is to preclude the various creative-accounting devices[65] which have enabled councils to get round spending restrictions.

---

* Over the period 1992/3–1997/8, credit approvals as a whole fell from £3.3 billion to under £2 billion.

† Where councils make it a condition of planning permission that a developer provides a community amenity (such as a leisure centre, shopping units or social housing).

Current reforms

Local authorities have long criticized capital controls (and especially the set-aside requirements) because they have deprived them of much-needed resources for new building, maintenance and renovation. But the capital finance system itself has been criticized on a number of grounds. Firstly, the system of annual allocations (which must be used within the year or they are lost) induces a short-term approach to expenditure and limits flexibility; this is increased by the uncertainty created by the competitive bids system. Secondly, capital allocations are increasingly for specific projects (via grants or SCAs) which limit or inhibit *local* decision-making; this is reinforced by the tendency for the guidelines (ACGs) to over-influence actual spending decisions,* i.e. the problem of virtual hypothecation (see, too, p. 377). Thirdly, there are the difficulties caused by multiple sources of funding, plus the complexities of Private Finance Initiatives (PFIs) and other undue regulations. Fourthly, there is often the inhibition arising from matched funding (by the council) requirements.

These problems, according to the Audit Commission† have been compounded by poor local management. 'Some councils have been criticised for lack of longer-term planning and priority setting, lack of effective corporate control over capital programmes, and poor property management'.‡

The government recognizes a number of these issues (and was itself critical of some aspects when in opposition, up to 1997). Consequently it is introducing a number of reforms which aim to give greater stability in the distribution arrangements, allow for flexibility and make the control system simpler to understand.

It has already committed itself to the doubling of public sector investment over three years (from 1998) for schools (under the New Deal for Schools programme), for local authority transport and roads,

---

* *Modernising Local Government: Capital Finance*, DETR, 1998, p. 40.
† *Just Capital* (1996) and *Capital Gains* (1997).
‡ *Modernising Local Government: Capital Finance*, DETR, 1998; Audit Commission, *Just Capital* and *Capital Gains*.

and for urban regeneration (through the Single Regeneration Budget and the New Deal for Communities programme); in addition, it released some £3.6 billion from capital receipts for repairs to council houses. In 1997 the government began to relax its controls over the recycling of property sales receipts (e.g. from sales of farms, car parks and airports) and some 'in-and-out' schemes are permitted (i.e. where a property is sold and the proceeds are dedicatedly used for replacement, such as a new school for a run-down one). The government has also set targets for the sale of local authority assets and to encourage this it has now abolished set-aside of receipts from asset sales other than housing and related land.

Perhaps the most important change is the intention to introduce a single capital 'pot' i.e. a cross-service rather than service-specific allocation for the bulk of central government capital support to councils. This would allow more autonomy for councils to decide allocation among services, thus providing more flexibility and more opportunity to address cross-cutting issues (such as social exclusion). However, certain individual programmes (such as schools) are to be protected initially (and some other more specific projects will continue to receive separate specific funding) and the 'single pot' will not be implemented before the year 2001.

Assessed need is a crucial factor in capital allocations and needs indicators are to be reformulated and these, together with total levels of government support will (like SSAs) be set out in three-year plans, thus providing greater stability and predictability. However, competitive bidding procedures will also continue,* especially to secure Best Value and optimum utilization of resources. Thus councils will be judged (and rewarded) according to their performance and achievements (with the best, the 'beacon' councils, being given additional credit approvals). To this end, councils and other public sector bodies are being encouraged to innovate in the use and management of assets

---

* In 1990/1 40 per cent central approvals and grants for local capital expenditure was targeted (i.e. related to specific programmes or schemes). By 1998/9 this had doubled to 80 per cent, especially as a result of initiatives and bidding regimes (SRB, Capital Challenge, New Deal for Schools etc.); see *Modern Local Government: Local Government Finance*, LGA, 1998.

through initiatives like one-stop shops, electronic service delivery, shared accommodation and single-site offices.

Finally, the government (now) sets great store by the Private Finance Intiative and Public/Private Partnerships Programme (the 4 Ps) – their development is 'a high priority'. The enactment of the Local Government (Contracts) Act 1997 has clarified the law on councils' powers in this respect and the use of PFIs is built into the Best Value regime. Government support for such schemes has been increased following the Comprehensive Spending Review (1997–8). Thus, for example, revenue support (in the RSG) was made available for £500 million of investment under such contracts in 1998–9.

A note on PFI

The Private Finance Initiative (PFI) is a new form of public service provision. Rather than provide, own and manage capital assets local (and other public) authorities purchase services from those who do, i.e. their private sector partners, who have successfully bid for the work involved in designing, building, financing and operating the service. Basically, the private sector provides the capital and the management skills and expertise (of design, construction, operation) and takes most of the risk involved. The private sector partner only gets paid if the asset works to specified levels of service (and there are financial penalties for under-achievement).

There are three types of PFI project: the financially free-standing, where it is provided on behalf of the public authority and people pay direct (e.g. toll roads or visitor centres). The second (known as Design Build Finance Operate) is where services are sold to the public sector (e.g. private prisons, where cells are 'rented'). And the third is joint ventures, where the costs are met jointly, but the control of the project rests with the private sector (e.g. urban regeneration or the Croydon tramlink). It is the last two methods which are mainly used in local government, for such facilities as IT services, schools, waste, transport, sports stadia and exhibition centres and economic development.

From the local government point of view, a major advantage is that the capital investment undertaken by way of PFI does not (since 1996) count against their quota in the capital control system (which is a real relaxation since the control system created in 1989 was established to prevent councils' various creative accounting methods of evasion, including leaseback, which is what many PFI projects amount to.

Banks and other private sector organizations had become wary of such ventures in view of the various cases* which resulted in some local authorities escaping from debts after the courts declared their actions to be *ultra vires* and the contracts involved therefore void, such that the banks could not reclaim the money they had loaned or guaranteed. The Local Government (Contracts) Act 1997 clarifies (though does not actually extend) local authorities' powers to enter into contracts and partnerships with the private sector, especially regarding capital finance.†

PFI has also become favoured by the Labour government because it chimes in with its concept of the 'stakeholder society' whereby more people are directly concerned with government activity. It also allows increases in public sector spending without adding to its borrowing, since capital spending is replaced by a stream of revenue payments to the private sector over a number of years.

Financial organization and procedures

Local authorities differ in their internal arrangements for dealing with financial matters. By law they are merely required to 'make arrangements for the proper administration of their financial affairs and ... secure that one of their officers has responsibility for the administration of those affairs'.[66] However, in practice local authorities

---

* Such as the interest rate 'swaptions' arrangement undertaken by Hammersmith and Fulham LBC in 1991, or the housing scheme of Waltham Forest LBC and the timeshare scheme of Allerdale DC. See *Credit Suisse v Allerdale*, 1996, *Credit Suisse v Waltham Forest*, 1996, *Hazell v Hammersmith and Fulham*, 1991. But see, too, *Kleinwort Benson Ltd v Lincoln City Council* (and other councils) 1998, where the House of Lords allowed that company to reclaim its money. It may also be noted that some of these inter-authority loan exchanges are acceptable, as a way of establishing a balance in the debt portfolio; but if it amounts to speculation, it is deemed illegal i.e. *ultra vires*.

† See A. Arden and S. Cirell, *The Journal of Local Government Law*, April 1998; also J. Bennett and S. Cirell 'PFI for local government', *FT Law and Tax*, 1997.

have adopted a number of common procedures from which it is possible to generalize, and they are all bound by the rules that the financial year begins on 1 April and that it is illegal to budget for a deficit.

As we saw in Chapter 9, local authorities generally have appointed a policy or Policy & Resources (P & R) committee. This committee plays a key role in the coordination and control of the local authorities' financial decisions and actions (for an illustration, see p. 391). However, it is also common practice for the council to create a separate finance committee which works closely with (and is often a sub-committee of) the P & R committee. To facilitate control and coordination, members of the P & R committee (and the finance sub-committee) are drawn from (and are often the chairs of) the service or 'spending' committees.

The chair of the finance committee is a key figure in the local authority, acting in the capacity of a minor Chancellor of the Exchequer and often making a dramatic 'state of the economy' speech at the council's annual budget and council tax-setting meeting. He or she is almost certainly a member of the P & R committee and as chair of the finance committee will have the power to authorize actions (by officers) on behalf of the committee between its meetings. In this respect he or she has a close working relationship with the chief financial officer of the authority (variously entitled the Treasurer or Director of Finance or, more recently, Director of Resources). The latter is the head of the Finance (or Treasurer's) Department, which comprises the senior officials, who are professionally qualified in accountancy, together with the more junior staff, who undertake the more routine processes of collecting money, checking bills and making payments on behalf of the authority.

Preparing the budget

The annual budget is a statement containing the details of the council's current and capital incomes and expenditures, together with plans for the coming year. The key decisions relate to level of spending, use of reserves or borrowing, and the level of council tax (or precept). While traditionally the budget is drawn up for one year at a time, it has become common practice to develop plans or 'continuation budgets' for several years ahead,[67] based tentatively on the authority's long-term corporate plans (and rolling programmes), together with population forecasts and estimates of need in the local community. This is known as the 'financial plan approach'. There are various methods of preparing the budget:

(i) the traditional or 'incremental' method, which involves the use of the existing 'base' budget of service expenditures, and adjusting these marginally up or down. The basic pattern or profile therefore alters slowly, if at all. The main defect is that it looks at monetary inputs rather than outcomes and effectiveness of expenditure.

(ii) zero-base budgeting (ZBB) involves starting from scratch – having a clean sheet, and requiring every service or programme to make a case for funds. This means they have to justify their 'bid', and no service just coasts along without appraisal. Few services these days are likely to have this latter luxury, and this procedure does make for rational decision-making and a proper consideration of priorities (though it does require much time, and cannot be undertaken frequently).

(iii) budget rationing is a process which begins by deciding what is the appropriate level of council tax. The total product or yield of that levy is then divided among the various services and functions – 'the coat is cut to match the cloth'. A variant of this is priority-based budgeting.

(iv) increasingly, councils are using public opinion, focus groups, referendums, surveys and questionnaires to shape their spending (and taxing) plans. A good example was Milton Keynes in February 1999, when residents held a referendum on three options for the council tax increase. Similarly, Oxfordshire invited residents to pay a higher council tax and choose its allocation among services (most went to education). This method will become more universal as, and in so far as, Best Value and community planning are implemented.

It is also common for local authorities to have (i) a Capital budget (setting targets for capital items which usually runs over a 3-to-5-year period), (ii) a Personnel budget (to monitor and control staffing levels) and (iii) a cash-flow budget (to monitor receipts and out-goings, e.g. to maximize interest income from loans).

A Planned Programme Budgeting System (PPBS) deals with programmes of activity (e.g. care of elderly) and objectives. It cuts across departmental boundaries and has a longer-term perspective. But it can require a lot of time to prepare and information is often lacking. (It is also said to ignore political realities.)

The budget cycle

Local authority procedures differ in detail, but broadly the budget cycle operates as follows:

April/June	Review of financial situation by Finance Officer/ Department and Policy and Resources Committee (PRC). Consideration of external factors: national events (new legislation/responsibilities, changes in interest/wage rates and charges for energy, insurances, etc.) and local circumstances (closure/ arrival of major business/employer, volume changes in client groups, school children, elderly, etc.), and internal policies: service standards and development, priorities, etc. Guidelines sent to departments/service committees
July/August	Departments start preparing estimates; committees consider priorities
September/ October	PRC considers and agrees priorities
November	Government's broad indication of its spending plans
December	Grant Settlement and UBR/NNDR announced by government, provides indicative figures, SSAs and 'guidelines' on expenditure (in place of 'cap', though Minister has reserve powers and may also place limit on subsidy for council tax benefit; appeals by council possible). PRC sets targets for services' expenditure

January	Service departments/committees finalize their estimates, taking account of the above information; may be bilateral discussions with finance department, and consultation with rate payers. Grant settlement (perhaps modified) figures confirmed (through Orders in Parliament)
February	P & R Committee collates and finalizes the figures for the council (including the use of reserves or balances) which then (at the annual budget meeting) determines the budget and sets the council tax (or precept), and perhaps local (supplementary) rate for businesses, in good time for the new financial year, starting 1 April. (By law this must be completed by the last day of February for precepting authorities and 10 March for others)
March	End of financial year; outturns compared to estimates, accounts are closed and prepared for audit (Spending is monitored throughout)

This sequence is subject to amendment as local authorities develop Best Value strategies, especially in so far as these involve fundamental reviews of services and liaison or joint-working with other bodies. Also the annual debacle of the Grant Settlement is modified since 1998 as broad grant figures and the SSA distribution now runs over a three-year period.

Control

The most important financial decisions – fixing the council tax and deciding borrowing policy – rest with the council; by law they cannot be delegated. Yet it often appears that the financial control exercised by the council as a whole is little more than a charade, since the estimates always seem to go through 'on the nod', without discussion or alteration. This may in part be due to their complexity and perhaps to the obscurity or esoteric nature of some of the language. Few councillors are financial experts and many feel at a loss.

However, many of the figures merely represent in money terms the nature of most of the local authority's activities: changes tend to be marginal (or 'incremental') and are usually well understood by members of the service committees. And members of the P & R or finance committee build up a familiarity and expertise which allows them to guide the council for purposes of control.

Indeed the whole purpose of the estimates and budgetary procedure is to allow the exercise of control from a central point – the P & R or finance committee. This committee will also monitor progress in the work and expenditure of the local authority. In this respect, at all stages the finance officer and his or her staff play a leading role – checking that expenditures are in line with targets, that cash flows are running according to plan and reporting on the local authority's finances and any difficulties to the appropriate committee or department.

Control is also exercised through standing orders (see p. 242, and, for illustration, Appendix 12), which are usually supplemented by special rules known as 'financial regulations'. Together these cover such procedures as the composition and role of the P & R and/or finance committee, the drawing-up and submission of estimates, special notification of proposals for large schemes, rules on virement (transfers of funds from one purpose to another) and on tenders (firms' quotations) and the placing of contracts. Another form of control which itself will be set down in standing orders (at least in part) is audit.

The *finance department* inevitably has close contact with all the departments of the authority and the *chief finance officer* (CFO or Treasurer/ Director of Finance) has close contacts with other chief officers (especially the chief executive officer)* and with the various service committees and their chairs. Under the Local Government Finance Act 1988 (following the Widdicombe Report), councils' chief finance officers are now required to be properly qualified. They also have the statutory duty to restrain what they see as unlawful expenditure or transactions by issuing a 'Section 114 report' to council members and the auditor. This enhanced role has already been exercised (e.g. in Brent London

---

* In 10 per cent of local authorities the posts of CEO and CFO are combined in one person.

Borough Council in November 1988 and Eastleigh in September 1990), but some people question the competence of treasurers to act in such a quasi-judicial fashion, while others feel such powers (and those outlined on p. 297) may engender unnecessary conflict between officers and members. (These empowering sections of the Finance Act 1988 were introduced because of the difficulties created by the 'hard Left' councils of the 1980s.)

It is the CFO's job to exercise a general oversight of the local authority's financial practices – methods of payment, timing cash flows, auditing and keeping within guidelines, checking virement, etc. In practice, much of this work will devolve on to senior officers while the CFO will concentrate on the other main role as financial adviser to the council. CFOs will be concerned with the financial implications of the council's overall policy and hence with the specific policies of the service committees and departments. While they may attend these committees or send reports to them, most of their attention will be focused on the finance committee and the P & R committee.

Like the finance officer, these two committees will have two broad roles: firstly, the more routine control function of approving the payment of bills, administration of the authority's superannuation scheme and insurance matters, supervision of the work of the finance department and investment arrangements, etc.; secondly, the more creative function of examining the spending plans and proposals of the service committees, with a view both to their coordination and to assessing their total impact on the resources of the local authority and its broad aims and priorities. This drawing-up of the council's budget is crucial to the operation of the local authority. It requires the close involvement of the P & R and the finance committees with other committees in order to strengthen the corporate approach to the authority's affairs. (A similar and parallel collaboration occurs between the finance department and other departments.) The result of their deliberations is a series of recommendations to the full council.

Control is also exercised externally by audit and by the general public. Under the Local Government Act 1972, the Local Government Finance Act 1982 and other statutes, local authorities are required to provide and/or reveal certain financial information to the public. During a three-week period (usually at the annual audit), the public may inspect and make copies of relevant documents. In practice, some councils make the latter very difficult (e.g. by refusing photocopying facilities or making extortionate charges).

Audit

Audit has a number of purposes – the detection of fraud, the propriety of accounting procedures, the legality of expenditure, value for money and to ensure that the accounts faithfully reflect the council's financial position. It takes two forms:

(1) *Internal*, undertaken by the officials of the local authority's own finance department. They will keep a regular check on incomes from rents, charges and other sources, the receipt of stores, claims for expenses, official receipts, etc. They will be checking the accuracy of stocks and accounts, together with the procedures involved, in order to prevent fraud and the misappropriation of council, property. (The most difficult area is housing benefit with an estimated 20 per cent fraudulent claims, costing some £2 billion. Detected benefit fraud was £78 million in 1998.*)

The purpose of internal audit is thus to ensure that the financial dealings of the local authority are undertaken in a proper manner. But, additionally, such audit will be concerned to ensure that departmental expenditures are being made in accordance with the approved estimates, and that money is not being unofficially transferred from one purpose to another (otherwise the whole idea of the budgetary procedure is undermined. Approved or permitted transfers are known as 'virement'.)

However, as is now the case with external audit (see below), the historical 'probity-centred' role of auditing has been joined by a more positive emphasis on auditing systems and operations, with auditors adding value to the authority by providing appraisal and advice on internal systems and processes.† A number of authorities are

* See *Protecting the Public Purse*, Audit Commission, 1998.
† See B. Hopkins, *The Nature of Quality Audit*, CIPFA, 1997.

reinforcing this role through the creation of Audit committees (a development encouraged by the Audit Commission).

(2) *External.* By law, all local authorities are subject to external audit. This itself may take two forms.[68] The first is 'District Audit', whereby the country is divided into districts and a district auditor is appointed to each to conduct audits of local authority accounts. Formerly these auditors were appointed by the Minister; since 1982 they are appointed by the Audit Commission (see p. 397), and are, in effect, public service employees. In 1994, District Audit became an arm's-length agency of the AC. With a staff of 1,200, it is responsible for about 70 per cent of local authority audits in England and Wales. In Scotland, external auditing is the responsibility of an independent Commission for Local Authority Accounts, appointed by the Scottish Executive. This Commission too recruits its own audit staff, but equally (like the Audit Commission) it also substantially (and traditionally) appoints private practitioners (see below).

The function of district auditors is to inspect local authority accounts in order to detect financial irregularities (fraud), to promote sound financial practices and procedures and to prevent or uncover unlawful payments. In this last capacity they are in effect reinforcing the *ultra vires* rule (see p. 76), for when they discover expenditure which is outside the legal powers of the local authority, they may refer the matter to the court for a judicial ruling on the legality or otherwise of the expenditure. The courts can thus disallow such illegal expenditure. Equally where there has been a failure to collect sums due to the council (such as rents or council tax) or there has been a loss to the council due to 'wilful misconduct' (knowingly doing something wrong or with reckless indifference, not just negligence, imprudence or error of judgement, or excessive zeal), the auditor alone (under the Local Government Finance Act 1982) may *surcharge* the responsible persons for the sums lost. Otherwise it is up to the court to disallow expenditures and perhaps order repayment by those members and officers who were responsible for the illegal expenditure (or for failure to collect any incomes due).[69] In the twenty-five years 1947–72 the number of cases of reported fraud or unlawful expenditure amounted to about fifty a year.[70] In 1997/8 there were 638 cases of fraud, worth some £4 million, and 40 cases of corruption (e.g. awarding planning consent, licences, grants, accommodation or contracts in return for cash, etc.) amounting to £7.4 million. Serious cases can result in a jail sentence (for councillors or officers).

Surcharge itself is quite rare – usually fewer than 5 cases a year. In 1985-6 councillors in Liverpool and Lambeth were 'surcharged' (heavily fined, at £5,000 each) and disqualified from office (for five years) for 'wilful misconduct in delaying the fixing of their councils' rates' (which is now statutorily timetabled).[71] It led to calls to have the surcharge penalty system (uniquely applicable to local government) abolished. In 1989 the district auditor successfully challenged the legality of some loan deals known as 'swaptions', i.e. where local authorities exchange interest rate charges (see p. 388).[72] And in 1988 ten councillors were surcharged for approving a budget containing an excess rate fund contribution to the housing account.[73] In the same case it was pointed out that councillors could be so penalized even if absent from the meeting; it would depend on the reasons for their absence. Officers too may be surcharged. The Westminster 'homes for votes' case (see p. 541) resulted initially (in 1994) in the surcharge of four councillors and two officers for over £31 million (subsequently appealed and scaled down to £27 million).

It was partly due to the enormity of the sums involved that surcharge is being abolished. Surcharge was being used as a penalty and, being unrelated to the means of the person being surcharged, could lead to bankruptcy. The system was also open the criticism that the auditor had excessive powers – formulating and prosecuting the case, judging guilt or innocence and determining the penalty based on estimated financial losses. Investigations could be costly too – the Redbridge case (see below) took 3 years and cost over £½ million, and the Westminster case took 7 years and cost £3 million. So, following the recommendation of the Nolan Report, surcharge is to be replaced with a system whereby the courts can order compensation from anyone (staff or councillor) who has gained personally from misconduct resulting in financial loss by the council.

Over the years, the district auditors (and internal auditors) have been focusing attention on wasteful expenditures or procedures (mode of borrowing, fuel consumption, cost controls over repairs expenditure, etc.) and increasingly on value for money (e.g. in the three years 1970–73, suggestions by the district audit saved an estimated £1.5 million).[74] For the latter purpose (under the Local Government Act 1992, and as part of the Citizen's Charter) the Audit Commission is required to publish 'performance indicators' (output divided by input) for comparing different services and different authorities (see Appendix 15).[75] And in 1979 the Advisory Committee on Local Government Audit was established, to consider the annual report of the Chief Inspector of Audit[76] and any questions arising from it which were of general interest, and to make recommendations to local authorities in respect of value for money (VFM).

The second form of external audit used to be called 'approved audit'. Here auditors (usually local firms of accountants) had to be approved by the Minister. Where these auditors found cases of illegal expenditure or losses, they had to report the matter to the Minister, who could order an *extraordinary* audit by the district auditor. Since 1982 the Audit Commission is responsible for this, and for the appointment of auditors from the private sector, who conduct about 30 per cent of all council audits. Thus in effect there are the Audit Commission's in-house 'district auditors' and private sector auditors working under contract for the Audit Commission.

Before each audit, the accounts and relevant documents must be available for public inspection for the previous fifteen working days, and may thus be examined and, if required, copied (for a fee). And electors may question the auditor about the accounts or make objections/allegations about illegality, losses due to mismanagement, misconduct, etc. It is also possible for the Minister (or Audit Commission, see below) to direct that there should be an additional or 'extraordinary' audit.

External auditors issue a report when they have completed their work, though if a matter is sufficiently important it may be issued beforehand. Audit is announced in advance in the press or public notice boards, and by law the local authority's accounts must be made available to the public. Members of the public are entitled to raise questions about the accounts with the auditors, and this can be an important aspect of local government accountability (seemingly under-utilized)[77] and, following the Nolan Report 1997, the district auditor can refuse to hear objection and challenges to the accounts if s/he considers them vexatious or identical to a previous objection. The auditor may issue a special *'public interest' report*, where the accounts appear to be unsatisfactory and things have gone wrong in some way (extravagance, fraud, inefficiency, faulty systems, etc.). There were thirty-six such reports in 1990; in 1996 there were ten, including Westminster LB. Furthermore, if an elector makes objections to the auditor about the accounts, the district auditor may refer the matter to the law court to rule on the lawfulness of expenditure. (In the Camden case, 1982, two members of the council's Conservative opposition party complained to the district auditor that the council had been 'illegally generous' in their pay settlement to striking workers during the 'dirty jobs' dispute in the 1978–9 'winter of discontent'. The auditor took the case to the High Court. The case was dismissed on the grounds that the settlement was within the council's discretion.*) Alternatively, the Minister could order the district auditor to hold an extraordinary audit, as in the Clay Cross case (see p. 103). If the district auditor refuses to submit an elector's objection to the court, s/he may go to court for a declaration and if necessary an injunction against the unlawful expenditure.

Other notable recent cases are those of Redbridge LBC (1997, which involved (early) retired staff being paid illegal pensions – triggered by an elector's objection), substantial financial irregularities in Doncaster (1997, Donnygate) and Blaenau Gwent (1998), and the Appleby Report on mismanagement and loss of funds in Lambeth LBC 1995.

The Audit Commission

Originating from the Layfield Report (1976), the Local Government Finance Act 1982 made local authorities in England and Wales subject to the 'Scottish' system of audit, with the creation of the Audit

---

* More recently, councils' DLOs have been under scrutiny as a result of several of them running into deficit. In 1998 there were allegations of some Scottish council workmen earning up to 5 times the basic wage through overtime, of a Liverpool street sweeper earning £25,000 with overtime, and a 'lollipop' man earning £370 per week for a 10-hour week.

Commission. The AC is a body – a 'quango' – of 13–17 members appointed by the government and drawn from industry, local government and trade unions. The aim of this change was to increase the apparent independence of audit, to bring in more private auditors and to increase the efficiency approach to local finances. The AC appoints auditors to inspect local authorities' accounts* (drawing on the District Audit service or, for about 40 per cent of councils, the private sector which local authorities themselves used to be able to choose), but it is specifically charged with promoting more value-for-money (VFM) auditing (for which purpose it absorbed the Advisory Committee). The AC issues auditors with a code of audit practice (approved by Parliament) for use in conducting audits.

In its mission statement (1993) it declares, 'The Audit Commission promotes proper stewardship of public finances and helps those responsible for the management and delivery of public services to achieve economy, efficiency and effectiveness.' It aims to be a 'driving force in the improvement of public services' which it seeks to achieve through 'auditing public service accounts to ensure their probity and regularity and producing national studies of value for money'.

The Commission produces regular and numerous VFM studies (e.g. 1,600 in 1985)[78] and performance indicators and comparisons:[79] see Appendix 15 for an illustration. Its reports cover all aspects of local government – housing, management, vehicle maintenance, parks, education, etc., and its various VFM studies have identified savings by local authorities amounting to some £2 billion a year.[80] Thus for example in 1988 the AC pointed to the falling school rolls and estimated that empty school places are costing some £250 million a year (though of course local politics and perhaps educational or social reasons may forestall closures of schools). In 1998, the Scottish Accounts Commission was highly critical of the 30 per cent of primary and 20 per cent of secondary schools with 40 per cent of empty places. It also revealed a council tax collection rate of only 87 per cent costing councils some £15 million a year. In 1989 the AC for England and

---

* Such scrutiny, unlike inspections, is not free, of course: the commission must cover its costs. Local authorities currently have to pay some £50 per hour (in addition to which there are audit fees for certifying/validating grant claims).

Wales criticized councils for allowing council tenants to fall into arrears* of some £500 million. In 1988 it criticized local authorities for allowing much of their accumulated land and property (worth £100 billion) to lie idle or under-used, and it suggested that in view of population changes and changing responsibilities (with contracting out, etc.) councils should dispose of some 25 per cent of their holdings. (The government responded by requiring councils to publish information on their unused land. And under the Local Government, Planning and Land Act 1980, the Minister has the power to require their disposal of land.)

The AC has been instrumental in drawing up (together with the local authority associations) a voluntary code of practice on 'a prudential approach to local authority commitments' to avoid risky financial transactions and the building up of excessive indebtedness (often the result of the creative accounting techniques used). And under the Local Government Act 1988 (Sec. 30), the AC was given a pre-emptive or 'stop' power† to prevent what it sees as questionable financial deals. This power has been criticized as excessive and undemocratic, and recent cases of surcharge and disqualification of councillors (see p. 394) have led to calls for auditors to shed their quasi-judicial role of initiating such proceedings. Indeed, some have seen the AC as an instrument of central government control.[81] Others raise questions about the Audit Commission's social and political composition (which could be significant in terms of their experience, knowledge, use of, and attitudes towards, local services). And thus there is the view that it uses too many business or accounting criteria in its scrutinies and reports; they are afraid that the work of the AC will (together with policies such as the national curriculum in schools) homogenize local authorities and that its tendency to develop a managerial role will impinge on the political aspects of councils' decision-making. Thus, among others, the National Consumer Council has expressed concern that service effectiveness is being neglected in favour of economy and efficiency,

* e.g. In 1996–7, Islington LBC was bottom of the league table for rents, with a collection rate of 94 per cent. At the top was Rushcliffe BC with 99.97 per cent, but it has only one-tenth the number of properties.

† Following the recommendations of the Nolan Committee in 1997, this 'stop power' is to be replaced by the AC's warning notices under the LG Bill 2000.

and that cost-effectiveness is only cost- and service-cutting.[82] Other critics have suggested that the Audit Commission has perhaps lost some of its traditional auditing cutting edge by focusing too much on VFM and, in view of the apparent recalcitrance of some authorities, that its powers should be increased.[83] However, the AC has rebutted a number of these criticisms (or 'myths'[84]) and now claims to have regard for outcome or quality of service,[85] and it recently declared that '1987–88 was a year in which the Commission's approach to value for money began to bear fruit on a large scale . . . local authorities are now responding positively and enthusiastically to our recommendations'.[86] Central government, too, has been the target of a number of the AC's critical reports, such as those concerning the former Block Grant system, SSAs and the capital control system. But, though it has removed its power to surcharge, the government has kept faith with the AC, enhancing its responsibilities in 1992 (in relation to the *Citizen's Charter*) and more recently in relation to Best Value audit.

In addition to the procedures for the audit of accounts, each local authority must supply annual financial returns to the Minister. These cover income and expenditure and details of rating/tax matters, and they provide an additional safeguard against improper financial activities and are a source of national statistics on local government finance.

Value for money (VFM)

The question of local government's efficiency was raised in Chapter 10. Efficiency may be defined as the maximum outcome or output from a given input of resources. But since the ultimate goal of local government is to enhance the general welfare of society, there can be no easy measure of its 'output'. And even if there were such a measure, allowance has to be made for political factors, both in the narrow (party) sense and in the broader (democratic) sense. Thus local government is subject to regular election, public funds must not be subject to risk, local authorities are subject to public accountability through open committee meetings and the publication of accounts (see above and Chapter 9) and to considerable oversight by the central government (see Chapter 12). On top of all this, local authorities are urged to encourage popular participation, and a number have introduced customer contracts with compensation for late or poor services.

Such features are in many ways very desirable, but they are not without some cost – such as the sudden reversals of policy following elections or the slowing-down of the decision-making process. Perhaps the best example of the latter is the two-tier structure of local government, which could be viewed as a deliberate sacrifice of efficiency for democracy, though others would argue that the large size of our local authorities sacrifices democracy to efficiency of service provision (see Chapter 3). However, as the Layfield Committee pointed out, the public are increasingly concerned at local government's efficiency and effectiveness in view of the steep rises in local taxes, while standards of service appear to fall in spite of the fact that manpower levels are stable. Consequently there have been calls for greater information to be made available to the general public about local government services,[87] a move enhanced by the *Citizen's Charter*, 1991. And under the Local Government, Planning and Land Act 1980 local authorities are required to publish annually their financial and manpower figures, together with information on performances, in order to strengthen local government's accountability to their electors and ratepayers (see too p. 394). This can be effective. For example in 1984–5 auditors received 730 questions and objections from members of the public. And the annual performance indicators (PIs)* are having the effect of improving performance, especially among those who have been doing worst and do not wish to be seen at the bottom of the table.†

Since the Rates Act 1984 councils must consult with local business. Best Value requires more substantial and sustained consultation with business and the local community of service users, taxpayers and citizens, i.e. the stakeholders.

---

* The local government accountancy body CIPFA also produces useful data. Its Statistical Information Service (SIS) compares councils' unit costs (per head of pupil or elderly client, etc.).

† See *The Local Performance Indicators 1995/6*, Audit Commission, 1997 (and 1998) which shows improvements in rent and council tax collection rates by poor performing councils (though the effect on better councils is uncertain; as Sir Jeremy Beecham, chairman of the LGA put it, 'measuring a horse does not make it run faster'. See *Sunday Times* 11 April 1999, p. 12 and *The Times*, 28 March 1996, p. 28).

Constraints

In the pursuit of value for money, local authorities should at least begin with a set of objectives, ranked in some sort of order of priority (based on rational criteria, such as need or expressed demand). Various ways of achieving those objectives should be considered and the most effective projects (those which maximize benefits) chosen and pursued. In Chapter 9 a number of management techniques which could help in this respect were outlined. In addition, local authorities are advised by their own management services units and by outside bodies such as the IDA (see pp. 284 and 390) or private consultants. And apart from the work of internal audit and budget monitoring techniques, many local authorities have established performance review committees.*

All of this, however, requires planning and reasonable stability. In practice, local authorities do not usually have this stability, partly as a result of local elections and changing party fortunes, which are paralleled at national level (with the consequence of significant changes in economic policy which can vitally affect local government), but also partly as a result of inconsistencies within central government (or at least a differing view on priorities) with some departments urging major local government restraint (e.g. the Department for the Environment, Transport and the Regions) while others urge greater provision (e.g. the Department of Health seeking greater local authority community care of hospital patients; or the ex-Department of Energy urging more expenditure on housing insulation grants by local housing authorities). Perhaps the area of greatest paradox has been within the DETR itself: on the one hand it has urged expenditure restraint through grant penalties, and on the other it sought expenditure on inner-city regeneration.

Furthermore, the central government can also regulate or require authority charges (for instance, for old people's homes and car-parks), and they can impose schemes on local authorities (such as rent and rate rebates or sale of houses) and more general commitments (such

* See *Portrait of Change*, LGMB, 1998.[88]

as minimum wages, maximum working hours, and initiatives on youth crime or the environment, etc.), all of which have significant cost, staffing and organizational implications for the authorities concerned. In this chapter we have seen how local government is subject to considerable financial control and influence, in particular through the RSG settlement and capping decisions (both of which have often appeared rather late for local authority financial planning purposes), cash limits, credit limits and public expenditure plans. In terms of value for money, therefore, local authorities are not entirely masters of their own fate. As the Layfield Committee commented, 'Our Report finds a lack of clear accountability for local government expenditure, which results from the present confusion of responsibilities between the government and local authorities.' This central–local relationship is considered in the following chapter.

12

CONTROLS AND INFLUENCES

Local authorities are political institutions: they exercise power. But they themselves are, of course, subject to a substantial degree of control and influence. Such control takes a number of different forms: some of these are widely accepted and cause little offence; others are regarded as exceptionable and give rise to substantial controversy. The most obvious are the controls imposed by elections and democratic opinion, by the law and by central government. Others are less clear and less firm – pressure groups, the ombudsmen, the media and Europe. Some of these are dealt with here, others in the next chapter.

Legislative/parliamentary control

In our system of government, Parliament is sovereign: an Act of Parliament becomes the law of the land and cannot be gainsaid. As a consequence, Britain has a 'unitary' constitution, in contrast to those 'federal' systems such as that of the USA, where power is divided and exercised coordinately (or in parallel) by both the central (federal) government and the individual states. In Britain legal authority emanates from Parliament and it may be convenient for Parliament to devolve power on to other bodies (such as local authorities or to regional assemblies). It may at any time rescind or withdraw that power from them (as indeed it did in the case of the Stormont Parliament, returning Ulster to 'direct rule' from Westminster in 1972).

Local authorities in Britain therefore exist by virtue of Acts of Parliament: legislation brings local authorities into existence, as the Local Government Act 1888 did (see p. 18), it gives them powers and duties, as the Education Act 1944 did (see pp. 80, 97), it will shape their composition and constitution, as the Local Government Act 1972 did, and it may pre-determine their internal arrangements, as the Local Authority Social Services Act 1970 did. Local government – with the exception of the City of London, which is technically a common law corporation rather than a statutory one – is thus the creature of Parliament.

Legal/judicial/quasi-judicial control

As a consequence of their being statutory bodies, local authorities are subject to a high degree of judicial control; that is, there are special remedies against local authorities because they themselves have special rights, powers and duties conferred by statute. We have already seen how they are subject to the principle of *ultra vires* (see p. 76) and how this is reinforced by the scrutiny of external audit (see p. 396). Where the auditor or an individual citizen believes that the local authority is acting *ultra vires* (including unreasonable expenditure) s/he can seek a declaration and injunction from a court of law, which might subsequently impose the requirement of recompense by repayment (see the London fares case, p. 121). Much of the legal challenge to local authorities arises from their use of discretionary powers – in particular whether their use has been 'reasonable'. This was established by the Wednesbury Corporation case (1948) when the authority imposed certain conditions on a cinema regarding the admission of children. The reasonableness of the conditions was challenged in court (unsuccessfully in this case). But more generally such powers are subject to judicial review to ensure that they are not being exercised improperly, that the purpose or objectives of the original statute are not being frustrated and that the local authorities are not taking decisions based, for example, on irrelevant considerations or without sufficient account of relevant facts. Thus were local authority decisions declared illegal in the cases of *Bromley v GLC* 1983 ('Fares fair'), *R v ILEA* 1986 (publicitity against government policy), *R v Lewisham LBC* 1988 (boycott of Shell re: South Africa), *R v Derbyshire CC* 1991 and *R v Ealing LBC* (1987; both concerning newpaper bans), *R v Somerset CC* 1995 (ban on hunting had involved irrelevant moral considerations), *Hazell v*

Hammersmith and Fulham LBC (interest rate swaps*), *Credit Suisse v Waltham Forest LBC* 1996 and *v Allerdale BC* 1996 (both involved improper raising of funds. Paradoxically in the latter cases the banks were unable to reclaim their loans because, being declared *ultra vires* (illegal), the contract was void; but see p. 79.) Current reforms are extending the general powers of local authorities and thus relaxing the *ultra vires* rule: see Chapter 15.

Judicial review is therefore an important means to check on the legality of local authority activities. But it can also help in the resolution of disputes as between local and central government (see p. 433) and among local authorities themselves; thus, some 20 per cent of cases brought by local councils are brought against other councils.†

However, legal remedy is not confined to cases of *ultra vires*[1] or illegal expenditure: it may be used where an individual's private right suffers particular damage or infringement, for instance against a council which erects a hoarding and blocks the light from a person's windows. Increasingly councils are facing claims for inadequate road maintenance or social care (especially community or domiciliary provision‡) or educational provision (poor, teaching, substandard buildings, school exclusion, etc.§) Individuals will usually conduct their own case. Where the aggrieved persons consist of the general body of ratepayers, as in the Fulham case,[2] court action is normally taken on their behalf by the Attorney-General. Such legal actions reflect a growing trend (the 'litigious society') which is likely to accelerate with the incorporation of the European Convention on Human Rights into UK law.¶ Thus local authorities now have to act in a way which is compatible with the Convention; this will require them to be more careful in such fields as education (rights to education, parental choice, education

---

* One such case involving Glasgow City council and Kleinwort Benson bank went to the European Court of Justice in 1995.

† M. Sunkin, 'The Judicial Review Caseload 1987–89', *Public Law*, 1991, pp. 490–8.

‡ An important precedent occurred in the House of Lords in 1997 when Gloucester CC won its case to reduce such provision on grounds of lack of resources (thus overturning the decision of the Court of Appeal in 1996).

§ See *Times Educational Supplement*, 20 June 1997, p. 14 and *Independent on Sunday*, 17 September 1995, p. 21.

¶ *Journal of Local Government Law*, vol. 1, no. 1, 1998, pp. 4–7. See too R. Clayton, *The Law of Human Rights*, OUP, 1999.

in accordance with parents' wishes, special needs, etc.); social care (avoidance of degrading treatment in residential homes, domiciliary services, etc.); the right to respect for family life (in matters such as removal of children into care, planning or housing provision/repair, etc.); freedom of expression and fairness (in relation to internal processes such as licence applications, benefit or education appeals and staff conditions). Some councils (under pressure from their insurance companies) have suppressed the reports of inquiries into their malpractices (such as sexual abuse of children in care) because the information could help victims in their legal claims (see, for example, *The Independent*, 27 March 1996, p. 1).

Actual remedies may take the form of injunctions (to cease the action) or payment of damages (to compensate). And there are a number of *prerogative orders*. These are High Court orders usually initiated by an aggrieved individual but pursued by the Crown. They take three forms: (1) the order of *mandamus* (the most frequently used) will require a local authority to carry out a duty imposed on it by law (e.g. to require an authority to issue a precept, invite tenders or to permit the inspection of its records); (2) the order of *prohibition* will restrain a local authority from proceeding further in a situation where it appears to be exceeding its jurisdiction, has disregarded the principles of natural justice or has not followed prescribed procedures (e.g. such an order was made to prevent a police doctor from determining the question of whether a police officer should be retired as disabled, as the doctor had prejudiced the issue in an earlier report[3]); (3) the order of *certiorari* applies, as does prohibition, in those situations where the local authority is acting in a judicial or semi-judicial – as opposed to purely administrative – capacity (as where it is hearing objections to one of its proposals, such as slum clearance). Under this order the action or decision-making procedure does not simply cease, as with the prohibition order. Instead the record or the decision of the authority is sent to the High Court to have its legality inquired into and if necessary to have the decision quashed. The decision of a rent assessment committee, for example, might be quashed on the grounds of bias by its chairman.[4]

The procedure involved in these prerogative orders is cumbersome; as a result there has been a tendency for aggrieved persons to seek judicial redress through actions for a declaration and injunction (as above) or through statutory remedies.[5] The latter may take the form of appeals to the Minister (see p. 423) or statutory appeals.

Since many of the powers conferred on local authorities may affect the interests of individuals, a safeguard is provided in the appeals machinery. In contrast to the procedure for injunctions or prerogative orders, *statutory appeals* are relatively simple and accessible. Under this procedure the individual has the right of appeal, stated in individual Acts of Parliament, against the improper or inequitable use of powers conferred on local authorities by the legislation, such as the granting of licences. Thus, under the Highways Act 1959 owners of properties abutting private streets may appeal to the Magistrates Court against the specification of works served on them by the council for making up the paving and drainage of the street. Similarly, under Housing Acts, property owners may appeal to the County Court against a local authority's order requiring the repair, demolition or closure of insanitary property. Finally, appeals may go to the High Court over such issues as clearance orders and compulsory purchase. In some instances, the court's powers will be limited, but in many cases it will be empowered to substitute its own discretion for that of the authority.

Local authorities are, in addition, subject to the control of the courts in much the same way as other organizations or individual people, so that if they are in breach of contract they may be sued or they may be sued in tort, i.e. for a civil wrong – e.g. negligence in constructing a sewer or in its duty of care (*Welton v North Cornwall DC* 1996) or in connection with special educational needs or child abuse investigations (*X (Minors) v Bedfordshire CC* 1995). In 1996, Hampshire CC had to pay damages of £16 million for the negligence of its fire service which caused destruction of property when the fire brigade, using their professional judgement, turned off water sprinklers (*Capital and Counties plc v Hampshire CC* 1996; see too *Duff v Highland and Islands Fire Board* 1995). A report by the CPS in 1999 estimated that litigation costs local authorities £1.2 billion. In 1996 a social worker and in 1999 a teacher won damages for stress from their local authority employers for £175,000 and £47,000 respectively. UNISON has estimated that in the first six months of 1999 alone there were £20 million worth of such claims, for accidents, etc., by staff.

In addition, of course, if a local authority (through one of its employees) commits a criminal offence, proceedings will be taken against it.

Despite their vast powers and responsibilities, however, local authorities are not often taken to court (though there are mounting actions and threats of action by parents on the grounds that expenditure cuts are causing LEAs to fail in their statutory duties to maintain minimum education standards[6], or provide adequate ESN statements, or fulfil the requirements of community care provision. It is also suggested that both citizens and lawyers have become more litigious, i.e. are more ready to make legal challenges these days, partly as a result of excessive or poorly processed legislation by Parliament.) Authorities are normally law-abiding bodies which keep careful track of the legality of their actions by appointing a monitoring officer or other legal staff to advise them. In addition, much control is exercised over them administratively (by Ministers – see below), which reduces the need for judicial control. And finally, judicial intervention occurs only when an aggrieved party (a citizen) institutes the necessary action, and this is not always easy: in spite of the apparently wide-ranging opportunities for redress, the judicial remedies for review and control of local government actions have long been the subject of criticism. The system is held to be confusing and the procedures complex. It is sometimes suggested that they should be consolidated and simplified. It is also felt that the ordinary courts of law are not always well suited to consider the technical issues which may arise in matters such as house repair or demolition or local government finance. (An alternative system would be a series of courts or tribunals which specialize in administrative justice, such as they have in France, though some of these do exist, such as the tribunals for valuation, employment, land, rent or school places.)

Notwithstanding these criticisms, judicial control can be justified on the grounds that it is impartial and not tied to policy matters. Consequently, it helps to secure public confidence that bias and corruption are not present in the administration of local government business. Such suspicions may linger where administrative control alone is involved. However, these suspicions may be further assuaged by the Local Government Commissioners ('ombudsmen') whose role it is to investigate and remedy maladministration.

The Ombudsman

Sometimes referred to as the 'citizen's defender' or 'speaker for the people', the ombudsman or 'referee' was introduced to deal with local government matters in 1974[7] (1976 in Scotland). The chairman (Edward Osmotherly) is the senior Commissioner and receives some £115,000 per annum. Officially called 'Commissioners for Local Administration' (CLA), there is one for Scotland, one for Wales and three for England (one of whom is a woman). Their function is to investigate and report on any claim by a member of the public that he or she has suffered *injustice through maladministration* by a local (or police*) authority[8] (except parishes), with a view to securing satisfactory redress for the complainant and better administration for the authorities. (A secondary objective is to encourage authorities to develop and publicize their procedures for the fair settlement of complaints and to settle as many of them as possible.)

'Maladministration' is not defined in the legislation, but refers generally to faulty administration in the *way* in which an authority's decision or action has been taken, rather than the actual merit of the decision. Thus maladministration is taken to cover administrative action (or inaction) based on or influenced by improper considerations (such as bias or unfair discrimination) or improper conduct (such as undue delay, failure to observe established procedures, giving wrong information, breaking promises or failure to take account of relevant considerations). Much is therefore left to the interpretation or discretion of the Commissioners themselves. This also applies to the concept of injustice, such as not getting an entitlement, being caused distress or suffering financial loss.

However, there are a number of areas from which they are explicitly excluded. These include complaints about commercial transactions (apart from the purchase or sale of land and buildings); job grievances and other personnel matters; certain education matters (including the giving of instruction and the internal organization of schools and colleges); and the investigation or prevention of crime (there is a separate machinery for dealing with complaints against the

---

* But not complaints against individual police officers.

police). Local Commissioners cannot investigate any matter about which the aggrieved person has appealed to a tribunal or to a government Minister or has taken proceedings in a court of law. Nor do they normally pursue the matter if the person has the right of appeal to a Minister, tribunal or court (though this rule may be waived if the Commissioners are satisfied that it is not reasonable to expect the person to use those other rights or remedies). Furthermore, the Commissioners may not look into cases where most or all of the local inhabitants are concerned – a complaint against the general level of rates would not be accepted for investigation. Finally, there is normally a time limit of twelve months within which the complaint must be made (unless there are special circumstances).

In 1988 one of the excluded areas was revised so that the CLA may now (except in relation to police authorities) consider matters concerning the investigation or prevention of crime, such as the way a council deals with matters involving a criminal offence under the trade descriptions and other consumer legislation.

The Commissioners will not normally investigate any complaint until it has been brought to the attention of the local authority or the council's complaints system and the authority has had a reasonable time in which to reply. If no satisfactory response occurs, the aggrieved person should put his or her complaint in writing and address it to a member (normally a councillor) of the relevant authority with a request that it be sent on to the ombudsman – thus does the local (like the Parliamentary) ombudsman seek to supplement the traditional democratic process rather than supplant it. Under the Local Government Act 1988, complainants may, if they prefer, complain direct to the local ombudsman. Either way, the complainant should send any relevant documents (or copies, such as letters from the council) with the complaint. It may also be the (unusual) case that the complainant wishes to employ a solicitor to help.

Unless the complaint is withdrawn or there is a local settlement, i.e. directly between the local authority and the complainant (rather like 'out of court' settlements in legal cases), and provided that it is within the legitimate scope of the CLA, an investigation takes place in which a CLA investigator interviews the complainant and will normally visit the local authority concerned, where he or she has, like the High Court, the power (within limits)[9] to examine internal papers and take written and oral evidence from anyone who can provide relevant information. However, all investigations are conducted in private. Sometimes investigation are not completed because the local authority offers to put things right during the course of the investigation, which thus ceases. There is no right of appeal against decisions of the CLA (though a challenge may be possible by way of judicial review, i.e. in the High Court).

When the investigation is completed, a report giving the CLA's findings will be sent to the complainant, the councillor (where appropriate) and the authority (and any person complained against). In addition, a copy is sent to the local media, and it is made available for public inspection. The report is made publicly available, but does not normally give names of individuals. Where the report finds that injustice (anxiety, financial loss, inconvenience, etc.) has been caused to the complainant by maladministration, the CLA will recommend what the council should do to put matters right (such as doing repairs, correcting council tax accounts, paying compensation or perhaps appointing an independent expert to advise the council on, say, the appropriate level of renovation grant). The council must then consider the report and recommended remedy and inform the CLA what action it proposes to take. If the council does not respond satisfactorily, the CLA must make a second report, which must be considered by the whole council. If there is another unsatisfactory response, the CLA may publish a statement in the local newspaper ('naming and shaming') or may require it to publish, at its own expense, an agreed statement explaining what has happened. In 1987/8, there were 8 such second reports and 5 published statements. (In 1996/7 there were a number of second reports and statements issued concerning Manchester City council and its special education needs (SEN) provision for four dyslexic children.)

Each year the CLA had to prepare a general report on the discharge of their functions. This was received by a body representing the local authority associations, which normally published the report together with its own comments.

In reviewing the effectiveness of the ombudsman system, one study has concluded that its impact on local authority procedures has been 'considerable'.[10] Between 1974 and 1978, the English Commissioners received nearly 7,500 complaints – about 2,000 a year (roughly the same, for example, as the South West Regional Gas Consumer Council received). By 1988, the figure had grown to 4,229 (of which half had been received direct and half via a councillor). In 1992 the figure had reached 12,123 and in 1997/8 the figure was 14,969 (a slight fall from the previous year's 15,322). It is difficult to determine whether the increase is evidence of growing maladministration or the result of greater public awareness of their rights and of the Commission's services. In 1997/8, the CLA actually considered 15,262 cases (i.e. including some from the previous year). Of these, the majority – 14,811 or 95 per cent – were not investigated beyond the stage of considering the authority's detailed comments on them, e.g. because the local authority itself settled the complaint satisfactorily (as in 2,438 of the cases). Or they were discontinued when it became clear that maladministration had not occurred (as in 6,529 cases). Or the issue was outside the CLA's remit. Out of the total of cases considered, only 451 were found to manifest maladministration (there was presumably a significant amount in those cases settled bilaterally by the councils, and perhaps in all of them). Thus, the findings of the 451 cases fully investigated were:

256 (57 per cent) injustice through maladministration (*58 per cent*);
107 (23 per cent) maladministration but no injustice (*4 per cent*);
88 (20 per cent) no maladministration (*38 per cent*).

(The figures in italics, for comparison, refer to the period 1974–8.[11] The figures for Scotland and Wales show similar amounts of maladministration to those for England.)

Examples of injustice caused through maladministration include the following: delay in processing housing benefit leading to eviction for rent arrears; unfair discrimination in awarding discretionary education grant; a piggery being used without relevant planning permission and the council taking little action in response to complaints about noise and smell; incompetence in granting planning permission for two houses adjoining the complainant's bungalow; failure to act to prevent the demolition of a listed building; failure or delays in assessing disability or special education needs*; and unreasonable delay in carrying out repairs to remedy dampness in a council house. The majority of cases (37 per cent) involve housing (especially repairs) or (for 22 per cent) planning matters (especially objections). Highways, education, social services and local taxation accounted for about 7 per cent each. (The CLA publishes annual digests of cases.) Among the complainants an estimated 14 per cent are from ethnic minorities and 25 per cent are disabled.

The CLA reports tend to be treated with respect by the local authorities. In nearly every case where injustice had been found, the CLA was satisfied with the subsequent action taken by the authority (an apology, provision of accommodation or financial compensation, alteration of procedures, etc.). In only a few cases do local authorities fail to take satisfactory action, as we have seen above. There are, on average (over the past ten years) about 20 to 30 such situations each year. (On at least one occasion the council went to court for a judicial review of the CLA's adverse report and was successful.) Normally, the CLA's only sanction here is a second report and reliance on the force of public opinion, though some councils argue that central government constraints on local expenditure and manpower are restricting their ability to provide adequate services or recompense. The CLA was also largely instrumental in the creation of the Code of Practice for receiving and investigating complaints (see p. 491). Since February 1992, it has encouraged the setting up of complaints systems, following the CLA's publication of guidance notes on good administrative practice, 'Devising a Complaints System'. It has since produced more guidance and codes including (in 1998) guidance on remedies. In 1978 legislation removed a considerable doubt and impediment on local authorities by allowing them to incur expenditure in order to recompense those who suffer injustice as a result of malad-ministration. And the 1980 Local Government, Planning and Land Act secured the CLA's right of access to relevant information and documents. In 1995, the CLA published a code of practice on access to information (a source of some of the complaints it receives).

---

* This is an area of increasing complaints, e.g. reports from the CLA on SEN have risen from 5 in 1988/9 to 37 in 1993/4.

The CLA has had a considerable impact on local authority procedures. But reviews of its work[12] have often been critical and have raised a number of questions: should the CLA be empowered to initiate investigations (as has been suggested in such areas as those of child abuse) instead of having to wait for a formal complaint? Should the scope be extended into some of those areas at present beyond the legal competence of the CLA? Is the continued mechanism of funnelling complaints through the councillor an impediment? Should the powers of the CLA be increased (either to insist on adequate – perhaps legally enforceable as in Ulster – redress or greater access to documents, etc.)? Are there too many ombudsmen (they exist separately for the civil service, for the NHS, for local government and users'/consumers' consultative committees/councils, plus the utility regulators as well as for non-public sector sector banking, insurance, pensions, building societies, investment, etc.) thus causing public confusion. This may be added to by the Freedom of Information Act 2000, since complainants may then be required or allowed to approach the proposed Information Commissioner (who will merge with the Data Protection Registrar). Is the system sufficiently well publicized and should other Commissioners appear on television to explain their work as the Scottish ombudsman has done?* Is the system (and is it held to be) sufficiently impartial? This last question arises from the fact that, though appointed by the Secretary of State, a number of the Commissioners have a local government background (as member or officer) and the whole system has been financed by the local authority associations. (The estimated cost of the CLA for England in 1997/8 was £7.4 million, i.e. about £450 per complaint received (a figure which has remained very constant since at least 1987). A final criticism concerns the time taken by the CLA to complete its investigations. In 1981 the average time taken to complete formal investigations was 40 weeks. Ten years later it had reached 75 weeks where it remains today. However, some of the apparent delay can be accounted for by such

---

* In 1995 the Welsh CLA was criticized as having too 'cosy' a relationship with local authorities and because correspondence and documents passing between the CLA and the council were not open to the complainant to see, especially where the CLA decided not to proceed with that case (when the only recourse was to seek judicial review in the High Court (see *Municipal Journal*, 18 August 1995, p. 9).

things as chronic illness by the complainant. Most cases do not go to full formal investigation and 90 per cent of these are completed within 40 weeks, with nearly half (45 per cent) within 10 weeks, giving an overall average for these (so-called Stage I) cases of 14.5 weeks. Nevertheless it has been suggested that the CLA is underfunded and that, if it had the power to charge or fine errant councils, it could afford to do more or speed up its investigations.* In view of its rising cost, at one time (in 1966) it was suggested that CLA be abolished and local authorities be required to set up effective complaints systems (as many had been).† This was reiterated in the Chipperfield Report, 1995, which also thought that the CLA was at risk of not being able to cope with the growing number of complaints, and further suggested that the CLA was usurping the responsibilities of councillors to deal with maladministration in their councils.

Criticisms like these were levelled at the Parliametary Commissioner for Administration (the ombudsman who investigates the civil service) when he was first established in 1967. Since then his role has been gradually amended so that he has evolved into a more effective and respected institution. The Commissioners for Local Administration appear to be developing in similar fashion. Apart from the developments mentioned above, the government introduced a number of changes under the Local Government and Housing Act 1989. These were largely in response to the Widdicombe Report,[13] a report by a Parliamentary committee[14] and in response to the pleas of the CLA itself, who refer to the continued 'discouraging feature . . . that a small minority of councils, with blatant disregard for the interests of complainants, were still defying the Local Government Ombudsmen by refusing to implement their recommendations.'[15] The Act now:

(1) requires councils found guilty of maladministration to inform the CLA what steps they are taking to prevent similar injustices occurring; where a council declines to comply with the remedies proposed in the CLA report, that decision must have been taken by the council (not just a committee) and they are required to publish a

---

* See P. Bibby and I. Lunt *Working for Children*, David Fulton, 1996.
† See *Municipal Journal*, 16 February 1996, p. 5, and *Local Government Chronicle*, 20 October 1995 and 16 February 1996.

statement in a local newspaper consisting of the action recommended by the CLA and, if they wish, their reasons for non-compliance;

(2) requires, in most cases, the CLA to name councillors who are involved in such cases and where they have broken the Code of Conduct (see pp. 224ff);

(3) allows the CLA to publish general guidance to local authorities on the principles of good administrative practice;

(4) abolished the representative bodies (for England and Wales; see p. 412) so as to remove the possible influence on the work of the CLA of local authorities who compose those bodies;

(5) changes the system of funding such that finance is raised by a deduction from the Revenue Support Grant;

(6) provides additional 'outside' members to the Commissions. Their role would be to help advise on CLA guidance to councils on efficiency and good administrative practice (as in (3) above);

(7) In addition, the government is reviewing the excluded area of commercial and contractual matters (partly in view of the fact that in some cases, such as market-stall allocations, the commercial aspect is secondary, while in other cases non-commercial considerations have obtruded into tendering/contracting-out procedures).

There is still unease at the refusal of some councils to implement the CLA's recommendations. There have been 76 cases since 1990/91 where the ombudsman has required the council to publish a statement (as in (1) above). But one of the Commissioners has stated that 'My experience so far is that the further step of producing a statement has had little effect on those public authorities which set themselves against accepting the referee's verdict.' The Widdicombe Committee and the CLA itself recommended that complainants should have a right to seek judicial enforcement of remedies through the courts. But this has been rejected by the government on the grounds that it would tend to make the investigations too inflexible, formal and legalistic, such that complainants might find the process more intimidating. This is one of the risks involved in developing the system. There is also the danger that administrators will become over-cautious[16] and that they will lose some of their valuable flexibility and informality (for example, by refusing to give 'off the record' advice to members of the public). However, in its White Paper, *The Citizen's Charter* (1991), the government states that if difficulties continue over ensuring that local ombudsmen's recommendations are implemented, 'we will take the further step of introducing legislation to make the . . . recommendation legally enforceable'.

The Citizen's Charter also raised the prospect of creating local lay adjudicators to deal with more minor claims of redress. But the CLA fears this may confuse citizens and possibly delay taking up complaints with itself. Meanwhile it is firmly of the view that current restrictions on its jurisdiction should be removed, and that (especially in the light of recent child-abuse cases) it should be able to undertake investigations on its own initiative without receiving a complaint. (In some of the child-abuse cases – such as that of Kimberly Carlile, 1987 – the inquiry lacked the power to compel witnesses to give evidence. The CLA has such a power.) On the other hand, there are those who have pointed to the costs which fall to local authorities as a consequence of CLA inquiries (the cost of officers' time, extra record-keeping, etc., quite apart from any compensation costs or the restructuring of procedures – for which reason even innocent local authorities are known to 'plead guilty' and settle with complainants, just to avoid the time and upheaval of an inquiry). And there is also resistance from councillors: some of them see the CLA as straying illicitly into areas of policy, while others, like MPs, claim that they are themselves 'ombudsmen' and that outside Commissioners are an intrusion.

There is some truth in this claim, as indeed the system originally recognized, by requiring complaints to be channelled initially through the elected representative. However, the evidence points to these representatives being inadequate to the task. This is partly because many have been poor at the constituency role (perhaps preferring to play the 'statesman' – see p. 204); partly because of lack of time (many MPs as well as most councillors are part-time); and partly because of a lack of expertise and power: councillors as individuals have little statutory authority and have until recently had limited access to internal documents[17] and perhaps limited support services. The CLA should therefore be seen as an adjunct or 'back-stop' to the councillor.

A recent study states that 'on almost any index, the LO had been a force for the good', and it reveals that in England 50 per cent of councils had amended their complaints procedures as a result of the local ombudsman's endeavours. But it went on to suggest that in some local government circles the work of the ombudsman was being taken less seriously than formerly.[18] There is also some concern about the lack of consistency among the different CLAs, while the existence of 'no-go areas' in their remit is felt to add to the public's confusion about the whole institution. Under the government's current reforms, the CLA is, in its reports, to comment more on the adequacy of local authorities' procedures and will publish general advice on good administrative practice. Judging from the evidence of the Widdicombe Report (see Table 25) there is a strong case for trying to raise people's awareness of, and confidence in, the role of the CLA: it appears that the ombudsman would only be people's fifth choice when considering how they would challenge a bad decision by the council, and is considered to be only the fifth most effective in remedying the problem.

Apart from the introduction of an Information Commissioner, there are other developments which may impact on the work of the CLA. First, as a result of the Woolf Report, *Access to Civil Justice* (1998), changes in legal aid are likely to reduce the number of people who are eligible for Legal Aid in civil cases. If this reduces people's access to remedies through the court, then the CLA may exercise its discretion (under the 1974 Act) to investigate complaints usually deemed ineligible. (It could be that an increase in 'no win no fee' agreements will compensate for a decline due to losses in legal aid.) Secondly, the government is to introduce legislation which will clarify and extend the powers of councils to pay compensation. Thirdly the CLA itself is considering the introduction of an 'ultimate rung' strategy. At the moment the CLA will not consider complaints which are 'premature', i.e. where councils have not had a reasonable opportunity to deal with them, but it does send the complaints to the councils concerned with a request that they investigate them. Under the new strategy, complainants would be expected to exhaust all their own councils' complaints procedures before the CLA will consider them. Finally, mention should be made of the fact that information about the CLA and access to it is now possible through the Internet (the Website of the CLA is http://www.open.gov.uk/lgo).

Administrative/governmental control

The closest and most continuous form of control over local authorities is that exercised by government departments. Such controls have come into existence piecemeal, as convenience and expediency required. Consequently, they are not uniform in their application and their scale varies from time to time and among the different services.

Government supervision of local authorities has always existed in some form – from the JPs of the Middle Ages, the Poor Law Commissioners of the 1830s and the school inspectors of the 1860s to the powers exercised by the modern Secretary of State. However, although the scale of this control appears to have fluctuated, there has been a more sustained increase since the 1920s and especially since the war.[19]

Justification of government control

Central control of local government may be justified on a number of grounds. Firstly, many of the services for which local authorities are responsible (education, housing, etc.) are national in character and need therefore to be sustained at some minimum standard at least. Secondly, in the interests of social justice the government will try to secure equality of standards and the avoidance of disparities. Besides, many local needs – traffic, fire safety, building controls, food safety, children's services, etc. – are common throughout the country. Thirdly, councils are substantial spenders and taxers (see Chapter II) and they control too many of the nation's resources to be left alone by the central government, which is generally held responsible for the management of the economy as a whole.

Thus, in general terms, the role of the central government is to secure the national interest over and above the purely local. For example, the Minister may intervene in matters of land use or development. It is sometimes held that central government control is justified because it is more efficient than local government ('auntie knows best'). This may have been true in the last century, when local authorities were far from competent or honest, or were often reluctant to spend ratepayers' money, but it is by no means demonstrably true today.

What is true is that the central government can act as a clearing house for useful ideas and good practices which it can disseminate among local authorities. Furthermore it is generally accepted that individuals and local authorities themselves need to have an accessible point of reference in cases of dispute (for example, between two councils regarding an overspill or development project, such as a waste-disposal site, or liability for homeless persons). In such cases the Minister can act as a referee.

These are the justifications for central government intervention in the affairs of local government. Whether they justify the present degree of control is another matter. But before examining the various forms which this intervention may take, it is worth pointing out that central intervention is inevitable, partly because the central government substantially finances local government (see p. 339), which provides a means of intervention; but also because political parties seek to apply their principles throughout the country and, since parties exist at both the national and the local levels, this will provide the necessary motive for intervention.

The forms of control

Acts of Parliament establishing local authority services give Ministers certain general powers to control the way in which councils act, and in some cases these powers may be quite sweeping. Thus the Education Act 1944 makes it the duty of the Secretary of State for Education 'to secure the effective execution by local authorities, under his control and direction, of national policy for providing a varied and comprehensive educational service in every area'. Similarly the Secretary of State for Health and Social Services is endowed with wide powers of *direction* and default (under the NHS and Community Care Act 1990 and most recently under the Carers (Recognition and Services) Act 1995). However such broad, almost autocratic powers are not found among all government departments, and in practice, it appears to be a convention that where they do exist they are rarely exercised. (This is not to deny that their mere existence and potential use may be a powerful influence. But see pp. 450ff.)

It is more usual for the legislation to specify the Minister's powers, and these specific forms of control are much more likely to be used.* For example the Local Government Act 1988 empowered the Secretary of State for the Environment to nominate additional services for compulsory competitive tendering. In most cases, too, Ministers have conferred on them the power to issue *regulations* and orders (generally called 'delegated legislation', 'statutory instruments' or 'SIs') to fill in the details of a service outlined in legislation or to bring in new elements and add to that service when circumstances suggest. For example, the Home Secretary issues regulations for the administration and conditions of service of fire services, and the Secretary of State for Social Services does the same for local authorities' arrangements for fostering children or for charges in old people's homes. (A number of Ministers have the power to specify the minimum and maximum charges which councils may levy.) It is usually by means of such regulations that Ministers try to secure the maintenance of standards in many local government services (as in the regulations concerning school buildings[21] or the qualifications of teachers or house-building). Ministers' powers to create regulations are quite discretionary (though technically subject to scrutiny and approval by Parliament). Thus under the Local Government (Politically Restricted Posts) Regulations 1990, the Minister determined which officers fell into that category. In 1993 the government unexpectedly scrapped the 1981 Education (Premises) Regulations which local authorities had been preparing for final implementation. While there were about sixty such SIs a year applying to local government in the 1960s, the average in recent years is over 200 (see Select Committee Report, p. 596 below).

---

* It is calculated that in 1988 the Local Government Finance Bill, the Education Bill and the Housing Bill gave 344, 366 and 110 separate statutory controls respectively to the Secretaries of State.[20] See too Sec. 53 of the 1990 Planning Act. The Education Act 1988 gave rise to over 1,000 such regulations, and the Local Government Act 1999 confers 25 extra discretionary powers on the Environment Secretary, including, for example, the decision to send 'hit squads' into under-performing councils. The Local Government Act 1999 gives considerable powers of intervention and direction to the DETR Secretary, especially in relation to the implementation of Best Value.

Alternatively, the government may vet and perhaps modify local authority *schemes* (and their standing orders; see Chapter 9). Many Acts of Parliament require local authorities to submit their schemes for the development of certain services. In the 1960s and 1970s a number of LEAs' schemes for 'going comprehensive' in their secondary schools were rejected as unsuitable by various Secretaries of State for Education. Similarly local authorities' structure plans (see p. 95) have to be approved by the Minister, and they may be altered.[22] So too must housing schemes. Under the Education Reform Act 1988 LEAs have been required to submit their schemes for the local financial management of schools (LMS) for approval. Needless to say, schools applying for opted-out/grant-maintained (GM) status required ministerial approval. Under the School Standards and Framework Act 1998, the LEAs have to submit their education development plans to the Minister.

Planning is an example (making by-laws is another) of an area where the Minister's *consent* or approval might be required for individual actions by the local authority. It is regularly needed for compulsory purchase orders and appeals over planning refusals. In the latter cases, an inquiry is usually conducted by a government official (or someone appointed by the government), known as the inspector. Inspectors' reports go to the Minister for his final decision, which in practice normally, but not always, endorses the recommendation of the inspector. As we have seen (in Chapter 4), Ministers take an interest in councils' local structure and development plans, and in recent years London boroughs have complained at the extent to which the former Department of the Environment has altered their unitary structure plans.

In this respect, the Minister is often acting as an *arbitrator* or judge in a dispute between the local authority and its citizens, such as there might be when parents object to the LEA's closure of a school. Or s/he may act to resolve a dispute between local authorities themselves, for instance over planning or overspill issues or financial liability for students or welfare clients. Similarly he may be called in to deal with disputes between a local authority and its staff over such issues as superannuation rights or conditions of service.

Some legislation gives Ministers important *default* powers over an authority which is failing to provide a service satisfactorily. For example under the NHS and Community Care Act 1990, the Secretary of State was given such powers in respect of local authorities' social care responsibilities. If a Minister is dissatisfied with an authority's provision of a particular service he may remove the responsibility from that authority, either taking it over himself (for instance by appointing a school's board of governors, or issuing new street by-laws, where the authority has failed to do so; a recent case involved Norwich council-house sales,[23] and in the 1980s there were plans for commissioners to take over responsibility from Liverpool council.);[24] or, more frequently, transferring responsibility to another local authority or to a special body, as in the Clay Cross case (see note 23). In each case, the financial liability remains with the defaulting authority. (The alternative procedure is for the Minister to issue directions or a default order enforceable through the courts – see p. 407). In practice, such events are rare, though the tendency of modern legislation to confer default powers on Ministers is increasing.[25]

Influences and informal controls

Besides these formal controls, there exist a number of other points of contact and influence between central and local government. They are less dramatic, but they are equally if not more influential on the operation of local authorities.[26] Thus Ministers may intervene in the *appointment* (or dismissal) of certain chief officers. For example, with the appointment of chief constables, fire officers and directors of social services, the local authority is normally obliged to submit its short list of candidates, many of whom may be vetoed by the Minister as unsuitable in an attempt to safeguard the quality of the service.[27]

Ministers will also seek to maintain the standards of certain services by means of *inspection*, which may be for purposes of securing compliance with statutory requirements (enforcement inspections) or to secure and maintain standards of performance (efficiency inspections). Inspection occurs in the following areas: trading standards/consumer protection, environmental health, ancient monuments and historic buildings, planning, building control, education, police, fire, social services and housing; Best Value inspection is the latest addition. Thus the police, fire and education services are subject to regular inspection by Her Majesty's Inspectors (HMIs) from the Home Office or by OFSTED, and social service departments are reviewed by the Social Service Inspectors (SSIs) of the Department of Health. (In Scotland until recently the relevant departments were the Scottish Education Department and the Scottish Home and Health Department. Responsibility now rests with the Scottish Executive.) These departmental inspectorates act as the 'eyes and ears' of the central government and can produce some very stern and critical reports (e.g. the Derbyshire police report, 1992 or the OFSTED report on Hackney 1996 or the SSI failures in 1999: see *The Times* 24 November 1999, p. 8). They collect and disseminate information and advice – 'local good practices' – on a large scale. Examples include educational organization and teaching methods, and sheltered housing schemes.

However, much of this *information* is collected from local government directly by the central government departments, for local authorities are required by law to 'send the Secretary of State such reports and returns, and give him such information . . . as he may require . . .'[28] Innocent as such data collection may seem, it might nevertheless have some influence on the methods and standards of council services, even if it only causes local authorities themselves to analyse and utilize their own findings.

Local authorities have the power (and in some cases the duty) to make *by-laws*. These must receive ministerial approval before they are valid and enforceable (e.g. in 1980 a number of councils failed to get Home Office approval of by-laws banning dogs in parks), but Ministers will usually short-circuit the process by issuing 'model' by-laws, which tend to be adopted by local authorities if only to save them time and effort. The same arrangement applies to the requirement that LEAs draw up and submit for approval their Instruments and Articles of Government for schools and colleges.[29]

Local authorities are influenced and persuaded by other central government documents. These include *memoranda*, research reports, White Papers, Green Papers[30] and statements (for instance, the statement on housing investment plans in 1979, which also said that councils would have to raise their rents by 60p per week in the following year, or the Minister's criticism of out-of-town superstores). In Scotland, devolved school management was the result of ministerial guidelines rather than of legislation.* Some departments regularly publish a news-sheet or bulletin (such as the Treasury's *Economic Progress Report*, the former DES's *Reports on Education*, DoE's planning guidance (PPGs) and Design Bulletins (for roads, footpaths, etc.), and the DSS's *Social Work Service*). All of these more or less help to shape local government activity.

Of particular importance in this respect are government *circulars*, which are sent out very regularly to local authorities explaining new legislation, suggesting new directions in policy or methods of administration, and perhaps explaining government policy. They vary from the relatively trivial circular concerned with minor matters of detail to the virtually mandatory, such as the DES circular 10/65, which requested LEAs to submit their schemes for comprehensive school reorganization, and the DoE circular 21/79, which explained the government's expectation of a 3 per cent fall in local government expenditure in 1979–80. (Other, less official, 'circulars' include those which are issued to local political parties by the party headquarters, and those which are sent to member authorities by the local authority associations.)

Finally, Ministers can exercise influence personally and directly when they meet local government members and officials at official visits or local government conferences. They can also make their views known through articles in local government journals (such as the *Local Government Chronicle*, the *Municipal Journal*, *Community Care*, *Public Finance and Accountancy* or *Municipal Engineering*) or through well-publicized statements. Two examples of the last include Anthony Crosland's declaration in 1975 that (for local government) 'the party's over' and Michael Heseltine's speech at the local government conference in September 1981 that it was 'closing time' for local authority growth – both of which helped to shape the psychological atmosphere in local government for the years ahead.

* See *Local Government Studies*, Summer, 1995.

Financial controls

The financial relationship between local and central government has been described as the iron fist in the velvet glove. It comprises a mixture of controls and influences. It was observed (on p. 396) how the external audit seeks to reinforce the judicial control of local authorities by its concern with the legality of local authority expenditure. Increasingly, however, the Audit Commission is exercising an administrative influence by widening its remit to cover value for money considerations, as a consequence of which it may attempt to guide and advise local authorities (e.g. on staff–pupil ratios, implementing care services, managing arrears). This will be overlain by the influence of Best Value inspections.

Stronger and more overt influence is exercised through government grants. This influence may be either particular or general in effect. 'Specific' grants (allocated to a particular service)[31] will tend to encourage the provision of that service, influencing the authority's pattern of service provision (and its corporate plan). It was suggested too (on p. 348) that such grants tend to bring with them rather closer central supervision. The substitution of a 'block' (non-allocated) grant for specific grants, which occurred substantially in 1958, was intended to release local authorities from such close oversight. However, a general grant brings with it the means of a more general control or influence, since all local authorities can be encouraged or discouraged from spending by the central government increasing or decreasing the proportion of expenditure it is prepared to finance.[32] The adequacy of the government's allowances for cost increases (known as 'cash limits') resulting from inflation and service growth is another factor. And there is a frequent tendency (wrongly) to regard service SSAs as an indication of the proper/required level of spending.

Local resources can be affected by central government in other ways. The government can delay carrying out the revaluation of property. It can determine (through legislation) the de-rating or re-rating of certain categories of property (see p. 356), both of which decisions will impinge on local authorities' tax/rates resources (especially before 1990 when domestic rates were replaced by the community charge). It may issue guidelines and even place upper limits ('capping') on local budgets/taxes. It determines, nationally, the level of the unified business rate (UBR or NNDR). And it can exercise some influence on local authorities' other main source of income – charges. In a general way it may seek to regulate all charges through a prices policy. More directly, the government can specify or restrict certain local authority fees, such as those for children in care, old people's homes, or (using heavy persuasion and altered subsidies) council rents. Councils are told what discount they must offer on their council house sales. In 1996 the government raised capital disregard limits for residential care (which increased councils' care costs and for which they were not fully compensated by way of grant).

In Chapter 11 we saw how local authority capital expenditure has long been subject to loan sanction. Apart from the control element inherent in such a process, additional influences flowed from the various conditions which often accompanied borrowing approval. Until recently, in seeking loan sanction to build houses, local authorities have had to follow certain building standards and conform to certain cost yardsticks.[33] Or in seeking loan sanction to develop nursery education, LEAs found Ministers more favourably disposed to approve certain kinds of project (such as nursery classes attached to primary schools) than others (such as separate nursery school buildings).[34] Finally, central government has an impact on local government's capital finance by changing its policy regarding access to the Public Works Loan Board (see p. 382) and through the interest charged on its loans, and by declaring moratoria on spending (as in 1982 and 1984). In recent years, Supplementary Credit Approvals have increased to about 35 per cent of total credit approvals and they are only allocated to specific services or projects. Similarly the increased use of the bidding process for government funds allows the government to shape local specifications. For new services or new policy requirements for example, the Crime and Disorder Act 1998 gives local authorities new responsibilities for young offenders and the School Standards and Framework Act 1998 has set lower class sizes and higher attainment targets for LEAs.

Other examples include the national policy of community care for the mentally disabled; and the imposition of the national curriculum in schools; or, through the device of inspection or new regulations, the urging of the expansion or improvement of existing services (police recruitment, fire regulations or schools building standards for instance). Equally, the central government is committing local government resources when it makes public statements on pay norms or sets up pay inquiries and commissions to determine appropriate wage increases, such as the Houghton Committee on teachers' pay in 1974 and the Comparability Commission (Clegg) which was involved in 1979 in the determination of the pay of teachers and other local government employees. It is difficult for councils not to be bound by the recommendations of these pay review bodies (though in 1999, the LGA did point out that every 1 per cent increase in teachers' pay cost local authorities some £120 million).*

Consequences of control

The vast array of controls and influences outlined above has given rise to deep concern about central domination and the subordination of local government. Professor Keith-Lucas suggests that local democratic self-government in Britain has become a 'romantic dream'.[35] And the Maud Committee (1967) concluded that British local government has, as a result of central government control, less discretion than local authorities in other countries. It also outlined the dangerous consequences of this excessive control, which it saw causing frustration and discouragement among local government councillors and officers, e.g. in 1993, the London Boroughs Association complained of the government's excessive interference in their unitary development plans, especially their use of new powers under the Planning and Compensation Act 1991.[36] They also believed that public interest in local government was diminished in so far as people perceived local authorities as little more than puppets dancing at the ends of central government strings with, for example, local authorities simply acting as cyphers or executors of central planning policy. Various inquiries into local voting and popular participation have suggested that

* *The Times*, 25 January 1999, p. 1.

excessive central control diminishes people's motivation and interest in local government. People's judgement on the extent to which local elections determine how things are run locally has fallen from 77 per cent (in the Maud survey 1965) to 54 per cent (in the *British Social Attitudes* survey 1994).[37] See p. 500 below.

Another consequence of controls is that local authorities' efficiency and corporate planning may be jeopardized, since different government departments could be pulling local authorities in different, even conflicting, directions. This view was confirmed to a certain extent by the government's own advisory 'think tank' in 1977[38] and more recently by the government itself in its 1996 White Paper, *Government response to the report of the House of Lords select committee on relations between central and local government, 'Rebuilding Trust'*. (The creation, in 1995, of Government Offices in the Regions had made a start in breaking down the departmentalist approach.) Furthermore, as the Bains and Paterson Reports pointed out (see Chapter 9), central requirements to appoint certain committees, such as social services, reduce local authorities' flexibility for internal organization; similarly, the requirement to appoint (and perhaps have vetted) certain chief officers, such as the director of social services, but not others, creates inconsistencies. The same issues were raised in the consultative paper on internal management of Scottish authorities (1993), and the working party report on English authorities (see p. 268 above) said, 'We believe that the statutory requirement to establish such committees does impose unnecessary constraints on local authorities and inhibits experiments; and that to allow local authorities greater flexibility in the way they carry out functions in no way detracts from their importance. On the contrary, local authorities should be enabled to carry them out in the way they consider most appropriate' (para. 4.26). The Private Member's Bill, introduced to Parliament by Lord Hunt in 1997 (but subsequently defeated) sought to give councils more freedom in this respect.

Apart from any costs which may be incurred (external Audit costs a local authority £50 per hour, amounting in Somerset CC for example to £100,000) inspections can take up a great deal of time for councils. They can also cause confusion by sending mixed messages – for example where the HMI from the Home Office offers a different view on the operation of the local Fire Service from that of the Audit

Commission (not to mention the Health and Safety Inspector). This problem is likely to increase with the proliferation of inspection regimes, unless there is some rationalization or more joint working.

A number of other remedies to these problems have been suggested. These are dealt with below (p. 441). But before examining them, it is important to be aware of the danger of exaggerating the central government's control of local government.

Hidden strengths?

It is easy to overstate and distort the image of the relationship between central and local government. Ministers do not have a free hand to interfere in local government affairs: local authorities are created by Acts of Parliament and these give them a substantially independent existence and range of powers. To intervene, Ministers must normally be able to point to a statutory power* to do so (e.g. giving them reserve powers to cap a local budget); in the absence of specific powers to the contrary, the government has no powers to intervene in the day to day affairs of a local authority. The wide powers of the Secretary of State for Education (see p. 423) are perhaps exceptional, but even here there are limits, as was shown by the Tameside case of 1976, when the Court of Appeal and the House of Lords decided that the Minister's direction to the LEA (which he believed was acting unreasonably in seeking to reintroduce selective secondary education) was invalid. A number of other legal challenges by local authorities have been successful, e.g. in 1994 in a case brought by Derbyshire and Lancashire CCs, the High Court declared illegal the Minister's revised guidance to the Local Government Commission; in 1997 Camden LBC in the Court of Appeal won its five-year claim against the Department of the Environment's withholding of £20 million housing subsidy and in the same year Dorset won £8 million from the Department of Social Security.[39]

Secondly, the central government is not monolithic. There is no unity or uniformity in the controls exercised by the various government

---

* Such powers are not always clear, as in 1998 when the Chief Constable of Grampian police resisted the Minister's call for him to resign.

departments: indeed there is considerable variation, even among the different services within the same department, for example between the police services and urban programmes within the Home Office. This may to a large extent be due to the existence of highly integrated vertical 'policy communities'. These are 'networks characterized by stability of relationships, continuity of a highly restrictive membership, vertical interdependence based on shared service delivery responsibilities'.[40] They consist of those people, especially professionals, working in the same field – housing, education, trading standards, environmental health, etc. – whose experience, training, and particular set of values (or ideology) gives them a commitment to their field or service area and allows them to exercise considerable power and influence on policy making across the central–local divide. These relationships are reinforced by local–central staff secondments.* And the Civil Service College runs courses on local government to enable staff to 'work more effectively in their dealings with local government' (though they do not always appear to do much for civil servants' generally negative view of local government.†

These networks arise essentially from the fact that the central government relies on local authorities to deliver services, for example the DfEE itself does not build schools, hire teachers, etc. nor does the DoH employ social workers or run care homes. There is what Rhodes[41] has described as a 'power-dependence' or exchange relationship between central and local government. Both levels of government have power and resources – consitutional/legal, financial, political, expertise and informational – it is not one-sided, and their relationship is not always strained. And, while ultimately the central government may predominate, it has to bargain and negotiate to avoid delays, adverse publicity, legal challenges, etc., where there is local resistance (as Dearlove points out central government 'cannot force local councils to do something *well*', if they are determined to be awkward). Besides, local authorities have much discretion in the design or format for the

---

* See *Municipal Journal*, 17 May 1996, pp. 20–1, *Local Government Chronicle*, 28 October 1994, pp. 16–17.

† See: G. Jones and T. Travers in L. Pratchett and D. Wilson, *Local Democracy and Local Government*, Macmillan, 1996.

implementation of policies, and quite often for their origination (vide LMS, sheltered housing, comprehensive schools, house sales, etc.).

Thirdly, while the central government may lay down certain minimum standards, councils have a substantial, though not unlimited, freedom to decide higher standards as they see fit; for example, while 53 per cent of three- and four-year-olds nationally have a place in an LEA nursery, over 90 per cent have a place in Knowsley, Walsall and North Tyneside, while in West Sussex, Oxfordshire and Wiltshire the figure is 25 per cent;* and local authority expenditure on youth services can vary between £18 per head to £292.†

This derives, in part, from the fact that local authorities themselves raise a significant proportion of their income from local taxes, charges and internal funds, which thus gives them a degree of financial independence (on occasion, some councils get no grant income).[42]

In addition to their financial and legal independence, local authorities have a considerable degree of political independence: they are, after all, elected bodies, which must carry some weight in the mind of the central government.[43] And where the party in power locally differs from that in power at the centre, there is a greater tendency to resist central dictates (in the 1970s, housing finance reform and council house sales policies were resisted by Labour Councils, while the subsequent Labour government's comprehensive education plans received filibuster treatment (i.e. deliberate delay) from many Conservative councils). The 1980s opened with much united hostility among councils of all political colours to the government's expenditure cuts, and the AMA mounted a national publicity campaign ('Keep It Local').

Such open hostility and defiance is rare, for central government and local authorities conduct much of their business informally (by means of letters, deputations to Whitehall, telephone calls, etc.) in an attempt to smooth differences and reach compromises. Local authority representatives sit on government advisory bodies (the Housing Services Advisory Group, the Schools Council, the Personal Social Services Council and so on), where they can expound the local government viewpoint. Local authorities (especially through their associations –

* *Times Educational Supplement*, 26 January 1996.
† *Times Educational Supplement*, 2 October 1998, p. 2.

COSLA in Scotland and the LGA in England and Wales – see p. 469 – are in regular and frequent contact and consultation with government departments over such matters as the annual RSG/grant negotiations, proposed legislation (and consequential regulations or SIs), the formulation of circulars* and guidance documents on new laws, the preparation of codes of conduct and practice (such as that dealing with publicity (1980), LEA–school regulations (1999) or that of 1997 dealing with the central–local relationship itself: see p. 568) and there is much written communication on a daily basis and especially following government Green and White Papers.† In 1996 the Associations were quite instrumental in the government's revision of its financial assistance to local authorities following the change in capital disregards limits for residential care), and in 1993/4 in restoring the threatened councillor membership to police authorities. And the local government professional associations, such as the Institute of Housing, the Institute of Revenues, Rating and Valuation or the Association of Directors of Social Services, are regularly called on to advise the government or participate in a working party which will shape government policy. Indeed, the official Housing Advice Unit in the DoE comprised former local government officers and members of the Institute of Housing. In 1997 a senior civil servant from the DETR became a senior executive of the LGA and the chairman of the LGA became a member of a government Cabinet committee, and regular discussions between Ministers and the LGA now occur following the formation of the Central/Local Partnership: p. 574.

In addition, local authorities may exercise their own influence on central government through their party machinery. The major parties have regular conferences on local government which provide an opportunity for central and local politicians to get together and exchange views. Both in and out of Parliament, the major parties have local government committees and advisory groups (the latter usually drawing on personnel from local government itself). Ministers are

---

* It took 6 months to negotiate the contents of Circular 10/65 (M. Kogan, *The Politics of Education*, Penguin, 1971, p. 189).

† The number of Green/Consultative Papers has increased from eleven in 1976 to 76 in 1981 and to 267 in 1990.

regularly receiving party delegations and deputations from local government (especially in recent years) and they may be similarly confronted when they return to their constituencies at weekends.

Some Ministers may have particular links, past or present, with local government.[44] So too do MPs, who can display their concern about local government through parliamentary questions and adjournment debates. About one third of MPs have had experience in local government, and some of them (for example 24 in 1980, 56 in 1983) have a 'dual mandate' and combine the role of councillor with that of MP*. A great deal of MPs' constituency (or 'surgery') matters concern local government, as does a significant proportion of their correspondence.[45] In 1981 Conservative MPs forced their own government to withdraw and substantially revise the Local Government Finance Bill (thereby dropping plans for local rates referenda).

Furthermore, some individual councillors and officers can be quite influential with Ministers and civil servants, on account of their personality, qualifications or expertise,[46] a situation which may be enhanced in so far as the elected mayor system is adopted. (In the recent past, senior local politicians could be regarded as 'more important than a junior minister . . . ministers would always find time to see them . . . The Director of Education for Liverpool, and in other cities, was a great figure'.)†

Local authorities may also exercise influence by forming regional groups and applying collective pressure. In some areas in the 1960s such groups pressed the government to speed up motorway building and reform the Selective Employment Tax (which was adversely affecting the tourist trade). In the 1970s pressure was used in bidding for government economic and industrial aid. And in the 1980s, on a number of occasions, local authorities successfully resisted central government policies.[47] Similarly in the mid-1990s, a number of local authorities caused the government to revise its housing projections and to shift the policy more towards brownfield sites.

Finally, what of the claim that local authority services are fragmented

---

* In the current Parliament, for example, five Liberal Democrat MPs are also active councillors.

† Quoted in Jones and Travers' chapter in L. Pratchett and D. Wilson, *Local Democracy and Local Government*, Macmillan, 1996.

and their corporate planning undermined by central government departments pursuing different policies and pulling local authority departments in different directions? In 1977 the government's 'think tank' (CPRS) did find some evidence for this claim – on occasion, the implementation by local authorities of multi-purpose capital projects had been hindered because different elements in the project received different responses – some approved, others refused – from different departments (see note 26). There was also a more general tendency to contradiction between the central spending departments (DSS, DfEE, Home Office, etc.) and the control departments (the Treasury and the Department of the Environment) (see note 38). Similar contradictions have arisen more recently with, for example, government education policy giving more parental choice (which requires more spare capacity in schools and therefore extra costs) and Treasury policy on public expenditure and cost-effectiveness in LEA spending. The policy of promoting school opt-outs also created cost and school planning problems.

However, the CPRS report concluded that the claim to lack of coordination was exaggerated, and that in many ways the central government was as well forward in the development and application of corporate management as most local authorities were. Nevertheless it did recommend that central government should deal with local authorities more on an inter-departmental programme basis than on a separate service-by-service basis. (The current government is pursuing just such a quest for 'joined-up' government – see below.) It also suggested that there should be more contact and mutual understanding between the central and the local authorities (the SIP scheme; see p. 449). And finally it suggested that the central government should reduce its interventions on matters of detail and concentrate instead on key matters, such as the overall size of capital allocations.

Local government expenditure restraint

In absolute terms, local government expenditure has grown continually in post-war years (e.g. from £2 billion in 1955 to £5½ billion in 1960* and £75 billion today). But much of this is due to inflation. To remove

---

* See *Royal Commission on Local Government*, 1969, vol. 1.

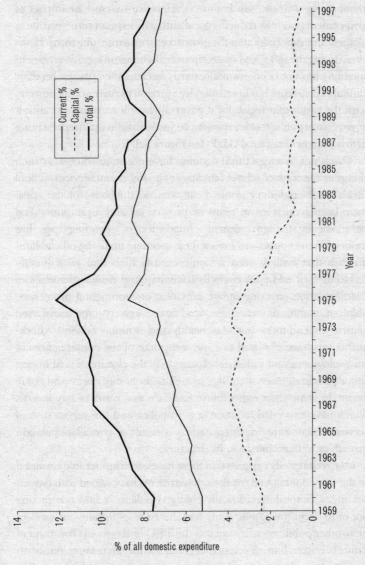

Figure 22 *Local government total revenue and capital expenditure, 1959–97*

the effect of rising prices, local expenditure can be compared to the economy as a whole: see Figure 22. Here we can see the impact of government policy in reducing local authority expenditure (relative to all spending) especially after the growth years up to the mid-1970s. However, during the 1980s and 1990s, the overall change in local government spending has not been dramatic, partly because the restraint on their capital expenditure has been offset by a growth in current expenditure, with the result that today local government still accounts for almost 25 per cent of public sector expenditure, just as it did in 1979 (representing nearly 10 per cent of total GDP, see Figure 22).[48]

This is not to suggest that councils have not suffered cuts, as such things as the state of school buildings or roads, social services, school meals or discretionary grants bear witness. But some of the 'cuts' have been reductions in plans or projections and aspirations. And paradoxically the government's imposition of spending caps has induced many councils to *increase* their spending up to the official limit (in case that limit is seen as unnecessarily high and subsequently reduced).[49] In addition, councils have acquired new responsibilities (*vide* legislation covering public nuisance, environmental protection, children, community care, etc.) and have received some transferred central expenditures (such as health and housing benefits). Local authorities have also had to cope with some of the consequences of unemployment and industrial change (e.g. the closure of coal mines, reductions in defence spending) as well as inner-city decay and rising crime. In some cases expenditure has risen as a result of pay awards which have exceeded inflation (e.g. in police and fire services). And service expenditure has increased as a result of overall population growth as well as change in its structure.

One recent study suggests that there has been considerable variation in the way councils and/or their departments have coped with limited resources. Some have radically changed policies – into contracting out or to decentralization; some had shifted responsibility for services on to other public agencies (such as the TEC or Regional Government Office); others had developed techniques for increasing resources (returns on cash surpluses for example; and some switched spending to maintain staff morale or to demonstrate the vitality of the council. Overall, it concluded that 'choice and discretion are still alive and well, constraints from central government are exaggerated'. See Appendix 16 for range of financial possibilities (and see *More for less: Managing limited resources*, LGMB 1997).

Overall, government policy has managed to slow or stabilize the growth of local spending (especially compared to the 1960s and 1970s). There have been efficiency savings and overall staff numbers have fallen from 2.3 million in 1980 to 1.8 million today. But there are unavoidable pressures for greater expenditure with the renewed growth in the school population and in the very dependent elderly. Crime figures suggest more spending on police and probation and school truancy programmes. There is also pressure from users of public services who, encouraged by the 'charters' of both central and local government, seek enhanced standards and quality of provision. Local authorities are now preparing for their new duty to promote the social, economic and environmental well-being of their areas, and are seeking to contribute to the government's social exclusion programme by increasing employment opportunities, reducing poverty and helping to improve health: see Chapter 15.

Proposed remedies

Clearly the CPRS report (above) was not content with the state of local–central relations. In this respect the report was echoing the sentiments of the Redcliffe-Maud and Wheatley Royal Commissions of 1966–9 and of the Maud Committee of 1967. It was the last which most clearly outlined proposals to improve the relationship of local government to central government. It recommended: (1) abolition of statutory requirements for the appointment of committees and officers; (2) abolition of ministerial control over the appointment and dismissal of officers; (3) abolition of the district auditor's power of surcharge (see p. 594), with its inhibiting effect on initiative by councillors; (4) simplification of Whitehall's machinery for dealing with local authorities: one department to be responsible for coordinating national policy relating to local government; (5) the setting up of a Central Office by the local authority associations to conduct negotiations with the central government; (6) abolition of the *ultra vires* principle; instead local authorities should be given general competence to do anything they considered to be for the good of their citizens; (7) freedom for local authorities to fix their scales for members' expenses; (8) greater financial freedom for local authorities, with additional sources of revenue to be devised and less detailed government involvement in local capital spending.

Most of these changes have now come to pass, more or less. But it is difficult to detect any great sigh of relief from local authorities. This is because central government still wields the 'big stick' – partly because (4) and (6) above have not changed,* and partly because in the 1980s there were fundamental changes in the central–local relationship, to the detriment of local government. Even before this, the Layfield Committee[50] (looking at local government finance) in 1976 declared 'a growing . . . propensity for the government to determine, in increasing detail, the pace and direction in which local services should be developed, the resources which should be devoted to them and the priorities between them' (Report p. 65). (It also pointed out that the 'drift towards centralization' was even more marked in Scotland than in England and Wales.) In particular, it found 'a lack of clear accountability for local government expenditure, which results from the present confusion of responsibilities between the government and local authorities' (p. xxv).

The Committee then posed a choice: that either an explicitly 'centralist' relationship should be instituted, giving clear and recognized responsibility to the central government for local government expenditure, both generally and among individual authorities; or a more 'localist' solution should be adopted. The latter was favoured by the Committee. It would involve local authorities taking greater responsibility for the conduct of local affairs, including more powers of decision in services such as education, social services, transport and housing. But above all, under this 'localist' solution, local authorities were to have an additional source of revenue in the form of a local income tax (LIT).

In practice, the central government has not accepted the recommendation of the LIT. Indeed, the then Labour government then did

---

* Though it is fair to say that important changes occurred when the government set up (in 1995) coordinating offices in the Regions (known as GOs) and the DoE was re-formed and expanded in 1997.

precisely what Layfield feared: it declared for a middle way between the two alternatives posed and argued in favour of a 'partnership' approach to the central–local relationship.[51] (Layfield thought this too vague and that it fudged the issue, and believed that it would only allow the centralist drift to continue.) In the meantime, there have been other developments.

Concern over central intervention in local government affairs is not new: it was expressed strongly in the early nineteenth century,[52] in the late nineteenth century[53] and in the early twentieth century.[54] However, it has been suggested that the situation became worse in the years following the Second World War.[55] In 1956 the government acknowledged the problem and sought to improve it by tidying the structure (via the Local Government Commissions of 1958–65; see p. 38) and by replacing a number of specific grants by a block grant in 1958 (converted into the RSG in 1966). In 1963 local authorities were empowered to spend up to a 1d. rate on anything which was in the general interests of their area. (Parishes were permitted to spend up to 0.2d. Scotland already had these powers.) In 1968 planning procedures were changed such that local plans (as opposed to the development plans) would no longer need government approval. At the same time there was some relaxation of central control over local authority transport planning, where, with the introduction of Transport Policies and Programmes (TPPs), the government gave approval for whole programmes of expenditure rather than individual projects (see p. 383). A similar development occurred in 1970 in the field of loan sanction for 'locally determined' schemes of capital development.

Further encouragement was given to local authorities in 1970 with the Conservatives' promise to abolish many of the 1,200 or so controls exercised over local government. Yet, in practice, it seemed that control was *increasing*: local authority social service departments were required to prepare ten-year plans; LEAs were obliged to stop supplying milk in schools to the over-7s (even if the LEA was itself prepared to pay for it); rate monitoring was undertaken by the central government; and the Housing Finance Act 1972 required local authorities to apply a universal system of rent rebates and to raise their rents in line with government policy (see p. 103).

However, the Local Government Acts 1972 and 1973 did remove many controls, including some quite significant ones: indeed one of the purposes of the local government reform was to strengthen and increase the independence of local government by eliminating the smaller and weaker authorities which were often held to be responsible for some of the government's controls (just as the speed of a convoy is dictated by the slowest vehicle).

Thus, apart from the reorganization itself, the legislation reduced the previous mandatory requirements on the appointment of officials and committees, and gave Ministers less power to intervene in appointment and dismissal procedures, including, in 1973, those of chief education officers. Secondly, the power of the district auditor was reduced, so that more issues of disallowance and surcharge are now decided by the courts (see p. 396). Thirdly, the 'free 1d.' was increased to 2p, now changed to a per capita maximum and with wider application (see p. 78). Finally, the Local Government Acts of 1972 (England and Wales) and 1973 (Scotland) empowered local authorities to pay members attendance allowances. (In the meantime, the giant Department of the Environment – now DETR – had been created, and acted, to a large extent, as the central department for coordinating relationships with English local authorities, rather as the Scottish Office and the Welsh Office have done.)

All this seemed to reflect a new faith in local government. But there was no real consistency, partly because of the impact of party politics. In 1975 the Labour government (1974–9) repealed much of the previous government's Housing Finance Act (freeing local authorities to a certain extent) but in 1976 it passed an Education Act which required all LEAs to introduce comprehensive secondary schooling. In addition, economic problems were imposing themselves on the relationship: the government's incomes policy in 1975 led to local authorities being threatened with a reduction in their RSG if they gave pay rises in excess of £6 per week. In 1978 a new form of control was introduced in the shape of 'cash limits' (see p. 429). And since the late 1970s, government inspectors have been becoming more directive (rather than merely advisory) in their approach. In broad terms, therefore, it seems that when national resources are scarce or under pressure the central grip tends to tighten.

In response to the economic and financial problems of 1974–5 (when there were numerous rate protests and sporadic rate strikes) the government established two new and important institutions. The first was the Joint Manpower Watch, whereby local authorities and the central government together began to collect and analyse information on local government employment numbers and patterns. The second was the Consultative Council on Local Government Finance (CCLGF). This was a joint central–local government committee, chaired by the Secretary of State for the (then) Department for the Environment. Its creation brought local authorities into the government's budgetary machinery through regular, annual (July) meetings of Ministers and officials from the DoE and the Treasury and the 'spending' departments (DSS, DFEE, HO, etc.) together with local authority members and officials drawn from the local authority associations. Its purpose was to provide 'consultations and cooperation . . . on major financial and economic issues of common concern, with special emphasis on the deployment of resources'. It was particularly concerned with matters of policy affecting local authorities which have major financial implications[56] – notably the effects of legislative changes, local authorities' spending plans and the government's SSAs/grants and their distribution. There was a similar council for Wales (though not for Scotland, where there were meetings between the Scottish Office and the (uniquely) single local authority association, COSLA).

The CCLGF arrangement ceased in 1997 with the creation of the Central/Local Partnership (see pp. 436, 574 and Appendix 31). This has a Finance sub-Group (plus specialist working groups) which discusses the same matters as the former CCLGF, together with policy iniatives on local government finance. It thus forms a key part of the annual local authority finance settlement (LAFS) process. There was considerable scepticism about the achievements of the CCLGF in certain respects – whether the local authorities' contributions were really heeded or influential, and whether there was any greater consistency among departments in their approaches to local authorities – and there was the view that having several local authority associations involved undermined cohesion.[57] With the creation of the single Local Government Association (largely Labour in composition) and the new rapprochement or concordat with the (new) Labour government there is more room for optimism of a real voice for local government – see Chapter 15.

The Conservative government, elected in 1979, sought to rationalize controls over local government. In a White Paper (see note 27) published in September 1979, it declared:

Democratically elected local authorities are wholly responsible bodies who must be free to get on with the tasks entrusted to them by Parliament without constant interference in matters of detail by the Government of the day. On the other hand there are certain national policies which it is the Government's duty to pursue even though they may be administered locally; for example, where by statute the responsibilities are shared between central and local government or where the Government of the day may have secured a particular mandate at a general election. It would be inappropriate therefore to abandon all control over local government; to do so would be an abdication of the Government's proper role.

Consequently its intention has been to remove or relax some 300 controls. These include often minor but still irritating controls over interest rates for various purposes; the hearing of appeals concerning the erection of bus shelters or against bridge restrictions or the provision of street lighting; the prescription of various fees (libraries, testing weights and measures equipment etc. and various licences); the approval of school development plans, of financial assistance to independent schools, of arrangements for the provision of PE clothing, of purchase of equipment for FE colleges; the power to require the submission of housing programmes and control over conditions attached to individual local authority mortgages; the confirmation of noise abatement orders; the consent to disposal of land by non-principal councils; the confirmation of new street by-laws; and the approval of plans for crematoria.

At the same time, the government reduced the volume of circulars and other papers issued to local government (e.g. they fell from 1,873 in 1978–9 to 592 in 1981–2, though see p. 424 above) and it has been reviewing its need for statistical information from local authorities. In addition, the government repealed the Education Act 1976, which means that LEAs were no longer obliged to introduce comprehensive schools and could themselves decide what form secondary schooling will take. In the field of housing (since 1981) local authorities are no longer bound by minimum (Parker-Morris) standards or maximum (yardstick) costings. And, more generally, the system of control over local authorities' capital expenditure now involves less detailed intervention (see p. 384).

Many people, especially those inside local government, were sceptical about the changes outlined above. Some saw them as aimed not so much at reducing the scope of government *interference* in local government affairs but at reducing the scope of *government* generally, in line with current Conservative philosophy. Others saw the government as giving with one hand and taking away with the other. As *The Times* put it, 'Where less government means more.'[58] Thus, under the same legislation which removes or relaxes many controls – the Local Government, Planning and Land Act 1980 – local authorities are required to: (1) publish key information about their finances and their performance generally; (2) to put services out to tender (CCT; see p. 344), and make more publicly accountable their direct labour organization (DLOs), some of which are prevented from undertaking work at the discretion of the Minister; and (3) prepare a register of unused land (following the repeal of the Community Land Act 1975). In addition (4) urban development corporations (UDCs) were set up, at the Minister's discretion, in eleven inner-city areas (such as Bristol, Liverpool and London), with wide powers to bypass ordinary planning procedures, and twenty-two tax- and planning-free 'enterprise zones' were established in inner-city areas. This is in addition to the Housing Act 1980, which obliged local authorities to sell (at discount) council houses. And while some local authorities were concerned at (5) the new capital expenditure controls procedure (see p. 384), many have been particularly incensed at (6) the form of the block/support grant system (see p. 349), which (together with the increasing tendency to develop specific grants; see p. 348) presented a further threat to local government's already limited freedom.

The legislation of 1980 in particular united the various local authority associations in their opposition to the (Conservative) government. This unity was unusual; equally unusual was their hostility to the government, as they were all at the time themselves Conservative-dominated in the composition of their own leadership (see p. 469). The chair of the Association of Metropolitan Authorities appeared to speak for them all when he said that the legislation presented 'the biggest threat to the constitutional independence of local government in this country since the nineteenth century'.[59]

Subsequent legislative developments increased this anxiety, as they eroded the base of local government. Thus under the Education Reform Act 1988, a national curriculum was imposed, schools could opt out of LEA control and the Minister's powers were substantially increased (and enhanced further by the Education Act 1993). Under the Housing Act 1988, council-house tenants can opt to transfer to a non-local-authority landlord, and the Local Government and Housing Act 1989 prevents councils from subsidizing their own rents. The Local Government Acts 1988 and 1992 required a large increase in competitive tendering (CCT) for council services (see p. 344). The legislation not only identified the service or function, but stipulated the form of tendering (through detailed regulations), rates of return and the publication of support service costs (which created the problem of revealing commercially sensitive information to competitors as well as increasing costs); it also gave the Minister powers to intervene, for example through the issue of Secs. 13 and 14 (1988 Act) notices, which may cancel contracts or require re-tendering. And in the field of finance, apart from the enhanced capital control system (p. 384) we have seen the replacement of local rates with the unified business rate and the council tax (p. 369) and a series of 'cat and mouse' manoeuvres regarding grants and penalties (p. 383 above and p. 547 below) and the introduction (under the Rates Act 1984) of rate-capping (or budget limitation) by the Minister (see p. 360).

If this legislation moved many councils to opposition, anger or anxiety over government policies, others were more favourably disposed because they saw the legislation (especially CCT and the new grant procedures) as a means whereby 'spendthrift' or 'profligate' Labour councils could be penalized and checked. Many of the latter, rightly or wrongly, were seen as actively sabotaging the government's economic policy by raising their rates/taxes and spending on public services. (In practice Conservative councils were hit too – see Chapter 14 – but many Conservatives still supported the controls, and often wanted more, especially if they lived in non-Conservative areas.)*

---

* See *Widdicombe Report*, vol. 3 and *Attitudes to Local Government*, JRF, 1990.

This argument illustrates the perennial question of 'democracy versus equality' – of how far individual authorities should be allowed to raise service standards above those of their neighbours, and face the consequent judgement of the electors at the next poll. The issue can be stated in a different way: is local government primarily a provider of services or of democracy?

The relationship between local authorities and the central government has been variously described as that of 'principal and agent', as power-dependency and as a 'partnership'. As *statements* or *prescriptions* of what is desirable or proper, this is clearly a matter of opinion and personal values. There is no formal or constitutional definition of the relationship, and there is no generally accepted theory or philosophy of local government.[60] Too often are local authorities regarded as no more than providers of services. Such a view is widespread, though it is perhaps best exemplified by the central government. For example, a recent government document, while stating that 'local government has a very important role in the democratic life of this country', goes on to state merely that 'local authorities provide or promote a wide range of public services', before it then considers their mode of operation for 'the effective delivery of services'.[61] Such a narrow view clearly forms the government's perception (and especially that of the civil service)[62] of its relationship with local government. However, a better understanding and greater cooperation may emerge from a scheme started in 1992 called the Secondment Initiative Programme (SIP). This aims to achieve 140 new secondments between Whitehall and local authorities over three years.[63]* In the White Paper *Modernising Government* (HMSO, March 1999) the government proposes further such secondments and interchange, together with joint training to prevent individuals becoming 'stuck in silos'.

Attempts to assess or *describe* the working relationship are very much a matter of individual judgement. Probably local authorities today are neither mere agents of the government nor equal partners: the relationship is somewhere between. But it is difficult to generalize. Politically, the government controls Parliament and thus can normally

* See too *Local Government Chronicle*, 28 October 1994, pp. 16–17, 17 January 1999, p. 3 and *Municipal Journal*, 17 May 1996, pp. 20–1

push through legislation which will affect the shape and substance of local government. Yet, in practice, local authorities too have a mandate (from their own electors), they have their own source of finance (from council tax and charges) and they have 'know-how' in the sense that they are 'in the field' and responsible for the delivery of a mass of services. As a result, the central government depends upon local authorities' knowledge, field experience and expertise (particularly that of local government officers). This applies more especially to some departments or divisions (education, social services, housing) than to others (the Treasury, agriculture or trade for example).

While relationships and influences vary among departments and different services, it is generally true to say that what is sought by both sides is agreement and amicable relations rather than hostility and the grudging acceptance of repugnant policies, for ultimately they both share a common concern: the public service. Clashes do occur and some of them become very public (such as Clay Cross UDC in 1972 and Tameside MBC in 1976 (see p. 431), the serious delay in settling the city's rate by Liverpool in 1984 and 1985, the GLC in the 1980s and, more recently, in the early 1990s, the mass revolt by teachers against school test and league tables). But the use of 'the big stick' can be awkward and embarrassing for central government as the Clay Cross (and the earlier Poplar 1921, Rotherham and Durham 1932 cases) well illustrated. And in practice, standards do vary considerably among councils: in spite of central government's apparent dominance, they have not been homogenized.[64] Disagreements are inevitable, since local authorities and central government have different perspectives, different party allegiances and different priorities.[65] This is most obviously illustrated where local authorities have their tax or budget 'capped' or reduced by the Minister (as did 21 councils in 1990; they subsequently took him to court to challenge its legality, unsuccessfully). What is needed is a clearer recognition of these differences and a better mutual understanding. There is some evidence that this is happening under the present (1999) Labour government (while in 1996, in office, and in 1998, in Opposition, the Conservatives have pledged a new, less interventionist relationship with local government.*

---

* See, e.g., *Municipal Journal*, 10 July 1998, pp. 14–15.

Not everyone in local government wants more 'freedom' from central controls: the removal of ministerial control over charges may cause authorities to turn basically free services into money-making ventures; standards of service may be jeopardized if ministerial intervention were to be removed; and certain controls may be welcomed as a means of sustaining local government employment (the need for ministerial approval may delay school closures, for instance). But above all, both inside and out of local government, is the view that real, local self-government is incompatible with social or territorial justice:[66] that social justice requires a high degree of equality in the standards of service from one part of the country to another. Such a view is widely held by Socialists,[67] though not exclusively or universally. It is more the Conservatives who have expressed the desire to 'get off the back' of local government though in practice this has not squared with Conservative local government legislation since 1979. Paradoxically, the Marxist Left also see a danger in centralization, with local authorities becoming little more than extensions of the capitalist state:[68] hence their frequent advocacy of local 'community politics'.

Local government and the European Community (EC)

Increasingly, British local government is having to look beyond the central government to the political institutions of the European Economic Community (EC). Ever since Britain formally joined the European Community in 1973 (under the European Communities Act 1972), local authorities, together with the rest of our society, have become subject to the international laws emanating from the European Commission in Brussels. For the most part these laws – generally referred to as 'Community law' – take the form of Regulations and Directives (or 'secondary legislation'). These regulations (which councils both obey and enforce), together with greater integration and the receipt of EU funds has been described as the 'Europeanization' of British local government.

The impact of Europe on British local government can be characterized[69] as fourfold: (1) organizational (2) functional (3) socio-economic and (4) constitutional. The first two effects are direct and factual; the other two are indirect, unclear and uncertain.

(1) Organizational effects are those aspects which affect the way in which councils operate (and their costs). These include (i) public procurement of works, supplies and services, where EU rules require that contracts are advertised and open to tendering and non-discriminatory competition across the Community; (ii) personnel matters which are subject to EU rules on equivalence of qualifications,[70] working conditions, part-time rights, consultation rights and freedom of movement (one of the 'four freedoms' of the EU); (iii) financial aspects including the freer movement of capital, fiscal harmonization, VAT on public services and EU grants.

(2) Functional effects cover a host of local services. This concerns some local authority departments and occupational groups more than others including education (European awareness, curricula, language and vocational training, student mobility and exchanges); technical services (construction, vehicle and engineering specifications and codes of practice, building control procedures); environmental services (air and water quality, harmonization of planning control and environmental impact assessment; noise, pesticide, fertilizer and waste management, fire safety); social services and housing (standards, safety, EU-wide access); consumer protection/trading standards (food inspection, product safety, control of product ingredients, packaging, labeling, weights and measures).

(3) Socio-economic effects have to do with the consequences (gains and losses) of the wider market and Britain's exposure to competition and to common policies (on agriculture, fishing, etc.). Clearly some communities suffer economic decline, de-industrialization and unemployment, much of the burden of which falls on local authorities. But other localities benefit from Europe's growth and lower inflation and, while local authorities may face extra burdens (e.g. costs of technical, legal, language training and information/library services or of larger lorries' damage to roads and bridges), they can gain from overseas investment and EU funding as well as tourism and local business growth.

(4) Constitutional consequences arise most obviously from the legal authority vesting in EU institutions, especially the Commission and

the Court of Justice. The UK Parliament has lost (or 'pooled') part of its sovereignty and for local government some key decision-making is thus more remote. There is also the fear that greater European harmonization reduces the scope of local discretion and choice. However, the EU has espoused the principle of 'subsidiarity' (i.e. local decision-making wherever possible) and the Commission has developed links with local authorities, both directly and through the Committee of the Regions (CoR)* and the Assembly of European Regions (which contain representatives of British local authorities who liaise with and lobby the Commission).† The regional dimension will become increasingly significant to Britain with devolution to Wales and Scotland and as England develops regional development agencies and assemblies (see p. 601). (Another constitutional element which should be mentioned is the right of EU citizens, under a Directive, to vote and stand for British local elections. In 1996 a Swedish woman was the first to be so elected, to Tendring District Council.)

Thus the EU has both specific and general implications for local government. Among the latter are those Community laws which raise questions about the legality of rate-subsidization such as de-rating agriculture or financial inducements such as low-rent land sites to attract business investment. But on the positive side is financial assistance. This takes the form of grants and loans, with some from the European Investment Bank, but most from Structural Funds (especially the Regional Development Fund and the Social Fund, for regional development, rehabilitation, training and job-creation) and to a lesser extent from community initiatives such as RECHAR (declining coal areas), KONVER (declining armaments), PESCA (fishing),

* Since local authorities have a major role in the implementation of EU regulations, the CoR provides an important mechanism by which their views can be taken into account in the early stages of legislation. It was set up in 1993 (replacing the Consultative Council of Regional and Local Authorities, founded 1989). In 1995 it made the 'thunderbolt' proposal that it has the right to bring proceedings before the Court of Justice for breaches of the principle of subsidiarity which affect the powers of local authorities; see *Local Government Chronicle*, 20 January 1991, pp. 14–15.

† Regional Development funding is provided mainly for large projects (transport, redevelopment, environmental protection etc.) with the result that councils tend to group together and cooperate in making applications.

RESIDER (steel) and from education programmes (such as LIN-GUA). Much depends on the nature or extent of the problems in the area/region, which determines whether they are recognized as having Objective 1 or 2 etc. status.

In the period 1989–93 the UK received some 5,500 million ECU (about £3,850 million) from EU Structural Funds[71]. In 1988 Birmingham City was selected to receive over £200 million over five years; Liverpool received £628 million of regeneration (Objective 1) funding 1993–9. But one problem has been that the money passes through the central government which has often made corresponding reductions in its own borrowing approvals or grant-aid to local authorities. However, since 1993/4, under pressure from the Commission, this has diminished as the principle of 'additionality' has become accepted (in the same way that government use of lottery funds for education, health and environmental projects is not to replace any mainstream funding for those services).

Many local authorities have appointed European Officers (and perhaps European Funding officers) and established European units, and a number of local authorities have set up offices in Brussels to build up links and sustain communications in order to help negotiate grant aid applications (thus seeking to bypass central government). In 1993 there were thirteen such offices representing individual councils (such as Birmingham, Kent and Strathclyde). Councils also form consortia to make bids for funds (e.g. East Midlands authorities) and they may join together to open offices in Brussels (e.g. as did Dorset, Hampshire and Lower Normandy in 1997, subsequently partnered by the Isle of Wight, Bournemouth University and several TECs).

Local authorities, therefore, may obtain substantial material benefit from the EU. And, as in its relations with the British central government, local government is not without influence: apart from briefing Members of the European Parliament (MEPs) (and perhaps influencing them through the party machinery) and sending deputations (lobbying) to the EU,[72] local authorities cooperate jointly with the EU through the International Union of Local Authorities (IULA) and the Council of European Municipalities and Regions (CEMR – see p. 457). They are also represented on various consultative committees. Evidently 'local government participation in Community affairs is not purely a matter of form. It can and does produce results.[73] But clearly this has not always been the case,[74] which may in part be due to inadequate information. Consequently, in 1979 the British section of the IULA and CEMR set up the European Information Service.

Peter John's study concludes that, 'On balance, European integration has been positive for British local government in the light of the deterioration of central–local relations and the loss of functions in the 1980s, but the gains are minor and the progress to greater European integration slow. Yet the development of faster integration might not benefit local authorities as it might lead to more centralization and greater controls over discretionary powers. The present balance of power between central government and European decision-making might be the most beneficial arrangement for local government.'*

The Local Government International Bureau (LGIB) is the European and International Affairs unit of the UK local authorities' associations and acts as the British Section of the International Union of Local Authorities (IULA) and the Council of Municipalities and Regions (CEMR) (see p. 454). The aims of the LGIB are to promote the knowledge and interests of British and European local government and of local government in general and to develop international links among local authorities. To these ends the Bureau has a number of specialist service team which provide information on: EU policy and legislation; links and networks with both the EU and other countries; support services for UK delegations to international forums (IULA, Committee of the Regions, CEMR) and to UK local authorities in their management of the European Structural Funds programme; international links teams (covering such aspects as twinning, the 'Know How Fund', exchanges and technical cooperation, links and coordination for overeseas projects, funding and environmental programmes).

Information on EU matters also derives from the consultative advisory machinery on EU affairs which exists inside many British government departments. And there is a six-monthly meeting of

* *The Impact of the EC on Local Government*, Joseph Rowntree Fund, June 1993. See, too, K. Taylor in *Political Quarterly*, March 1995.

representatives from British local and central government in the European Joint Group, which meets to consider EU legislation and to act as an information clearing house for local authorities. Together these devices enhance coordination, so that lines do not get crossed when local and central governments are in direct but separate contact with the EU. Thus there is developing another area of common ground between the central government and local authorities.

13

LOCAL GOVERNMENT AND THE LOCAL COMMUNITY

We have seen in the last chapter how local government has a close relationship with the central government, and that British local authorities are subject to international (EU) controls as well as the benefits of financial aid (mainly for industrial development). Local authorities have long had other international links, mainly through the International Union of Local Authorities (IULA), an organization, based in the Netherlands, which acts as a spokesman for local government on the international level, provides a forum for the exchange of views on local government policies and supplies services (training, research, information, etc.) for over ninety member countries. The last are particularly useful to the developing countries, but the regular bi-annual conference (which has considered such themes as urbanization, leisure and conservation) is well attended by the membership generally. The last conference (in 1997) was held in Mauritius.

The relationship of the IULA with the EU is handled by the Council of European Municipalities and Regions (CEMR) which has 38 national sections in 25 European countries. It aims to promote the interests of local authorities and inter-relations between them within Europe. It arranges a congress for members every two years (the latest in Finland in 2000) and other *ad hoc* conferences dealing with European themes, often in collaboration with European institutions. The CEMR holds regular meetings with the European Commission (on regional policy, transport, the environment, social policy, etc.). It also has links with the European Parliament and the Committee of the Regions (CoR).

Local authorities are also brought together internationally by such organizations as the Commonwealth Association of Town Clerks, the International City Management Association and (rather more specialized) the Federation of Nature and National Parks of Europe and the International Federation for Housing and Planning. There are similar organizations for recreation administration, for conservation and for public cleaning. Cooperation at a very practical level takes place through the Standing Technological Conference of European Local Authorities (STCELA). This is a development for the exchange of technical know-how and the benefits of centralized purchasing.'[1]

Local government perspectives are thus by no means as narrow as many people imagine. Perhaps the best illustration of this is the involvement of officials from British local authorities in the first elections in Zimbabwe (Rhodesia) in 1980, in Eastern European countries in 1989–90 and most recently in elections in Bosnia (1997). British local authorities have also been much involved in the provision of technical help, advice and cooperation for the latter as they emerge from their former communist regimes (though such local authority assistance to developing countries is not always applauded).[2]

However, in this chapter, our primary concern is with the *local* community and local government's varied relationship with its inhabitants.

Local government and other local public bodies

Apart from government departments, the other form of public authority with which local authorities are likely to have contact is the 'quango' or semi-independent government agency. There are many such agencies and, collectively, they present a vast and rather ill-defined area of government. Indeed, as many of them are regional or local in scale and character, they might even be regarded as another form of local government and certainly as an important part of local governance. All local authorities have some working relationships with them, especially the public corporations (waterways, post office, etc.), in such fields as rating (or payments in lieu), housing and other development, planning controls and amenity arrangements (such as under-grounding power cables). There are also disputes and even legal entanglements (for instance with the post office or the MoD, for failing to make good damage to a property or a road it has dug up). And there is substantial cross-membership, with, for example, local authority representatives sitting on electricity, transport, etc. consumer councils. Local authorities also meet together and with other public, private and voluntary bodies (NHS, power and communications industries, etc.) at courses and conferences (e.g. at the Home Office's Emergency Planning College).

Some local authorities have especially close relations (and overlapping membership) with particular government bodies such as the tourist boards, the Countryside Agency and New Town corporations or nuclear power stations (via liaison committees). For example, Somerset County Council has close links with the Highways Agency, Norfolk County Council has close links with the Broads Authority, Cumbria County Council with the Lake District Planning Board, and Scottish and Welsh local authorities with their respective Development Agencies. There are also frequent contacts with the Department of Social Security and the Benefits Agency, especially by local social services and housing departments. In recent years a number of councils have signed service-level agreements (SLAs) with local benefits offices to provide quick and efficient processing of council tax and housing benefits.

The *Probation Service* is not a mainstream local government service but there are close links with local authorities. England and Wales is divided into 54 probation areas and each is administered by a Probation Committee comprising magistrates and co-opted members of the community, including councillors (under the Probation Service Act 1993). Probation committees are statutory corporations for which the Home Secretary (assisted by the Probation Inspectorate) is responsible to Parliament. Expenditure (mainly for paying salaries to probation officers) is met by local authorities who receive a specific grant to cover 80 per cent while they themselves fund the remaining 20 per cent; they also provide accommodation and administrative support to the Probation Committee.

Health and water

There are two services which have been particularly important to local government. This is because they used to be services provided directly by local authorities and partly because the services are closely related to those still provided by local authorities. The first is the *National Health Service*. Local authorities have provided health services since the nineteenth century. Under the NHS Act 1946 their hospitals were transferred to Regional Hospital Boards and local Management Committees, all appointed bodies but containing local authority representatives. This arrangement continued under the NHS Reorganization Act 1973 when Regional and Area Health Authorities were created, subsequently replaced (in 1982) by 201 English and Welsh District Health Authorities and 15 Scottish Health Boards. Local authority representatives comprised a third of the membership of these bodies, but this ceased altogether under the NHS and Community Care Act[3] 1990. Meanwhile local authorities lost their personal health responsibilities (clinics, vaccination, health visiting, ambulances) to the Health Authorities under the 1973 Act. However, local authority members continue to constitute half of the membership of the Local (Scotland) or Community (England and Wales) Health Councils (the consumer 'watchdogs').

There also continue to be day-to-day working relationships, with local authority social workers employed in hospitals or attached to general practitioners; there are close links and joint appointments between the community physician[4] and local authorities' public analysts and environmental health officers; and there is close collaboration between local authority social services and local health authorities – through what are known as 'joint care planning teams' – to plan and finance local health and welfare projects, such as hostels or sheltered accommodation for patients from psychiatric hospitals. These links are facilitated by the common geographical boundaries of many local authorities and NHS authorities (often now called 'Commissions' because they commission or contract for services from the independent NHS hospital Trusts). The government has recently become very critical of the liaison (or lack of it) between the NHS and local authority social services (Frank Dobson, the Secretary of State for Health, described it as 'a Berlin wall' and a report by the Select Committee on Health in 1999 described the relationship as 'tribal'). Consequently there is to be closer collaboration between them, particularly with a view to releasing hospital bed spaces by transferring more patients to local authority social care, i.e. to reduce the problem of 'bed-blocking'.* Some councils have anticipated such developments, forming joint health commissioning boards (e.g. Somerset CC, Somerst HA, Avalon Trust and Bath Mental Health Care Trust). Indeed it has also been mooted that local authorities themselves should commission services from the NHS. Apart from meeting particular problems, this joint working is one aspect of community leadership and 'joined-up government' which the government is seeking to develop.

The other public service with which local government has close contact is *water supply*. In the past water services were provided by individual local authorities and some private companies. In the 1950s there were a number of amalgamations and many local authority joint water boards were formed. This was brought to an end in England in 1989. Scottish local authorities lost their responsibility for water under the Local Government (Scotland), etc. Act 1994, when water services were transferred to three water authorities. However, local authority representatives constitute part of those authorities' membership. And, more generally, local authorities have a continuing interest.

Local authorities also work closely with the Countryside Agency (formerly the Countryside Commission) and with the *National Parks*. In 1997 the National Parks became independent free-standing local authorities or 'qualgos', i.e. they operate independently of other local authorities, whereas previously they had been run by joint committees of constituent local authorities (e.g. the Exmoor National Park was run by a joint committee of members from Somerset and Devon County Councils). However, the constituent local authorities still provide the majority of members (in Wales two thirds, in England 50

---

* The Government White Papers, *Our Healthier Nation* (1998) and *The New NHS: Modern, Dependable* (1997) place a duty on health and social services authorities of partnership working (and propose a place for local authority chief executives on health authorities). This is particularly so in the Health Action Zones and in the pursuit of Health Improvement Programmes. (See the White Paper *Modern Social Services* 1999.)

per cent plus 1, which must include parish council members; the Minister appoints the remainder). And those councils provide 25 per cent of the finance, the government meeting the other 75 per cent.

The notion that local authorities are responsible for more than just a narrow range of services and specific needs, that they should develop the role of 'consumer advocate'[5] and have responsibility for the coordination and development of the community overall – the concept of 'community leadership' – has been gathering support since the 1980s. The result has been a growing interest and interaction with local (and private) bodies. Councils have instigated a 'Quango Audit' or 'Quango Watch' and regularly send observers to the meetings of the various local non-elected quangos and their reports form part of the councils' formal business. There may also be some cross-membership. The motivation for this is two-fold. On the positive side it is an attempt to monitor and bring together the various elements of service and programme delivery in the locality. On the negative side, local authorities have become increasingly concerned or alarmed at the growth of local 'quangos'* – quasi-independent non-elected public bodies – and what has been described as 'the new magistracy' (i.e. reminding us of the origins of local government when, in the nineteenth century, most local functions were in the hands of the appointed Justices of the Peace). Such bodies have existed since the eighteenth century but it is their recent prolific growth which causes concern. Thus apart from long-established health and water boards, we have seen the creation of Urban Development Corporations, Training and Enterprise Councils, Careers Service Companies, Housing Action Trusts, FE and HE Corporations, Housing Associations, Grant Maintained schools and a host of national quangos which impact on local areas – such as the utility regulators (OFWAT, OFGAS – now OFGEM, etc.), the Food Standards Agency, the Health and Safety Executive, the National Council for Vocational Qualifications, the Sports Council, the Rural Development Commission, the Arts Council, the Tourist Board, the

---

* quango = quasi non-governmental organization. They are also known as 'para government', EGOs (extra-governmental organizations), NDPB (non-departmental public bodies). At local level they may be known as 'qualgos', as they form part of local government or governance, or perhaps as specialized local authorities.

CLA, British Waterways, the Audit Commission, the Charities Board, the Millennium Commission, Research Councils, the Environment Agency, the Regional Development Agencies, etc. Their total number ranges from 1,000 to 5,500 according to definition.[6] Similarly their total expenditure ranges from an estimated £18 billion to some £60 billion or a figure approaching that of local government itself.[7] Certainly their expenditure locally can exceed that of local authorities, e.g. in 1995 Dorset County Council spent £500 million, while quangos in Dorset spent an estimated £600 million.[8] In 1994 Somerset County Council identified over 90 relevant local quangos.

A study of local authorities in the Midlands showed that, while the number of elected councillors remained constant at 600 over the period 1986–94, the number of appointees on local bodies grew from 200 to 1,000.* Altogether there are now an estimated 65,000 'quangocrats' – nearly three times the number of elected councillors. In Scotland there are 372 such appointed bodies, spending over £6.2 million a year and containing some 6,000 members (cf. 1,200 elected councillors; see COSLA report 1997).

Hence the policy – national and local – of seeking to develop a more collaborative approach. But, while close and continuous links between local authorities and these other agencies is crucial for a truly corporate and community approach to service planning and management, there are difficulties because of differing boundaries, separate and jealously guarded budgets, particular interests are pursued rather than the general interest and there is a certain amount of resentment on the part of local authorities who, only a few years ago, were themselves responsible for many of these services. Their differing responsibilities sometimes create tensions and indeed legal conflicts (as when Wirral Council sought to prosecute the North West Water Authority in 1989 for its failure to exercise its anti-pollution responsibilities). However, the government aims to alter this situation to the extent of giving local authorities a new duty of promoting the social and economic wellbeing of the community and requiring them to draw up community development plans (see Chapter 15).

Being appointed bodies, quangos have the advantage of continuity

---

* See *Local Government Studies*, February 1996.

and stability. They can also specialize on one area of activity (health, training, broadcasting, etc.) and board members can be appointed for their specialist knowledge and experience. Such members can also be more impartial, objective and avoid party political bias, as a result of all of which local authorities themselves find it appropriate to create their own semi-independent units, trusts, companies, etc. But a major criticism has been precisely that of patronage and appointments being biased for party advantage. In addition they are less open and account-able – John Stewart describes them as 'the unknown government'. The Nolan Committee on Standards in Public Life (see p. 229) expressed concern at the way they are appointed and the dangers inherent in the lack of democratic control over them. Hence its recommendation that they be made more open and politically balanced in composition. And, from a local government point of view, not only have councils lost some of their responsibilities* to them, but quangos fragment services and make a coordinated, community-wide approach more difficult to achieve. (In one case, for example, a large hotel development was planned by a public agency just yards from one planned by a different development agency.) A further difficulty is that in many cases the policies of quangos are centrally determined; only their strategies are localized (see *Public Administration*, 2, 1999).

Some have seen the bypassing and weakening of local government as part of a 'Thatcherite hegemonic project'. But the Labour Party has created its own share of quangos; indeed the creation of public corporations is attributed to Herbert Morrison (in the 1940s), and Richard Crossman, in the late 1960s, deliberately sought to avoid placing health services in the hands of local authorities because their elective/ democratic nature would make it difficult for them to resist pressure to continuously increase expenditure on health. It might also be added that local authorities also create their own quangos, such as companies and enterprise boards; 40 per cent have an interest in at least one company.

---

* Including some less obvious aspects: see p. 340. See too H. Davis and D. Hall, *Matching Purpose and Task: The Advantages and Disadvantages of Single- and Multi-purpose Bodies*, JRF, 1996.

Local authority inter-relationships

Such a community approach demands no less of a close working relationship among local authorities than it does between local government and other public bodies. Unfortunately, the history of local cooperation has not been an entirely happy one in that respect. One survey of local authorities found only 14 per cent of councillors reporting good relations among local councils, and 67 per cent considered the two-tier structure a mistake.[9]

Historically, there were frequently strained relations between the GLC and some London boroughs, Greater Manchester and some constituent districts (especially Manchester City). Merseyside County and Liverpool City, and Lothian Region and Edinburgh City Council.[10]

The reorganizations of the 1980s and 1990s removed some of the inter-tier stresses (indeed these were one of the stated reasons for the abolition of the GLC and metropolitan county councils). But new resentments were generated (particularly in the struggles for unitary status), and assistance and cooperation with the newly (re)empowered unitary councils is sometimes grudging. (There is also an undercurrent caused by the continuing aspiration of the towns – such as Exeter and Norwich which failed to achieve unitary status in the 1990s reorganization.) And a further irritation can arise where 'tier-skipping' occurs, i.e. where a local authority incurs expenditure (under Section 137; see p. 78) on an activity which is the primary responsibility of another tier of local government without the consent of the other authority. And even at the lowest tier, there are occasions when relations have become so embittered that parishes seek (via the Local Government Boundary Commission) to opt out of their 'host' district and into another.[11]

To some extent conflicts are inevitable: old identities and loyalties underlie the new structures; some of the responsibilities are split; precepting arrangements can cause ill-will; and frictions arise from differences in party control. But perhaps above all each council exists in its own right and will therefore seek jealously to guard its independence. (Although it is usual to refer to the 'tiers' of local government, this does not imply a relationship of authority or power. Counties do not have authority over the district councils, except for emergency planning situations; nor, except for minor matters like filling vacant seats, do the districts exercise any legal authority over parishes and communities.) In such cases of conflict, the Minister may be called in to arbitrate (see p. 425), or another third party (person) may be engaged, for instance to decide which authority is responsible for a particular homeless family. Sometimes the issue is settled in the law courts.[12] Otherwise if it is a dispute of general interest, it may be carried upwards to the local authority associations (see below).

Fortunately, most local authorities seek cooperative and amicable relations with their neighbours: after all, they have in so many cases to work together – where powers are shared (as in planning),[13] or where powers are exercised concurrently (as in the provision of amenities), or where agency arrangements exist (as in much highway maintenance; there was a diversification here in the 1990s, during the reorganization process as counties devolved more functions to districts (or perhaps parishes), such as day centres, playschemes, women's refuges, family centres, and the administration of ('orange') disabled car badges). In Scotland, the Local Government Act 1994 specifically allows for joint arrangements for service provision and requires the production of schemes of decentralization. Even where functions are apparently quite separate, there is much need for close consultation. For example, the county social services departments will from time to time have to consult with the districts – the housing authorities – concerning the nature and extent of the special accommodation (sheltered housing) needed for infirm people. Another example is where counties, under their transport role, need to liaise with districts to, say, encourage them to provide car parking and approve their car parking charging policies. Indeed, one recent study[14] of county–district relations has shown that while the amount of contact between counties and districts is surprisingly large, the more extensive contacts are confined to a few services. The same study concluded:

The reality is that inter-tier relationships in a metropolitan area (or elsewhere) are neither intrinsically difficult and conflictual nor intrinsically straightforward and consensual. It all depends on the contextual circumstances impinging upon a particular county–district network and upon individual links therein, particularly the attitudes and interests of key participants . . . Several examples were discovered of 'difficult' county–district relationships, in which non-cooperative or indeed obstructive strategies were used; but equally several examples were discovered of relationships which were successful, in that a positive outcome was produced which would not have been possible without inter-tier co-operation . . . Conflict in inter-tier relationships is the exception rather than the rule. Most inter-tier relationships work smoothly most of the time . . . The defunct metropolitan system was more prone to conflict than the non-metropolitan one . . . Handling county–district relations successfully is still a major challenge.

Liaison, coordination and mutual understanding are facilitated by the overlapping of membership among the various tiers of local authorities. This cross-membership at council level, unlike that which occurs at committee level (see below), is not deliberate or consciously planned, yet it does occur on a substantial scale, both between district and county and between parish or community and district. Such councillors are said to have a 'dual mandate' (some may belong to three sets of authorities and thus have a 'triple' mandate). The number of councillors with such a dual membership (excluding parishes) is some 13 per cent[15] (ranging between 2 per cent in London boroughs to 28 per cent in county councils though it is as much as 50 per cent in some councils, having been boosted in the 1990s by fears of loss of seats with reorganization). In addition, mutual understanding is facilitated by the common background and professional values and attitudes of the officials involved (and overall most of the inter-authority relationships are between officials rather than councillors).

Local authorities form joint committees or establish forums to discuss common problems and matters of mutual interest – conservation, structure plans, transport subsidies, libraries, tourism, crime prevention, provision for the arts, etc. Typically, there are county joint committees comprising representatives from the county council and from the constituent district councils. They can be much wider in scope,[16] with the local authority developing a true community leadership role (see Chapter 15).[17] Where these committees are responsible for allocating capital expenditure approvals (see Chapter 11), the parish and community councils will also send representatives.

Such joint committees were strongly advocated by the Bains Report[18] as a means to 'coordinate the interaction of all county and district functions and policies for the locality' and for 'coordination and joint planning of the broad overall policies of the county and the districts within it'. Some of them take the form of 'area' committees or 'district joint committees'. These may comprise district and county councillors for the particular area (together with a team of officers from both tiers) or just the relevant members of the county council. Their purpose is to take a community or corporate approach to the problems of the particular area and the coordination of the local services. However, these committees are usually non-executive and are not directly responsible for the provision of services, but are rather a means of reviewing the services provided and of inviting local public participation, comment and 'feedback'.[19] But they are not always so positive and constructive; they may simply vent inter-authority grievances, jealousies or party differences, and thus languish.[20]

Some of these advisory or consultative committees may specialize in a particular service, e.g. education, where many LEAs have established district advisory groups, and subsequently area development groups, to replace the former divisional executives;[21] these often comprise head teachers and officers as well as county and district councillors. They may also contain representatives from the local schools' governing bodies. And these bodies themselves are another example of inter-authority contact, the LEA appointing members to governing bodies from local district and parish or community councils.

Not all of these joint committees are merely consultative or advisory. Some of them are executive; they may specialize in a particular service, such as planning or highways, and they may appoint staff and be given substantial amounts of delegated power. They may thus come to resemble 'quangos' (see p. 462), the best-known example of which was (until its abolition in 1990) the Inner London Education Authority (ILEA), which was a statutory body; but more general examples include those joint authorities established for services such as police, airports or crematoria. The abolition in 1986 of the metropolitan county councils and the GLC led to the creation of a number of joint committees and joint boards (see pp. 52, 109, 123). However, while such bodies bring local authorities together, there is some disagreement about their ability to get results.[22]*

More informal groupings may also take place at a local level, particularly among officers, though often on a purely professional rather than a strictly inter-authority basis. Local authorities also frequently share premises and equipment, such as computers, and engage in joint purchasing schemes – in 1970 the Consortium for Purchasing and Distribution (CPD) was formed to provide joint purchasing facilities for a group of local authorities in the south-west of England (the GLC was the main purchaser for London local authorities). There are also a large number of local authority consortia for education system building (such as CLASP), and for housing. Local authorities sometimes join forces to submit joint bids for EC funding (as did Avon, Gloucester and Wiltshire County Councils in 1993 to help counter the impact of defence job cuts).

Local authority associations[23]

Local authorities have common interests and common problems. It is therefore not at all surprising that they should join together to consider them. However, their interests and problems are not identical, and as a result they have formed into a number of separate groupings, each representing a different type or tier of local authority though some individual councils do not join. In England and Wales there was an association for the (non-metropolitan) county councils (the ACC), another for all metropolitan authorities (the AMA) and a third for the district councils (the ADC). However, in 1997 (and stimulated by reorganization) they merged into the one Local Government Association (LGA) which describes itself as 'the *national* voice for local communities'. Welsh authorities too are members but they also have a separate Welsh LGA. Single service authorities (such as Police Authorities) are also members. In Scotland too there is a single association for the principal local authorities, the Convention of Scottish

---

* cf. T. Travers *et al.*, *Joint Working between Local Authorities*, BKT, 1995.

Local Authorities (COSLA), which was formed in 1975 at the time of reorganization.

Parish and community councils are represented in the National Association of Local Councils and the Association of Scottish Community Councils, and there is a separate association for 'neighbourhood councils' (see p. 526). In addition to these national associations, there are some area and regional groupings such as the Association of London Government, the East and the West Midlands LGAs, the Surrey LGA, the Welsh Association of Community and Town Councils and there are county- and unitary-wide Associations of Parish Councils, together with various specialized bodies such as the Federation of Economic Development Authorities (FEDA), the Council of Local Education Authorities (CLEA), the British Fire Service Association and the British Resorts Association.

Negotiations on the LGA merger were protracted because of fears about party political advantage – the ACC was usually Conservative dominated and the AMA Labour dominated. In the LGA there are four political groups – Labour, Conservative, Liberal Democrat and Independent – some with a formal whip system. The Conservatives having lost so many seats in local government in the 1990s, the LGA has been dominated by Labour members. But the LGA – through its Assembly, regional groupings and committees (education, housing, etc.) – operates on a cross-party basis with places being allocated according to proportional electoral support to reflect types of authority and regions as well as political party.

The purpose of these associations is (like pressure groups) to protect and advance the interests and powers of member authorities, especially as these may be affected by legislation. Some also have the explicit objective of promoting high standards of administration and service delivery in local government (e.g. in 1998 the LGA sent a team of specialist education advisers to assist the long-troubled education service of Calderdale MBC, and thereby forestalled government intervention). For these purposes they nominate members to the various staff negotiating bodies (see Chapter 10) and have formed a number of joint bodies to advise on or provide central services, such as training, management, etc.[24] all largely integrated into the Local Government Management Board in 1991 and the IDA in 1999 (see p. 284). But above all, the associations exist to deal with issues of common concern to their members, and to network, support, advise, lobby, publicize, monitor and negotiate with the central government on matters of local government policy and finance. They may sometimes try to promote legislation to enhance the powers of local government[25] and usually establish a special relationship with certain MPs who will be expected to speak on their behalf in Parliament. The local authority associations often work with the central government, e.g. in drafting codes of conduct and regulations.

Their most important role concerns negotiations with the central government (mainly the Department of the Environment/DETR or, for Scotland, the Scottish Office, and the Welsh Office in Wales, though these latter are now largely superseded by the home nations' Executive and Parliament/Assembly, see pp. 68–9). And the LGA was created in the belief that one strong voice for local government can present the case better than three separate organizations (though not everyone is convinced about this).[26] Thus the declared aims of the LGA are to:

increase the role and influence of local government
provide a national democratic leadership for local government
seek more control for local government over its affairs
establish better and more effective relationships with government and the European community*

More specifically, it has two policy agendas. First, to improve the quality of life, by raising educational standards, promoting healthier and safe communities and regenerating local economies. Second, to improve the running of the country, by improving (even equalizing) the local–central partnership, promoting value and quality in public services, lobbying to restore local financial discretion, encouraging more people to become involved in local democracy, demanding greater powers to enable local community initiatives and developing new models of regional government. The LGA has already established a new, more positive rapport with the (equally new) Labour government and it applauds and supports most of the government's local government reforms (and indeed has contributed and is contributing

---

* *This is the LGA*, LGA, 1997.

to them). In 1996 the LGA appointed a senior civil servant (from the then DoE) to become its Finance Director, and in 1998 the LGA's chairman (Sir Jeremy Beecham) became of member of a Cabinet ('Better Government') committee and helped to negotiate a concordat of good relations (see Appendix 31).

Thus the associations seek to persuade and influence. They may do this collectively, in the interests of local government as a whole, or they may act separately, where an association presses the interests of its particular group of authorities. For example, in 1995 the ADC claimed to have successfully negotiated council tax modifications/ exemptions, additional district-based unitaries and extended lead times for the latters' introduction. Other examples of apparently successful lobbying include extending the de-trunking of roads, preventing some of the unitary authority proposals of the English Royal Commission (see pp. 42ff), amending the proposals for the composition and status of the new police authorities, the greater use of brownfield sites for housing, improving grant compensation for costs arising from changes in the capital-disregard limits for residential care. There have also been the regular meetings of the Consultative Council on Local Government Finance where grant levels and distribution are (or were: see p. 445) negotiated and altered (though some are sceptical about the significance of the associations' input).[27] They are able to exercise influence through their experience, knowledge and expertise, and their research capability is considerable (*vide* their numerous publications). One Minister declared that '. . . the Associations have now virtually become part of the constitution of the country'.[28] But they also have the power to be awkward and non-cooperative (as with local government reform; see Chapter 3) or positive and helpful in the implementation of specific policies (community care, best value, standards of conduct).

However, it is not easy to assess their impact, since much of their work occurs behind closed doors. The apparent success of the LGA today stems largely from the party outlook and policy agendas which it shares with the government: they are 'singing from the same – or at least a similar – hymnsheet' in many respects. But the government is refusing to accede to certain of their misgivings (such as beacon councils) or demands (such as a return of business rates to local control or the complete abolition of capping). In the end, associations are powerless to stop a determined government, as various disputes have shown (e.g. over capping; abolition of the GLC/metropolitan counties; aspects of the Local Government, Planning and Land Act 1980; reorganization in Scotland in the 1990s.*) And in a number of areas, usually concerning the bigger issues, the pressure of the LGA may be countered by that of others (such as the CBI or the British Retail Consortium, e.g. regarding responsibility for business rates). In addition, the voice of the LGA may be weakened by the formation of separate groupings within the LGA – to represent the interests of London authorities, the metropolitan counties and the shire counties†, and largely reflecting their differences over grant or SSA weightings and distribution (i.e. as between rural/urban or Northern/Southern authorities).‡

Collectively or individually, then, local authorities act as pressure (or interest) groups. In turn, however, they themselves are often on the receiving end of pressure-group politics.

Voluntary organizations and pressure politics (or 'lobbies')

The variety of groups

Most of us belong to a pressure group, though we may not normally think of it as such: it may be the tennis club; the AA; the British Legion; the Church; the Red Cross; the RSPCA; the Old Boys' Association; the WRVS; the Parent–Teachers' Association; the WI; the Embroiderers' Guild . . . each going about its own business and not interfering in the pursuits of others. We belong because it is convenient: it helps to meet one of our needs or interests.

---

* Some people see COSLA as having 'shot itself in the foot' by refusing to negotiate – or even have a dialogue – with the government over reorganization in 1994, including their demurring at the nomination of members to the proposed water authorities. COSLA argued they had tried to negotiate in the past – and failed – over the introduction of the poll tax.

† Thus SIGOMA is the Special Interest Group of Municipal Authorities and CCN is the County Councils Network. There is also the Most Sparsely Populated Councils Group and the Rural Partnership Services.

‡ See *Local Government Chronicle*, July 1998.

Some members, however, will want more than this: they will wish to see their interests not merely provided for but also defended against any threats from outside and positively promoted in terms of facilities and resources. This aspect is perhaps most obviously displayed by such groups as trade unions or professional and business associations (such as the Chamber of Commerce or the Licensed Victuallers' Association), but even seemingly innocuous groups like the Old Boys' Association or the PTA can be stung into 'political action' or protest against a local authority proposal to change a school's status, or the badminton club can be moved to write to the local paper about the unreasonable increase in the hall letting charges.

For the latter groups, such political action is an occasional event, a by-product of their existence.[29] For the other groups such as trade unions or commercial associations (and, through their associations, local authorities themselves), protecting and furthering the interests of their members is their *raison d'etre* and their use of political pressure as a method is commonplace. Consequently we may refer to voluntary organizations as 'interest groups' where they seek to protect and promote the interests of their members by the use, occasional or otherwise, of political methods, i.e. by bringing pressure or influence to bear on governmental authorities to achieve (or resist) changes in public policy. At local level, common examples include teachers' and students' unions, civic societies, residents' or ratepayers' associations, tenant groups, allotment holders, market traders' groups, etc.

A second broad type of pressure group is the 'cause group' – of those who share an attitude and pursue a goal which is not confined to the immediate interests of members of the group but is of more general benefit. Notable examples at national level include Age Concern, CND, Friends of the Earth, the League Against Cruel Sports, Oxfam, the Society for the Protection of the Unborn Child, Liberty, Shelter, the Lord's Day Observance Society and CAMRA. At local level, there may exist branches of these national organizations, and there will be many of purely local origin, for example: a bypass or motorway action group, a women's aid group, an association for homeless men, an anti-fluoridation group and a host of other amenity and conservation ('green') groups.

Some groups may overlap and be difficult to categorize into one broad type or the other: for example, the trade union UNISON will primarily seek to protect their sectional interests through campaigns against local authority expenditure cuts, but it will also undertake a cause role in so far as it presses (perhaps through the TUC) for better universal retirement pensions or greater priority to be given to the educational provision for the sixteen- to nineteen-year-olds. Other varieties of pressure group may be found locally. Some, such as community groups and Councils of Voluntary Service, are inaugurated by local authorities themselves; others are substantially funded by local authorities or receive material assistance, such as free printing and postage, the use of rent-free property, and some are statutory, for example Community Health Councils and the Transport Users Consultative Committees. Some 'pressure groups' are no more than a local but important employer (Clarks of Street or Fords at Dagenham, or a major local leisure attraction (football club, holiday camp). Many groups, such as those formed for rent strikes or anti school-closure campaigns, are short-lived, temporary 'flashes' which wither away once their goal has been gained (or lost). Others are barely organized at all and hardly amount to a pressure group in the normally understood sense, like the 'Grocks [i.e. Outsiders] Go Home' sentiment-cum-movement in Cornwall. (Local and other public authorities may, of course, act upon one another; but it is uncertain whether such official bodies may be regarded as pressure groups).

The spread of pressure groups

Pressure groups, like political parties, are by no means a new phenomenon in local government, although it does seem that their activities have been increasing in recent years (in contrast to, and perhaps, causally, in place of parties). Nearly 500 civic societies were founded between 1957 and 1970; nearly 200 local consumer groups between 1961 and 1970; and some 16,000 charities in England and Wales alone since 1960. The NCVO has referred to the striking development over the past ten years of 'the growing number and type of self-help organizations particularly in urban areas'[30] so that today there are over 181,000 charities registered with the Charities Commission. Clearly, many of these are only 'partial' pressure groups, in that their principal focus of activity is not their relations with local authorities and other public bodies. However, in so far as many of them do try to exercise some influence, it is pertinent to ask why their numbers have grown so substantially. Besides, half of the groups listed in the *Guardian Directory of Pressure Groups* have come into existence only since 1960.

A number of reasons can be suggested for the growth in pressure groups, such as the greater leisure, education and affluence of society generally, and the emergence of new specialist services and occupations. It is also perhaps a consequence of the widely reported decline in deference or traditional respect for authority, i.e. of no longer accepting what is decided or provided and asking no questions. Equally it may be a response to the growth in concentration of power as the state has assumed greater responsibilities and business units have become bigger and more impersonal. Moran suggests it has to do with the decline of party–class politics.[31] (Certainly party membership has declined since the 1950s.) A study of parties for the Commission on Local Democracy (1995) talks of 'severely depleted memberships, decreasing or limited numbers of ageing activists and their [parties'] "relevance" challenged by ever proliferating numbers of single-issue groups'. Gyford points to 'the emergence of a more assertive public attitude towards politicians and professional experts, and in the wider society a shift towards greater fragmentation and diversity [has] produced an increasingly sectionalist politics.' The trend seems to flow clearly in the direction of according greater recognition to sectional interests'.[32] There has also been a growing concern with the state of public services (education, youth provision, housing, transport, social care), partly in response to actual or perceived cut-backs, but also as a result of rising expectations and growth in consumer rights and consumerism generally (encouraged by local authorities' own greater attention to marketing and customer service). Concern with the environment and conservation* has been another driving force in recent years (partly the consequence of greater home-ownership and home-centredness: people have more to protect and built environments

---

* Friends of the Earth grew sixfold 1981–94, to 112,000 and Greenpeace grew tenfold in the same period; 1971–94 saw the RSPB grow from 98,000 to 877,000, and the National Trust currently has over 2 million members.

are more fundamental in that they last longer than, say, changes in school organization or social care arrangements). A further such increase in activism is forecast due to 'rising levels of educational attainment and a growth in the proportion of the population in middle-class occupations ... [And] ... increased "environmental awareness" will lead to increasing levels of public organisation and protest against perceived threats (such as highways building) with "major public health alarms" being the most likely catalyst for action.'* Finally, it might be suggested that pressure groups are self-generating in that their presence in society has come to be taken for granted and, as their activities and successes are given wide coverage in the media, so other groups are encouraged to form.

Because of their volatility and the problems of definition, it is difficult accurately to determine their number in any particular area, but it is likely to be substantial. In his study of Birmingham, Newton gave a figure of over 4,000 voluntary organizations[33] operating in that city. Of these about one third were politically active, that is 'making demands on public policy and resources', and most (63 per cent) of these were only involved over a single issue. Since they are usually quite specific and limited in their demands, being mostly concerned with individual decisions, they tend to be more sporadic and less institutionalized than those groups which operate at national level.[34] Wilson and Stoker show that in 1990 some 685 voluntary bodies received grants (of £2.2 million) from a single committee (Recreation) of Leicester City Council;[35] in 1995 that council provided a total of £8 million in grants (14 per cent of its budget) while Birmingham council awarded £22 million (2.4 per cent of its budget).[36] A national survey (by the NCVO) estimated a total of £687 million of financial support by local authorities, representing 12.5 per cent of voluntary sector income for 1995, plus an estimated £500 million in rate relief.

---

* *Social and Economic Trends to 2005*, LGMB, 1996.

A comparison with parties

In many ways pressure groups are like political parties, especially newly founded, local or single-issue parties such as the United Country Party, the Wessex Regional Party, the Campaign for a More Prosperous Britain Party, the NHS Supporter Party or the Anti-Poll Tax Party.

However, pressure groups are normally distinguished from parties in that they do not generally seek office but only seek to influence the actions – the authoritative decisions – of those holding office. But with all definitions and classifications there are marginal cases – after all the Labour Party itself is the product of the trade unions' aim to get direct representation for themselves in Parliament, and locally there are close ties between local Labour council groups and trades councils. There may even be factions or pressure groups within the parties, for example CAER – Conservative Action for Electoral Reform. And sometimes pressure groups field candidates for elections to protest at such things as town centre development or sites for BSE incineration, nuclear waste, travellers or oil exploration, etc. Furthermore, there is substantial overlap (some deliberate, some fortuitous) between elected members of local authorities and members of voluntary organizations: in 1967 the Maud Committee showed that 99 per cent of councillors belong to organizations outside the council,[37] and the average councillor belongs to six or seven such organizations. The LGMB Census (1998) shows 60 per cent of councillors are school governors and nearly 70 per cent work for voluntary organizations. Dearlove talks of interests being 'built into the very heart of the council'[38]* partly because of who the councillors are (farmers, businessmen, etc.) and partly because group representatives sit on council committees (perhaps by legal right/requirement and they may even have voting powers, as do church co-optees or appointees to education committees). The Birmingham survey showed that one third of politically active organizations had a member serving on at least one statutory, advisory or other public body in the city, and 40 per cent had at least one council member or MP

---

* as does Saunders in his study of Croydon council which 'has sought to integrate business interests into the local political system' (P. Saunders, *Urban Politics*, Penguin, 1980, p. 324).

holding an official position in the organization. Such cross-membership will colour the local authorities' attitudes to organizations, and will influence the way the latter operate politically.

How pressure groups operate

Like pressure groups at national level, local groups can engage in public politics in a variety of ways. They may approach the council as a whole (by letter or petition). They may contact and 'lobby' individual councillors, especially committee chairmen and those who show sympathy with their cause (perhaps members of their organization), and ask them to press the matter at council/committee level. Alternatively, they may negotiate directly with the local authority departments and their officers (again, by letter, petition or delegation; research shows that groups are rather more likely to approach officers than councillors.[39] This is in contrast to approaches made by individuals; see Table 25, p. 497).[40] All this implies an initiative by the group itself. In fact, organizations may be approached by the local authority, or they may be automatically consulted in so far as they are represented on advisory bodies: for example teachers' organizations or non-LEA education bodies may be represented on committees through the process of co-option (see p. 232), and amenity groups and the Country Landowners Association are consulted on development and planning matters.

Some groups will act by seeking the support of other groups ('coalition-building') or the local political parties,[41] especially where the group's cause seems to fit into the party's ideology, or where they can promise or threaten electoral repercussions for the party.[42] Quite often organizations will call on the local MP to intervene, perhaps to prevent transfer of a local authority home or the closure of a local hospital or school, and possibly they will appeal to the government (see p. 425), the 'ombudsman' (see p. 411) or even the law courts (see p. 408). At the same time such groups may resort to publicity (via the press, television, leaflets, meetings) and in the last resort take direct action such as demonstrations, sit-ins, squatting, rent strikes or disrupting council meetings. Other informal influences may result from shared networks of clubs and other bodies.[43]

Which of these different approaches a group will take will depend on a variety of factors:

(a) Is the group attempting to influence policy or just details of administration? Such a distinction is not always easy to make, but the orientation is likely to have some influence on the group's mode of operation. Broadly speaking, if it is a question of administrative detail it might seem reasonable for the group to approach the administrators (the officials), and where policy is involved to approach the policy-makers (the members).[44]

(b) One would expect pressure groups to operate at those points in the local government system where they will be most effective, that is where the power lies. But local authorities will show variations in the locus and diffusion of power (as between committee chairmen, the majority party group, the officers, particular committees and the council as a whole). And pressure groups will vary in their knowledge and understanding of the mechanics of the local government decision-making, both in local government generally and in their own local authority in particular. Some organizations will therefore know who to approach; others will not and may thus simply focus on the most visible or apparently accessible point in the system.

(c) Knowledge of the appropriate 'pressure points' will be aided by having knowledgeable members, especially 'insiders', such as councillors or officers of the council. Newton[45] shows (and the author can confirm from his experience) how these insiders may sometimes find themselves 'wearing two hats'; as members of an outside body they may have to communicate with themselves as members or officers of the local authority! Such a situation should result in at least a declaration of interest (see Chapter 8 above).*

(d) Effective contact with the local authority need not be confined to cross-membership. The extent to which an outside organization is 'established' or held to be respectable will help to determine the attitude and receptiveness of the authority towards them; that is

---

* See too *Quangos Just Grow*, CPS 1985, for critical comment on this.

whether they are regarded as 'in-groups' or 'out-groups'. Their respectability (or 'legitimacy') very much depends on the social standing of their membership, or at least of their officers. Having an MP or other local notable as chairman or committee member is an asset to any group wishing to exercise some influence with the local authority.

In this respect a study by Dearlove[46] suggests that the attitude of local authorities to outside organizations will be based not just on the character of the group but also on the nature of its demands and its methods of communicating those demands. Some groups are accepted because their membership contains the 'right' people, or because of the moderateness or usefulness of their cause, or because of the propriety of their methods or 'style'. Other groups become alienated and forfeit their chances to influence the council by appearing too radical, supporting questionable causes (such as 'gay lib', licensed prostitution or topless beaches) or resorting to unacceptable methods such as direct action.[47] As a result some groups – out-groups – can find themselves in a very difficult position: if they have the wrong 'image' they will not have the 'ear' of the council and will have to use aggressive publicity-seeking methods which will be less acceptable to the council and will thus further diminish the group's standing and frustrate the achievement of its cause. The Widdicombe Committee expressed concern at the way in which some councils discriminated against certain groups on party political grounds.[48]

Apart from their attitude to individual groups, councillors may have a general judgement on pressure groups. This will be coloured no doubt by their experience of particular groups, but it is likely to be generally influenced by the councillor's perception of his/her own role. We have referred (p. 205) to the 'trustee', 'delegate' and 'politico' types of councillor. One might expect the trustee/chair/leader type to resist sectional interests on principle and conversely the politico/backbencher to be more accommodating and there is some evidence for this view, but it is not conclusive.[49]

One might also expect Conservative councillors to look quite favourably on pressure groups (especially the welfare, service-providing groups) because they exemplify self-help as well as helping to keep down the council tax. Labour councillors on the other hand might well be expected to cavil at the distortions and inequalities which such groups may introduce. The evidence is, however, conflicting.[50]

(e) While councillors have attitudes towards groups, so do groups have opinions about councillors, and this can affect the way they seek to influence the authority. It is evident for example that many groups operate through the official side of local authorities (e.g. the Widdicombe Committee showed 50 per cent of approaches were to officers compared to 20 per cent to members). Newton shows a similar differential. This could be due to a lack of confidence in councillors.[51]

(f) The timing of the issue (whether it is near an election for example) and the stage at which the outside organization comes to hear of it (whether before or after the relevant committee meeting) will obviously have a bearing on the group's approach. And the nature of the issue itself can be critical: for example, if there is conflict over a local authority's promotion of a Private Bill (see p. 80), pressure groups may have the opportunity for a public hearing before a Parliamentary committee.

(g) The nature of the local party system can be an important factor. If there is a party monopoly or dominance (see p. 160), it would be appropriate for the pressure group to concentrate its efforts on that majority party and perhaps withdraw from any other approaches. It may be the case, however, that the development and consolidation of political parties in local government has made life more difficult for pressure groups as parties' agendas are likely to be more firm and resistant to influence compared to largely or wholly Independent councils.

It has been suggested that the more conspicuous their activities are, the less influence pressure groups are likely to exert.[52] This is largely because, as we have seen, local authority members feel there is a 'right' and a 'wrong' way for groups to approach them. The evidence from the Birmingham study suggests that

the local pressure group system seems to operate in such a way that the best-established groups . . . are able to work through their close ties with decision-makers . . . and . . . operate in a relatively quiet and unnoticed way . . . Paradoxically, the noisier and more visible the group the greater the likelihood of its being powerless in the political system.[53]

However, where the group or the issue cannot be accommodated in this behind-the-scenes fashion, the only alternative is for it to go beyond the council and make the matter more public and more obviously political.

The effectiveness of pressure groups

It is clearly difficult to judge the effectiveness of pressure groups at local level since their success will vary with the local authority, the issue or cause and the standing, resources and style of the groups themselves.[54] Slightly more specifically, we can say that a group will succeed or fail according to such variable factors as:

(a) the size of the membership, income and full-time staffing of the group;
(b) the extent of cross-membership and other contacts with the local authority, and its degree of acceptance or establishment;
(c) the general attitude of the local authority to pressure group politics;
(d) the methods used by the group and the quality of their arguments;
(e) the extent of public and media sympathy with their cause;
(f) the organization, methods and arguments of counter-groups (such as developers v. conservationists);
(g) the 'direction' of its cause, that is whether it runs with, against or across established council policy. This will help to shape the authority's perception of the pressure group as 'helpful' or 'unhelpful'.[55]

This last point is crucial. Political activity through pressure groups is an exchange process, and just as it takes two to tango (or salsa) so the success of a pressure group depends on the recipients – the councillors (and officers) and their values, ideologies, policy preferences, pro-grammes: are the group's demands congruent and in harmony with these? Indeed, are they contributing to the aims of the council? Dearlove's study of Kensington and Chelsea Council showed that certain 'in-groups' were deemed responsible, helpful or legitimate because they helped the council to achieve its policies (housing, social provision, promoting charitable activity) and they saved some council expenditure. By contrast groups which made demands which were considered out of order, expensive or to which they themselves made little material contribution were decidedly 'out-groups' and received less recognition, accommodation and support. The Birmingham survey suggests that pressure groups are well satisfied with the local authority response. But this may have been due to the fact that their aims were limited to single issues or issues that were congruent with council policy. Nevertheless, Newton suggests that in Britain pressure groups are accepted much more willingly than they are in the USA;[56] 80 per cent of his sample of councillors were described as 'facilitators' rather than 'resistors' of pressure groups. And throughout Britain the extent of support for such groups (especially welfare groups) is indicated by the substantial and increasing financial and material assistance which is provided by local authorities.

However, certain developments in local government have both helped and hindered pressure groups. Thus the growth of party politics in local government has probably made councils somewhat more resistant to pressure-group influence. Conservative policies to 'roll back' the public sector imply a reduced dependence on the consent and goodwill of (some) pressure groups and, insofar as the government has taken powers from local authorities and taken more power (especially financial) over them, this too reduced the incentive, scope and influence of local groups. Life has also been made more difficult as local government has been fragmented (through tenant and school opt-outs and devolved budgets (LMS)), the creation of local quangos (TECs, UDCs, Housing Associations, and separate authorities or joint arrangements for fire, police and transport) and the outsourcing and contracting out of services to commercial businesses, voluntary bodies and not-for-profit organizations (and even families themselves).

On the other hand, contracting out and an increasing readiness to involve or utilize the voluntary sector in the delivery of local services has produced considerable opportunities for insider group pressure.[57] Young, who calls them Third Force Organizations, cites tenants' management co-ops, and groups running community centres, playgroups, OAP centres, youth clubs and regeneration projects as examples,[58] and this is likely to increase as councils focus on the 'wicked issues' of crime, poverty, regeneration, and the environment, greater commitment to 'customer care' creates a more listening and learning council which provides more opportunities for clients and citizens and their sectional groups. Changing councillors' roles and management structures and the development of Best Value are already increasing the community consultation process. And, arguably, the reformed (and re-reformed) structure of local government has removed some of the earlier organizational and communication problems facing local pressure groups such as those identified by the Royal Commission.[59]

In the end, of course, it is a two-way process:

Groups need government to deliver authoritative decisions and governmental policy makers need groups to facilitate the formulation of a workable and effective policy. A group has a set of political goals. It will depend on the nature of these goals whether these could be better advanced in the interest group/bureaucratic world of 'logic of negotiations' or in the more overtly political world of a public protest campaign. Thus groups who wish to pursue radical policy change exclude themselves by definition from participating in the insider, political accommodation game. The pursuit of 'incremental' style goals gives a group eligibility for legitimate insider status. The key variable . . . is . . . that of resources. The group–government relationship is exchange-based; government offers groups the opportunity to shape public policy, while groups provide government with certain resources.[60]

These resources include knowledge, technical advice, expertise, representative base, membership compliance or consent, credibility, information, implementation guarantees. Consequently, in determining status (in- or out-) the primary factor for public bodies is the possession or offer of resources. 'In determining status, strategies are secondary (while nevertheless significant) to questions of resources'.[61]

Pressure groups – threat or promise?

Pressure groups then, like political parties, are a fact of life. If they did not exist, perhaps they would have to be invented, since they bring with them a number of distinct advantages to the administration of local affairs: they provide expertise;[62] they act as a funnel or filter between the local authority and the various individuals, families, firms etc. who might otherwise separately convey their views and thus deluge the authority; they can scrutinize local government expenditure to detect value for money; they help to smooth administration by securing cooperation and acceptability of policy; or (as in the case of a local government trade union) the implementation of a policy (such as contracting out or selling houses).

These groups also provide an additional method or source of involvement for the community: anyone can engage in pressure politics; it does not necessarily involve heavy expense, especially since the media seem so ready to provide free publicity for the sake of a story. Armed with the support of others in a group, the individual need no longer feel powerless against the juggernaut local authority. And membership of such a group does not bring with it a continuing commitment which public office or party membership normally requires. Where people feel alienated or estranged from their elected representatives, they can find an alternative voice in the form of a pressure group.

A large proportion of the general public belongs to voluntary organizations. A survey published in 1967[63] showed that some 60 per cent of adults belong to one, and a significant proportion of these seem to be active members (though mainly in the non-political aspects of their group). In so far as these organizations do become politically active and establish contacts with the local authority, bridges are being built between the authority and the wider community: the authority has an additional means of gauging public reaction to their proposals and can explain their actions more fully than they could hope to do through the columns of the local press.[64] This mutual exchange of views and information may help to weaken the attitude of 'them and us' which unfortunately bedevils so much of local government's relationship with the public (see pp. 495ff).

Casting a vote is a very generalized expression of opinion about policy: the most conscientious citizen can turn out to vote at every election and yet still have his or her particular interests overlooked in the manifestos and official policies. Besides, in many areas there are no elections, or the result is a foregone conclusion, and so there is little opportunity for influence. Pressure politics can articulate minority views and injustices which might otherwise go unheard and unacknowl-edged; in this respect they act as an educative force in society. Professor Richards suggests that pressure groups 'are a particularly valuable element in maintaining a spirit of local democracy as they frequently promote causes that cut across the lines of political party policies'.[65]

Finally, in favour of pressure groups it can be argued that they help to strengthen the democratic process by augmenting the resources of elected members. For those who take a somewhat conspiratorial view of the role of the official in local government, it may be reassuring to see pressure groups helping to restore the balance in favour of the elected member by supplying him or her with information which can augment that provided by the officers of the authority and may, wittingly or not, be biased.

We all have interests and attachments – personal, religious, racial, local, national. We reflect these, or an amalgam of them, when we cast our vote. Voting is thus an individualized registration of our interests. Pressure groups are simply a group or collective form of the same process. As such, they are hardly anti-democratic, and most of them do not deserve the bad name which has derived from the lurid exposures of the influence which some of them have exercised on political decisions during this century (mainly at national level and especially in America).

However, there are certain aspects of pressure groups which do give rise to serious and widespread concern. Principally, they are criticized for distorting or undermining the democratic process of government in its traditional form, in which policy reflects the wishes of the public as expressed through their elected representatives. Through pressure groups, certain interests – especially powerful economic inter-ests – are able to get an unreasonable amount of attention and so distort the balance of local provision, to the detriment of genuine needs. Thus we have a situation 'in which a minority of determined people are able to organize themselves into groups, apply pressure to the right quarter, and so influence decisions which affect us all. Parliamentary democracy has given way to politics by pressure.'[66] Essentially the criticism here is that the interests covered by pressure groups are too limited in scope, and that the already powerful groups accrue extra power through group pressure tactics.[67]

The uneven coverage of interest groups is partly due to the unequal distribution of wealth and other resources in society. It is also due to the fact that overwhelmingly pressure groups are created and run by people from a middle-class background, whose education and ambitions are said to make them 'born organizers'. Thus it could be argued, notwithstanding the prevalence of trade unions, that the working class is under-represented in the pressure group area of politics.[68] This is the general conclusion drawn by individual case studies.[69] Since those studies were completed there have been increased opportunities for the business interests to prevail – through the development of Business in the Community (BiC) and Business Links, the revised composition of local boards and committees, the creation of TECs, UDCs etc., competitive tendering and contracting out and public–private partnerships; PFI, local authority consultation with business re: local financial plans and a more commercial culture within local authorities together with a more market-orientated way of managing local authority business. However, Wilson and Stoker suggest that there are limits to such business hegemony and that local authorities have become or are becoming more open and approachable in the range of pressure-group politics. They show that, in their case study of Leicester City Council, there is a decidedly Leftward bias in group support. The same was clearly true in the case of support for voluntary groups in the latter days of the GLC. And in a more general sense it follows that council composition and bias will be crucial in determining the groups which are 'in' or 'out' with the council.

Furthermore, although it has been said that pressure groups provide an opening for greater community involvement in public decision-making, in fact, while many people belong to organizations, most do so for their social, economic or spiritual functions rather than their political activities. A relatively small percentage – 14 per cent[70] – are involved in the organizational or bargaining aspect of their association or society. As Gyford says, '. . . the various groups and individuals which engage in local politics outside the ranks of the national political parties . . . represent a modest widening . . . of the area of debate'.[71]

The other main criticism of pressure groups is their mode of operation: their secrecy. In discussing 'the lobby' at parliamentary level, Professor Finer expressed the concern thus:

When we realize ... that the debates upstairs [at private meetings of the parties] are conflicts between the claims of the rival lobbies in the parties concerned, surely it is clear that we, the general public, the people who have a right to know, are being denied the opportunity to judge between the true contestants – between the prime movers – between the real issues? Instead we are treated to the premasticated speech, tossed back and forth across the floor of the House, of blocs who have already formed their opinions in secrecy. This secrecy, this twilight of parliamentary debate envelops the lobby in its own obscurity. Through this, above all, the lobbies become – as far as the general public is concerned – faceless, voiceless, unidentifiable; in brief, anonymous.[72]

Room for reform?

Thus may pressure groups exercise power without responsibility, and many councillors feel that if such people wish to press their 'rights' they should also accept duties and responsibilities, and become more open and accountable, perhaps by helping to shoulder the burden of office as elected members of a public authority. In practice, of course, many pressure groups do shoulder responsibility – for example in providing voluntary services to the community. Nevertheless, one simple reform could help to meet this criticism: the introduction of a register in each local authority area for all pressure groups which are in contact with the local authority. This could be available for inspection by the public and perhaps contain details of the organizations' aims, membership and funding.

Local authorities might also encourage the formation of groups and provide them with information and resources. This would enable a wider cross-section of the community to be represented and act as a counter-weight to the big battalions already well placed. Some authorities already do this, for example by appointing community development officers and associations. And while in their own way, parish and community councils act as community 'watchdogs', some areas are establishing even more local 'neighbourhood' councils (see p. 526). As regards planning, local authorities are required to publicize their plans, to make people who might be affected aware of their rights, and to give them an adequate opportunity of making representations. In 1969, largely in response to the Skeffington Report of the same year,[73] the government recommended to local authorities that 'the formation of residents' associations should also be encouraged'.[74] In the wake of the Taylor Committee[75] many local education authorities encouraged community participation by appointing parents to school governing bodies (now mandatory under the Education Act 1980 and enhanced in 1986).

However, the opportunities for group formation and participation must be real: they need encouragement as well as resources. Participation 'involves doing as well as talking and there will be full participation only where the public are able to take an active part throughout the plan-making process'.[76] Or, in the words of the Seebohm Committee:

Community development in this country is seen as a process whereby local groups are assisted to clarify and express their needs and objectives and to take collective action to attempt to meet them. It emphasizes the involvement of the people themselves in determining and meeting their own needs. The role of the community worker is that of a source of information and expertise, a stimulator, a catalyst and an encourager . . . Community identity may also be developed through organizations such as community centres, clubs, play centres and tenants' associations, where the social service department could provide technical and professional help, information, stimulation and grant-aid.[77]

The Seebohm Committee was aware that 'there is certainly a difficult link to be forged between the concepts of popular participation and traditional representative democracy'.[78] But it also implied that the growth of the Welfare State has altered the relationship between state and people and requires something of a review or revision. The promotion of local groups is one such development. Furthermore, if sufficient such groups are created, then rather than adversely distorting local provision, they may instead provide an invaluable source of information about 'real' needs in the community. Councils have become more accessible to a wider range of groups, and established groups no longer have such a predominance for a number of reasons. First, as we have seen, councils rely more on voluntary groups for their service provision. Secondly, there is a greater assertiveness and confidence by community groups, who are also perhaps more able and willing to use legal argument and tactics. On the other hand there is a greater receptiveness by councils as a result of education and enlightenment (plus the stimulus of a greater volatility in voting). Thirdly, councils have become more user-conscious and subject to more targets and indicators: Best Value and community leadership require/imply much more consultation and stakeholder involvement – thus providing greater opportunities for 'voice' by local groups.

In the last resort, of course, it is the responsibility of the local decision-makers to strike the right balance between the various claims, and there is always the sanction (real or imagined) of the next election if they are seen to be failing in this respect.

The citizen with a grievance

Politics at local or national level is about the resolution of conflicting claims. Inevitably, where interests clash, someone wins and someone else loses, or more likely (in the event of compromise) both win something and lose something.

Local authorities mediate the conflicting claims and interests of the community. Theoretically, they attempt to promote its collective interests as expressed through the ballot box. In practice, owing to a host of imperfections both in the mechanism and in the very concept of representation,[79] the pursuit of the public interest leaves a lot to be desired.

But even with a perfect system of representation (plenty of candidates, perfect communications, high voting turnout, etc.) and with the best will in the world, local authorities are bound to upset some people: the 'general will' takes precedence over the individual in such matters as the compulsory purchase of property, the levying of taxes or the allocation of children to schools. But in a liberal-democratic society, while the majority may rule, they must not ride roughshod over minority interests. The individual must be given a chance to have his or her grievance investigated and redressed.

How should aggrieved individuals seek redress from their local authority? Much will depend on the nature of their grievance: they may have been refused a licence or a council house; they may find that the council has given approval to an objectionable development near their home; they may object to the excessive amount of money being spent on local sports facilities or the inadequate amounts going to the home help service; they may protest generally about the level of the council tax.

We have already indicated some specific means of remedy – addressing questions to the district auditor (p. 395); presenting objections to the Minister (p. 425); taking legal action (p. 407); or contacting the local MP or ombudsman (p. 409). But the most obvious and sensible starting point is to contact the appropriate councillor, especially through his or her 'surgery'. In practice, it seems that councillors have one such contact per day, on average.[80] However, for various reasons (see p. 514) there may be problems in doing this. The alternative is to approach the local authority itself, though for many people this is a daunting prospect, overlaid with the problem of finding the right department or officer: in the last resort they can simply write to the chief executive officer or the chair of the council. Table 22 shows the differing pattern of contact.

Failing satisfaction here, or if they are uncertain of their case or the correct procedure, complainants may turn to less formal channels: contacting their local or neighbourhood council (if there is one), approaching a local political party, getting in touch with a relevant pressure group or voluntary organization, informing (or just threatening to inform) the local media, starting a petition.

Although local authorities are not normally deliberately perverse or more self-defensive than other organizations, they have been criticized for their inadequate machinery for dealing with complaints. The authors of one study have said:

From our experience of representing members of the lower socioeconomic groups, we have found local authority departments particularly difficult to deal with, not because of any unusual obstinacy on the part of officials or members, but because of a singular lack of adequate and visible procedures, the existing mechanisms frequently being convoluted and Byzantine to a degree.[81]

And a former head of the Local Government Information Office states:

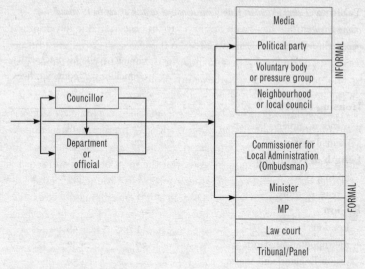

Figure 23 *Channels of redress*

Unless something is done to alleviate the public's suspicions that local government is just another part of the bureaucratic machine, resenting criticism and setting itself apart from the community it represents, then it is unlikely that it will survive for very much longer in present form [*sic*].[82]

And it seems that amongst those members of the public (a small minority) who do complain to their councils, over half (54 per cent) proclaim themselves dissatisfied with the way the complaints are handled. (This is a higher proportion than is the case of those complaints going to large firms, the NHS, the central government or the gas and electricity boards.)[83]

However, some of these criticisms are losing their force as local authorities follow the recommendations of their local authority associations and the Commission for Local Administration in England. In 1978 they jointly issued a 'Code of Practice' for local authorities receiving complaints. Among other things, this suggests:

Authorities should ensure that effective and continuing information is available to the public about channels through which queries can be raised or complaints made . . . There should be easy access by the public to those responsible for

Table 22 *Extent of contact with councillors and council offices by locational characteristics*

	Contact with councillor %	Contact with council offices %
Housing tenure		
owner occupier	18	50
council tenant	32	47
Length of residence		
up to 5 years	11	44
5 years or more	24	50
Region		
London	14	49
metropolitan England	20	52
rest of England and Wales	22	50
Scotland	21	32
Ratepaying		
pays rates in full	23	53
rates partly rebated	25	50
does not pay rates	18	43
All respondents	20	49

Source: The Conduct of Local Authority Business: Research Vol. 3: The Local Government Elector, HMSO, 1986, Table 2.12.

dealing with queries and complaints whether officers or Members . . . Contact points should be widely publicized, including the names and addresses of Members and appropriate officers. The procedure(s) should ensure that those raising queries are not unnecessarily passed from one place or person to another and that they are dealt with as locally and conveniently as possible . . . Responsibility for dealing with queries and complaints must be firmly established . . . There should be a willingness to see enquirers and complainants particularly when the issues are complicated or the facts need to be clarified . . .[84]

And local authorities have since developed a more conscious 'public service orientation' and reminded staff to 'put people first'.[85] This is partly in response to the pressure or threat presented to local government by increased competitive tendering, by greater opportunities for groups (parents of schoolchildren, council house tenants) to opt out of local authority control and by increased numbers of people paying more explicitly for services through the community charge and the council tax. The central government has also required local authorities to set up appropriate complaints procedures, e.g. on education matters under the Education Reform Act 1988 and the NHS and Community Care Act 1990. And local authority associations issue 'model' procedures. In the meantime, local authorities have been improving their general administrative procedures[86] as a result of the reports issued by the Commission for Local Administration (CLA) – the citizen's local 'ombudsman' (see p. 411 above). And increasingly local authorities are seeking to involve the community in their policy and decision-making processes.

Participation

Political participation has been defined as involvement in the decision-making process or, more comprehensively, as 'the taking part in the processes of formulation, passage and implementation of public policies'.* In practice this refers to activities such as voting, contacting a politician or official, standing as a candidate, joining a party, canvassing, signing a petition, writing a letter of complaint/protest/support, etc., attending a meeting, joining a pressure group, going on a march or 'demo'. Tables 22 to 24 give some indication of the scale of such involvement. Using these conventional measures, British local government does not seem to enjoy a high degree of public participation, though some consider it to be 'substantial' (and for others, it is at least adequate).[87]

Parry concluded that 'there is no single avenue for participation and a society of "specialists" can have much to commend it'. And, while the 'complete' participant will always be a relatvely rare creature, 'this is not to say that, in the right conditions, far more people might not find the time and opportunity . . . to keep the authorities on their toes'. The report also shows that participation is subject to substantial

* G. Parry *et al.*, *Political Participation and Democracy in Britain*, CUP, 1992.

Table 23 *Range of involvement in local politics (1)*

Level	Estimated number of people	Estimated % of electorate
Consumer of local government services	40,200,000	98
Votes at local election	17,000,000	42
Knows name of council chairman/mayor	11,500,000	28
Very interested in local affairs	8,000,000	20
Ever contacted local councillor	6,800,000	17
Confident of influencing local council	5,000,000	12
Knows date and place of council meeting	3,200,000	8
Member, principal local authority	21,695	0.05

Source: R. Rose, *Politics in England*, Faber, 1984 (adapted).

Table 24 *Range of involvement in local politics (2)*

Involvement (over previous 5 years)	% of population	
Just votes (regularly)	51.0	
Almost inactive (sometimes vote)	25.8	
Activists (= 10 million)	23.2	
(collective – with organized or informal group		8.7)
(contacting – councillors, MP, town hall, media*		7.7)
(direct – protest, confrontational		3.1)
(party – party-based activity		2.2)
(complete – several or all of these activities		1.5)

Source: G. Parry *et al.*, *Political Participation and Democracy in Britain*, CUP, 1992.
*See Appendix 31 for further detail.
Note on Parry: Also with nearly a quarter of the adult population 'relatively participatory', we have nearly 10 million people politically active in one way or another (quite apart from voting). While this was a general survey, most of the participatory activity was concerned with local matters (planning, housing, schools, etc.). In this respect it could be argued that local government keeps the democratic/participatory flame alive!

Table 25 *Actions to be taken when faced with a 'really wrong' council decision and 'most effective' action*

	Would take[1] %	Most effective %
Respondent would contact:		
councillor	49	18
council officers	28	4
ombudsman	8	3
MP	47	22
district auditor	2	1
local newspaper/radio	25	15
other people	4	1
Other actions:		
sign petition	53	12
go on protest demonstration	7	1
take council to court	6	4
vote against council	19	4
Other	2	1
None of these	4	6
Don't know	3	9

Source: Widdicombe Report, vol. III, HMSO, 1986, Table 4.7.
[1]Multiple responses.

local variations, in the same way that voting preferences and turnout varies;[88] this is not surprising considering the unique nature of each local area and culture.*

Just 1 per cent of people have stood for election as a councillor and a further 4 per cent have considered doing so (cf. 2 per cent and 6 per cent respectively 30 years earlier),[89] a high proportion of seats go uncontested (e.g. 70 per cent in Powys CC, 1985) and the average turnout at local elections is only 40 per cent or less (see p. 146). A survey for the Maud Report[90] found that: between one fifth and one half of the informants were unable to name any service provided by

* *Getting On With It*, LGMB, 1991.

their local authority; and that situation has worsened since.[91] In the Maud survey two thirds said they had not heard of anything which their council had done during the previous month; less than one fifth had ever been in touch with a councillor for help or advice; only 7 per cent (1 per cent in counties) had ever been to a council meeting (it was 8 per cent in 1990),[92] and nearly one quarter felt alienated from the local authority. A different survey[93] found that amongst those who were aware of any participation exercise conducted by their local authority only 12 per cent had in fact participated by returning questionnaires, visiting an exhibition or attending a public meeting (9 per cent did the last in 1990), and 42 per cent had declared themselves little or not at all interested in who wins local council elections. In 1999 a MORI survey showed 71 per cent knew 'just a little or hardly anything' about their local council (though nearly 50 per cent felt they did have a say in how their community is run), and 50 per cent wanted to get more involved in it (see *Local Government Chronicle*, 14 May 1999, p. 21). A social survey for Matthew Parris MP (April 1981) showed 57 per cent could not name any councillor for their area; 56 per cent could not name their own local authority; two out of three did not know which layer of local government was responsible for different services. Research for the Widdicombe Committee (Vol. 3) found that only 30 per cent could name any of their councillors (only 15 per cent in London) and only half could correctly name their county or regional council. Many people still believe hospitals (59 per cent in the Widdicombe survey) and job centres are run by local government.[94] British local government is often held to compare unfavourably with other countries in these respects.

These are important findings, but their importance must not be exaggerated. Comparisons with general election turnouts can be misleading, for at national level there is more publicity, the issues are usually much clearer, with perhaps more at stake, and the MP will (unlike many local councillors) live in the constituency. Similarly, comparisons with local government elections in other countries must take account of their laws on compulsory voting, polling on Sundays or holidays, or the fact that voters may be electing candidates to national as well as local office. Besides, having a high level of turnout does not necessarily imply a high level of interest, concern or understanding of what the councils are doing. Furthermore, as the Maud Committee itself pointed out,

It is of no particular significance that the public do not throng the public galleries of the councils; at any rate this does not seem to be peculiar to this country . . . Local authorities provide a wide range of services to the community and relatively few people need to make contact with their authorities unless things go wrong. The lack of public interest in the work of local authorities may well suggest that the public are satisfied with the services which the local authorities provide. The Social Survey's findings in fact do not show that there is any high degree of dissatisfaction with the services or with the way in which local authorities are run.[95]

Other measures suggest a reasonable level of interest in and commitment to local affairs and there has been recent improvement in some aspects (aided by rising educational standards)[96]. Thus an American survey found that in Britain 70 per cent of those interviewed felt that they ought to play an active part in local affairs and 78 per cent felt that they could if necessary alter 'an unjust local regulation'.[97] In another, two thirds of people say they would take action if their council proposed something they strongly disapproved of.[98]

In another survey, some 65 per cent claimed to be 'quite interested' or 'very interested' in the work of their local council,[99] though a later figure is only 27 per cent (see note 89). And in the survey for the Maud Report 52 per cent said that they wanted to know more about their local council.[100] The Widdicombe inquiry found over 50 per cent could correctly name their council's or councillor's political party, and that more generally 52 per cent were well or quite well informed about local government. This latter figure has since increased to 57 per cent according to the DoE survey, *Public Perceptions of Local Government*, 1992; this also showed that more people (73 per cent) could now correctly name their county/regional council and it also revealed considerable knowledge about local finance (sources and expenditures). Other evidence shows over 3 in 4 people can correctly identify the provider of local services (such as schools, housing, street cleaning and refuse collection, though the figure has declined somewhat).* The

* *Attitudes to Local Government*, JRF, 1990.

Widdicombe inquiry also showed a very high (72 per cent) general level of satisfaction with the performance of local authorities.[101] Evidence since suggests further overall improvement here (though there is some variation among different services, e.g. opinions on refuse collection are up, those on libraries and playgrounds are down.* There is also evidence to suggest that on balance (just) more people want to see less central control of local authorities.[102]

Furthermore, as we have seen (p. 486), some studies suggest that as many as two thirds of electors claim to belong to at least one voluntary organization (though a later figure is only 20 per cent: see note 92), and some 80 per cent of local electors are readers of the local press.[103] Other evidence of a 'rising tide of public involvement' is to be found in the growth of local groups, inquiries at Citizens' Advice Bureaux and in swelling complaints to the CLAs.[104] As a consequence, it may well be that many people are interested in particular aspects of a council's work, rather than have an enduring interest in local government as a whole.[105] Besides which, the governing bodies of schools and colleges, together with the tribunals set up to hear appeals over school admissions or curriculum matters (under the Education Act 1980 and the Education Reform Act 1988 respectively), involve many thousands of such 'lay' members. (There are some 300,000 school governors.) And there are some 10,000 parish and community councils.

Notwithstanding what is said above, the apparently low level of active interest in local government is regrettable, especially with the quite large proportion of people who believe it is not even worth bothering to complain[106] and the increase in those who seem to be losing faith in the value of local elections: in 1965, 77 per cent believed elections 'decide how things are run locally', but by 1995 the figure was only 54 per cent (see *Local Government Chronicle*, 6 August 1999, and Table 26 below). The figures are provided by Professor Hambleton, who suggests that a major factor is the fall in the *local* funding of councils. Consequently, it is perhaps not enough to cry 'apathy', since some of the explanations lie in the machinery or procedures of local government itself rather than its citizens. The situation is therefore capable of improvement.

* See *Consumer Concerns*, NCC, 1995.

Table 26 *Attitudes to the local electoral process: 1965–94 (%)*

	1965	1985	1994
The way that people vote in local elections is the main thing that decides how things are run in this area	77	60	54
Local council elections are sometimes so complicated that I really don't know who to vote for	29	34	30

Source: Maud Committee, vol. 3, 1967; Widdicombe Committee, vol. 3, 1986; *British Social Attitudes*, 1995.

Improving participation

The Maud Report made a number of recommendations to raise the level of public interest and participation in local government affairs:

(a) removal of some of the confusing features of local government, such as the aldermanic system and the varying systems of electing councillors;

(b) more education of schoolchildren (and their teachers) in the role and responsibilities of local government in the community;

(c) the development of closer relationships between local authorities and voluntary organizations;

(d) more in the way of advance information to the public on major issues or proposals coming before the council (that is something analogous to government Green and White Papers);

(e) better arrangements at council offices for the public to gain access to responsible officers to raise matters which affect them personally or be put in touch with members if they are dissatisfied with the official response;

(f) easier access for the press to committee meetings; the press should be regarded as partners in the process of informing the public and should be given adequate facilities.

A number of these proposals have been implemented – aldermen have been abolished; public access to meetings and council documents has been increased (under the 1985 Act); while the local electoral system is still complex, it has (arguably) been simplified, and elections at least now all occur on the same day. Some of the proposals have been left to the discretion of local authorities themselves such that some allow much greater direct access to officers, or allow people to raise questions at council meetings; in 1986 Lambeth Council began to pay out baby-sitting fees (using Section 137 of the Local Government Act 1974) to enable more of the public to attend its meetings. Many councils have created strong links with voluntary organizations by establishing volunteer liaison officers and through grants. But in terms of education in schools, there has until recently been no obvious move towards local government or political studies, despite the efforts of the Politics Association and a recommendation in 1978 by HMIs.*

However, while government policy has been firmly in the direction of the core curriculum and/or a vocational (work-related) approach, there is renewed interest in civic or political education following the 1998 Advisory Group (Crick) Report, *Education for Citizenship*. And in 1999, the government agreed that citizenship is to form a part of the secondary school curriculum. This has also been recommended by the McIntosh Commission: see Chapter 15 below.

Other suggestions and developments are dealt with below. But before turning to these it is appropriate to mention that there is evidence to suggest that public understanding of local government is greater in single-tier authorities.[107] If this is so, then the recent (1990s and 1986) reorganization in the direction of unitary authorities may have helped, though it is likely to have been offset by the creation of various joint authorities and boards[108] (compounded in these and other areas by the formation of Urban Development Corporations, Housing Action Trusts, Grant-Maintained Schools, College Corporations and Training and Enterprise Councils.

Local authorities have attempted to make themselves more access-ible and open to the public, for example, by holding public question sessions and open forums, producing community videos, setting up decentralized information points and by creating charters of rights

---

* In fact the number of pupils studying politics has fallen significantly and Politics at GCSE has virtually ceased to exist. See, too, G. Stoker in H. Davis, *New Perspectives on Local Governance*, JRF, 1997, p. 121.

(or contracts of service), together with channels for comments and complaints systems. They have sometimes run into legal problems, as when the Audit Commission has, on the grounds of illegal expenditure, barred councils from holding public opinion polls or referendums on the question of local reorganization proposals. A further development has been local devolution and decentralization where 'within a corporate policy framework, managerial and sometimes political decisions are made nearer to the point of service delivery, where the aim is to make services "accessible" in every sense of the term and where a basic aim is to stop "buck-passing" and to work with and on behalf of the local community.'* Increasingly, in the 1990s, it has been about improving responsiveness, tailoring services to local needs and making links to other local organizations, although the various manifestations (in Walsall, Islington, Basildon, Fife, Strathclyde, Rochdale, Harlow, Hackney, Tower Hamlets, South Somerset, Kingston on Thames, etc.) show wide variations in form and purpose, and consequently, of community involvement and participation.[109] Seven out of ten councils have developed initiatives which involve the users of services in finding ways of improving them.†

While most have been voluntary, local decisions/policies, some decentralization has been the result of legislation, most obviously in Scotland (under the 1995 reorganization Act) where unitary councils have been obliged to consult local communities and draw up schemes for decentralization. Elsewhere, as a result of the Local Government and Rating Act 1997, it has become easier to form parish councils (including in urban areas – hitherto parish-free zones) and for principal councils to devolve more function downward. As a result the form that decentralization can take is highly variable: one recent study distinguishes seven such types, including single-issue forums (housing, environment, etc.), neighbourhood issue meetings, information-exchange networks and focus groups/task teams.‡

In 1993, the government invited local authorities to follow its lead in being more open, allowing greater access to personal files and

---

* Gaster and Mo O'Toole, *Local Government Decentralization*, SAUS, 1995.
† *Celebrating the Launch of the Local Government Association*, LGA/MJ, 1997, p. 4.
‡ See *Enhancing Local Democracy*, LGMB, 1996.

providing information about health and safety matters (such as the safety of transport and public places). But they have also been pushed to become more accountable and responsible to their ratepayers and consumers (or users) by the government: thus the 1980 Local Government, Planning and Land Act requires them to publish information on staffing and finance as well as annual general reports; the Local Government Finance Act 1982 gave ratepayers enhanced powers to inspect and challenge the accounts at audit time; the 1980 Housing Act requires information for tenants; the 1980 Education Act requires information on schools (to allow real choice), which is reinforced by the publication of HMI reports and the involvement of parents in school governing bodies (which now incorporates some 300,000 more people into the political process); the 1986 Disabled Persons (Services, Consultation and Representation) Act requires the greater dissemination of information on services; the 1987 Access to Personal Files Act allows access to housing and social services files (education files became more accessible under the 1980 Education Act); and the 1985 Local Government (Access to Information) Act has made available minutes, agendas and other official documents as well as giving greater public access to committees,

However, local authorities retain discretionary powers to declare certain items as confidential and therefore exempt from disclosure (there are fifteen such categories in the 1985 Act; see p. 246). And there is evidence that some councils seek to avoid disclosure by abusing discretionary powers, by charging unreasonably (e.g. up to £25) when clients want copies of documents, by setting up 'advisory' bodies or working parties (i.e. not proper, and therefore accessible, committees), or by circulating information informally rather than reporting it to committees. In terms of general information, some reports are inappropriate in content or design to be useful to members of the general public. And there is perhaps too often insufficient explanation about complaints procedures.[110] The Freedom of Information Act 2000 should improve matters here.

Stoker suggest that participation became prominent in the 1960s and 1970s, but declined in the 1980s, due largely to the New Right agenda of markets and consumerism[111] (and, it may be added, the 'quango explosion' and the increase in central control). However, it was not an absolute decline in that some consumers were empowered (such as parents, who were given more information and choice on schools and more school-management opportunities) and many more have become the focus for consultation, charters and sampling, etc., for the purposes of improving service standards. This will increase, as it is unlikely that the (New) Labour government will turn back the clock and it is already creating additional motivations in the form of Best Value, community leadership and planning, and a new role or direction for backbench councillors – all of which call for increased consultation (see Chapter 15). Thus, while 'the evidence available from the 1960s suggests that public interest and confidence in the local political process was not that deep . . . There never was a golden age of participation with respect to local government . . . the 1990s has seen a revival of interest in participation.'[112]

We have also witnessed the emergence of what has been called a 'new politics', in which thousands have become engaged in periodic waves of political expression and activism. These are motivated by causes such as feminism, ecologism, anti-consumerism, and they have often involved less conventional methods – civil disobedience, demonstrations, even violence or squatting. Another new form of participation may be encouraged by the revolution in communications and information technology: see below.

Communications

Communication is a prerequisite of participation. It has been described as the 'lifeblood of democracy', as it is a vital element in transparency, accountability and control. In its broadest sense, communication between the local authority and the community occurs by way of elections, co-option, political parties, pressure groups, area committees and neighbourhood groups, lobbying, open committee meetings, official notices, the media, letters, telephone* and direct action. In this section, we are concerned with the latter aspects of communications.

---

* Seventy-five per cent of councils' contact with the public is by telephone (*Local Government Talkback*, July 1999, p. 6).

Public relations. Communication is a two-way process: from the local authority to the community and vice-versa. It is commonly referred to as 'public relations' (PR), which has been defined as 'the deliberate, planned and sustained effort to establish and maintain mutual under-standing between an organization and its public' (Institute of Public Relations). The Maud Committee stated that

Public relations are not just a matter of the mechanics of giving information to the public either through the press or over the radio, but also of individual behaviour and attitudes on the part of all who serve the local authority.[113]

This was endorsed by the Bains Report, which said,

. . . the public have a right to information about the affairs of their local council . . . local authorities should themselves adopt an outgoing and positive attitude to the members of the community which they serve and should provide adequate resources, both finance and staff, to finance this.[114]

But it is said that PR is harder to define in local government than elsewhere because it has to promote the many, often divergent, people who make up the council rather than a single person (such as a Minister) or a single commercial product.

The Local Government Act 1972 empowers local authorities to provide information about their functions and services and the Local Government, Planning and Land Act 1980 places a duty on local authorities to publish information about the discharge of their func-tions, such as minutes of meetings, expenditures, financial accounts, notices of road alterations or school closures, etc. The 1980 Act empowered the Minister to issue codes of recommended practice and a number of such codes (and sometimes accompanying regulations) have been issued regarding tax demands, annual reports, staffing, planning applications, underused land and performance standards. In practice, local authorities provide more information than this (though there is considerable variation among them). Since the 1970s, there has been a significant increase in the number of civic or council-sponsored newspapers,[115] progress reports, open days, exhibitions and councillors' open forums. Moreover the number of local authorities appointing a specialist officer – the public relations officer (PRO) has increased. In the early 1970s just 50 councils made special provision for public relations. By 1980 the number had increased to 200. Many more specialist PR units were created in the early 1990s in view of the pending reorganization, with the result that the vast majority of local authorities in Britain now have specialist/dedicated PROs:* of the 82 which do not, 74 are district councils and 8 are unitaries.

Briefly stated, the task of PROs is to supply information to the press and public, to instruct those staff responsible for dealing with the public and to organize open days, tours, exhibitions and displays of local services. They might also be involved in the investigation of complaints and the mounting of local campaigns (such as road safety or 'use your vote'). Some, however, are no more than advertising devices for encouraging industrial development or attracting tourists.

Such developments are advocated as a means of bridging the gap and creating a sense of partnership between the citizen, the elected member and the official. Others have seen it as a means of improving the image of local government, of marketing, of preventing or remedying misunderstandings, of bringing before the public how much they owe to local government (by way of services) and of encouraging greater interest and participation.

However, many of these initiatives in communication have not always been sustained. Some have been abandoned as an economy measure – in 1974 the Local Government Information Office, working on behalf of local government generally, was closed down – and others have become piecemeal exercises instead of being systematic and comprehensive. In some (fewer) authorities there is a long-standing scepticism about public relations: a feeling that it is a waste of officers' time and the council's money; on the other hand there are officers and members (and perhaps journalists) who dislike the centralizing role of the PRO, whom they feel may 'steal their thunder'; some are also fearful of having more 'open' government.[116] Equally, there are members of the public who suspect that it is only a propaganda exercise (or 'whitewash machine') and that PROs (often ex-journalists) have developed a cosy relationship with the local media, with the latter

---

* Variously known as communications, publicity, media, liaison, marketing, promotions, external relations, or information manager. See too H. Davidson, 'Communication Out of the Box', *Local Government Voice*, July 1999, pp. 11–12.

publicizing the councils' conveniently prepared and predigested statements and other releases.

Meanwhile, as we have seen, local authorities have been obliged to publish more information about their finances and their general 'stewardship' and about their responses to ombudsman reports. The Local Government (Access to Information) Act 1985 has taken this further, as has the Education Act 1980 (by requiring more information on schools to facilitate greater parental choice). The Local Government Acts of 1988 and 1992 involved more publicity (about DLOs etc.) for purposes of competitive tendering – though this cut both ways, with councils becoming less open as certain aspects of their business became more confidential (to consider tenders, etc.). Overall, the aim is to help council-tax payers, electors and councillors make comparisons and judgements on their authority's performance, especially since the publication in 1992 by the Audit Commission of performance indicators for local authorities (see p. 317). However, it is fair to say that some authorities and services have been doing something like this for many years. Greater openness should result from the Freedom of Information Act 2000. It requires councils (among others), over a five-year period, to publish annual booklets outlining the information they have to provide, subject to exemptions for information which may 'prejudice' the operations of the authority. The arrangements are supervised by the Commissioner for Information (which now incorporates the Data Protection Registrar). Appeals can be made to the Commissioner and thereafter to the Freedom of Information Tribunal (and if necessary to the courts).

The media

The local media are the public's main source of information about their council.* The development of local broadcasting has increased the importance of radio and television in the reporting and reflecting of local affairs (including phone-in discussion programmes and the broadcasting of live or recorded extracts from council debates).[117]

* *Representing the People*, Audit Commission, 1997.

Local radio was seen as a great opportunity for councils to explain their policies and to have councillors and election candidates give their views. 'We would hope that interest in local politics would be stimulated in this way as well as by the reporting of council meetings' (BBC Director General, 1961). Such hopes were expressed again in the 1988 White Paper on broadcasting in the 1990s, though a study in 1982 was sceptical and concluded that 'local radio had exercised a minimal effect' in this regard.[118] A similar conclusion has been drawn for local television[119] despite its acknowledged general impact on peoples' lives[120] and its making political information accessible to a wider section of the community than represented by the newspaper-reading public. However, the development of video boxes and community programmes provide more opportunities for public debate.[121] Local authorities could help too by providing more adequate facilities, though local authorities are increasingly going on-line and setting up Websites (see below).

Consequently, the local press appears to remain the most important communication link between the local authority and the community,[122] some four out of five electors being regular readers of local newspapers which have been augmented in recent years by free local newspapers – e.g. these increased in number from 39 in 1975 to 344 in 1985.

Important as they clearly are, local newspapers have been subject to a number of criticisms. In the first place, they tend to present local government affairs in somewhat raw terms: committee meetings are summarized or extracts are culled from official minutes with little or no attempt to interpret them or place them into a wider context of council policy or community development. Consequently, so many of these items tend to become discrete snippets, devoid both of background or sustained interest.[123] Secondly, it has been argued that the local press (especially the weeklies) tends to create an artificial or distorted image of the locality as being essentially united and at harmony with itself, unaffected by social or political division.[124] On the other hand, the press may go to the other extreme and exaggerate the antagonisms which exist in the council and so understate the consensus which may exist on many issues (in the same way as the national press virtually ignores the work of the all-party committees of Parliament). Of councils' own newspapers, it has been said that they 'can be in the unique situation of having 100 per cent penetration (all households get one) but extremely low appeal' – low because they tend to be written by public relations staff rather than journalists, and are consequently too often left unread (although more local, neighbourhood office versions are often successful).*

In general, the press appears to give local government affairs a low priority, devoting few staff or only more junior staff to its reporting. And there is the temptation to seek reader-appeal by sensationalizing news items – good news is no news: after all, they are profit-seeking enterprises (mainly owned by large national companies), not philan-thropic bodies working to promote democracy. In so far as the national press has less need than the local press to have a positive relationship with local government, it is 'freer to highlight the negative or sensational as well as the cases of genuine injustice or political and policy ineptitude . . . in the national rather than the local press, local government receives a more negative coverage'.[125] It has been suggested that the media were a significant element in the public disquiet and unrest over the poll tax.[126] And it was the national press which targeted the activities of certain Labour councils during the 1980s and led to a number of 'loony left' council stories whose effects were long-lasting.[127] The national press also tends to give local elections national rather than local significance and 'spin'. As some editors recognize, the press does and should have a broadly educational and democratizing role, encouraging and leading an interest in civic affairs, rather than simply following or reflecting it.

However, the press is not altogether to blame, since to a large extent it is dependent on the local council for much of its information on local government matters[128] and it may not wish to jeopardize this relationship by being too critical or incisive in its reporting. The press has to walk something of a narrow path between too cosy, bland and passive a relationship with the local authority and a more critical stance which may result in upset, hostility and a closing up of the channels of communication.† Furthermore, in contrast to national

---

* See *Enhancing Local Democracy*, LGMB, 1996.

† In 1991 the *Sunday Times*' critical reporting of the way Derbyshire CC dealt with its pension fund led to the paper being sued for libel. In February 1992 the Court of Appeal dismissed the claim and emphasized that criticism of the conduct of authorities should be free.

politics there are fewer obvious leaders for the media to focus on in local government. Conversely, there are too many local authorities, so that coverage becomes more diffuse and more superficial. And the national media either report local politics for what they infer is its significance for the national scene or they simply do not report local events. There is no television or radio programme that regularly covers local government issues* and only one national newspaper has a Local Government correspondent. In 1998 the BBC decided to cut its local government correspondents from seven to just one (in London, thus adding to the so-called 'dumbing down' image of the BBC).

Councils have been accused of being too secretive:[129] as Barbara Castle explained it, 'The tendency is always for the public to be told too little, not too much, because by their very nature, executives tend to be secretive.'[130] A number of recent surveys suggest that the situation has not sufficiently changed and that councils are failing to keep their publics sufficiently informed. They also indicate that councils are better regarded where they publicize themselves more.[131]

In her maiden speech to Parliament, Margaret Thatcher introduced a Private Member's Bill which subsequently became the Public Bodies (Admission to Meetings) Act 1960. This clarified and secured the right of admittance of the press and the public to meetings of local authorities. This right was apparently extended by the Local Government Act 1972 (for England and Wales) and 1973 (Scotland) to allow access to committees of local authorities. However, much of the work of local government occurs in sub-committees and there has been considerable doubt and variation of practice concerning the public's right of access to these[132] (see p. 234). Furthermore, the public and press can be excluded from full council and committee meetings if those bodies go into 'camera' or closed session by passing a resolution that 'publicity would be prejudicial to the public interest by reason of the confidential nature of the business to be transacted or for other special reasons'.[133] As a consequence of taking decisions in private session or at sub-committee level, it may be that the press and public become aware of an issue at a stage too late for them to exercise any influence.

---

* The first regular TV broadcasts of council meetings began in September 1998 from Reading Borough Council.

In 1975 the central government showed its concern by issuing a circular to local authorities[134] which emphasizes that ready access to full information about a local authority's activities is essential if democracy is to flourish. It pointed out that the legislation of 1960 and 1972–3 sets out minimum requirements only, and it expressed disappointment at the limited moves by authorities to increase their freedom of information in dealing with the press and public. Since then local authorities have opened up more of their meetings, especially sub-committees, and made much more information available, often under government insistence. Some authorities have raised objections to these impositions as yet another example of central interference, often suggesting that central government should put its own house in order.[135] Other councils see opportunities rather than threats – that greater publicity can be put to advantage. It can provide local authorities with an opportunity to blow their own trumpets, to display their achievements, to show they are giving value for money and to rally public support. In addition, by providing more information, they can give the public greater opportunities for comment and for airing views, and thus perhaps avoid frustration and resentment, and forestall outbursts of protest and various forms of direct action. It may also prevent the media providing only one side of a story and the public being given the wrong impression. This often happens in cases where confidentiality is important (as, for example, when children are taken into care), though in such cases the scope for greater explanation will clearly be limited.

In 1995 local authorities in England and Wales were spending some £158 million a year on public relations (about half by PR units and half by service departments).* The Local Government Act 1986 requires that such spending is separately reported. This was part of the government's restrictions on councils' spending for political purposes (such as support for a particular political party or for anti-capping and anti-abolition campaigns, like the GLC's in 1985/6.† It sought to reinforce the idea that councils could only seek to inform

---

* *Talk Back*, Audit Commission, 1995.
† See *R. v ILEA* 1986, *R. v GLC* 1984 and 1985.

people, not to persuade them (no 'propaganda on the rates'*). But it is a fine difference. Local authorities cannot help being concerned with their image and reputation (some have had to re-build the latter following financial and political scandals and cases of gross mismanagement). Some authorities, like Manchester and Birmingham, have sought to promote themselves on an international scale (Olympic bids, etc.). The publication of Performance Indicators and evidence of pursuing Best Value provide regular occasions or opportunities for 'reputation management' (encouraged by the Audit Commission's *Read All About It* model) and the introduction of elected mayors is likely to add to this (as may the Freedom of Information legislation). Indeed '. . . an important part of the success of the democratic renewal project rests on the nature of the interaction between council, media and local communities'.† One of the problems for the local media had been the fact that the key decision-making process occurs behind the closed doors of the party groups. 'Bland, sensationalist or negative reporting . . . of local government rests partly on the secrecy of the political, managerial and policy process.'‡ In so far as such processes are made more open and transparent by the current modernizing reforms so may communications truly enhance democratic accountability.

Information technology is playing an increasingly important role here. Most councils have a website; e-mail, electronic noticeboards, interactive touch screens etc. are becoming more available, not just to convey basic information, but to facilitate self-service, feedback, opinion polling and perhaps soon, for voting.§ One obvious problem here is that of ownership or access to the technology. At the moment some 12 per cent of homes are connected to the Internet; this is forecast to rise to 80 per cent by 2010.

---

* The propaganda is not confined to party politics; the Local Government Act 1988 prohibits councils' promotion of homosexuality.
† C. Copus, *Local Government and the Media*, LGMB, 1999.
‡ Ibid.
§ See 'Interface', *The Times*, 22 September 1999, p. 10. In 1996, only 40 per cent of councils had a website: see G. Jackman, *The State of Local Government on the Internet*, URL, 1996.

Community politics

Communication is, or should be, a two-way process. Local government should be open to the receipt as well as the delivery of information. In the broadest sense this occurs through elections, pressure groups etc.

How, and how successfully, do local authorities receive the community's messages in the narrower, ordinary sense of the term? Ideally, the councillor is the main channel. But in practice there are severe limitations: there is substantial ignorance, lack of esteem, dissociation and even hostility towards councillors[136] due, in part, to the complexity of the local government system and its greater remoteness after reorganization in 1974–5 and since not all councillors are open to, or adept at, the constituency or 'tribune' role (see p. 203); and difficulties can arise where the councillor lives outside the area or belongs to the 'wrong' party.

There is evidence to suggest that, people prefer to deal with officers.[137] But there are problems here too: crossing the threshold of the town or county hall, locating the appropriate officer, dealing with receptionists, etc. But in general, the main problem is the citizens' (the amateurs) lack of time, knowledge and resources: the local authority (the professionals) has all three. According to the Parris survey (see p. 498), 50 per cent of people feel too ignorant about the system to know who to complain to. And a further survey (Sobol[138]) showed that a majority thought it not worthwhile complaining. The consequence may be a sullen acceptance of or resignation to council policies. But sometimes frustration breaks out into confrontation and direct action – demonstrations, rent strikes, occupation of nurseries or schools or squatting in houses, disturbing council meetings and inquiries or even rioting.[139]

Such events, have often been, at least partly, a reaction to the current economic situation, with cuts in expenditure following years of growth in services and rising aspirations. In part, too, they may be a result of the quickening in the pace of social change, of urban redevelopment and loss of established communities. But it also reflects a reaction to the growth of government and an apparent lack of receptiveness on the part of the authorities. As the Skeffington Report put it:

In the past, local authorities have been more successful in informing the public than involving them. Publicity is comparatively easy, but effective participation is much more difficult . . . We understand participation to be the act of sharing in the formulation of policies and proposals. Clearly the giving of information by the local authority and of an opportunity to comment on that information is a major part in the process of participation but it is not the whole story. Participation involves doing as well as talking and there will be full participation only where the public are able to take an active part throughout the plan-making process.

The report recommended the creation of greater opportunities for public participation in the planning processes of local government (they were largely enacted in the Town and Country Planning Act 1972). But the results have been disappointing in terms of public response. This may be partly due to the language (or jargon) used by the planners; it may be that the public are unprepared for consultation ('Participation does not come naturally, it has to be learned');[140] there is the suspicion too that the consultation is a sham, that the policy is crystallized and more than half decided, or at least the options (or parameters) have been pre-determined.[141] Consequently public meetings which aim to sound out public feeling often leave the public more confused or frustrated.

It is sometimes suggested that information and consultation are not enough: that real participation calls for real partnership, for the delegation of power to neighbourhoods and groups, for citizen control. The argument thus becomes more obviously about the distribution of power and resources in the community. And if the gulf between the governors and the governed becomes too wide, the latter may turn to direct action.

Consequently a number of other participative devices have been developed or suggested. Apart from the establishment of a variety of advice and aid centres (for such services as housing, planning, education, welfare and litigation) there is the encouragement of active involvement of clients in the provision or management of various services. These include mothers helping in nursery classes or playgroups, residents or members helping to run old people's clubs and homes, and volunteers helping in youth clubs or adventure playgrounds. In the field of education, there is more information and choice of schools, and there has been a significant growth in the number of parent–teacher bodies (PTAs) and of parent representation on school governing bodies.[142] As advocated by the Plowden Report[143] there has been some movement towards the development of 'community education' in which schools and colleges are more open to the general public and become a resource for the wider community rather than exclusively for children between the hours of 9 am and 4 pm. In some areas there have been developments in tenant management of estates or tower blocks (and in some cases the establishment of tenant cooperatives). Legislation, such as the Housing Act 1980 (the 'tenants' charter') and the NHS and Community Care Act 1990 provide more opportunities.[144]

Some of these developments have been quite unofficial and due entirely to local initiative, such as the setting up of action groups to monitor redevelopment or rehabilitation programmes, luncheon clubs, 'good neighbour' schemes or community bus services. They may be purely local or indigenous, or they may be an offshoot from a national organization (such as Shelter or Age Concern). The Seebohm Report drew particular attention to the importance of voluntary organizations in community development work (instancing the community projects taking place in North Kensington in London, Sparkbrook in Birmingham and Toxteth in Liverpool).

Similar developments have been started or encouraged (through cash or equipment) by local authorities, especially in response to the creation of educational priority areas (EPAs) and the urban aid programme.[145] Of particular interest has been the appointment of 'Community Development Officers' (sometimes known as social development or social relations officers). Some are appointed by local authorities or other statutory bodies,[146] and others by voluntary organizations including neighbourhood councils. (Many are self-appointed in that youth workers, adult education organizers, librarians or social workers may develop a strong commitment to the community and adapt their role accordingly – in some cases adopting a radical stance and thus placing themselves and the authority in an awkward position.)

Apart from giving information and advice to local residents, their function is to identify the needs and problems of the community and to help to deal with these either by calling on official resources or particularly by encouraging local self-help and initiatives. In this latter sense the community worker is acting as a catalyst.

A more radical approach to community work is being developed in areas such as Walsall and Kirklees through multi-purpose and greatly decentralized 'neighbourhood' – virtually walk-in – housing departments.[147] And a number of social service departments are developing the 'patch' system approach to social work services.[148] The aim is to try to 'de-paternalize' services and make them more a real community resource.

An analysis by John Gyford[149] for the Widdicombe Committee has identified two explanations for this increased activism and partici-pation: (i) a more assertive public, which is less prepared to accept the judgements of local politicians and professionals; and (ii) greater social fragmentation and diversity (as a result of changing employment patterns and composition, significant local ethnic concentrations, changing family formations and more individual or customized con-sumption behaviour). Together, these have 'produced an increasingly sectionalist politics' and a growth in single-issue politics and pressure-group activity. This in turn has been accommodated (at least to some extent) by more open and accessible procedures – in particular by (a) greater consultation with council tenants (especially following the 1980 Housing Act), with business (following the 1984 Local Government Finance Act), with ethnic minorities (through community relations councils and race relations committees), through the establishment of committees dealing with women's issues, and more general schemes involving area/district consultation meetings, advice centres and com-munity newsletters; and (b) various forms of decentralization such as area committees (as in Tower Hamlets LB or South Somerset DC), community development projects, neighbourhood management and patch systems outlined above.

Thus 'the history of local government over the past two decades has ... been, in part, one of continuing attempts to supplement the institutions of representative democracy and professional service departments'.[150] Such developments challenge what Professor John

Stewart sees as the three traditional or common organizing principles of local government in Britain, i.e. hierarchy, uniformity and functionalism (or departmentalism), and consequently they may meet resistance from chief officers, leading councillors, trade unions and political parties. And some see a risk of these developments going too far, that 'an elaboration of consultative mechanisms somehow devalues and even endangers the traditional institutions of representative democracy itself [since] their existence may . . . lead to the establishment of a network of consultations and liaison whose existence is rarely visible to the voters at large' and which increases the complexity of the machinery of government and thus its remoteness.[151] However, the current reform programme is building community involvement into the very heart of local authorities, and the aim is to change the processes and general culture of local government (see Chapter 15).

Most of the initiatives in participation have occurred in urban areas. This is partly because urban community problems are more obvious or overt (though not necessarily greater)[152] than rural ones, and also because communication links are easier. But another reason is that urban areas lack local bodies (local councils) to represent them.

Local councils

In this book the emphasis throughout has been on the so-called 'principal' authorities, the boroughs, unitaries, counties and districts. In this section attention is drawn to the more local, grassroots councils. These consist of parishes (in England) or community councils (in Wales and Scotland). In urban areas (formerly boroughs and UDCs) they are usually called 'town' councils (entitling them to a 'town mayor'). Collectively, they are all known as 'local councils' and their interests are promoted by the National Association of Local Councils (NALC), which is a federation of county associations (in England and Wales), and the Association of Larger Local Councils (ALLC).

Under the Local Government Act 1972, parish (or town) councils were formed in England from existing parishes. Elsewhere in England (except London) parish councils would be formed (by order of the Minister) (1) where the population contained 200 or more electors; (2)

where there were 150–200 electors and a parish meeting passed a resolution to have a council; or (3) in a parish of under 150 electors if the district council agrees. Where there is a parish or (in 6 per cent of cases) town council, there must be an annual meeting open to all electors. A council consists of a chairperson (or perhaps town mayor) and at least four other councillors. Where there is no council, there must be such a meeting at least twice a year (though quite often in practice this does not happen). The parish meeting may appoint a committee. Altogether there are about 10,200 parishes in England, of which 8,159 have a council (containing over 70,000 councillors), about 150 of which comprise group or joint councils, each administering two or more parishes. Local councils cover 14 million people in England (i.e. about 25 per cent of the population). Parishes are to be found predominantly in rural areas and range widely in area (from a few acres to nearly 100 square miles), in population (from 0 to 40,800, with half below 500) and in resources (from a few pounds to around £300,000 (Swanlea, Kent) or £400,000 (East Grinstead, West Sussex) from their council tax precept, which itself ranges from under £10 to £100 per council tax Band D property). Over the past 30 years, more 'urban' areas (especially in the freestanding towns) have become parished. However, there are still few in metropolitan areas,* and even in rural England their coverage is not universal – though their formation is made easier by the Local Government and Rating Act 1997. Under this Act, the Minister (in England) has the power to create a new parish in response to a petition of 10 per cent of electors in the proposed parish area (provided there are at least 250 signatures). It is anticipated that most expansion will occur in metropolitan areas, though a major problem is identifying appropriate communities; neighbourhoods and housing estates are likely areas.

In 1974, Wales was divided up into communities – about 800 in all – based on previous parishes or (where they were requested) urban districts and boroughs. Under conditions similar to those in England they have formed councils in about 750 of them. In certain areas (the larger urban areas)[153] community councils were not permitted; just as

---

* There are 229, of which 173 are in the two Yorkshire metropolitan counties. They pre-existed the 1974 reorganization.

in England, it was felt appropriate that no community (parish) should have normally a population in excess of 20,000 (or 20 per cent of the population of the parent district). As a result only about 300 such councils in England and 90 in Wales were created in urban areas. (No parishes were allowed in London.)

The boundaries, status and electoral arrangements of these local councils are likely to change (marginally) as they are subject to review. This is the responsibility of the district or unitary councils, who must channel their recommendations though the Local Government Commission (England) or (in Wales) through the Local Government Boundary Commission (see p. 73) to the Secretary of State who makes the final decisions, though this may change as the Welsh Assembly and Executive take greater effect. Thus new parishes may be created (in England) by the Local Government Commission, by district/unitary review and by petition. In England it is the district council which determines the number of councillors on a parish council (though the minimum must be five) and (both in England and Wales) the district council has the power to co-opt members on to the parish or community council where they are seriously deficient.

Parish and community council elections take place every four years, the most recent being in 1999. Councillors are bound by the same conditions (in terms of qualifications, disclosure of interests, etc.) as those in principal authorities, though not subject to the jurisdiction of the local ombudsmen, and they may claim certain allowances. Interest in becoming a parish councillor has increased over the past thirty years, and this is reflected in the higher number of contested elections[154] and an improvement in turnout (which now stands at 44 per cent). Parish councils also have a better representation of women (at 30 per cent). The councils themselves feel their role as the voice of their communities is enhanced by the fact that they operate independently of party politics, though this is diminishing, especially in the larger and more (sub)urban parishes (and some of the non-party parishes are accused of being somewhat 'cliquish').[155]

These local councils are currently estimated to have over fifty legal powers.* Their functions are broadly four-fold. Firstly, they provide

* *Local Government Chronicle*, 24 April 1998, p. 8.

certain services (playing fields, community halls, bus shelters, etc. – see Appendix 10), many of which are run concurrently with the district council or in partnership with private or voluntary organizations. Secondly, they have the discretionary power to spend Section 137 or 'free resource' money (of up to £3.50 per head; see pp. 77–8). Thirdly, they must be consulted about certain matters (such as footpath surveys by the county council and the appointment of governors to local primary schools) and they must be notified by the district council about certain other matters (including local planning applications, particular bylaws, etc.). Fourthly, and perhaps above all, their function is to act as a forum for the discussion of local affairs and to represent the interests of the local community to the district council and other local and national bodies generally. In 1980, this latter function was graphically illustrated in a number of parishes in East Anglia, such as Brandon and Thetford, when under Schedule 12 of the Local Government Act 1972 they conducted local referendums (see footnote p. 529) on the siting of American 'cruise' missiles in their area. More recent issues have been the government's plans for housebuilding on greenfield sites and the closure of hospitals and schools. For all of these purposes, local councils have the power to precept* (see p. 354) upon the district council (the authority responsible for collecting the council tax. For figures see Appendix 11). Indeed this is overwhelmingly their main source of income as they receive no government grants.

The total revenue expenditure of parish councils in England is over £200 million (in 1997). An estimated 26,400 people work for these local councils, one third of them on a voluntary basis. Of the remainder who are paid, only 7 per cent are full-time paid staff.[156] The government currently approves capital borrowing of £6.25 million p.a. by English parishes. In the past there was some disquiet about the financial accountability of local councils.[157] As a result they were brought into the District Audit system in 1997 (though this is causing considerable problems in terms of the charges for audit† and the extra time to the council staff, which may be exacerbated by the auditors' lack of familiarity with local government).

---

* Which ranges from under £10 to over £100 per council tax Band D property.
† For some parishes this can amount to one third of their whole budget!

The Local Government (Scotland) Act 1973 set up a totally different kind of community council system in Scotland. Although the community councils here have a statutory existence, they do not really form local authorities, since they have no statutory powers or any access, as of right, to public funds.

Initially the Scottish district and island councils were required to consult the public in their areas, then draft schemes for the creation of community councils (which were then submitted to the Secretary of State for Scotland for approval). Fifty-six such schemes were approved, covering all local authority areas. As in England and Wales, there is considerable variation in the population coverage of the councils: most (75 per cent) have populations of under 5,000 (and 30 per cent have under 1,000), but twenty councils (in the cities) have populations of over 20,000. The schemes also vary in other respects – frequency of meetings and of elections, qualifications of candidates and of electors, methods of balloting, etc.

The schemes also laid down certain conditions for the creation of the councils: at least twenty electors have to sign a requisition for elections to be held, and usually a minimum number of candidates must stand. Since the schemes provide for (potentially) 1,343 community councils, some 15,300 councillors could be required (in effect, 1 for every 340 people in Scotland). In practice, there are currently 1,100 such councils. This is in contrast to the 1,600 councillors then (and 1,200 now) in the principal councils. It presents a tall order and provides a sure test of community commitment. In practice, the response has been sufficient for 85 to 90 per cent of the proposed councils to have been successfully formed, though in most cases there have not been enough candidates to hold elections and only about one quarter of the council seats have been contested.[158]

According to the 1973 legislation, the general purpose of the community councils is:

to ascertain, coordinate and express to the local authorities for its area, and to the public authorities, the views of the community which it represents, in relation to matters for which those authorities are responsible, and to take such action in the interests of that community as appears to it to be expedient and practicable.[159]

For these purposes, the principal councils have been empowered to provide the community councils with finance and other assistance such as may be agreed between them, though this may change with the advent of the Scottish Assembly and Executive.

The community councils in Scotland, like the local councils in England and Wales, are intended to be broadly based organizations of official standing with which local communities as a whole can identify and through which they can speak and act. Unlike those in England and Wales, they are not a third tier of local government and have no statutory responsibilities: 'their purpose being to complement local government, not compete with it'.[160] They have the important job of assessing and expressing local opinion, thus bringing to the attention of local authorities and other public bodies any matters of concern to their particular locality. In addition they can collaborate with local authorities in the organization and management of local facilities and services, and initiate community projects. It was a novel scheme in terms of public participation, and one which could appeal to many people in (urban) England who feel relatively deprived of a 'voice' at local level.

As part of the reorganization process in England in the 1990s, the role and structure (including elections and finance) of local councils, was subject to review, and to this end the government published a consultation document in *The Role of Parish and Town Councils in England* (HMSO, 1992). This invited views on how they may become more effective as representatives of their communities and raised expectations of their having an enhanced role – an idea endorsed by the counties (ACC) and the districts (ADC) as well as the local councils themselves (though a significant number said they neither wished nor were able to take on additional primary responsibilities). In 1993 the government announced that it felt it inappropriate to enlarge their area of responsibility.

However, spurred on by reorganization* prospects, (and in keeping with notions of 'subsidiarity' and 'getting closer to the customer') there was a flurry of activity by districts and (especially) counties to explore the

---

* Some saw such decentralization as way of staving off change; others saw it as a way of bidding for unitary status which did not involve remoteness.

possibilities of devolving powers (of decision-making and/or function) from districts (and counties) to parishes. Such devolution did occur (by way of agency agreements, involving such services as youth services, nursery and community education and school management). In some areas it was limited because districts felt their own existence to be under threat and it could be awkward where the district had a large number of parishes. (CCT regulations were an added impediment to delegation.) But in other cases it was quite substantial, particularly after an agreement in 1996 between NALC and the districts' ADC which sought to extend agency agreements for a range of services (including libraries, litter, noise control, leisure provision and street cleaning, maintenance, lighting and parking). Then in the same year the (Conservative) government, seeking to boost (or, with 41 per cent of parishes without a shop, in many cases revive) village and rural community life,* applauded and advocated such devolution and reinforced it with legislation. Under the Local Government and Rating Act 1997 the government can use reserve powers to require principal councils to consult more with parishes on planning and other matters (i.e. where there are inadequate voluntary agreements). This arrangement is based on that established in Wales under the Local Government (Wales) Act 1994. Subsequently the Welsh Office issued guidance on consultation mechanisms and subjects.

The 1997 Act also increased the powers of parishes in relation to transport and to crime. Under the former, parish councils can now set up car-sharing schemes, arrange concessionary taxi-fare schemes, make grants to voluntary bus services and install traffic-calming measures (in conjunction with principal councils). Under the latter they can install CCTV cameras, run community policing schemes and make grants to the local Police Authority for the purpose of having a village bobby. (There was no grant-aid for this extra spending as such.) Business rates were reduced (50 per cent mandatory, plus up to 50 per cent at the discretion of the district council) for village post offices and shops (depending on their merchandise) and saving them some £500 a year (the cost of which falls on the national Exchequer and the districts). In 1998 the Charities Commission said it was

* See White Paper, *Rural England*, 1996.

considering conferring charitable status on organizations helping rural communities to improve retail and other services and this might extend to shops.*

A number of parishes (especially the larger ones) had anticipated some of these changes and sought agency powers (e.g. for CCTV or for deciding planning applications). And there can be real cost reductions (e.g. by having grass cut by the local farmer). But there is still some reluctance or hesitation because, although the parish council is reimbursed by the district council, it is often below cost.† District councils (such as South Norfolk) have called on support from the Rural Development Commission and the private sector, and others have created multi-agency forums and partnerships to address rural issues and development.‡

Collectively, parish and community councils have considerable potential to enhance the life of the communities they are elected to serve. As the government has recently declared, 'Parish councils will continue to play a key role in many of our towns and villages. They have a vital role in helping principal councils keep in touch with the smallest communities in their areas. Parish councils can work in partnership with their principal council to bring government closer to the people, and to establish the decentralized delivery of local government services. It is important therefore that parish councils everywhere embrace the new culture of openness and accountability, putting their local people first' (*Modern Local Government: In Touch with the People*, HMSO, 1998).

Yet, puzzlingly, there are reports suggesting that the government is now considering the actual abolition of parishes, with the possibility of neighbourhood forums being created to take their place (see *Sunday Times*, 3 October 1999, p. 1).

* See *Promotion of Urban and Rural Regeneration*, Charities Commission, 1998.

† Not all parishes wish to take on more service responsibilities, partly because of the added complications and time involved and/or because (rather like the Scottish community councils) they do not see their proper role as service providers (see Report on parishes by Peterborough City Council, 1998).

‡ See, e.g., *Local Governance*, vol. 24, no. 1, Spring 1998, pp. 67–76.

Neighbourhood councils

The Royal Commissions in 1969 on local government in England and Scotland each emphasized the necessity of local councils both to provide certain services and to represent the wishes of the inhabitants on matters that affect the local community. These roles were seen as crucial in view of the substantial reduction in the number of councils and councillors which would result from their proposals.

As we have seen, local councils have been established (or re-established) throughout much of Britain. However, in England the local councils predominate in the rural areas and the smaller towns. Very few exist in the large urban areas (e.g. there are just two in Manchester, and they are not legally permissible in Greater London) with the result that 75 per cent of the population of England live in 'unparished' areas. (In March 1990 Simon Hughes MP introduced a Bill to allow parish councils in London, unsuccessfully.) A further anomaly is that within the same district council some areas are entitled to have a local council while others are not. Consequently, there is strong pressure from many groups in the community for an extension of local councils to the urban, especially metropolitan, areas. This may occur naturally, as districts or unitaries undertake their parish review (see pp. 515–16). However, such an extension may meet resistance from many existing councillors, partly on the grounds that it would involve a further upheaval in local government so soon after the reorganization of the 1990s. There may also be opposition (as indeed there has been) arising from the fear of party political rivalry.

In the meantime an alternative is being pursued in the form of 'neighbourhood councils', otherwise known as 'urban parish councils'. These are non-statutory bodies which 'belong to the underworld of local government'.[161] They are based, as the name implies, on a neighbourhood of about 10,000 people (though ranging from under 3,000 to over 20,000). Their existence predates reorganization and they are often the product of local community issues and local action groups which sprang up in response to those issues (see below). They received added impetus from the reorganization of local government, with its creation of larger and what many feel to be remoter forms of local authority.

The government in the mid 1970s considered giving them statutory status, and has sought mildly to encourage their formation.[162] The Association for Neighbourhood Democracy (AND) is a pressure group founded in 1970 (and based in Brighton). It comprises individuals, groups and neighbourhood councils, and seeks to promote participation in local affairs and to achieve local government which provides effectively for the needs of urban neighbourhoods (including parish councils).[163] The AND (in contrast to the Scottish community councils) also wishes to see neighbourhood councils with financial independence (that is, with the right to precept on the rating authorities) and the power to provide certain services and amenities. The AND publishes a monthly magazine, *Anchor*.

There were 150 neighbourhood councils in 1975 when hopes were high of statutory recognition. But their numbers have dwindled as they lost heart or won recognition as parish/town councils (and host district councils have not always encouraged them). Because they are non-statutory, their size, finance, form and purposes vary considerably.[164] But typically a neighbourhood council has the following objectives: (1) to represent to other organizations (such as government departments, local authorities, public corporations and local industry) the needs and wishes of the local community. In this respect it will act as the 'ears, eyes and mouth' of the community on all aspects of community development. It may campaign for local amenities such as sports facilities, a shopping area, a play space or a community hall; or it may try to protect the local environment by scrutinizing local development plans or raising questions about derelict land or empty properties in the area; (2) to organize or stimulate self-help within the local community in order to improve the quality of life for the residents as a whole. This may include the clearing of dumped material from derelict sites, helping to set up holiday play schemes or 'good neighbour' arrangements; (3) to help those in the community in need of special facilities by providing services and amenities (such as voluntary playgroups, school crossings or youth clubs) and providing advisory services (such as 'problem shops'); (4) to foster or preserve community spirit or identity, and help to create a sense of community responsibility among residents. In other words, the neighbourhood councils may perform roles which are part social and part political. As regards the latter, this does not seem either in practice[165] or in theory[166] to imply party politics.

Neighbourhood councils are potentially an important development in local government. Like the statutory parish and community councils they provide a 'voice for the neighbourhood'. Research has shown that most people identify with, or are conscious of belonging to, a definable area known as the 'home area'[167], a point recently confirmed during the Local Government Review 1994–7* (though not without challenge).†

Local councils and neighbourhood councils cover such areas. And, being so local, these councils should be more accessible to the community and their members less anonymous than most councils, boards and commissions. Some people even envisage the development of sub-units based on groups of streets.

The Chairman of the National Consumer Council (in 1981) spoke[168] of the 'smouldering discontent' among consumers over public services, and how for many people 'life involved banging their heads against the brick wall of bureaucracy'. In this context there is 'a very high level of unhappiness' with the attitudes of council staff. (In August 1991, the NCC found 40–49 per cent of people were fairly or very satisfied with their council. The figure for British Rail was 51 per cent.) Such public feelings were felt to be dangerous at a time of mounting unemployment and simmering unease. He advised making public services more accountable to the public they serve by establishing and publicizing adequate complaints and redress systems. A similar warning that 'the monster machine of local government' needs to be geared to the real day-to-day needs of individual people has been expressed by the president of the Association of Directors of Social Services.[169] Neighbourhood councils can play a vital part in this.

We must, however, beware of over-stating their value, actual or potential. There is the danger that yet another council will confuse people or dilute their loyalties to existing local authorities. If they are to be a genuine and effective vehicle for the expression of community or grassroots feeling, they must not become or *appear* to become too

* *In Search of Community Identity*, JRF, 1996.
† See *Local Government Chronicle*, 11 October 1996, p. 8.

formal, bureaucratic or cliquish. Some people may be put off if they see the council becoming too much a part of 'the establishment' and the machinery of consensus politics. Democratic structures do not necessarily pass power over to the people, but too often the power falls into the hands of small groups adroit at committee work (which is essentially a minority skill and interest). Furthermore, it may be that there is less need for neighbourhood councils as such since the Local Government and Rating Act 1997 now makes it easier for parish councils to be formed (including in urban areas).

Apart from elections therefore, there must be regular open meetings, newsletters, questionnaires and other means of allowing individuals to express opinions and raise questions – questions which might otherwise go by default because the individual feels overawed, powerless or bemused, or because he or she feels that the matter may be regarded as too petty. Like a speck of dust in the eye, seemingly small matters – litter, dogs, traffic, trees, transport – can loom large in the life of an individual or a small community. Over the past 20 years, local Liberal parties have built up strong support through their policy of taking a deliberate interest in such matters, including broken pavements – hence the term 'pavement (or community) politics'.[170] (During their brief period of political control in Islington in 1982, it was the SDP which initiated an opinion survey of public attitudes to that council and its services.)

Maintaining open channels of communication with the whole community, the neighbourhood and local councils can encourage the 'non-joiners' to participate, and this may be especially important in the inner-city areas. In this way, these councils can put community politics on a more regular basis by enabling ordinary people to band together to exert some influence on the decisions being made every day in town halls, government departments and company offices – decisions which may vitally affect their (our) lives.* This is increasingly important as the scale and penetration of these decisions increase.

---

* A parish poll can be called to hold a referendum where requested by ten people or one third of those present at the meeting. The issue needs to be one arising from the meeting (presumably notified beforehand and on the agenda). The District Council would need to be informed and it would provide the necessary administration, though the parish would foot the bill (*Parish and Community Meeting (Polls) Rules*, 1987, SI no. 1).

The neighbourhood and other local councils, in acting both as 'watchdogs' and 'caretakers', can be a means of fusing or combining the old concept of representative democracy with the newer and particularly urban concept of participatory democracy.

All this will be affected by the current reform and modernization of local government – especially as local authorities are required to increase their consultation procedures and improve popular participation (see Chapter 15). This provides both a threat and an opportunity to neighbourhood and local councils: they could benefit as instruments in the process of democratic renewal – or they could be superseded by their larger principal authorities.

Closely related to neighbourhood councils is the development of *neighbourhood management* initiatives. Defined as 'the local organization and delivery of core urban services within a small, recognizable built-up area of under 5,000 homes* (often based on housing estates), they are usually originated by central or local government, often to stimulate regeneration or the prevention of decay. But they are managed variously by housing associations, residents or tenants groups, local authorities directly or through companies. While they often involve one-stop shops and neighbourhood offices for dealing with core services and problems (damage, housing repairs, nuisance etc.) there is much liaison, collaboration and coordination of other local services (education, police, libraries, transport, health) as well as private business.

* A. Power and E. Bergin, *Neighbourhood Management*, ESCR/CASE Paper 31, 1999.

14

OUT OF THE NINETIES: TAKING STOCK

Local government is part of the 'body politic' and as such it is in a state of continuous change and development – indeed, 'The 1980s and 1990s were periods of more rapid change in local government than at any other time in recent history.'*

It has its critics – what social institution has not? In an educated, democratic society criticism is to be expected and welcomed, especially where it is constructive. Consequently, there are many opinions about the shape and direction that local government should take in the twenty-first century.

Firstly, there is the question of *structure*. The reorganization in 1972 (England and Wales) and 1973 (Scotland) created much dissent and left many elements disgruntled, though a new revision was out of the question in the 1970s. However, there was some (actual or proposed) change by stealth, involving the reallocation or readjustment of functions among local authorities. There was the Labour government's plan for 'Organic Change' in 1979 (see p. 60) which sought to restore to a number of district borough councils the responsibilities they had previously enjoyed as county boroughs. Under the Local Government, Planning and Land Act 1980, certain planning functions were removed from the counties and consolidated into the districts. There was a similar rationalization of concurrent functions under the Local Government and Planning (Scotland) Act 1982. More generally, both the Labour and the Liberal Democratic parties have advocated the abolition of the *ultra vires* rules, and propose that councils have 'general competence' powers (see p. 79).[1]

In the 1980s, both the Labour and the Social/Liberal Democrat

* *Portrait of change*, LGMB, 1997.

parties developed policies for a more substantial restructuring of local government. Both opposition parties proposed a regional tier of government, and a single-tier system of 'unitary' authorities based broadly on enlarged districts. This gained increasingly widespread support (including that of many Conservatives who wished to simplify accountability for local taxes). Meanwhile, the Conservative government (in power 1979–97) implemented a major reorganization in 1986 through the abolition of the metropolitan counties and the GLC, with their functions transferring to component district/borough councils or to *ad hoc* joint boards. It was argued by the government that changed circumstances and practical experience had revealed these top-tier authorities to be unnecessary and wasteful[2] (see pp. 51, 121); they had also been Labour-controlled – often stridently so – since 1980–1. Opposition parties criticized this hastily devised restructuring and promised at least to restore a London-wide body – which the present Labour government has put in place (since May 2000) under the Greater London Authority Act 1999.

The abolition of the metropolitan county councils threw into greater relief the contrasting (and many would say illogical) status and role of boroughs such as Barnsley, Kirklees, Tameside or Doncaster and such comparable (but relatively functionless) cities such as Bristol, Nottingham, Hull, Plymouth and Southampton. This was compounded by the abolition of the ILEA (under the 1988 Education Reform Act) and the transfer of its functions to the inner London boroughs, whose populations are often smaller than many non-metropolitan boroughs (such as Bristol etc., above). Meanwhile, in Scotland, there appeared to be a growing consensus for the abolition of the regions. Consequently, as we have seen above (pp. 53ff), the government inaugurated a full-scale review of the structure of local government in England, Wales and Scotland which resulted in a uniform unitary system for Scotland and Wales and a partial reorganization in and of some of the English shire counties (and resulted in 46 unitary councils). There is currently no enthusiasm – in local or central government – for further local restructuring, and some of the original motivation for unitaries has gone (e.g. with the scrapping of the GMS/school opt-out policy). But the issue of reorganization is not settled, not least because the emergence of Regional Assemblies in England is likely to see the removal of a tier of local government (Labour has already envisaged this, indeed Jack Straw as Shadow Minister made it a precondition and this was confirmed by the Secretary of State John Prescott).* A significant, and growing, number of towns (currently 18, such as Exeter, Gloucester, Norwich, Northampton, Oxford) are still pursuing unitary status and have formed the Local Governance Review Group to press their case with the government. There are also some counties which aspire to unitary status. In Scotland, the reorganization was accused of gerrymandering ('fiddling' the boundaries for party advantage) so there could be some local and piecemeal revision – but that will be up to the new Scottish Parliament and Executive to decide.

Secondly, local authorities are still trying to settle their *management* structures and procedures of committees, 'cabinets' and departments,[3] and the appointment and role of their officers. A number of councils are breaking out from the Bains pattern of management by dispensing with the post of chief executive (in some cases (currently 10 per cent) by amalgamating it with the treasurer's or by operating at the top with a small corporate team of chief officers). Others are revising (often reducing) their committees and committee roles (such as separating service-based, decision-making and relatively routine-dominated committees from more open, non-decision-making committees that review and explore policy and strategy, or deal with general (or 'horizontal') issues through area, health, or women's committees etc.). They and others are amalgamating departments (such as housing and social services or architect's, valuation and property) and creating (or reinventing) multi-service or multi-functional directorates. And a small but growing number are moving away from the bureaucratic top-down model to a more decentralized pattern of core–periphery, in which the centre provides a policy framework for, and monitors the performance of, the outer executive units and local committees which have devolved powers and contacts with the community grassroots (see pp. 514ff). (In the context of the English unitary councils, it has been suggested that the simultaneous development of corporatism and community governance presents potential problems.†

* See *Local Government Chronicle*, 17 February 1991, p. 51 and *New Labour, New life for Britain*, Labour Party, 1996 and *Observer*, 29 August 1999.
† See *Local Governance*, no. 2, 1998, pp. 91–9.

Local authorities have been driven to consider the way they go about their business by management thinking, by the need for savings, by CCT, Best Value, outsourcing and partnerships, etc. and by one another; and they are being encouraged by organizations such as the Audit Commission, the Efficiency and Improvement and Development Agency (the ex-LGMB), the Joseph Rowntree Foundation and not least by the government – both the previous Conservative and above all, by the present Labour one: see Chapter 15. Consequently there is considerable movement and diversity among councils in their internal arrangements.[4]

Furthermore, with the introduction (in 1974–5) of payments to councillors (for attendance at meetings, for special responsibilities and, now, flat-rate payments for all members), the full-time local politician has become more widespread – from something like 100 in 1990 to 4,850 (or 25 per cent) today.* Some would argue that such a development is long overdue, since British local authorities are of a generally higher average size than in most European and North American countries, and their budgets exceed those of a number of independent sovereign states. Also, elected members are having to become semi-business managers and develop a familiarity with the complexities of the local authority financial system (grants, multipliers, indicators, etc.) and elements of financial management (performance measures, zero-base budgeting, etc.). One further consequence will be the increased need to develop different links between members and officers (and a clearer understanding of their respective and changing roles).

Away from the policy area, there are developments in service delivery, with decentralization and community-based administration. Some of this is purely administrative, some involves decision-making and policy development or feedback. There is more devolution of management responsibility to the point of service provision (residential homes, leisure centres, etc.) – and compulsory in the case of community care management, and in schools and colleges in the form of the local management of schools or LMS, whereby LEAs must delegate some 90 per cent of the education budget to schools. As a result, there is a need for clarification of policy and specification of what managers are

* *First National Census*, LGMB, 1998.

expected to achieve and with what resources, as well as appraisal or review of performance (upon which pay and perhaps renewal of contract of employment may depend). A further consequence of such accountable-management developments (or 'Volvo-ization') is the reorganization of individual departments, often involving shortened hierarchies. Some have developed market or commercial methods internally, so that service departments 'buy' (through charges) central support services (management, legal, training, computing).

There is also a growth in public–private partnerships (PPPs) (e.g. for housing, leisure or sports facilities or for urban (re)development. These are often the result of Private Finance Initiatives (PFI) or are encouraged by the Single Regeneration Budget (SRB) and other government funding opportunities (City Challenge, Estates Renewal, etc.) and may involve other local authorities and voluntary and public agencies such as housing associations, TECs or government departments. Such developments, together with the growth in non-elected public bodies (see p. 555), mean that the government of local areas – local governance – is far less the preserve of local authorities than it used to be; local governance is now more fragmented. Contracting out – voluntary and compulsory – has obviously increased and extended (perhaps as contract management) into areas such as the management of welfare homes or financial services (auditing, staff wages/pensions, rent/tax collection, etc.). And in response to competitive tendering, councils have appointed Directors of Contract Services or created their own companies or semi-autonomous trusts, and there have been employee/management buy-outs (MBOs). In these circumstances the local authority becomes the 'client', which 'buys' services from outside sources or from its own service or works department (DLO/DSO, where the function is kept in-house). Thus it is suggested that 'compulsory tendering is arguably the most important influence this century on local authorities and the way they operate.'[5] As a consequence, the local authority 'becomes more service-orientated,* consumer- and

---

* In terms of its effects a survey of local authority CEOs showed: 71 per cent believe it has increased concern for quality and 46 per cent it has raised service standards, 69 per cent it increased concern for customer satisfaction; 65 per cent it has reduced costs of service provision. But 60 per cent thought it has reduced pay and conditions (*Portrait of change*, LGMB, 1998).

client-led and sharper in its objectives of serving the public'.[6] Overall, in 1998 DSOs had won 55.5 per cent of contracts tendered (equal to 73 per cent of their value) of which the most successful was in housing management (88 per cent of contracts) and the least successful was building cleaning (41 per cent).

The purpose of such developments is to improve economy, efficiency and effectiveness, through more flexible and quicker response and through greater commitment, as managers 'own' the decisions and priorities because they have determined them (within the limits set down); thus they can exercise judgement, initiative and enterprise. But equally important is the political purpose: empowerment. This means greater access, accountability and control by the community (as clients, consumers or users of services), and it is achieved (alongside the neighbourhood or area offices, multi-service centres or 'one-stop shops', 'patch' social work and neighbourhood repair teams, etc.) by means of neighbourhood or area committees, local forums, charters, service agreements, user-group control or management participation (e.g. tenants, residents or users of leisure facilities). In the future the government sees communities being empowered by the clearer accountability of the executive, the enhanced representative role of councillors and the requirement of greater consultation (see Chapter 15). Meanwhile, a survey by INLOGOV[7] showed a doubling (from 9 to nearly 20 per cent) in the number of councils using neighbourhood service outlets between 1980 and 1988 (especially in metropolitan authorities). The same survey showed that over 25 per cent had established a system of devolved budgetary control – again double the 1980 figure – and another study concludes, 'Our analysis suggests that decentralization (broadly defined), far from being a passing fad, can be shown to be a deep-seated trend in the development of the social and economic organization of western democracies which will be of major significance in the 1990s and beyond.'[8] Clearly, in contrast to the recent past, small, not big, is beautiful – although some people are concerned at the cost and others fear for corporate management and coordination of services and unequal treatment/provision (which may be compounded by the quest for local authorities to become 'enablers'; see below).

Clearly local authorities have not all behaved in the same way or to the same extent. A number of authorities take a positive approach to change and are, in the process, helping to 'reinvent' our system of local government. One recent survey by the Local Government Management Board identifies 'leading edge' or pro-active authorities who have recognized the need to develop a capacity to manage change:

Leading-edge authorities embrace the concept of strategic management the better to manage change. Their organizational and management structures recognize the integrated nature of many of the functions they perform. They set up working parties to examine specific issues which are seen to require a corporate approach. Middle-rank officers orchestrate networks across departments. The role of the elected member and the nature of political management assumes a different form . . . Formal committee processes are slimmed down in favour of strategy groups and ad hoc working parties, while small groups of prominent members act as custodians of the authority's values and strategic purposes . . . They take seriously the dialogue with local residents and service users . . . and seek to work . . . with other agencies in the public, private and voluntary sectors.[9]

On the other hand (in 1993), 'many authorites seek to avoid wholesale change. They tackle issues incrementally . . . In more than half of all authorities, members were seen as reluctant to respond to change or not fully aware of the pressures.' Thus, for example, only one authority in five had an authority-wide policy on Europe (two in five by 1996) and only a quarter have put their chief officers on a fixed-term contract or performance-related pay.

Overall, however, the impressions from the LGMB survey are 'of sustained rapid change, and of a cumulative impact powerful enough to transform the operations of the local authority . . . [amounting to] a transformation of local governance and of local government management', with, for example, almost half of authorities having recast their departments. Moreover, four out of five have cut their subcommittees (down to 12 in 1996) and slimmed down their management team (down to 6 in 1996); four out of five now frame 'mission statements' and have put in place arrangements for performance review; a third of authorities have created special posts in strategic management and an authority-wide policy on quality (with a further 40 per cent actively preparing the latter).

Nearly all have revised their structures during the 1990s, though the unitary councils have perhaps been best placed to do so owing to their novel creation, and they have tended to adopt a more explicitly corporate system.* But such an approach is not confined to them: many councils have sought to develop such an approach in response to the new areas of concern and activity which have emerged – employment, economic development, the environment (areas also in which councillors have been able to develop initiatives because they were less subject to government control).† Two thirds of authorities have revised their structures in the last three years.

These developments both reflect and propel the new 'managerial revolution' in the public and private sectors. And a 1993 report on change, drawing on interviews with chief executives, concludes, 'If chief executives have got it right, local government faces more of the same over the next three years.'[11] The follow-up survey in 1996 confirmed this prediction, and concludes that not only are local authorities coming to terms with change but they are 'looking outwards and seeking to learn and improve rather than trying to cope or survive'.‡

One of the consequences of these (and other) changes has been the increase in staff (and member) turnover, especially among chief officers. In the years 1990–94, twenty-three out of thirty-three London chief officers changed; in the metropolitan boroughs it was twenty-one out of thirty-six. Whilst this may be a cause for concern, there is also evidence of gain, in that 'the new ranks of chief executive are certainly more attuned to the new agenda' of putting client needs first and developing new ways of delivering services.[12] The 1996 survey showed that member turnover 'is bringing in cohorts of councillors who are already attuned to the new world of local government'§; they are also playing a larger role as 'change drivers' in their local authorities. Consequently, the new (and changing) local government is here to stay: there can be no going back (indeed local change is being pressed further by the government: see below Chapter 15). One indication of

* See *Local Governance*, no. 2, 1999.
† *Portrait of change*, GMB 1998.
‡ ibid.
§ ibid.

this is that councils are no longer driven by compulsion to submit their services to competition: eight out of ten would do so voluntarily.* Competitive tendering is now firmly entrenched and has changed the pattern of public service management probably for ever.†

Thirdly, *party politics* are providing a motive force for some of these developments (including the turnover, and perhaps politicization of officers.[13]‡ But the party system itself is experiencing important changes. In the last twenty years party politics have obtruded into more council chambers (see Table 10), especially in urban areas.[14] One consequence of this has apparently been the reduction of the number of uncontested seats (e.g., in English county councils, the figures have fallen from 376 in 1977 to sixty-three in 1981 and a mere thirty-three in 1985). Since 1981, we have seen the emergence of the Social Democratic Party which has sought, in alliance with the Liberals, to 'break the mould' of British politics. They have scored some notable election successes (described as 'political earthquakes'), and their achievements at local level have been impressive. In 1981 they had nine council members: in 1986 they had 420. Following their amalgamation into the Liberal Democrat party in 1987, their success continued so that today they have some 4,750 councillors. In 1993 they dominated and ran 53 councils and either ran or shared power in more than a quarter of all councils, though in 1998 their control of councils had fallen to 47. Their success has led to an increase in the number of balanced or 'hung' councils (where there is no overall control by any one party; see p. 248). Thus, for example, in 1977 there were just five hung county councils; in 1989 there were fourteen and in 1998 there were 17 (out of 34). Altogether there are now some 170 such councils without a majority – over a third of the total.

Meanwhile the Conservatives have had very mixed fortunes. For example, in 1989 they regained control of nine counties, and in 1992 they had (outside London) their best results since 1977. But 1993 was calamitous as they lost control of sixteen county councils (losing 500 seats) and leaving them with control of just one (Berkshire). They now

---

* *Portrait of change*, LGMB, 1998.
† *Competition, Contracts and Change*, JRF, 1995.
‡ *Local Government Chronicle*, 27 January 1995, p. 9, and 26 July 1991.

(1999) control six counties, but only 17 others (or 5 per cent in all, though with 4,500 councillors). For its part, after a succession of defeats in general elections (1992 saw its worst election result in ten years), the Labour Party reviewed its policies and drew back from its earlier left-wing stance; the moderates gained the ascendancy (hence 'New' Labour) and have restored the party's fortunes locally and nationally. Although down from over 200 councils in 1997 it now (1999) controls 167 of the 441 councils in Britain (with some 9,000 councillors). For a time in the 1980s the Green Party seemed to be making something of a breakthrough into local politics, but their popularity has waned, probably as a result of the economic recession; though they have won some twenty seats recently. In Wales and Scotland, the nationalist parties (Plaid Cymru and the SNP) control four councils (out of 54), but they have some 300 councillors and anticipate further progress after 1999 with the establishment of their national Assembly/Parliament.

All such developments have important consequences for the organization and management of local authorities,[15] especially the hung council. In different fashion, the party-dominant/monopoly situation affects council management. The stranglehold is open to abuse (see p. 174) and there is justified criticism. But, in practice they are relatively short-lived: only some 14 per cent of councils have been under unbroken one-party control for the last 20 years.[16]

Of equal significance, however, are the changing trends *within* the major parties. In the 1970s and 1980s they became more polarized and assertive than they had been for over thirty years.[17] This is partly because, under Mrs Thatcher, the Conservatives pursued a very market-centred or 'monetarist' approach to public policy, which involved the privatization of state industries and cuts in taxes and in public sector expenditure. Labour on the other hand, moved to the left, as a result of having lost the 1979 general election on what was felt to be a weak socialist programme and performance in office (1974–9), and because of the emergence of more radical, egalitarian and intellectual middle-class activists.[18] Voters witnessed the results of these latter changes in the 'de-selection' by local Labour parties of some long-standing and moderate councillors. The councils became more involved in national and international issues, with local authorities declaring themselves 'nuclear-free zones' (seeking to ban the deployment of nuclear weapons or the transportation of nuclear waste), calling for boycotts of South African products and investments or holding controversial talks with Provisional Sinn Fein.[19]

Labour has since changed almost out of recognition to become New Labour (in which there are so many elements from the previous Conservative regime that it has been dubbed 'Blatcherism' – by Simon Jenkins).

Officers too are feeling the effects of the more ubiquitous and committed party politics: not only is their professional advice often being spurned* or challenged (perhaps on the counter-advice of 'imported' party advisers) but so too (as we saw on p. 182) is their impartial selection and tenure[20] – though some officers themselves have enthusiastically embraced the party commitment, and (in contrast to civil servants) have sought to combine the dual roles of officer and member.[21] As we have seen above (pp. 183, 296ff) such 'twin-tracking' and other political activity is (under the 1989 Local Government and Housing Act) now prohibited for senior officers. And the combination of tight budgets, assertive party politics, current destabilized conventions,[22] government policies (e.g. on education, housing, finance, reorganization, numerous initiatives and Task Forces or CCT) and seemingly perpetual change has caused many senior staff to seek jobs outside local government, or early retirement.[23] While government policies may be causing some officers to leave, others are developing a more openly critical, though not necessarily party political, stance,[24] and some have been encouraged to do so by their professional body.[25]

---

* Party extremism of the urban Left (the 'loony Left') has been mirrored in some councils by the new (or 'raving') Right. One chief officer (in charge of the sale of Westminster's cemeteries in 1988) has declared that, 'I've never had to work in a climate like I worked here – ever, and I've dealt with some pretty difficult Socialist councils before I came here . . . If you put any opposition up, you were either "not one of them", you were opposed to them politically, or you were "negative".' (BBC, *Panorama*, 20 July 1989.) Westminster LB council underwent a special inquiry by the District Auditor and the cemetery sale was subsequently declared unlawful. This council was subject to a further inquiry into its manipulation (under the policy known as 'Building Stable Communities') of council house sales to engineer the location of Tory-inclined voters into key marginal wards – otherwise known as gerrymandering or 'houses for votes'. Subsequently Dame Shirley Porter, the then council leader was surcharged over £20 million (subsequently subject to lengthy appeal).

However, this situation is being modified with the emergence of de-radicalized New Labour.

The fourth and most crucial area of change or contention in local government is *finance* and its consequences for local autonomy and local–central relations.

Local authority expenditure grew significantly up to the mid-1970s as a result of general economic growth, population growth, new and expanded responsibilities (community care and domiciliary services, child care, housing, schools) and the increase in client groups (the elderly, children, disabled, household formation, etc.) together with the quest for improved standards. In 1975, a senior Minister (Anthony Crosland) declared 'the party's over'. Local authorities (not alone) became regularly and continally subject to 'resource squeeze' and 'fiscal stress'[26] – mainly because of reductions in government grant (from 66 per cent in 1976 to 45 per cent 1986–9), coupled with an inadequate, un-buoyant rates system (see p. 357). Meanwhile, economic changes – de-industrialization, unemployment, inflation – created new problems to those from social change (above) and the increasing obsolescence of capital, buildings and sewerage, etc. (e.g. in 1990 the Audit Commission referred to a 'maintenance time bomb' for schools).

One strategy developed in the 1980s was to maximize the use of resources and/or augment them through 'privatization'. This might take the form of total withdrawal of council provision and the transfer of a service to the private sector (e.g. sports facilities) or to individuals (e.g. selling council houses); or it might involve joint provision of a service with a voluntary or private agency (e.g. homes for the elderly). But most commonly, it consisted of competitive tendering by local business and the council's own workforce (or 'direct labour organization') and 'contracting out' council services to private firms or voluntary organizations where it was appropriate (i.e. cheaper). As we have seen (pp. 75ff and 345) these services may be for the public, e.g. refuse collection (whose privatization was pioneered in 1981 by Southend council) or for the local authority itself (such as legal services, auditing, management consultancy, etc.). Such practices are by no means new: local authorities have long engaged private firms for such things as architecture, building, engineering, industrial waste disposal, school transport, etc. (though some are new, such as private security patrols).

The main advantage of this outsourcing arrangement is a possible lowering of costs, easier budgeting (with fixed-price contracts) and flexibility for work involving irregular work flows. But critics are fearful of a lowering of standards, of redundancies, of worse pay and conditions, of loss of service (through bankruptcies), or being held to ransom over subsequent charges, and above all of the adequacy of control and accountability; there are also doubts about the possible savings to be gained.[27] In 1989 it was estimated that 213 local authorities had contracted out at least one service (40 per cent of refuse and cleaning in London), and the estimated annual savings were £42 million.[28] However, by 1993, only an estimated 17 per cent of the value of contracts had been won by the private sector, and in the area of building cleaning, for example, local authority workforces retain 62 per cent of the contracts;[29] by 1996 this had not altered.

Compulsory tendering became an issue because it was pressed on local authorities by the Conservative government (under the Local Government Acts of 1980, 1988 and 1992; see p. 345) – realizing some of the fears expressed by critics (e.g. the reduction in pay and conditions for local authority cleaners, refuse collectors and catering staff.)* Cat and mouse games – or 'creative management' – developed as some councils (especially in Scotland) allegedly sought to obstruct tendering by demanding excessive performance bonds with unreasonable penalties, time limits or documentation. And others have sought to counter privatization (as well as promote their own social policies such as equal opportunities) by 'contract compliance', i.e. insisting that private firms that have contracts with the council observe certain non-commercial considerations and fulfil stringent conditions regarding health and safety, trade union recognition, fair wages, and the employment of women, immigrants and the handicapped. (For example, before abolition, the GLC had contracts worth some £200 million, and nineteen

---

* 60 per cent of councils believe that competition has reduced pay and conditions (*Portrait of change*, LGMB, 1998).

It is an odd coincidence that, while Westminster LB was one of the first councils in Britain to introduce competition and 'new public management' methods, Westminster in California was the first city in California to contract out its fire service (with estimated savings of £7m over five years (W. Eggars, *Cutting Local Government Costs through Competition and Privatisation*, California Chamber of Commerce, 1997).

firms were refused business on grounds of alleged discrimination, compared with 130 firms which did comply with the employment practices requirements.) Such requirements became subject to strict limits under the Local Government Act 1988, and under the Local Government Act 1992 the Minister obtained the power to define and forbid anti-competitive behaviour. An alternative strategy in some councils has been to set up 'enterprise boards' (such as Greater London Enterprise, Merseyside Enterprise Board, Lancashire Enterprises Ltd, West Midlands Enterprise Board, West Yorkshire Enterprise Board), to establish or invest in local companies for the purpose of control, to secure local employment and economic growth, as well as providing income. These boards are free of some of the legal constraints which apply to a local authority, though the Local Government and Housing Act 1989 limits the powers of such companies in which local authorities have an interest. Some critics have regarded them as highly dubious, publicly funded political bodies.

The present government has applauded some of the results of CCT*. But it condemns its compulsory nature and is critical of its inflexibility and effects on service quality. It also points to the costs to staff, to their demoralization and to the whole atmosphere of antagonism which was created. Consequently, it is now abolished, though competitve tendering will live on in Best Value (see below p. 591).

One uncertainty casting a shadow over the policy of competitive tendering and the contracting out of services is that of European law in relation to contracts of employment. Under EC law – the Acquired Rights Directive (77/187) of 1977 – when an undertaking is transferred to another owner, existing employment conditions are also transferred. This was integrated into British law in the Transfer of Undertakings (Protection of Employment) Regulations 1981, often called 'TUPE'. There have been a number of cases which have gone before industrial tribunals or the employment appeals tribunal (EAT) whereby public sector workers have claimed unfair or illegal loss of employment or pay/pensions as a result of contracts being awarded to private companies. The most celebrated case, in August 1993, was that of the successful Eastbourne dustmen, who had been made redundant when

* See Green Paper, *Improving Services through Best Value*, DETR, 1998.

their council's cleansing contract was privatized in 1990. But there have been other cases that have gone against the employees and their unions*, and the legal situation remains unclear. Individual cases may turn on the details of the actual procedure involved at the time of the transfer. The general principle hinges on the definition of 'undertaking' (whether it must include premises, goodwill, etc.) and the extent to which it may be deemed to be commercial in nature. (There are other problems: see *Local Government Studies*, Autumn, 1998.) The position is likely to remain unsatisfactory until there is a definitive ruling, though the government is now seeking to clarify and confirm employees rights (see *Staff transfers in the public sector*, Cabinet Office, 1999). In the meantime TUPE is likely to deter many private contractors from getting involved in council-service provision.

Whatever the overall savings from privatization have been they have not been sufficient to free local authorities from dependence on central grants. And such grants provide a means if not a motive for central control.

Central–local government relations should be seen as a major constitutional issue for the 1990s, as it was for the 1980s. It raises fundamental questions about the place of local government in Britain, accountability and the clash of democratic mandates, and the future of Britain as a liberal–democratic state.

The problem has always existed because there is no clear statement of what the relationship is or should be. Britain has no written or codified constitution and, like so much else in our governmental system, the relationship of local government to central government is left to general understandings or conventions, usually characterized as partnership, cooperation or power-sharing. As far as the law was concerned, Loughlin says its role was

to establish a general framework for the conduct of central/local relations: the work of policy development and policy implementation was channeled through the policy and professional communities with very little active legal regulation, and the courts have played only a marginal role in policing local action, with the active supervisory work being undertaken by central

---

* Such as the Suzen case at the European Court in 1998.

government agencies. (M. Loughlin, *Legality and Locality*, Clarendon Press, 1996, p. 76)

But subsequently, he goes on to say, legislation changed from being facilitative to regulatory with, ultimately, local authorities being 'treated merely as agencies for delivering centrally determined policies'.

It is often held (even amongst Ministers) that in the course of this century, local government has been increasingly subject to central control. This is difficult to evaluate – like the alleged fall in standards of education or morality, measures are difficult to agree or calibrate. But there is now widespread agreement that the longstanding consensus or concordat between central and local government has been broken in recent years – especially since the advent of Conservative rule in 1979. Indeed this was acknowledged by the government itself in 1996.*

It has been suggested that in post-Second World War years, the relationship between local and central government has fallen into three phases. In the first, during the period of economic growth, the relationship was one of consultation and easy-going incremental growth based on a perception of common interests. The second began in the mid-1970s with a tightening of resources and a more 'corporatist' approach (especially via the CCLFG). The third phase, from 1979, was more polarized and confrontational, which resulted in much litigation and a number of dysfunctional or unintended effects, described in total as 'a policy mess'.[31] Strains began to show in the 1970s as both the Conservative and Labour governments sought to reduce the growth of state (including local government) expenditure, but the underlying consensus remained. Since 1979, this has been shattered.

The Conservative government of Margaret Thatcher (elected 1979 and re-elected 1983 and 1987) adopted an unusually forthright and rigid framework for its policies – to the extent that members of the Conservative Party (the so-called 'wets') expressed concern at this uncharacteristic adoption of an ideology. The basis of this doctrinaire approach ('Thatcherism') has been *monetarism*, which implies anti-

* See White Paper, *Government response to the report of the House of Lords select committee on relations between central and local government*, '*Rebuilding Trust*'.

Statism – or getting the state 'off people's backs'. It is held that the private sector would be more thrusting if there were fewer regulations and controls (over employment, planning, etc.), and it could more effectively and efficiently utilize the resources absorbed (especially through taxation) by the public (state) sector.[32] In addition, monetarism involves curbing the money supply to control inflation. This involves reducing state expenditure – including that of local government.

The latter policy has been conducted largely through restrictions on local capital expenditure and through changes in the government grant system – partly by placing tight cash limits on grants (see p. 429); partly by reducing the proportion of grant support (in England from 61 per cent in 1979–80 to 52 per cent in 1984–5 and 46 per cent from 1987 to 1990); and partly by changing the nature of the Rate Support Grant to include (up to 1990) a block grant element (see pp. 348ff). The block grant provided a diminishing proportion of grant aid (the 'taper') for expenditure which exceeded a given 'threshold' level (based on GREAs (i.e. central assessments of local spending needs; see p. 51)). Where there was a wholesale crossing of thresholds, then local authorities' grant entitlements were 'clawed back' to allow total grant entitlements to match the total grant available.

Soon after this system was inaugurated (1981) the Secretary of State (Michael Heseltine) announced (volume) 'target' expenditures for local authorities. Where a local authority's expenditure exceeded this guideline figure, it paid the penalty in lost grant (known as 'holdback'), the result of which was to reduce the actual grant proportion (e.g. in 1985–6, 2.8 per cent of the original grant of 48.8 per cent was held back in penalties). These targets were altered so much that councils protested at the difficulty of 'hitting a moving target' (others called it 'Block Grant Bingo'). But the real cause for concern was that rather than monitoring the overall grant figure, the government was telling each council what it should spend, and further, that it was indicating what councils should spend on particular services. This was compounded by the resurgence of specific grants (see p. 346) (including one for aspects of education and for the new community care) and by the legislation which gave the government power to limit or prohibit councils' subsidies for transport (under the Transport Act 1983) and for council house rents.[33]

Many councils 'overspent' the government's target figures and lost all or some grant (e.g. nearly £800 million during 1982–4). However, they were often able to make good the loss by raising a supplementary rate (or precept). This avenue was closed by the Local Government Finance Act 1982 which abolished the right of councils in England and Wales to raise supplementary rates/precepts, as was already the case in Scotland. The Act also clarified grant 'holdback' powers[34] and dropped plans for rates referendums.[35]

In Scotland, the Local Government (Miscellaneous Provisions) (Scotland) Act 1981 allowed the Minister to reduce the grant to any Scottish council which was planning levels of expenditure (i.e. in the budget estimates) which he regarded as 'excessive and unreasonable'. Thus facing a loss of grant, councils were expected to cut expenditure and so reduce the rates. In practice a number of (Labour) councils (e.g. Lothian) opted for losing grant. So under the Local Government and Planning (Scotland) Act 1982 the screw was tightened and the Minister could actually limit (or 'cap') the rate of any particular council – thus providing another example of 'fiscal centralism'.[36] These powers were augmented when the scheme was extended to England and Wales (under the Rates Act 1984) though it was only applied *ad hoc*, to councils selected by the Minister. In 1991 it became a generalized system so that every council whose planned budget exceeded a stated level of increase or of expenditure would be capped. This regime applied to the community charge/poll tax (which replaced domestic rates 1989/90) and thence to the council tax (in 1993), though councils could appeal to the Minister.[37] In 1988–9, seventeen councils (plus nineteen joint authorities) were capped (amounting to some 20 per cent of current expenditure).[38] In 1990, twenty-one were charge capped and in 1998 there were two. Altogether it is estimated that, if capping had never existed, councils could have spent an extra £1.2 billion on services (though local tax bills would have been around 13 per cent higher, equivalent to an extra £90 a year on an average band D property.)*

Altogether these are massive central powers – the result of what Professors Jones and Stewart call 'panic ad-hocery'.[39] The balance

---

* *The impact of capping on local service provision*, Institute for Fiscal Studies, 1998.

of the constitution is being changed such that, in relation to local government, central government has come to resemble the Big Brother of George Orwell's *Nineteen Eighty-Four*: indeed rate-capping has been called 'knee-capping'. But before considering the significance of these powers, we should consider why the government thought them necessary.

The 1983 White Paper *Rates* gives the following reasons. Firstly to protect ratepayers in general against 'excessive levels of expenditure and therefore of rates' (in October 1985, the government estimated that rate-capping was saving some £300 million per annum). Secondly, the cost of local government is felt to be 'too great a burden on the private sector' and is jeopardizing the economic regeneration of Britain: a reduction in rates would help to reduce the tax burden, increase incentives, increase competitiveness and reduce inflationary pressures. Thirdly, 'the government necessarily have a major interest in local authority services which are national in character, such as education, or of national importance, such as the police . . . [and in] the balance between these and other services'. Fourthly, and above all, the government is responsible 'for the broad conduct of the economy' and is 'determined, through firm control, to reduce public expenditure as a proportion of the Gross Domestic Product' so as to permit a reduction in public sector borrowing (PSBR*, part of which is the LABR) and thus a lowering of interest rates (to encourage investment).

In response, critics have made the following observations: (1) rates form a small part (2–3 per cent) of business costs, and business taxation in Britain (including rates) is comparatively light by international standards; and the effect of selective rate-capping in reducing the tax burden has been estimated at only about 0.5 per cent; (2) rates had been rising no faster than the retail price index, and have reflected the inflation rate rather than contributed to it; (3) rate increases have largely been a reflection (as indeed intended) of the government's own policy of withdrawing grants – both the penalty withholdings (amounting to £260 million during 1983–4) for 'overspenders' and the general reduction in the rate support grant (e.g. in England from

---

* Now known as Public Sector Net Cash Requirement.

61 per cent in 1979 to 46 per cent in 1986–9),[40] as well as central decisions on such matters as the development and pay of police, local government implementation of community care and the statutory sick-pay scheme, keeping redundant schools open, the 1981 Education Act, the introduction of the youth training scheme (YTS) and reduced subsidies for housing benefit; in addition local authorities were affected by high interest rates, and the heavy bill for housing renovation (estimated ultimately at some £20 billion); (4) the 'overspend' (at £900 million in 1984 and £700 million in 1988) was equivalent to little more than 0.5 per cent of total public sector expenditure, and local authorities as a whole did not stray far from the government's targets (despite the latter's arbitrary nature and frequent inadequate allowance for inflation);[41] indeed as a proportion of the GDP local spending fell from 15.9 per cent in 1974–5 to under 13 per cent in 1982–3 and 11.4 per cent in 1987 (such that the local government spending in Britain was below the average for developed countries);[42] meanwhile central government's spending only changed from 33.3 per cent to 31.6 per cent (largely as a result of significant cuts in capital expenditure, especially housing, its proportion of debt also rose while that of local government fell);[43] (5) some of the biggest overspending (and therefore penalized) councils faced some of the greatest problems of unemployment and deprivation, and capping hit many communities in terms of such vital services as schools, libraries, home helps, residential care and housing improvements;[44] (6) the capping mechanisms were unnecessary – indeed they amount to overkill since the worst offenders of overspending (the GLC and the metropolitan counties) had been abolished; and the doubling of the abatement penalties[45] in 1984 had a noticeably cautionary impact on local authorities; (7) there are considerable costs attached to the control process itself, with costs arising from the numerous meetings and mass of communications involved, the production and submission of information, the calculations and assessments, the appeals mechanism, the delays, the legal challenges, the altered timetables and the overall uncertainty and demoralization with the whole procedure engenders: capping manifested the twelfth financial system experienced by local government between 1979 and 1984.[46] Indeed, a report[47] by the Audit Commission attacked the block grant system as confusing and perverse. (The

Commission has also criticized the capital control system as wasteful.)[48]

The government subsequently acknowledged the problems of this grant support system – a large part of what Rhodes calls 'the policy mess' in local–central relations.[49] In 1986, the system of targets and penalties was abandoned (partly, it is alleged, to soothe the shires, which this system hit rather more than the previous GREA mechanisms of tapers and clawback). Domestic rates were abolished and replaced with the community charge/poll tax in 1989 (Scotland) and 1990 (England and Wales), and business rates (UBR/NNDR) were placed under central government control. In a move to lessen the impact of the community charge/poll tax, local authorities were given an additional grant of £4.3 billion; thus local authorities became more reliant on central funding, so that, broadly, over half of local expenditure (net of fee income) was met by government grants, and the remainder from business rates (UBR determined by the government) and from poll tax. When the council tax was introduced to replace the poll tax (in 1993), the balance of local to central funding was unchanged.

In the context of central–local relations, there are a number of points to observe about these financial changes. First it means that some 85 per cent of local finance comes from the government, i.e. RSG + UBR. The remaining 15 per cent (apart from fee income) relies on the council tax.* The council tax therefore finances any expenditure beyond that covered by government funding and revenue from charges, and any increases are likely to be steep because they face the effect of 'gearing' (see p. 367). Councils may well therefore curb their spending for this reason (let alone budget-capping). But it

---

* The precise figure varies according to definition. In the first place, some identify the business rate as a local tax while others see it as a form of government funding/grant. More specifically there are different definitions, conventions and practices regarding accounting periods, capital items, income and expenditure, etc. For example for technical reasons (see *Local Government Financial Statistics*, HMSO) 'current' expenditure is not quite the same as 'revenue' expenditure. 'Expenditure' itself may be treated as 'gross' or 'net' of fee income and perhaps, of specific grants; but 'gross' may *also* mean net of fee income but including capital charges/debt interest, transfers (such as council tax benefit) and perhaps double–counted items (as between services and authorities). Then there are considerations such as inclusion/exclusion of capital depreciation, sale of assets, whether the figures are money figures or 'real' (i.e. allowing for inflation) etc.

may be at the cost of crucial services*. Another consequence may be further increases in fee-charging for services (the scope for which has been increased by recent legislation)[50] and/or an off-loading of council services to the central government or into private hands.[51]

There are some who question the whole need for central involvement in local government expenditure (see below p. 597), arguing that local spending has not been excessive nor damaging to the economy. Critics also argue that the government intervention, both in financial matters and more generally, not only undermines local government but threatens overload and inefficiency at the centre†. Others acknowledge that the government does have a legitimate concern with total expenditure and with local expenditure as a component. But they argue that the government need only control local government expenditure financed by borrowing and central grants; that expenditure financed by rates or the local tax does not impinge on money supply and interest rates,[52] and has a nil or only marginal impact on aggregate demand in the economy.[53] As the *Economist* put it:

One of the few pluralist aspects of the British constitution is the right of elected local councils to decide what level of local services they deem desirable for their areas, and to levy rates accordingly. The proof of this autonomy is that occasionally such services, and such rates, are more lavish than is considered appropriate by central government. Mrs Thatcher regards this autonomy as an offence against her doctrine of public spending restraint and intends to end it.[54]

Furthermore, as Diane Dawson has stated, 'To identify the particular policy objectives of a government with the centre's responsibility for managing the economy is a red herring frequently invoked by governments of both parties.'[56]

Government intervention is also criticized because it confuses accountability. With such a high proportion of local government

* One study suggests that council tenants have been relatively unconcerned about increases in rates[55] and other studies suggest a readiness to face higher taxes for more or better services, e.g. in 1999 Milton Keynes UA and in 1992 and 1993 Tower Hamlets LBC staged referendums with just such results). See too 'Society', p. 15, *Guardian*, 5 January 2000.

† See for example *Local Government Studies*, September 1987, p. 11.

income coming from the government, a small change in grant can have a dramatic effect on the level of local services and council tax – but who is held responsible? This is particularly the case in so far as Standard Spending Assessments are (wrongly) taken to indicate what councils ought to spend on particular services (i.e. hypothecation). 'Accountability to the Secretary of State is substituted for accountability to the local electorate,'[57] for if the government 'allocates' a particular council an expenditure (i.e. having determined its needs) and a rate or local tax level to cover it, what accountability is there left between the local council and its citizens? Whitehall has displaced Town Hall. Why bother to vote for the council? And how can one vote sensibly when it is impossible, for example, to know whether the tax level is the product of council decisions, outdated property valuation, a government decision to alter the business rate (or delay revaluation), a change in the grant or tax limitation,[58] or inadequate allowance for inflation in the SSA or RSG? In effect, in practice local authorities take responsibility or for the actions of the government. (The SSA system has recently been criticized on the grounds of its distortion, inefficiency and injustice[59] and is currently under review by the DETR.)

Furthermore, there is considerable doubt about the validity and wisdom of the whole policy of deflation through public sector expenditure reductions. Some (neo-Keynesian) economists have argued that such a policy could cripple Britain's industrial base and have intolerable social consequences – in terms of crime, family stress, health and social unrest (such as the urban riots of 1981 and 1985).[60] And standards of basic services have suffered, including housing, roads, transport and education. Basically they argue for more state expenditure, and conclude that even if the monetarist policy is right in the long run, the price might be too high.

Some would go further and argue not just that the policy represents the political opportunism of the Conservative central government sequestering Labour councils (e.g. none of the twenty-one councils capped in 1990 was Conservative), but also that it manifests blatant class war: that the attack on local spending is an attack on the welfare services of the working class to provide tax cuts for the rich. (The left-wing Liverpool councillors were determined to resist cuts in local services, but they also sought to avoid penalizing the rate-payers as their view was that it was really the government at fault for 'robbing' the city of £350 million in grants since 1979: hence the deficit budget in 1985–6. For local government as a whole, the estimated loss of grant support for 1979–87 was £17,500 million: See S. Douglas and I. Lord, *Local Government Finance*, LGIU, 1986.)

The price of the attack on local government may be too high in another sense. Local government is a system which diffuses power; it provides local opportunities for choice; and it provides alternative solutions (right or wrong) to local problems. It is the existence of local government which provides part of the 'checks and balances' of our unwritten constitution. Its existence helps to render inaccurate Lord Hailsham's description of our political system as an 'elective dictatorship'. Local government is part of the pluralism which characterizes the liberal-democratic state. Indeed Parliament itself provides inadequate checks and balances on the government: there is much official secrecy and there is Crown or 'public interest' privilege. By contrast, local government is more open, it can be taken to court more easily, local people can challenge local decisions, there is more audit and backbench councillors (including the opposition members) have rights of access to officials and information. It is this which is at risk as local decision-making is circumscribed and centralized. 'In effect, local government has been regarded by the Conservative government and perhaps by past governments not as a basic element in the system of government, but as a subordinate piece of administrative machinery.'[61] As Professors Jones and Stewart have said, with reference to the rate-capping legislation: 'The proposed Bill makes a constitutional change of the greatest significance. It removes from the local authorities that Parliament has set up as elected authorities the right of control over their own tax. It concentrates power to an extent unparalleled in this country since local authorities were created.'[62] In Parliament, the centralizing implications of the rate-capping legislation caused ex-Prime Minister Edward Heath to vote against his Conservative Party and defy a three-line whip: he was the first Prime Minister this century to do this.

Local government and the democratic deficit

We referred on pp. 540, 546 to Conservative (Thatcherite) monetarist policy as seeking to reduce the role of the state. This occurred in a number of areas: sale of state industries and assets, deregulation of employment and transport, market testing and contracting out services and reductions in public sector spending. Local authorities have been a major element in this, having to sell much of their housing stock, to contract out services, to limit their subsidies to transport and, above all, to live within severe constraints on resources. A tier of local government (covering 40 per cent of the population) has been abolished, with many functions being transferred to non-elected or indirectly elected boards. These were augmented (e.g. with fire authorities) when unitary councils were created in 1995–8 (which took some 2,000 councillors out of the system), and (under the Police and Magistrates Courts Act 1994) police services were further detached from local authorities. In the meantime a number of other local non-elected bodies (quangos or qualgos) were being created – Urban Development Corporations (UDCs), Training and Enterprise Councils (TECs or LECs), Housing Actions Trusts (HATs), Grant Maintained Schools (GMS), housing associations, education corporations – all forming part of what John Stewart has referred to as 'the New Magistracy'[63], and contributing to the 'democratic deficit' in Britain. More specific (or 'ring-fenced') grants were introduced (in education and social services), some 35,000 pupils were centrally funded for (assisted) places in private schools, and the determination of teachers' salaries was taken over by the government.

Thus the role and size of the state has diminished. But democratic control has also shrunk partly through privatization and the transfer of services, but partly too because, where the state continues to provide, control is increasingly indirect and tenuous. The latter is evident in central government, where ministerial responsibility has become diluted or blurred as activities are hived off to departmental (internal or 'Next Step') agencies or to the numerous (see p. 355) quangos (including Health Authorities, some of whose functions have subsequently been devolved on to health service trusts). In between lie the contracted-out public services (national and local), and it is a moot point as to how far such an arrangement reduces control and accountability. The Conservative government denied (see below) the democratic deficit – indeed it proclaimed the opposite,[64] particularly in the field of local government where it has been most active. Thus:

(1) The Education Reform Act 1988. This removed polytechnics and colleges from LEA control; introduced a compulsory national curriculum and allowed schools to opt out of LEA control alongside the separately created City Technology Colleges; required LEAs to admit pupils to schools up to their maximum capacity; delegated control of finance (85 per cent, since increased) and staffing to schools' governing bodies (LMS). The Education (Schools) Act 1992 requires schools to be inspected every four years and to publish annual performance indicators (exam results, truancy rates, etc.). The Further and Higher Education Act 1992 removed sixth form and FE colleges from LEAs and gave them independent corporate status (financed through the Further Education Funding Council).

(2) The Local Government Act 1980 introduced the compulsory sale of council houses, and the Housing Act 1988 allows council tenants to opt for an alternative landlord and, where appropriate, for estates to be taken into the hands of Housing Action Trusts. Meanwhile, councils were encouraged to transfer their houses to housing associations (though not encouraged to build). The Housing, Land and Urban Development Act 1993 extended the sale of council houses and set up the Environment Agency.

(3) The Local Government Act 1980 introduced compulsory competitive tendering (CCT) for certain local authority building, roads and other works/services and the Local Government Act 1988 extended this to include catering, grounds maintenance, vehicle maintenance, refuse collection, cleaning and (subsequently) sports/ leisure facilities; others could be added by the Minister. It also strengthened the ban on political advertising (see p. 186); gave district auditors powers to issue 'stop orders' to prevent unlawful expenditure. The Local Government Act 1992 extended competitive tendering to the 'white collar' activities of local authorities. And under the Trade Union Reform and Employment Rights Act 1993, LEA careers services were put out to tender.

(4) The Local Government Planning and Land Act 1980 introduced the block grant, with explicit expenditure assessments and grant reduction thresholds. The Local Government Finance Act 1988 replaced domestic rates with the community charge or poll tax; non-domestic (or business) rates were taken over and redistributed by the government; the Rate Support Grant become the Revenue Support Grant, which is a fixed amount per annum; the chief finance officer is given the duty to enforce prudence in their council's financial affairs. The Local Government Finance Act 1992 replaced the community charge/poll tax with the council tax, but at the same (low) level of 15 per cent of contribution to local revenue and under the continued risk of capping.

(5) The Local Government and Housing Act 1989. This was the government's main reponse to the Widdicombe Report on 'The Conduct of Local Authority Business' (1986). It regulates the appointment and management of staff and restricts their right to engage in political activity; creates a 'monitoring officer' and requires the designation of a head of the paid service; regulates local authorities' interests in companies; controls capital expenditure by limiting borrowing (or credits) and councils' use of their own assets sales receipts; prevents councils from subsidizing their housing rents; permits local authorities to charge for a wider range of services.

It is calculated that since 1979 local authorities have been subjected to some 200 pieces of legislation (though some have been inspired by local government itself) and in the words of the Controller of Audit, local government has been 'under siege'.[65] Local authorities are being told what do to (impose the national curriculum, raise rents, contract our services, etc.). And they are being bypassed as functions are transferred to other, non-elected, bodies – development corporations, training councils, housing associations and trusts, governing bodies, funding councils, careers companies, the National Parks Commission and the Environment Agency. Thus in 1995, of the estimated 5,750 quangos (with some 66,000 appointees) 5,207 were operating at local level. Altogether they were spending £60 billion, compared to local government's £73 billion and compared to their expenditure of £42 million in 1979.* 'Quangocrats' thus outnumber elected councillors (22,000).† What has made the situation more objectionable is the apparent, though understandable (party-preference) mode of appointment.[66] They often receive higher allowances than councillors too.[67]

The government has not denied the magnitude of the changes. But it has denied the democratic damage.[68] Many of the changes were being made in the name of the citizen and taxpayer, in pursuit of effectiveness, efficiency and economy. They also sought liberation – 'setting the people free' – through the provision of opportunity, ownership and choice. Under Conservative reforms tenants have been given choice, patients have choice, parents of school children have choice. The Minister responsible for overseeing the implementation of the Citizen's Charter, William Waldegrave, proclaimed that the government's public service reforms were 'helping to restore a proper balance to the relationship between State and citizen'.[69] He said that accountability was being increased because more information on service procedures and outcomes was being made available, and that there was a greater clarity or transparency of the link between policy formulation and its implementation (i.e. through the purchaser/provider split).

He also asserted that 'the key point is not whether those who run the service are elected, but whether they are producer or consumer responsive. Services are not necessarily made to respond to the public simply by giving citizens a diffuse democratic voice in their makeup.'[70] However, one recent study has thrown considerable doubt on this; that consumers – parents, tenants, patients – had gained little or nothing owing – paradoxically – to central intervention.[71] Also where there is a lack of real choice (as with, say, hospitals or community psychiatric services), the only means of influence is through the political

---

* See *The Untouchables*, Democratic Audit Paper 3, 1996.
† A century ago, 12,000 people were elected to govern London. The same number still govern the capital, but only 1,000 are elected: the rest are appointed: Simon Jenkins, *The Times*, 20 September 1995. However, many councillors are themselves members of quangos – indeed the government is said to have appointed many ('thousands') to NHS Trusts (*Local Government Chronicle*, 6 August 1999, p. 12). Some 43% of councils have taken, or are taking action to hold quangos to account (*Modern local government – taking the initiative*, LGA, 1999. See too p. 462 above.

process. In the area of local authority social services, the opportunity for meaningful choice is often extremely limited in practice. It is also suggested that many of the changes only transfer power from one set of professionals to another.[72]

The enabling council

The Conservative government increasingly saw local authorities as 'enablers' rather than 'providers'. This concept was most evident in the field of housing, where government policy reduced council housing stock through sales of over 1 million dwellings since 1979. It also provided the rationale for the policy of compulsory tendering. It was given added impetus by the government's acceptance (in July 1989) of the main recommendation of the Griffiths Report on community care of the elderly and the mentally disabled. Under the NHS and Community Care Act 1990, local authorities were given the leading role in assessing needs and designing, organizing and purchasing care services and not acting primarily as direct providers. 85 per cent of expenditure had to be channelled through non-council agencies.*

To many people, especially those who believe in the collective or State provision of goods and services, the concept of the enabling authority represents a threat to local government; it is perceived as a means of lowering or cheapening service standards, of eroding the welfare state (in line with the Conservative government's policy of changing the 'culture of dependency' to a 'culture of enterprise') and of weakening local authorities' political role or 'clout'.[73] Yet the notion is not entirely new; to some extent local authorities have been 'enabling' for many years[74] and it has increasingly wide support (including that of the Labour Party). But it is a matter of scale, emphasis and, above all, meaning. Certainly there are many officers who welcome the managerial freedom which 'the competitive council' has provided, and there are those who support the view that local government has been too 'cocooned by protective legislation'.[75] Nicholas Ridley, when Secretary of State, once declared that his ideal council would be one

* This requirement ceased in 1998 under the Labour government.

that met once a year to award contracts for all its services to the private sector (a view which, apart from anything else, overlooks the council's role in drawing up the service/contract specifications and monitoring its implementation and outcome, together with its role in securing adequate coordination). Later he acknowledged that councils should have a providing role,[76] but within a more diverse service provision, with a variety of agencies working alongside councils. Thus:

The role of the local authority will no longer be that of the universal provider. But it will have a key role in ensuring there is adequate provision to meet needs, in encouraging the various providers to develop and maintain the necessary services, and where necessary in providing grant support or other assistance to get projects started, and to ensure that services are provided and affordable for the clients concerned.[77]

Arguably, the essence of government is control or regulation of the community – originally (in the case of local government) in the shape of law and order and, in the nineteenth century, environmental health, slums, etc. Provision of services came later. In this respect, it is perhaps worth recalling the original reasons for the state provision of services: the family and voluntary sector cannot always provide sufficiently or consistently; the private enterprise or market system can fail to meet the needs (welfare, education, etc.) of those without money and it can exploit its (often) monopoly situation;[78] and there are aspects of society (conservation, public health, etc.) which can only be dealt with on a collective basis.

A broader view of the enabling role sees it as an opportunity to develop more creative local government, with councils more responsive to the needs of their communities and placing themselves at the centre of a network of formal and informal links with local groups, businesses and individuals. Councils here have the role 'to identify and articulate the collective needs and aspirations of its own community' through actions as a lobbyist, promoter, coordinator, managing agent and service provider.[79] This view is expressed by Michael Clarke and John Stewart as one where:

The local authority accepts that its direct provision of services is but one means of providing for the community among many. Its role as an 'enabling' council is to use all the means at its disposal to meet the needs of those who live within its area.[80]

Local authorities are having to learn that they can be local government even where they cannot act directly. The management of influence is required as well as the management of action.[81]

They suggest councils have become so immersed in the business of ensuring services are provided day by day that they have often lost sight of a wider role – acting with and speaking on behalf of their community on issues other than local government services:

In the past local authorities have defined their role by the services provided. Committees, departments and professions have been structured around them. The business of the authority has been to deliver them. Councillors' attention has focused on service production as the main expression of the interface with the community. At times, many seem to have become more absorbed in the problems of production than the needs of the community . . . Freed from the assumption of self-sufficiency and the need to produce all it does directly, the enabling council can define its role not by the services it produces but by a broader agenda of concerns . . . Councillors will focus on whether needs are being met rather than on the detailed problems of production . . . It is a recognition that the role of the local authority can be one of *local government* with concerns for its community which extend beyond service provision . . . It needs to recognise the resources that lie within communities and to develop them.[82]

As a result, local authorities would have the task of constantly searching for gaps and weaknesses in community provision; they would continue to make some direct provision, but they would also work through and with other organizations; aiding, stimulating, pump-priming, advising, guiding, regulating, inspecting.[83] Local authorities should break with their tradition of direct provision or 'self-sufficiency' and analyse 'what local government bureaucracy is good at providing, as well as what it is not so good at accomplishing'.[84] The Audit Commission, as a result of the Education Act 1988, envisages the reorganization of LEAs as they change to become 'leaders, partners, planners, informers, regulators and bankers'.[85]

Local government has been understandably cautious and on the defensive; but it need not be, since 'in reality significant opportunities have opened up which will relieve it of the burden of day-to-day management of services to focus on broader policies'.[86] They should 'share the ownership of problem-solving with others'.[87]* In the latter respect councils have been urged to form partnerships with, and contract out services to, other local or public authorities and trusts, the private sector, or voluntary and cooperative organizations; to devolve more management to users (e.g. tenants) and help communities to solve their problems, providing vouchers to enable customers to buy services both within and outside the local authority; to conduct surveys to find out what the public thinks, creating forums for discussion of issues, giving publicity to issues of concern, linking groups together. Their overview role is seen as particularly important since, with many and various agencies involved, there will be problems of coordination and steerage as well as the risk of unequal treatment and user access.

Many councillors have become concerned about their future not just because of local authorities' reduced role in direct service provision but also because of the changes in the management of councils: the widespread introduction of local authority 'cabinets', political mayors and two-tier councillors is unsettling.[88] In the light of this Professor Jones suggests councillors should develop the role of consumer proponent and promote consumer democracy:

In the new era they could take on the role of representing consumers, acting as their champions as they draw up policy and the specification of performance for different services and as they monitor and evaluate the performance of the providers, whoever they are. Councillors would act on behalf of consumers. In this sense 'consumers' means not just those who receive a particular service, but also potential consumers who may be denied access.

Councillors could see themselves as advocates of consumers in their wards, districts and areas, expressing in council and committee meetings (and other

---

* There is a close parallel between this and what has been happening in the field of education, where teachers have become 'facilitators' in the new, 'wired-up' student-centred classroom. Teachers are still very much involved in the education process – perhaps more so – but they too are finding it difficult to adjust to a culture in which they are no longer centre-stage with talk and chalk. Similarly, under the NHS reforms, health authorities plan and purchase rather than directly provide medical services.

settings) the concerns of their constituents. But they need not constrain themselves to services for which the council is or was responsible but may also become involved in other public services . . . and even voice concerns about providers . . . So, instead of championing their 'own' services, councillors could play a lead role in championing their consumers.[89]

But to fulfil this role properly, councils themselves need to be 'enabled'; they need freedom from central controls, less circumvention and unilateral transference of responsibilities by the government, and more financial resources that are truly local. Some councils, in pursuit of the 'consumer watchdog' role, have run into the problem of *ultra vires* (in relation to conducting opinion polls). Thus local authorities also need to be given the power of 'general competence'[90] or something similar such as the power of local initiative.*

So far they can be quite encouraged by the words and deeds of the present Labour government (elected 1997) many of whose ideas and aims chime closely with those expressed above (indeed the government has drawn substantially on them.) As Prime Minister, Tony Blair has promised to restore power to local authorities but 'there can be no return to the bygone era of big local government, where the council tried to do everything . . . We will bring decision-making back to people – though for councils to get more powers they must modernise, and change.'†

They also need the support, confidence and goodwill of the public. This can be enhanced by the process of enabling, and at the same time it provides one of the motives for this new approach. For it can be seen as a response to the changing environment of local government – the growth of private provision (of welfare, health, housing, transport, etc.) and the trend to 'consumerism', where the 'customer is king', increasingly aware of his or her rights, becoming less grateful for services received, seeking variety and quality or value for money (including in taxes, national and local) and exercising choice to express or achieve individual identity through customized design, specialization and 'post-Fordism'.[91] This has thrown into relief the form and

* See, for example, J. Stewart, *An Experiment in Freedom*, IPPR, 1991 and, D. King and J. Pierre, *Challenges to Local Government*, Sage, 1990.
† *Local Government Voice*, LGA, July 1998, p. 4.

content of state provision, and has given rise to the criticism that public services are, variously, too bureaucratic, unresponsive, inflexible, wasteful, impersonal, uniform, paternalistic and professions- or union-dominated.[92] It can be argued that 'it is not merely a matter of building support for local services, but rather that services might not deserve to survive unless they are made more accountable and user-friendly. It may be that the final battle for the future of local government will lie between the decentralisers and the privatisers.'[93] The head of the Audit Commission believes that 'The best of local authority service provision has nothing to fear from competition,'[94] and councils are becoming much more public-service orientated and are 'putting people first' through decentralization, customer contracts, user panels, increased information, consumer (and staff) surveys[95] and other 'marketing' devices.[96] Again such developments are very much in tune with the government's current vision and proposals for local government (see below).

However, while there are undoubted gains, there are also risks attached to this new competitive environment. In seeking to protect or promote the interests of themselves or their profession, service or council, local authorities and their staff should not lose sight of the public interest nor their sense of public service. The traditions of British public service are something of which we can be proud – integrity, professionalism, fairness and a sense of service. A more commercial culture can soon erode these values and create a more instrumental and selfish attitude and approach.

The challenge of a changing environment

We have seen how local government is responding to changes in its environment or context. Some of these changes (such as the penetration of parties or the greater assertiveness of councillors) are more or less self-induced; others (more limited resources, contracting out, loss of domain) are largely the result of government policies; and still others, such as enhancing participation and democratic renewal, partnerships and Best Value derive from both central and local government. But there are developments which are effectively beyond control, though they have important implications for local government. These are dealt with briefly below.

Population changes are affecting local authorities in a number of ways. The changing age structure in the 1980s brought a 25 per cent fall in secondary-school rolls and a 50 per cent increase in the frail and vulnerable elderly (over-85s). The former is now being reversed (accompanied by a growth in further and higher education students though, with a likely surplus of primary schools (Henley 1996)) but the latter is likely to continue. So too is the fall in the population of working age, and local authorities have experienced shortages of professional staff (such as accountants, lawyers, planners, IT staff, social workers). This may lead to greater contracting out of services; it may have an impact on personnel policies, such as pay, training and retention, and above all on the recruitment of and greater opportunities for women (with its consequential withdrawal of unpaid, informal care in the community and its increasing demand for nursery school places and child-minding facilities). It is also likely to influence industrial relations and trade union power. Increasing early retirement is providing opportunities for more people to become involved in their local communities.

The traditional family continues to decline and a wider range of household formations is emerging. The most significant growth here is for single-parent families and people living alone – with consequential effects on the demand for housing and child-care provision. There is also an increasing demand for leisure/recreational facilities, particularly in the fastest-growing middle-aged group of the population. And there are a number of broader, so-called 'wicked issues' facing local authorities – 'greening' and environmental sustainability, traffic congestion, rising levels of crime and fear of crime. Such problems are increasingly being addressed by authorities adopting a community governance approach by working with other councils, public agencies, voluntary and private organizations, etc. – a pattern which will accelerate under government plans.*

Globalization has many aspects. The 'world village' created by high-speed communications and transport means that problems and solutions cross national boundaries, and national governments are

---

* See Chapter 15 below; also M. Clarke, *Handling the Wicked Issues*, INLOGOV, 1996.

often powerless to intervene – whether it involves transfer of money, of capital, of information, of workers, of refugees, of environmental hazards, etc. Globalization and the revolution in technology, coupled with fierce economic competition (including in such areas as education or retailing, which, with the Internet, need not even involve travel), are helping to create a different view of the world. One consequence is that left-of-centre governments are reconciling themselves to market mechanisms (known in Britain as 'the Thatcherization of the Labour Party'), with consequences for policies in such areas as low taxation, restricted public expenditure, scaling down the welfare state, and increasingly adopting the management methods and ethos of private business. It has been suggested that Britain is particularly vulnerable.*

The reach of international organizations (IMF, WTO/GATT, World Bank, International Labour Office, the UN) and sub-global arrangements (such as the European Union) is wide and growing. The consequences range from decisions on debt write-off to regulation of asylum-seeking and working conditions/pay, citizenship rights (see p. 408) and international welfare and redistribution (such as EU structure funds). Local authorities will gain or lose as their local economies succeed or fail. Councils themselves will face competition (from French streetcleaners or Taiwanese word/data-processing services, for example). And they will continue to feel the effects of constraints on public expenditure, as well as being held to ransom (over planning matters, etc.) by businesses which can easily transfer elsewhere, or coping with the additional costs of inward migration and asylum-seeking.

In general, the Henley Centre see that global forces will require local authorities to intervene in the local economy, especially

to secure competitive advantage . . . through appropriate supply-side measures to enable local producers to achieve higher levels of value added through innovation . . . [However,] the imperative for local government is to prevent the attraction of inwards investment becoming a game in which some local authorities benefit at the expense of others, through renewed emphasis on

---

* Because of our universal language, our large inward investment, our large stock of capital at home and overseas, and our special relationship with the USA.

social justice and judicious supply-side intervention. (*Social and Economic Trends 2005*, LGMB, 1996.)

They also forecast that economic internationalism and European integration is likely 'to reinforce the cycle of "cumulative causation" that structurally favours the south'. These forces are also

leading to the emergence of a network society in which traditional patterns of power, and of organisation based around the fixities of territory . . . are overlaid by a continuously changing kaleidoscope of cross-cutting patterns . . . The new paradigms and patterns of governance are multi-level, multi-nodal and multi-national. And the more imaginative local authorities know that change and innovation is not an option, but a necessity, and that inter-organisational networks provide an opportunity not only to share the risks and pool the findings from experiment, but also to create powerful learning networks to support the processes of continuous change and adaptation. (J. Benington, 'Saints or Sinners?', the *Guardian*, 24 June 1998.)

Population is also on the move, drifting from north to south and moving out of the inner urban areas to the suburbs and beyond – with social, economic and political consequences, and bringing problems of planning, transport, de-industrialization, dereliction and unemployment to local authorities. Over 40 per cent of jobs in manu-facturing and mining were lost during the 1980s.[98] Traditional com-munities are altering with the changing ethnic composition and more generally with the growth of divorce (at 170,000 per annum), reconsti-tuted families and single parents (one in seven families) – all amounting to what has been described as an 'imminent threat to our social ecology'.[99]

Information technology is not new to local government. But it is beginning to affect its operation in new ways. First it is changing the relationship between local authorities' central departments and their service departments as the latter become better informed and less dependent on the former, particularly as service managers are caught up in competitive tendering.[100] It also allows for decentralization without loss of control. Secondly, elected members increasingly have the facility to key in to council mainframe computers and gain access to reports and appropriate data. Some authorities provide their councillors with micro computers for this and related purposes: in a recent survey 16 per cent of councils said they gave members access to information technology to aid their decision-making and casework activities.[101] And thirdly, service users are being informed and empowered by the provision of high street viewdata (in libraries etc.), where they can check such things as their eligibility for benefits, education grants, etc., opening times of council facilities, waiting lists, charges, names of councillors, etc. The survey showed 40 per cent of the councils in the north made such provision compared to only 18 per cent of southern councils.[102]

Finally the European Union has an increasing number of implications for local government. Local authorities are increasingly called upon for information about the EU in general and on particular aspects, e.g. the significance for business of standards, competition and State subsidies. Businesses and local trading standards/consumer protection departments are at the moment affected by some 600 Acts and Regulations, 20 per cent of which emanate from the EU. Since 1993 about 80 per cent of the consumer protection legislation is affected by harmonization within the EU. There are literally dozens of EU directives just dealing with additives and materials in contact with food, responsibility for which falls on local authority trading standards officers. There will be new rules governing waste disposal (restricting land-fill for example) and other environmental controls (such as transport and highways). There will be new rules governing employment and health and safety; these alone will cost local authorities millions of pounds to implement[103] (just as the Working Time Directive which, since 1999 limits working hours, has in local authority social care provision for example).

However, local authorities' principal interest in Europe concerns finance* and they have derived substantial funding from the EU. This is diminishing as funds are diverted to other agencies (such as voluntary organizations, universities, etc.). It is also likely that in future fewer funds will be flowing to Britain as a result of the changing identification of Objective 2 status (and perhaps as a result of new members joining). In 1999 there were discussions within the EU about reducing Britain's

---

* K. Young, *Portrait of change*, 1998, LGMB.

annual contributions rebate. There is also European Monetary Union and its implications for local authorites' pension funds and investment portfolios, financial transactions, accounts, staff training, etc. as well as for a number of the aspects mentioned above. These will intensify if (when?) Britain does join the Euro.*

Another concern is that 'the development of the European Community . . . seems to be having a centralizing impact upon member-states . . . the institutions of the Community are likely to take greater powers upon themselves. Therefore, unless the position of local government is more firmly entrenched, there could be a real shift of power away from the individual citizen to institutions which seem remote to him or her.'[104] Paradoxically, while the Prime Minister, John Major, argued for greater independence or safeguards for the UK (through opt-out clauses) in the Maastricht Treaty of 1992, he was less willing to apply the same principle (of 'subsidiarity')† to local government within Britain.

Inevitably, complex problems require complex solutions. How well local authorities will provide solutions to the problems outlined above remains to be seen, though many have already displayed initiatives in, for example, supporting their local economy and helping to reduce the impact of unemployment.[105] In the words of the Audit Commission, 'In any period of uncertainty and change, the well-managed organization survives more successfully than the rest. That will be true of local authorities in the next decade.' The AC then provides a checklist of advice for well-managed councils.[106] But their capacity to respond to problems has been hindered by the actions of the government, with the reorganizations, the loss of functions, the creation of special agencies, the reduced resources and the increased steerage of their general and particular expenditure.

Local government has not been alone in this assault by the 'strong State': legislation has significantly curbed the power of trade unions, the church has been attacked for 'interference' in social affairs, the

---

* See *Public Treasurer*, January 1999.

† 'Government should be provided at the smallest, most local level possible which is consistent with the efficient and acceptable delivery of services' (Treaty of Maastricht).

media have been issued 'stop notices' and a standards watchdog for broadcasting, the institutions of higher education have been squeezed financially and placed at risk of losing their autonomy with the loss of academic tenure and the creation of less independent finance bodies, and the legal institutions similarly threatened. There is an 'apparent drift towards authoritiarianism',[107] government policies are moving Britain towards a 'mass society' – where intermediate bodies, between the government and the people, are weak and vulnerable (as they were in Germany prior to Hitler's rise to power).[108] Thus Professor Newton feels that Britain stands within sight of a form of government which is 'more highly centralised than anything this side of [pre-1990] East Germany'.[109] Referring to the financial settlement for local authorities, the *Guardian* in 1993 said 'Central controls over local government in the UK now rival the old Eastern command economies. This is centralism gone mad'.[110] It was to get worse, with the controls resulting from the local authority financial and grants system being described as actually *greater* than those exercised under the Soviet regime.[111]

Local government has been especially hit because it does not operate on the basis of the dominating principle: market forces. Local authorities manifest so much of the 'positive' state for it is not government ministers and their departments which build schools or employ teachers and social workers or plan cities. In so far as the state and its expenditure has been rolled back, local authorities have found themselves in the front line. Lord Jenkins has called it 'civic degradation'.[112]

Thus we return to the opening theme of this book; the proper role of local government in Britain. It is this which has recently been under threat[113] (and now under review, and perhaps renewal?). But local authorities have not received much defensive support from the general public – perhaps because the national government gets its own message across more successfully and there is too great a readiness to allow local matters to be subsumed by national.

At one time it was assumed that local government would be 'safe' from excessive central interference because, ultimately, the central government depends upon the goodwill and expertise of local government for the delivery of national environmental, economic and social services (i.e. the relationship of power-dependence: see p. 434). This safeguard has now become less certain as the central government's commitment to such service provision diminished. Central government has become less reliant on local authorities as there are more alternative suppliers/providers – the private sector, appointed bodies and voluntary organizations. Local government is now part of a more mixed local economy of provision, and indeed local authorities are themselves frequently commissioners of services. Yet local government is robust and still has a large, if perhaps changing, part to play. Local authorities have shown adaptability and resilience especially in the way they have coped with the changes in finance (from rates to poll tax to council tax), with reorganizations, with the development of CCT and with the implementation of many complex policies on education, community care, children's services and housing. They have also displayed imagination and innovation in their internal management structures, in listening and responding to their communities (see below) and in creating decentralized policy and management structures and delivery systems.

Despite what is often said, there is evidence of a considerable reservoir of support and goodwill towards local government.[114] A MORI survey in 1996 revealed that more people think of their local council than any other service when they hear the term 'public services'. Opinion polls have shown that 55 per cent of electors disapprove of capping[115] and a large majority (up to 75 per cent) want local taxes to be determined by local councils rather than by central government,[116] 39 per cent want less central control of councils (against 14 per cent who want more) and twice as many people are satisfied with the performance of local government as with that of central government.[117] In 1995 49 per cent of people were very or fairly satisfied with the way their councils were doing thier job (cf. 28 per cent for/with Parliament and 18 per cent EU;[118] in 1997, the figure for local government was 52 per cent and for Parliament only 23 per cent.* And two thirds of the public think they get good value for money from local government.[119]† Local authorities can build on this – indeed they are bound to with the opportunities and encouragement of the new government.

* *Speaking for Communities*, LGA/MORI, 1997.

† Young injects a note of caution about figures such as these when he suggests that positive levels of satisfaction might simply be extensions of feelings of contentment with life in general.[120]

15

NEW LABOUR: NEW DEAL FOR LOCAL GOVERNMENT?

A Report on local government by a Parliamentary Committee recently stated that:

Over a long period local authorities have lost powers, whether to central government or quangos, not to conform to some over-arching philosophy but in a way which has incrementally soured relations, weakened democracy and blurred accountability. (*Rebuilding Trust*, Report by the House of Lords' Select Committee on Relations Between Central and Local Government, HMSO, 1996.)

Similarly, after a ten-year programme of research into the relations between central and local government, by the Joseph Rowntree Trust, Charles Carter concluded that 'The long years of rancour and mistrust must be brought to an end through measures that strengthen democracy and allow local diversity to flourish'.*

In May 1997, the Labour government was elected. It won its highest ever number of Parliamentary seats (with 418 MPs) and a huge majority (of 179) over the other parties (among whom the Conservatives polled their lowest share of votes since 1832). Labour therefore had a clear mandate† to govern and implement its manifesto proposals. Among these was commitment to revise and modernize the constitution of Britain by introducing some fundamental changes – to the House of Lords, state secrecy, regional devolution, Human Rights, the electoral system and to local government. When elected it was described as having 'hit the ground consulting'.

In Opposition the Labour Party had promised to restore freedom and power to local authorities and to redress the situation portrayed

* *Members One of Another*, JRF, 1996.
† Though its share of the vote has only 43 per cent.

above. The shadow Environment Minister (Frank Dobson) said that the 'Labour Party wishes to give greater political weight to local government in its general decision-making. We want to enter the new century with a bigger role for councils'.[1] A Labour Party document declared that

'We will act to decentralize power, to lift decisions ... out of Westminster and Whitehall and bring them closer to the people they affect. Subsidiarity is as good a principle in Britain as it is in Europe ... Local civic government in Britain should be revived. It should be less constrained by central government, but at the same time more accountable to local people.'*

Labour's 1997 Election Manifesto declared,

Over-centralisation of government and lack of accountability was a problem in governments of both left and right. Labour is committed to the democratic renewal of our country through decentralisation and the elimination of excessive government secrecy ... Local decision-making should be less constrained by central government, and also more accountable to local people.

And in government, the Minister (Hilary Armstrong) said that the government wanted 'to reinvorate local government, to rekindle and reignite the energy that is so patently there to provide energetic local solutions to local problems'. Consequently, as Tony Travers put it, for local government: 'Labour's victory seemed like the end of a nightmare.'† However, disturbed sleep may precede (perhaps displace) sweet dreams

One of the new government's first actions was to sign the Council of Europe's Charter of Local Self-Government (created in 1985), which seeks to lay down basic safeguards for protecting the role of local government within state systems.[2] The previous government had resisted the call to do so and, although the membership of the Charter is more symbolic than substantive, it does recognize in writing for the first time local government's consitutional legitimacy. It was an indication of Labour's attitude to local government.

Within days of the election, the government met local government

---

* *New Labour, New Life for Britain*, Labour Party, 1996.
† The *Guardian*, 24 April 1998, p. 7.

leaders (via the LGA) and soon established the Central/Local Partnership (of Ministers and councillors). This forum meets several times a year and discusses and negotiates issues and policies of mutual concern (finance, local government reform, health, education, regeneration, etc.). It is an attempt to create more coherent and constructive contacts to replace the 'old-style ... formal, ritualistic gatherings'.[3] Consequently, at the second meeting, the two sides signed a concordat setting out the terms of the (closer) working relationship between them and included details on joint working arrangements, consultations and the exchange of information. This 'framework document', laying down six main principles (see Appendix 31) was substantially based on that devised by the LGA in 1996 (and urged in the House of Lords' Committee Report) to address the (then) government's lack of consultation. (It might also be noted that in August 1997 a new Cabinet Secretary – the most senior civil servant – was appointed: Sir Richard Wilson, who is familiar with and well disposed to local government.)

At an LGA conference in 1997, the Minister for local government (Hilary Armstrong) declared that 'We are not just a new Government, we are a new type of Government. Our decisions will not be handed down from on high. Nor will we abuse our position and impose solutions and policies dreamt up behind closed doors . . . We want to hear your ideas and we want you to tell us what you think of ours.' In practice, the government has listened and it has acted, and quite quickly: in the form of the Local Government (Supplementary Credit Approvals) Act 1997, it has begun the phased release of house-sales receipts, and under the Local Government (Contracts) Act 1997 it has removed the doubts surrounding local authorities' powers to enter into contracts with companies. It also plans to allow councils more scope to trade, by revising the Local Authorities Goods and Services Act 1970. And it also eased the cap on local spending levels.

Modernizing local government

In 1998, the government issued six consultative (or green) papers containing its proposals for modernizing and renewing local government.

Our agenda is the renewal of local democratic government, leading local communities and serving local people. We want councils to gain a new democratic legitimacy. We want them to follow new ways of working and to adopt new disciplines. We want councils, renewed in this way, to have the new powers they need to lead their communities. And we want finance systems which match their roles and responsibilities. (Preface to the DETR papers)

The subsequent White Paper, *Modern Local Government: In Touch with the People* (Cmd 4014) was published in July 1998. It contains the government's strategy for reform and modernization stretching over ten years or more. The Secretary of State, John Prescott, described it as the most comprehensive package of reforms for generations, one which will lead to 'the rebirth of democratic local government'.

A number of these reforms have been dealt with (in passing) in the chapters above. Here we shall examine them more fully and provide some assessment. They fall into three broad aspects – *political, managerial, financial*. And, while to a large extent the changes all hang together, they will be dealt with separately.

The *political* reforms range from the broad objective of 'community leadership' to the rather narrower, though still important, one of increasing voter turnout. Councils are being urged to break out of 'the old culture of paternalism and inwardness' and to develop new attitudes since 'there is no future in the old models of councils trying to plan and run most services. It does not provide the services which people want, and cannot do so in today's world.' Furthermore, as directly elected bodies, 'they are uniquely placed to provide vision and leadership to their local communities'.

Community leadership is at the heart of the role of modern local government. Councils are the organisations best placed to take a comprehensive overview of the needs and priorities of their local areas and communities and lead the work to meet those needs and priorities in the round. Modern Britain faces a number of key challenges . . . such as sustainable development, social exclusion, crime, education and training. Councils are at the centre of local public service and local action to tackle these difficult issues . . . Councils are ideally placed to work with government, their communities and the wide range of public, private and voluntary sector bodies who operate at local level and who need to come together if these challenges are to be successfully addressed. (*Modern Local Government: In Touch with the People* (White Paper 1998) para 8.1–8.4)

Consequently local authorities are to have a new power 'to promote the economic, social and environmental well-being of their areas . . . in taking decisions . . . councils will have to weigh up the likely effects . . . against the three objectives – economic, social and environmental – and if necessary strike a balance to ensure that the overall well-being of their area is achieved. The new duty . . . will include a requirement for councils to secure the development of a comprehensive strategy for promoting the well-being of their area' (paras 8.8, 8.10, 8.12).

In order to fulfil this new role, local authorities will have to get 'in touch with their local people'; they need to become outward-looking, listening and responsive – often by following the lead given by those 'many councils [which] have already adopted new and imaginative measures' (such as those dealing with the environment under Local Agenda 21)*. While there are material advantages to councils in consulting their local communities (such as the conferment of 'beacon' status and the avoidance of failing Best Value inspection) there is to be a statutory duty on councils to consult and engage with their communities such that consultation and participation become 'embedded into the culture of all councils'. Councils will thus become less paternalistic in their outlook and mode of operation.

Clearly, they will also have to work more in partnership with others as 'there is an overwhelming need for greater cohesion and coherence at the local level of all those – public sector, business, voluntary bodies – whose activities and efforts can affect local communities'. Thus, apart from coordinating their own (education, transport, land-use, etc.) development plans and fitting them into the 'wider picture', local authorities will have to ensure coherence with those of other agencies (such as Health Improvement Programmes, Welfare to Work etc.).

Such community planning implies a 'vision', core values and an

---

* See too Appendices 20–23, those described in *Leading Communities*, LGMB, 1998 and *Local Government and Community Leadership*, LGMB, 1993.

overall aim for the community, together with a comprehensive strategy for their realization. In developing corporate objectives, 'most authorities recognise that providing everything themselves is both unrealistic and unnecessary. Nor can they achieve all that they want to do in a single or even in several years' (White Paper IP7.8). Consequently they need to establish priorities as well as service objectives. All of this 'will flow from engagement with the wider community' and, while making it a necessarily joint or cooperative endeavour, the government is allowing councils flexibility in how they approach it (though consultative devices such as public forums, consultation papers, public meetings, and committees of inquiry are suggested;* so too is the increased use of referendums for which purpose the law is to be clarified).†

A number of councils have already exemplified many of these – such as the committee of inquiry by Cambridge, 1997; the residents' and business opinion surveys by Chester, 1992 and 1997/8; the citizens' jury in South Somerset and in Lewisham, 1996 or Plymouth 1999; the citizens' panel and a residents' forum in Somerset, 1998; the referendum in Strathclyde, 1994; public questions in Braintree, 1993; the focus group in Sheffield, 1994; neighbourhood committees in Rochdale and in Kingston, 1996; the video box in Lewisham, 1995; inter-active IT, Bedfordshire, 1995; on-line information and services in Cumbria, 1997 (and indeed most councils now have web sites).

They are also to have additional flexibility in that they will be given clear discretionary powers to make partnership arrangemnts, including

---

* Other methods are outlined in the consultation paper, *Local Democracy and Community Leadership*, DETR, 1998. These include citizens' juries, focus groups, survey panels, conferences, public opinion polls and deliberative opinion polls (the latter involving informed debate), citizens' panels (e.g. youth councils, tenant panels, etc.) and public question times. Attention is also drawn to other methods and approaches, including cross-membership and standing conferences of all providing or partner bodies, and those found in the report *Enhancing Public Participation in Local Government*, DETR, 1998. As John Stewart has put it, in recent years a lot of attention has been given to improving management; now it is time to attend to the improvement of local democracy: see his series *Innovation in Democratic Practice*, INLOGOV, 1995, 1996 and 1997; also *Towards a Deliberative Democracy*, INLOGOV, 1999.

† It may be noted that the government itself is increasingly embracing the referendum, and it regularly canvasses opinion on policies and service quality by use of a 'people's panel' of 5,000 people.

such things as sharing resources (staff, IT, accommodation), the delegation of decision-making and the formation or participation in companies. (In all these developments, a key role will be played by local authority chief executive officers[4] and clearly their mandatory appointment to health authorities announced in the NHS 1998 White Paper is significant (though some may regard this as introducing an element of inflexibility).

Furthermore, in the longer term, there is the promise of greater autonomy, of substantial additional freedoms and powers – even taking over responsibilities from other bodies. Those councils (and not just the 'beacons': see below) which demonstrate their capacity to innovate and to manage a greater range of responsibilities will be given greater scope to meet local needs, to experiment with service provision and to pilot new ideas (such as those emerging from the Action Zone* and Better Government projects). The government sees such arrangments providing an incentive to councils to modernize and improve their performance and to local people and business to press councils to so improve.

In many ways, these resemble the 'trust councils' idea floated by the Conservative government as an aspect of deregulation in 1994, and also the Scandinavian 1980s experiment in 'free councils'.[5] But there is some scepticism from those who dislike the notion of selectivity, elites and differential treatment, and from those who are suspicious of the criteria for selectiom (such as party bias, civil service or accountancy values, etc.). The government abandoned the idea of 'trust councils' because of the problems associated with determining appropriate criteria.

Clearly the councils best fitted to lead their communities are those with the strongest democratic base or legitimacy. Apart from seeking

---

* Action Zones are areas of multiple deprivation or social exclusion. The aim of government policy is to concentrate resources (through partnerships of government, local councils, community groups and business) to improve health, education and employment. They resemble earlier policies such as the Education Priority Areas of the 1960s (under Labour) and the Task Forces and Urban Development Corporations of the 1980s (under the Conservatives), though the latter were more focused on economic regeneration. See G. Smith, *Area-based Initiatives*, CASE Paper 25, STICERD/LSE, 1999.

to enhance public participation in general, the government wants to bring about a renewal of local democracy by improving the electoral element. As we have seen above (Chapter 6) the government is increasing the frequency of elections by applying the 'thirds' system of annual elections to all unitary councils and London Boroughs. In the shire counties and districts, elections are to be alternated, with half of each council being elected every other year. In all cases, councillors retain their four-year term of office (currently, in 1999, three in Scotland). The objective is to make councils more accountable and to keep them in touch with current public opinion, i.e. voters have an opportunity every year to give their verdict on the council's performance. It can also encourage a more ordered approach to financial planning as councils are no longer able to leave any tax increases to the year after the (fourth year) election. However, some see a risk of 'voter fatigue' in more frequent election. And it is suggested that annual elections may jeopardize longer-term planning by favouring 'short-termism'. It may also exacerbate the evident strained relations between councillors and officers in some councils as local councillors' or their parties' time-horizons are shortened.* It is also pointed out that existing councils which operate the annual/thirds system are not obviously better managed, have less corruption or enjoy higher voting turnout.

Less straightforward are reforms to change (improve) electoral procedures. It has been estimated that two to four million people are absent from the electoral register – some deliberately seeking to avoid the (then) poll tax, others simply being uninterested or too mobile to bother. The government suggests that local authorities learn from the best among them and seek to increase registration by such methods as starting the annual registration process earlier in the year and being more assiduous in following up non-respondents (through reminders by post/telephone or by rewarding canvassers who reach performance targets, and through the mass media); perhaps threatening prosecution or, more positively, by pointing to advantages to registration (such as increased credit-worthiness). For those who are reluctant to appear on the open, public register, the government is considering allowing anonymous registration; it is also considering the possibility of 'rolling'

* *Municipal Journal*, 29 November 1996, pp. 14–15.

registers, which are open to amendment throughout the year (rather than just once a year as now).

A bigger problem than non-registration is non-voting, with an average turnout of around 40 per cent – although in 1998 the overall average was a mere 30 per cent (one urban ward registering 8 per cent. There was even one polling station where no one voted!) To improve turnout the government's Local Government Act 2000 allows councils to experiment with electoral procedures, which could include electronic voting, tele-voting, postal voting (as in New Zealand where some local elections were conducted entirely by post and doubled turnout to 60 per cent);* having mobile polling stations, using unorthodox polling stations (supermarkets, places of employment, etc.); improving access for people with disabilities; extending voting hours or changing to Sunday voting or perhaps allowing voting over a number of days; and quite simply increasing publicity and making the polling card more eye-catching. However, in the opinion of some, these changes are just tinkering with the system, in that it is argued that there is a fundamental lack of interest in local government because it lacks real power (MORI 1998) or autonomy – and this arises from its over-dependence on central funding.† Without greater financial autonomy, it is argued (by LGA and others)[6], councils cannot demonstrate that they can make a real difference to people's lives and so turnout will remain low: see below. (The 1998 Local Government White Paper also says the 'framework of controls has weakened public interest' (para 1.14), hence its proposals to relax some restrictions (on capping, on entering partnerships and contracts, on internal structures and, for the 'best performing councils', more generally; see below).

One method the government does not favour, however, is the idea of compulsory voting. Another is proportional representation (PR), though it does not rule this out in the longer term – especially since it is now operative to a significant extent: in elections for the Greater London Authority, for the European Parliament and for the Assembly/

---

* See C. Rallings and M. Thrasher, *Enhancing Local Electoral Turnout*, JRF, 1996. See too Appendix 17, MORI on voting.

† This dependence is greater than in most European countries: see Select Committee (Environment) Eighth Report on LG Finance, March 1999, para. 21.

Parliament in Wales, Scotland and Northern Ireland (in the last of which it is used for local elections too; Scotland is likely to follow suit – see below). Following the Jenkins Commission *Report on the Voting System* (July 1998) the government is at least considering some form of PR for the Westminster Houses of Parliament. The government does acknowledge that PR could help to reduce the virtual one-party councils which exist (in nearly 25 per cent of councils; see p. 160) and which are consequently at risk of becoming complacement and incompetent, if not anti-democratic and corrupt. PR also appears to enhance turnout (perhaps by some 7 per cent).[7]

Critics of PR fear that it will lead to more indecisive results and hung councils, with attendant risks of delay and/or weak decision-making, together with loss of accountability (for eventual compromise, coalition-type policies). The government also cherishes the close links between councillors and citizens which exist under our current 'first past the post' or simple majority system.

Such direct, if not so close, links can be achieved under the directly elected mayor system. It is also likely that it improves voting turnout. In the case of the GLA elections the 11 of the 25-member Assembly are elected by a proportional system and the victorious candidate for mayor is determined by the Supplementary Vote system.*

This brings us to the *management* aspect. We looked at the question of the elected mayor in Chapter 9. But the current management reforms go further than the creation of this new (for Britain) institution.

Ever since the Maud Report of 1967 (see p. 252) there has been periodic concern about the internal management of local authorities and particularly the committee system. There have been a number of general attempts at reform (such as those of Maud, Bains and Paterson; see pp. 250ff) and numerous reviews and revisions by individual councils (especially in recent years, due at least in part, to loss of functions, competitive tendering and reorganization). But dissatisfaction has

---

* Under this system, all candidates are listed on the ballot paper; voters mark the ballot paper with a X in either or both of two (first and second choice) columns. Any candidate with over 50 per cent of first votes is elected. If not, all but the top two candidates are eliminated and their second preference votes are redistributed. Whoever of the two remaining candidates has the most votes is the winner.

continued to be expressed, for example by the Widdicombe Committee (1986), by the Environment Secretary in 1991 (see p. 267), by a prestigious Working Party (see p. 270) and by the Audit Commission, as well as by academic researchers.* It is perhaps best encapsulated in the title of an Audit Commission paper, *We Can't Go On Meeting Like This* (1990).†

The consultative paper, *Modernising Local Government: Local Democracy and Community Leadership*, is quite blunt:

The way local government currently operates with its traditional committee structure is inefficient and opaque. This committee system was designed over a century ago for a bygone age; it is no basis for modern local government (para 5.1).

This is the crux of the problem. Councillors in general are spending an increasing amount of time on council duties, from 52 hours a month in 1967 to 80–90 today (and perhaps even more, with some well in excess of 100 hours; see p. 204). But the problem is not just the amount of time; it is also its allocation and its efficient use. Between 50 per cent and 65 per cent of councillors' time is spent on committee and council meetings.‡ Yet 70 per cent of them feel that representational work directly with the community is a more important role, so the 30 per cent of their time they are actually able to devote to this is inadequate. Furthermore, committee work is often a waste of time because the real decision-making is more often taken behind closed doors at political group meetings – perhaps just by key leaders – with the result that many councillors feel unable to provide any input or exercise any significant influence on behalf of their consitituents. Thus too often their function is to explain council decisions to the public rather than explain the public's views to the council.

A further consequence is that political leadership is unclear and people do not know who is really taking the decisions. 'They do not know who to praise, who to blame or who to contact with their

* Such as K. Young and N. Rao, *The Local Government Councillors in 1993*, JRF, 1994 and N. Rao, *Managing Change*, JRF, 1992.
† Updated in 1997 in *Representing the People*.
‡ See Young & Rao op. cit.

problems. People identify most readily with an individual, yet there is rarely any identifiable figure leading the local community. This is no basis for modern, effective and responsive local government'.* And in addition, the system is expensive in terms of officer/staff time: for example, councillors' allowances, plus staff time (exluding senior management) on committee work can cost over £1 million p.a. in a large authority.†

The government commends the growing number of councils which have been reforming their procedures – reducing the number of committees and replacing them with short-term working parties, shrinking committee membership, shortening meetings, improving the structure or content of committee cycles or committee agendas (e.g. by eliminating information-only items),‡ delegating more to officers, altering councillors' allowances etc. It also applauds those which have sought to open up their decision-making processes, and make the system more transparent and easier to access – for example through open public debates, and forums etc., and also with different forms of decentralization (such as area and neighbourhood committees) which can help communities to identify with those who represent them: see Appendix 20 for illustration. But overall progress here is felt to be inadequate, partly because of old cultures and attitudes, but partly too because of legal constraints (e.g. regarding single-party committees or cabinets).

Consequently, the Local Government Act 2000 removes a number of statutory requirements from councils (such as social services committees) and allows them to radically recast their internal political management structures. To this end, the government has provided three optional models from which councils can choose to make their own decision-making arrangements (see Appendix 24). These are (i) a directly elected (or 'strong') mayor with cabinet, under which the mayor selects a cabinet from one or more party members of the

---

* White Paper, *Modern Local Government: In Touch with the People*, 1998, para 3.7.
† *Representing the People*, Audit Commission, 1997, p. 100
‡ For example in a council of 60 members, a reduction of committees from 25 to 23, in meetings from 10 to 8, in membership from 25 to 20 and in meeting time from four to three hours, would reduce the average time-commitment for councillors from 417 to 184 hours a year! (*Representing the People*, p. 19.

separately elected council. Like Ministers the cabinet members would have specific areas of responsibility and could take individual executive decisions. The mayor would be the political leader for the community, proposing policy for approval by the council and steering implementation by the cabinet through council officers; (ii) a cabinet with a leader, either both elected by the council or with a leader elected by the council (an 'indirectly elected mayor') who then appoints the cabinet (single or multi-party). The mayor's powers are likely to be narrower than those of a strong mayor as his/her authority or mandate does not derive from the electorate but from the council, who can replace him/her; (iii) a directly elected mayor and a council manager, whereby the mayor is like the non-executive chairman of a company giving a political lead and guidance to the manager/chief executive officer who has delegated powers of strategic policy and day to day decision-making. (See Appendices 24 and 25. In practice there are many variations on such models.)*

The aim is to distinguish and separate the *executive* role of the local authority from its *non-executive* (or scrutiny/supervisory/representative) role, rather on the broader model of the 'separation of powers' (most explicitly manifested in the Presidency and Congress of the USA). As the White Paper explains:

Both the executive and backbench roles of councillors are vital to the health of local democracy and to effective community leadership. Each role can only be fully effective when it is separated from the other. These roles therefore need to be separated and each given its rightful place and powers. The executive role would be to propose the policy framework and implement policies within the agreed framework. The role of backbench councillors would be to represent their constituents, share in policy and budget decisions of the full council, suggest policy improvements, and scrutinise the executive's policy proposals and their implementation. The precise balance between the roles of the executive and the backbench councillors in initiating policies will depend on the detail of the arrangements in place (paras. 3.12, 3.13).

* See *New Forms of Political Executive in Local Government*, LGMB, 1998, and *Community Leadership and Representation*, DoE, 1993. The LG Bill 2000 allows for possible direct election of members of the executive cabinet, either collectively or individually to identified posts or responsibilities (like directly elected local 'Ministers').

However, like the British Cabinet system, the separation of powers is not complete (except in the mayor/manager model). But the separation of roles is clear, as individual councillors are not allowed to participate in both the executive (mayor/cabinet) and the non-executive (scrutiny/oversight) functions. Thus the role of the executive is broadly two-fold: (i) to exercise political leadership on behalf of the council, and to represent the council and the community's interests to the outside world and (ii) to translate the wishes of the community into action through policy development, decisions on the allocation of resources (through the annual budget, approved by the council), forming partnerships with other bodies (both in and outside the local community) and securing the effective delivery of the programme on which it was elected.

The non-executive (or backbench) role is broadly to 'check and balance' and inform the executive. More specifically councillors are to review and question the performance and general direction of the authority, and to articulate their constituents' or stakeholders' concerns – raising local issues, submitting proposals and scrutinizing the draft budget and voting on it. This would occur in the light of the councillors' greater contact with the community (through residents' meetings, councillors' surgeries, etc.) for which they would have more time (and indeed a duty, under other aspects of the modernization process such as Best Value, business rates, etc.).

Each councillor will become a champion of their community defending the public interest in the council and channelling the grievances, needs and aspirations of the electorate into the scrutiny process. In-touch local councillors, aware of and responsive to the needs of those they represent, will have a greater say in the formulation of policy and the solving of local problems than they could have within current committee structures . . . This enhanced role will provide new opportunities to backbench councillors. The role could be less time-consuming but it will be high profile, involving real and direct responsibilities for the well-being of their community and will be more challenging and rewarding. [White Paper paras 3.43, 3.45]

In any of these systems with a separated executive there must be one or more scrutiny committees, each having the explicit duty to review and question the decisions, policies and performance of the executive, to which they can propose changes and additions. Membership of these committees must exclude members of the executive and must (unlike the executive) reflect the political balance of the council (and opposition members are expected to chair at least some committees). The committees are empowered to call members and officers to appear before them for questioning. All councillors are to benefit from greater administrative support/facilities and training,* and some will be entitled to pensionable salaries.

All councils (except parishes) are required to produce detailed proposals for reforming their decision-making structures together with a timetable for implementation. Following the precedent of the GLA (in 1998) there is to be a statutory referendum in those areas which have opted for the directly elected mayor system in order to test public opinion. Where a council does not opt for such a system a referendum may be called (if required by 5 per cent or more of the electorate) to put the idea forward. And where a council is dragging its feet over the reform process, the government has reserve powers to require a referendum asking the public to vote on one of the approved options, though if there is a 'no' vote, the council can continue unchanged or can bring forward alternative proposals.

The government argues that the new streamlined system has three main advantages. It will be more (i) *efficient* as the small executive can act more quickly and responsively, (ii) *transparent* since it will be clearer who is responsible for decisions and the rationale behind them, and (iii) *accountable* as greater transparency will enable people to measure the executive's actions against its manifesto promises: it will be clear(er) who 'carries the can'. The new system may also increase public interest in local affairs and perhaps improve voting turnout and participation generally.† The government prefers the elective mayor system, and two ESRC surveys (for the Local Governance Programme of the Economic and Social Research Council)

---

* Less than 50 per cent of councils provide an ongoing programme of member training and development, and the expenditure overall amounts to £5 a year per councillor; see *Supporting Councillors*, LGIU, 1998.

† A MORI poll in April 1998 showed that 21 per cent said they would be more likely to vote if there was a directly elected mayor system (though it also showed that others – over 10 per cent – would thereby be less likely to vote. See Appendix 17).

revealed 65–70 per cent public support for such a system[8] – though a subsequent survey indicated only 26 per cent support,[9] and the referendum (in 1998) for the GLA/mayor system only produced a 32 per cent turnout. In practice most councils so far (November 1999) have opted for a Leader–Cabinet system (see *Modern Local Government*, LGA, 1999).

One of the biggest problems with the proposals is the fear, by many councillors, of losing power and role – in short, of being side-lined. See, for example, the experience claimed by councillors on Hammersmith and Fulham LBC (which pioneered the executive/scrutiny committee format in 1998).[10] Despite the government's reassurances, and their own sway (see *Voice*, September 1999), most backbenchers appear sceptical about having an 'enhanced role' and there are fears that their perception (of a diminished role) will reduce the attraction of standing for election. Besides, there is a risk of 'throwing the baby out with the bathwater' in that the traditional committee system has much to commend it (see the Audit Commission's *Representing the People* and the 1999 Report of the Joint Committee on the Local Government (Organisation and Standards) Draft Bill,) though in many councils there may be a need to review their number, frequency, agendas, etc.

Some of the fears have been confirmed to some extent by practical experience and recent research. A report (*Political Management Arrangements in Local Government*, IDA/LGA, 1999) indicates that in many of the 175 councils which are adopting the executive cabinet/scrutiny committees system, there are some serious weaknesses in implementation or operation. These include the inadequate development of the committees and their roles; it is reminiscent of much experience in the 1970s (see Chapter 9) when councils adopted the forms of the new (Maud/Bains/corporate) management, but not the substance, spirit or culture. There is also some concern that cabinets are being less than open, and are taking too much advantage of the 'closed meeting' facility (see *Local Leadership, Local Choice*, DETR, 1999, para. 3.61). The campaign for FOI is particularly fearful here.

The successful operation of the executive/non-executive split will also depend on some relaxation in party discipline (otherwise the scrutiny committees become 'poodles' rather than guard-dogs. The

Labour Party has begun such a revision – on the role of whips, codes of conduct among members, etc*) and in October 1999, the party declared that whipping will not apply (for its own members at least) in the new committees. And with regard to the elective mayor system, there is concern about the ability to remove them from office (for incompetence or loss of public confidence, etc.). Other aspects of the elective mayor system are dealt with on p. 275.

The success of management in local government in general also depends on proper standards of behaviour. Under the Local Government Act 2000, the proposals for a new ethical framework, with revised Codes of Conduct and mandatory standards committees, are given effect. So too is the abolition of surcharge (p. 396.)

Sooner or later, the modernizing changes to local government will have *financial* implications for local authorities. But a number of the reforms themselves are specifically financial and economic. Some of these have been indicated in earlier chapters (especially Chapter 11). Thus the government is reforming the capital finance system (releasing assets, developing the 'single pot', etc.); it is encouraging closer collaboration with business through PFI; it is altering the law to facilitate partnerships, etc.

Perhaps the greatest disappointment to local government is the government's failure to restore business rates (NDR) to local authorities as it (in Opposition) had pledged to do. In 1998 the Minister (Hilary Armstrong) ruled this out for at least ten years.[11] Local government wants NDR 'de-nationalized' to facilitate greater independence, and to enable local authorities to re-engage and bond more genuinely and effectively with business stakeholders, and thus enhance their community leadership role and credentials. And indeed, as the White Paper points out, councils are vital to the competitiveness of business in respect of such aspects as education standards, services for carer-employees, crime, regeneration and transport/traffic management, so there needs to be something to substantiate the dialogue between them. In 1997, Hilary Armstrong wrote, 'The "nationalization" of the national non-domestic rates has made it much harder to construct genuinely local partnerships with businesses . . . Labour plans to return

* See *Modernising Labour groups and local governance*, Labour Party, 1999.

the business rate to local control precisely because it recreates the relationship between local business and local government'.* And in their policy document *Renewing Democracy, Rebuilding Communities*, the Labour Party said:

... the business rate has no relation to local needs or services and so breaks the link between local business, their local councils and local communities ... The basis of the statutory consultations between business rate payers and councils has also been destroyed ... Labour is committed to returning the business rate to local control (p. 19).

But most obviously local government seeks the return of business rates in order to reduce its dependence on central funding, currently some 80–85 per cent. Instead, local authorities are to be allowed to raise some marginal revenue from a supplementary rate on business (conversely, they may individually allow reductions or rebates).

Councils are already expected to consult local businesses in their budget planning. This will be a specific requirement where they propose to impose a local supplement to the NDR; they will be expected to agree the level and objectives of such an increased rate. The supplement cannot exceed 1 per cent† in any one year, nor 5 per cent over a period of time; it may also be linked to the council tax. Business cannot block the increase, but where there is disagreement about the use of the proceeds, the government may require their being put into the national pool. The 'Beacon' councils (i.e. those identified by the government as deserving special consideration) will have the power to raise an *additional* supplementary rate by up to another 1 per cent (and 5 per cent maximum), and they have some flexibility in applying it to all or some businesses in all or part of the area. (Small businesses – with rateable values of under £5,000 – will get special consideration because rates form a disproportional share of their profits

---

* *Local Government Chronicle*, 4 April 1997, p. 8. She also pointed to the added gain of a lower gearing effect: see *Municipal Journal*, 9 February 1996, p. 12.

† In practice, the financial return to a local authority may be outweighed by the time involved in consulting with businesses, and in two-tier (plus police?) authority areas, there are further complications, such as the share of the 1 per cent. A 1 per cent supplementary business rate would, for example, raise about £1 million for Plymouth City Council alone, or about 0.5 per cent of its budget.

– up to 30 per cent compared to just 10 per cent or perhaps even 3 per cent for the larger businesses.

Council tax is to stay unchanged, despite the fact that it 'betrays the haste with which it was introduced . . . after the failure of the poll tax . . . [by] the Tory government'* and despite what many – including the Labour Party (in Opposition) – see as its regressive or unfair nature† (which could be reduced through the creation of more, especially higher, bands and/or adjusting the ratios between them, as the LGA has proposed).‡ Nor is there any intention (unlike business properties) to conduct a revaluation of domestic properties at least until the next Parliament – which postponement is likely to undermine the credibility of the system (as it did with rates in the past: see Chapter 8).

However, perhaps more importantly, universal budget capping is abolished (under the Local Government Act 1999) and councils will no longer be told in advance what they may spend. Restraint on spending will be exercised through the greater accountability which this greater freedom provides. Responsibility and discipline will be enhanced by the various modernizing reforms – in particular, the improvements to the democratic process (of increased voter turnout, more frequent elections, greater consultation by freed-up representative councillors, etc.) and the statutory requirements within the Best Value, community leadership and business rates mechanisms. Councils are thus freer to determine their own local tax-and-spend policies (subject to 'gearing effects'; see pp. 367, 378). And this clarity of responsibility is reinforced by a three-year freeze on SSA adjustments and changes in the aggregate allocation of central funds to local government.

Yet, in case the democratic disciplines fail or are not sufficiently reformed and mobilized by local authorities, the government retains a reserve power to cap individual councils. Such a power will be used selectively – where spending or its increase is deemed excessive (or the concomitant level of service is inadequate). But there will be no

---

* *Renewing Democracy, Rebuilding Communities*, Labour Party, 1995, p. 20.
† See *Renewing Democracy*, p. 20: J. Gibson in *Local Governance*, 2, 1999; also IRRV.
‡ *Modernising Local Government: Reforming Local Government Finance*, LGA, 1998.

automatic trigger for capping and account will be taken of the council's recent experience, community views on the level of its council tax, the absolute size of the budget and council's general performance. And if necessary a capping condition for a council can be phased in rather than be applied all at once. Nevertheless, there is uncertainty about the arbitrary nature of the Minister's ability to select, and the general impression is still one of lack of trust or faith in local government. (In Scotland, the regime is less selective in that councils are given a 'guideline' spending or tax increase limit, currently 5 per cent. If this is exceeded significantly, the Minister will use his/her capping powers.)

There is also hostility to another aspect of capping, which is general in its application; this is the limit on council tax benefit. This is funded by central subsidy, with the result that part of the cost (about a fifth) of any increase in council tax (to pay benefit) falls on the government. (In some local authorities, with high proportions of citizens on low incomes, the benefit can amount to over 30 per cent of council tax revenue.) Consequently, there is now an upper limit to budget/council tax increases which will be so subsidized. Currently, a council tax rise beyond 4.5 per cent (5 per cent in Scotland) is not fully eligible for subsidy (this is known as 'clawback') so the council tax payers meet more of the bill. Those receiving council tax benefit are not affected, but the scheme has been criticized, among other things, as 'the nearly poor paying for the really poor.'*

Local authorities now have the duty to obtain 'Best Value' in all their activities; they are required 'to meet the aspirations of local people for the highest quality and most efficient services that are possible at a price that people are willing to pay'.†

Best Value is concerned with value-for-money in the use of council resources. While its focus is on Efficiency, Economy and Effectiveness – the 'three Es' – its remit is wider in that it includes Equitable considerations (such as equal opportunities in accessing services or at

---

* LGA in December 1998; see *Municipal Journal*, 4 December 1998.
† *Modernising Local Government: Improving Local Services Through Best Value*, DETR, 1998, para 1.2. It derives from the government's general programme of Better Quality Services and the New Charter programme. (Sceptics have suggested that 'Best Value' is just a 'spin' nomenclature to reduce association with the previous regime.)

work, and good employment practice). Indeed in their capacity as 'community leaders' and with the new power to promote economic, social and environmental wellbeing, local authorities will have to have a wider concern with the roles and resources of other agencies:

Best value will also help councils to address the cross-cutting issues facing their citizens and communities, such as community safety or sustainable development, which are beyond the reach of a single service or service provider. These issues can only be tackled successfully with cooperation between partners ... The community leadership role gives [councils] an opportunity to shape the agenda across the board, so that efforts are focussed and combined effectively. One of the most significant causes of failure to achieve a best value service is the lack of consideration of how resources are used in relation to common objectives. Best value will support improved performance measurement when council services need to be integrated with those delivered by other ... agencies ... Whatever the shared aim – it might be to reduce social exclusion, raise standards of public health, or improve air quality – the best value process will help councils to decide on priorities in consultation with their communities and other partners, build consensus on what needs to be achieved, and measure how their own programmes and services are contributing to the shared objective. (White Paper para 7.3)

Part of the objective should be to reverse the recent fragmentation of local government into business units which has had an adverse effect on their concern with the council's wider objectives and on the general sense of community. CCT has created adversarial relations between different parts of the authority and secretive behaviour within and between local authorities.[12] Ultimately, poor provision can threaten society itself. 'Efficient and effective public services are an essential part of the fabric of a healthy democratic society'.* But, obviously, resources are limited and they need to be put to best use. There are wide variations in standards of services (as shown by Audit Commission reports, CIPFA, etc.) and the government is concerned at the inefficiencies revealed most blatantly in the gross failures in some councils' services – residential care for the elderly or children,

---

* *Modernising Local Government: Improving Local Services Through Best Value*, DETR, 1998, para 1.2.

failing schools, substantial council tax or rent arrears, loss-making DLOs, etc.

The aim of Best Value is therefore to even-up performance and to bring the worst up to the best. Furthermore,

... Continuous improvements in both the quality and cost of services will therefore be the hallmark of a modern council, and the test of best value ... [It] will be a duty to deliver services to clear standards – covering both cost and quality – by the most effective, economic and efficient means available. In carrying out this duty local authorities will be accountable to local people and have a responsibility to central government in its role as representative of the broader national interest. (White Paper paras 7.1, 7.2)

Thus under the Local Government Act 1999, CCT is abolished (in the year 2000, though councils are still subject to the procurement/ tendering rules of the EU) and local authorities (except small town/ parish councils) have the wider obligation to obtain Best Value. This is to be achieved by councils following a set sequence of steps; see Appendices 27 and 28. The essence of the process is the setting of both national and local objectives and performance measures (standards and targets). Most of these will be determined by local authorities themselves and will flow from their corporate/community plans (see above) since, in effect, Best Value is a negotiated concept:

... best value is primarily a matter for individual local authorities in consultation with local people ... Best value is about the cost and quality of services that meet the aspirations of local people. (*Best Value in Housing Framework*, DETR, 1999, paras 1.3, 2.4)

But, in devising their standards, local authorities have to take account of those set nationally. Thus, the government is establishing a set of performance indicators (PIs) for the effectiveness and quality of major services (see Appendices 15 and 29 for examples) as well as some broader 'general health' PIs which deal with the overall capacity* of

* These include democratic vitality (voting turnout, registration, etc.); quality of service management (susceptibility to litigation claims, complaints to the Ombudsman, etc.); human resource management (days lost through sickness, compliance with equal opportunities codes, etc.); financial management (collection rates, debt interest costs, etc.)

local authorities as democratic and public spending institutions. As well as PIs, in some cases, the government sets performance standards against which councils have to report performance, e.g. national standards for educational attainment for different age groups (or Key Stages).

Local authorities set targets in respect of the PIs and they must publish these targets together with their subsequent performance in an annual local Performance Plan. They are also required, as a minimum, to set *quality* targets over a five-year period which are consistent with the performance of the top 25 per cent of all councils and *cost and efficiency* targets consistent with the performance of the top 25 per cent of councils in the region. Councils are also required to undertake a fundamental performance review of all services over a five-year period (normally dealing with the weakest first). These reviews entail the 'four Cs':

(i) Challenge the current situation by asking *why* the service is being provided, whether it is still relevant, and *how* and at what cost is it being provided (e.g. may new technology or others' good/best practice suggest changes?).

(ii) Compare with others' performance (councils, private sector, etc.) and perhaps using benchmarks (exemplary or model standard of performance).

(iii) Consult the community (users, providers and other stakeholders) in conducting the reviews (such as already occurs with council tenants, under the National Framework for Tenant Participation Compacts).

(iv) Compete with the best in terms of quality, relevance and cost through tendering and market testing, which may lead to contracting out, but is more flexible and substantiated than CCT (though any trading losses where a service is kept in-house will be jumped on by the government, e.g. requiring CCT or transfer to another council or body, etc. The government is clarifying and extending the application of TUPE regulations (see p. 544) to make competition less threatening.

New performance targets will result from these reviews and these are incorporated each year in the annual Performance Plan which reports on current performance (including comparisons), identifies annual and longer term targets and comments on the means to achieve the Plan (including capital projects, etc.). Such Plans also show how the corporate strategy is operating and relating to other agencies (especially where there are explicitly shared responsibilities such as with the Health Improvement Programme, Youth Offending Partnerships, etc.).

All this is subject to an extensive and rigorous regime of external audit and inspection. The former is largely concerned with compliance and accuracy, while inspection is more concerned with achievement and quality (e.g. are the targets sufficiently demanding? If not there can be a requirement to review and revise). For this purpose, there is a new Best Value Inspectorate (within the Audit Commission). This contains lay members to represent service users. The BVI, of which the Housing Inspectorate is part, works alongside and together with the specialist inspectorates (SSI, OFSTED). Where there are serious failings in performance, the government may intervene and require a new action plan or it may impose competiton or outside assistance or perhaps even remove and transfer responsibility, though this is seen as a last resort, and local authorities have sought to minimize or obviate such central involvement. At the meeting of the Central–Local Partnership (p. 574), Ministers and LGA leaders agreed a series of protocols (or ways of working) to guide the use of ministerial intervention and directive powers contained in the Best Value (1999) and education (1998) legislation. The protocols recognize that, except in the most urgent cases, councils should be given the chance to put their own houses in order with the help of the Local Government Association (such as in the case of Calderdale LEA 1996–9) and from the self-help, 'troubleshooting' Improvement and Development Agency (IDA) (see p. 282). In fact, the IDA is playing a major role in the Local Government Improvement Programme, and, by invitation, it sends small teams to councils to provide peer-group reviews.

Thus in summary the achievement of Best Value requires a long-term commitment to a stakeholder-focused culture of continuous improvement. It is a demanding regime, which involves a substantial change of approach in service provision (though some aspects are not new – PIs, policy/service objectives, performance review, etc.). But there are potentially considerable rewards: (i) extra resources from savings (estimated at 2 per cent), from more successful bids and from agreement on supplementary business rates, (ii) additional powers and freedom from regulations, (iii) conferment of 'beacon' status for the council (or, in the beginning, some of its services) which brings further autonomy and resources, (iv) success at the polls and re-election!

Much detail has yet to be worked out. But a number of concerns have already been expressed – Is there a danger of 'consultation fatigue'? Will there be sufficient public response, and what will it cost? How much weight will be given to social or qualitative considerations such as democratic accountability, quality, employment practices, etc? How to assess quality, especially as Best Value involves much subjective judgement as well as quantitative measurement, and how much weight is to be given to local community views? Are the auditors/inspectors too accountancy orientated? Might CCT be reimposed 'through the back door', by stealth? Or, conversely, might the greater flexibility on competition provide fertile ground for corruption?[13] Has the government too many (and too arbitrary) powers of intervention and statutory guidance? Is Best Value 'another Whitehall hoop to jump through'?[14] Does Best Value represent a rigid 'statutory management system, which will reduce local innovation'?[15] Will it fail to achieve the efficiency gains of CCT?[16] UNISON regards Best Value as a greater threat than CCT to local services and to working conditions,[17] and similar fears have been expressed by Professor Sanderson, who sees it (especially the 'Challenge' element) as a 'more rigorous test of performance than councils have faced in the past . . . councils may face pressure to externalize services that are far more radical than CCT . . . continuing the withdrawal of government from our lives'.[18]

More generally, while local government has found much to welcome in the government's reform/modernization programme, with over half of local authorities applying for Beacon Status, and much action on the organization and standards front (see *Modern Local Government: Taking the Initiative*, LGA, 1999), there is disappointment too, especially regarding finance (and stemming largely from the government's conforming to the previous government's spending plans).

The last twenty years has seen an unprecedented increase in the level of central control over local government expenditure, and with the government's current reform proposals, it is not clear that this will change significantly, though there are some changes at the margin as we have seen above. There are some who would argue that such control is unnecessary and that the effects of local spending on the economy in general are not proven.[19] Others may concede that the government has a legitimate interest in certain aspects of local spending, such as capital (because it may affect borrowing levels and interest rates) or to the extent that national/government taxes, via grants, pay for much local spending – though even here there is concern about such aspects as the fairness of SSA/grant allocation or challenge funding (requiring bids) as, apart from the uncertainty and costs involved, it is often unclear why applications have failed (or succeeded) and it can give rise to suspicions about political favouritism. But most contested is the case for controlling local authority self-financed expenditure, i.e. charges and council tax. Yet capping is to be retained by this government (albeit selective) which in effect means controlling that aspect of local spending which is self-generated and makes councils most (potentially) accountable to their communities and voters.

The Select Committee on Environment, Transport and the Regions' *Report on Local Government Finance*, March 1999, declares bluntly that 'local government finance is in a mess' (para 67). The Committee was critical of the limited scope of the government's changes to the system of local finance and said 'we are concerned that without a major reform its modernizing agenda will be undermined'.

It was very concerned at the erosion of local government responsibility over the years – with the loss of functions, increased reliance on grants, lack of financial discretion and increased central regulation, and felt that local authorities were in danger of becoming 'merely central government agents'. It condemned the introduction of limits on council tax subsidy and the retention of (reserve) capping powers, and it urged the government to improve local autonomy and accountability* by increasing the proportion of finance raised locally through the return of the non-domestic rate to local control and an extension of council tax banding.

The government rejected the Committee's conclusions on the

---

* Though it did acknowledge that the link between local taxation and local automony/ accountability is uncertain; see para 18.

grounds that taxpayers needed to be protected and that local autonomy was unaffected by the proportion of funding raised locally (plus, councils would in the future be able to negotiate supplementary rates with business, thus raising (potentially) an additional £650 million).

For the first time since it began, there was no capping in 1999–2000 despite significant increases in spending and council taxes (some of which were substantially above the government's guideline figure, though twelve councils were issued with a 'yellow card' government warning). And it may be that, unannounced, the government is prepared to allow such increases whilst holding its own contributions constant. This will gradually change the balance of local funding (and accountability) towards locally based sources, and there is evidence of this beginning to happen in recent years: for example, in Scotland between 1993 and 1997, while the index of local spending rose by 100, grants rose by 95.5 and council taxes by 117.[20]

In general, local autonomy is going to have to be earned. And many (notwithstanding devolution) are concerned about what they see as centralist or autocratic tendencies, or continuities, in the new government – as evidenced, in the case of local government, by such actions as the imposition of national standards and targets, the extension of performance indicators and league tables, use of improvement or development teams ('hit squads'), inspections 'overload'* (including the extension of OFSTED to LEAs themselves and to councils' day care for children), the imposition of Health Improvement and Education Action Zones, compulsory health and social services partnerships, abolishing GM schools (and prejudicing the existence of Grammars), reinforcing the national curriculum (with compulsory reading hours, extending SATs, instructions on teaching methods – even for nursery classes), imposing performance-related pay for teachers, reinforcing LMS by squeezing the cap on funds retained by LEAs, replacing local authority Social Services inspection with regional commissions, continued privatization, excessive guidance and regulation (including the submission of detailed local service plans), the failure to reduce quangos or to democratize them, greater use of

* *The Times*, 6 May 1998.

specific grants and the retention of capping powers. Simon Jenkins says that, under Labour, 'the centralism of the Thatcher–Major Government is not yet a spent conviction. Ministers . . . have, if anything proved even more centralist than the Tories.'*

The government is being quite forceful in getting local authorities to revolutionize their political management arrangements and equally prescriptive regarding the details. Local authorities are to have, in effect, new constitutions, and the government is laying down detailed requirements such as the posts and roles of key members and officers, their mode of appointment and inter-relationships, the size and composition of cabinets, the roles of committees, etc. There is still some element of choice and local discretion, but the government paper *Local Leadership, Local Choice* (1999) which accompanied the Local Government (Organisation and Standards) draft Bill confined itself to the three models outlined in the 1998 White Paper. How much room for manoeuvre councils have in practice remains to be seen.

Parallel developments have occurred in Wales and Scotland. Reform proposals like those in England were produced for Wales by the Welsh Office. There were a series of consultative papers covering the same aspects of local government and these too resulted in a White Paper (*Local Voices: Modernising Local Government in Wales*, Cm 4028, Stationery Office, 1998). Consequently, the local government legislation on Capping and Best Value (see p. 591) and Organization and Standards (see p. 583) applies to Wales as well as England.

In Scotland, the devolution of power to the new Parliament and Executive was accompanied by the setting up of a Commission to consider (i) the relationship between them and local authorities, and (ii) methods of improving local democracy and accountability. The (McIntosh) Commission produced two consultative papers and a final report, *Moving Forward: Local Government and the Scottish Parliament* (Scottish Office, 1999). In its final report, the Commission sought to modernize local government and make local authorities more open, efficient and accountable. Consequently, it recommended: (a) a Covenant and a

---

* See M. Power, *The Audit Explosion*, Demos, 1999, and S. Jenkins, *The Times*, 3 February 1997 and 13 January 1999; see also M. Taylor, *The Times*, 13 September 1999, p. 17.

Joint Conference to establish a dialogue and working relationship between Parliament/Ministers and the councils; (b) a power of general competence for councils; (c) an inquiry into local government finance; (d) a review of local elections, to consider a rolling register, postal and electronic voting, a 4-year term (from 2005) and proportional representation (from 2002); (e) a review, by all councils, of their committees, workloads and meeting times and other management arrangements, especially to consider clarifying accountability by formalizing the political leadership (possibly by direct election); (f) the formalization and moderation of party whipping; (g) a review of councillor training and remuneration and perhaps the provision of a job description; (h) the retention and strengthening of community councils, with the possibility of extending their election to 16-year-olds; and (i) the development of civic education.

The Scottish Executive has responded positively to this report, declaring that 'Local government has a rightful place at the heart of the New Scotland. There should be "parity of esteem" between central and local government, with mutual trust and respect on either side' (Scottish Executive Press Release, 9 July 1999). It has declared an acceptance of the majority of the recommendations, and, while councils are expected to review (by 2001) their own decision-making processes, the Executive has established the Renewing Local Democracy Working Party to look at attracting and rewarding councillors and at local election systems. It is also taking some action on finance – a review of the grant distribution and capital finance systems, a revaluation of business rates, developing local links with business (through private finance and BIDs and by developing the pooling of funding streams between central, local and other agencies to secure savings and joined-up delivery. In the meantime, the policy of Best Value (in the delivery of services) is being developed, and the Scottish Parliament is processing the Standards in Public Life Bill to implement a new ethical framework for local authorities (and quangos) in Scotland.

Local government was changed radically under the Conservative governments of 1979–97. The election of the Labour government has started a transformation in the context and culture of local (and national) government in Britain. There is an obligation and drive for change and innovation – in the direction of a more citizen/ community-oriented participation and provision, a more collaborative and integrated ('joined-up') approach to local (and national) governance, and a more consultative rather than confrontational relationship between the two levels of government.

There is a serious challenge to local government. It is underpinned by what has been called 'the carrot and the Semtex'. In five years, no council will be quite the same. If Best Value fails to deliver significant and measurable improvements in the quality of services (and Labour's local reputation) responsibilities can be lost to other agencies; indeed several education authorities such as Islington LB and Hackney LB are already having to transfer some of their responsibilities to private companies. Then there is the uncertain impact on local authorities of devolution (though the Government of Wales Act 1998, for example, imposes a statutory duty on ther Assembly to promote and foster local government). In England, the creation of unaccountable Regional Development Agencies (despite their having some councillor input/membership) is causing some concern. They currently spend some £2 billion a year (see *RDA News*, 2, 1999) and the nine RDAs have been described by John Prescott as 'powerful and influential bodies with substantial budgets, able to make a real mark on the economies of the regions'. Regional assemblies or chambers may help to balance and check the Agencies, but ultimately, these are accountable to the Minister. And furthermore, the chambers may themselves draw powers away from local councils – indeed they could displace shire counties.

In general, the behaviour of the Labour government has been something of a surprise. It has not expanded the state, significantly increased taxation, taken over private businesses, restored trade union powers. The Chancellor of the Exchequer, Gordon Brown, has pursued consistent ('responsible') fiscal and monetary policy and 'prudent' spending! This is contrary to many people's expectations – hence, 'New' Labour or the 'Third Way', which seeks to steer between the old Labour top-down, centralized/Fordist state approach and the Conservative/Thatcherist free market system, to pursue economic growth and social cohesion through a 'synthesis of public values and private dynamism' (involving stakeholding, partnerships, social

inclusion, improved education, modernization and rewarded achievement and enterprise, etc.)*

While the public sector has not received any particular favours,
neither has it been the particular object of attack; while it is being
pressed to reform and modernize, the government has also applied
this policy to other organizations such as its own party and, through
admonition, to private business.

This quest to modernize – 'a mission to transform the public
services'† – is perhaps most thoroughgoing in the case of local government. It has a number of worrying features, as indicated above – in
particular, the extent of central control, direction and regulation.‡
There are renewed references to the command and managerial state
and analogies with the USSR (e.g. in the *Local Government Chronicle*,
10 September 1999, p. 3) and suggestions that local authorities are
becoming merely instruments for implementing the government's
election manifesto. There is also concern at the uniformity and homo-
genization of local services and processes, with consequential loss
of innovation.[22] Indeed, the government has been characterized as
'control freaks'.

For the government, the end – better and more equal health,
education, safety, etc., and reduced poverty and social exclusion –
justifies the means; (see Environment Select Committee Report, p. 597
above, para 8). And in another sense, councils 'must be forced to be
free'.

It is to be hoped that this is a short phase. And every threat can

---

* Though Professor Sanderson, for one, sees it as a sell-out to New Right thinking: see
Local Government Chronicle, 3.9.99, p. 16.

† Tony Blair, *The Times*, 2 September 1999. He also declared that 'change is not an
option', (*Local Government 'Voice'*, July, 1998, LGA). But it is not, apparently, pain-free,
even for the Prime Minister, who revealed (6 July 1999) that he bore 'scars on his back'
in his efforts to change the public sector which he described as manifesting the 'forces
of conservatism' (Labour conference, September 1999). On the other hand, at the
Labour Party conference in September 1999, John Prescott declared that 'we have a
new, positive partnership . . . No longer is local government treated as the enemy
within. We value public services . . .'

‡ For example, it has been estimated that government education policy has resulted
in the processing of over 2,600 school plans: see *The Times*, 6 September 1999; also 8
July 1998.

also be an opportunity. There is much to be optimistic about in the government's programme, for it has promised that if local authorities demonstrate their ability to deliver the required changes, then the rewards are potentially substantial. Power will be devolved when councils show responsibility; in effect, modernization earns freedom and resources. In anticipation of that, under the Local Government Act 2000, local authorities are being freed up and given the power to promote the economic, social and environmental wellbeing of their communities. And there is in the government's reform programme for local government an important recognition that local government is more than efficient service delivery and consumer/user satisfaction – a recognition that local government is about local governance and democracy. The programme is centred around getting 'in touch' with the people and strengthening local democracy. Alongside the concern for the quality of local *services* is a concern for the quality of *government*, and a recognition of local authorities' political and governmental role. It is very much a programme of democratic renewal. Alongside (even beyond?) the self-interest of the service user/consumer, there must be consideration of common purpose and the common good.

The various proposals to enhance participation, public consultation, community leadership and citizenship education, together with the promise of the general power to promote the well-being of their areas, will help to redress the balance of the purpose and place of local government. In so far as this becomes a reality, local government will be 'walking on two legs'.

APPENDIX 1

Birmingham Elections and the National Swing

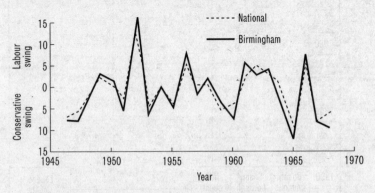

(Note: Swing = [% gain by major party + % loss by other] ÷ 2)

APPENDIX 2

The Changing Pattern of Local Government

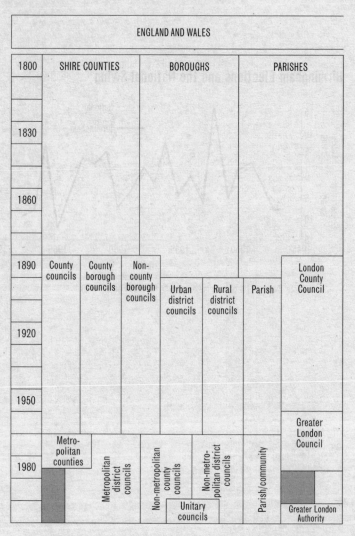

ENGLAND AND WALES

1800	SHIRE COUNTIES	BOROUGHS	PARISHES

1800
1830
1860
1890
1920
1950
1980

County councils

County borough councils

Non-county borough councils

Urban district councils

Rural district councils

Parish

London County Council

Metro-politan counties

Metropolitan district councils

Non-metropolitan county councils

Non-metro-politan district councils

Unitary councils

Parish/community

Greater London Council

Greater London Authority

		SCOTLAND			

| | | COUNTIES | BURGHS | KIRK/ PARISH | 1800 |

Ad hoc bodies associated with local government – considerably absorbed by local authorities during this period though some reappear on a national or regional basis in the period since the Second World War

1830

1860

County councils

1890

Burgh councils — Parishes

London borough councils

1920

County councils — Burgh councils — District councils — Counties of cities councils

1950

Greater London borough councils — Regional councils — District councils — (Community) councils

1980

Unitary councils

APPENDIX 3

Election Contests and Turnout 1945–70

Average % polls at government elections (England and Wales)

Year	County councils	County boroughs	Non-county boroughs and UDCs	RDCs
1945	30.1	45.6	46.4	47.9
1949	42.5	52.2	47.0	51.6
1952	43.2	49.9	50.9	52.0
1955	36.5	43.8	45.0	48.2
1958	33.3	40.3	42.9	46.2
1961	35.7	40.6	42.3	45.0
1964	41.0	40.5	42.0	45.1
1967	38.7	40.3	42.8	42.8
1970	33.8	37.6	40.4	42.3

Uncontested seats (%) at local government elections (England and Wales)

Year	County councils	County boroughs	Non-county boroughs and UDCs	RDCs
1945	43.5	7.8	7.3	59.2
1949	52.1	7.7	19.2	66.5
1952	55.3	12.4	25.4	67.2
1955	60.7	18.5	31.5	72.7
1958	60.9	18.6	32.1	75.2
1961	61.2	12.8	28.5	73.9
1964	55.6	8.8	19.7	69.9
1970	55.0	6.0	23.0	70.0

Source: Registrar General's Statistical Review of England and Wales 1970, Part II; and the Maud Report, Vol. I, p. 93 (amended).

Scottish local authorities 1970

	Uncontested seats (%)	Voting turnout (%)
Scottish local authorities	50	44.1
Counties of cities	0	39.4
Large burghs	14	43.8
Small burghs	40	46.9
Landward areas	67	53.6
Districts	80	53.3

Source: Registrar General of Scotland: Annual Report 1970, Part II.

APPENDIX 4

An Example of a County Council Agenda

Please sign the Attendance Book in the vestibule of
the Shire Hall before entering the Council Chamber

WESSEX COUNTY COUNCIL

LOCAL GOVERNMENT ACT 1972

YOU ARE HEREBY SUMMONED to attend a Meeting of the
Wessex County Council to be held in the Council Chamber, Shire
Hall, Selmer, on Wednesday next, the 23rd June, 1999, at 10.30 a.m.
The business is specified in the following Agenda.

Anyone requiring further information about the meeting or wishing
to inspect any of the background papers used in the preparation of
the reports referred to in the Agenda is requested to contact Mr
Lionel Hampton, County Secretary and Solicitor's Dept, County Hall,
Selmer.

Dated this 14th day of June, 1999

Charles Mingus

Chief Executive
County Hall, Selmer

To: The Meeting of the Wessex County Council

AGENDA

1. The Meeting to be opened with Prayer.
2. To sign the Minutes of the meeting of the Council held on 28 April,
   1999.
3. Apologies for absence.

4. Chairman's announcements.
5. Notice of Motion – Hunting.

Mrs E. Fitzgerald to move, in accordance with notice duly given:

(i) That the Council welcomes the recent decision of the National Trust to limit the number of occasions that land within their control is hunted over together with the banning of motorized hunt followers, and in indicating its support for these policies, seeks to make provision for similar measures over council-owned land.

(ii) That this motion be treated as urgent for the purposes of Standing order 26.

6. To consider the reports of the following Committees: –

A Policy and Resources Committee
B Planning and Transportation Committee
C Public Protection Committee
D Social Services Committee
E Libraries, Museums and Records Committee
F Education and Cultural Services Committee

(Copies of these reports have already been circulated.)

Note: All the reports mentioned above, including any documents circulated previously or with this Summons, are to be considered and taken as part of the Agenda.

APPENDIX 5

An Example of a Committee Agenda: Wessex County Council Social Services Committee – 8 June 1999

A meeting of the Social Services Committee will be held in the Brubeck Room, County Hall, Selmer, on Tuesday 8 June 1999 at 2.15 pm. This meeting will be open to the public and press, subject to the passing of any resolution under Section 100A(4) of the Local Government Act 1972.

Charles Mingus
County Secretary and Solicitor

1. Minutes of the meeting held on 4 May 1999.
2. Public Question Time: to allow members of the public to ask questions or make statements about any matter on the Agenda.
3. Community Services Sub-Committee: to consider the quarterly report of the Sub-Committee.
4. Planning and Resources Sub-Committee: to consider the quarterly report of the Sub-Committee.
5. Grants to outside bodies: to consider a report by the Director of Social Services.
6. Proposed Strategies for the Care of the Mentally Disabled: to consider the consultation document prepared jointly by the Director of Social Services and the Wessex District Health Authority.
7. Benefit Payments to People in Voluntary and Private Residential Care Homes: to consider a report by the Director of Social Services.
8. Best Value Position Statement: to consider a report by the Director of Social Services regarding the Social Service Department's response to Best Value proposals.
9. Report of the Gypsy and Traveller Sites Panel.

10. <u>Annual Report on Complaints about the Social Services Department</u>.

11. <u>Report of the Director of Social Services – Part 1</u>: to consider the quarterly report of the Director on matters (a) for decision and (b) for information.

12. <u>Action agreed by the Chairman</u>: to report the action taken in consultation with the Chariman, as set out in the schedule to be laid on the table.

13. To seal and to authorize the County Solicitor to sign any necessary documents arising out of the matters dealt with at the meeting.

14. <u>Any other business</u>.

15. <u>Confidential Business: Exclusion of the Press and Public</u>: to consider passing a resolution under Section 100A(4) of the Local Government Act 1972 that the public be excluded from the remainder of the meeting, on the grounds that if the public were present during that item of business there would be a likelihood of disclosure of information on the following descriptions:–

    'Information relating to the financial or business affairs of any particular person (other than the authority).'
    'The amount of any expenditure proposed to be incurred by the authority under any particular contract for the acquisition of property or the supply of goods or services.'

16. <u>Report of the Director of Social Services – Part 2</u>.

APPENDIX 6

An Example of Committee Structure (County Council)

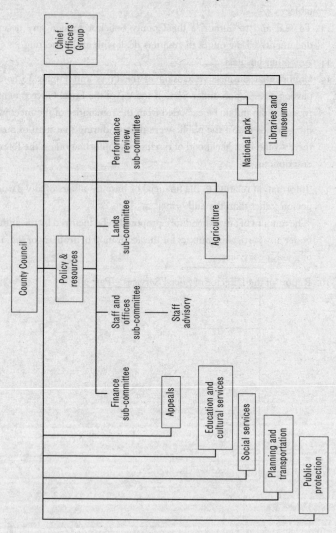

APPENDIX 7

An Example of Departmental Structure (County Council)

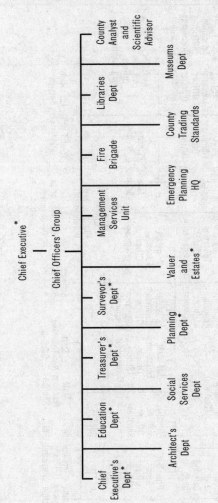

Chief Executive *

Chief Officers' Group

| Chief Executive's Dept * | Education Dept * | Treasurer's Dept * | Surveyor's Dept * | Valuer and Estates * | Management Services Unit | Fire Brigade | Libraries Dept | County Analyst and Scientific Advisor |

| Architect's Dept | Social Services Dept | Planning Dept * | Valuer and Estates * | Emergency Planning HQ | County Trading Standards | Museums Dept |

* Indicates permanent membership of the Chief Officers' Group (COG)

APPENDIX 8

A County Council's Education Department

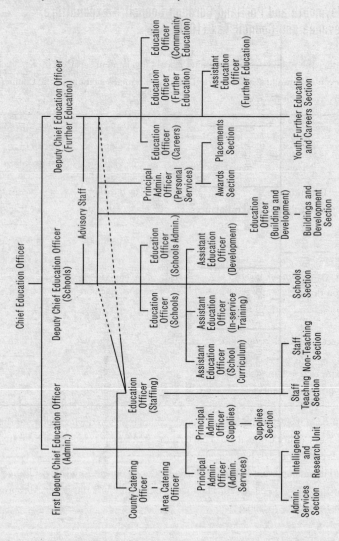

APPENDIX 9

Weymouth and Portland Borough Council – Expenditure, Revenue and Council Tax (1998)

Under the new system of financing Local Government services, the Revenue Estimates are converted into the Council's element of the Council Tax as set out below:

	1997/98 £	Amount per head of population
Net Expenditure	6,948,650	110.54
Less Contributions from Balances	460,650	7.33
	6,488,000	103.21
Less:		
Revenue Support Grant	2,554,000	40.63
Non-domestic Rates Pool	1,995,000	31.74
Collection Fund Adjustment	165,550	2.63
Precept on Collection Fund	1,773,450	28.21
Expressed as Council Tax Base	20,600	
Expressed as Band D	86.09	

This can then be expanded to include all tax bands and when added to the Dorset County Council and Police Authority elements gives the total sum collectable for each band, as shown below.

The total amount levied by Dorset County Council from this Authority for 1997/98 is £11,457,926. The total amount levied by the Police Authority for 1997/98 is £1,309,954.

	Weymouth and Portland B.C.	Dorset Police	Dorset County Council	Transitional Reduction	Total (£)
Band A	57.39	42.39	370.81	17.29	453.30
Band B	66.96	49.46	432.61	20.17	528.86
Band C	76.52	56.52	494.41	23.05	604.40
Band D	86.09	63.59	556.21	25.93	679.96
Band E	105.22	77.72	679.81	31.69	831.06
Band F	124.35	91.85	803.41	37.45	982.16
Band G	143.48	105.98	927.02	43.22	1,133.26
Band H	172.18	127.18	1,112.42	51.86	1,359.92

NOTE: The total payable for Council Taxpayers resident in Portland is slightly higher due to a precept of £15,000 from Portland Town Council.

APPENDIX 10

Functions of Parish Councils in England and Community Councils in Wales

A. Powers to provide facilities and/or to contribute towards the provision of facilities by others

1. Allotments
2. *Arts and Recreation*

   Arts and Crafts, support and encouragement

   Community halls, provision

   Recreational facilities (e.g. parks and open spaces, playing fields, swimming baths etc.)

   Tourism, encouragement
3. *Burials* etc.

   Cemeteries and crematoria†

   Closed churchyards, maintenance†

   Mortuaries, provision†
4. *Environmental Health*

   Cleaning and drainage of ponds etc.

   Litter control

   Public conveniences

   Wash houses and launderettes
5. *Footpath, Roads and Traffic*

   Bus shelters*

   Footpaths – creation and maintenance; signposting*

   Footway lighting, provision*

   Parking facilities – cycle and motor cycle parks, off-street car parks*

   Rights of way, acquisition and maintenance

   Roadside verge, provision, maintenance and protection*

6. Public Clocks
7. War Memorials†

B. Specific powers to receive notifications and represent parish interests to other authorities
  1. District councils must notify parish councils in England and community councils in Wales of the following –
    a. planning applications received by them where the parish or community council asks to be so notified;
    b. intention to make by-laws relating to hackney-carriages, music and dancing, promenades, sea shore, registry of servants and street naming;
    c. intention to provide a cemetery in a parish or community;
    d. proposals to carry out sewerage works.
  2. County councils must consult parish councils in England and community councils in Wales about footpath surveys.†
  3. Parish councils in England and community councils in Wales may in certain circumstances withhold consent to proposals for stopping up unclassified highways and footpaths.
  4. Parish councils in England and community councils in Wales are 'minor authorities' for the purpose of appointing managers of primary schools serving their area.†
  5. Parish councils in England and community councils in Wales may often act as trustees or make appointments to the trustees of local charities.
  6. In England, the district councils may confer any power of a parish council on to a parish meeting.

* The exercise of these powers is subject to the consent of the county council.
† These powers or rights, as appropriate, are also available to parish meetings.

NOTE: *There may be additional responsibilities as a result of agreements with District and Unitary councils, with County councils and perhaps Police Authorities. Some of these result from the Local Government and Rating Act 1997*

APPENDIX 11

Income and Expenditure Pattern of Parish Councils 1990

Expenditure		
Finance charges & insurance – 6.8%	Bank charges	0.3%
	Loans	4.7%
	Other	0.6%
	Insurance	1.2%
Office administration – 26.9%	Clerk's salary	11.0%
	Audit fee	0.7%
	Other	15.2%
Activities – 66.3%	Parks & open spaces	20.4%
	Village/community hall	12.8%
	Burials/crematoria facilities	6.8%
	Indoor recreation	6.6%
	Tourism	4.1%
	Lighting	3.4%
	Footpaths	2.5%
	Public amenities	1.4%
	Car & cycle parks	1.3%
	Allotments	1.1%
	Communications	0.8%
	Litter bins	0.8%
	Competitions	0.2%
	Other	4.1%

Revenue

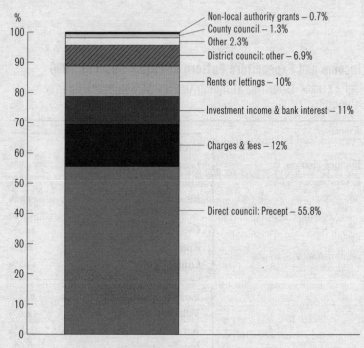

Source: The Role of Parish and Town Councils in England, HMSO, 1992.

APPENDIX 12

An Extract from the Standing Orders of Somerset County Council

(reproduced by kind permission)

POLICY AND RESOURCES COMMITTEE

86(1)(a) The Policy and Resources Committee shall consist of 19 councillors, including the Chairman and Vice-Chairman of the Council and the Chairmen of [all the Council's committees]

(2) It shall be the duty of the Committee

(a) to consider and advise the Council regarding:

(i) their strategic policies, and for such purposes to consider the broad social and economic needs of the county (having regard also to any relevant national and regional considerations), to take into account (and to be consulted in the preparation of) any structure plans for the county, and to advise the Council on what their aims and priorities should be, and on methods and programmes for the achievement of those, either in whole or in part;

(ii) their overall level of expenditure both on capital and revenue account, their forward capital programme and the allocation and control of the financial, manpower and land resources of the Council;

(b) (i) to regulate and control the financial affairs of the Council and for such purpose from time to time to embody their directions relating to financial matters in a code of procedure which shall be observed by all committees of the Council;

(ii) to present to the February meeting of the Council each year estimates of income and expenditure of the Council for the next financial year together with a recommendation as to the amount which will be required to be raised by means of precepts in respect of that financial year;

(c) to keep under review the progress of any of the Council's work and services, the effectiveness of such work and services, and the standards and levels of, and the necessity for, existing services;

(d) to examine and make recommendations to either the Council or the committee concerned as the Policy and Resources Committee consider appropriate, on any proposal or decision of a service committee for new major policies or services or for any material changes in existing major policies or services, with due regard to any impact upon the Council's strategic policies or resources, for which purpose each service committee is hereby directed to refer any such proposal or decision to the Policy and Resources Committee before it is implemented;

(e) to keep under review the main policies and aims of the Council and the arrangements for their implementation;

(f) to ensure that the organization and the management processes of the Council are designed to make the most effective contribution to the achievement of the Council's aims; and to keep them under review, making recommendations as necessary for change in either committee or departmental structures, or the distribution of functions and responsibilities, or Standing Orders;

(g) to advise the Council on the carrying out of any major building development schemes by the Council in association with any other local or public authority or private developer;

(h) to ensure that the Council maintain effective liaison with other local authorities and appropriate bodies in respect of matters within the purview of the Commitee;

(i) to ensure the maintenance of an effective public relations service;

(j) to determine polling districts for County Council elections;

(k) to recommend to the Council the appointment of the Chief Executive, the Deputy Chief Executive and County Solicitor, the County Treasurer, the County Architect and the County Valuer and Estates Officer;

(l) to make recommendations to the Council regarding the appointment of:
(i) councillors to serve on the various committees (including the Staff Advisory Committee and the County Joint Committee);
(ii) persons to serve as additional members of committees;
(iii) councillors and other persons to serve on statutory and other outside

bodies or committees thereof under whose constitutions the Council are entitled to representation except in those cases where this power is specifically reserved to another committee;

(m) to act as the controlling committee in relation to the Departments of the Chief Executive, the County Solicitor and the County Architect.

FINANCE SUB-COMMITTEE

87(1)(a) The Policy and Resources Committee shall appoint a Finance Sub-Committee consisting of ten councillors including the Chairman of the Council, the Chairman and four other members of the Policy and Resources Committee;

(b) the Chairman shall be elected from members of the Sub-Committee who are also members of the Policy and Resources Committee.

(2) Subject to the overall control of the Policy and Resources Committee, it shall be the duty of the Sub-Committee

(a) to advise the Committee as to
– the methods and procedures for controlling the financial affairs of the Council and to supervise their implementation and, where appropriate, give directions;
– the Council's annual capital and revenue budgets and forward capital and revenue estimates for successive years;
– members' allowances.

(b) to make recommendations regarding the granting of supplementary estimates, provided that the Sub-Committee may in their discretion approve any supplementary estimate which the Council are obliged by law to incur or suffer or which is required to meet an unforeseen increase in the level of costs, prices or remuneration; [and in respect of certain other items].

(c) to examine estimates of the cost of proposals by committees and to draw the attention of the Policy and Resources Committee to any points in connection with such estimates or proposals as they may think fit;

(d) to act as the controlling sub-committee in relation to the County Treasurer's department.

APPENDIX 13

An Example of a Schedule of Delegation of Powers to Officers

The Director of Social Services and in his absence or where appropriate, a Deputy Director (and where specifically mentioned, other officers) have delegated to them the powers set out below, subject to the overall policy of the Council, its Committees and sub-Committees, and the expenditure involved being within the overall estimate provision and to the amounts expended on any individual client (residential placements excepted) not exceeding £250.

(1) To authorize the payment of boarding-out allowances in accordance with the Scale approved by the Committee.

(2) Area Officers to approve or refuse applications from persons wishing to become foster parents to children in care, subject to a report being made to the Care and Community Services Sub-Committee stating the reasons where application is not approved and to the Director of Social Services seeking the observations of any member of the Committee living in that locality.

(3) To authorize, subject to reporting to the Chairman and Vice-Chairman of the Social Services Committee, at the first available opportunity, to grant or refuse permission for a period in secure accommodation in accordance with the law in respect of the children in care of the County Council but admitted to Homes not under the management of this authority, and to authorize the County Solicitor, in consultation with the Director of Social Services, to apply to the Juvenile Court where appropriate for an Order under Section 21(a) of the Child Care Act 1980, enabling a child to be kept in secure accommodation. (Also exercisable by the Principal Assistant, Children and Families.)

(4) To authorize the County Solicitor or the persons designated in Standing Order 107(a), in consultation with the Director of Social Services or the Deputy Director, Operational Services, to issue a complaint to the junevile court under Section 43 of the Adoption Act 1958 that a child be removed to a place of safety subject to the action taken being reported to the next meeting of the Care and Community Services Sub-Committee.

(5) To make decisions on or give effect to the recommendations of the Adoption Panel in relation to the acceptance, placement and freeing of children for adoption and to authorize the County Solicitor to make application to Court, on the recommendation of the Adoption Panel and Director of Social Services for a Freeing Order. (Also exercisable by the Principal Assistant, Children and Families and Area Officers as appropriate.)

(6) To give or withhold consent to an application for custodianship, including the payment of allowances. (In disputed cases, the power to hear representations and determine the question will be delegated to the Care of Children Panel).

(7) To deal with the question of charges for children attending day nurseries on the basis of social need. (Also exercisable by the Principal Assistant, Children and Families).

(8) To vary the assessed charge for parental contributions on the basis of social need. (Also exercisable by the Principal Assistant, Children and Families).

(9) To decide the dates of terms and holidays at Day Centres for the handicapped.

(10) To issue permits under the Minibus Act 1977 where appropriate.

(11) To authorize the issue of child employment permits in compliance with County Council Bye-Laws under the Children and Young Persons Act 1933 and to issue licences to perform under the Children (Performances) Regulations, 1968. (Also exercisable by Senior Administrative Assistant, Support Services under the direction of Principal Assistant, Children and Families.)

(12) The County Solicitor acting in consultation with the Director of Social Services be authorized to institute care proceedings under Section 1, Children and Young Persons Act 1969, other than under Section 1(2)(e) on grounds of education where a recommendation is required to the

Special Services Sub-Committee for the Education and Cultural Services Committee by the County Solicitor acting in consultation with the Director of Social Services and the Chief Education Officer.

APPENDIX 14

Council Tax Valuation Bands

Range of values	Valuation band	Range of values	Valuation band
England		*Scotland*	
not exceeding £40,000	A	not exceeding £27,000	A
£40,001–£52,000	B	£27,001–£35,000	B
£52,001–£68,000	C	£35,001–£45,000	C
£68,001–£88,000	D	£45,001–£58,000	D
£88,001–£120,000	E	£58,001–£80,000	E
£120,001–£160,000	F	£80,001–£106,000	F
£160,001–£320,000	G	£106,001–£212,000	G
exceeding £320,000	H	exceeding £212,000	H
Wales			
not exceeding £30,000	A		
£30,001–£39,000	B		
£39,001–£51,000	C		
£51,001–£66,000	D		
£66,001–£90,000	E		
£90,001–£120,000	F		
£120,001–£240,000	G		
exceeding £240,000	H		

APPENDIX 15

An Example of an Audit Commission Profile

For purpose of performance review, local authorities receive this information, comparing them with a group (or family) of similar authorities. In this case, for Somerset, the 'family' consists of eighteen county councils.

	Somerset	Family Average	Cost of Difference
PRIMARY SCHOOLS			£000
Pupil/teacher ratio	22·2	21·9	(478)
Salary and oncosts per teacher (£)	12,126	12,711	(859)
Cost per pupil	£	£	
Teaching costs	558	599	(1·336)
Education support staff	32	26	223
Other employees	76	78	(58)
Premises	104	106	(74)
Books and educational equipment	31	25	202
Home to school transport	14	17	(114)
Other costs less income	7	11	(129)
	823	862	(1,286)

Pupils per school	140	142
Pupils per 1,000 population		
Under 5	11·2	7·1
5 and over	60·8	65·5
Number of schools		
Nursery	0	2
Primary	234	243
Percentage of primary schools		
50 or less pupils	21%	22%
51–200 pupils	50%	52%
201–400 pupils	28%	24%
401 or more pupils	1%	2%
Number of FTE Teachers	1,511	1,625

How well do our councils perform? – Examples of the main Audit Commission's performance indicators (1996)

Somerset County Council

37 per cent of three and four-year-olds with school places (county council national average 49 per cent).

Spending per primary pupil £1,651 (av £1,624); secondary pupil £2,171 (av £2,150).

44 per cent special needs statements prepared within 18 weeks (av 47 per cent).

11 per cent of over 75s helped to live at home (av 10 per cent).

89 per cent of minor items of equipment to help people live at home provided within three weeks (av 77 per cent).

The district authorities

THE Audit Commission figures for Taunton Deane and West Somerset District councils (WSDC):

Average time to re-let council homes – 2 weeks; West Somerset District Council – 3.9 weeks (South West district council average 4.8 weeks).

1 per cent tenants with rent arrears 13 weeks or more; WSDC 2 per cent (av 3 per cent).

6 per cent household waste recycled; WSDC 14.1 per cent (av 6 per cent).

73 per cent householder planning applications dealt with in eight weeks;

100 per cent of people entering residential care offered single rooms (av 87 per cent).

76 per cent of children in council care in foster homes (av 68 per cent).

11 books and other items per person borrowed from libraries (av 9.7).

0.25 trading standards inspections per high and medium risk premises (av 0.36).

99.5 per cent fire calls at which attendance standards were met (av 95 per cent).

Cost of fire service per person £20 (av £24).

Total county spending per person £551 (av £592).

WSDC 75 per cent (av 79 per cent).

91 per cent land searches carried out within 10 working days; WSDC 98 per cent (av 87 per cent).

73 per cent council tax benefit applications processed in 14 days; WSDC 85 per cent (av 85 per cent).

98 per cent council tax collected; WSDC 98 per cent (av 96.1 per cent).

71 per cent inspections of food premises of total inspections which should have been carried out; WSDC 100 per cent (av 84 per cent).

Total net spending per head of population £80; WSDC £112 (av £95).

APPENDIX 16

Strategic Financial Options and Tactics

Strategic policy options	Fiscal tactics
Services shift	A1: contract out to private business
	A2: contract out to voluntary agencies
	A3: contract out to other public agencies
	A4: shift responsibility to other governmental units
Service reduction	B1: reduce inter-agency funded services (e.g. joint financing, matching grants)
	B2: limit demand/reduce service eligibility
	B3: reduce provision of low priority services
	B4: cut least effective services
	B5: across-the-board service cuts
Limit expenditure	C1: reduce overhead expenditure
	C2: reduce capital expenditure
	C3: reduce spending on supplies
	C4: spend below inflation rate
	C5: defer maintenance expenditure
	C6: compulsory and voluntary redundancies
	C7: hiring freeze
	C8: reduce workforce through attrition
	C9: reduce overtime
	C10: early retirement

	C11: more flexible pay structures
	C12: more flexible service conditions
	C13: across-the-board efficiency savings
Productivity shift	D1: strategic productivity techniques
	D2: capital/labour substitution (e.g. IT)
	D3: joint purchasing arrangements
	D4: training
	D5: customer service
	D6: quality improvement
	D7: employee motivation
	D8: performance management
	D9: business process redesign
Revenue generation	E1: diversify funding sources
	E2: increase prices or user charges
	E3: draw down reserves/surpluses
	E4: explore new intergovernmental revenue sources (SRB, EU)
	E5: explore ways of increasing RSG/UBR
	E6: increase long-term borrowing
	E7: increase new sources of long-term capital (e.g. PFI)
	E8: sell assets
	E9: improve treasury management/return on investment portfolio
	E10: increase council tax

Source: More for Less, LGMB, 1996 and S. E. Clarke, *Urban Innovation and Autonomy*, Sage, Newbury Park, California, 1989.

APPENDIX 17

Improving Voter Turnout?

'Which of the following suggestions would make you personally more likely to vote in the next council elections?'

	All	Rarely vote	Never vote	18-24 year olds
Voting from home using the telephone	40	56	36	49
Having polling stations at shopping centres	38	45	35	46
Having polling stations at the supermarket	37	46	35	45
Polling stations being open for more than one day	32	40	36	53
Voting by post	26	48	23	29
Voting from home using digital television or the Internet	26	47	24	35
Polling stations being open 24 hours	24	39	27	37
Voting from work using digital television or the Internet	24	36	23	35
Voting on Saturday, instead of Thursday	22	28	20	28
Voting for a directly elected mayor who will run the council	21	29	19	19
Voting on Sunday, instead of Thursday	16	26	17	21
Having polling stations at train stations	14	14	11	12

Source: Market Opinion Research International (MORI), April 1998. See too *Local Government Chronicle*, 26 June 1998.

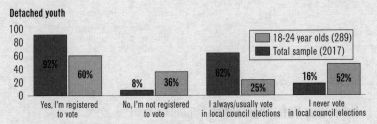

Detached youth

Source: Market Opinion Research International (MORI), April 1998.
See *Local Government Chronicle*, 26 June 1998.

APPENDIX 18

Calculation of the Revenue Support Grant

	Authority X (Low need, high resource)	Authority Y (High need, low resource)
Population	540,000	540,000
Standard Spending Assessment	£310 million	£360 million
Council Tax base (number of band D equivalent properties)	190,000	140,000
Council Tax for Standard Spending	£635	£635
Distributable Amount per head (from UBR/NDR pool)	£250	£250
Population × Distributable Amount per head =	540,000 × £250 =	540,000 × £250 =
Income from redistributed business rates	£135 million	£135 million
Council Tax base × Council Tax for Standard Spending =	190,000 × £635 =	140,000 × £635 =
Income from Council Tax if set at the standard rate	£120.65 million	£88.90 million
Standard Spending Assessment	£310·00 million	£360·00 million

less income from redistributed business rates	−£135·00 million	−£135·00 million
less standard Council Tax income	−£120·65 million	−£88·90 million
= Revenue Support Grant	**£54·35 million**	**£136·10 million**

NOTE: Both authorities have the same population. However authority X has a lower need (as measured by the Standard Spending Assessment) but a higher resource (in terms of the Council Tax it should receive if it sets its Council Tax at the same level as Council Tax for Standard Spending). So authority X needs less Revenue Support Grant to make up the difference between its need and its resources.

Source: A Plain Guide to the Local Government Financial Settlement, HMSO, 1998. Crown copyright is reproduced with the permission of the Controller of Her Majesty's Stationery Office.

APPENDIX 19

Calculation of Council Tax

	Authority X (Low need, high resource)	Authority Y (High need, low resource)
Scenario 1: Assuming budget requirement set at Standard Spending Assessment		
Budget requirement	£310·00 million	£360·00 million
less income from redistributed business rates	−£135·00 million	−£135·00 million
less Revenue Support Grant	−£54·35 million	−£136·10 million
= Actual Council Tax sum needed	£120·65 million	£88·90 million
divided by the council's estimate of Council Tax base (this assumes they will collect Council Tax from 97% of their Council Tax base)	÷ 184,300	÷ 135,800
***equals* Council Tax level for band D**	=£654·64	= £654·64

NOTE: The budget requirement is equal to the Standard Spending Assessment, and both councils make the same estimates of the proportion of the Council Tax base they will successfully collect Council Tax from, so the Council Tax level set is identical. This is achieved because the Revenue Support Grant equalizes the different levels of need and resource.

Scenario 2: Assuming budget requirement set 5% above Standard Spending Assessment

Budget requirement	£325·50 million	£378·00 million
less income from redistributed business rates	−£135·00 million	−£135·00 million
less Revenue Support Grant	−£54·35 million	−£136·10 million
= Actual Council Tax sum needed	£136·15 million	£106·90 million
divided by the council's estimate of Council Tax base (this assumes they will collect Council Tax from 97% of their Council Tax base)	÷ 184,300	÷ 135,800
equals **Council Tax level for band D**	=£738·74	= £787·19

NOTE: With the budget requirement 5% above Standard Spending Assessment, Authority Y has to raise an extra £18 million (compared with authority X's £15.5 million), and has a smaller Council Tax base from which to raise it. So, the Council Tax level for Authority Y is higher than that for Authority X.

Scenario 3: Assuming budget requirement set 5% below Standard Spending Assessment

Budget requirement	£294·50 million	£342·00 million
less income from redistributed business rates	−£135·00 million	−£135·00 million
less Revenue Support Grant	−£54·35 million	−£136·10 million
= Actual Council Tax sum needed	£105·15 million	£70·90 million
divided by the council's estimate of Council Tax base (this assumes they will collect Council Tax from 97% of their Council Tax base)	÷ 184,300	÷ 135,800

equals **Council Tax level for band D** $=£570\cdot54$ $=£522\cdot09$

NOTE: If budget requirements are set below Standard Spending Assessment, the Council Tax level for Authority Y will be lower than for Authority X.

Source: A Plain Guide to the Local Government Financial Settlement, HMSO, 1998. Crown copyright is reproduced with the permission of the Controller of Her Majesty's Stationery Office.

APPENDIX 20

The Transformation of South Somerset District Council

(i) Committee and management structures in 1991

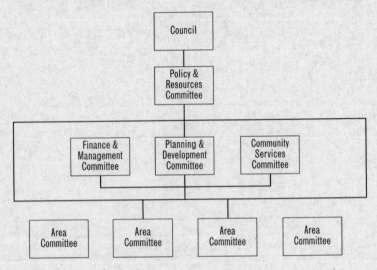

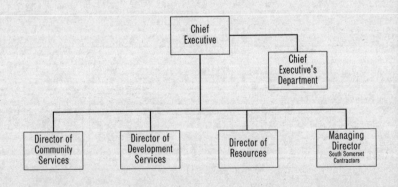

(ii) Committee and management structures in 1996

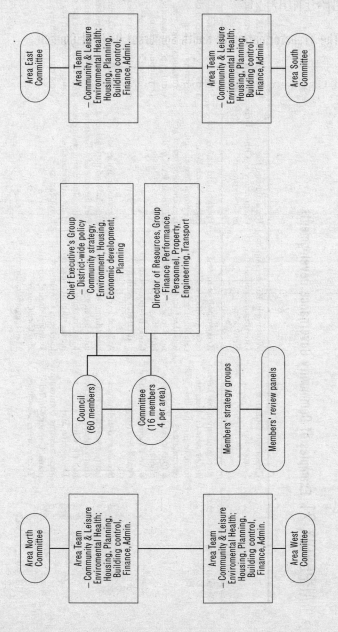

APPENDIX 21 Examples of Community Governance Developments

	Grassroots Community Leadership	Working in Partnership & Inter-organizational Networks	Representing the Community to Other Tiers of Government	Managing the L.A. & Giving Clear Strategic Direction
Cheshire County Council	Reorganization has been a major spur to closer and more responsive links with communities • Quality of Life Survey (1996) • Area Committees to be established (1998)	Recognition of missed opportunities to date: establishing better links with District Councils; need to win, e.g., SRB bids. Good relations with TECs and Health Authority	Political and managerial role in North West Regional Association. Less encouragement at European level to date	Structural reorganization of authority to support elected members in their community roles, e.g. setting up Community Development Dept. covering a range of community-focused services
Coventry City Council	Six area co-ordination teams focused on high disadvantage – covering half the City. Developing and implementing community plans. Capacity-building. Teams are cross-agency	At local level, area co-ordination teams are inter-agency. Joint working in partnership at corporate level, e.g. Coventry & Warwickshire Partnership, also City Centre Management company	Various activities at regional and national level. Part funding of a Brussels office. Increasing awareness of the importance of European issues	Political reorganization to enable elected members to have a stronger community focus through the use of panels focused on key cross-cutting themes.

London Borough of Islington	Innovations in decentralization in 1980s. • 23 neighbourhood offices serving 11 areas. • Each neighbourhood has a forum. Offices now under review as part of organizational review.	Partnerships with business community over economic regeneration are being developed for focus on life-long learning. Relationships with voluntary sector could be more strategic – being reviewed on both sides.	Links to national government – in part because of location in London. Part fund a Brussels office (through Association of London Government) and active in some European policy networks.	Neighbourhood services dept. was established at same time as Neighbourhood offices and forums. Now under structural review to create a strategic focus and co-ordinating relations with external agencies.
South Somerset District Council	Strong commitment to community governance through: • decentralization of political decision-making; • organizational restructuring; • promotion of a culture concerned with meeting community aspirations.	Working with town and parish councils, e.g. town centre for Yeovil.	The emphasis on area working has meant less political attention to other tiers of government, though this will be a focus of future work.	Clear community focus for the vision of the authority, supported by structural and cultural change.
Torfaen County Borough Council	Reorganization has encouraged the articulation of a vision and values statement to underpin a stronger community focus.	Partnership will be important for the new authority – but with an emphasis where possible on providing services directly.	Links with Welsh Office are important for economic and social regeneration. Links with the Welsh Assembly will become important in the future.	Vision and values to support a stronger strategic purpose. A clear Human Resource strategy to counter possible staff demoralization following reorganization.

Source: Leading Communities, LGMB, 1998. Copyright © The Improvement and Development Agency for Local Government.

APPENDIX 22

Reformed Organization and Management of London Borough of Redbridge (1998)

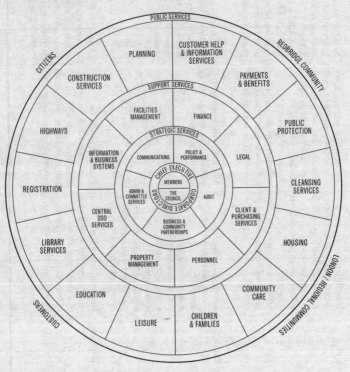

APPENDIX 23

Strategic Choices in Public Service Management

Public service ethos	Public innovation ethos
Concern for procedures	Concern for results – quality of service, efficiency, impact
Controlling	Steering – clear guidance, local autonomy, valuing staff
Conformance	Performance – creative, inventive, risk-taking
Consistency	Diversity – responsive to differences, customized, flexible
Traditional councillor roles	New councillor roles – strategists, scrutineers of performance, community advocates
Service the public	New council roles – empowering consumers, citizens, communities

Source: Freedom Within Boundaries, LGMB, 1997. Copyright © The Improvement and Development Agency for Local Government. As the authors say, 'aspects of the public service ethos are in tension with elements of the emerging public innovation ethos . . . there are great strengths on both sides. It is for each authority to consider, in relation to particular issues and services as well as in relation to its overall stance, where it wishes to locate itself on the six dimensions.'

APPENDIX 24

Cabinet Models

(i) cabinet with a leader

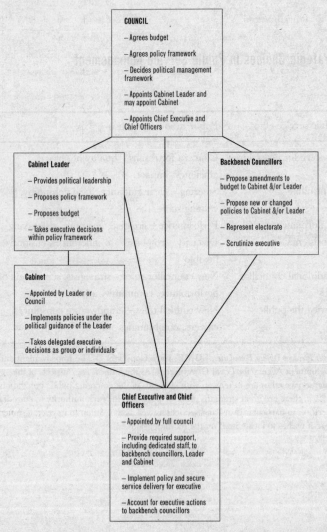

COUNCIL

- Agrees budget
- Agrees policy framework
- Decides political management framework
- Appoints Cabinet Leader and may appoint Cabinet
- Appoints Chief Executive and Chief Officers

Cabinet Leader

- Provides political leadership
- Proposes policy framework
- Proposes budget
- Takes executive decisions within policy framework

Cabinet

- Appointed by Leader or Council
- Implements policies under the political guidance of the Leader
- Takes delegated executive decisions as group or individuals

Backbench Councillors

- Propose amendments to budget to Cabinet &/or Leader
- Propose new or changed policies to Cabinet &/or Leader
- Represent electorate
- Scrutinize executive

Chief Executive and Chief Officers

- Appointed by full council
- Provide required support, including dedicated staff, to backbench councillors, Leader and Cabinet
- Implement policy and secure service delivery for executive
- Account for executive actions to backbench councillors

(ii) directly elected mayor with cabinet

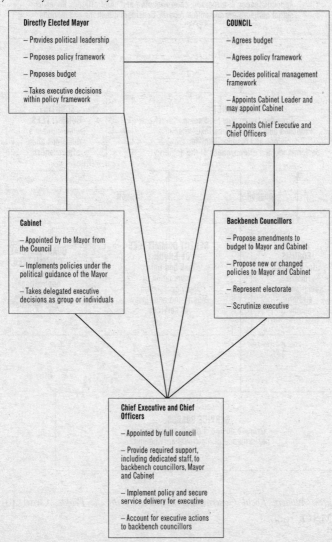

Directly Elected Mayor

– Provides political leadership

– Proposes policy framework

– Proposes budget

– Takes executive decisions within policy framework

COUNCIL

– Agrees budget

– Agrees policy framework

– Decides political management framework

– Appoints Cabinet Leader and may appoint Cabinet

– Appoints Chief Executive and Chief Officers

Cabinet

– Appointed by the Mayor from the Council

– Implements policies under the political guidance of the Mayor

– Takes delegated executive decisions as group or individuals

Backbench Councillors

– Propose amendments to budget to Mayor and Cabinet

– Propose new or changed policies to Mayor and Cabinet

– Represent electorate

– Scrutinize executive

Chief Executive and Chief Officers

– Appointed by full council

– Provide required support, including dedicated staff, to backbench councillors, Mayor and Cabinet

– Implement policy and secure service delivery for executive

– Account for executive actions to backbench councillors

(iii) executive cabinet: a draft member structure

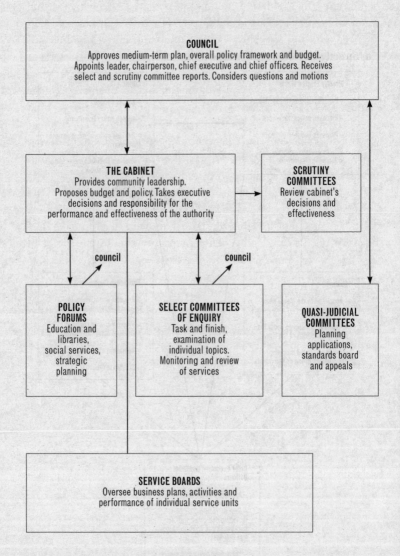

COUNCIL
Approves medium-term plan, overall policy framework and budget.
Appoints leader, chairperson, chief executive and chief officers. Receives
select and scrutiny committee reports. Considers questions and motions

THE CABINET
Provides community leadership.
Proposes budget and policy. Takes executive
decisions and responsibility for the
performance and effectiveness of the authority

SCRUTINY COMMITTEES
Review cabinet's decisions and effectiveness

council

council

POLICY FORUMS
Education and libraries, social services, strategic planning

SELECT COMMITTEES OF ENQUIRY
Task and finish, examination of individual topics. Monitoring and review of services

QUASI-JUDICIAL COMMITTEES
Planning applications, standards board and appeals

SERVICE BOARDS
Oversee business plans, activities and performance of individual service units

Source: Modern Local Government: In Touch with the People, Cmd 4014, HMSO, 1998.

APPENDIX 25

Devising the New System for Decision-making

Whichever precise system is adopted (as between, and within, the mayoral, cabinet, manager, etc.), there are similar fundamental issues facing all councils in developing the division or 'split' between 'executive' and 'non-executive' functions:

1. Who is to exercise 'executive' functions – full council, cabinet &/ or mayor &/or manager, etc., officer delegations +?
2. Who is to exercise non-executive functions – committees, boards, panels, area partnership committees?
3. Numbers, composition, specialized, mixed (e.g. single- or multi-party cabinet)?
4. Precise roles of each (especially of committees/panels re: scrutiny, policy initiatives, feedback) and power relationships (e.g. powers to call-in executive decisions for review; access by individual councillors to raise consituency issues, etc.).
5. Duplication, and possible disagreement, between Council and cabinet/mayor or between cabinet and overview committees/panels.
6. Appropriate level of delegation to officers.

More generally, the new split between 'executive' and 'non-executive' functions will have a dramatic effect on the culture of local authorities, and on roles and relationships. These are difficult to plan and prepare for, and there will inevitably be huge variations.

APPENDIX 26

People Making Contact

Percentage of people making contact over 5-year period with:

Local councillor	20.7
Town Hall	17.4
MP	9.3
Civil servant	7.3
Media	3.8

Source: G. Parry et al., *Political Participation and Democracy in Britain*, CUP, 1992.

APPENDIX 27

Principles of Best Value

Best Value – 12 Provisional Principles (June 1997)

---

1. The duty of Best Value is one that local authorities will owe to local people, both as taxpayers and the customers of local authority services. Performance plans should support the process of local accountability to the electorate.

2. Achieving Best Value is not just about economy and efficiency, but also about effectiveness and the quality of local services – the setting of targets and performance against these should therefore underpin the new regime.

3. The duty will apply to a wider range of services than those covered by CCT.

4. There is no presumption that services must be privatized, and once the regime is in place there will be no compulsion for councils to put their services out to tender, but there is no reason why services should be delivered directly if other more efficient means are available. What matters is what works.

5. Competition will continue to be an important management tool, a test of Best Value and an important feature in performance plans. But it will not be the only management tool and is not in itself enough to demonstrate that Best Value is being achieved.

6. Central government will continue to set the basic framework for service provision, which will in some areas as now include national standards.

7. Detailed local targets should have regard to any national targets, and specified indicators to support comparisons between authorities.

8. Both national and local targets should be built on the performance information that is in any case needed by good managers.

9. Audit processes should confirm the integrity and comparability of performance information.

10. Auditors will report publicly on whether Best Value has been achieved, and should contribute constructively to plans for remedial action. This will include agreeing measurable targets for improvement and reporting on progress against an agreed plan.

11. There should be provision for intervention at the direction of the Secretary of State on the advice of the Audit Commission when an authority has failed to deliver Best Value.

12. The form of intervention should be appropriate to the nature of failure.

Source: Modern Local Government: In Touch with the People, Cmd4014, HMSO, 1998. Crown copyright is reproduced with the permission of the Controller of Her Majesty's Stationery Office.

APPENDIX 28

The Best Value Performance Management Framework

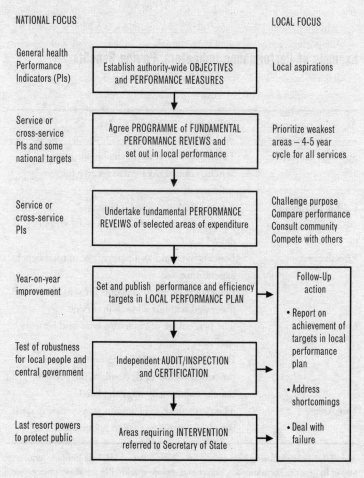

NATIONAL FOCUS

LOCAL FOCUS

General health Performance Indicators (PIs)

Establish authority-wide OBJECTIVES and PERFORMANCE MEASURES

Local aspirations

Service or cross-service PIs and some national targets

Agree PROGRAMME of FUNDAMENTAL PERFORMANCE REVIEWS and set out in local performance

Prioritize weakest areas – 4-5 year cycle for all services

Service or cross-service PIs

Undertake fundamental PERFORMANCE REVEIWS of selected areas of expenditure

Challenge purpose
Compare performance
Consult community
Compete with others

Year-on-year improvement

Set and publish performance and efficiency targets in LOCAL PERFORMANCE PLAN

Follow-Up action

• Report on achievement of targets in local performance plan

Test of robustness for local people and central government

Independent AUDIT/INSPECTION and CERTIFICATION

• Address shortcomings

Last resort powers to protect public

Areas requiring INTERVENTION referred to Secretary of State

• Deal with failure

Source: Modern Local Government: In Touch with the People, Cmd4014, HMSO, 1998. Crown copyright is reproduced with the permission of the Controller of Her Majesty's Stationery Office.

APPENDIX 29

Example of Performance Indicators: Paying Benefits

Aspect of performance	Indicators
Strategic Objectives	To ensure ×% of those eligible for housing benefit/council tax benefit receive full entitlement
Cost & Efficiency	Administration cost per claimant
	Percentage of new claims processed within 14 days
Effectiveness	Benefits overpaid as a percentage of total benefit expenditure
	Percentage of renewal claims for rent allowance processed without a break in service
Quality	The percentage of claimants who said benefits staff were helpful
	Percentage of new Housing Benefit claims processed within 14 days where the correct benefit entitlement was calculated
Fair Access	The percentage of claimants surveyed who said the claim form was easy to understand

Source: Best Value in Housing Framework (Consultation Paper) DETR, January 1999.
NOTE: In general, the nationally prescribed service specific PIs are likely to embrace the following aspects of performance:
1. Strategic objectives – what the service is trying to achieve so as to provide a focus for the service and in order to monitor achievement.

2. Cost and efficiency – of provision, to reassure people, managers and the government that the service is being provided at a price comparable with other authorities.
3. Effectiveness – of service delivery and the systems therefor.
4. Quality – of service, as indicated by user satisfaction and in relation to cost.
5. Fair access – to services, in terms of ease and equality, regardless of race, gender, etc.

APPENDIX 30

Proposed General Principles of Conduct
(to be incorporated in each council's Code of Conduct)

Councillors of local authorities in England are expected to behave according to the highest standards of personal conduct in the performance of their duties. In particular, elected councillors must observe the following principles of conduct.

Community leadership

You should promote and support these principles by leadership and example, always acting in such a way as to preserve public confidence in the council.

Duty to uphold the law

You have a duty to uphold the law, and to act on all occasions in accordance with the public trust placed in you.

Constituency

You have a duty to assist the council to act as far as possible in the interests of the whole community that it serves. Where constituents' interests are in conflict with those of other groups or areas, you should help to ensure that the council is aware of them and that constituents are able to pursue their concerns, but you are not obliged to put the interests of constituents above the general interest.

Selflessness

You should act solely in the public interest. You should never use your position as a councillor to gain for yourself, your family or your friends any financial benefits, preferential treatment or other advantage, or to confer such benefits, treatment or advantage improperly on others.

Integrity and propriety

You should not put yourself in a position where your integrity is called into question by any financial or other obligation. As well as avoiding actual impropriety, you should avoid any appearance of it.

Hospitality

You should record all gifts and hospitality received in connection with membership of the council. You should not accept gifts or hospitality that might reasonably be thought to influence, or be intended to influence, your judgement; or where to do so could bring discredit upon the council.

Decisions

Whilst you may very properly be influenced by the views of others, including your political group, it is your responsibility to decide what view to take, and how to vote, on any question which councillors have to decide.

Objectivity in decision-taking

In carrying out public business, including making public appointments, awarding contracts, or recommending individuals for rewards and benefits, you should make decisions on merit.

Accountability

You are accountable to the electorate and the council's wider community for your actions and your part in reaching decisions, and must submit yourself to whatever scrutiny is appropriate to your office.

Openness

You should be as open as possible about all your actions and your part in reaching decisions. You should seek to ensure that reasons are given for decisions of your council and that disclosure of information is restricted only in accordance with the law.

Confidentiality

You should also ensure that confidential material, including material about individuals, is handled in accordance with the law and – having regard to the public interest – any decisions on such handling taken by the council; and is not used for private purposes.

Stewardship

You have a responsibility to play your part in ensuring that the council uses its resources prudently and in accordance with the law.

Participation

You may take part in the consideration of questions which come before councillors unless you have a private interest of a kind which, in accordance with this Code, precludes you from participation.

Declarations

You have a duty to declare any private interests relating to your public duties and to take steps to resolve any conflicts arising in a way that protects the public interest. You should make relevant declarations of interest at meetings of the council, its committees and working groups, or any outside body to which you are appointed or nominated by the council, during informal contacts, and meetings of your political party, and in all circumstances where you are active in your role as a councillor.

Relations with officers

You should respect the role of the council's officers and employees and treat them in a way that engenders mutual respect at all times.

Source: Modern Local Government: In Touch with the People (White Paper), Cmd 4014, HMSO, 1998.

APPENDIX 31

The Central–Local Accord

The Framework for Partnership document (November 1997)

The Government and the Local Government Association are committed to work together in order to strengthen and sustain local elected government in England.

Central government, by the authority of Parliament, has responsibility for determining the powers and duties of local government, and for setting the framework for local government and local service provision. The Government and the LGA have agreed that the framework should:

Ensure that local decision-making reflects both national priorities and the views of local communities, becoming less constrained in matters of details by central government and more responsive and accountable to local people.

Increase the discretion and local accountability of local authorities on expenditure and revenue-raising matters, within such disciplines as are essential to national economic policy.

Ensure best value in the provision of public services.

Enable and encourage local authorities to modernize and revitalize their structures and working practices so as to provide accountable and responsive leadership for local communities.

As a general principle, provide for services and decision-making affecting local communities to be undertaken at the level which is closest to the people and area to be served, consistent with competence, practicality and cost-effectiveness.

Uphold standards of conduct in public life, founded on principles of selflessness, integrity, objectivity, accountability, openness, honesty and leadership.

Central and local government are mutually dependent and these objectives can best be delivered by a partnership in which central and local government support and respect each other's roles and work together in the development and implementation of policy. In recognition of the independent democratic legitimacy of local government, the Government has signed and intends to ratify the Council of Europe's Charter of Local Self-Government.

NOTES AND REFERENCES

1 WHAT LOCAL GOVERNMENT IS

1 See *Sunday Times*, 19 September 1993, p. 15. In 1978 P. Holland MP estimated there were 3,000: see P. Holland and M. Fallon, *The Quango Explosion*, CPC, 1978. See also *What's Wrong with Quangos?*, Outer Circle Policy Unit, 1979, D. N. Chester, 'Fringe Bodies, Quangos and All That', *Public Administration*, Spring 1979, A. Barker, *Quangos in Britain*, Macmillan, 1982 and W. Hall and S. Weir. *The Untouchables*, Democratic Audit Paper 8. Scarman Trust, 1996.

2 Estimates vary according to definition. See the *Independent*, 17 March 1994 and *Labour Party News*, January 1994. Cf. *The Times*, 29 January 1994, p. 8. See too P. Holland, *Quelling the Quango*, CPC, 1993.

3 F. A. Hayek, *The Road to Serfdom*, Routledge, 1946, pp. 174–5.

4 See for example J. S. Mill, *Representative Government*, 1861, Chapter XV, and J. Toulmin Smith, *Centralisation or Representation?*, 1848, and *Local Government and Centralisation*, 1851.

5 *The Conduct of Local Authority Business* (Widdicombe Report), HMSO, 1986, p. 47.

6 P. Blair in R. Batley and G. Stoker (eds), *Local Government in Europe*, Macmillan, 1991, pp. 47, 49. See too G. Stoker, *The Role and Purpose of Local Government*, CLD, 1994.

7 See also *Local Government Studies*, December 1984, and G. Jones and J. Stewart, *The Case for Local Government*, Allen & Unwin, 1985.

8 See A. Henney, *Inside Local Government*, Sinclair Brown, 1983.

9 See for example 'Abolish Local Authority Funding', *The Times Educational Supplement*, 19 May 1992; 'Honouring Town Hall Humbug', *The Times*, 23 February 1988. It appears that the government was indeed minded to abolish local government: see *The Times*, 1 May 1996, p. 18 and the introduction to *Taking Charge*, CLD, 1995.

2 AN EVOLVING SYSTEM

1 This reluctance was a consequence of the prevailing philosophy of *laissez faire*, which implied that the state should not interfere with private interests, especially in business. See D. Fraser, *The Evolution of the Welfare State*, Macmillan, 1973; A. J. Taylor, *Laissez Faire and State Intervention in Nineteenth-Century Britain*, Macmillan, 1972; and E. J. Evans, *Social Policy 1830–1914*, Routledge, 1978.

2 For example, Liverpool promoted nine such Bills in Parliament in the period 1858–83.

3 The population of Britain, in the years 1801–51, increased from 10.5 million to 20.8 million. Over the same period, individual towns experienced the following population growths: Birmingham 71,000 to 233,000; Liverpool 82,000 to 376,000; Glasgow 77,000 to 345,000; Manchester 75,000 to 303,000; London 865,000 to 2.8 million.

4 Some counties, Yorkshire and Sussex for instance, were divided into separate administrative areas (North Riding, East Riding and West Riding; East Sussex and West Sussex) because of their size or shape. England's fifty-two geographic counties were thus divided into sixty-two administrative counties.

5 This figure included four towns – Canterbury, Worcester, Burton and Chester – which achieved county borough status despite having populations of less than 50,000.

6 A number of individual towns had acquired a variety of powers, for example to establish free libraries, museums, police forces, housing and tramways, largely through private Acts of Parliament.

7 See the *Report of the Committee on the Management of Local Government* (the Maud Report), HMSO, 1967, Vol. 1.

8 It has been suggested that some of the functions of the Countryside Commission, the Housing Corporation and the Scottish Development Agency could be taken over by local authorities. See N. and H. M. Drucker, *The Scottish Government Yearbook 1979*, Paul Harris, 1978.

9 There were eight of these in England; Wales and Scotland had councils with similar functions. They were all abolished in 1980.

10 *Report on Social Insurance and Allied Services*, Cmd 6404, HMSO, 1942.

11 J. Wiseman, 'Local Government in the Twentieth Century', *Lloyds Bank Review*, January 1966.

12 G. Jones and J. Stewart, 'Against Centralism', *Local Government Studies*, December 1984.

13 The population of Scotland rose from 1.5 million in 1801 to 3 million in 1851. By 1861, nearly one third of Scotland's population was living in one-room dwellings, and Glasgow was described as 'possibly the filthiest and unhealthiest of all British towns in the period'. See M. W. Flinn, *Chadwick's 'Report on the Sanitary Condition of the Labouring Population of Great Britain'*, pp. 10, 99.

14 Following the Parliamentary Reform Act 1832, a number of non-burghal towns were designated 'parliamentary boroughs', entitling them to elect MPs and set up town councils.

3 THE STRUCTURE OF LOCAL GOVERNMENT

1 See, for example: W. A. Robson, *Local Government in Crisis*, Allen & Unwin, 1968; *Report of the Royal Commission on Local Government in England* (the Redcliffe-Maud Report), Cmd 4040, HMSO, 1969; *Report of the Royal Commission on Local Government in Greater London*, Cmd 1164, HMSO, 1960.

2 *Report of the Royal Commission on Local Government in Scotland* (the Wheatley Report), Cmd 4150, HMSO, 1969, Vol. 1, paras. 1 and 2.

3 Parishes did not exist in Scotland, having been abolished in the Local Government (Scotland) Act 1929.

4 Some shared the provision of services through joint schemes, or they 'borrowed' from their neighbours.

5 *Ad hoc* provision includes such things as gas, electricity and National Assistance. Delegation occurred (usually) when an upper-tier authority arranged for services to be provided by lower-tier authorities (for example education or planning in 'excepted' districts with populations of over 60,000).

6 *Local Government: Areas and Status of Local Authorities in England and Wales*, Cmd 9831, HMSO, 1956, p. 4.

7 ibid., p. 6.

8 See H. V. Wiseman, *Local Government in England 1958–69*, Routledge, 1970, p. 30.

9 The Local Government Commission for England produced separate Reports and Proposals for: West Midlands Special Review Area (1961); West Midlands General Review Area (1961); East Midlands General Review Area (1961); South Western General Review Area (1963); Tyneside Special Review Area (1963); North Eastern General Review Area (1963); West Yorkshire Special Review Area (1964); York and North Midlands General Review Area (1964); Lincolnshire and East Anglia General Review Area (1964); and Lincolnshire and East Anglia General Review Area (1965). (All published by HMSO.)

10 Wiseman, op. cit., p. 1.

11 This did not apply only to seats on local councils: as Richard Crossman recorded in his diary when writing about his decisions on the reports of the Local Government Commissions and their possible impact on his parliamentary colleagues, '. . . each of them knows that as Minister of Housing [and

Local Government] the decision I make may be life or death for them in terms of representation at Westminster'. See R. H. S. Crossman, *Diaries of a Cabinet Minister*, Cape, 1975, Vol. 1, pp. 87, 88. See also F. Mount, 'The History of a Mistake', *Spectator*, 6 October 1979.

12 Crossman (op. cit. above) explains how he took the initiative in setting up the Royal Commission in the fortuitous absence of his strong-willed and sceptical Permanent Secretary. The paradox is that this civil servant became a member of the Royal Commission!

13 Local Government Commission for Wales, *Report and Proposals for Wales*, HMSO, 1963, paras. 14, 16.

14 *Local Government in Wales*, Cmd 3340, HMSO, 1967.

15 Originally this was to be elected and executive – a response to the growing nationalist feelings in Wales at the time.

16 The Redcliffe-Maud Report, Vol. 1, para. 28.

17 *Local Government Reform in England*, Cmd 4276, HMSO, 1970.

18 *Report of the Royal Commission on the Constitution* (the Kilbrandon Report), Cmd 5460, HMSO, 1973. This report produced a number of schemes for devolving power to the regions of Britain, and led ultimately to legislation to set up elected assemblies in Scotland and Wales (subsequently repealed, see note 46 below).

19 The Redcliffe-Maud Report, Vol 11, Memorandum of Dissent, Cmd 4040–41, HMSO, 1969.

20 It is estimated that the reorganized structure transferred twenty seats from Labour to Conservative. See F. Mount, 'The History of a Mistake', *Spectator*, 6 October 1979; B. Keith-Lucas and P. G. Richards, *A History of Local Government in the Twentieth Century*, Allen & Unwin, 1978, pp. 223–4; and P. Hall, 'The Country Fights Back – and Wins', *New Society*, 17 September 1970.

21 *Local Government in England*, Cmd 4585, HMSO, 1971.

22 *The Reform of Local Government in Wales*, HMSO, 1971.

23 Some district councils – former boroughs and UDCs – are entitled to call themselves 'boroughs' and some parishes are known as 'town councils'. In addition, some authorities have retained the title of 'city'.

24 *Local Government in England* (op. cit.), para. 13.

25 The adoption of certain business practices ('corporate management' – see Chapter 9) might be regarded as a further move in this direction. However, for the main thrust of the argument, see J. Dearlove, *The Reorganisation of Local Government: Old Orthodoxies and a Political Perspective*, CUP, 1979. See also the references in note 65, Chap. 12. While the Maud Report of 1967 (Vol. 2, p. 20) showed that 55 per cent of councillors were managers, farmers, professional workers or employers, and the Redcliffe-Maud Report of 1969 (Vol. 3, p. 132) quotes a similar figure of 51 per cent, the more recent Robinson Report (*Report* *of the Committee of Inquiry into the System of Remuneration of Members of Local Authorities*, HMSO, 1977, Vol. 2, Tables 10 and 11) shows that at least 65 per cent of councillors are from non-manual occupational backgrounds, and that over 60 per cent of male councillors who are working are from just four groups of occupation (sales, clerical, administration/management and professional/technical). This change may please those who bemoaned the poor calibre of councillors, but it adds credence to those who, like Dearlove, interpret the reorganization of local government in class terms.

26 See G. Jones, 'The Local Government Act 1972 and the Redcliffe-Maud Commission', *Political Quarterly*, April 1973.

27 These services have been transferred into the hands of separate boards and authorities under the NHS Reorganization Act 1973 and the Water Act 1973.

28 Redcliffe-Maud Report, Vol. I, para. 576 (iv).

29 N. Flynn *et al.*, *Abolition or Reform*, Allen & Unwin, 1985.

30 E.g. boroughs have had difficulties reaching joint decisions because of different party control in Merseyside, W. Yorkshire and Greater London.

31 *Streamlining the Cities*, Coopers & Lybrand Ltd, December 1983 and February 1984.

32 S. Bristow *et al.*, *The Redundant Counties?*, Hesketh, 1983.

33 S. Leach in S. Leach *et al.*, *Enabling or Disabling Local Government*, Open Univ. Press, 1996.

34 T. Travers and G. Jones, *The Government of London*, J. Rowntree, 1997; also *Local Government Studies*, Autumn 1997 p. 53.

35 J. Sharland, *A practical approach to Local Government Law*, Blackstone, 1997.

36 D. Wilson in *Parliamentary Affairs*, July 1996; also D. Wilson and C. Game, *Local Government in the UK*, Macmillan, 1997.

37 C. Game in *Parliamentary Affairs*, January 1997.

38 D. Wilson as note 36 above.

39 S. Leach in *Local Government Studies*, Autumn 1997.

40 *Local Government Studies*, Autumn 1997.

41 op. cit.

42 'The Whitehall farce hits town', *Local Government Agenda*, July 1995; also *Local Government Chronicle*, 5 May 1996.

43 *Organic Change in Local Government*, Cmd 7457, HMSO, 1979. The philosophy behind organic change is that the structure of local government should not be rigid but should vary between different parts of the country, taking into account local circumstances. However, it may be that the original proposals were a first step towards a general pattern of most-purpose district councils; see J. Stewart *et al.*, *Organic Change*, Institute of Local Government Studies, 1978, p. 4.

44 *Devolution and Regional Government in England*, Labour Party, 1975, p. 8. See also *Regional Authorities and Local Government Reform*, Labour Party, 1977.

45 There were some reservations by members about the allocation of planning functions and the structure of the island councils.

46 N. and H. M. Drucker, eds., *The Scottish Government Yearbook 1979*, Paul Harris, 1978. A. Dawson, 'The Idea of the Region and the 1975 Reorganization of Scottish Local Government', *Public Administration*, Autumn 1981.

47 'The imbalance of size has been a natural target for criticism, but the boundaries of the Strathclyde region correspond broadly to a distinctive area with regional characteristics and large-scale problems. Any sub-division would have meant a weakening of administrative cohesion and an impairment of strategic opportunities' (*Brief on Local Government Reform*, Scottish Office, HMSO, 1974).

48 Elections were held in 1974 in readiness for the 1975 start.

49 It has been suggested that this was to give the districts a worthwhile role (see *Municipal Journal*, 16 May 1975).

50 The Commission on Local Government and the Scottish Parliament (McIntosh), Consultation Papers 1 and 2, 1998.

4 THE SERVICES OF LOCAL GOVERNMENT

1 Attorney General *v.* Fulham Corporation (1921). Local authorities are 'corporations', i.e. they have corporate status. This means the collection of individuals (councillors) becomes one body, with a name and with 'perpetual succession' (i.e. even though actual members change) and with legal rights and duties. Thus it is a legal *persona*, an artificial person, which is itself (rather than individual, constituent members) capable of holding property, making contracts, suing and being sued.

The powers expressly stated or implied in an Act are in practice extended, in that local authorities may legally also do whatever is 'reasonably incidental' to them (such as employing staff, acquiring property, etc.). But it does not mean 'in connection with', which is too broad or vague.

In the exercise of their powers (particularly their discretionary powers – granting licences etc.), local authorities are expected to act 'reasonably'; otherwise they may be deemed to be acting *ultra vires*. In the Wednesbury Corporation case (1948) it was suggested that reasonableness implies that relevant matters are taken into account and irrelevant ones are excluded, and that decisions are not made in bad faith or for improper purposes; nor should they be just plain arbitrary or perverse.

2 In reality the distinction is not very important since, as the Layfield Committee (1976) pointed out, the bulk of local activity is a mixture of free choice, formal requirements and various pressures and influences: see *Layfield Committee on Local Government Finance*, pp. 403–5.

In practice even some mandatory responsibilities may not be fulfilled by local authorities, or they may be undertaken in purely token fashion, as the provision of county colleges after the 1944 Education Act and provision of health centres after the 1946 Health Service Act were. In other cases there may be uncertainty whether the responsibility is mandatory or not, as in the case of the provision of adult or nursery education. *Note*: legislation may also be required where a local authority wishes to cease a function (e.g. close a dock).

3 Scottish authorities also have the power to spend 'common good' funds: see *Public Finance and Accountancy*, 11 November 1988, p. 14.

4 See 'Aspects of Local Democracy', *The Conduct of Local Authority Business* (Widdicombe), Research Vol. 4, HMSO, 1986. See also C. Crawford and V. Moore, *The Free Two Pence*, CIPFA, 1983. Also *Public Finance & Accountancy*, May 1985, which shows that Lancashire spent 99 per cent and Tyne & Wear only 18 per cent of permitted expenditure.

5 *Qualgos just grow*, Centre for Policy Studies, 1985.

6 'Local Government Today and Tomorrow', *Municipal Journal*, 1962, p. 27.

7 The Maud Report, Vol. 1, Chapter 4. See also the Redcliffe-Maud Report, Vol. 1, para. 323, and the Wheatley Report, Vol. 1, para. 640.

8 See for example *Local Government Chronicle*, 13 March 1991, p. 26; *Reducing Uncertainty – The Way Forward*, CIPFA, 1992; *The Power to Act*, LGIU, 1991; S. Cirell and J. Bennett, *Municipal Trading*, 1992. See too C. Crawford and C. Grace, '*Conducive or Incidental to*', INLOGOV, 1993; J. McFadden, *A Power of General Competence: The Time Has Come*, Scottish LG Information Unit, 1997; *A Power of General Competence for Local Authorities in Britain*, Commission for Local Democracy, 1995 and in L. Pratchett, *Local Government and Local Democracy*, Macmillan, 1997; M. Loughlin, *Fifty Years of Municipal Decline*, Unwin, 1985.

9 For example the York Corporation Act 1969 cost £6,000. Today such an Act could be ten times that: some opposed Bills may cost over £1 million. However, under the Local Government Act 1972 (sec. 262) it was intended that certain powers conferred by local Acts should be made generally available to local authorities.

10 There are various types of order, and procedures differ for each. For further details, see C. A. Cross, *Principles of Local Government Law*, Sweet & Maxwell; W. O. Hart and J. F. Garner, *Hart's Local Government and Administration*, Butterworth, 1973; or J. A. G. Griffith and H. Street, *Principles of Administrative Law*, Pitman.

11 The Redcliffe-Maud Report, Vol. 1, paras. 257–8.

12 The Wheatley Report, Vol. 1, paras. 361–9.

13 Joint committees are sometimes formed here too – e.g. Somerset County Council and Taunton Deane Borough Council had a joint planning committee until 1980 when under the Local Government Planning and Land Act 1980 counties lost most of their control responsibilities over 'county aspects' of planning. Note the intention to scrap structure plans, proposed in 1988; see note 19.

14 In some areas, in order to avoid the messy administration which can sometimes occur when responsibilities are claimed, 'excepted districts' have been created whereby the district authorities may, for example, become responsible for the road maintenance of whole areas.

15 A *statutory joint authority* or *board* is a body with its own legal existence, made up of councillors nominated by a number of local authorities, and with the power to precept on those authorities, to employ its own staff and hold its own property.

A *joint committee* is a voluntary, but formal, combination of authorities, having no separate legal existence. It is able to discharge functions but has no power to precept, employ staff or hold property.

A *joint forum* is an informal combination of authorities, such as a regional association or county tourism forum. It has no power to discharge functions, which stays with the individual authorities.

A *lead authority* is one authority acting on behalf of others. It can only be used for service provision and not for deciding another authority's service policy, since the latter is a statutory responsibility of the individual authorities.

An *arm's-length supplier* is a company or other organization under the nominal ownership of one authority but supplying also to others.

16 K. Newton and T. J. Karran, *The Politics of Local Expenditure*, Macmillan, 1985.

17 In England the Department of the Environment, Transport and the Regions in Wales the Welsh Office and in Scotland the Development Department of the Scottish Office, until 1999 when the Scottish Parliament took over.

18 Under the Transport Act 1968, certain areas of Britain were designated 'passenger transport areas' within which municipal transport was managed by 'passenger transport executives' (PTEs), full-time experts who worked under the control of 'passenger transport authorities' (PTAs), comprising part-time members, mainly representatives of the local authorities in the area. In 1974 the role of the PTAs was taken over by metropolitan county councils and the Strathclyde Regional Council. With the abolition of the Metropolitan counties (1986) the PTAs became joint boards formed from the constituent metropolitan boroughs.

19 Largely a result of *People and Planning* (the Skeffington Report), HMSO, 1969.

20 This includes public as well as private developments, so that local authorities themselves have to make applications. However, certain government departments and government properties are excluded. In addition, certain aspects of 'permitted' development do not require specific applications for permission. These occur under a statutory instrument (the General Development Order) and include, for example, small house extensions.

21 Apart from private health provision, the health service provided under the Employment Medical Advisory Service, and health services in prisons and the armed forces, are technically outside the NHS.

22 See, for example, the Redcliffe-Maud Report, Vol. 1, paras. 259–367.

23 See, for example, the *Report of the Royal Commission on the National Health Service*, Cmd 7615, HMSO, 1979, para. 16.22; *Community Care: Agenda for Action* (Griffiths Report), HMSO, 1988.

5 LONDON'S LOCAL GOVERNMENT

1 They were in fact called 'Progressives' and included many Liberals and some Conservatives. They were sometimes also known as 'Municipal Socialists', as they sought to emulate and surpass the achievements of Joseph Chamberlain, mayor of Birmingham in the 1870s.

2 This notion was examined by the Royal Commission on Greater London (Ullswater) in 1921–3. It lacked unanimity, producing three conflicting reports, and consequently no action was taken on its various recommendations.

3 From some 600,000 per day in the 1920s to nearly 1 million in the 1950s. See K. B. Smellie, *A History of Local Government*, Allen & Unwin, 1968.

4 Of these counties perhaps Middlesex was the most notable in this respect, having a number of boroughs which by the criterion of population size merited promotion to county borough status, except that this would have emasculated the administrative county.

5 The London boroughs were given some traffic management responsibilities.

6 See, for example, Professor Griffith's evidence to the Royal Commission (para. 192). See also W. A. Robson, *Local Government in Crisis*, Allen & Unwin, 1967, Chapter XXXI.

7 G. Rhodes (ed.), *The New Government of London: The First Five Years*, Weidenfeld & Nicolson, 1972; see also the *Local Government Chronicle*, 4 March 1972.

8 *The Times*, 6 July 1978. See also R. Freeman, 'London through the Looking Glass', *New Society*, 27 March 1980.

9 See *Hansard*, 12 April 1982; *The Times*, 24 June 1982, 29 July 1982.

10 White Paper, *Public Transport in London*, Cmd 9004, 1983.

11 *Local Government Review*, no. 8, ACC, 6 May 1994, p. 3. See too M. Hebbert and T. Travers, *The London Government Handbook*, Cassell, 1988.
12 See *The Times*, 20 April 1990 and *Sunday Times*, 25 February 1990. Also D. Walker, 'London cries out for a voice again', *The Times*, 15 January 1988; D. Walker, *Capital Welfare*, RIPA, 1988; P. Kelly, 'London isn't Working', *Midweek*, 27 October 1989; *After Abolition*, NCVO, 1987. Conversely, there is evidence of success; see *Municipal Journal*, 19 February 1989. There were suggestions that London was treated favourably in the RSG settlement to make the reorganization more of an apparent cost-cutting success.

6 LOCAL GOVERNMENT ELECTIONS

1 Such as voting twice by impersonating someone else, etc. Anyone found guilty of such offences is debarred from voting in the local area in which the offence was committed for five years from the date of conviction.
2 See W. Miller, 'Local electoral behaviour', in 'The Local Government Elector', *The Conduct of Local Authority Business* (Widdicombe), Research Vol. 3, HMSO, 1986; M. and S. Pinto-Duschinsky, *Voter Registration: Problems and Solutions*, Constitutional Reform Centre, 1987.
3 See A. Wigram and E. Lyon, *Local Government Elections – the Case for Proportional Representation*, CAER, 1979; B. Keith-Lucas, *Local Elections – Let's Get Them in Proportion*, Parliamentary Democracy Trust, 1978; V. Bogdanor, 'Why the Local Elections System Makes Us Appear More Divided', *The Times*, 19 May 1980; 'Putting the Local Government Vote in Proportion', *Local Government Chronicle*, 17 December 1982; *Electoral Systems in Local Government*, INLOGOV, 1986.
4 See *Local Government Chronicle*, 28 June 1996, p. 8.
5 By-elections take place when vacancies occur on the council owing to resignation, death or disqualification of councillors. A councillor may be dismissed as a result of his unauthorized absence from council meetings over a continuous period of six months. However, a by-election would not take place in any of these situations if normal elections were due within six months, unless the council was deficient in membership by a third or more.
6 Up to 1979, members could be disqualified on the grounds of having been surcharged (in effect fined) the sum of £500 or more by the District Auditor. This power ceased as such under the Local Government Act 1972, but see p. 395 and note 69, Chap. 11.
7 This principle implies that those who make the law should be different from those who operate it and from those who adjudicate when it is broken. For a rather fuller treatment, see C. Padfield, *British Constitution Made Simple*, Heinemann, 1987.

8 See *Municipal Journal*, 2 February 1990. Other estimates put the figure at 130,000; see *Hansard*, 13 June 1989. This Parliamentary debate revealed that twenty-four out of forty Greenwich councillors would be affected by this ban.

9 *Candidates' Expenses at Local Government Elections*, Home Office circular, RPA 263. Also Representation of the People Act 1985.

10 These electoral areas are reviewed from time to time by the Local Government Boundary Commissions (see p. 73), though the local authorities themselves may initiate alterations, counties seeking to change divisions and districts revising wards and parishes/communities. In the case of GLC elections, the boroughs assumed the role of electoral areas.

11 'The Local Government Elector', *The Conduct of Local Authority Business* (Widdicombe), Research Vol. 2, HMSO, 1986.

12 The Conduct of Local Authority Business (Widdicombe Report), HMSO, 1986, p. 170.

13 The Maud Report, Vol. 3, pp. 72–80.

14 See, for example, A. H. Birch, *Small Town Politics*, OUP, 1959; W. Hampton, *Democracy and Politics*, OUP, 1970; F. Bealey *et al.*, *Constituency Politics*, Faber, 1965. Information has also been drawn from L. J. Sharpe, *Voting in Cities*, Macmillan, 1967, and *Power in Britain*, BBC, 1965.

15 See note 11. See also W. Miller, *Irrelevant Elections?*, OUP, 1988.

16 See C. Rallings *et al.*, *Community Identity and Participation in Local Democracy*, CLD, 1994; also C. Rallings and M. Thrasher, *Enhancing local electoral turnout*, JRF, 1996.

17 P. Lynn, *Public Perceptions of Local Government*, HMSO, 1992.

18 *Electoral Roll: Unintended Consequences?*, University of Warwick, 1992: See too *Local Government Chronicle*, 25 April 1995, p. 16.

19 See, for example, Hampton, op. cit., and P. Fletcher, in Sharpe, op. cit.

20 See *Local Government Studies*, Summer 1992, pp. 2–3.

21 C. Rallings and Thrasher, op. cit., p. 20.

22 R. Masterson in *Local Government Studies*, 1980, pp. 63–82.

23 J. Stanyer, *Understanding Local Government*, Fontana, 1976, pp. 272, 284.

24 J. Stanyer, 'Why Does Turnout Vary?', *New Society*, 13 May 1971.

25 What these average figures do not show is the wide range of turnout among local authorities. For example, in the 1973 local elections the districts of Ceredigion and Dwyfor, in Wales, had turnouts of 93.9 per cent and 82.8 per cent respectively, while those in Middlesbrough and Stoke-on-Trent were 18.1 per cent and 22 per cent. On the other hand, high voting turnouts can disguise the fact that a high proportion of seats have gone uncontested, and vice versa. See Appendix 3.

26 As note 16 above.

27 Such a view is at least implicit in the Government's White Papers *Local*

Government in England, Cmd 4585, and *Reform of Local Government in Scotland*, Cmd 4583, both HMSO, 1971. See also the Redcliffe-Maud and Wheatley Reports. Some election figures for the old local government system are given in Appendix 3.

28 The Maud Report, Vol. 3, Table 113, p. 82.

29 K. Young, 'Attitudes to Local Government', in 'The Local Government Elector', *The Conduct of Local Authority Business* (Widdicombe), Research Vol. 2, HMSO, 1986.

30 As note 16 above.

31 As note 16 above and Widdicombe Report, Vol 4, HMSO, 1986.

32 *Attitudes to Local Government – A Survey of Electors*, Joseph Rowntree Foundation, 1991.

33 R. Jowell and J. Curtice *British Social Attitudes*, Gower, 1995.

34 J. G. Gibson, 'Rate Increases and Local Elections', *Policy and Politics*, Vol. 16, no. 3, 1988; J. Ferry, 'Rates and Elections', *Centre for Environmental Studies Review*, Vol. 5, 1979; C. Game, 'Local Elections', *Local Government Studies*, Vol. 7, 1981.

35 G. W. Jones, 'Varieties of Local Politics', *Local Government Studies*, April 1975.

36 C. Game and S. Leach, *The Role of Political Parties in Local Democracy*, CLD, 1994.

37 See, for example, W. H. Morris-Jones, 'In Defence of Apathy', *Political Studies*, Vol. 2, no. 1, 1954. See also L. J. Sharpe, 'Instrumental Participation in Urban Government', in J. A. Griffiths, *From Policy to Administration*, Allen & Unwin, 1976.

38 *Taking Charge*, CLD, 1995, para. 115, c.f. para 3.18 and Table 7 above; see too *The Times* leader 5 May 1994, and *Sunday Times*, 12 May 1996.

39 J. M. Bochel, *The Scottish Regional Elections 1986*, Dundee University, 1986. There is a tendency in rural areas towards a lack of contests because the incumbent councillor is often known personally by the electors, who may not wish to give offence by opposing him. Subsequently, many rural councillors become well entrenched and almost irremovable. This has been well illustrated in the study of the Scottish Communities – see R. Masterson and E. Masterman, 'The Scottish Community Elections, the Second Round', *Local Government Studies*, January 1980.

40 *Local Government Studies*, Annual Report 1983.

41 'The Local Government Councillor', *The Conduct of Local Authority Business* (Widdicombe), Research Vol. 2, HMSO, 1986, Table 4.2., and G. Courtnay, *The Impact of Releasing People for Council Duties*, DETR, 1998.

42 The Maud Report, Vol. 1, p. 134; see also p. 93.

43 The Maud Report, Vol. 5, pp. 48–9.

44 The last time there was an uncontested parliamentary seat in Britain was in 1951, when four constituencies went uncontested. See A. J. Allen, *The English Voter*, English Universities Press, 1964, p. 13.

45 See the Maud Report, Vol. 3.

46 Maud Report, Vol. 1, 1967; M. Hodge *et al.*, *More than a flower show*, Fabian, 1997; *Enhancing Turnout*, JRF, 1996; *Enhancing Local Democracy*, LGMB, 1995; J. Stewart, *Innovation in Democratic Practice*, University of Birmingham, 1995, 1996, 1997; J. Stewart, *Towards a Deliberative Democracy*, University of Birmingham, 1999; M. Geddes, *Extending Democratic Practice in Local Government*, Warwick University, 1996; *Enhancing Public Participation in Local Government*, De Montfort University DETR, 1998.

47 J. G. Bulpitt, in *Participation in Politics*, ed. G. Parry, Manchester University Press, 1971, p. 290. There has been some change in composition since then (see Chapter 8) and some would argue that Bulpitt's warnings were justified: see J. Dearlove, *The Reorganisation of Local Government*, CUP, 1979.

48 Parties are not entirely unwritten elements in local government operations. Many councils' Standing Orders contain references to them; they were recognized in the Representation of the People Act 1969 (which allowed affiliations or labels on ballot papers), the Local Government Act 1985 requires constituent local authorities to reflect the balance of parties in their appointments to joint authorities (sec. 33) and the Local Government and Housing Act 1989 requires proportional representation of parties on committees (though this is now changed, under the Local Government Act 2000).

7 THE POLITICAL PARTIES

1 The 'Shetland Movement', an erstwhile party, contains any so-called Independents: see J. M. Bochel and D. T. Denver, *The Scottish Regional Elections 1982*, Dundee University, 1982. In order to cover these various situations, J. Stanyer has suggested a classification as follows: a 'developed' party system exists where parties contest elections and control the council; a 'semi-party' system is where they contest elections but hardly refer to their party labels while in office; a 'concealed' system is one where members are partisan behind the scenes of council work, but do not contest elections using party labels; a council is 'non-partisan' where parties are absent from elections and the council. J. Stanyer, *Understanding Local Government*, Fontana, 1976, p. 136.

2 See H. V. Wiseman, *Local Government at Work*, Routledge, 1967, and the Maud Report, Vol. 5, p. 100.

3 In 1956 Liverpool (Labour) city council took it upon itself formally to condemn the British invasion of Suez. In June 1981 the GLC declared a boycott on South African goods as a protest against apartheid.

4 A five-fold classification is suggested by L. Corina, 'Elected Representatives in a Party System', *Policy and Politics*, Vol. 3, no. 1, 1974.

5 Political culture has been defined as 'orientations towards political objects' – A. Almond and S. Verba, *The Civic Culture*, Princeton, 1963. In the local government context, it implies the amalgam of people's judgements and attitudes about political institutions (the council, parties, the town hall, etc.), personalities (the chairman, the officers, social workers) and processes (elections, rate collection, etc.). It also entails an element of how individuals see or feel about their own role in the local political system. e.g. Strathclyde provides an illustration with its tradition of left-wing distrust of voluntary organizations and a preference for working through the Labour Party. For a concise account of the general concept, see D. Kavanagh, *Political Culture*, Macmillan, 1972.

6 Some of them could be said to have begun with the Birmingham Liberals under Joseph Chamberlain in the 1860s. See A. Briggs, *Victorian Cities*, Penguin Books, 1968; C. Game and C. Skelcher, 'Manifestos and other Manifestations of Local Party Politics: The Spread of Party Politics since Reorganisation', *Local Government Studies*, 1983.

7 J. Redlich and F. W. Hirst, *A History of Local Government in England*, ed. B. Keith-Lucas, Macmillan, 1958; K. Young, 'Party Politics in Local Government: an Historical Perspective', in 'Aspects of Local Democracy', *The Conduct of Local Authority Business* (Widdicombe), Research Vol. 4, HMSO, 1986.

8 A nice illustration of the resistance to state provision was given by *The Times* in 1854 when it stated, 'We prefer to take our chance of cholera and the rest than be bullied into health.'

9 See W. Thornhill, *The Growth and Reform of English Local Government*, Weidenfeld & Nicolson, 1971, pp. 106–8, 112–13. See also Chapter 5 above.

10 Just as at national level more than half of the seats in Parliament went uncontested prior to the emergence of national parties. See T. Lloyd, 'Uncontested Seats in British General Elections 1852–1910', *Historical Journal*, Vol. viii, no. 2, 1965; J. M. Bochel, *The Scottish Regional Elections 1986*, Dundee University, 1986.

11 It is true that some councillors are deterred by the existence of political parties, but these appear to be few in number. See the Maud Report, Vol. 1, pp. 109, 145; Vol. 3, Table 207.

12 See for example J. G. Bulpitt, *Party Politics in English Local Government*, Longman, 1967; H. V. Wiseman, *Local Government at Work*, Routledge, 1967; W. Hampton, *Democracy and Community*, OUP, 1970; K. Newton, *Second City Politics*, OUP, 1976; G. W. Jones, *Borough Politics*, Macmillan, 1969. This concentration of study may also be justified on the grounds that, while it may not cover a lot of local authorities, it does cover a lot of Britain's population.

13 See H. V. Wiseman, 'The Party Caucus in Local Government', *New Society*, 31 October 1963.

14 See the Maud Report, Vol. 5, p. 105.

15 See too *New Society*, 4 April 1986, and *Local Government Chronicle*, 3 January 1986, and 24 October 1997, p. 13.

16 There have been some bitter episodes with party groups disowning or de-selecting councillors; e.g. see *Economist*, 3 October 1981.

17 In addition they may also determine the choice of co-opted members. See p. 235. Indeed, well-established majority parties could change the number and structure of committees and to a large extent even the internal organization of the authority if they wished. See the *Guardian*, 27 May 1981.

18 See the Maud Report, Vol. 5, p. 98.

19 *The Role of Political Parties in Local Democracy*, CLD, 1994.

20 See note 19 above.

21 J. Gyford and M. James, *National Parties and Local Politics*, Unwin, 1983.

22 See note 19 above.

23 Maud Report, Vol. 5, p. 104.

24 See J. Gyford, *Local Politics in Britain*, Croom Helm, 1976, pp. 78, 84.

25 The Maud Report, Vol. 5, p. 193.

26 J. Gyford *et al.*, *The Changing Politics of Local Government*, Unwin, 1989.

27 Gyford, op. cit., p. 82.

28 See the Maud Report, Vol. 5, p. 100.

28a As quoted by Camden Labour councillors in BBC *Panorama*, 16 March 1981.

29 See Gyford, op. cit., pp. 86–7, G. W. Jones' article in *Local Government Studies*, April 1975, p. 31, and Table 7.5 in Bennett, *Central Grants to Local Government*, CUP, 1982.

30 See Chapter 8. The October 1974 Parliament comprised only 4 per cent women and 7 per cent working-class members, while the middle-age groups (35–54), with 63 per cent, were well over-represented, and the younger (21–34) and older (55 plus) groups were under-represented with 8 per cent and 29 per cent respectively. See C. Mellors, *The British MP*, Saxon House, 1978; also 'The Times' *Guide to the House of Commons 1974*. On a wider perspective, the role of local politics as a stepping stone to national politics should be noted: Mellors shows that one MP in three has local government experience.

31 See L. J. Sharpe, *Why Local Democracy?*, Fabian Society, 1965; J. M. Bochel, note 39, Chap. 6.

32 MEP G. Watson has said 'There are five non-party councils in the South West. None has a good report from the Audit Commission.' *Somerset County Gazette*, 25 September 1998.

33 See J. D. Stewart, 'The Politics of Local Government Reorganisation', in K. Jones, *The Yearbook of Social Policy 1973*, Routledge, 1974.

34 The Maud Report, Vols. 1 and 2.

35 Source: K. Newton, *Second City Politics*, OUP, 1976, fig. 2.2. Newton declares that 'local elections are a sort of annual general election'. Another recent study concludes: 'On the whole . . . municipal voting in big cities is a product of whatever factors happen at the time to be salient nationally.'

36 W. Miller, note 2, p. 673 and *Irrelevant Elections*, OUP, 1988.

37 *The Times*, 3 May 1990.

38 S. Jenkins, *The Times*, 1 February 1995: also 1 May and 24 July 1996.

39 *Political Studies*, 28, 1980; *Local Government Chronicle*, 20 June 1997; D. Wilson and C. Game, *Local Government in the UK*, Macmillan, 1997, p. 211. For 1997 see C. Rallings and M. Thrasher in D. Denver (ed) *British Elections and Parties Review*, Cass, 1998 and *Talking Politics*, Winter 2000.

40 See *Local Government Chronicle*, 19 May 1997.

41 C. Rallings and M. Thrasher in *Parliamentary Affairs*, October, 1997; see too P. Norris (ed.) *Britain Votes*, 1997.

42 *Local Government Chronicle*, 26 May 1995, p. 8.

43 E.g. the 'Lothian effect', see J. M. Bochel and D. T. Denver, *The Scottish Regional Elections 1982*, Dundee University, 1982.

44 See C. Game, 'Local Elections', *Local Government Studies*, March/April 1981, and references therein; J. Ferry, 'Rates and Elections', *Centre for Environmental Studies Review*, January 1979; G. Jones and J. Stewart, 'The Local Factor in a Local Election', *Local Government Chronicle*, 18 June 1982; see also *Local Government Chronicle*, 17 June 1983, and *Municipal Journal*, 3 June 1983. In May 1979 the local elections happened to coincide with the General Election, and the authors of the second study mentioned in note 35 above show that electors (at least in Liverpool) made use of that unique opportunity to 'split' their vote and separate national issues from local by voting for one party in parliament and a different party in their local council: see W. Harvey Cox and M. Laver, 'Local and National Voting in Britain', *Parliamentary Affairs*, Autumn 1979. C. Rallings and M. Thrasher in *The 1985 County Council Election Results in England* conclude that 'while there might be some national trends evident in local voting behaviour they are by no means the only . . . influences . . . [a] scan through the results should reveal considerable variation and demonstrates that local elections must be viewed in the light of both national and local circumstances.' See also their article in *Local Government Studies*, January/February 1990. See too G. Green, *Policy and Politics* 1 (1), 1972, and A. Bruce and G. Lee, *Political Studies*, June 1982.

45 W. Miller, note 2, p. 673.

46 See J. C. Gibson, note 34, p. 675 and W. Miller, op. cit.

47 E.g. see *Economist*, 12 May 1990, pp. 35–6.

48 *Parliamentary Affairs*, January 1999.

49 See too *Local Government Chronicle*, 22 July 1994.

50 The adversary or 'yah-boo' system as it occurs nationally is also heavily criticized: see S. E. Finer, *Adversary Politics and Electoral Reform*, Wigram, 1975.

51 *Municipal Journal*, 4–10 June 1993, p. 15.

52 See *Local Government Chronicle*, 5 March 1982, 18 September 1981.

53 C. Collus 'Herd instincts', *Local Government Chronicle*, 3 July 1998, p. 15.

54 See note 19 above.

55 *It's our party*, LGMB, 1998

56 ibid.

57 V. Bogdanor, 'Town Hall v Whitehall,' *Fair Votes*, Summer/Autumn 1987.

58 See *The Times*, 24 March 1990, and 7 December 1990.

59 The Maud Report, Vol. I, p. 110.

60 K. Young, *The Conduct of Local Authority Business since Widdicombe*, Rowntree Trust, 1989

61 ibid., Vol. 5, p. 109, and the Widdicombe Report.

62 Gyford, op. cit., p. 68.

63 Source: *Municipal Year Books*.

64 See, for example, *Local Government Chronicle*, 12–26 April 1991.

65 See *The Conduct of Local Authority Business*, Committee Report and Research Vol. 1, HMSO, 1986.

66 *The Conduct of Local Authority Business: The Government Response*, HMSO, 1988.

8 THE COUNCILLORS

1 *Councillor Recruitment and Turnover*, LGMB, 1993.

2 By the Committee on Management of Local Government (Maud), 1967. See also C. Rallings and M. Thrasher, 'Disillusion, Age and Frustration – Why Councillors are Calling it a Day', *Local Government Chronicle*, 9 October 1981.

3 Councils are free to determine the timing of their meetings. Consequently, there are variations, but in very general terms county and regional councils and Scottish districts meet in the daytime (mornings or afternoons); other districts meet in the afternoon or evenings; and the London boroughs meet in the evenings.

4 A local study by Peter Beresford (1983) suggests that the Act is quite effective.

5 *Municipal Journal*, 8 March 1996, p. 21.

6 *Community Leadership and Representation: Unlocking the Potential*, DoE, 1993, para. 4.24.

7 G. Courtnay, *The Impact of Releasing People in Council Duties*, DETR, 1998.

8 See *The Times Educational Supplement*, 28 April 1989.

9 See *Local Government Studies*, Sept/Oct 1982.

10 R. V. Clements, *Local Notables and the City Council*, Macmillan, 1969.

11 C. Rallings and M. Thrasher *Community Identity and Participation in local Democracy*, CLD, 1994.

12 *Local Government Chronicle* 23 January 1998, p. 3.

13 *Municipal Journal*, 13 December 1996, p. 13.

14 *Local Government Chronicle*, 6 February 1998, p. 71.

15 The Maud Report, Vol. 2.

16 As with MPs, this normally means that the union agrees to make a contribution towards the candidate's election expenses (in effect to the local party funds). However, in local government it is less systematic (e.g., agreements are not signed) and the sums involved are small. Sponsorship normally occurs where the candidate is a member of the union and displays this fact on his election material.

17 *Local Government Chronicle*, 6 June 1997, p. 81.

18 The Maud Report, Vol. 1, p. 139.

19 See note 7, above.

20 This information is drawn from *The Remuneration of Councillors*, Vol. 2, HMSO, 1977, the Maud Report, Vol. 2, the Widdicombe Report, 1986, and *The First National Census*, LGMB, 1998.

21 See note 7, above.

22 J. M. Bochel, *Scottish Local Elections 1995*, University of Dundee, 1995.

23 See G. Courtnay op. cit., and *First National Census*, LGMB, 1998.

24 Widdicombe Report, vol. II, 1986.

25 *Local Government Chronicle*, 24.3.95, p. 8.

26 See J. Gyford, 'Our Changing Local Councillors', *New Society*, 3 May 1984, and 'The Local Government Councillor', *The Conduct of Local Authority Business* (Widdicombe), Research Vol. 2, HMSO, 1986.

27 See note 11, above.

28 See G. Almond and S. Verba, *The Civic Culture*, Princeton University Press, 1963, and Little Brown, 1981: W. H. Morris-Jones, 'In Defence of Apathy', *Political Studies*, vol. 2, no. 1, 1954.

29 The Maud Report, p. 143.

30 Thus local authorities' conventions vary in such matters as drawing up agendas, officers attending party meetings, members appointing officers, etc.; See Widdicombe Report. See also K. Young, *The Conduct of Local Authority Business since Widdicombe*, Rowntree Memorial Trust, 1989. For a good illustration see the Statement of Conventions by Cheshire County Council in Widdicombe Report, Annexe H.

31 Thus the chairmen of committees may take decisions on behalf of their committee, for example where the matter is urgent. Furthermore, it would appear that just one person may legitimately constitute a committee – see *Local Government Chronicle*, 30 March 1979, 13 April 1979, 4 May 1979.

32 This dilemma is made no easier when councillors are given such guidance as: 'Your over-riding duty as a councillor is to the whole local community. You have a special duty to your own constituents . . .' (Circular on the National Code of Local Government Conduct, 1975. See note 83 below.)

33 See *Towards a New Governance?*, LGMB, 1993, and *Local Government Chronicle*, March 1993, p. 13.

34 *Community Leadership and Representation*, para. 4.10 (iv).

35 For various studies of this aspect, see K. Newton, *Second City Politics*, OUP, 1976; I. Budge *et al.*, *Political Stratification and Democracy*, Macmillan, 1972; J. Dearlove, *The Politics of Policy in Local Government*, CUP, 1973; J. M. Lee, *Social Leaders and Public Persons*, Oxford, 1963. In his study 'The Functions and Organisation of Councillors', *Public Administration*, Vol. 51, 1973, G. Jones suggests that, at that time, councillors broadly fell into three groups – 75 per cent mainly concerned with representing the ward and constituents' interests, about 5 per cent acting as general policy-makers and 20 per cent being policy-makers in particular service areas. See also *Local Government Studies*, Sept/Oct 1982.

36 *Community Leadership and Representation*, para. 5.5.

37 *First National Census*, LGMB, 1998.

38 *Report of the Committee of Inquiry into the System of Remuneration of Local Authorities*, HMSO, 1977, Vol. 2.

39 *Municipal Journal*, 13 December 1996, p. 12.

40 J. Barron, *Councillors in Crisis*, Macmillan, 1991.

41 The chairman of the council is sometimes known as the 'mayor'; in Scotland he is known as either the 'convenor' or the 'provost'.

42 *Municipal Journal*, 13 December 1996, pp. 13–15.

43 A. Bloch, *The Turnover of Local Councillors*, Rowntree Trust, 1991.

44 K. Young and N. Rao, *Councillors and the New Local Government*, Rowntree Trust, 1992; see too *The Times*, 29 July 1993, p. 14.

45 See notes 11, above: also *The Role of Political Parties in Local Democracy*, CLD, 1995.

46 See note 11, above.

47 See note 45, above.

48 See note 11, above, and *Local Government Chronicle*, 8 April 1993, p. 6; also *Local Government Studies*, Summer 1992, pp. 5–6.

49 See note 43 and 45 above.

50 See note 7, above.

51 R. Boyson, *Speaking My Mind*, Peter Owen, 1995.

52 See notes 43 and 45 above.

53 See note 11 above.

54 *Community Leadership and Representation*, para. 4.10 (ix).

55 See Addenda to the *Report of the Royal Commission on Standards of Conduct in Public Life* (the Salmon Report), Cmd 6524, HMSO, 1976.

56 The Robinson Report, Vol. 1.

57 The Maud Report, Vol. 3.

58 *Community Leadership and Representation: Unlocking the Potential*, HMSO, 1993, para. 4.18.

59 See, for example, *Municipal Journal*, 28 May 1993, pp. 26–7.

60 *The New Local Authorities*, HMSO, 1972, para. 7.52. Concern at the calibre of members is still being expressed: see R. Garson, 'What Direction Should Local Government's Leaders Take Now?', *Local Government Chronicle*, 2 May 1980.

61 *Support Services for Councillors*, Association of Councillors/Charles Knight, 1988.

62 T. Eddison *et al.*, *Strengthening the Role of the Elected Member*, LGTB, 1979; *Support Services for Councillors* (Thomas Report), Association of Councillors, 1982. In recent years, the University of Bristol has run some courses for councillors, as indeed it did in 1979 for newly elected MPs.

63 *The Conduct of Local Authority Business* (Widdicombe Report), HMSO, 1986, p. 163.

64 N. Rao. *The Making and Unmaking of Local Self-Government* Dartmouth, 1994.

65 E. L. Hasluck, *Local Government in England*, CUP, 1948. However, it should be noted that such complaints are not a new phenomenon, having been made at various times in the nineteenth century. See E. P. Hennock, *Fit and Proper Persons: Ideal and Reality in Nineteenth-Century Urban Government*, Arnold, 1973; G. Jones, *Borough Politics*, Macmillan, 1969.

66 Dame E. Sharp in a speech quoted in the *Municipal Review*, November 1960. See also *Public Administration*, Winter 1962.

67 Professor B. Keith-Lucas, *The Mayor, Alderman and Councillors*, Liberal Publications, 1961.

68 The Maud Report, Vol. 5, p. 458; see also pp. 40–46 of the report.

69 ibid., p. 196.

70 The Salmon Report, p. 11.

71 See note 51 above; also *The Times* 11 or 12 March 1995; and note 64, above.

72 See for example *Local Government Chronicle*, 23 May 1992, p. 8.

73 Maud Report, vol. 1, p. 143

74 The various relevant nineteenth-century laws were consolidated in the 1933 Local Government Act and are found in the Local Government Act 1972 (secs. 94–98) and the Local Government (Scotland) Act 1973 (secs. 38–42).

75 *Conduct in Local Government*, Cmd 5636, HMSO, 1974.

76 *Report of the Royal Commission on Standards of Conduct in Public Life 1974–6* (the Salmon Report), Cmd 6524, HMSO, 1976.

77 *Conduct in Local Government*, p. 3.

78 *Report of the Royal Commission on Standards of Conduct in Public Life*, p. 11.

79 *Conduct in Local Government*, p. 11.

80 *Report of the Royal Commission on Standards of Conduct in Public Life*, Addendum by Mrs Ward-Jackson, p. 117.

81 An interesting illustration of this is provided by the former Chief Executive Officer of Wandsworth Borough Council who said that he was sacked for calling in the police to investigate suspected corruption. 'There is an immense amount of corruption going on and it is got away with because people know there is no thank you for reporting it' (*Local Government Chronicle*, 20 April 1979).

82 *Report of the Royal Commission on Standards of Conduct in Public Life*, p. 19.

83 Joint circular, *The National Code of Local Government Conduct*, HMSO, 1975.

84 *The Times*, 20 June 1973.

85 See A. Doig in *Local Government Studies*, Spring 1995; also A. Doig, *Corruption and Misconduct in Contemporary British Politics*, Penguin, 1984. This book provides a number of useful case studies of corruption in local government.

86 Victims of reported fraud are shown below. The Audit Commission report *Protecting the Public Purse* (1994) concluded that 'probity in local government is generally in good order, especially with regard to the honesty of staff.' But it has also revealed many cases of fraud and corruption, totalling £25 million. To counter the greater risks associated with CCT, LMS, etc., some councils are appointing an officer whose sole responsibility is fraud investigation.

87 *Local Government Chronicle*, 17 September 1999.

Victims of reported fraud (1987–1992)

	Number	amount £m	% of total amount
Banking and finance	105	490	31
Commercial companies	58	473	29
Public (including investors)	77	230	15
Pension funds	2	147	9
Inland Revenue/Customs & Exise	26	99	6
Local and Central Government	**37**	**17**	**1**
Other	31	129	8
Not known	13	20	1
	349	1605	100

Source: Local Government Agenda, ICSA, September 1993.

88 See ACE Bulletin Nov/Dec 1985.

89 In England and Wales, this system started under the Municipal Corporations Act 1835 and did not apply to many later types of local authority, including UDCs, RDCs and parishes.

90 However, it was not a clean break, as aldermen did not disappear from London until 1977 (GLC) and 1978 (London boroughs); and the City, being exempt from the 1972 Act, still has its aldermen. Furthermore, under that Act, principal local authorities in England and Wales are empowered to confer the title of 'honorary alderman' on anyone who has given eminent service as a past member of the council. He/she may then be invited to attend civic ceremonies, but that is all.

91 Equally co-opted members are disqualified like councillors, the one notable exception being teachers, who since 1902 have been regularly co-opted on to LEA education committees.

9 INTERNAL ORGANIZATION: THE COUNCIL AND ITS COMMITTEES

1 Standing orders (SOs) are the set of rules by which local authorities conduct themselves. They are rather like a written constitution, explaining the composition, powers and procedures of the local authority's component parts. For example, they would lay down the quorum required for meetings, the procedures for entering into contracts or those matters upon which committees or officers could make (delegated) decisions on behalf of the council. The central government issues 'model' standing orders for the benefit of individual local authorities. An example of a local authority's standing orders is given in Appendix 12. New model SOs are emerging as a result of recent legislation (and under the Local Government and Housing Act 1989, the Minister can require local authorities to make certain types of SOs, known as 'core' standing orders).

2 See P. Cousins, 'Council Leaders: the New Strong Persons in Local Government', *Administrator*, July, 1984.

3 See *Local Government Chronicle*, 19 July 1985.

4 See the Bains Report, *The New Authorities*, HMSO, 1972, para. 4.34.

5 See *The local government councillor in 1993*, Rowntree, 1994.

6 See too S. Leach in *Parliamentary Affairs*, January, 1999.

7 C. Game and S. Leach *The Role of Political Parties in Local Democracy*, CLD, 1995.

8 See C. Meltors, *Managing without a majority*, LGMB, 1996; S. Leach and J. Stewart, *The politics of hung councils*, Macmillan, 1992; *Working with the balance*, LGMB, 1995.

9 The Maud Report, Vol. 1.

10 The Paterson Report, *The New Scottish Local Authorities: Organisation and Management Structures*, HMSO, 1973, para. 3.10, found some 20 per cent of their sample of local authorities reported having made significant changes in organization since the Maud Report.

11 For details of surveys of local authorities see Occasional Papers by the Institute of Local Government Studies (INLOGOV), 1969, 1970.

12 A. L. Norton and J. D. Stewart, 'The Bains Impact', *Local Government Chronicle*, 9 March 1973.

13 The Bains Report, p. xv and para. 2.3; the Paterson Report, para. 4.3.

14 See for example E. F. L. Brech, *Management: Its Nature and Significance*, Pitman, 1967.

15 See the Bains Report, Appendix J.

16 With the possibility of joint meetings (ibid., para. 5.42).

17 The Paterson Report, para. 4.9.

18 ibid., para. 4.6.

19 J. D. Hender, *Municipal and Public Services Journal*, 15 September 1972.

20 This reflects the view of Sir Andrew Wheatley when he dissented from the Maud Committee Report on the grounds that this would keep council members generally better informed and would avoid the danger of the management board members becoming too remote or detached (see the Maud Report, Vol. 1, pp. 156–6). Bains did, however, follow Maud in pointing out that members have different interests, and implied that some of them could be satisfied in pursuing a purely constituency (rather than policy-making) role. (See the Bains Report, Chapter 3.)

21 For example, whether monitoring should be undertaken by the P & R committee or should form a separate sub-committee function; or whether the chief executive should develop a small inner 'executive office'. See too R. Greenwood *et al.*, *The Organisation of Local Authorities in England and Wales 1967–75*, INLOGOV, 1975.

22 See R. Greenwood *et al.*, *In Pursuit of Corporate Rationality: Organisational Developments in the Post-Reorganisation Period*, INLOGOV, 1977.

23 Greenwood, op. cit., p. 18.

24 Greenwood, op. cit.

25 Greenwood op. cit.

26 Maud Report, vol. 5, 1967.

27 *Portrait of change*, LGMB, 1998.

28 See note 15.

29 Note Avon's battle (May 1990) with the Minister for Education over Beechen Cliff school's opting out of LEA control and thereby upsetting the authority's plans for rationalizing its school usage. Also, see B. Chilton,

'Enabling Local Government to Survive', *Journal of Public Finance*, 1 June 1990.

30 N. Hepworth in *Public Finance and Accountancy*, 9 September 1988.

31 *Local Government Today*, LGMB 1996: also *Municipal Journal* 8 March 1996, pp. 26–7.

32 Speech to the Conservative Party Annual Conference, October 1991.

33 See Chap. 15; also *Representing the People*, Audit Commission, 1997, and K. Young and M. Rao, *The Local Government Councillor in 1993*, Rowntree, 1994.

34 'Invent a Problem', *Local Government Chronicle*, 16 July 1993, p. 13; also M. Rao, 'Representing the People? Testing assumptions about local government reform', *Public Administration*, 2, 1999; *Taking the initiative*, LGA, 1999; *Political management arrangements in local government*, IDA/LGA, 1999.

35 J. Mc Leod and M. Lee, *Towards a New Governance*, LGMB, 1993.

36 See N. Rao, *Managing Change*, Rowntree Trust, 1993.

10 INTERNAL ORGANIZATION: THE OFFICERS

1 See J. H. Warren, *The Local Government Service*, Allen & Unwin, 1952.

2 This is augmented by general legislation such as the Contracts of Employment Act 1972, the Health and Safety at Work Act 1974, the Employment Protection Act 1975 and the Sex Disqualification Act 1975.

3 See *Local Government Chronicle*, 10 April 1992, p. 7.

4 *Municipal Journal*, 7 November 1997, p. 16; *Local Government Studies*, Spring 1998 and Autumn 1993.

5 See the *Report of the Committee on the Staffing of Local Government* (the Mallaby Report), HMSO, 1967.

6 See the *Report of the Royal Commission on Standards of Conduct in Public Life 1974–76* (the Salmon Report), Cmd 6524, HMSO, 1976.

7 See A. Spoor, *White Collar Union*, Heinemann, 1967.

8 *Public Finance and Accountancy*, 2 April 1993.

9 K. P. Poole, *The Local Government Service*, Allen & Unwin, 1978, p. 114; also *Public Finance and Accountancy*, February 1980, p. 26.

10 Nolan Committee in *Standards in Public Life: Local Government*, Stationary Office, 1997.

11 See the Salmon Report; also 'The Dangerous Ground in Public Life', *Local Government Chronicle*, 20 April 1979, pp. 425–7.

12 See K. Young, *The Conduct of Local Authority Business since Widdicombe*, Rowntree Memorial Trust, 1989.

13 Nolan, op. cit.

14 *The Conduct of Local Authority Business* (Widdicombe Report), HMSO, 1986, para. 6.161; 'The Political Organisation of Local Authorities', *The Conduct of*

Local Authority Business (Widdicombe), Research Vol. 1, HMSO, 1986. See too note 30, Chap. 8.

15 See *Local Government Chronicle*, 11 March 1996, pp. 10–11 and 27 March 1997, p. 3.

16 See Chapter 6. Teachers are an exception: they can be (and in Scotland must be) co-opted on to education committees.

17 E.g. in 1984 Camden council appointed the left-wing chairman of the social services committee of the neighbouring borough, Hackney, to the post of Director of Social Services. *The Times* declared it to be an 'example of degenerating civic culture'. (See note 21, Chap. 14.)

18 'The Political Organisation of Local Authorities', *The Conduct of Local Authority Business* (Widdicombe), Research Vol. 1, HMSO, 1986, Table A49.

19 *Local Government Chronicle*, 23 October 1998, p. 16.

20 *Political leaders and chief executives*, LGMB 1997.

21 White Paper, *The new NHS: Modern and Dependable*, 1998.

22 See R. Greenwood *et al.*, *In Pursuit of Corporate Rationality*, INLOGOV, 1977.

23 B. Wood, in *Party Politics in Local Government*, RIPA/PSI, 1979.

24 See R. Greenwood *et al.*, *The Organisation of Local Authorities in England and Wales 1967–75*, INLOGOV, 1975, and R. Greenwood and J. Stewart, *Local Government Studies*, October 1972.

25 Greenwood *et al.*, op. cit. (1975). Since then several local authorities have dropped their chief executive posts.

26 In the reports by Maud (1966), Mallaby (1967), Bains (1972) and Paterson (1973).

27 See R. Greenwood, 'The Recruitment of Chief Executive Officers', *Local Government Chronicle*, 19 October 1973. See also Alexander, op. cit.

28 See Greenwood *et al.*, op. cit. (1977) and op. cit. (1975).

29 J. Stewart, *The New Management of Local Government*, Allen & Unwin, 1986.

30 See too LGTB, *Breakout from Bains*, 1987.

31 See for example *Municipal Journal*, 13–19 August 1993, pp. 16–17, and 18 September 1992, pp. 25–6.

32 J. Hunt, CEO of Ealing LB. See *The Times*, 20 May 1993, p. 14.

33 *Municipal Journal*, 11 June 1993, p. 18.

34 See *Local Government Chronicle*, 11 June 1993, p. 15.

35 See *Municipal Journal*, 7–13 December, 1990, p. 7.

36 See *County News*, ACC, October 1992, p. 186, and *The Citizen's Charter. First Report 1992*.

37 BS 5750 is a national standard for quality assurance systems. It is awarded through certification (after assessment by an independent certification body). The aim of the standard is 'to establish, document and maintain an effective and economical quality assurance system that will enable an organization to demonstrate to its customers that it is dedicated to quality and has the ability to meet customers' needs. The principles of BS 5750 ... identify the basic principles and specify the procedures to ensure that its services meet customers' requirements.' In practical terms, this requires the creation (involving staff) and maintenance of a quality manual which concerns procedures. Over 50 per cent of local authorities use the BS 5750 criterion in awarding contracts, which made it a logical step for them to apply the same quality assurance system to their own departments.

Total Quality Management (TQM) is more concerned with attitudes in the organization, and its aim is for everyone to 'get it right first time, every time'. It has four basic principles: (i) the vision and drive for quality has to be led and demonstrated from the top; (ii) TQM is about satisfying customer needs, both internally and externally, at the right cost; (iii) quality is everyone's responsibility; (iv) quality has to be designed and built into a product or service and not just inspected out at delivery stage. It therefore involves finding out what customers want and what the organization can best provide; turning those requirements into written objectives and specifications; and setting up procedures to ensure the specifications are met. See *Municipal Journal*, 21 January 1994, p. 20.

38 See for example *Municipal Journal*, 30 October 1992, pp. 14, 16; 7 May 1993, pp. 18–19; and 13 August 1993, p. 19. See also M. Jacques, 'Britain's Dinosaurs Must Adapt to a Competitive New World', *Sunday Times*, 1 August 1993, and D. Osborne and T. Gaebler, *Reinventing Government*, Plume/Penguin, 1993.

39 H. Davies, *Fighting Leviathan*, Social Market Foundation, 1992.

40 See *Public Finance and Accountancy*, 11 June 1993, pp. 12, 14, 27, 29; *Local Government Chronicle*, 15 June 1990, pp. 17, 26.

41 D. Prior *et al.*, *Is the Citizen's Charter a Charter for Citizens?*, LGMB, 1993. See also *Local Government Chronicle*, 8 April 1993, p. 15.

42 See *Municipal Journal*, 2 October 1992, p. 22; *Local Government Chronicle*, 23 April 1993, p. 16.

43 See for example F. Analoui and A. Kakabadse, *Sabotage: How to Recognise and Manage Employee Defiance*, Mercury, 1991; C. Cockburn, *In the Way of Women*, Macmillan, 1991; C. Hakim in *Work, Employment and Society*, 4(2), pp. 157–88; J. MacInnes, *Thatcherism at Work*, Open University, 1987; J. Newman and J. Clarke, *Doing the Right Thing?*, Open University, 1993.

44 Further details may be found in the Treasury's *Glossary of Management Techniques*, HMSO, 1967. See too *Public Finance and Accountancy*, April 1983.

45 See, for example, *Output Measurement – Discussion Papers*, published by CIPFA (and previously by the IMTA).

46 See, for example, the Local Government Operational Research Unit report,

Evaluating Alternative Housing Management Strategies, HMSO, 1973; *Information Techniques in Local Authority Supplies Organisations*, HMSO, 1979; and *Planning Remedial Work on Local Authority Buildings*, HMSO, 1979.

47 ZBB implies abandoning the normal 'continuation' budget and examining the whole basis of funding a service by relating its budget to objectives and levels of service. Thus a service, e.g. fire, is broken into functional components (such as Operations Prevention, Transport, Administration) for which objectives can be set. Alternative levels of service can then be considered, including a minimum or zero-base level. Options can be evaluated and priorities determined.

48 See A. Seldon, 'Local Government Imperialism', *Economic Affairs*, January 1984.

49 See, for example, *Performance Management in Local Government*, published by Epping Forest District Council.

F. McNulty, *Ethic Cleansing, Headless Chickens and all that*, Paper presented to the Second International Conference on Managers and Professionals, Stirling University, August, 1995, and *Ethic Cleansing Revisited*, Paper presented at the International Symposium on Public Service Management, Aston University, March, 1996.

50 See the Layfield Report; also Walker and Henney (Further Reading, Chap. 9).

51 In 1974 the DES established the Assessment of Performance Unit to monitor national levels of pupil achievement. See *Output Budgeting for the Department of Education and Science*, Education Planning Paper I, HMSO, 1970, and *Performance Indicators in the Education Service*, CIPFA, 1984.

52 *Which?*, March 1989.

53 MORI 1986.

54 *The Conduct of Local Authority Business* (Widdicombe), Research Vol. 3, HMSO, 1986.

55 W. Miller, *Irrelevant Elections?*, OUP, 1988.

56 *Public Policy and Administration*, November 1996; *LGC*, 11 September 1998; 13 November 1998; *Municipal Journal* 28 March 1997, 12 September 1997.

57 For a more general appreciation, see N. Johnson, *In Search of the Constitution*, Pergamon, 1977.

58 Other notable legal cases such as Attorney-General *v.* De Winton (1906) and *Re* Hurle Hobbes ex-parte Riley and another (1944) seem to imply that officers have a duty to the electors and may disobey council instructions. However, this would seem only to apply in cases where the legality of the council's instructions was in serious doubt.

59 The Maud Report, Vol. 5, p. 196. Elsewhere in that report officers are reported to say that 'only a minority of members on their committees make any real contribution' and 30 per cent to 40 per cent of the committee members 'were useless' (p. 42). The Royal Commission on London also noted that a good education officer 'is normally immensely influential in policy as well as in administrative questions' (*Report of the Royal Commission on Local Government in Greater London 1957–60*, Cmnd 1164, HMSO, 1960, para. 469). An example of LAMSAC's work concerned the computerization of refuse collection in 1982.

60 The Maud Report, Vol. 1, para. 109. See also *Local Government Chronicle*, 4 May 1990, p. 19.

61 K. Young and M. Davies, *The Politics of Local Government since Widdicombe*, Rowntree Trust, 1990.

62 ibid., Vol. 1, para. 145.

63 *We Can't Go On Meeting Like This: The Changing Role of Local Authority Members*, Audit Commission, 1990.

64 *Competition, Contracts and Change*, JRF 1995 and *Portrait of change* LGMB, 1996 and 1998.

65 See *The Times*, 20 May 1982.

66 See *Community Care*, 4 March 1982.

67 See *Municipal Journal*, 21 May 1982. Also article by D. Peschek in *Local Government Chronicle*, 24 April 1981.

68 *The Conduct of Local Authority Business* (Widdicombe), Research Vol. 1, p. 133, HMSO, 1986.

69 *Aspects of Administration in a Large Local Authority*, INLOGOV, 1967. At one time during the 1984–5 Militant-dominated Labour administration of Liverpool City Council, every item of expenditure had to be approved personally by the Chairman of Finance.

70 B. Keith-Lucas, 'Who Are the Policy Makers?', *Public Administration*, Vol. 43, 1965.

71 J. Gyford, *Local Politics in Britain*, Croom Helm, 1976, p. 43.

72 See, for example, M. Kogan and W. Van Der Eyken, *County Hall LEA*, Penguin Books, 1973. It is perhaps not without significance that this study of policy-making was based upon interviews with the *officers*, while the parallel study at national level (*The Politics of Education* by M. Kogan, Penguin Books, 1971) concentrated on elected *politicians*.

73 It is sometimes felt by some chief officers that education gets an unreasonably favourable share of the authority's resources because it has a powerful lobby behind it – parents. However, this can lead to those other officers reacting by 'ganging up' against the chief education officer.

74 See Kogan and Van Der Eyken, op. cit., and K. Wheare, *Government by Committee*, Oxford, 1955, Chapter 7.

75 See G. W. Jones, 'Varieties of Local Politics', *Local Government Studies*, April

1975. Another writer suggests that there may be differences between the political parties when it comes to keeping a rein on officers: see J. Sharpe, 'American Democracy Reconsidered', *British Journal of Political Science*, Vol. 3, no. 1, 1973. See too M. Bichard, 'The Tale of Two Councils', *Municipal Journal*, 21 April 1989, and 'Managing in a Political Environment', *Administrator*, January 1986.

76 J. Gyford *et al.*, *The changing politics of local government*, Unwin, 1989.

77 *Party Politics in Local Government*, RIPA/PSI, 1979.

78 *Municipal Journal*, 29 November 1996, pp. 14–15.

79 See, for example, the clerk who wrote, 'in any cases where officials have tried to interfere with policy I have rapped them firmly over the knuckles' (Maud Report, Vol. 5, p. 268).

80 See *Municipal Journal*, 8–14 May 1992, p. 7.

81 See *Local Government Chronicle*, 15 June 1990, p. 17.

82 See P. Saunders, *Urban Politics*, Hutchinson, 1979, A. Blowers, *The Limits of Power*, Pergamon, 1980, and C. Cockburn, *The Local State*, Pluto, 1977.

83 See, for example, the interpretation in S. Barrett and C. Fudge, *Policy and Action*, Methuen, 1981, and C. Ham and M. Hill, *The Policy Process in the Modern Capitalist State*, Wheatsheaf, 1984.

84 *The Conduct of Local Authority Business* (Widdicombe), Research Vol. 1, p. 125, HMSO, 1986.

85 Ibid. p. 130.

86 Ibid. pp. 137, 141.

87 C. Game and C. Skelcher, 'Manifestos and other Manifestations of Local Party Politics: The Spread of Party Politics since Reorganisation', *Local Government Studies*, 1983.

88 *The Conduct of Local Authority Business* (Widdicombe Report), HMSO, 1986.

89 See R. Wendt, 'Decision-making in Central and Local Government in the Absence of Political Majority', *Public Administration*, Autumn 1986.

90 On the grounds that there are other strong influences and inputs – see G. Stoker and D. Wilson, 'Intra-organizational Politics in Local Authorities', *Public Administration*, Autumn 1986.

91 The Paterson Report recommended the provision of offices for committee chairmen (and perhaps party leaders), interviewing rooms at headquarters and local offices, libraries and information rooms, assistance with research, dictating, typing, copying and other secretarial services and adequate telephone facilities. See also T. Eddison, *Strengthening the Role of the Elected Member*, LGTB, 1979.

92 Under the reorganization of 1974–5, the number of members (excluding parishes and communities) fell from 42,000 to 26,000; the number of employed staff remained constant at over 2 millions (having risen from a figure of 1.4

million in 1952 and 1.8 million in 1962). A similar problem occurred at central government level with a virtually constant number of ministers having to control a greatly expanded (post-war) civil service.

11 FINANCE

1 See A. T. Peacock and J. Wiseman, *The Growth of Public Expenditure in the United Kingdom*, OUP, 1961, and the *Report of the Committee on Local Government Finance* (the Layfield Report), Cmd 6453, HMSO, 1976.

2 In Scotland, teacher training and advanced further education (and mandatory grants) are not local authority functions and are financed directly by the central government.

3 See *UK National Accounts*, Central Statistical Office, HMSO; *Annual Abstract of Statistics*, Central Statistical Office, HMSO; *Social Trends*, Central Statistical Office, HMSO; and the *Local Government Trends*, CIPFA.

4 For example, the London Lotteries Club comprising the GLC and twenty-one boroughs) raised £2½ million up to the beginning of 1980. See the *Local Government Chronicle*, 8 June 1979 and 1 January 1980.

5 The Community Land Act 1975 gave local authorities substantial powers to acquire land for development. This was being implemented slowly by councils, but under the Local Government, Planning and Land Act 1980 the 1975 Act was repealed and the scheme has ceased to operate.

6 A possible fourth group concerns the inter-local authority charges which occur under 'pooled' expenditure arrangements (see p. 94) and where the residents from one local authority benefit from the services provided by another; for example, students travelling to another LEA's college or children being placed in care outside the native local authority.

7 Individual councils may decide to adopt such a policy, but in some services (e.g. for free school meals) it may be laid down by the central government (as indeed might the actual scale of charges; e.g. those for residents of old people's homes).

8 See *Housing Policy Technical Volume 3*, HMSO, 1977. Local authorities are obliged to keep a separate housing account.

9 See *Local Charges as a Source of Local Government Finance*, IMTA, 1968; A. Seldon, *Charge*, IEA, 1979; A. Maynard and King, *Prices and Rates*, IEA, 1972; M. Beasley, 'How Rates Can Be Abolished', *Local Government Chronicle*, 4 January 1980; *Alternatives to Domestic Rates*, HMSO, 1981; *Service Provision and Pricing*, HMSO, 1981; Economic Affairs, July 1984; and S. J. Bailey, 'Paying for Local Government: Charging for Services', *Public Administration*, Winter 1986. Another regular suggestion was that students be paid loans instead of grants. In February 1981, the High Court ruled that Hereford and Worcester LEA was breaking the law in charging for individual music lessons in school time: see *Where*, March 1981.

10 An Audit Commission report (August 1984) was sceptical about the savings achieved by private refuse collection. Yet savings of 3 per cent p.a. are claimed: *LGC Supplement*, 5 July 1985.

11 *Paying for Local Government*, HMSO, 1986, para. 7.3.

12 See note 9.

13 Bailey *et al.*, *Local Government Charges*, Longman 1993 S. Baldwin *Charging ahead*. Policy Press, 1998, P. John, *Charging for Local Service*, JRF, 1996.

14 Bailey in note 9.

15 *Municipal Yearbook 1985*.

16 LGMB CCT Report, May 1993.

17 *Local Government Chronicle*, 13 November 1992, p. 10.

18 S. Szymanski and T. Jones, *The Cost Savings from CCT of Refuse Collection Services*, London Business School, 1993.

19 *Realising the Benefits of Competition*, Audit Commission, 1993.

20 *Impact of CCT on refuse collection*, Imperial College, 1996.

21 *LGMB Service Delivery and Competition Information Service Report*, No. 16, Spring 1998.

22 See K. B. Smellie, *A History of Local Government*, Allen & Unwin, 1946, pp. 112–14. Their expansion was mainly hindered by jealous Chancellors.

23 Some of these – police, education, roads – were paid on a percentage basis; others, such as housing, were paid on a unit basis, for instance £5 per house p.a.

24 See the White Paper on Local Government, 1929. In fact this is not easy to determine: it is very much a matter of judgement. For example the police services are closely overseen, but they probably would be even if there were no specific grant. On the other hand there is some evidence that the specific grants which go to housing and transport do bring with them a significant degree of central intervention. (See, for example, P. G. Richards, *The Reformed Local Government System*, Allen & Unwin, 1978, p. 104.) The House of Commons Select Committee (Environment) Report on local government finance (March 1999) recognized that the evidence was conflicting, but it concluded that there is a 'link between the proportion of finance raised locally and democratic accountability/local autonomy' (para. 20). See also *Local Government Chronicle* articles 1 May 1998, p. 8; 20 Nov. 1998, p. 8; 11 December 1998, pp. 16–17; 30 July 1999 and 6 August 1999.

25 See *Public Finance and Accounting*, 3 August 1990.

26 In England and Wales, they meet under the auspices of the Consultative Council on Local Government Finance. See Chapter 13. 'Relevant' expenditure covers most local authority expenditure but excludes housing subsidies and student mandatory grants, which are paid separately.

27 The percentage figure is higher in Scotland for historical reasons: the amalgam of general and specific grants in 1966 amounted to a higher proportionate figure in Scotland than it did for England and Wales. Also, in Scotland relevant expenditure is differently determined. Scotland's costs are greater too (e.g. harder winters, etc.).

28 See, for example, *Local Authority Needs and Resources*, Centre for Environmental Studies Research Paper no. 12, December 1974; also F. Cripps and W. Godley, *Local Government Finance and Its Reform*, CUP, 1976.

29 *Local Government Finance*, Cmd 6813, HMSO, 1977.

30 This implies a common, uniform precept across the county. In fact (essentially in London) there may be local additions to the basic precept where services are not evenly provided over the whole area.

31 E.g. 97 per cent of spending in 1990 was funded from rates in Harlow cf. 8 per cent in Rhondda.

32 A further consideration is whether neighbouring district authorities do so. Any such decision will automatically affect the yield of the county precept from which *all* county inhabitants benefit.

33 In Scotland the regions and islands appointed independent assessors (the Scottish Assessors Association). Their revaluations have been fairly regular (occurring in 1961, 1966, 1971, 1978 and 1985). This is in contrast to England and Wales, which since a partial revaluation in 1956 has only had a revaluation in 1963 and 1973. It was Scotland's 'efficiency' in carrying out a revaluation in 1986–7 that produced some shock increases and led to the introduction of the community charge a year before England and Wales.

34 Site values are said to have the merit of encouraging the development of empty sites. Capital values are said to be more realistic and easier to determine. The Government accepted the advantages of the capital valuation method. See *Local Government Finance*, Cmd 6813, HMSO, 1977.

35 As an illustration, if the local authority's

estimated expenditure is		£40,000,000
and its estimated income is:		
grants ⎤	£20,000,000	
charges ⎦	5,000,000	25,000,000
then the rate-borne expenditure is		15,000,000
If the total rateable value is		20,000,000
then the rate poundage is		

$$\frac{15,000,000}{20,000,000} = 75\text{p per } £ \text{ R.V.}$$

In actual practice, councils determined the rate on the basis of the 'product of a 1p. rate'. In the example, if 1p rate raises £200,000, then to raise the required £15 million (which is 200,000 × 75) the local authority must charge 75 times the 1p rate. See too Appendices 9 and 19.

36 There are some 28 million income earners compared to (in 1990) 20 million ratepayers. Under the Local Government Act 1980 elderly ratepayers in arrears could arrange to have their debts settled from their estate when they die. Source: *Alternatives to Domestic Rates*, Cmnd 8449, 1981; *Economic Progress Report*, January 1982; *Lloyds Bank Review*, July 1982.

37 In 1963 the *Report of the Committee on the Impact of Rates on Householders* (Allen), Cmd 2582, HMSO, suggested that while rates were regressive, they were broadly proportionate to incomes. It was this report which led to the rate rebate scheme in 1967. The Layfield Report (1976) said that rates were progressive up to £40 per week income, were proportional between £40 and £60 and were less than proportional over £60 per week. See also *Alternatives to Domestic Rates*, HMSO, 1981. In addition 2.45 million of those receiving Supplementary Benefit had their rates paid.

38 See the Allen Report and the Layfield Report, Annexe 19; also *The Times*, 19 April 1980, *Alternatives to Domestic Rates*, HMSO, 1981. K. Newton and T. J. Karran, *The Politics of Local Expenditure*, 1985.

39 S. Weir, 'The Citizen and the Town Hall', *New Society*, 4 March 1982; T. Travers, 'Local Government is More Popular than Politicians Realise', *Local Government Chronicle*, 13 June 1980; C. Game, 'Budget Making by Opinion Poll', *Local Government Studies*, March/April 1982; 'Islington's Rates Survey', *Local Government Review*, 13 March 1982; Coventry's referendum, *The Times*, 26–28 August 1981; Layfield Report (Appendix) 1976.

40 Another case in point is the rate rebate scheme under which the central government reimburses local authorities 90 rather than 100 per cent.

41 See P. Self, in *From Policy to Administration*, by J. A. G. Griffith (ed.), Allen & Unwin, 1978. Thus, it is estimated that while half of the 42 million voters pay rates, only one-third pay full rates.

42 *New Sources of Local Revenue*, RIPA, 1956; S. Hindersley and R. Nottage, *Sources of Local Revenue*, RIPA, 1958; IMTA studies covering, individually, rates, sales tax, local income tax, charges and motor tax (1968–9); *The Future Shape of Local Government Finance*, HMSO, 1971. Britain would appear to be the only country where local authorities rely on only one local tax.

43 *The Future Shape of Local Government Finance*, HMSO, 1971; *Local Government Finance*, HMSO, 1973.

44 *Local Government Finance*, HMSO, 1977, para. 6.12.

45 In 1934 and 1948 Public Assistance was transferred to the central government partly because of the burden on local authorities, but mainly for other reasons (uniformity, equity and to de-stigmatize the service).

46 *Alternatives to Domestic Rates*, HMSO, 1981.

47 *Rates*, HMSO, 1981.

48 *Paying for Local Government*, HMSO, 1986.

49 J. Gibson in *Local Governance*, 2 February 1999, p. 123.

50 See W. J. Blum and H. Kalven, *The Uneasy Case for Progressive Taxation*, Macmillan, 1960; Antony Flew, 'Inequality is not Injustice', *Economic Affairs*, IEA, June 1987.

51 See J. LeGrand, *Strategy for Equality*, Unwin, 1982, and *Not only the Poor*, Newtones, 1988; also the study of Cheshire County Council in G. Bramley, 'How Far is the Poll Tax a "Community Charge"?', *Policy and Politics*, July 1989. See too G. Bramley and G. Smart, *Who Benefits from Local Services?*, LSE/ STICERD, 1993. The suggestion that non-ratepayers vote themselves (free) services paid for by ratepayers is discounted by Miller on the grounds that very few people realized or regarded themselves as non-ratepayers, and 'when it came to voting in actual elections . . . turn-out bias toward left or right, rich or poor, council tenant or house-owner was very small or non-existent. In particular, ratepayers and non-ratepayers were almost equally likely to vote.' W. Miller, *Irrelevant Elections?*, OUP, 1988.

52 See *Municipal Journal*, 5 May 1989, p. 9, and *Local Government Chronicle*, 23 June 1989. In the USA this was one of the purposes of the poll tax – hence its abolition (in 1963) as a condition of voting. But it remains as a Residents Tax, e.g. in New Hampshire.

53 The 'safety net' mechanism involves transferring funds such that local authorities, and their local taxpayers, are eased into the new tax system: thus local taxed/rated areas will be 'subsidized' at a decreasing level over four years to avoid the sudden increase in tax. Similarly, the higher-rated areas will find their situation improves over four annual stages. The higher-rated areas are critical of their having to thus support many high-spending authorities. Many critics see the device as a political ploy by the Government to make the scheme's introduction more acceptable as we approach a general election. Clearly, accountability during the four-year period will be compromised. See M. Cowan in *Municipal Journal*, 12 February 1988, and R. Hale in *Public Finance and Accountancy*, 22 February 1988.

54 See W. Miller, *Irrelevant Elections?*, OUP, 1988.

55 See note 49 above.

56 Compare figure in *Local Government Financial Statistics*, ONS (95%), with that in *Improving Financial Accountability*, DETR (98%).

57 See *Local Government Chronicle*, 29 May 1998, p. 11, and *Municipal Journal*, 23 October 1998, pp. 16–17.

58 See *Local Government Chronicle*, 26 July 1991, pp. 16–17; *Passing the Bucks*, Audit Commission, 1993; *Public Finance and Accountancy*, 14 September 1990, pp. 16–21; *Local Government Policy Making*, July 1993, pp. 67–9.

59 *The Times*, 14 June 1991.

60 The (Conservative) government was wedded to a monetarist (or deflation-ary) economic policy: this implies a commitment to reduce the money supply which itself involves substantial reductions in borrowing by public authorities in particular (the 'Public Sector Borrowing Requirement'). However, apart from this there is a broad (party) difference of general philosophy regarding capital expenditure, with Labour largely seeking to spread the benefits and costs of capital projects over a number of years by borrowing, and Conservatives, broadly, believing in living within one's means and seeking to minimize borrowing. Furthermore, the move towards greater revenue financing may be seen as a further move towards the adoption of business methods, since much business finance is raised internally, including sale of assets.

61 Such legislation may for example set limits on local authorities' short-term borrowing as a percentage of its long-term, or it may govern their arrangements for the issue of bonds, mortgages, etc. The Local Authority (Mortgages) Regulations 1974 are an example.

62 Partly because local authorities have been able to spend without approval from their own (revenue) resources and partly by leasing, but also because approved borrowing may run over a long period and become out of phase as capital projects get held up (or suffer what is called 'slippage').

63 See, for example, the critical report of the Audit Commission, *Capital Expenditure Controls*, HMSO, 1985.

64 See *Capital Expenditure and Finance*, HMSO, 1988.

65 See *Local Government Chronicles*, 13 November 1992, p. 3.

66 Local Government Acts 1972 (Sec. 151) (England and Wales) and 1973 (Sec. 95) (Scotland). Under previous legislation some local authorities were required to appoint a finance committee.

67 Especially for capital expenditure. However, in practice this has become extremely difficult because of the uncertainties regarding government grants, economic policy, interest rates and inflation.

68 They could also choose (as did eight local authorities in England and Wales) to have partial audit by both district and approved auditors. In England and Wales 90 per cent had chosen district audit pre-1982.

69 Before 1972–3, the district auditor himself could actually disallow and 'surcharge' (fine). This was felt by many, for example the Maud Committee (1967), to be excessive, inhibiting local authority activities. Consequently, under the 1972 Act, leniency will be exercised where the persons concerned acted reasonably or in the belief that the expenditure was authorized by law.

The Minister retains his discretionary power to approve expenditure of questionable legality. In the Camden wages case (Pickwell *v.* London Borough of Camden, April 1982) the auditor's claim of excessive and illegal expenditure was refused by the court.

70 R. Minns, 'The District Audit', *New Society*, 10 July 1975.

71 The charge was that by delaying the collecting of rate income, they had lost potential interest on the revenue. See *The Times*, 6 March 1986. The Local Government Act 1986 now requires councils to fix a rate by April. On surcharge abolition see *Local Government Chronicle*, 14 February 1986.

72 Some of these are acceptable, as a way of establishing a balance in the debt portfolio; but if it amounts to speculation it is deemed illegal, i.e. *ultra vires*.

73 See *Public Finance and Accountancy*, 22 July 1988.

74 See note 70.

75 See E. C. Thomas, 'The District Audit Since Reorganisation', *Telescope*, November 1976; also L. Tovell, 'The District Auditor and His Place in Local Government', *Local Government Chronicle*, Supplement, 8 June 1979. W. Werry, 'What Does an Auditor Add Up To?', *Local Government Chronicle*, 29 January 1982.

76 See, for example, *The Local Government Audit Service*, the report of the Audit Inspectorate 1979, which makes critical remarks on bonus schemes, building contracts and pooling arrangements for polytechnics. In April 1982 the report criticized overtime payments.

77 See note 75.

78 And found improvement opportunities of about £500m. *Annual Report*, HMSO, 1985.

79 *Audit Commission Performance Review in Local Government*, HMSO, 1988.

80 See *How Effective is the Audit Commission?*, 1991.

81 Its independence was cast in doubt because it made a presentation to the Cabinet in 1985. Also over surcharging in 1985 – see *Local Government Chronicle*, 13 September 1985, 25 April 1986, 2 May 1986, 20 April 1990 and 7/14 June 1991.

82 *Measuring Up: Consumer Assessment of Local Authority Services*, NCC, 1986.

83 *Public Finance Accounting*, 16 April 1993, pp. 11–13.

84 See *Local Government Chronicle*, 20 November 1990, p. 16.

85 'Howard's Way', *Municipal Journal*, 25 March 1988.

86 *Annual Report for 1987–88*, HMSO.

87 For example, *The Consumer and the State – Getting Value for Public Money*, National Consumer Council, 1979. See also 'Value for Money in the Public Sector', CIPFA, 1980; C. Holtham and J. Stewart, *Value for Money*, INLO-GOV, 1981.

88 With a view to keeping their committee structure within reasonable proportions, a number of authorities have had second thoughts about these.

12 CONTROLS AND INFLUENCES

1 *Ultra vires* may be procedural as well as substantive: thus if a council has not followed proper procedure in exercising its rightful powers (such as obtaining magistrates' approval before implementing a nuisance abatement order), the action is unlawful. See too note 1, Chap. 4.

2 Attorney-General *v*. Fulham Corporation (1921), in which the council went beyond its powers to provide washing facilities by providing a laundering service.

3 R. *v*. Kent Police Authority (1971).

4 Metropolitan Properties Ltd *v*. Lannon (1969).

5 See H. W. Clarke, 'The Prerogative Order', *Local Government Chronicle*, 23 August 1974.

6 Recent cases include the GLC (December 1981) and the West Midlands MCC (January 1982), both of whose supplementary precepts (for subsidized transport) were quashed; similar protests by BL (*v*. Birmingham MCD, February 1982) and GUS (*v*. Merseyside MCC, December 1981) failed.

7 Local Government Act 1974 and Local Government (Scotland) Act 1975.

8 Except parish and community councils. The addresses of the CLA are: 21 Queen Anne's Gate, London; Portland House, 22 Newport Rd, Cardiff; 125 Princes St, Edinburgh. Contact normally takes place in the first instance through a member of the local authority.

9 Local authorities have some discretion to withhold records or information and can refuse to allow their officers to be interviewed by the ombudsman on grounds of confidentiality.

10 N. Lewis and B. Gateshill, *The Commission for Local Administration*, RIPA, 1978.

11 See Lewis and Gateshill, op. cit.

12 *Your Local Ombudsman. Report for the Commission for Local Administration in England*, 1978. Published annually, the Report for 1981–2 responded to the 'Justice' appraisal (p. 633 below), endorsing its recommendations that CLA should be able to: receive complaints direct; secure legally enforceable remedies; deal with New Towns, school matters and contractual/commercial matters. The CLA also seeks the power to initiate investigations, while 'Justice' wanted independent (central) funding for the CLA. The 1983 Report was highly critical of the negative or inadequate council responses to findings of maladministration. This was reiterated in 1985.

13 *The Conduct of Local Authority Business* (Widdicombe Report), HMSO, 1986.

14 Report of the Select Committee on the Parliamentary Commissioner for Administration, HC (1985–86), 448.

15 CLA, *Annual Report 1991–2*.

16 E.g. see Audit Commission Report, August 1984 (in Further Reading, Chap. 10).

17 For example R. *v* Hampstead BC ex-parte Woodward (1917); R. *v* Barnes BC ex-parte Conlan (1938); R. *v* Lancashire CC Police Committee ex-parte Hook (1980). Also C. Webster, 'What Right to Know Has the Member?', *Local Government Chronicle*, 9 November 1979; C. Cross, 'March with the Lawyers', *Local Government Chronicle*, 25 April 1980; H. W. Clarke, 'The Legal Right to Look at Local Authority Documents', *Local Government Chronicle*, 9, 16 July 1982; *Local Government Review*, 1983, pp. 226 and 451.

18 *Complaints Procedures in Local Government*, Centre for Criminological and Socio-Legal Studies, Sheffield University, 1986. See too *Administrative Justice: Some Necessary Reforms*, Report of the Committee of the Justice-All Souls Review of Administrative Justice in the United Kingdom, Oxford, 1988.

19 See W. A. Robson, 'The Central Domination of Local Government', *Political Quarterly*, January 1933; B. Keith-Lucas and P. G. Richards, *A History of Local Government in the Twentieth Century*, Allen & Unwin, 1978; the Maud Report, Chapter 4; and the Layfield Report.

20 *What Future for Local Government?*, AMA, 1988. See also *The Times Educational Supplement*, 1 April 1988.

21 For example *Standards for School Premises Regulations 1972*. Strictly speaking such regulations are a legislative form of control as much as administrative.

22 E.g. see *Local Government Chronicle*, 11 April 1980, p. 404. Another instance concerned Manchester's sixth forms: see the *Guardian*, 12 January 1981.

23 In 1972 the Clay Cross Council refused to apply the new (Conservative) Housing Finance Act to its tenants: consequently eleven councillors were surcharged (£63,000) and disqualified from holding office. In 1974 the council went out of existence as a result of local government reorganization, but in the meantime the Minister established a Housing Commission to take responsibility for the housing functions of the local authority. The council refused to cooperate with the Commission and made its work rather difficult.

An earlier case of a commission being sent in to replace a local authority occurred in 1927, when the Tredegar Board of Guardians was found to be too generous with poor relief. Outside local government, a more recent example concerned the Lambeth, Southwark and Lewisham Area Health Authority, which was replaced by Health Commissioners between 1979 and 1980. Most recently (November 1981–February 1982), the Minister was about to send his own agents in to administer the sale of council houses (and he had won a case in court to prove his right to do so) when the council, Norwich DC, acceded to the Minister's pressure to carry out the responsibility under the Housing Act 1980. In March 1986 the Government appointed a commission ready to assume responsibility for Belfast City Council where members ceased conducting business as a protest against the Anglo-Irish agreement, 1985.

24 See K. Baker, *The Turbulent Years*, Faber and Faber, 1993.

25 W. O. Hart and J. F. Garner, *Hart's Local Government and Administration*, Butterworth, 1973, p. 371.

26 See *Relations between Central Government and Local Authorities* by the Central Policy Review Staff, HMSO, 1977.

27 In 1970, for example, half of the lists of candidates for posts of director of social services were altered following submission to the Minister. See Lord Redcliffe-Maud and B. Wood, *English Local Government Reformed*, OUP, 1974, p. 127. In 1979, the Government issued a White Paper, *Central Government Controls over Local Authorities* (Cmd 7634), which proposed to drop the ministerial vetting of candidates for such posts; this was not legislated for, however. In May 1990 Derbyshire Police Authority proposed to challenge in the High Court the Home Secretary's veto of their choice of John Weselby as Chief Constable.

28 Local Government Act 1972 (Sec. 230) and Local Government (Scotland) Act 1973 (Sec. 199).

29 The 'Instruments' deal with the procedures of governing bodies – their size, membership, meetings, etc. The 'Articles' are concerned with their powers and duties – appointing staff, the conduct of the school, its curriculum, lettings, etc.

30 A White Paper is a government document declaring its policy; a Green Paper is a consultation document indicating the Government's tentative ideas on policy, for discussion purposes.

31 Student grants, for example, within the education service. Such grants may take the form of 'percentage' grants (as in the case of the police, where the central government pays for half of the cost of local police forces – 51 per cent since 1985–6). Alternatively, grants may be paid on a unit basis (such as the traditional form of housing subsidies, where a fixed amount of grant is given to local authorities for each house built).

32 If the government's allowance for inflation (the cash limits) is less than the actual rate of inflation, local authorities will find their resources stretched. Another constraint is the amount of planned expenditure which the government is prepared to recognize as 'relevant' for grant purposes, that is upon which it is prepared to make its proportionate contribution.

33 The building standards have been known as 'Parker Morris' standards after the committee which determined them in 1961. Cost yardsticks are in effect the maximum expenditure per house which the government recognizes as reasonable. In 1980, the Government began to dismantle these controls.

34 See the White Paper, *A Framework for Expansion*, Cmd 5174, HMSO, 1972.

35 B. Keith-Lucas, 'What Price Local Democracy?', *New Society*, 12 August 1976. See also W. A. Robson, *Local Government in Crisis*, Allen & Unwin, 1968; *Local Government Chronicle*, 9 October 1981, pp. 1041–2; the Maud, Wheatley, Redcliffe-Maud and Layfield Reports.

36 See *Municipal Journal*, 16–22 June 1993, p. 10.

37 *British Social Attitudes: Twelfth Report*, Gower, 1995.

38 See the Central Policy Review Staff's *Relations between Central Government and Local Authorities*, HMSO, 1977; the Layfield Report; and J. A. Taylor, 'The Consultative Council in Local Government Finance', *Local Government Studies*, March/June 1979.

39 Secretary of State for Education and Science *v.* Tameside Metropolitan District Council (1976). See also A. Bradley, 'The Tameside Affair', *Listener*, 5 May 1977. In 1980, a similar event occurred in that the courts declared as unlawful the Minister's appointment of Health Commissioners in place of the Lambeth, Southwark and Lewisham Area Health Authority. In October 1981, the court held that the Minister had acted illegally (on a technicality) in withholding grant from six London Boroughs; in December Hackney successfully challenged his right to withhold part of their inner city 'partnership' grant. In 1990 the High Court initially found against the Minister's approval of Beechen Cliff School to opt out of Avon LEA.

40 R. Rhodes, *Beyond Westminster and Whitehall*, Unwin, 1988. See also J. A. G. Griffith, *Central Departments and Local Authorities*, Allen & Unwin, 1966.

41 R. Rhodes *Control and Power in Central–Local Government Relations*, Gower, 1981.

42 See D. E. Ashford, 'The Effects of Central Finance on the British Local Government System', *British Journal of Political Science*, Vol. 4, no. 3, 1974; K. P. Poole, 'England and Wales', *Studies in Comparative Local Government*, Vol. 4, no. 1, 1970. Cf. E. Page, 'Grant Dependence and Changes in Intergovernmental Finance', Strathclyde Studies in Public Policy, 1981; article by D. Wardman in *Local Government Chronicle*, 2 July 1982; A. Robinson, 'The Myth of Central Control', *Listener*, 19 June 1982.

43 It is said that Richard Crossman resisted the proposals to place the NHS in the hands of local authorities (or any other separately elected bodies) because they were too successful in spending money, having the force of 'active' public opinion behind them. A similar point is made in L. J. Sharpe, *Why Local Democracy?*, Fabian Society, 1965.

44 Previous Ministers include Attlee, Morrison and Bevan. The one-time

Conservative Party Chairman, Kenneth Baker, is an ex-councillor as was Patrick Jenkin, a past Environment Secretary. The Minister for Consumer Affairs until 1981, Mrs Oppenheim, was also Vice President of the Association of District Councils. Lord Bellwin, once the Minister for Local Government, was a prominent councillor and leader of Leeds City Council before the Conservative election victory in 1979, and John Major was a prominent councillor in Lambeth LB.

45 For this information, I am grateful to Edward du Cann, MP, and also the House of Commons Public Information Office. See also F. Willey, *The Honourable Member*, Sheldon Press, 1974; P. Richards, *The Backbenchers*, Faber, 1972; A. Barker and M. Rush, *The Member of Parliament and His Information*, Allen & Unwin, 1971; 'The Times' Guide to Parliament 1979. However, it may be added that MPs are not always the allies of local government: by passing on complaints to the Minister rather than the local authority, the MP (perhaps unwittingly) draws the central government into local affairs. See G. Jones, 'MPs – Eroding the Independence of Local Government?', *Municipal Review*, July 1972.

46 It is claimed that they may carry more influence with Ministers than do MPs: this was suggested by the ex-leader of the Liverpool Council ('Brass Tacks', BBC, 17 July 1979).

47 See H. Drucker *et al.*, *Developments in British Politics 2*, Macmillan, 1986, pp. 142–3.

48 See *The Times Educational Supplement*, 5 May 1989, pp. 14–16, and *Local Government Chronicle*, 4 September 1992, pp. 13–15, and 27 March 1992, pp. 16–17.

49 See *Local Government Chronicle*, 31 July 1992, p. 13.

50 *Local Government Finance* (1976).

51 *Local Government Finance* (1977), para. 2.9.

52 In 1854 *The Times* declared 'we prefer to take our chance of cholera and the rest than be bullied into health'.

53 In 1873, the town of Nottingham published an open letter to the president of the Local Government Board criticizing the degree of ministerial control: see Keith-Lucas, op. cit.

54 See Robson, op. cit.; L. T. Hobhouse, *Liberalism*, HUL, 1910, p. 233.

55 See Keith-Lucas, op. cit.; Robson, op. cit.; and see R. Darke and R. Walker (eds.), *Local Government and the Public*, Leonard Hill, 1977, Chapter 1.

56 Denis Healey, Chancellor of the Exchequer, House of Commons debates (*Hansard*), cols. 296–7, 15 April 1975.

57 See Taylor, op. cit. Also A. Alexander, *Local Government in Britain Since Reorganisation*, Allen & Unwin, 1982 who sees it more as a consultative rather than a negotiating body.

58 *The Times*, 19 February 1980.

59 *The Times*, 20 March 1980.

60 Though there are a number of theories: see W. J. M. Mackenzie, *Theories of Local Government*, LSE, 1961. See also L. J. Sharpe, 'Theories and Values of Local Government', *Political Studies*, no. 80, 1970; O. A. Hartley, 'The Relationship between Central and Local Authorities', *Public Administration*, Winter 1971; *The Times*, 8 July 1972.

61 *The Conduct of Local Authority Business: The Government Response*, HMSO, 1988.

62 See G. Jones and T. Travers, 'Attitudes to Local Government' in *Westminster and Whitehall*, CLD, 1994.

63 See *Municipal Journal*, 2 July 1992, p. 7.

64 Variations in the standards of local authority services are well documented. For example, see: the *Report of the Committee on Local Authority and Allied Social Services*, HMSO, 1968; S. Sainsbury, *Registered as Disabled*, Bell, 1970; B. Davies, *Variations in the Services for the Elderly*, Bell, 1971; B. Davies *et al.*, *Variations in Children's Services Among British Urban Authorities*, Bell, 1972; N. Boaden, *Urban Policy-Making*, CUP, 1971; Newton and Sharpe (Further Reading, Chap. 8). The Chartered Institute of Public Finance and Accountancy (CIPFA) regularly provides useful analyses of local authority expenditures through Statistical Information Service, from which the following examples are taken:

Estimated expenditure per primary pupil (1984–5)

Dudley MD	£623	Powys CC	£926
Newcastle MD	£850	Kent	£639

Estimated expenditure per pupil in special education (1976–7)

Somerset	£930	Gwent	£2,154

Estimated expenditure per head for planning functions (1984–5)

Solihull MD	£2.63	Manchester MD	£12.75

Estimated expenditure per head for social services (1984–5)

Cleveland CC	£46.30	Shropshire CC	£27.81
Manchester MD	£99.62	Dudley MD	£32.44

Expenditure on consumer services (1975–6)

Powys CC over £1 m   Hertfordshire CC less than £200

Home help contact hours per 1,000 over 65 (1984–5)

Gwent CC	17,152	Surrey	5,069
Sunderland MB	26,582	Wirral MB	10,763

Meals delivered to pensioners (1976–7)

Doncaster MD provided four times those provided by Sheffield

Overall spending per head (1983–4)

Haringey LB	£697	West Sussex CC	£315
South Cambs. DC	£24.75	Blackburn BC	£122

It is unwise to draw too hasty conclusions from these figures: such 'league tables' can be misleading unless other factors are taken into account (such as need, costs, alternative provision, etc.). A useful discussion of the reasons of variations is to be found in Boaden, op. cit., A striking example emerged from a report of the Public Accounts Committee. This expressed concern at the substantial variations in expenditure among police forces – hardly the least centrally supervised local service. (See *Fifth Report from the Committee of Public Accounts: Procurement of Police Equipment*, House of Commons Paper 445, HMSO, 1980.)

65 See also P. Saunders, 'Local Government and the State', *New Society*, 13 March 1980; and P. Saunders, *Urban Politics: A Sociological Interpretation*, Penguin Books, 1981.

66 B. Davies, *Social Needs and Resources in Local Services*, Michael Joseph, 1968, and K. Judge, *Rationing Social Services*, Heinemann, 1978. But cf. Darke and Walker (eds.), op. cit., Chapter 14.

67 Darke and Walker (eds.), op. cit.

68 Saunders, op. cit. See also C. Cockburn, *The Local State*, Pluto, 1977; W. K. Tabb and L. Sawers, *Marxism and the Metropolis*, OUP, 1978; and M. Castells, *City, Class and Power*, Macmillan, 1978.

69 See P. Bongers, *Local Government and 1999*, Longman, 1992.

70 E.g. some of the work of British environmental health officers and meat inspectors is carried out in Europe by vets. This may have career implications.

71 A. Norton, 'Local Government and Europe', *Local Government Studies Annual Review*, 1979; J. Redmond and G. Barrett, 'The European Regional Development Fund and Local Government', *Local Government Studies*, September 1988; A. Davison, *Grants from Europe: How to Get Money and Influence Policy*, Bedford, 1988; C. Maclure 'A minefield of opportunity', *Local Government Chronicle*, 29 January 1999.

72 E.g. see 'European Pay Off', *Local Government Chronicle*, 14 March 1980; 'How to get Brussels working for you', *The Times*, 23 February 1991.

73 R. A. W. Rhodes, *Local Government and the European Community*, INLOGOV, 1973, p. 7. See too J. Glasson, *Local Authorities Access to EEC Aid*, Oxford Polytechnic, 1984.

74 A. Norton, 'Relations between the European Commission and British Local Government', *Local Government Studies*, January/February 1980, p. John, *The impact of the EC on local government*, JRF, 1993, *Regional strategy and partnership in European programmes*, JRF 1996, *The Europeanisation of British Local Government*, LGMB, 1995 and M. Goldsmith and K. Klausen, *European Integration and Local Government*, Elger, 1997.

13 LOCAL GOVERNMENT AND THE LOCAL COMMUNITY

1 See D. Peschek, 'Local Authority Technology Co-operation in Europe', *Local Government Chronicle*, 19 October 1979.

2 See *Scottish Government Yearbook*, 1991.

3 See *Working for Patients*, HMSO, 1989.

4 This post replaces that of the old Medical Officer of Health. Doctors are appointed by the health authorities, but since they work in and with the district councils, they have to be formally 'adopted' by those local authorities. Local authorities are required to appoint Public Health Officers (under the Public Health (Control of Diseases) Act, 1984; in practice appropriate NHS consultants are usually designated as the council's 'Proper Officer' for that purpose.

5 See *Local Government Chronicle*, 12 March 1993, p. 13, and *Local Government Agenda* (ICSA), July 1993.

6 For example compare *The Quango State*, CLD, 1995; W. Hall and S. Weir, *The Untouchables*, Democratic Audit Report, 1996; *Local Government Chronicle*, 30 August 1996, p. 12; *EGO Trip*, 1994; *Public Bodies*, HMSO (annual); *The Governance Gap*, JRF, 1994; *Second Report of the Committee on Standards in Public Life* (Nolan), 1996.

7 J. Kilfoyle *Times Educational Supplement*, 1994; *Local Government Chronicle*, 30 August 1996, p 12.

8 *Bournemouth Evening Echo*, 22 April 1995.

9 C. A. Collins, 'Councillors' Attitudes', *LG Studies*, April 1980, p. 36.

10 E.g. the GLC fares issue was started by Bromley council. On Manchester see: 'Greater Manchester 78', *Guardian*, 27 November 1978; 'Metropolitan Review', *Local Government Chronicle*, 14 March 1980; H. Elcock, 'English Local Government Reformed', *Public Administration*, Summer 1975; and M. Fitzgerald, 'Politics', *Local Government Chronicle*, 28 September 1979. The inquiry into the Toxteth riots in 1981 referred to the strained relations between the two tiers of local government on Merseyside.

11 See, for example, the *Somerset Express*, 24 May 1988.

12 For example, Manchester City Council *v.* Greater Manchester Council (1979) and Kensington and Chelsea LB *v.* GLC (1982).

13 One area of potential conflict in the field of planning is being somewhat diminished by the removal of many of the counties' planning control functions (known as 'county matters') to the district councils, under the Local Government, Planning and Land Act 1980.

14 S. Leach *et al.*, *Two-Tier Relationships in British Local Government*, INLOGOV, 1987. They go on to suggest how these authorities may work together via aligned service boundaries, rearranged departmental responsibilities (including lead departments) and joint provision.

15 'The Local Government Councillor', *The Conduct of Local Authority Business* (Widdicombe), Research Vol. 2, HMSO, 1986.

16 In 1993 Somerset County Council inaugurated an Environment Forum of some fifty representatives from local councils, government departments and statutory undertakings (rail, waterways, tourism, forestry), the CBI and Chambers of Commerce (and local industries such as quarrying, farming, construction), voluntary organizations (for sport, leisure, youth, conservation) and interest groups (Country Landowners Association, Archaeological Society).

17 See *Local Government – The Community Leadership Role*, LGMB, 1993.

18 The Bains Report, Chapter 8.

19 Some are executive in nature: see, for example, T. J. Phillips, 'Area Planning Committees in Walsall', *Local Government Studies*, January 1979. See also Barbara Webster, 'Area Management', *Local Government Studies Annual Review*, April 1979; L. Corina, 'Area Councillors Committees', *Public Administration*, Autumn 1977; and R. Greenwood *et al.*, *The Organisation of Local Authorities in England and Wales 1967–75*, INLOGOV, 1975, section III.

20 A. Alexander, *Local Government in Britain Since Reorganisation*, Unwin, 1982.

21 Divisional executives were a form of decentralization within counties for the purpose of educational administration. They comprised members of the (county) local education authority and members of the district councils within the divisional area, together with some co-opted members. Their functions varied from county to county, but they normally exercised some powers delegated by the LEA.

22 See *Strategic Government*, Winter 1992, ACC.

23 Apart from the local authority associations, there are some separate associations representing members (the Association of Councillors, for example) and officers (the Society of Education Officers and the Association of Directors of Social Services, for example). These are professional bodies: they do not negotiate pay or conditions of service, for which they may have separate bodies, such as the Association of Local Authority Chief Executives. There are also party groupings, e.g. Association of Liberal Councillors.

24 For example, the Local Government Training Board (LGTB); the Local Authorities Management Services and Computer Committee (LAMSAC); the Local Authorities Conditions of Service Advisory Board (LACSAB); the Local Authorities Mutual Investment Trust (LAMIT).

25 Such as the Bill drawn up by the AMA in 1979 seeking extensive powers for local authorities to help small firms in inner cities.

26 See D. Peschek, 'Can the Associations Become One Body?', *Local Government*

Chronicle, 14 September 1979. However, one of the objectives of the ACC is the setting-up of a single body to speak for local government in England and Wales. J. Kellas, *The Scottish System*, CUP, 1975, p. 143; the Layfield Report, p. 87. Though this contrast has diminished with the Local Government Acts of 1980 and 1982. See D. Heald, 'The Scottish Rate Support Grant', *Public Administration*, Spring 1980.

27 See note 20 above.

28 Mr Duncan Sandys in a speech reported in the *County Councils Gazette*, September 1956, pp. 195–6. See also A. C. Hetherington, *Local Government Studies*, April 1980, who notes the increasing readiness to hold talks with local authority association representatives at ministerial level.

29 As such they are 'partial' or semi-pressure groups. In practice many people belong indirectly to 'overt' pressure groups in so far as local (or first-order) groups may become members of a regional or a national network (second-order groups). For example, a local sports club may become affiliated to a regional/ national body or standing conference which in itself provides no sporting facilities but seeks solely to further sporting interests.

30 D. Hill, *Participation in Local Affairs*, Penguin Books, 1970, p. 200; *Westminster Bank Review*, August 1979; *The Voluntary Sector*, NCVO, 1985. See too S. Lowe, *Urban Social Movements*, Macmillan, 1986; The Wolfenden Report: *The Future of Voluntary Organisations*, 1977; and *Social Trends*, 1989.

31 M. Moran, 'The Changing World of British Pressure Groups', in L. Robins, *Political Institutions in Britain*, Longman, 1987.

32 J. Gyford in 'Aspects of Local Democracy', *The Conduct of Local Authority Business* (Widdicombe), Research Vol. 4, HMSO, 1986.

33 K. Newton, *Second City Politics*, OUP, 1976. He adds (p. 36) that there might well be another 5,000 which he had not included. There are about 400 such organizations in the area of Taunton, Somerset.

34 See J. Stanyer, *Understanding Local Government*, Fontana, 1976. But see also W. Hampton, *Democracy and Community*, OUP, 1970, p. 244.

35 D. Wilson and G. Stoker in *Public Policy and Administration*, Summer 1991, pp. 20–34.

36 D. Wilson and C. Game, *Local Government in the UK*, Macmillan, 1997, p. 301.

37 The Maud Report, Vol. 2, pp. 184–5.

38 J. Dearlove, *The Politics of Policy in Local Government*, CUP, 1973.

39 See, for example, Newton, op. cit. and R. Davis and P. Hall, *Issues in Urban Society*, Penguin, 1978, p. 265.

40 See too R. Hambleton *et al.*, *New perspectives on Local governance*, JRF, 1997, p. 134.

41 For example, the groups resisting the local introduction of nuclear power production may seek the aid of the energy-saving or alternative energy producers.

42 See Hampton, op. cit., Chapter 10.

43 See P. Saunders, *Urban Politics*, Penguin, 1980.

44 Councillors in Britain, however, have been traditionally and notoriously involved in administrative details. See the Maud Report, Vol. 1.

45 Newton, op. cit. He also points to the very large amount of informal contacts, lunchtime chats, etc. It must be quite obvious to councillors or local government officers why they are invited to social occasions or to act as speakers at meetings of local organizations. Nevertheless, even if their goodwill is not thereby engendered, such occasions do provide opportunities for them to be buttonholed or 'lobbied'.

46 J. Dearlove, 'Councillors and Interest Groups in Kensington and Chelsea', *British Journal of Political Science*, Vol. 1, no. 2, 1971, and *The Politics of Policy in Local Government*, CUP, 1973.

47 An example at national level is the RSPCA, which Professor Birch suggests has maintained its parliamentary reputation as a responsible body by successfully restraining the extremists within its ranks who would like to oppose blood sports. A. H. Birch, *The British System of Government*, Allen & Unwin, 1967.

48 *The Conduct of Local Authority Business* (Widdicombe Report), HMSO, 1986, Chap. 8.

49 Newton, op. cit., pp. 132–3.

50 See Dearlove, Hampton and Newton, studies cited above.

51 Newton, op. cit., Chapters 4 and 9. But cf. Hampton, op. cit., pp. 215 and 244.

52 Birch, op. cit., p. 99.

53 Newton, op. cit., p. 88.

54 Some interesting case studies are provided in Hampton, op. cit., Chapters 9 and 10, and in R. Darke and R. Walker (eds.), *Local Government and the Public*, Leonard Hill, 1977.

55 Dearlove's terms.

56 Newton, op. cit., p. 132. Cf. Hill, op. cit., p. 199.

57 G. Stoker, *The Politics of Local Government*, Macmillan, 1991.

58 See G. Stoker and K. Young, *Cities in the 1990s*, Longman, 1993; see also publications by Aldbourne Associates (1994), J. Gibson (1993), M. Taylor (1995), S. Thake (1995), S. Thake and R. Staubach (1993), J. Wilson (1994) all published by J. Rowntree Trust.

59 A study for the Royal Commission on Local Government in England 1968 suggested that the effectiveness of pressure groups in the field of local government was hindered by 'the multiplicity of areas and the division of functions between them [which] makes the organisation of such groups difficult, the fact [that] many existing local authority areas do not in any way correspond to communities . . . [and] the way in which many local authorities run their affairs through elaborate committee and sub-committee structures does not make it easy for the views on the development of services as opposed to particular cases or issues to be voiced and properly considered (Royal Commission, Research Study 1).

60 W. A. Maloney *et al.*, 'The insider and outsider Model Revisited', *Journal of Public Policy*, vol. 14, No. 1, 1994

61 Ibid.

62 In mobilizing the skills and energies of their members in the design and execution of local projects, pressure groups are acting rather like co-opted members at one remove.

63 The Maud Report, Vol. 3, pp. 114–17.

64 The need for this is well illustrated in Hampton, op. cit., pp. 206–13, where he shows significant differences between what councillors perceive to be issues and what the ordinary electorate thinks.

65 P. G. Richards, *The Reformed Local Government System*, Allen & Unwin, 1978, p. 157.

66 P. Rivers, *Politics by Pressure*, Harrap, 1974, p. 7.

67 See Rivers, op. cit., pp. 16–20, and Hampton, op. cit., p. 216.

68 See, for example, Newton, op. cit., pp. 83–4; the Maud Report, Vol. 3, Table 159; Hill, op. cit., pp. 53, 89; G. M. Aves, *The Voluntary Worker in the Social Services*, Allen & Unwin, 1969, para. 38.

69 See Dearlove, Newton, Saunders cited above; also R. King, *Capital and Politics*, Routledge, 1983, and W. Grant, *Political Economy of Corporation*, Macmillan, 1985.

70 The Maud Report, Vol. 3, p. 167, Table 167.

71 J. Gyford, *Local Politics in Britain*, Croom Helm, 1976, p. 109.

72 S. E. Finer, *Anonymous Empire*, Pall Mall Press, 1969, p. 145.

73 *People and Planning: Report of the Committee on Public Participation in Planning*, HMSO, 1969.

74 Ministry of Housing and Local Government, Circular 65/69.

75 *A New Partnership for Our Schools*, HMSO, 1977.

76 The Skeffington Report, para. 5.

77 *Report of the Committee on Local Authority and Allied Personal Social Services*, HMSO, 1968, para. 480.

78 Ibid., para. 494.

79 A. H. Birch, *Representation*, Macmillan, 1972.

80 Darke and Walker (eds.), op. cit., p. 73.

81 N. Lewis and P. J. Birkinshaw, 'Local Authorities and the Resolution of Grievances', *Local Government Studies*, January 1979.

82 Laurence Evans, 'Review of Public Relations', *Municipal Year Book*, 1975.

83 *Report of the Royal Commission on the Constitution* 1969–73 (the Kilbrandon Report), Study no. 7, Table 25.

84 *Complaints Procedures: A Code of Practice for Local Government and Water Authorities for Dealing with Queries and Complaints*, Commission for Local Administration in England, 1978.

85 See *The Public Service Orientation*, LGTB, 1985; *Learning from the Public*, LGTB, 1989; *Getting Closer to the Public*, LGTB, 1987.

86 N. Lewis and B. Gateshill, *The Commission for Local Administration, a Preliminary Appraisal*, RIPA, 1978.

87 See G. Stoker, p. 159 in Hambleton, at 40 above: also Morris-Jones at reference 37, Chapter 6, and A. Ryan, 'Why I don't vote', *New Society*, 16 July 1981, p. 111.

88 See C. Rallings *et al.*, *Community Identity and Participation in local Democracy*, CLD, 1994.

89 See *British Social Attitudes 1994*, Gower, 1995 and *Maud Report*, vol. 3, 1967.

90 The Maud Report, Vol. 3. A later figure is 25 per cent: *New Society*, 4 March 1982. But see *Attitudes to local government*, JRF, 1990.

91 See p. 121 of Hambleton, note 40 above.

92 *Public Perceptions of Local Government*, HMSO, 1992.

93 National Opinion Polls, 'Public Participation in Local Government', *Political Economic Social Review*, no. 1, 1975. For 42 per cent figure see *Local Government Chronicle*, 13 June 1980.

94 *New Society*, 4 March 1982.

95 See the Maud Report, para. 323 and Table 91.

96 See Hambleton, op. cit., p. 150.

97 G. A. Almond and S. Verba, *The Civic Culture*, Princeton, USA, 1963.

98 Widdicombe Report, vol. III, 1986: Hambleton, op. cit. p. 134; *British Social Attitudes 1994*, Gower 1995; *Attitudes to local government*, JRF, 1990.

99 The Kilbrandon Report, 1973, Research Paper no. 7, Table 4.

100 See the Maud Report, Vol. 3, Table 38.

101 *The Conduct of Local Authority Business* (Widdicombe Report), Vol. 3, HMSO, 1986.

102 See note 98.

103 The Maud Report, Vol. 3.

104 See K. Newton and T. J. Karran, *The Politics of Local Expenditure*, 1985.

105 J. Bonner, 'Public Interest in Local Government', *Public Administration*, Winter 1954.

106 That is 30% of those who did not complain: see *Public Perceptions of local Government*, HMSO, 1992: also Widdicombe, vol. III, 1986.

107 The Maud Report, Vol. 3, Chapter 1. Also *Attitudes to local government*, JRF, 1990 and Hambleton, p. 150, op. cit.

108 See C. Game, 'Public Attitudes to the Abolition of the Mets', *Local Government Studies*, September 1987.

109 See D. Burns *et al.*, *The Politics of Decentralisation*, Macmillan 1994; J. Chandler *et al.*, *Decentralisation and devolution in England and Wales*, LGMB, 1995; *Local government policy making*, 1994; *Freedom within boundaries*, LGMB, 1997

110 See B. Walker, 'Client's Choice', *Social Services Insight*, 20 February 1987. See too P. Birkinshaw, *Open Government, Freedom of Information and Local Government*, Local Government Legal Society Trust, 1986.

111 Hambleton, op. cit., p. 158.

112 Ibid. pp. 158–9.

113 The Maud Report, Vol. I, para. 448.

114 The Bains Report, paras. 7.35, 7.39.

115 See S. Jackson (p. 636 below) for an interesting case-study.

116 H. Benham, *Two Cheers for the Town Hall*, Hutchinson, 1964, suggests that local authorities do not aim to maximize their communications with the public because they can administer services more smoothly without publicity. In particular it appears that some Labour councils are suspicious, rightly or wrongly, of press publicity because they feel that newspapers are Conservative in general outlook: see D. Hill, *Participating in Local Affairs*, Penguin Books, 1970; D. Murphy, *The Silent Watchdog: The Press in Local Politics*, Constable, 1976.

117 See A. Wright, *Local Radio and Local Democracy*, IBA, 1982.

118 A. Wright, 'Local Broadcasting and the Local Authority', *Public Administration*, Autumn, 1982.

119 C. Copus, *Local Government and the Media*, LGMB, 1999, p. 14.

120 J. Corner, *Television Form and Public Address*, ed. Arnold, 1995.

121 R. Kilborn, 'Shaping the Real', *European Journal of Communication*, Vol. 13, 2 June 1998.

122 *Publicity for Work of Local Authorities*, Department of the Environment Circular 47/75. Also see the Maud Report, Chapter 1, and the Royal Commission on Local Government in Scotland (Wheatley) Research Study 2, HMSO, 1969, p. 22, and S. C. Sobol, in *Local Government Studies*, September/October 1981.

123 H. Cox and D. Morgan, *City Politics and the Press*, CUP, 1974; Hill, op. cit., Chapter 6.

124 I. Jackson, *The Provincial Press and the Community*, Manchester University Press, 1971.

125 Copus, op. cit.

126 See *Local Government Studies*, Summer 1993.

127 J. Gyford *et al.*, *The Changing Politics of Local Government*, Unwin, 1989.

128 For example, while the Public Bodies (Admission to Meetings) Act requires local authorities to supply agenda and other papers to the press it does not lay down how far in advance. And the Local Government Act 1972 was silent on the issue of papers for committee meetings, so that local authorities vary in their practices here. See now Local Government (Access to Information) Act 1985.

129 'Participation', *Studies in Comparative Local Government*, Vol. 5, no. 2, International Union of Local Authorities, The Hague, 1971.

130 R. Burke, *The Murky Cloak: Local Authority–Press Relations*, Charles Knight, 1970, p. vii.

131 *Public Policy and Administration* November 1996; *Local Government Chronicle*, 13 November 1998, 5 December 1997; *Municipal Journal*, 12 September 1997.

132 A. Harding Boulton, 'Councils, Public and the Press', *Local Government Chronicle*, 31 March 1978.

133 Public Bodies (Admission to Meetings) Act 1960, sec. 1.

134 *Publicity for the Work of Local Authorities*, Department of the Environment Circular 47/75.

135 Referring not just generally to more open government and freedom of information etc. but also specifically to the government's sharing information with local authorities in particular. Local authorities frequently show their frustration at being given too little information too late: they should therefore well understand the public outbursts of those who feel local government is playing the cards too close to its chest. Thus in fairness to the central government, it must be said that some local authorities do lack initiative and do need prodding.

136 See, for example, the Maud Report, Vol. 3, Tables 98, 99; L. Corina, 'Area Councillors Committee', *Public Administration*, Autumn 1977, p. 335; Lewis, op. cit., p. 13.

137 The Redcliffe-Maud Report, Research Study 9; the Wheatley Report, Research Study 2; Hampton, op. cit., pp. 87–8.

138 The Maud Report, Vol. 3, Chapter 1.

139 The riot in the St Pauls district of Bristol in April 1980 and in Brixton in April 1981 led some to suggest that 'no go areas' were beginning to develop in certain (especially immigrant) areas of mainland Britain.

140 Hill, op. cit., p. 150. See also Darke and Walker (eds.), op. cit., Chapter 10.

141 While planning is *not* easy and its results are distant in time, it has nevertheless been suggested that the participation element has been jeopardized by its being left in the hands of the professional planners to arrange: see Darke and Walker (eds.), op. cit., p. 83.

142 Under the Education Act 1980, it is now to be a legal requirement that parents be appointed to school governing/managing bodies. This follows the recommendations of the Taylor Report, *A New Partnership for our Schools*, HMSO, 1977.

143 *Children and Their Primary Schools*, HMSO, 1967. Current legislation is seeking to extend parental choice of schools and also to give greater publicity to their activities – see the Education Act 1980.

144 The Housing Act 1980. In 1975, forty-six local authorities had introduced schemes for tenant participation and a further forty were considering doing so. See Darke and Walker (eds.), op. cit., Chapter 12.

145 Following the recommendations of the Plowden Report certain inner urban areas were given priority (or 'positive discrimination') in obtaining resources to improve their schools and educational opportunities: these were known as 'educational priority areas'. The 'urban programme' started in 1969 when special financial assistance was directed from the central government to certain local authorities containing areas of special social need. While early attention was focused on facilities for children, part of the funds have been used for 'Community Development Projects' which involved more intensive approaches by specially appointed staff who sought to gain the cooperation of all the local central and local social service agencies. Action zones represent the latest approach: see Chap. 15.

146 For example in rural areas many community development officers are funded by the Development Commission.

147 See *Guardian*, 16 March 1982; *New Statesman*, 19 March 1982.

148 See R. Hadley and S. Hatch, *Social Welfare and the Failure of the State: Centralized Social Services and Participatory Alternatives*, Allen & Unwin, 1981; *Barclay Report*, 'Social Workers: Their Role and Tasks', Bedford, 1982.

149 J. Gyford, 'Diversity, Sectionalism and Local Democracy' in 'Aspects of Local Democracy', *The Conduct of Local Authority Business* (Widdicombe), Research Vol. 4, HMSO, 1986.

150 Ibid.

151 Ibid.

152 See A. Walker, *Rural Poverty*, CPAG, 1978.

153 Cardiff, Swansea, Newport, Port Talbot, Merthyr Tydfil and Rhondda. There could be changes here as a result of the current special review.

154 *Parish and Town Councils in England: A Survey*, Aston Business School, 1992.

155 *Role and Activities of Parish and Town Councils in England: Case Studies*, HMSO, 1993.

156 See *Public Finance and Accountancy*, 14 May 1993, pp. 12–14.

157 Ibid.

158 *Community Councils in Scotland*, Central Research Unit Paper, Scottish Office, September 1978. Early analysis of some of the second round of elections suggests an even smaller proportion of contested seats: see M. Masterson and

E. Masterman, 'Elections of the Second Generation of Community Councils', *Local Government Studies*, January/February 1980;*Local Government Chronicle*, 22 March 1984.

159 Local Government (Scotland) Act, Sec. 51.

160 *Local Government in Scotland* (Scottish Office Brief), p. 7.

161 M. Minogue, *The Consumer's Guide to Local Government*, Macmillan, 1977, p. III.

162 *Neighbourhood Councils in England*, Consultation Paper LG4/743/4, Department of the Environment, HMSO, 1974.

163 B. Dixey, *A Guide to Neighbourhood Councils*, The Association for Neighbourhood Councils, 1975.

164 J. Talbot and S. Humble, 'Neighbourhood Councils Defined', *Local Government Studies*, July 1977. Also *An Investigation into Neighbourhood Councils*, INLOGOV, 1977.

165 See note 164.

166 *A Voice for Your Neighbourhood*, Department of the Environment, 1977.

167 The Redcliffe-Maud Report, Vol. I, p. 99 and Research Study 9; and the Wheatley Report, Research Study 2.

168 At an ICSA–CIPFA conference in November 1981. See also NCC publications, 'Bureaucracies', 1981, and 'The Neighbourhood', 1982.

169 See *Community Care*, 19 November 1981, p. 3.

170 See A. Godfrey, 'More Pavement Politics', *Local Government Review*, 28 November 1981.

14 OUT OF THE NINETIES: TAKING STOCK

1 See *Renewing democracy rebuilding communities*, Labour Party, 1995; *Local Government Chronicle*, 21 June 1991.

2 Reports by management consultants Coopers & Lybrand, *Streamlining the Cities*, suggest that savings will be negligible or nil. A later report by PA Management Consultants (1984) condemns the reorganization for other, non-financial reasons. See too N. Flynn *et al.*, note 29, Chapter 3 above.

3 E.g. in Bournemouth: see *Local Government Chronicle*, 17 February 1984.

4 See *Getting On With It*, Vols. 1 and 2, LGMB, 1992.

5 *Solicitor's Journal*, 16 February 1990.

6 *Public Finance and Accountancy*, 29 January 1993.

7 *Challenge of Change in Local Government*, INLOGOV, 1988; see too R. Pearson and C. Miller, 'Laying the foundations', *Insight*, 21 February 1989.

8 R. Hambleton, 'The Decentralisation of Public Services', *Local Government Studies*, January 1989.

9 *Survey of Internal Organizational Change in Local Government*, LGMB, 1993.

10 *Local Government Chronicle*, 12 February 1993, p. 16.

11 *Survey of Internal Organizational Change in Local Government*, LGMB, 1993, p. 1.

12 See note 10.

13 *Local Government Chronicle*, 27 January 1995, p. 9 and 26 July 1991.

14 K. Young and M. Davies, *The Politics of Local Government since Widdicombe*, Rowntree Foundation, 1990.

15 See *Local Government Studies*, August/September 1982; *Local Government Studies*, May/June 1983; *Local Government Chronicle*, 3 January 1986; *Managing Hung Authorities*, LGTB, 1985; *Local Government Chronicle*, 12 July 1985.

16 See S. Leach, *It's our party* LGMB, 1998.

17 See K. Young, *The Conduct of Local Authority Business after Widdicombe*, Rowntree Memorial Trust, 1989.

18 R. Dahrendorf, *On Britain*, BBC, 1982. See also J. Gyford, *New Society*, 3 May 1984.

19 The GLC did all three, arguing that London's population has a large Irish element, and has suffered the effects of IRA terrorist bombings, or that London is especially susceptible in the event of nuclear attack, i.e. that foreign policy is a quite legitimate pursuit. Others have justified their actions by arguing that national policies may have direct effects on their localities' welfare (e.g. housing or education in immigrant areas) or their economy or community (e.g. in mining or industrial areas) or that (nuclear) civil defence expenditure wastes part of their budgets. A contrary view has been expressed by Prof. Regan. He points to the expenditure of such councils, e.g. on anti-nuclear propaganda and subsidies to unilateralist groups. (Some 'nuclear free zone' councils have blacked firms involved in building or supplying nuclear sites.) He concludes that, 'even if this expenditure is within the law [using the Section 137/free 2p] it is a distortion of the status and role of local government in our political system. For local authorities to conduct a multi-million pound propaganda campaign on defence is as inappropriate as it would be for a local authority to open an embassy in Albania or purchase anti-aircraft missiles. Some local authorities are now being exploited to serve political ends far removed from their responsibilities' (*The Times*, 5 August 1985).

20 See B. McAndrew, 'Complications of Overtly Political Officers', *Local Government Chronicle*, 22 July 1984, and M. Clarke, 'What Has Happened to the Ground Rules?', *Local Government Chronicle*, 3 August 1984. The resignation or suspension of a number of chief officers in the 1980s may have been prompted, in whole or part, by party-political considerations, e.g. James Pailing, Director of Education, Newham LB (1985); Keith Bridge, Humberside MCC Chief Executive (1983); Alf Parrish, Chief Constable, Derbyshire CC (1985-6).

21 In a number of authorities, officers have been encouraged (e.g. by granting/withholding paid leave) to participate in activities of a party political nature. In a number of London Boroughs, an estimated 1 in 8 councillors (known as 'twin-track politicians') works as an officer in another authority; *Sunday Times*, 14 April 1985. See too p. 325 above.

22 Many of the old certainties, traditions and conventions are being challenged and overturned due to the erosion of mutual trust and toleration between members and officers. This is due to the mounting polarization of the parties, the greater assertiveness of the new, younger, more highly educated and less deferential members, and to the strains thrown up by diminished resources (and its incidental politicization of staff). Officers are often having to shed their traditional caution in implementing policies; and if they turn to COG for support or protection, they risk being perceived as conspirators.

The emergence of hung councils is causing similar or other problems – longer meetings, more tortuous consultation, etc. Local authorities are having to devise new procedures and ground rules with regard to drawing up agendas, officer's advice to opposition and minority party groups, the selection and role of chairs, etc. The Widdicombe Committee may well have an impact here, though there is a strong case for leaving local authorities to determine their own arrangements (after all very little of our central cabinet/parliamentary/party government is based on legislative provisions). See C. J. Davies, 'The Changing Roles of Officers and Members', *Local Government Studies*, January/February 1986; K. Walsh, *Ethics and the Local Government Officer*, LGTB, 1984; M. Laffin and K. Young, 'The Changing Roles and Responsibilities of Local Authority Chief Officers', *Public Administration*, Spring 1985; D. Kennedy, 'Officers can support members without being labelled', *Local Government Chronicle*, 14 February 1986. See Cheshire County Council's conventions in the *Widdicombe Report*, HMSO, 1986, Annexe H. See also *The Times*, 17 February 1990, p. 3.

23 See *The Times Educational Supplement*, 24 November 1989, p. 22, and *Local Government Chronicle*, 21 August 1992, p. 4.

24 See, for example, *The Times Education Supplement*, 16 June 1993.

25 See SOLACE report in *Municipal Journal*, 1 May 1992, p. 6.

26 See K. Newton in L. J. Sharpe (ed.), *The Local Fiscal Crisis in Western Europe*, Sage, 1981; also P. Jackson *et al.*, 'Urban Fiscal Decay in UK Cities', *Local Government Studies*, September 1982.

27 See note 10, Chapter 11, above.

28 See *Public Service Review*, January 1990, and *Public Finance and Accountancy*, 26 January 1990.

29 *Institute of Public Finance*, August 1993.

30 *Quangos Just Grow*, Centre for Policy Studies, 1985.

31 See D. Marsh and R. A. W. Rhodes, *Implementing Thatcherite Policies*, Open University Press, 1992.

32 See R. Bacon and W. Eltis, *Britain's Economic Problem: Too Few Producers*, Macmillan, 1978.

33 Under the Rating and Valuation (Amendment) Scotland Act 1984, and the Local Government and Housing Act 1989.

34 There had been some uncertainty about the Minister's legal power to withhold grant from overspending councils; this was unsuccessfully contested (January 1983), e.g. by Camden council. It might be added, too, that at one stage the Bill included powers allowing the Minister to penalize councils on conditions drawn up retrospectively, i.e. after the financial year had begun: this was dubbed 'super-holdback'.

35 The original Local Government Finance Bill 1981 would have allowed the Minister to require a local authority to hold a local referendum before it could impose a supplementary rate/precept (as some thirty councils had done that year, including the GLC for its 'Fares Fair' transport subsidies). The Bill was withdrawn in November 1981 after vehement opposition from the local authority associations and a number of MPs: they argued that (i) a referendum was difficult to validate if there was a low poll (it was only 26 per cent in Coventry's experimental rate referendum of August 1981) and if the wording was over-simplified; (ii) that if adopted, referendums should become applicable to central government extra-budgetary tax changes; and, above all, (iii) that referendums would emasculate local responsibility by undermining the value of the ordinary electoral process and reducing councillors to mere delegates and cyphers.

36 See R. Jackman, 'Does Central Government Need to Control the Total of Local Government Spending?', *Local Government Studies*, May 1982; also D. Walker in C. Jones and J. Stevenson (eds.), *Yearbook of Social Policy 1980–81*, Routledge, 1982.

37 Derogation was not taken up by the rate-capped councils in 1985–6, partly in protest at the whole new regime of rate control, and partly because it would involve the central government in detailed scrutiny and approval of individual service levels of the authorities. But a number of councils did negotiate a re-assessment or re-determination the following year.

38 T. Travers, in M. Parkinson (ed.), *Reshaping Local Government*, Policy Journals, 1987.

39 *The Times*, 7 November 1981.

40 This was confirmed and detailed in the report of the Comptroller and Auditor-General, *Operation of the Rate Support Grant System*, HMSO, 1985. And a report by LACSAB, *The Effects of Central Government Initiatives on Local Government* (1984) shows how central policies have themselves added some 16,000 council jobs over five years. In 1985 the Government gave some acknowledgement of the impact of its own policies on local expenditures, e.g. by increasing the police grant from 50 per cent to 51 per cent.

41 P. Smith, 'How Targets Went Wrong', *Public Finance and Accountancy*, December 1983; K. Young, *National Interests and Local Government*, Heinemann, 1983; P. Jackson in *Economic Affairs*, IEA, October 1988.

42 See K. Newton and T. J. Karran, *The Politics of Local Expenditure*, Macmillan, 1985, p. 8.

43 Thus while local government debt fell from 21.7 per cent (of the total public sector) to 18 per cent the Government's rose from 59.7 per cent to 65 per cent over the period 1980 to 1983. It has been suggested that the Government focuses attention on local expenditure and its cuts in order to draw attention away from its inability to control its own spending. The *Financial Times* has said, 'With one or two well publicized exceptions, the local authorities have a record of sound budgetary control which Whitehall should envy' (see Newton and Karran, op. cit., p. 17).

44 It puts things into perspective when we see that as a nation we spend more on alcohol than LEA education, on tobacco than personal social services and on hair and beauty care than refuse collection.

45 For 1984–5 the penalties involved a 2p rate poundage holdback (or abatement) for the first 1 per cent of overspend, 4p for the second 1 per cent, 8p for the third 1 per cent and 9p for each subsequent 1 per cent. In 1983–4, the figures were 1p, 2p, 3p, 5p. For 1985–6 they were 7p, 8p, 9p, etc.

46 G. Jones, J. Stewart and T. Travers, 'Rate Control: the Threat to Local Government', *Local Government Chronicle*, December 1983. A senior civil servant, Sir Antony Part (Permanent Secretary to the Department of Trade and Industry, retired), has commented in relation to the various grant formulae, 'They've got themselves so snarled up they hardly know what they're doing at the moment' ('Who Rules Britain?', BBC, 19 October 1982).

47 Referring to the uncertainties engendered by fluctuations of the block grant, in targets, in penalty systems and in the GRE assessments, the Report of the Audit Commission, *The Impact on Local Authorities' Economy, Efficiency and Effectiveness of the Block Grant Distribution System* (1984), says that 'The conflicting signals which the grant system contains and the variations in these signals from year to year cause authorities to protect themselves by building up substantial reserves.' This exaggerates apparent overspending, so that in fact 'real overall local government spending last year was probably in line with target'.

The Report also comments critically on (i) the reliability of the information on which GREAs are based, so that some councils receive substantially more or less than their circumstances might warrant; (ii) the divergence of targets from GREAs, so that local authorities lose grant though their spending does not exceed GREA; (iii) the targets which, being related to past expenditure, provide a perverse inducement to spend more (i.e. at least up to target) since spending below target in one year may be 'rewarded' by a lower target (but the same penalties) next year: consequently, (iv) the grant system provides few incentives for local authorities to increase efficiency; (v) the fact that changes in local rates are not a reliable guide to individual councils' changes in expenditure; (vi) the continued central involvement in local affairs which has not been reduced as intended by the new system; (vii) the number of people (over 800) in local government alone who are occupied in grappling with the complex grant system, and (viii) the intricacies of the grant arrangements that (inevitably?) distract too many of the recipients into 'playing the system'. This was reiterated in the report of the Auditor-General: see note 40 above. See also *Public Money*, September 1983.

48 *Capital Expenditure Controls*, HMSO, 1985.

49 R. Rhodes, *Beyond Westminster and Whitehall*, Unwin, 1988, p. 254.

50 The Local Government and Housing Act 1989.

51 D. Mason, 'Slimming for Survival', paper to IEA Conference, 27 April 1988, and P. Minford, in *Economic Affairs*, IEA, October 1988.

52 Indeed the main impact of public sector borrowing seems to be on the exchange rate rather than on interest rates, and the latter are largely influenced by external factors anyway, especially US interest rates.

53 G. Jones, 'How to Save Local Government', in *Town Hall Power or Whitehall Pawn?*, IEA, 1980, and J. Barlow, in *Local Government Studies*, May 1981. R. Jackman, in *Local Government Studies*, March 1982.

54 *Economist*, 6 August 1985.

55 *The Future of Local Government in Britain*, ICL, 1988.

56 D. Dawson in K. Young (ed.), *National Interests and Local Government*, Heinemann, 1983.

57 *Municipal Journal*, 29 July 1983. Such increased direct intervention is evident in the new (1986) joint boards and authorities, e.g. the Transport Minister has imposed a 10 per cent reduction in the expenditure of the new Passenger Transport Authorities 1986–7 (to provide 'a reasonable balance between the interests of public transport users and ratepayers').

58 Indeed, the Auditor-General declared that the grant system was so complex 'that many officers and members had abandoned the attempt to fully understand it' and accountability had diminished because of its ambiguities and confusions: see note 40 above.

59 J. Gibson, *Increasing the Efficiency of the SSAs*, INLOGOV, 1993; see too *Local Government Chronicle*, 8 April 1993, p. 15, and *Public Finance and Accountancy*, 14 May 1993, p. 9.

60 See SOLACE report in the *Observer*, 18 July 1982; T. Blackstone in *The Times Educational Supplement*, 24 September 1982; and a MORI poll (*Sunday Times*, 6 September 1981) which found that nearly half of young unemployed respondents believed that violence to bring about political change is justified. See also B. Stevenson, 'Cleveland's Crazy Cuts', *Local Government Chronicle*, 14 January 1983, and B. Simon, *Marxism Today*, September 1984 (compare with the survey in the *Economist*, 4 July 1982).

61 J. Stewart, *The Role of Local Government in the UK*, INLOGOV, 1995.

62 *Municipal Journal*, 29 July 1983.

63 *Accountability to the Public*, European Policy Forum, 1992. See also *The New Local Governance*, European Policy Forum, 1993.

64 The whole issue was investigated: see D. Beetham, *Auditing Democracy in Britain*, Charter 1988, 1993. See too *Taking Charge: the Rebirth of Local Democracy*, CLD, 1995.

65 Howard Davies, 'Local Government Under Siege', *Public Administration*, Spring 1988.

66 See *Independent*, 24 March 1994, p. 8; K. Morgan, *Quango Report*, University of Wales, 1994; Committee on Standards in Public Life (Nolan), Vol. 2, 1996. M. Flinders and M. Cole 'Opening or Closing Pandora's Box? New Labour and the Quango State', *Talking Politics*, Summer 1999.

67 *Local Government Chronicle*, 19 April 1996, pp. 14–16.

68 See note 64.

69 W. Waldegrave, *Public Service and the Future: Reforming Britain's Bureaucracies*, Conservative Political Centre, 1993.

70 *The Times*, 5 August 1993. See too *Public Finance and Accountancy*, 16 June 1993, pp. 6–7.

71 *Municipal Journal*, 31 January 1997, p. 3.

72 M. Kogan, in M. Parkinson (ed.), *Reshaping Local Government*, Policy Journals, 1987.

73 Dawn Oliver, 'Law, Convention and Abuse of Power', *The Political Quarterly*, January 1989.

74 Through grants to voluntary bodies (such as CABx, Relate, etc.), support to informal carers (such as respite, bathing attendance, laundry, etc.) and contracting out. An estimated 1 million people receive welfare services from the non-statutory sector.

75 Hepworth, op. cit. note 51. The possibilities have been illustrated enthusiastically by one housing manager. 'Just passive enabling will be an inadequate response; the Council must assume the role of strategic housing authority, set the parameters and direct the resources; make things happen in the way and in the timescale it needs. Most of all it must try to ensure that what gets built meets the needs of the locality . . . it is a case of exploiting the volatile and lively environment, forging partnerships and putting up workable ideas. It is a new form of brokerage . . .' D. Hawes, *Municipal Journal*, 10 June 1988.

76 'The Governing Principle', *Municipal Journal*, 10 June 1988.

77 N. Ridley, *The Local Right: Enabling not Providing*, CPS, 1989.

78 See, for example, S. Mohun, in A. Cochrane and J. Anderson, *Restructuring Britain: Politics in Transition*, Sage, 1989.

79 D. Jackson, 'Analysing the Nature of Local Government Today', *Public Finance and Accountancy*, 7 October 1988.

80 M. Clarke and J. Stewart, *The Enabling Council*, LGTB, 1988.

81 M. Clarke and J. Stewart, *Managing Tomorrow*, LGTB, 1988.

82 M. Clarke and J. Stewart, *The Enabling Council*, LGTB, 1988.

83 Some suggestions for the enabling (housing) role were given by the Minister, Michael Howard, in a speech to the IEA, 27 April 1988, such as the assessment of demand and supply, development control, land assembly and site provision, subsidies to the private rented sector, lending to housing associations, repair and improvement grants, allocation of tenancies, monitoring and regulating, and the coordination and provision of housing-related social services and amenities.

84 K. Spencer, *Alternatives to the Direct Delivery of Services by Local Government*, INLOGOV, 1986. It should be noted that indirect provision or administration of services was quite common in the nineteenth century; see, for example, J. Stanyer, p. 636 below.

85 *Losing the Empire, Finding a Role: The LEA of the Future*, Audit Commission, 1989.

86 Hepworth, 'What Future for Local Government', *Inquiry*, IEA, 1988.

87 M. Clarke and J. Stewart, *The Enabling Council*, LGTB, 1988; see too *Partners or Rivals?* [voluntary organizations], LGTB, 1988.

88 N. Rao, *Managing Change*, LGMB, 1993.

89 *Local Government Agenda*, ICSA, March 1993. See too *The Councillor and the Enabling Council*, LGTB, 1990.

90 See the Widdicombe Report, HMSO, 1986; *The Enabling Council*, LGTB, 1988; Maud Report, HMSO 1967; the Local Authorities (General Powers) Bill 1988, a Private Member's Bill introduced by Tony Benn in 1988.

91 P. Hoggett and R. Hambleton, *Decentralisation and Democracy*, SAUS, 1987.

92 R. Harris and A. Seldon, *Over-ruled on Welfare*, IEA, 1979; P. Taylor-Gooby, *Public Opinion, Ideology and State Welfare*, Routledge, 1985; see too *Journal of Social Policy*, October 1983.

93 J. Gyford, in M. Parkinson, *Reshaping Local Government*, Policy Journals, 1987.

94 Howard Davies, 'Local Government Under Siege', *Public Administration*, Spring 1988.

95 E.g. *Tell Us What It's Really Like*, Age Concern, Norfolk, 1989.

96 Marketing is about selling and publicity, and local authorities are having to do their share of these, for example to boost their falling college rolls. But marketing is also about satisfying customer needs, and this applies, as 'social marketing', whether services are free or are charged for. See K. Walsh, *Marketing in Local Government*, Longman, 1989, and *Has Marketing a Role in Local Government?*, LGTB, 1987.

97 *A Glimpse of the Future: Social and Economic Trends for Local Government in the 1990s*, LGMB, 1992.

98 A. Coulson, in *New Directions for INLOGOV*, INLOGOV, 1988.

99 See Professor R. Whitfield in the *Sunday Times*, 4 June 1989.

100 N. Hepworth, 'Changing Relations between Local Government Officers', *Public Finance and Accountancy*, 9 September 1988.

101 *The Challenge of Change in Local Government*, INLOGOV, 1988.

102 Ibid.

103 See, for example, *Municipal Journal*, 5–11 June 1992, p. 20.

104 *Against the Over-mighty State*, Federal Trust for Education, 1988.

105 The Audit Commission is more sceptical here; see its *More Equal Than Others*, in which it points to local authorities' budgetary crises and problems with handling falling school rolls as signs that local government may not be so able to make the necessary decisions to be credible as a centre of genuine discretion.

106 See *The Competitive Council*, 1988, where it advises the well-managed council to: (1) understand its customers; (2) respond to the electorate; (3) set and pursue consistent and achievable objectives; (4) assign clear management responsibilities; (5) train and motivate people; (6) communicate effectively; (7) monitor results; and (8) adapt quickly to change. These principles are also dealt with by M. Clarke and J. Stewart, *Managing Tomorrow*, LGTB, 1988, though they also emphasize the need to work through political processes and to 'rediscover local government'.

107 *Political Quarterly*, January 1989.

108 W. Kornhauser, *The Politics of Mass Society*, Routledge, 1960.

109 K. Newton and T. J. Karran, *The Politics of Local Expenditure*, Macmillan, 1985.

110 The *Guardian*, 3 December 1993; also S. Jenkins, *The Times*, 30 April 1999.

111 T. Travers in the *Guardian*, 3 December 1996.

112 'LGTB Conference', *Insight*, 14 March 1989.

113 It has been suggested that a Bill of Rights for local government may provide protection: see J. Stewart, 'Now is the time for our Bill of Rights', *Municipal Journal*, 5 June 1981; J. Raine (ed.), *In Defence of Local Government*, INLOGOV, 1981; P. Self, 'Rescuing Local Government', *Political Quarterly*,

July 1982; Federal Trust, op. cit., note 104; *Political Quarterly*, January 1989.

114 See R. Greenwood *et al.*, 'Making Government More Local', *New Society*, 25 February 1982. However, a Gallup poll in 1981 showed only 27 per cent were in favour of more decentralization from London to regional and local authorities.

115 See *British Social Attitudes*, Gower, 1985; Chris Game, 'Opinion Polls can be a Real Asset', *Local Governments Chronicle*, 13 September 1985; *Local Government Chronicle*, 20 September 1985. See also Commission on the Constitution Research Paper 7, *Attitudes Survey*, 1973.

116 *British Social Attitudes*, 1994, Gower, 1995

117 See note 115.

118 See MORI in *Local Government Chronicle*, 10 May 1996.

119 *Which?*, March 1989. This was confirmed by a MORI Poll in 1991.

120 K. Young in H. Davies (ed.), *New perspectives in Local governance*, JRF, 1997, p. 152.

15 NEW LABOUR: NEW DEAL FOR LOCAL GOVERNMENT?

1 *Municipal Journal*, 31 January 1997, p. 7.

2 The charter is reproduced in the report of the Commission on Local Democracy, *Taking Charge: The Rebirth of Local Democracy*, CLD, 1995.

3 *Municipal Journal*, 6 June 1997, p. 3; *Local Government Chronicle*, 18 July 1997, p. 1.

4 See M. Clarke and J. Stewart, *Community governance, community leadership and the new local government*, JRF, 1999.

5 See J. Stewart, *An experiment in freedom*, IPPR, 1991; also *Local Government Chronicle*, 15 May 1998, p. 8.

6 See R. Hambleton in *Local Government Chronicle*, 11 December 1998, pp. 16–17, though cf. G. Stoker in *Local Government Chronicle*, 1 May 1998, p. 8 and 27 November 1998, p. 8.

7 See *European Journal of Political Research*, 18, 1990, pp. 167–81; E. Lakeman, *How Democracies Vote*, Faber 1974; G. Powell in R. Rose, *Electoral Participation*, Sage, 1980.

8 W. Miller and M. Dickson, *Local Governance and Local Citizenship*, ESRC, 1996; New Local Government Network, *Municipal Journal*, 30 October 1998, p. 3.

9 See *Local Government Chronicle*, 29 January 1999, p. 3.

10 See *Local Government Chronicle*, 20 November 1998, p. 4.

11 See *Local Government Chronicle*, 18 December 1998, which believes this is the result of pressure by the CBI: see *Local Government Chronicle*, 20 November 1998.

12 L. Pratchett and M. Wingfield, *The Public Service Ethos in Local Government*, CLD, 1994; A. Alexander and K. Orr, *Managing the Fragmented Authority*, LGMB, 1993.

13 See Fenwick in *Local Governance*, 2, 1998, pp. 111–18.

14 *Local Government Chronicle*, 29 May 1998, p. 9.

15 Rita Hale, *Local Government Chronicle*, 6 August 1999, p. 11.

16 See P. Vincent-Jones, 'Compulsory Contracting in the transition from CCT to Best Value', *Public Administration*, No. 2, 1999 and P. Riddell, *The Times*, 27 September 1999, p. 18 cf., J. Arnold-Foster who regards BV as far more detailed and far-reaching, and also gives the Government greater powers of intervention. *Local Government Chronicle*, 6 August 1999, pp. 12–13.

17 *Municipal Journal*, 18 June 1999, p. 10.

18 *Local Government Chronicle*, 3 September 1999, p. 16.

19 See R. Jackman, *Local Government Studies*, May/June 1982; C. D. Foster *et al.*, *Local Government Finance in a Unitary State*, Unwin, 1980; D. M. King, *Fiscal Tiers*, Unwin, 1984; P. Watt and J. Fender, *Local Government Spending and the Macroeconomy*, LGMB, 1998.

20 A. Midwinter, 'The Fiscal Crisis in Scottish Local Government', *Local Governance*, 1, 1998.

21 Rita Hale, *Local Government Chronicle*, 6 August 1999, p. 11, though the head of the civil service, Sir Richard Wilson, acknowledges the contribution of local government to central policies and insists that the Government cherishes the experience, expertise and the ideas of local authorities; see *Local Government Chronicle*, 1 April 1999, p. 20; see too *Local Government Chronicle* special supplement, October 1999, p. 1.

FURTHER READING

Serious students cannot rely upon a single book for their knowledge of local government. Yet they face the problem that the literature on local government is constantly growing in volume and diversity: new areas and themes are being explored and older ones are being revisited and researched and perhaps re-interpreted. And with the advent of the CD Rom and the Internet, it is also expanding its format. All this is both inevitable and desirable, for our understanding of local government cannot be fixed once and for all, and, in particular, it should not be based simply on an understanding of the statutory and other legal provisions (important though these are).

However, as a bibliography, a long list of sources can be off-putting – and academics do get carried away (what enthusiast doesn't?). In what follows, therefore, I have aimed to provide a range of suitable reading from which students can make selections (bearing in mind that a number of the titles listed are alternatives). It is very difficult deciding what to leave out: even authors whose ideas are unacceptable can stimulate lines of thought and provide interesting insights and perspectives. Also, while some may appear dated, they are included because of the continuing relevance of their general analysis, their identification of abiding issues or their value in illustrating changing perspectives and policies.

The list is essentially a list of books, though some important articles are included. Other articles and books are mentioned in the chapter references. And I have also identified some useful websites.

Finally, those who wish to keep themselves up to date with developments in local government should regularly consult the journals mentioned in the last section of this list, as well as newspapers (especially the *Guardian*'s weekly 'Society' supplement) and radio programmes such as 'File on Four' and 'Analysis and TV programmes such as 'Panorama', 'Dimbleby', 'On the Record', 'West in Westminster'.

Local authorities issue local newsletters, annual reports and make available their council papers (in public libraries and at their committee and full council meetings, which are open to the public).

1 GENERAL REFERENCE

Annual Abstracts of Statistics, HMSO (annual).

Finance and General Statistics, CIPFA (annual).

M. J. Gafour, *Researchers' Guide to Sources of Official and Unofficial Local Government Information*, Europulse, 1995.

Local Authorities Research and Intelligence Association (LARIA).

Local Government Financial Statistics (published separately for England, Scotland and Wales), HMSO (annual).

Local Government Information Service, Hampshire County Library (Winchester).

Local Government Trends (annual statistical digest, CIPFA).

M. Minogue (ed.), *Documents on Contemporary British Government*, Vol. 2: *Local Government in Britain*, CUP, 1977.

Municipal Year Book (annual).

Public Authorities Directory, LGC/CSL, 1999.

Public Domain, CIPFA (annual).

Public Services Yearbook, Pitman.

UK National Accounts, HMSO (annual).

Who's Who in Local Government, LGC/CSL, 1996.

Useful Websites especially for White Papers, Parliamentary Bills, reforms etc.:

Parliament at www.parliament, uk

The Department of the Environment, Transport and the Regions (DETR) at www.detr.gov.uk/ *and* www.local.detr.gov.uk

The Office of the Secretary of State for Wales at www.wales.gov.uk

The Scottish Office at www.scotland.gov.uk

and www.scottish-devolution.org.uk

The Government Information Service (GIS) at www.open.gov.uk

See also www.local.gov.uk/

And www.brent.gov.uk/other/uklg/lginfo.htm

www.hmso.gov.uk

The Local Government Association at www.lga.gov.uk/

The Improvement and Development Agency (I&DeA, formerly the Local Government Management Board) at www.idea.gov.uk

Joseph Rowntree Foundation has summaries of its local government research publications at www.jrf.org.uk/

University of Plymouth (for politics course information) at www.politics. plymouth.ac.uk

Audit Commission at www.audit-commission.gov.uk

Individual local authorities have websites, as do related/relevant quangos.

Comprehensive Spending Review White Paper at www.hm-treasury.gov.uk/ pub/htm/csr.index.html

Best Value at www.local-regions.detr.gov.uk

Charter Mark, at www.servicefirst.gov.uk

Excellence in Schools as well as Education Action Zones at www.dfee.gov.uk

Better Government for Older People Programme at www.cabinet-office.gov.uk/servicefirst/index/opmenu.htm

New Deal for Disabled People at www.disability.gov.uk

New Commitment to Regeneration as well as Community Planning at www.lga.gov.uk

Lewisham/Camden One-Stop Shop at www.dss.gov.uk/cgis/ndlp/index.htm

No. 10 Downing Street at www.number-10.gov.uk

Cabinet Office at www.cabinet-office.gov.uk

Public Appointments Unit at www. open gov.uk/pau/pauhome.htm

Public Bodies at www.official-documents.co.uk/documents/caboff/pb98.htm

International Union of Local Authorities at www.cvapp.udel.edu/iula

2 GENERAL AND/OR THEORETICAL

Modern Local Government: In Touch with the People, Cmd 4014, Stationery Office, 1998. (This is the White Paper on local government in England which analyses and outlines reforms to management and internal organization, elections, accountability, ethical standards, functions, finance and efficiency. It derives from the 1998 consultation papers, especially *Modernising Local Government – Local Democracy and community*; others are identified under the relevant chapter headings below.)

Local Leadership, Local Choice, Cmd 4298, DETR, 1999 (a government paper which reiterates and refines some of the key elements of the White Paper *In Touch with the People*. It urges councils to start introducing reforms – to management, standards, participation, etc. – and encourages local people to get involved in the process).

Local Voices: Modernising Local Government in Wales, Cmd 4028, Stationery Office, 1998. (This is the White Paper on local government in Wales; similar to that for England, above.)

Moving Forward: Local Government and the Scottish Parliament, Scottish Office, 1999. (This is the final report of the McIntosh Commission set up to consider (i) relations between local government and the new Scottish Parliament and Executive and (ii) methods of improving local democracy and accountability. It deals with many aspects covered/contained in the White Papers above.)

The Conduct of Local Authority Business, HMSO, 1986 (the Report of the Widdicombe Committee). (Considers the purpose of local government, the impact of party politics, member–officer relationships and conduct, decision-making, elections, discretionary spending, audit and public challenge.)

'Aspects of Local Democracy', *The Conduct of Local Authority Business* (Widdicombe), Research Vol. 4, HMSO, 1986. (Includes chapters on discretionary spending, rate-setting in Liverpool, history of local party politics, decentralization and local government abroad.)

A. Alexander, *Local Government in Britain since Reorganization*, Allen & Unwin, 1982.

J. Bulpitt, *Territory and Power in the United Kingdom*, Manchester UP, 1983.

C. Gray, *Government Beyond the Centre*, Macmillan, 1994.

J. Stanyer, *Understanding Local Government*, Fontana, 1976.

W. Hampton, *Local Government and Urban Politics*, Longman, 1992.

G. Stoker, *The Politics of Local Government*, Macmillan, 1991.

J. A. Chandler, *Local Government Today*, Manchester UP, 1997.

H. Elcock and M. Wheaton, *Local Government: Politicians, Professionals and the Public in Local Authorities*, Methuen, 1996.

C. Mellors and N. Copperthwaite, *Local Government in the Community*, ICSA, 1987.

D. Wilson and C. Game, *Local Government in the United Kingdom*, Macmillan, 1997.

Local Government: A Councillor's Guide 1999/2000, LGMB, 1999.

Councillor's Handbook, Municipal Journal, 1996.

Local Government, COI Aspects of Britain Series, 1997.

Introducing Local Government (interactive computer-based programme), LGMB, 1992.

Welcome to Local Government, LGMB, 1992.

S. Leach and M. Stewart, *Local Government: Its Role and Function*, Joseph Rowntree, 1992.

S. McNaughton, *Local and Regional Government in Britain*, Hodder, 1998.

G. Stoker, *The Role and Purpose of Local Government*, CLD/Municipal Journal, 1994.

J. Stewart, *The Nature of British Local Government*, Macmillan, 1999.

J. Stewart, *The Role of Local Government in the UK*, Univ. of Birmingham, 1995.

L. Pratchett and D. Wilson, *Local Democracy and Local Government*, Macmillan, 1996.

J. Stewart and G. Stoker (eds.), *Local Government in the 1990s*, Macmillan, 1995.

D. King and J. Pierre (eds.), *Challenges to Local Government*, Sage, 1990.

Changes in the role and function of local government, Joseph Rowntree, 1992.

G. Stoker (ed.), *The New Politics of British Local Governance*, Macmillan, 2000.

J. Stewart and M. Clarke, *Developments in Local Government*, Univ. of Birmingham, 1996.

H. Atkinson and S. Wilks-Heeg, *British Local Government since 1979: the End of an Era*, Sheffield Hallam Univ., 1997.

D. Blunkett and K. Jackson, *Democracy in Crisis: The Town Halls Respond*, Hogarth, 1987.

S. Leach in S. Leach *et al.*, *Enabling or Disabling Local Government*, Open UP, 1996.

N. Rao, *The Making and Unmaking of Local Self-Government*, Dartmouth, 1994.

L. Byrne, *Local Government Transformed*, Baseline, 1997.

A. Cochrane and J. Anderson, *Restructuring Britain: Politics in Transition*, Sage, 1989.

'Symposium on Local Government', *Contemporary Record*, Summer 1989.

'What is happening to Local Government?', *Local Government Studies*, November 1989.

H. Davis *et al.*, *New perspectives on local governance*, Joseph Rowntree, 1998.

D. Osborne and T. Gaebler, *Reinventing government*, Plume/Penguin, 1993.

E. Butler and M. Pirie (eds.), *Economy and Local Government*, Adam Smith Institute, 1981.

Wiser Counsels, Adam Smith Institute, 1989.

D. Hill, *Democratic Theory and Local Government*, Allen & Unwin, 1974.

W. J. M. Mackenzie, *Theories of Local Government*, LSE, 1961.

L. J. Sharpe, 'Theories and Values of Local Government', *Political Studies*, June 1970.

D. Judge *et al.*, *Theories of Urban Politics*, Sage, 1995.

W. Magnusson, 'Bourgeois Theories of Local Government', *Political Studies*, Vol. XXXIV, no. 1, 1986.

G. Boyne, *Public Choice Theory and Local Government*, Macmillan, 1998.

J. Stewart, *Understanding the Management of Local Government*, Longman, 1995.

J. Stewart, *Local Government: the Conditions for Local Choice*, Allen & Unwin, 1983.

G. Jones and J. Stewart, *The Case for Local Government*, Allen & Unwin, 1985.

J. Raine *et al.*, *In Defence of Local Government*, INLOGOV, 1981.

D. King and G. Stoker, *Rethinking Local Democracy*, Macmillan, 1996.

A. Phillips, *Local Democracy: the Terms of the Debate*, CLD Municipal Journal, 1994.

J. Percy-Smith, *Submissions to the Commission on Aspects of Local Democracy*, CLD/ Municipal Journal, 1994.

S. Duncan and M. Goodwin, *The Local State and Uneven Development*, Polity, 1988.

M. Boddy and C. Fudge, *The Local State: Theory and Practice*, SAUS, 1981.

P. Dunleavy, *Urban Political Analysis*, Macmillan, 1980.

K. Young, *Essays in Urban Politics*, Macmillan, 1975.

C. Cockburn, *The Local State*, Pluto, 1977.

P. Saunders, *Urban Politics*, Penguin, 1979.

J. Dearlove, *The reorganisation of local government*, CUP, 1979.

M. Goldsmith, *Urban political theory*, Gower, 1986.

Coopers and Lybrand Deloitte, *The Constitutional Role of Local Government*, ACC, 1991.

3 HISTORY

K. B. Smellie, *A History of Local Government*, Allen & Unwin, 1968.

J. Redlich and F. W. Hirst, *The History of Local Government in England*, ed. B. Keith-Lucas, Macmillan, 1970.

B. Keith-Lucas and P. G. Richards, *A History of Local Government in the Twentieth Century*, Allen & Unwin, 1978.

W. Thornhill (ed.), *The Growth and Reform of English Local Government*, Weidenfeld & Nicolson, 1971.

N. Rao and K. Young, *Local Government since 1945*, Dartmouth, 1997.

H. V. Wiseman, *Local Government in England 1958–69*, Routledge, 1970 (structure, management, finance and a chapter on 1945–58).

V. D. Lipman, *Local Government Areas 1834–1945*, Blackwell, 1949.

C. J. Pearce, *The Machinery of Change in Local Government*, Unwin, 1982.

D. Fraser, *Municipal Reform and the Industrial City*, St Martin, 1982.

M. Loughlin (ed.), *Half a Century of Municipal Decline*, Allen & Unwin, 1985.

F. Dolman, *Municipalities at Work, The Municipal Policy of Six Great Towns and its Influence on their Social Welfare*, Godard, 1898, reprinted 1985.

4 THE LEGAL CONTEXT

A. Arden, *Local Government Constitutional and Administrative Law*, Sweet & Maxwell, 1999.

S. Bailey, *Cross on Principles of Local Government Law*, Sweet & Maxwell, 1997.

H. L. A. Hart, *Administrative Law*, OUP, 1994.

J. McEldowney, *Public Law*, Sweet & Maxwell, 1998.

J. Sharland, *A practical approach to Local Government Law*, Blackstone, 1997.

R. Clayton, *Judicial Review of Local Government*, Wiley, 1997.

M. Supperstone and J. Goudie (eds.), *Judicial Review*, Butterworths, 1992.

'Judicial Review', a special edition of *Public Administration*, Summer 1986.

S. A. de Smith, *Judicial Review of Administrative Action*, Stevens, 1973.

O. Lomas *et al.*, *Legality and Local Politics*, Dartmouth, 1987.

L. Bridges *et al.*, *Local Politics and Legality*, Gower, 1987.

M. Loughlin, *Local Government and the Modern State*, Sweet & Maxwell, 1986.

K. Puttick, *Challenging Delegated Legislation*, Waterlow, 1988.

S. A. de Smith, *Constitutional and Administrative Law*, Penguin Books, 1979.

R. Morris, *Local Government Ground Rules*, Longman, 1994.

M. Loughlin, *Administrative Accountability in Local Government*, Joseph Rowntree, 1992.

C. Crawford and C. Grace, *Conducive or incidental to: Local Authority Discretionary Powers in the Modern Era*, INLOGOV, 1993.

L. E. Rockley, *Public and Local Authority Acts*, Heinemann, 1978.

J. Garner, *'Ultra vires* principle', *Local Government Studies*, 1973.

Ultra Vires *in the Public Sector: Final Report of the Legal Risk Review Committee*, Bank of England, 1992.

J. McFadden, *A Power of General Competence: The Time Has Come*, Scottish LG Information Unit, 1997.

H. Kitchin, *General Competence for Local Authorities in Britain in the Context of European Experiments*, CLD/Municipal Journal, 1995.

R. Jeffries, *Tackling the Town Hall*, Routledge & Kegan Paul, 1982.

M. Loughlin, *Local Government, the Law, and the Constitution*, Local Government Society Trust, 1983.

V. Bogdanor, *Local Government and the Constitution*, SOLACE, 1994.

M. Loughlin, *The Constitutional Status of Local Government*, CLD/Municipal Journal, 1994.

The Constitutional Status of Local Government in other Countries, Scottish Office, 1998.

5 STRUCTURE

Report of the Royal Commission on Local Government in England 1966–1969 (the Redcliffe-Maud Report), 3 vols., Cmd 4040, HMSO, 1969.

Report of the Royal Commission on Local Government in Scotland 1966–1969 (the Wheatley Report), 2 vols., Cmd 4150, HMSO, 1969.

Local Government in England: Government Proposals for Re-organization, Cmd 4584, HMSO, 1971.

The Reform of Local Government in Scotland, Cmd 4583, HMSO, 1971.

C. Arnold-Baker, *The Local Government Act 1972*, Butterworth, 1973.

P. G. Richards, *The Local Government Act 1972: Problems of Implementation*, Allen & Unwin, 1975.

K. Newton, 'Is Small Really So Beautiful? Is Big Really So Ugly?', *Political Studies*, June 1982.

B. Wood, *The Process of Local Government Reform 1966–74*, Allen & Unwin, 1976.

J. A. Brand, *Local Government Reform in England 1888–1974*, Croom Helm 1974.

J. Dearlove, *The Reorganisation of British Local Government*, CUP, 1979.

G. Jones, 'The Local Government Act 1972 and the Redcliffe-Maud Commission', *Political Quarterly*, April 1973.

S. L. Bristow, 'Criteria for Local Government Reorganisation and Local Authority Autonomy', *Politics and Problems*, December 1972.

R. A. W. Rhodes, 'Local Government Reorganization: Three Questions', *Social and Economic Administration*, no. 8, 1974.

J. M. De Grove, *The Reorganization of Local Government in England 1972–77: An assessment*, Transaction, 1978.

S. Bristow *et al.*, *Redundant Counties?*, Hesketh, 1983.

N. Flynn *et al.*, *Abolition or Reform?*, Allen & Unwin, 1985.

The Structure of Local Government in England, DoE, 1991.

S. Leach and C. Game, 'English Metropolitan Government since Abolition: An Evaluation of the Abolition of the English Metropolitan County Councils', *Public Administration*, Summer 1991.

N. Flynn and S. Leach, *Joint Boards and Joint Committee: an Evaluation*, INLO-GOV, 1984.

S. Leach *et al.*, *After Abolition*, INLOGOV, 1992.

S. Leach *et al.*, *The Heseltine Review of Local Government*, INLOGOV, 1992.

The Structure of Local Government: Shaping the Future – The New Councils, Cmd 2267, HMSO, 1993.

Local Government Studies, special issue on reorganization, Autumn 1997.

S. Leach, *Local Government Reorganisation: The Review and its Aftermath*, Cass, 1990.

R. Leach, 'Local Government Reorganisation', *Political Quarterly*, January 1998.

G. Boyne, 'Local Government Structure and Performance: Lessons from America?', *Public Administration*, Autumn 1992.

G. Boyne, *Local Government Reform: A Review of the Process in Scotland and Wales*, LGC Communications, 1995.

M. Stewart, *The Work of the Local Government Commission for England*, Joseph Rowntree, 1997.

M. McVicar, *The process of local government reform (Wales and Scotland)*, Joseph Rowntree, 1995.

Decentralisation in the Counties, LSBM/LGA, 1994.

A. Harding *et al.*, *Regional government in Britain: an economic solution?*, Joseph Rowntree, 1996.

B. Hogwood, *Regional boundaries, coordination and Government,* Joseph Rowntree, 1996.

K. Donnelly and R. Hazell, *Regional government in England,* Joseph Rowntree, 1996.

Regionalism, LGMB, 1996.

Regionalism: The Local Government Dimension, AMA, 1995.

Regionalisation and its Effects on Local Self-government, Council of Europe, 1998.

Regional Government in England, Constitution Unit, 1996 (also JRF Findings no. 50).

B. Hogwood and M. Keating (eds.), *Regional Government in England,* Clarendon Press, 1982.

The new regional agenda, LGUI, 1999.

B. Hogwood and B. Keating (eds.), *Regional Government in England,* Clarendon Press, 1982.

R. Ball, *Local Authorities and Regional Policy in the UK,* Paul Chapman, 1995.

Devolution and Local Government, LGMB/LGA, 1998.

6 FUNCTIONS AND SERVICES

The Functions of Local Authorities in England, HMSO, 1992.

J. Percy Smith and I. Sanderson, *Understanding Local Needs,* Institute for Public Policy Research, 1992.

The Impact of Population Size on Local Authority Costs and Effectiveness, Joseph Rowntree, 1992.

Local Government Community Leadership, LGMB, 1992.

S. Savage, *Public Policy in Britain,* Macmillan, 1997.

S. Savage and R. Atkinson (eds.), *Public Policy Under Blair,* Macmillan, 1999.

A. Byrne and C. Padfield, *Social Services Made Simple,* Heinemann, 4th ed., 1992.

P. Lloyd, *Services Administration by Local Authorities,* ICSA, 1985.

G. Stoker (ed.), *The New Management of British Local Government,* Macmillan, 1999.

O. Hartley, 'The Functions of Local Government', *Local Government Studies,* February 1973.

R. Hambleton, *Beyond Excellence: Quality Local Government in the 1990s,* SAUS, 1990 (the governmental/political function of councils).

D. Hill, *Urban Policy and Politics in Britain,* Macmillan, 1999.

S. Horton and D. Farnham (eds.), *Public Services Management in Britain,* Macmillan, 1999.

N. Ellison and C. Pierson (eds.), *Developments in British Social Policy,* Macmillan, 1999.

P. Gooby-Taylor and R. Lawson, *Markets and Managers: New Issues in the Delivery of Welfare*, Open UP, 1993.

From Providing to Enabling, Local Authorities and Community Care Planning, JRF, 1991.

White Paper: *Caring for People (Community Care in the Next Decade and Beyond)*, DHSS, 1989.

White Paper: *Modernising Social Services*, HMSO, 1998.

Partnership in Practice: New Opportunities for Joint Working between Health and Social Services, DoH, 1998.

Health Promotion and Local Government, HEA, 1996.

R. Drake, *Understanding Disability Policies*, Macmillan, 1999.

Essential Local Government, LGC, 1996.

R. Means and R. Smith, *Community Care*, Macmillan, 1998.

Coopers and Lybrand Deloitte, *Caring for the Community*, ACC, 1992.

Report of the Committee on Local Authority and Allied Personal Social Services (Seebohm Report), Cmd 3703, HMSO, 1968.

Working Together under the Children Act 1989, DHSS, 1991.

Local Management of Schools, Coopers and Lybrand, 1988.

E. Lister, *LEAs – Old and New*, CPS, 1991.

S. Maclure, *Education Reformed: A Guide to the Education Reform Act*, Hodder, 1988.

E. Morris, *Central and Local Control of Education after the Education Reform Act 1988*, Longman, 1990.

Education Reform Act, 1988.

Education Framework and Standards Act 1998.

R. Bell and N. Grant, *Patterns of Education in the British Isles*, Allen & Unwin, 1978.

M. Kogan, *Educational Policy Making*, Allen & Unwin, 1975.

M. Kogan, *The Politics of Educational Change*, Fontana, 1978.

N. Rao, *Educational Change and Local Government: The Impact of the Education Reform Act*, Joseph Rowntree, 1990.

S. Ransom, *The Role of Local Government in Education: Assuring Quality and Accountability*, Longman, 1992.

M. Kogan and J. Cordingley, *Caring for Education: The Functioning of Local Government*, Jessica Kingsley, 1983.

D. Regan, *Local Government and Education*, Allen & Unwin, 1977.

J. Pratt *et al.*, *Your Local Education*, Penguin Books, 1973.

J. Driscoll, 'Public housing after the Local Government and Housing Act 1989', *Modern Law Review*, 54.

DoE, *Homelessness: Code of Guidance for Local Authorities*, HMSO, 1991.

K. Gibb *et al.*, *Housing Finance in the UK*, Macmillan, 1999.

J. Demaine (ed.), *Education Policy and Contemporary Politics*, Macmillan, 1999.

P. Malpass and R. Means, *Implementing Housing Policy*, Open UP, 1993.

P. Malpass and A. Murie, *Housing Policy and Practice*, Macmillan, 1999.

N. Rao, *The Changing Role of Local Housing Authorities*, Joseph Rowntree, 1990.

Coopers and Lybrand Deloitte, *Housing*, ACC, 1992.

D. Donnison and C. Ungerson, *Housing Policy*, Penguin Books, 1982.

J. B. Cullingworth, *Essays on Housing Policy*, Allen & Unwin, 1979.

Coopers and Lybrand Deloitte, *Protecting the Community*, ACC, 1992.

T. A. Critchley, *A History of the Police in England and Wales*, Constable, 1978.

S. Elkin, *Politics and Land Use Planning* CUP, 1974.

J. Gyford, *Town Planning and the Practice of Politics*, University College London, 1978.

J. B. Cullingworth, *Town and Country Planning in Britain*, Allen & Unwin, 1976.

Y. Rydin, *Urban and Environmental Planning in the UK*, Macmillan, 1998.

M. Burton and D. Nicholson, *Local Planning in Practice*, Hutchinson, 1987.

Managing the Local Environment – Local Authorities in Action, LGMB, 1990.

Environmental Practice in Local Government, LGMB, 1990.

The Environmental Role of Local Government, LGMB, 1990.

G. Ashworth, *The Role of Local Government in Environmental Protection*, Longman, 1992.

P. Hall, *Urban and Regional Planning*, Routledge, 1992.

Coopers and Lybrand Deloitte, *Leisure and Recreation*, ACC, 1992.

Coopers and Lybrand Deloitte, *Planning and Transport*, ACC, 1992.

S. Glaiser *et al.*, *Transport Policy in Britain*, Macmillan, 1998.

Local Government on the Move: A New Agenda for local Transport, LGMB/LGA, 1995.

R. Bennett and G. Krebs, *Local Economic Development: Public–Private Partnership Initiatives in Britain and Germany*, Bellhaven, 1991.

M. Campbell (ed.), *Local Economic Policy*, Cassell, 1990.

J. Benington and M. Geddes, *Restructuring the Local Economy*, Longman, 1992.

M. Campbell *et al.*, *Local responses to long-term unemployment*, York, 1998.

I. Sanderson *et al.*, *Back to Work: Local action on unemployment*, York, 1999.

J. A. Chandler & P. Lawless, *Local Authorities and the Creation of Employment*, Gower, 1985.

A. Coulson, *Managing Local Economic Development*, LGMB, 1990.

M. Kane and P. Saw, *Economic Development: what works at the local level*, LGC Communications, 1997.

G. Bramley *et al.*, *Local Economic Initiatives*, SAUS, 1978.

Implementing Anti Poverty Strategies, AMA, 1995.

T. Clark *et al.*, *Does Council Tax Benefit work?*, Joseph Rowntree, 1999.

G. Smith, *Area-based Initiatives: The rationale and option for area targeting*, Centre for Analysis of Social Exclusion, 1999.

D. Robinson *et al.*, *Social Enterprise Zones*, York, 1998.

Coopers and Lybrand Deloitte, *Economic Partnerships*, ACC, 1992.

M. Hughes *et al.*, *Local government regulation of business*, Univ. of Birmingham, 1999.

K. Ennals and J. O'Brien, *The Enabling Role of Local Authorities*, Public Finance Foundation, 1990.

Local Authorities' Activity under Section 137, DETR, 1998.

Local Councils' Use of Section 137, DETR, 1998.

7 ELECTIONS AND COUNCILLORS

C. Rallings and M. Thrasher, *Local Elections in Britain*, Routledge, 1997.

C. Rallings *et al.*, *Enhancing Local Electoral Turnout*, Rowntree, 1996.

A. Adonis, *Voting in proportion*, Fabian Society, 1998.

P. Dunleavy and H. Margetts, *Electoral reform in local government: alternative systems and key issues*, Joseph Rowntree, 1999.

Encouraging People to Vote: A MORI survey of people's attitudes to local elections, LGMB, 1998.

A. Adonis and S. Twigg, *The Cross We Bear – electoral reform for local government*, Fabian Society, 1997.

W. Miller, *Irrelevant Elections?*, OUP, 1988.

M. and S. Pinto-Duschinsky, *Voter Registration: Problems and Solutions*, Constitutional Reform Centre, 1987.

R. Gregory, 'Local Elections and the Rule of Anticipated Reactions', *Political Studies*, March 1969.

P. Fletcher, 'An Explanation of Variations in Turnout in Local Elections', *Political Studies*, March 1969.

L. J. Sharpe, *Voting in Cities*, Macmillan, 1967.

'The Local Government Elector', *The Conduct of Local Authority Business* (Widdicombe), Research Vol. 3, HMSO, 1986.

C. Martlew, *Local Democracy in Practice*, Avebury, 1988.

J. Stewart and C. Game, *Local Democracy – Representation and Election*, LGMB, 1991.

C. Rallings and M. Thrasher, 'The Impact of Local Government Electoral Systems', *Local Government Studies*. Summer 1992.

C. Rallings and M. Thrasher, *Electoral Reform for Local Government*, Electoral Reform Society, 1991.

The influence of electoral procedures on voting turnout, DETR, 1999.

C. Rallings *et al.*, *Community Identity and Participation in Local Democracy*, CLD/Municipal Journal, 1994.

C. Rallings and M. Thrasher, *Explaining Election Turnout*, HMSO, 1994.

University of Plymouth Local Government Elections unit – produces annual statistical analyses in *The Local Elections Handbook*. See also *Local Elections in Britain: A Statistical Digest (1973–1992)*, LGC, 1995.

Report of the Committee on Management of Local Government (the Maud Report), Vols. 2, 3 and 5, HMSO, 1967.

Why Bother?, LGMB, 1991.

People and Places (the Boundary Commission), HMSO, 1989.

V. Bodganor, *Electoral Systems in Local Government*, INLOGOV, 1986.

C. Game, 'How local are local elections?', *Social Studies Review*, 6, 5, 1991.

Modernising Local Government: local democracy and community, DETR, 1998.

H. Bochel and D. Denver, *Scottish Local Government Election: Results and Statistics*, Election Studies, 1995.

J. Prophet, *The Councillor*, Shaw, 1994.

A. Young, *Councillor's Handbook*, Harrap, 1995.

Association of Councillors, *Support Services for Councillors*, Knight, 1988.

Councillor's Handbook, Municipal Publications, 1996.

First National Census of Councillors in England and Wales, LGMB, 1999.

'The Local Government Councillor', *The Conduct of Local Authority Business* (Widdicombe), Research Vol. 2, HMSO, 1986.

A. Brown *et al.*, *The 'representativeness' of councillors*, Joseph Rowntree, 1999.

Support Services for Elected Members, LGMB, 1997.

M. Morag, *Support Services for Scottish Elected Members*, Scottish LGIU, 1997.

Supporting councillors, LGIU, 1999.

N. Rao, *Managing Change: Councillors and the New Local Government*, Joseph Rowntree, 1993.

R. Brown, *An Independent Councillor*, Pentland Press, 1994.

Representing the People: The Role of Councillors, Audit Commission, 1997.

A. Bloch, *The turnover of councillors*, Joseph Rowntree, 1992.

R. Kerley, *Councillors' turnover in Scotland*, Joseph Rowntree, 1992.

K. Young and N. Rao, *The Local Government Councillor in 1993*, Rowntree, 1994.

Exit survey of local authority councillors in England, IDEA, 1999.

P. Vestri, *The Changing Role of Councillors*, Scottish LGIU, 1997.

The Councillor's Representative Role, LGMB, 1994.

We Can't Go on Meeting Like This: the changing role of local government members, Audit Commission, 1990.

The Impact of Releasing People for Council Duties, DETR, 1998.

J. Barron, *Councillors in Crisis – The Public and Private Worlds of Local Councillors*, Macmillan, 1991.

Political Leadership in Local Government, LGMB, 1990.

The Remuneration of Councillors, Vol. 2, HMSO, 1977.

G. Jones, 'The Functions and Organisation of Councillors', *Public Administration*, Winter 1973.

H. Heclo, 'The Councillor's Job', *Public Administration*, Summer 1969.

D. Denver, *British Elections and Parties Review*, Cass, 1999.

P. Corrigan, *New roles for council members*, JRF, 1999.

T. Harrison, *Danger Zones: A Guide for Councillors and Officers*, LGC Communications, 1999.

S. Leach *et al.*, *All you need is Trust? The changing relationship between members and officers*, LGMB, 1998.

Consultation Paper: *Modernising local government – A new ethical framework*, DETR, 1998.

Third report of the Committee on Standards in Public Life: Standards of Conduct in Local Government (Nolan Report), Cmd 3702, Stationery Office, 1997.

8 PARTIES AND POLITICS

G. Stoker (ed.), *The New Politics of British Local Governance*, Macmillan, 2000.

C. Game and S. Leach, *The Role of Political Parties in Local Government*, CLD/ Municipal Journal, 1995.

Modernising Labour groups and local governance, Labour Party, 1999.

'The Political Organisation of Local Authorities', *The Conduct of Local Authority Business* (Widdicombe), Research Vol. 1, HMSO, 1986.

'Aspects of Local Democracy', *The Conduct of Local Authority Business* (Widdicombe), Research Vol. 4, HMSO, 1986.

K. Young, *The Conduct of Local Authority Business since Widdicombe*, Rowntree Memorial Trust, 1989.

It's our party, LGMB, 1998.

J. Gyford *et al.*, *The Changing Politics of Local Government*, Unwin Hyman, 1989.

J. Gyford and M. James, *National Parties and Local Politics*, Allen & Unwin, 1983.

J. Gyford, *Local Politics in Britain*, Croom Helm, 1984.

J. G. Bulpitt, *Party Politics in English Local Government*, Longman, 1967.

Report of the Committee on Management of Local Government (the Maud Report), Vol. 5, HMSO, 1967.

A. H. Birch, *Small Town Politics*, OUP, 1959.

P. Saunders, *Urban Politics: A Sociological Interpretation*, Hutchinson, 1979.

W. Grant, *Independent Local Politics in England and Wales*, Saxon House, 1978.

A. Richards and A. Kuper, *Councils in Action*, CUP, 1971.

B. Wood, *The Political Organisation of Local Authorities*, RIPA, 1971.

S. Lansley *et al.*, *Councils in Conflict: The Rise and Fall of the Municipal Left*, Macmillan, 1989.

M. Boddy and C. Fudge, *Local Socialism*, Macmillan, 1984.

J. Gyford, *The New Urban Left*, Town Planning Discussion Paper no. 38, University College, 1983.

Local Government Handbook, Labour Party, 1977.

Conservative Political Centre, *Party Politics in Local Government*, 1962.

G. Jones, 'Varieties of Local Politics', *Local Government Studies*, April 1975.

G. Green, 'Politics, Local Government and the Community', *Local Government Studies*, June 1974.

W. Grant, 'Non-Partisanship in British Local Politics', *Policy and Politics*, 1973.

J. Alt, 'Some Social and Political Correlates of County Borough Expenditure', *British Journal of Political Science*, 1971.

K. Newton and J. Sharpe, 'Local Outputs Research', *Policy and Politics*, 5, 1977.

J. Sharpe and K. Newton, *Does Politics Matter? The Determinants of Public Policy*, OUP, 1984.

K. Ascher, *The Politics of Privatization*, Macmillan, 1987.

M. Cowan, *Politics and Management in Local Government*, RIPA, 1983.

J. Barry, *The Women's Movement and Local Politics*, Avebury, 1991.

J. Edwards, *Local Government Women's Committees: A Feminist Political Practice*, Avebury, 1995.

Women and Local Government: A Directory of Local Authority Initiatives, AMA, 1993.

S. Halford and S. Duncan, *Implementing Feminist Policies in British Local Government*, Univ. of Sussex, 1991.

S. K. Mitra *et al.*, *Local Government and Urban Poverty*, Sangam, 1991.

S. Saggar, *Race and public policy: a study of local policies*, Avebury, 1991.

G. Ben-Tovin *et al.*, *The Local Politics of Race*, Macmillan, 1986.

W. Ball and J. Solomos, *Race and Local Politics*, Macmillan, 1990.

Race, equality and local governance, ESRC, 1996.

J. Richardson and G. Jordan, *Governing Under Pressure*, Martin Robertson, 1979.

G. Stoker and D. Wilson, 'The lost world of British local pressure groups', *Public Policy and Administration*, 6:2, 1991.

J. Dearlove, *The Politics of Policy in Local Government*, CUP, 1973.

Parliamentary Affairs, July 1998 issue devoted to pressure groups plus case studies.

C. Mellors, *Managing Without a Majority*, LGMB, 1996.

M. Temple, *Coalitions and Cooperation in Local Government*, Electoral Reform Society, 1996.

S. Leach and L. Pratchett, *The management of Balanced Authorities*, LGMB, 1996.

N. Carter, *Is There Life After Hanging?* (a study of three counties), Univ. of Bath, 1986.

9 MANAGEMENT, ORGANIZATION AND PROCEDURES

J. Stewart, *Understanding the Management of local Government*, Pitman, 1995.

White Paper: *Modern Local Government: In Touch with the People*, chapter 3, Cmd 4014, Stationery Office, 1998.

Community Leadership and Representation: Unlocking the Potential, DoE, HMSO, 1993.

The Internal Management of Local Authorities in England, DoE, HMSO, 1991.

New forms of Political Executive in Local Government, LGMB/LGA, 1998.

We Can't Go on Meeting Like This, Audit Commission, 1990.

Representing the People, Audit Commission, 1997.

P. Whitford-Jackson, *New Management Structures in Local Government*, LGC Communications, 1998.

Report of the Committee on Management of Local Government (the Maud Report), Vols. 1 and 5, HMSO, 1967.

The New Local Authorities: Management and Structure (the Bains Report), HMSO, 1972.

The New Scottish Local Authorities: Organisation and Management Structures (the Paterson Report), HMSO, 1973.

R. Greenwood *et al.*, *Patterns of Management in Local Government*, Martin Robertson, 1980.

Portrait of Change 1997, LGMB, 1998 (local government management).

The Conduct of Local Authority Business (Widdicombe Report), HMSO, 1986.

The Conduct of Local Authority Business: The Government Response, HMSO, 1988.

More than a flower show, Fabian Society, 1997 (elected mayor).

G. Stoker and H. Wolman, *A Different Way of Doing Business: The Experience of the US Mayor*, LGMB, 1991.

D. Regan, *A Headless State*, University of Nottingham, 1980.

M. Clarke *et al.*, *Executive Mayors for Britain?*, Univ. of Birmingham, 1996.

J. Stewart, *The Responsive Local Authority*, INLOGOV, 1974.

J. Stewart, *The New Management of Local Government*, Allen & Unwin, 1986.

M. Clarke and J. Stewart, *General Management in Local Government: Getting the Balance Right*, Longman, 1990.

R. Hambleton, *Beyond Excellence: Quality Local Government in the 1990s*, SAUS, 1990 (the governmental/political function of councils).

T. Caulcott, *Management and the Politics of Power: Central and Local Government Compared*, LGC Communications, 1996.

P. Minford, 'How to De-politicise Local Government', *Economic Affairs*, 9 January 1988.

P. Joyce *et al.*, *Managing in the New Local Government*, Kogan Page, 1999.

P. Corrigan, *Shaping the Future: managing new forms of local democracy*, LGMB, 1997.

G. Stoker (ed.), *The New Management of British Local Governance*, Macmillan, 1999.

J. Wilson and P. Hinton, *Public services and the 1990s*, Tudor, 1995.

S. Leach *et al.*, *The Changing Organisation and Management of Local Government*, Macmillan, 1994.

T. Cutler and B. Waine, *Managing the welfare state*, Berg, 1994.

'The New Public Management', special issue of *Public Administration*, Spring 1991.

'A public management for all seasons?', *Public Administration*, Spring 1992.

'From public administration to public management', *Public Administration*, Spring 1996.

E. Ferlie, *New Public management in Action*, OUP, 1996.

The Competitive Council, Audit Commission, 1988.

The Enabling Council, LGTB, 1988.

K. Walsh, *Marketing in Local Government*, Longman, 1989.

N. Ridley, *The Local Right: Enabling not Providing*, Centre for Policy Studies, 1988.

Coopers and Lybrand Deloitte, *The Changing Style of Local Government – Enabling in Practice*, ACC, 1991.

K. Ennals and J. O'Brien, *The Enabling Role of Local authorities*, Public Finance Foundation, 1990.

C. Hislop, *The enabling council: a critique*, LGIU, 1994.

T. Sheppard, *Enabling authorities: the new privatisation*, LGIU, 1994.

R. Brooke, *Managing the Enabling Council*, Longman, 1989.

The Councillor and the Enabling Council: Changing Roles, LGTB, 1989.

Realising the Benefits of Competition, Audit Commission, 1993.

Competition and Local Government, LGMB, 1996 (effects on attitudes and management).

Competing for Quality, Cmd 1730, HMSO, 1991.

Competition for local government services, INLOGOV for DoE, 1990.

D. Whitfield, *The welfare state*, Pluto, 1992 (privatization/deregulation).

B. Jordan, 'Are New Right Policies sustainable?' in *Journal of Social Policy*, July 1995.

K. Walsh, *Public services and market mechanisms*, Macmillan, 1996.

S. Ransome, *Management for the public domain*, Macmillan, 1994.

M. Mullard, 'The Politics of Trusteeship' in *Talking Politics*, Vol. 9, (Winter 1996–7), pp. 124–8.

G. Jones, *Local Government: The Management Agenda*, LGC/ICSA, 1995.

G. Jones, *The New Local Government Agenda*, LGC/ICSA, 1998.

G. Hollis, *Transforming Local Government*, Longman, 1994.

From Providing to Enabling: Local authorities and community care planning, Joseph Rowntree, 1991.

T. Cutler and B. Waine, *Managing the Welfare State: The Politics of Public Sector management*, Berg, 1994.

J. Fenwick, *Managing Local Government*, Chapman & Hall, 1996.

M. Clarke and J. Stewart, *Diversity and Choice*, Univ. of Birmingham, 1998 (the role of the chief executive in local government).

M. Clarke, *Renewing Public Sector Management: An Agenda for Local Government*, Pitman, 1996.

S. Leach *et al.*, *The Changing Organisation and Management of Local Government*, Macmillan, 1994.

L. Keen and R. Scace, *Local Government Management: The Rhetoric and Reality of Change*, Open UP, 1998.

P. Gooby-Taylor and R. Lawson, *Markets and Managers: New Issues in the Delivery of Welfare*, Open UP, 1993.

T. Butcher, *Delivering Welfare*, Open UP, 1995.

Cross-cutting Issues Affecting Local Government, DETR, 1999.

Getting Closer to the Public, LGMB, 1987.

Learning from the Public, LGMB, 1988.

Innovation within local government, DETR, 1999.

D. Rosenburg, *Accounting for Public Power: Power, Professionals and Politics in Local Government*, Manchester UP, 1989.

Political Leaders and Chief Executives, LGMB, 1997.

Innovative models of local authority working, LGMB, 1997.

Practical Implications of New Forms of Political Executive, LGMB, 1998.

Professionalism and the Management of Local Authorities, IDeA, 1999.

M. Laffin and K. Young, *Professionalism in Local Government; Change and Challenge*, Longman, 1990.

T. Travers *et al.*, *The role of the local authority chief executive*, Joseph Rowntree, 1997.

A. Norton, *The Role of the Chief Executive in British Local Government*, INLOGOV, 1991.

The Role of the Chief Executive, LGMB, 1991.

A. Norton, *The Town Clerk*, LGC Communications, 1997 (history and role).

M. Clarke and J. Stewart, *Diversity and Choice: Reflections on the Role of the Chief Executive in Local Government*, Univ. of Birmingham, 1998.

R. Morris and R. Paine, *The Chief Executive in Local Government*, ICSA, 1995.

Audit Commission, *More Equal Than Others: the Chief Executive in Local Government*, HMSO, 1989.

K. P. Poole, *The Local Government Service*, Allen & Unwin, 1978.

M. Laffin and K. Young, 'The Changing Roles and Responsibilities of Local Authority Chief Officers', *Public Administration*, Spring 1985.

L. Pratchett and M. Wingfield, *The Public Service Ethos in Local Government*, CLD/Municipal Journal, 1994.

Public Service Ethos Towards 2000, LGMB, 1998.

K. Walsh, *Ethics and the Local Government Officer*, INLOGOV, 1984.

Paying the Piper: People and Pay Management in Local Government, Audit Commission, 1995.

Politicians and Professionals, LGTB, 1988.

C. Collins *et al.*, 'The Officer and the Councillor', *Public Administration Bulletin*, December 1978.

A. Alexander, 'Officers and Members', *Local Government Studies*, 1981.

D. Rosenburg, *Accounting for Public Policy: Power, Professionals and Politics in Local Government*, Manchester UP, 1989.

J. Greenwood, 'Facilitating Officer/Councillor Relationships – Meeting the Post-Widdicombe Challenge', *Local Government Studies*, November 1990.

S. Leach *et al.*, *All you need is Trust? The changing relationship between members and officers*, LGMB, 1998.

R. Kerley, *Managing in Local Government*, Macmillan, 1994.

C. Tomkins, *Achieving Economy, Efficiency and Effectiveness in the Public Sector*, Kogan Page, 1987.

A. Lawton and A. Rose, *Organisation and Management in the Public Sector*, Pitman, 1994.

N. Flynn, *Public Sector Management*, Prentice-Hall/Wheatsheaf, 1997.

J. Wilson (ed.), *Managing Public Services: Dealing with Dogma*, Tudor, 1995.

M. Clarke and J. Stewart, *Developing Effective Public Service Management*, LGMB, 1990.

CCT Survey Reports, LGMB, (annual).

Quality and Competition, LGMB, 1990.

I. Sanderson, *Management of Quality in Local Government*, Longman, 1993.

C. Skelcher, *Managing of Service Quality*, Longman, 1992.

Innovations in Service, LGMB, 1991.

L. Gaster, *Quality in Public Services*, Open UP, 1995.

L. Gaster, *Quality at the Front Line*, SAUS, 1992.

A Local Authority's Options for Service Delivery, LGMB, 1990.

J. Stewart and M. Clarke, *The Search for Quality*, LGMB, 1990.

IT Trends in Local Government, SOCITM, 1990.

Fitness for Purpose, LGMB, 1993.

Audit Commission, *Performance Review in Local Government*, HMSO, 1988.

Audit Commission, *Managing Services Effectively – Performance Review*, HMSO, 1989.

S. Rogers, *Performance Management in Local Government*, Longman, 1990.

B. Tanner and D. Rawlinson, *Financial Management in the 1990s*, Longman, 1989.

R. Knowles, *Effective Management in Local Government*, ICSA, 1988.

Challenge and Change: Characteristics of Good Management in Local Government, LGMB, 1993.

Managing Change, LGMB, 1992.

N. Rao, *Managing Change*, Joseph Rowntree, 1993.

Strategic Role of Local Government in the Community, LGMB, 1992.

On Merit: recruitment in Local Government, Audit Commission, 1995.

A. Fowler, *Human Resource Management in Local Government*, Pitman, 1995.

S. Halford, *Gender, Careers and Organisations*, Macmillan, 1997.

K. Young and L. Spencer, *Breaking down the barriers: Women Managers in Local Government*, LGMB, 1991.

The Management of Hung Councils, LGTB, 1985.

Working with the Balance, LGMB, 1993.

M. Temple, 'Power Distribution in Hung Councils', *Local Government Studies*, July/August 1991.

M. Temple, 'Political Influence in Hung and Non-Hung Councils', *Local Government Policy Making*, July 1993.

S. Leach and J. Stewart, *The Politics of Hung Authorities*, Macmillan, 1992.

A. Doig, *Corruption and Misconduct in Contemporary British Politics*, Penguin Books, 1984.

D. Walker, *Municipal Empire*, Temple Smith, 1983.

A. Henney, *Inside Local Government*, Sinclair Browne, 1983.

C. Goodson-Wickes, *The New Corruption*, CPS, 1984.

C. Pollitt *et al.*, *Decentralising Public Service Management*, Macmillan, 1998.

D. Burns, *The Politics of Decentralization*, Macmillan, 1995.

B. Hogget and R. Hambleton, *Decentralisation and Democracy*, SAUS, 1989.

V. Lowndes and G. Stoker, 'An Evaluation of Neighbourhood Decentralisation', *Policy and Politics*, 1992.

Decentralisation in the Counties, LGMB, 1994.

Decentralisation of Social Services Departments, DHSS, 1988.

Decentralisation and Accountability, LGMB, 1998.

Leading Communities: Competencies for effective community leadership, LGMB, 1998.

Local Government Community Leadership, LGMB, 1993.

Leadership in urban governance, LGMB, 1998.

Political leadership and public management, IDA, 1999.

10 FINANCE

A Councillor's Guide to Local Authority Finance, CIPFA, 1998.

Guide to Local Government Finance, LGIU, 1997.

S. Bailey, *Local Government Economics*, Macmillan, 1999.

W. Birtles and A. Forge, *Butterworth's Local Government Finance*, Butterworth, 1999.

Eighth Report of the House of Commons Environment, Transport and Regional Affairs Committee, 'Local Government Finance', HMSO, March 1999.

Government's Response to the Committee's Report 'Local Government Finance', Cmd 4402, HMSO, July 1999.

Paying for Local Government, Cmd 9714, HMSO, 1986.

Alternatives to Domestic Rates, Cmd 8449, HMSO, 1981.

The Future Shape of Local Government Finance, Cmd 4741, HMSO, 1971.

Local Government Finance: Report of the Committee of Enquiry (Layfield), Cmd 6453, HMSO, 1976.

G. Pola, *Developments in Local Government Finance: Theory and Practice*, Elgar, 1996.

H. Glennester, *Paying for the Welfare*, Prentice Hall, Wheatsheaf Harvester, 1997.

I. Sanderson, *Current Issues in Local Government Finance*, CLD/Municipal Journal, 1995.

P. Watt and J. Fender, *Local Government Spending and the Macroeconomy*, LGMB, 1998.

N. P. Hepworth, *The Finance of Local Government*, Allen & Unwin, 1984.

C. D. Foster *et al.*, *Local Government Finance in a Unitary State*, Allen & Unwin, 1980.

L. J. Sharpe (ed.), *The Local Fiscal Crisis in Western Europe*, Sage, 1981.

K. Newton, *Balancing the Books: Financial Problems of Local Government in Western Europe*, Sage, 1980.

R. Rose and E. Page, *Fiscal Stress in Cities*, CUP, 1983.

A. Midwinter, *The Politics of Local Spending*, Mainstream, 1984 (esp. Scotland).

T. Travers, *The Politics of Local Government Finance*, Allen & Unwin, 1986.

S. J. Bailey and R. Paddison, *The Reform of Local Government Finance*, Routledge, 1988.

K. Newton and T. J. Karran, *The Politics of Local Expenditure*, Macmillan, 1985.

G. Jones *et al.*, *The Way Ahead for Local Government Finance*, INLOGOV, 1982.

R. Hales and T. Travers, *Sources of Revenue for Local Authorities*, LGMB, 1997.

A. Midwinter and N. McGarvey, *From Accountability to Control? New Council Tax in Practice*, Certified Accountants Education Trust, 1995.

From Rates to Council Tax, INLOGOV Informs, Univ. of Birmingham, 1994.

C. Harrington and M. Lee, *Council Tax: Your Guide*, IRRV, 1997.

L. Eastham, *Council Tax*, Citizen's Advice Notes Service Trust, 1993.

Responses to the Government's Consultation Paper, 'A New Tax for Local Government', Audit Commission, 1991.

Alternatives to the community charge, Joseph Rowntree, 1990.

A. Midwinter and C. Main, *Rates Reform: Issues, Arguments and Evidence*, Mainstream, 1987.

A. Midwinter and C. Monaghan, *From Rates to the Poll Tax*, Edinburgh University Press, 1992.

A. Midwinter, 'The Poll Tax in Practice: The Distributive and Political Consequences of Rates Reform in the Scottish Highlands', *Local Government Studies*, January 1989.

G. Hollis *et al.*, *Alternatives to the Community Charge*, Joseph Rowntree, 1990.

J. LeGrand and G. Bramley, *Who Uses Local Services: Striving for Equity*, LGMB, 1992.

D. Butler *et al.*, *Failure in British Government: The Politics of the Poll Tax*, OUP, 1994.

D. Dunn, *Poll Tax: The Fiscal Fake*, Chatto & Windus, 1990.

J. Gibson, *The Politics and Economics of the Poll Tax: Mrs Thatcher's Downfall*, EMAS, 1990.

B. Jones, *Financing Local Government: The Erosion of Autonomy*, PAVIC/Politics Association, 1994.

M. Ridge and S. Smith, *Local Taxation: The options and arguments*, Institute for Fiscal Studies, 1991.

S. Smith and D. Squire, *Local Taxes and Local Government*, Institute for Fiscal Studies, 1987.

J. Owens, *Local Government Taxation*, IRRV, 1991.

P. John, *A new tax for local government*, Joseph Rowntree, 1991.

J. Isaac, *Options for a local income tax*, Joseph Rowntree, 1992.

R. Bennet, 'The Local Income Tax in Britain: A Critique of Recent Arguments Against Its Use', *Public Administration*, Autumn 1981.

J. Hall and S. Smith, *The feasibility of a local sales tax*, Joseph Rowntree, 1995.

A Plain English guide to the Local Government Finance Settlement, DETR, 1999.

Passing the Bucks, The Impact of Standard Spending Assessments on Economy, Efficiency and Effectiveness, Audit Commission, 1993.

R. Hale and T. Travers, *The effect of Standards Spending Assessments*, Joseph Rowntree, 1993.

The SSA Tables for local authorities are available at www.local.detr.gov.uk

R. J. Bennet, *Central Grants to Local Governments*, CUP, 1982.

Standard Spending Assessments: A Reappraisal, Society of County Treasurers, 1992.

Audit Commission, *The Impact on Local Economy, Efficiency and Effectiveness of the Block Grant Distribution System*, HMSO, 1984.

K. Judge, *Pricing the Social Services*, Macmillan, 1980.

Charging for Services, LGMB, 1996.

S. J. Bailey, *Local Government Charges: Policy and Practice*, Longman, 1993.

S. J. Bailey, *Practical Charging Policies for Local Government*, Public Finance Foundation, 1988.

Survey of Charges for Social Care 1993–5, AMA, 1995.

Too High a Price? Examining the Cost of Charging Policies in Local Government, LGIU, 1991.

S. Baldwin, *Charging ahead*, Policy Press, 1996 (charging for social care).

M. Chetwynd, *The cost of care*, Policy Press, 1996.

P. John, *Charging for local government services*, Joseph Rowntree, 1995.

Charging policies in local government, CIPFA, 1984.

M. Loney, *The State or the Market?*, Sage, 1991.

P. Self, *Government by the Market? The politics of public choice*, Macmillan, 1993.

R. Harris and A. Seldon, *Pricing or Taxing*, IEA, 1976.

K. Judge and J. Mathews, *Charging for social care*, Allen & Unwin, 1980.

A. Seldon, *Charge*, Temple Smith, 1977.

A. Maynard and D. King, *Rates or charges?*, IEA, 1972.

S. Bailey, 'User charges for urban services', *Urban Studies*, 32, 1994.

Impact of Rates on Businesses, DETR, 1995.

Local partnerships: A Research Review of Local Authorities' Statutory Duties to Consult with Business, DETR, 1995.

'Why the Rate Burden on Business is a Cause for Concern', *National Westminster Quarterly Bank Review*, February 1984.

R. Hale and T. Travers, *The operation of the non-domestic rate*, Joseph Rowntree, 1994.

K. Denny, *Options for business rate reform*, Joseph Rowntree, 1995.

Consultation Paper: *Modernising local government – Improving local services through best value*, DETR, 1998.

Consultation papers: *Modernising local government: Improving local financial accountability; Capital finance; Business rates*, DETR, 1998.

Achieving Best Value Through Partnership, DETR, 1999.

Achieving Best Value Through Public Engagement, DETR, 1999.

Achieving Best Vale Through Quality Management, DETR, 1999.

Organisation-wide approaches to Best Value, DETR, 1999.

Achieving Best Value Through Competition, Benchmarking and Performance Networks, DETR, 1999.

Achieving Best Value Through Performance Review, DETR, 1999.

Towards Best Value, Open University, 1999 (case study of Newham LBC approach to Best Value).

T. Travers, *Change for Local Government: Commentary on the Government's Proposals for Local Authority Finance*, York, 1999.

K. Walsh and H. Davis, *Competition and Service: The Impact of the Local Government Act 1988*, HMSO, 1993.

K. Desai and J. Sealey, *The Provision of White Collar and Professional Services by Local Authorities: voluntary exposure to market forces*, DETR, 1996.

Competitiveness and contracting out of local authority services, Audit Commission, 1987.

N. Adnett and S. Harding, 'The Impact of TUPE on Compulsory Competitive Tendering', *Local Government Studies*, 24, 3, Autumn 1998.

W. Eggers (ed.), *Cutting Local Government Costs through Competition and Privatization*, California Chamber of Commerce, Sacramento, 1997.

N. Rao and K. Young, *Competition, Contracts and Change: The Local Authority Experience of CCT*, Joseph Rowntree, 1995.

K. Walsh, *Public Services and Market Mechanisms*, Macmillan, 1995.

J. LeGrand, *Quasi markets and social policy*, Macmillan, 1993.

'Internal markets – the road to inefficiency' in *Public Administration*, Autumn 1990.

F. Foldarvy, *Public goods and private communities: the market provision of social services*, Elgar, 1994.

R. L. Kemp, *Privatisation: the provision of public services by the private sector*, McFarland, 1991.

G. Boyne, *Public Choice Theory and local Government*, Macmillan, 1998.

J. Walker and R. Moore, *Privatisation of Local Government Services*, WEA, 1983.

D. Whitfield, *Making it Public: Evidence and Action Against Privatisation*, Pluto, 1983.

T. Bovaird *et al.*, *More for Less*, LGMB, 1997.

C. Bone, *Achieving Value for Money in Local Government*, Longman, 1992.

C. Tomkins, *Achieving Economy, Efficiency and Effectiveness in the Public Sector*, Kogan Page, 1987.

Local Authorities' Activity under Section 137, DETR, 1998.

Local Councils' Use of Section 137, DETR, 1998.

Auditing Local Government: A Guide to the Work of the Audit Commission, Audit Commission, 1986.

Protecting the Public Purse, Audit Commission, 1997.

How effective is the Audit Commission?, Audit Commission, 1992.

R. Stanton, *Access to capital for local services*, Joseph Rowntree, 1995.

Local Authorities' Involvement in Companies, DETR, 1997.

Local Authorities' Attitudes to Private Sector Funding, DETR, 1998.

B. Jones, *Local Government Financial Management*, ICSA, 1995.

D. Rawlinson and B. Tanner, *Financial management in the Public Sector*, Pitman, 1997.

P. Cook, *Local Authority Financial Management and Accounting*, Longman, 1993.

B. Blake *et al.*, *Local Budgeting in Practice: Learning from Two Case Studies*, SAUS, 1991.

H. Elcock *et al.*, *Budgeting in Local Government: Managing the Margins*, Longman, 1989.

H. Elcock and G. Jordan, *Learning from Local Authority Budgeting*, Avebury, 1987.

Worth more than money, Audit Commission, 1998 (role of CFO).

C. Farringdon, *Local Government Taxation in Europe*, IRRV, 1991.

G. Hollis *et al.*, *Local Government Finance: An International Comparative Study*, LGC
    Communications, 1994.
Economics textbooks often have a chapter on Local Government finance.

11 CENTRAL GOVERNMENT AND OTHER RELATIONSHIPS

P. John, *Recent Trends on Central–Local Relations*, Joseph Rowntree, 1992.
Local–Central government relations: a compendium of research findings, Joseph Rowntree,
    1997.
House of Lords Committee on relations between Central and Local Government, Report,
    Vol. 1, HMSO, 1996.
White Paper: *Improving Central–Local Government Relations*, HMSO, 1996.
C. Carter, *A New Accord, Promoting Constructive Relations between Central and Local
    Government*, Joseph Rowntree, 1992.
S. Jenkins, *Accountable to None: the Tory Nationalisation of Britain*, Penguin Books,
    1995.
P. John, 'Central and Local Government Relations in the 1980s and 1990s',
    Local Government Studies, 20, 3, 1995.
Local–Central Government Relations: A Compendium of Research Findings, Joseph
    Rowntree, 1997.
A. Seldon and S. Ball, *Conservative Century: the Conservative Party since 1900*, OUP,
    1994.
M. Loughlin, *Legality and Locality: the role of law in central/local relations*, Clarendon
    Press, 1996.
Two to Tango? Charting the central-local relationship and its legal framework, LGMB,
    1998.
M. Clarke, *Rebuilding trust?*, European Policy Forum, 1998 (Labour party, LG
    and the LGA).
G. Jones and T. Travers, *Attitudes to Local Government in Westminster and Whitehall*,
    CLD/Municipal Journal, 1994.
M. Laffin, *Professionalism and Policy: the Role of the Professions in the Central–Local
    Government Relationship*, Gower, 1986.
M. Clarke, *Breaking down the barriers: inhibitions to secondment between central and
    local government*, LGC publications, 1995.
H. Butcher *et al.*, *Local Government and Thatcherism*, Routledge, 1990.
A. Cochrane, *Whatever Happened to Local Government?*, Open University, 1993.
Against the Over-mighty State: A Future for Local Government in Britain, Federal Trust
    for Education and Research, 1988.
N. Lewis, *Inner-City Regeneration – Demise of Local Government*, Open University,
    1992.

R. Rhodes, 'Inter-governmental Relations in the post-War Period', *Local Government Studies*, November 1985.

R. Rhodes, *Beyond Westminster and Whitehall*, Unwin, 1988.

M. Parkinson (ed.), *National Interests and Local Government*, Heinemann, 1983.

A. McPherson and C. Raab, *Governing Education: A Sociology of Policy since 1945*, Edinburgh University Press, 1988.

A. Midwinter and N. McGarvey, *From Accountability to Control? New Council Tax in Practice*, Certified Accountants Education Trust, 1995.

J. Swaffield, 'Local Government in the National Setting', *Public Administration*, Autumn 1970.

N. Boaden, 'Central Departments and Local Authorities: The Relationship Re-examined', *Political Studies*, 28, 1970.

S. Ranson (ed.), *Between Centre and Locality*, Allen & Unwin, 1985.

M. Loughlin (ed.), *Half a Century of Municipal Decline*, Allen & Unwin, 1985.

R. Rhodes, *The National World of Local Government*, Allen & Unwin, 1986.

J. A. G. Griffith, *Central Departments and Local Authorities*, Allen & Unwin, 1966.

Report of the Committee on Management of Local Government (the Maud Report), Vols. 1 and 5, HMSO, 1967.

Local Government Finance: Report of the Committee of Enquiry (Layfield), Cmd 6453, HMSO, 1976

W. Robson, *Local Government in Crisis*, Allen & Unwin, 1968.

D. N. Chester, *Central and Local Government: Financial and Administrative Relations*, Macmillan, 1951.

M. Thrasher, 'The Concept of a Central–Local Government Partnership', *Policy and Politics*, 9 April 1981.

T. Travers, *Joint Working Between Local Authorities*, LGC Communications, 1995.

K. Young, 'Inter-tier Political Relations in a Metropolitan System', *Local Government Chronicle*, 9 October 1971.

Local Government Studies, May/June 1982 (issue devoted entirely to central–local relations).

G. Jones, *Introduction to Central–Local Government Relations*, SSRC, 1980.

G. Jones (ed.), *New Approaches to the Study of Central–Local Government Relationships*, Gower, 1980.

Rhetoric and Reality, Society of Education Officers, 1982.

D. Mellor, *The Effects of Central Government Initiatives on Local Government Manpower and Expenditure*, LACSAB, 1984.

M. Goldsmith, *New Research in Central–Local Relations*, Gower, 1985.

R. Rhodes, *Control and Power in Central–Local Government Relations*, Gower, 1981.

C. Crouch and D. Marquand (eds.), *The New Centralism*, Political Quarterly/ Blackwell, 1989.

G. Jones, 'The Crisis in Central–Local Government Relations', *Governance*, April 1988.

B. Houlihan, *Housing Policy and Central–Local Government Relations*, Avebury, 1988.

O. Hartley, 'The Relationship between Central Government and Local Authorities', *Public Administration*, Winter 1971.

Auditing Local Government: A Guide to the Work of the Audit Commission, Audit Commission, 1986.

Sir F. Hill, 'The Partnership in Practice', *Political Quarterly*, 2, 1966.

J. Boynton, 'Local Councils in Confrontation: the Current Conflict with the Centre', *Policy Studies*, April 1982.

P. Carmichael, *Central–Local Government relations in the 80s*, Avebury, 1995 (compares Glasgow and Liverpool).

M. Loughlin, 'Understanding Central–Local Government Relations', *Public Policy and Administration*, 11/3, 1996.

G. Stoker, 'Understanding Central and Local Relations: a reply', *Public Policy and Administration*, 11/3, 1996.

M. Laffin, *Professionalism and Policy*, Gower, 1986.

D. Marsh and R. Rhodes, *Policy Networks in British Government*, OUP, 1992.

P. Dunleavy, 'Professions and Policy Change', *Public Administration Bulletin*, 36, 1981.

M. Thrasher, 'The concept of central–local government partnership', *Policy and Politics*, April 1981.

R. Rhodes, *Understanding Governance: Policy Networks, Governance, Reflexivity and Accountability*, Open University, 1997 (changes in service delivery and organization in central and local government).

R. Rhodes and D. Marsh, 'The Concept of Policy Networks in British Political Science', *Talking Politics*, Spring 1996, pp. 210–22.

J. A. Chandler, *Public Policy-Making for Local Government*, Croom Helm, 1988.

C. Lamb and M. Geddes, *Scope for Choice and Variety in Local Government*, LGC Communications, JFR/LGC, 1995.

G. Boyne, 'Central Grants and Local Policy Variation', *Public Administration*, Summer 1990.

Local Freedom and Accountability: learning from America and Australia, LGMB, 1996.

R. Hambleton *et al.*, *The Collaborative Council: A Study of Inter-Agency Working in Practice*, LGC Communications, 1995.

R. Means *et al.*, *Making partnerships work in community care*, Policy Press, 1997.

Working Across Organisational Boundaries, LGMB, 1992.

Community Leadership, LGMB, 1992.

C. Carter, *Members one of another: the problems of local corporate action*, Joseph Rowntree, 1996.

Whose Zone is it Anyway? The Guide to Area Based Initiatives, IDeA, 1999.

S. Hall and J. Mawson, *Challenge funding, contracts and area regeneration: A decade of innovation in policy management and coordination*, Policy Press, 1999.

Listening to Business: Building Stronger Partnerships between Local Government and Business, IDeA, 1999.

Local Authorities' Statutory Duty to Consult with the Business Community, DoE, 1995.

M. Hughes *et al.*, *Local government regulation of business*, Univ. of Birmingham, 1999.

C. Bemrose and J. Mackeith, *Partnerships for Progress: good practice in the relationship between local government and voluntary organisations*, Policy Press, 1996.

Freedom Within Boundaries: Developing Effective Approaches to Decentralisation, LGMB, 1997.

Local Partnership for Economic and Social Regeneration, LGMB, 1995.

History, Strategy or Lottery? The Realities of Local Government/Voluntary Sector Relationships, IDeA, 1999.

What Price Charity?, LGMB, 1996 (LA support for voluntary hospices).

C. Skelcher *et al.*, *Creating effective Community networks in Urban regeneration*, Joseph Rowntree, 1996.

N. Boaden, *Public Participation in Local Services*, Longman, 1982.

T. Gibson, *People Power: Community and Work Groups in Action*, Penguin Books, 1979.

H. Davis and D. Hall, *Matching purpose and task: the advantages and disadvantages of single- and multi-purpose bodies*, York, 1996.

R. Rhodes, *The Europeanisation of the Sub-Central Government*, Centre for European Studies, Oxford, Discussion Paper no. 13, 1992.

W. Hall and S. Weir, 'The rise of the quangocracy', *Local Government Chronicle*, 30 August 1996.

S. Weir and W. Hall, *Ego Trip and Extra Governmental Organisations in the UK*, Democratic Audit Paper 2, Univ. of Essex, 1994.

P. Hirst, 'Quangos and Democratic Government', *Parliamentary Affairs*, 48/2, 1995.

The Quango File, LGIU, 1995.

J. Plummer, *The Governance Gap*, Joseph Rowntree, 1994 (quangos).

The Changing Face of Quangos, AMA, 1994.

H. Davis, 'Quangos in local government: a changing world', *Local Government Studies*, 22/2, 1996.

Local quangos and local governance, LGA, 1998.

C. Skelcher and H. Davis, *The membership of local appointed bodies*, Joseph Rowntree, 1995.

Qualgos just grow, Centre for Policy Studies, 1985.

J. Stewart *et al.*, *Democracy and appointed bodies*, CLD, 95.

J. Stewart *et al.*, *The Quango State: An Alternative Approach*, CLD/Municipal Journal, 1995.

W. Hall and S. Weir, *The Untouchables: Power and Accountability in the Quango State*, Univ. of Essex/Scarman Trust, 1996.

A. Greer and P. Hoggett, *The governance of local spending bodies*, Rowntree, 1997.

Secret Services? Handbook for Investigating Local Quangos, LGIU, 1995.

A. Greer and P. Hoggett, *Patterns of Accountability with Local Non-elected Bodies*, York, 1997.

H. Davis, *Quangos and Local Government: A Changing World*, Cass, 1996.

'Local authorities and non-elected agencies', *Public Administration*, Summer 1997.

C. Skelcher, *The Appointed State*, Open UP, 1998.

Developing local compacts: Relationships between local public sector bodies and the voluntary sectors, YPS/York, 1999.

W. Waldegrave, *The Reality of Reform and Accountability in Today's Public Service*, Public Finance Foundation, 1993.

C. Skelcher and H. Davis, *Opening the Boardroom Door: membership of local appointed bodies*, LGC Communications, 1995.

M. Flinders and M. Smith (eds.), *Quangos, Accountability and Reform: the Politics of Quasi-Government*, Macmillan, 1998.

C. Painter *et al.*, *Changing Local Governance: Local Authorities and Non-Elected Agencies*, LGMB, 1997.

A. Greer and P. Hoggett, *Patterns of Accountability within non-elected bodies*, York, 1997.

J. Benington, *Local Democracy and the European Union*, CLD/MJ, 1994.

M. Cini, *Local Government and the European Community*, Polytechnic of North London, 1990.

C. Crawford, 'European Influence on Local Self-Government, *Local Govt. Studies*, Spring 1992.

M. Goldsmith, 'The Europeanisation of Local Government', *Urban Studies*, nos. 4/5, 1993.

M. Goldsmith and K. Klausen, *European Integration and Local Government*, Elgar, 1997.

P. Johns, *The Europeanisation of British Local government*, LGMB, 1994.

R. Rhodes, *Local Government and Europe*, Univ. of Birmingham, 1973.

A Rough Guide to Europe, HMSO, 1993.

Europe: A Guide for Public Authorities, FIS/CIPFA, 1993 (annual subscription).

C. Hull and R. A. W. Rhodes, *Intergovernmental relations in the European Community*, Saxon House, 1978.

P. Bongers, *Local Government and 1992*, Longman, 1991.

1992: The Impact on County Councils' Services, CECSNET, 1991.

E. Bomberg and J. Peterson, *Decision-making in the EU: Implications for Central–Local Government Relations*, York, 1996.

J. Bachtler and I. Turok, *The coherence of EU regional policy*, Jessica Kingsley, 1997.

S. Martin and A. Healy, 'EU funding and local authority capital funds', *Final Report to the Audit Commission*, LG Centre Univ. of Warwick, 1997.

E. Bomberg and J. Peterson, *The impact of regional and local authorities on EU decision-making*, Joseph Rowntree, 1996.

S. Pyecroft, 'The Organisation of Local Authorities' European Activities', *Public Policy and Administration*, 10/4, 1995.

P. Roberts and T. Hart, *Regional strategy and partnership in European programmes*, Joseph Rowntree, 1996.

Building the new Europe: The Role of local authorities in the UK, ACC, 1994.

Towards 2006: European Union Regional Policy and UK Local Government, LGIU, 1998.

Other People's Local Government, LGMB, 1997 (links with other countries).

12 LOCAL COUNCILS

Local Governance, Winter 1998 – special issue on parish councils.

Report of the Royal Commission on Local Government in England 1966–1969 (the Redcliffe-Maud report), Vol. III, Appendix 8, HMSO, 1969.

C. Arnold-Baker, *Local Council Administration*, Longcross, 1989.

W. H. Ousby and B. G. Wright, *A Practical Guide to Local Council Administration*, Knight, 1976.

S. Ellwood *et al.*, *A Survey of Parish and Town Councils in England*, HMSO, 1992.

R. Harrop, *Parish, Town and Community Finance – A Practical Guide*, Knight, 1991.

Coopers and Lybrand Deloitte, *Making the Most of Parish and Town Councils* ACC, 1992.

Department of the Environment, *Neighbourhood Councils in England*, HMSO, 1974.

Department of the Environment, *A Voice for Your Neighbourhood*, HMSO, 1977.

J. Seabrook, *The Idea of Neighbourhood – what local politics should be about*, Pluto, 1984.

H. Clarke, *Parish, Town and Community Councils: a Guide to Law and Administration*, Knight, 1992.

Role and Activities of Parish and Town Councils in England: Case Studies, HMSO, 1993.

Making the Most of Parish and Town Councils, ACC-Coopers and Lybrand Deloitte, 1992.

Local Council Review (bi-monthly).

Local Councils' Use of Section 137, DETR, 1998 (discretionary spending).

J. Prophet, *The Parish Councillor's Guide*, Shaw, 1993.

B. Greaves and G. Lishman, *The Theory and Practice of Community Politics*, Association of Liberal Councillors, 1980.

13 PARTICIPATION

D. Hill, *Participating in Local Affairs*, Penguin Books, 1970.

G. Parry (ed.), *Participation in Politics*, Manchester UP, 1972.

G. Parry *et al.*, *Political Participation and Democracy in Britain*, CUP, 1992.

G. Stoker, *Democratic Renewal: issues for local government*, LGMB, 1998.

Democratic Practice: A Guide, Democratic Network, 1998.

J. Stewart, *Innovation in Democratic Practice*, Univ. of Birmingham, 1995, 1996 and 1997; 1999 version entitled *Towards Deliberative Democracy*.

M. Clarke, *Renewing Citizenship and Democracy*, Univ. of Birmingham, 1997.

Citizens' attitudes and knowledge of local government, DETR, 1999.

Who Asked You? The Citizen's Perspective on Participation, IDeA, 1999.

K. Young *et al.*, *Community identity and local government*, Joseph Rowntree, 1996.

A. Bloch and P. John, *Attitudes to local government*, Joseph Rowntree, 1991.

G. Stoker, *Politics and Local Government: Testing Public Opinion*, New Local Government Network, 1998.

Enhancing Public Participation in Local Government, DETR, 1998.

C. Rallings *et al.*, *Community Identity and Participation in Local Democracy*, CLD/Municipal Journal, 1994.

G. Higgins and J. Richardson, *Political Participation*, Politics Association, 1976.

V. Lowndes *et al.*, *Enhancing Public Participation in Local Government*, DETR, 1998.

M. Geddes, *Poverty, Excluded Communities and Local Democracy*, CLD/Municipal Journal, 1995.

Enhancing Local Democracy, LGMB, 1997.

M. Geddes, *Extending Democratic Practice in Local Government*, CLD/Municipal Journal, 1996.

C. May, *Citizen's Democracy: Theory and Practice*, Scottish LGIU, 1997.

M. Barnes *et al.*, *Citizens' Participation: A Framework for Evaluation*, Univ. of Birmingham, 1997.

Consulting and Involving the Public: Good Practice and Local Authorities, LGIU, 1998.

Participation Works! 21 techniques of community participation for the 21st Century, New Economics Foundation, 1998.

S. Baine, *Community Action and Local Government*, Bell, 1975.

W. Harvey Cox, *Cities: The Public Dimension*, Penguin Books, 1976.

A. Brier and T. Hill, 'Participation in Local Politics: 3 Cautionary Case Studies' in L. Robins, *Topics in British Politics*, Politics Association, 1982.

G. Jones, *Local Community*, Harrap, 1983.

J. Smith, *Public Involvement in Local Government*, Community Rights Foundation, 1984.

Participation in Public Life at Local Level, EOC, 1985.

P. Lynn, *Public Perceptions of Local Government*, DoE, 1992.

R. Jowell and J. Curtice (eds.), *British Social Attitudes: the Twelfth Report*, Gower, 1995.

Committee on the Management of Local Government (Maud Report), HMSO, 1967, Vols. 3 and 5.

Committee on the Conduct of Local Authority Business (Widdicombe Report), HMSO, 1986, Vols. 3 and 4.

Royal Commission on Local Government in England, Research Study 9, *Community Attitudes Survey*, HMSO, 1969.

Royal Commission on Local Government in Scotland, Research Study 2, *Community Survey*, HMSO, 1969.

People and Planning: Report of the Committee on Participation, HMSO, 1969.

R. Benewick and T. Smith (eds.), *Direct Action and Democratic Politics*, Allen & Unwin, 1972.

D. Jones and M. Mayo, *Community Work*, Routledge, 1974.

A. Lapping, *Community Action*, Fabian Society, 1970.

W. Hampton and R. Walker, *The Individual Citizen and Public Participation*, Sheffield UP, 1978.

C. Ward, *Tenants' Takeover*, Architectural Press, 1974.

S. Arnstein, *A Ladder of Citizen Participation*, Royal Town Planning Institute, 1971.

Citizens and Local Democracy: Empowerment – A Theme for the 90s, LGMB, 1992.

J. Stewart, *Accountability to the Public*, European Policy Forum, 1992.

W. Hampton *et al.*, 'Public Participation in Planning Within a Local Representative Democracy', *Policy and Politics*, 7, 1979.

Towards a New Governance? Local Authorities as Democratic Advocates, LGMB, 1993.

D. Prior *et al.*, *Is the Citizen's Charter a Charter for Citizens?*, LGMB, 1993.

Administrative Responsibility in Local Government, Joseph Rowntree, 1992.

Measuring Up: Consumer Assessment of Local Authority Services, NCC, 1986.

L. J. Sharpe, 'Instrumental Participation and Urban Government' in J. A. G. Griffith (ed.), *From Politics to Administration*, Allen & Unwin, 1976.

P. Willmot, *Community Initiatives, Patterns and Prospects*, PSI, 1989.

Tenant Participation in Housing Management, Institute of Housing, 1989.

Citizens and Local Democracy: A Resources Guide, LGMB, 1993.

G. Mulgan, *Politics in an Antipolitical Age*, Polity, 1994.

Listening to Communities: How Councils are involving people more directly in local government, LGMB/LGA, 1998.

A. Mabileau *et al.*, *Local Politics and Participation in Britain and France*, CUP, 1990.

J. Gyford, *Does Place Matter?: Locality and Local Democracy*, LGMB, 1991.

J. Gyford, *Citizens, Consumers and Councils: Local Government and the Public*, Macmillan, 1991.

D. Prior, *Citizenship, Rights, Community and Participation*, Pitman, 1995.

W. Miller and M. Dickson, *Local Governance and Local Citizenship: A Report on Public and Elite Attitudes*, ESRC, 1996.

D. McNulty, *Referenda and Citizens' Ballots*, CLD/Municipal Journal, 1995.

Local Referendums and Citizens' Ballots, LGA, 1999.

E. Lee, 'Can the British Voter be Trusted? The Local Referendum and Tax Reform', *Public Administration*, Summer 1988.

Citizen's Juries in Local Government, LGMB, 1997.

Twelve good neighbours: the citizen as juror, Fabian Society, 1997.

R. Bailey, *Access to Local Government Information*, LG & Health Rights Project, 1983.

A. Maidment and J. Steele, *Public Access to Information about Local Government*, DoE, 1995.

P. Birkinshaw, *Government and Information: The Law Relating to Access, Disclosure and Regulation*, Butterworth, 1990.

J. Percy-Smith, *Digital Democracy: Information and Communication Technologies in Local Politics*, CLD, 1995.

Getting Closer to the Public, LGTB, 1987.

The Public Service Orientation, LGTB, 1985.

Learning from the Public, LGTB, 1989.

Hearing the Voice of the Consumer, PSI, 1988.

P. McCarthy, *Grievances, Complaints and Local Government*, Avebury, 1992.

D. Burns *et al.*, *The Politics of decentralisation*, Macmillan, 1994.

M. Barnes *et al.*, *User Movements and the Local Governance of Welfare*, Policy Press, 1999.

D. Burns, *Decentralisation: Towards a New System of Accountability in Local Government*, COSLA, 1997.

L. Gaster and M. O'Toole, *Local Government Decentralisation: An Idea Whose Time Has Come*, SAUS, 1995.

Local Government Policy Making, No. 4, 1994 – special issue on decentralization.

V. Lowndes and G. Stoker, 'An Evolution of Neighbourhood Decentralisation', *Policy and Politics*, 1992.

P. Hoggett and R. Hambleton, *Decentralisation and Democracy*, SAUS, 1987.

P. Wilmott, *Local Government, Decentralisation and Community*, PSI, 1987.

K. Spencer, 'Decentralisation and Neighbourhood Management – Is the Mood Changing?', *Local Government Studies*, 1983.

T. Duncan, 'Community Councils in Glasgow', *Local Government Studies*, March 1990.

Community government and local government, Joseph Rowntree, 1996.

M. Clarke and J. Stewart, 'Empowerment: A Theme for the 1990s', *Local Government Studies*, Summer 1992.

14 COMPARATIVE

H. J. Teune, *Local Governance Around the World*, Sage, 1995.

Other People's Local Government, LGMB, 1996.

A. Norton, *International Handbook of Local and Regional Government*, Elgar, 1994.

K. Young, *Local leadership and decision-making: international comparisons*, Joseph Rowntree, 1994.

D. Hirsch, *A positive role for local government: lessons from other countries*, Joseph Rowntree, 1994.

C. Carter, *Local government: the lessons from other countries,* Joseph Rowntree, 1995.

M. Bowman and W. Hampton (eds.), *Local Democracies: a Study in Comparative Local Government*, Longman Cheshire, 1986.

R. Batley and A. Campbell, *The Political Executive: Politicians and Management in European Local Government*, Cass, 1992.

E. Page, *Localism and Centralism in Europe*, OUP, 1991.

J. Chandler (ed.), *Local Government in Liberal Democracies*, Routledge, 1992.

Coopers and Lybrand Deloitte, *The New Europe*, ACC, 1992.

L. Gain and J. Richardson, *Citizenship and Local Democracy: A European Perspective*, LGMB, 1992.

R. Hambledon, *Urban Government Under Thatcher and Reagan*, SAUS, 1988.

'Financing European Local Governments', special edition of *Local Government Studies*, Winter 1992.

'The Political Executive: Politicians and Management in European Local Government', special edition of *Local Government Studies*, Spring 1992.

O. Borraz, *Local leadership and decision making*, JRF, 1994.

K. Young *et al.*, *Local Leadership and Decision-making* (a study of France, Germany, USA and Britain), Joseph Rowntree, 1994.

Committee on the Management of Local Government (Maud Report), Vol. 4, HMSO, 1967.

Local Government Studies, March 1993, special edition on Financing European Local Government. (See also references in Finance, above.)

R. Batley and G. Stoker, *Local Government in Europe*, Macmillan, 1991.

J. Stewart, 'The Internal Management of Local Authorities in Britain – The Challenge of Experience in Other Countries', *Local Government Studies*, Spring 1992, pp. 5–17.

15 PUBLIC RELATIONS AND THE OMBUDSMAN

D. Walker, *Public Relations in Local Government*, Pitman, 1996.

J. Steel, *Public Access to Information: An Evaluation of the Local Government (Access to Information Act)*, PSI, 1995.

M. Fletcher, *Managing Communication in the New Local Government*, Kogan, 1999.

Talkback: Local Authority Communication with Citizens, Audit Commission, 1995.

T. F. Richardson, *Public Relations in Local Government*, Heinemann, 1988.

Public Relations in Local Government, Institute of Public Relations, 1993.

D. Fedorcio *et al.*, *Public Relations for Local Government*, Longman, 1991.

D. Deacon and P. Golding, 'Barriers to Centralism: Local Government, Local Media and the Charge on the Community', *Local Government Studies*, Summer 1993.

B. Franklin, *Public Relations Activities in Local Government, A Research report*, Centre for Television Research, Univ. of Leeds, 1990.

Effective Communication: A Guide to Public Relations in Local Government, ACC, 1990.

K. Walsh, *Marketing in Local Government*, Longman, 1989.

Complaints Procedures in Local Government, Centre for Criminological and Socio-Legal Studies, Univ. of Sheffield, 1986.

Administrative Justice: Some Necessary Reforms, Report of the committee of the Justice – All Souls Review of Administrative Law in the UK, Clarendon Press, 1988.

M. Simey, *Government by Consent: The Principles and Practice of Accountability in Local Government*, Bedford, 1985.

F. Laws, *Guide to the Local Government Ombudsman Service*, Longman, 1990.

C. O. Bell, 'Local Government Ombudsmen: Progress Through Persuasion', *New Law Journal*, 11 June 1981.

D. Murphy, *The Silent Watchdog: The Press in Local Politics*, Constable, 1972.

A. Sherman, *Councils, Councillors and Public Relations*, Barry Rose, 1973.

A. J. Morris, 'Local Authority Relations with the Local Press', *Public Law*, Autumn 1969.

Justice Report, *The Citizen and His Council*, Stevens, 1969.

Justice Report, *The Local Ombudsmen: A Review of the First Five Years*, Stevens, 1980.

N. Lewis and B. Gateshill, *The Commissioner for Local Administration: A Preliminary Appraisal*, RIPA, 1978.

I. McLeod, *Local Government Ombudsman: A Casebook*, Barry Rose, 1991.

Annual reports of the CLA.

K. Thompson, 'Conciliation or Arbitration'? The Place of Local Settlements in the Work of Local Ombudsmen', *LG Studies*, Vol. 17, 1991, 15.

R. Hall, 'New Electronic Communication from Local Government – Marginal or Revolutionary?', *Local Government Studies*, Summer 1998, pp. 19–33.

F. Laws, *Guide to the Local Government Ombudsman Service*, Longman, 1990.

C. Copus, *Local government and the media*, LGMB, 1999.

M. Hepworth, 'The Municipal Information Economy'?, *Local Government Studies*, Autumn 1992.

16 REFORM AND THE FUTURE

The White Paper *Modern Local Government: In Touch with the People*, Cmd 4014, Stationery Office, 1998 outlines a reform programme stretching over ten years and indicating changes in management and internal organization, elections, accountability, ethical standards, finance and efficiency, each of which received more detailed attention in separate DETR consultation papers.

Regional Government in England, DETR, 1997.

T. Blair, *Leading the Way: A New Vision for Local Government*, IPPR, 1998.

M. Clarke, *Handling the Wicked Issues*, Univ. of Birmingham, 1997.

M. Clarke and J. Stewart, *Community Governance, Community Leadership and the New Local Government*, YPS, 1999.

Social and Economic Trends 2005, LGMB, 1996.

K. Young, *Local Government research: future issues*, York, 1997.

'New Futures for Local Government', *Public Policy and Administration*, Autumn 1996 (special edition).

The Renaissance of Local Government, SOLACE, 1995.

S. Leach and H. Davis, *Enabling or Disabling Local Government: Choices for the Future*, Open UP, 1997.

Local Government Community Leadership, LGMB, 1993.

Leading Communities, LGMB, 1998 (nature, competencies and examples of community governance).

M. Clarke and J. Stewart, *Choices for Local Government for the 1990s and Beyond*, Longman, 1991.

M. Clarke and J. Stewart, *The Future of Local Government: Issues for Discussion*, LGTB, 1989.

M. Clarke and J. Stewart, *The Future of Local Government: Some Lessons from Europe*, LGTB, 1990.

V. Bogdanor, *Against the almighty state: a future for local government*, Federal Trust, 1988.

F. Terry, *The Future Role of Local Government*, Public Finance Foundation, 1990.

J. Stewart and G. Stoker, *The Future of Local Government*, Macmillan, 1989.

H. Davis (ed.), *Reports on the Future of Local Government*, INLOGOV, 1986.

Change and Challenge, LGMB, 1993.

What Future for Local Government?, IEA, October, 1988.

The Future Role and Organisation of Local Government, INLOGOV, 1987.

The Future of Local Government in Britain, ICL, 1988.

G. Hollis *et al.*, *The Future Role and Structure of Local Government*, Longman, 1992.

G. Filkin *et al.*, *Starting to Modernise*, New LG Network/JRF, 1999.

Making a Difference: A White Paper for Local Government, LGA/IDeA, 1999 (a review of how local authorities are responding to the modernization proposals).

P. Gordon, *New Start? Local Government Agenda for the Incoming Government*, CIPFA, 1997.

M. Hodge and W. Thompson, *Beyond the Town Hall: Reinventing Local Government*, Fabian Society, 1994.

J. Stewart and G. Stoker, *From Local Administration to Community Government*, Fabian Society, 1988.

Commission for Local Democracy, *Taking Charge: the Rebirth of Local Democracy*, Municipal Journal Books, 1995.

Re-inventing Local Government: Policies for the Reform of Local Government, Liberal Democratic Publications, 1998.

M. Irvine, *Stakeholding; Putting Local Democracy at Stake?*, Scottish LGIU, 1998.

S. Savage and R. Atkinson, *Public Policy under Blair*, Macmillan, 1999.

J. Lane, *Public Sector reform*, Sage, 1997.

M. Chisholm *et al.*, *A Fresh Start for local Government*, PFF/CIPFA, 1997.

New Statesman, special supplement on Local Government, 27 July 1997.

Renewing Democracy: Rebuilding Communities, Labour Party, 1995.

M. Goldsmith (ed.), *Essays on the Future of Local Government*, Univ. of Salford, 1986; *Options for the Future? Local Democracy Abroad*, LGMB, 1992.

Modernising Government, HMSO, 1999 (mainly central government but some relevance/application to local government).

J. Percy-Smith, 'Downloading democracy?' *Policy and Politics*, 24 January 1996.

M. Powell, *New Labour, new welfare state*, Policy Press, 1999.

J. Hartley and J. Bennington, *Community governance in the information society*, LG Centre, Warwick Univ., 1998.

17 CASE STUDIES

(While some of the following works deal with a particular area, others deal with a particular policy or aspect of policy-making. Where this is not self-evident, it is indicated in brackets.)

A. Henney, 'The Cost of Camden', Camden Commercial Ratepayers Group, 1981.

G. Jones, *Borough Politics: A Study of the Wolverhampton Town Council 1888–1964*, Macmillan, 1969.

J. M. Lee, *Social Leaders and Public Persons*, OUP, 1963 (Cheshire).

J. M. Lee *et al.*, *The Scope of Local Initiative*, Martin Robertson, 1974 (Cheshire).

W. Hampton, *Democracy and Community*, OUP, 1970 (Sheffield).

K. Newton, *Second City Politics*, OUP, 1976 (Birmingham).

M. Stacey, *Tradition and Change*, OUP, 1960 (Banbury).

M. Stacey *et al.*, *Power, Persistence and Change: A Second Study of Banbury*, Routledge, 1975.

A. Clipson, *Public Trust – Public Property: Open Government in Bradford*, Bradford Council for Voluntary Service, 1986.

M. Parkinson, 'Decision Making by Liverpool City Council: Setting the Rate, 1985–6', *The Conduct of Local Authority Business* (Widdicombe), Research Vol. 4, HMSO, 1986.

F. Ridley, 'Liverpool is Different', *The Political Quarterly*, 57, 1986.

H. V. Wiseman, *Local Government at Work*, Routledge, 1967 (Leeds).

R. Reiner, *Chief Constables*, OUP, 1991.

Tower Hamlets and Decentralisation, LGMB, 1991.

G. Jones and A. Norton, *Political Leadership in Local Authorities*, INLOGOV, 1978 (a selection of personal portraits).

N. Dennis, *People and Planning*, Faber, 1970.

N. Dennis, *Public Participation and the Planner's Blight*, Faber, 1972 (redevelopment).

J. Beishon, *A Local Government System*, Open University, 1973 (Brighton Marina project).

J. Gower-Davis, *The Evangelistic Bureaucrat*, Tavistock, 1972 (redevelopment).

R. Minns, 'The Significance of Clay Cross', *Policy and Politics*, 4, 1974.

R. Mitchell, 'Clay Cross', *Political Quarterly*, 2, 1974.

S. Ranson, 'Changing relations between Centre and Locality in Education', *Local Government Studies*, November/December 1980.

R. Farrel, *Local Planning in Four English Cities*, Gower, 1983.

Efficiency in Public Services, CBI, 1984 (privatization).

Local Government and Racial Equality, Commission for Racial Equality, 1982.

D. Rowlands, 'The Impact of the Introduction of Corporate Management on the London Borough of Waltham Forest', Polytechnic of the South Bank, 1981.

D. Skinner and J. Langdon, *The Story of Clay Cross*, Spokesman Books, 1974.

M. Gillard and M. Tomkinson, *Nothing to Declare*, Calder, 1980 (the Poulson affair).

A. P. Brier, 'The Decision Process in Local Government: A Case Study of Fluoridation in Hull', *Public Administration*, Winter 1970.

D. G. Green, *Power and Party in an English City*, Allen & Unwin, 1981 (Newcastle).

A. Blowers, *The Limit of Power: The Politics of Local Planning Policy*, Pergamon, 1980 (Bedfordshire).

R. Glasser, *Town Hall*, Century, 1984 (St Albans).

S. Jackson, *The Anatomy of a Local Government Newspaper*, Welwyn and Hertford District Council, 1984.

A. Alexander, *Borough Government and Politics 1835–1985*, Allen & Unwin, 1985 (Reading).

P. Beresford, *Good Council Guide: Wandsworth 1978–87*, CPS, 1987.

J. Carvel, *Citizen Ken*, Chatto & Windus, 1985.

F. Reeves, *Race and Borough Politics*, Avebury, 1989 (Wolverhampton).

J. Stanyer, *The History of Devon County Council 1889–1989*, Devon Books, 1989.

M. Harloe *et al.*, *Place, Policy and Politics: Do Localities Matter?*, Unwin Hyman, 1990 (seven case studies: Swindon, Teesside, Merseyside, SW Birmingham, Cheltenham, Lancaster, Isle of Thanet).

J. Barry, *The Women's Movement and Local Politics*, Avebury, 1991 (London).

S. Goss, *Local Labour and Local Government*, Edinburgh UP, 1988 (a study of social change and local politics in Southwark 1891–1982).

K. Davidson and J. Fairley, *Local Government in Aberdeen 1975–96*, Scottish Cultural Press, 1999.

M. Parkinson, *Liverpool on the brink: one city's struggle against government cuts*, Policy Journals, 1985.

G. Stoker (ed.), 'Reflections on Neighbourhood Decentralisation in Tower Hamlets', *Public Administration*, Autumn 1991, pp. 373–84.

Many county councils published a history of their authority in the centenary year 1989.

R. Turton and H. Woodall, 'The Debureaucratised World of Local Government: The Case of Halton Borough Council', *Local Government Studies*, September 1987.

M. Boddy *et al.*, City for the 21st Century? Globalization, Planning and Urban Change in Contemporary Britain, Policy Press, 1997 (Swindon).

18 LONDON

The LBA Handbook 1992–3: A Guide to Local Government in London, LBA, 1993.

G. Rhodes (ed.), *The New Government of London: The First Five Years*, Weidenfeld & Nicolson, 1972.

G. Rhodes, *The Government of London: The Struggle for Reform*, Weidenfeld & Nicolson, 1970.

D. Foley, *Governing the London Region*, Univ. of California Press, 1972.

Report of the Royal Commission on Local Government in Greater London (Herbert Report), Cmd 1164, HMSO, 1960.

Royal Commission on Local Government in England, Research Study 2, *The Lessons of the London Government Reform*, HMSO, 1968.

D. Donnison and D. Eversley (eds.), *London: Urban Patterns, Problems and Policies*, Heinemann, 1973.

E. Wistrich, *The First Years of Camden*, Borough of Camden, 1972.

W. E. Jackson, *Achievement: A Short History of the LCC*, Longmans, 1965.

A. Saint (ed.), *Politics and the People of London: The London County Council 1889–1965*, Hambledon, 1989.

J. Davis, *Reforming London: The London Government Problem, 1855–1900*, Clarendon, 1988.

P. Hall, *Radical Agenda for London*, Fabian Society, 1980.

H. Cutler, *The Cutler Files*, Weidenfeld & Nicolson, 1981.

D. Owen, *The Government and Victorian London 1855–89*, Harvard UP, 1982.

M. Hebbert and T. Travers, *The London Government Handbook*, Cassell, 1988.

Governing London (weekly).

Audit Commission, *The Management of London's Authorities*, HMSO, 1987.

S. James, 'A Streamlined City: The Broken Pattern of London Government', *Public Administration*, Winter 1990.

T. Travers *et al.*, *The Government of London*, Joseph Rowntree, 1991.

A Mayor and Assembly for London, Cmd 3897, 1998 (White Paper).

J. Davis, *Reforming London 1855–1900*, Clarendon Press, 1988.

T. Travers and G. Jones, *The New Government of London*, Joseph Rowntree, 1997 (see also *Local Government Studies*, Autumn 1997, p. 53).

Annual Abstract of Greater London Statistics, London Research Centre.

New Leadership for London, Cmd 3724, HMSO, 1997.

19 SCOTLAND

Local Government in Scotland, Factsheet 12, Scottish Office, 1998.

Moving Forward: Local Government and the Scottish Parliament, Scottish Office, 1999. (This is the final report of the McIntosh Commission set up to consider (i) relations between local government and the new Scottish Parliament and Executive and (ii) methods of improving local democracy and accountability. It deals with many aspects covered/contained in the White Papers above.)

P. Vestri and M. Brown, *A Guide to Scottish Local Government*, Scottish LGIU, 1995.

G. Monies, *Local Government in Scotland*, Green, 1996.

K. Ferguson, *An Introduction to Local Government in Scotland*, Planning Exchange, 1984.

Shaping the New Councils, HMSO, July 1993 (White Paper on structure of Scotland).

Report of the Royal Commission on Local Government in Scotland 1966–1969 (the Wheatley Report), 2 vols., Cmd 4150, HMSO, 1969.

J. P. Mackintosh, 'The Royal Commission on Local Government in Scotland 1966–1969', *Public Administration*, Spring 1970.

D. Sinclair, *Scottish Local Government: Beyond 1996*, Univ of R. Gordon, 1996.

D. Sinclair, *Review of Scottish Local Government: Challenges and Constraints*, Scottish LGIU, 1997.

G. Boyne, *Local Government Reform: A Review of the Process in Scotland and Wales*, LGC Communications, 1995.

M. McVicar, *The process of local government reform*, Joseph Rowntree, 1995 (changes in Wales and Scotland).

A. Midwinter, *Local Government in Scotland – Reform or Decline?*, Macmillan, 1995.

M. Keating and A. Midwinter, *The Government of Scotland*, Mainstream, 1983.

Guide to Local Government Finance in Scotland, CIPFA, 1988.

A. Midwinter, 'The Fiscal Crisis in Scottish Local Government', *Local Governance*, Spring 1998.

J. McCormick, *The Green and the Tartan: Business Rates after Devolution*, IPPR, 1996.

A. Midwinter *et al.*, *Politics and Public Policy in Scotland*, Macmillan, 1991.

V. D. Lipman, 'Some Contrasts between English and Scottish Local Government', *Public Administration*, 3, 1949.

H. M. Drucker and M. G. Clarke or N. Drucker (eds.), *The Scottish Government Yearbook*, Paul Harris (annually since 1978). D. McCrone (ed.), Edinburgh UP since 1984. A. Brown (ed.) since 1990.

J. M. Bochel and D. T. Denver, *The Scottish Local Government Election 1974*, Univ.

of Dundee, 1974 and subsequent years, the latest being *The Scottish Local Election: Results and Statistics*, Election Studies, 1995.

C. Himsworth, *Local Government Law in Scotland*, T. Clark, 1995.

Butterworth's Scottish Local Government Handbook, Butterworth, 1997.

A. Whetstone, *Scottish County Government in the 18th and 19th Centuries*, John Donald, Edinburgh, 1981.

D. Cepok, 'Decentralisation: power to the people?', Report of the fourth seminar: From *Wheatley to What?*. Univ. of Edinburgh, 1996.

Scotland's Parliament, Cmd 3658, HMSO, 1997.

A useful Internet address is the Scottish Office at www.scotland.gov.uk and www.scottish-devolution.org.uk

20 WALES

Local Government in Wales: A Charter for the Future, HMSO, 1993 – the White Paper on reorganization of local government structures.

Local Voices: Modernising Local Government in Wales, Cmd 4028, HMSO, 1998 – the White Paper outlining the reform programme for local authorities. The various aspects were dealt with in separate Consultative/Green Papers drawn up by the Welsh Office in consultation with the Welsh Local Government Association (WLGA), namely:

The Agenda

Local democracy and community leadership

Options for managing capital

Improving local services through best value

Business rates

Improving local accountability for council tax

A new ethical framework

Local Democracy in Wales: Implications of the Welsh Assembly, Welsh LGA, 1997.

G. Boyne, *Local government in Wales: its role and function*, Joseph Rowntree, 1992.

G. Boyne, *Local Government Reform: A Review of the Process in Scotland and Wales*, LGC Communications, 1995.

M. McVicar, *The process of local government reform*, Joseph Rowntree, 1995 (changes in Wales and Scotland).

M. Cadwallader, 'Councillors in Wales', *Local Government Studies*, Autumn 1995.

M. Griffiths and A. Lawton, 'Community Councils in Wales', *Local Government Studies*, Summer 1992.

I. B. Rees, *Government by Community*, Knight, 1971.

P. Madgwick *et al.*, *The Politics of Rural Wales*, Hutchinson, 1973.

A useful Internet address is the Office of the Secretary for Wales at: www.wales.gov.uk

An Assembly for Wales, HMSO, 1997.

Local Democracy in Wales: Implications of the Welsh Assembly, Welsh LGA, 1997.

21 JOURNALS

Local Government Chronicle (weekly)

Municipal Journal (weekly).

Local Governance (quarterly).

Local Government Executive (bi-monthly).

Local Government and Law (monthly).

Local Council Review (bi-monthly).

Local Government Talkback (monthly).

Local Government Voice (quarterly).

Local Government Annotations Service: LOGA (bi-monthly).

Local Government Studies (bi-monthly).

The Local Economy (quarterly, Longman).

Public Money and Management (quarterly, Blackwell).

Local Government News (monthly).

Local Government Comparative Statistics (annual, CIPFA).

Local Government Management (quarterly).

New Economy (quarterly).

New Statesman (weekly).

Policy and Politics (quarterly).

Public and Social Policy (quarterly).

Public Finance (weekly).

Public Policy Review (monthly).

Public Policy and Administration (quarterly).

Research Link, LGMB (quarterly).

Stakeholder (bi-monthly).

Teaching Public Administration (bi-annual).

Contemporary Record (quarterly).

The Economist (weekly).

Urban Studies (quarterly).

Public Law (quarterly).

INDEX